THE RUSSIAN JEW
UNDER TSARS AND SOVIETS

SECOND EDITION, REVISED AND ENLARGED

WITH A NEW FOREWORD BY THE AUTHOR

SALO W. BARON

The Russian Jew
Under Tsars and Soviets

The
Russian Jew
Under
Tsars and
Soviets

SECOND EDITION
REVISED AND ENLARGED

Salo W. Baron

With a New Foreword by the Author

SCHOCKEN BOOKS • NEW YORK

First Schocken paperback edition 1987
10 9 8 7 6 5 4 3 2 1   87 88 89 90

Copyright © 1964, 1976, 1987 by Salo W. Baron
All rights reserved. No part of this book may be reproduced or
transmitted in any form or by any means, electronic or mechan-
ical, including photocopying, recording or by any information
storage and retrieval system, without permission in writing from
the Publisher.

Library of Congress Cataloging-in-Publication Data
Baron, Salo Wittmayer, 1895–
The Russian Jew under Tsars and Soviets.
Reprint. Originally published: New York:
Macmillan, c1976.
Bibliography: p.
Includes index.
1. Jews—Soviet Union—History.   2. Soviet Union—
Ethnic relations.   I. Title.
[DS135.R9B28   1987]   947′.004924   87–9601

Manufactured in the United States of America
ISBN 0–8052–0838–0

Acknowledgments

Every effort has been made to secure permission for quotation from the copyright owners, but in some cases it has been impossible to locate the owners. Grateful acknowledgment is due to the following for permission to quote selections from the works cited:

American Academy for Jewish Research, New York: Philipp Friedman, "Wirtschaftliche Umschichtsprozesse . . . ," 1935.

The American Jewish Committee, New York: Solomon M. Schwartz, *Jews in the Soviet Union*, reprinted by permission from *Commentary*, Copyright © 1951 by the American Jewish Committee. *The American Jewish Yearbook for 5667, 1906–1907. The Jews in the Eastern War Zone*, 1916.

Behrman's Jewish Book Shop, New York: Simeon Samuel Frug's "Resurrection" in Edmund Fleg's edition of *The Jewish Anthology*, 1925.

Chapman and Hall, Ltd., London: Julius F. Hecker, *Religion and Communism: A Study of Religion and Atheism in Russia*, 1933.

Chatto & Windus, Ltd., London: Alexander Herzen, *My Past and Thoughts*, translated by Constance Garnett.

Columbia University Press, New York: Zbigniew Brzezinski, *Dilemmas of Change in Soviet Politics*. Oscar I. Janowsky, *The Jews and Minority Rights*, 1933. Isaac Levitats, *The Jewish Community in Russia, 1772–1884*, 1943.

Acknowledgments

Conference on Jewish Social Studies, New York: R. Ainzstein, "Jewish Tragedy and Heroism in Soviet Literature," XXIII (1961). Paul Berline, "Russian Religious Philosophers and the Jews," IX (1947). Alfred A. Greenbaum, "Hebrew Literature in Soviet Russia," XXX (1968). Moshe Perlmann, "*Razvet* 1860–1861: The Origins of the Russian Jewish Press," XXIV (1962). Koppel S. Pinson, "Arkady Kremer, Vladimir Medem and the Ideology of the Jewish Bund," VII (1945). Zosa Szajkowski, "How Mass Migration to America Began," IV (1942).

Crown Publishers, New York: B. Z. Goldberg, *The Jewish Problem in the Soviet Union: An Analysis and a Solution,* © 1961 by B. Z. Goldberg. Used by permission of Crown Publishers, Inc.

Dawar, Tel Aviv: Elisha Rodin, *Bi-fe'at Nekhar,* 1938. Author's translation.

Howard Fast, "A Matter of Validity," *Midstream,* IV (1958).

Fordham University Press, New York: N. S. Timasheff, "Russian Nationalism under the Soviets," from *Izvestia* of April 17, 1939; *Thought,* XX (1945).

Harcourt, Brace and Jovanovich, New York: Corliss Lamont, *The Peoples of the Soviet Union,* 1946.

Harper and Row Publishers, New York: Harrison E. Salisbury, *To Moscow and Beyond: A Reporter's Narrative,* 1959.

Harvard University Press, Cambridge: E. J. Simmons, *Continuity and Change in Russian and Soviet Thought,* 1955.

Hebrew Union College—Jewish Institute of Religion, Cincinnati: David Philippson, "Max Lilienthal in Russia," *Hebrew Union College Annual, XII–XIII.*

Herzl Press, New York: Theodor Herzl, *Complete Diaries of Theodor Herzl.*

Hoover Institution Press, Stanford, California: H. H. Fisher, *Out of My Past: Memoirs of Count Kokovstov,* reprinted by permission of the publishers, Hoover Institution Press. Copyright © 1935 by the Board of Trustees of the Leland Stanford Junior University.

Horovitz Publishing Company, Ltd. (East and West Library), London: *Ahad Ha-Am: Essays, Letters, Memoirs,* translated by Leon Simon, 1946.

Institute of Jewish Affairs, London: J. A. Newth, "A Statistical Study of Intermarriage. . . ," *Bulleting of Soviet Jewish Affairs,* No. 1 (1968). L. Kochan, ed., *Jews in Soviet Russia,* 2nd edition.

International Publishers, New York: Maxim Gorki, *Culture and People,* 1939. Nicolai Lenin, *On the Jewish Question,* 1936.

The Jewish Historical Society of England, London: Albert M. Hyamson, ed., *The British Consulate in Jerusalem,* 1939–41.

Jewish Publication Society of America, Philadelphia: Joseph Baron, *Stars and Sand,* 1943. A. L. Eliav (Ben Ami), *Between Hammer and Sickle,* 1967. Joseph Nedava, *Trotsky and the Jews,* 1972.

Acknowledgments

Journal of the History of Ideas, Philadelphia: Hans Kohn, "Dostoyevsky's Nationalism," VI (1945).

Alfred A. Knopf, Inc., New York: Alexander Herzen, *My Past and Thoughts*, translated by Constance Garnett, © 1924–26.

Ktav Publishing House, New York: Elias Shulman, *A History of Jewish Education in the Soviet Union*. Zosa Szajkowski, *Jews, Wars and Communism*, 1972–74.

Little, Brown and Company, Boston, in association with the *Atlantic Monthly*: Catherine Drinker Bowen, *"Free Artist": A Story of Anton and Nicholas Rubinstein*, published by Random House, New York, 1939.

Macmillan Publishing Co., Inc., New York: Michael T. Florinsky, *Russia: A History and an Interpretation*, 2 vols., © 1954; Paul B. Anderson, *People, Church and State in Russia*.

Mediaevel Academy of America, Cambridge: *Russian Primary Chronicle*, translated by Samuel H. Cross and Olgerd P. Sherbovitz-Wetzor, from *Publications*, LX (1953).

The New York Times Company, New York: Harry Schwartz, "Moscow Papers Assail Writer" (English translation of an excerpt from Yevtushenko's *Babii Yar*), *New York Times*, September 28, 1961. Copyright © by the New York Times Company. Reprinted by permission.

Martinus Nijhoff's Boekhandel, The Hague, The Netherlands: March Raeff, *Michael Speransky*, 1957.

Oxford University Press, London: L. Kochan, ed., *Jews in Soviet Russia*, 2nd edition.

Frederick A. Praeger, Inc., New York: Bertram Wolfe, *Krushchev and Stalin's Ghost*, copyright © 1957.

Princeton University Press, Princeton, New Jersey: Zvi Y. Gitelman, *Jewish Nationality and Soviet Politics: The Jewish Section of the CPSU*, © 1972. Reprinted by permission of Princeton University Press.

Sheed and Ward, London: Nicholas Berdyaev, *The Russian Revolution*, 1931.

Universe Books, New York: Leonard Schroeter, *The Last Exodus*, 1974.

Yale University Press, New Haven: Louis Greenberg, *The Jews in Russia*, 1951.

Avrahm Yarmolinsky, *Literature under Communism*, © 1960.

Contents

Contents

Contents

Foreword

Much has happened in the life of the Soviet Union and its Jewish population during the two decades since the publication of the first edition of this work in 1964. Unexpected even by close observers of the Soviet scene, the "thaw" from extreme Stalinist tyranny, which had partially begun during the Khrushchev era, for the first time in two generations enabled a number of freedom-loving thinkers to make known their dissent from the official party line. Through its *samizdats*, small as their circulation may be, this minority has become a force in Soviet society much beyond the numerical strength of its adherents.

Jews, too, almost totally silenced by the repression of the last Stalin years, now found a number of courageous and self-sacrificing spokesmen who, to some extent, succeeded in reversing the governmentally promoted denial of Jewish identity by many of their fellow citizens. By publicly identifying themselves with the fate of the State of Israel, at a time when the Soviet regime had officially severed its diplomatic relations with that country and become the leader in a world campaign against "Zionism" (which also served as a cloak for a vociferous general anti-Jewish propaganda), they testified to the eternal self-rejuvenating vitality of the Jewish people. With the aid of an aroused world opinion and the spreading demand for the universalization of the Human Rights Covenant under the auspices of the United Nations—which the Soviet Union had formally to accept, though it has thus far successfully evaded the implementation of these safeguards—they forced the authorities to allow more than 250,000 Soviet Jews to breach the anti-emigration walls and to find their way to their old "Jewish homeland" and other countries. An entirely new chapter (18), written for the revised edition of this book published in 1976, is devoted to an analysis of the transformations that took place in the preceding decade.

This relatively favorable situation did not last, however. As early as the regime of Brezhnev (1960ff.), there had been a considerable deterioration in the attitude of the government to the Jewish question. Yet, at first the decade of 1977 to 1986 continued with the earlier general policy of moderation. This was evidenced most graphically by the number of Jews who were allowed to emigrate to Israel and indirectly to other countries. The figures of annual departures increased from 16,831 in 1977 to 28,993 in 1978, and reached a climax of 51,547 in 1979. At that point there was a change in attitude, and the figures dropped to 21,471 in 1980 and to 9,400 in 1981. They continued to decline thereafter to almost nothing worthy of recording. In those years the Western world's concentration was mainly on individuals, especially distinguished scholars who, as *refuseniks*, were often imprisoned and sent to harsh labor camps. An outstanding example was Anatoly Shcharansky, whose liberation after several years of suffering was celebrated the world over. But such individual exceptions merely underscored the practical cessation of Jewish emigration during the years 1980–86.

The changing attitudes of the Soviet regime were to a large extent a reflection of the ups and downs in the international relations—particularly the degree of détente—between the two superpowers, the United States and the Soviet Union. The moderation of the Soviets in the 1970s was primarily the result of foreign pressures in the field of human rights. On occasions, the Soviet Union found itself constrained to cosign a *Universal Declaration of Human Rights* by the United Nations for the newly proclaimed principle of every citizen having the right to leave his country or to return to it at his own will. True, the Soviet regime always found ways to evade the practical application of such principles to itself. At one particular point the Soviets made use of the human rights issue as an instrument for obtaining from the United States a number of concessions, including the formal recognition of the annexation of the Baltic states (Estonia, Latvia, and Lithuania) in a pact concluded in Helsinki in 1975. This concession, which ended three decades of a twilight situation in the international position of these important lands after World War II, was largely secured by a Soviet promise of fully honoring the human rights proclaimed by the United Nations. As before, the Soviets did not have any intention of fulfilling that promise in the way expected by the West. It shared in this respect the fate of many other international Soviet commitments, including the very fundamental law granting self-government to the numerous nationalities constituting the Soviet Union. From its creation on, the leaders adopted Lenin's principle recognizing the right of self-determination of each nationality. This provision, included in 1918 in the first Constitution of the Soviet Union, has been repeated in the subsequent texts of the Constitution down to the last published in 1977, and remains valid to the present. Yet in practice, throughout the seven decades since its first enactment, any person trying to exercise that right was considered to have "committed a crime against the state" punishable by death.

In the case of other human rights, too, the Soviets have consistently refused to implement them in the Western meaning of this term by offering an entirely different interpretation. Even after leaving the Helsinki Conference, attended by representatives of thirty-five nations, in an exhilarated mood and fully satisfied with the promises of the "Final Act of the Conference on Security and Cooperation in Europe"—the text of which Brezhnev speedily distributed in 20,000,000 copies—they apparently did not intend to apply them to the satisfaction of the West. In a speech at the conference, the Soviet leader only emphasized that "we trust that all countries represented at the Conference will abide by the accords reached here. The Soviet Union will do precisely that." In practice, however, the Soviets merely continued applying those human rights that they had long before proclaimed as desirable: for instance, the laws promising to provide full employment and affordable housing to their population and thereby avoid the problem of homeless people. This difference in interpretation was debated back and forth, especially at the important East-West Conference in Madrid from 1980 to 1983.

In the ultimate sense, the actions of the Soviet rulers did not depend on their interpretations but on the facts of life in the ever deteriorating relationship between the two superpowers. If the early concessions of the 1970s were partly enforced upon the Soviet Union by the economic measures taken by the United States in the Jackson-Vanik and Stevenson amendments to the Omnibus Trade Reform Bill—which greatly undermined commercial exchanges between the two powers so long as the Soviet Union seriously prevented the emigration of Jews—further deterioration on the international scene was occasioned by the invasion of Afghanistan, the Soviet attack on the Korean jetliner, and the frequent verbal attacks on the "evil empire" by President Reagan. Rarely in the history of the world did the problem of the emigration of a part of a country's population play such an extensive role in international relations. The Soviet Union argued that handling emigration was part of domestic policy in which other countries should not interfere. But Israel, the United States, and Western Europe pleaded that it was a stark disregard of human rights to prevent the reunification of families, as was the case of Soviet Jews seeking to rejoin relatives abroad. At times human rights became intertwined with the fundamental problems of world peace and thus became a major subject of political discussion, especially in American presidential and congressional election years.

In the Soviet Union, on the other hand, aspects of international trade connected with the Jewish emigration issue had some impact on the Soviet economy. On the whole, in the 1970s and early 1980s the Soviet Union suffered from growing economic stagnation, which contrasted vividly with the tremendous innovations and expansions in the economies of the West, particularly the United States, and Japan. The great economic strides made during that period by China and such Third World countries as Taiwan, Korea, and Hong Kong also contrasted sharply with the retardation of the Soviet economy. Yet any innovation in the Soviet Union or Eastern Europe could only be achieved by seriously changing the existing system at the expense of the traditional holders of power (as witnessed in Hungary). It has long been observed that, in the Soviet power structure, the Politbureau decreed but the bureaucracy enforced. Because of widespread lack of discipline on the productive scene, corruption in the higher echelons, and the problem of alcoholism, the Soviet economy fell increasingly behind, although the standard of living improved slightly from year to year. The total output, however, remained behind the needs of the country, especially aggravated by the concentration on armaments and military expenditures. The result was that, although officially economists attributed to the Soviet economy an annual growth of two percent, it but barely kept pace with the population growth.

From another angle the character of this population growth ran counter to the wishes of the Great Russian populace. Population increases were particularly pronounced among the Muslim sections of the country. Even in their less fertile decade of 1970–79, when the more than 45,000,000 Muslims in the Soviet Union increased at the rate of 2.47 percent (rather than the 3.25 percent of the preceding decade), their demographic advance was four times that of the Great Russians (0.6 percent). Moreover, the statistical figures for the Great Russian population include many "pseudo-Russians" culled from Jews and members of other minorities without religious or national feelings who, like Leon Trotzky in contrast to Maxim Litvinov, registered themselves as belonging to the Great Russian nationality.

As a result, for the first time in its history, the Great Russian population found itself to be a declining minority in the country. At the same time, the Jewish population was actually diminishing in absolute numbers from one census to the next. The chances are that, in addition to the émigrés, all along there have been numerous Jews who denied their Jewishness and joined the majority, for the most part without a formal conversion to another religion. These demographic realities, usually overlooked, may in part explain the strong resistance of the Soviet rulers to a Jewish mass emigration.

In general, Russia's domestic policies toward Jews have not changed very much. They may be characterized as a combination of assimilation and anti-Semitism. The Soviet state continued in this area much of the anti-Jewish behavior maintained by the tsarist regime. When in 1939 the Soviet Union shared with Nazi Germany the occupation of Polish territories, it immediately started remodeling the local population, including Jews, in order to integrate them into the Soviet system. Here the racial aspect also played a considerable role. The new masters tried to convert Jews, Germans, and others to the Slavic culture by entrusting the administration to either Russians, Ukrainians, or Belo-Russians. One could not evaluate the success of that brief experiment, since it was brought to an abrupt end with the German invasion of 1941. However, when the Russians returned during and after the war, their policy of assimilating Jews to Soviet culture continued unabated. It was intensified under the Stalinist Terror of the late 1940s and early 1950s, which easily suppressed all overt opposition. At the same time, anti-Semitism, which had formally been condemned in the early years of the Soviet Union as a crime against the state, had already become an acceptable weapon in assimilating Jews and in gaining approval from the anti-Jewish population by allowing the publication of anti-Semitic books and pamphlets and cultivating anti-Jewish policies in practice. The government did not discourage the populace from treating its Jewish neighbors as scapegoats for the spreading black markets or from frequently complaining about the numerically disproportionate Jewish participation in higher occupations.

On their part, the authorities gradually eliminated Jews from government posts. The participation of Jews in the bureaucracy receded from year to year, as did the admission of Jewish students to more select universities and other schools of higher learning. While the census of 1926 revealed that Jews held about eight percent of posts in the bureaucracy reaching up to the high offices in Moscow, which amounted to four times their percentage of the population, in later years their elimination proceeded even in areas of their special competence, such as foreign policy, international trade, and their often creative political and ideological partisanship. Ultimately they were completely eliminated from the Politbureau, the higher ranks of the army, and other areas of leadership. Much of that elimination took place in Stalin's lifetime, but it continued, although at a slower pace, under his successors. For example, the number of Jews in the U.S.S.R. Supreme Soviet was reduced from forty-seven in 1937 to five in 1950 and to three in 1958, though before long Brezhnev raised the total to six. Membership in the enormous Communist Party, generally needed for jobs above the lowest categories, at first included disproportionately many Jews. But the growing availability of educated non-Jews with good training in special occupations reduced Jewish membership from 294,724 in January, 1976, to less than 260,000 in 1982, or only 1.9 and 1.4 percent of the population, respectively. This was less than the Jewish ratio in the population. Simultaneously, the opponents to admitting Jews to higher education, higher-ranking jobs, and particularly to positions of power forgot that they were thereby counteracting the regime's primary objective of assimilating the Jews away from their Jewish heritage. For this objective, during the entire postwar period a literature debasing Jewish virtues from antiquity to the present was allowed to sprout not only in the Ukraine, but also in the central Great Russian areas, including Moscow. At the same time, the Jews were deprived of all their schools, press, and literature, except for the Yiddish journal *Sovetish Haimland*, which printed only materials agreeable to the authorities. Even private instruction in Hebrew was forbidden and could only be obtained surreptitiously.

The resulting lack of Jewish education and familiarity with Jewish traditions of a great many Soviet Jews, especially among the younger generation, became a major problem for the new emigration. It aggravated for them the other difficulties confronting newcomers deriving from the differences between the general Soviet lifestyle and that of the countries of immigration. Jews arriving in Israel, the United States, and other Western countries were often overwhelmed by the necessary adjustments to the new lands. They found that, while at home they obtained dwellings and occupations by government assignment, in their new countries of settlement they were often at a loss as to how to obtain a residence, look for a job, or even perform such simple tasks as shop for food. While in some countries relatives or members of aid societies proved very helpful in overcoming such obstacles, the strangeness of that dependence was often very disheartening. Needless to say the comment made by the First Deputy Premier, Frol Kozlov, in the midst of the Stalin terror in 1959, that "the Jews live better in Russia than in any other land, including Israel," was a great exaggeration. But it also contained a grain of truth, considering the difficulties of adjustment of émigrés in their new countries. Even a recent Jewish emigrant in New York was overheard complaining that "we Soviets are not like the East Europeans, we have had fifty-seven years of isolation and brainwashing. . . . We are from another planet." It is not surprising, therefore, that Kozlov's assertion was indeed the accepted notion, shared by the Russian government and public for generations. Russian writers generally took for granted that as a rule emigrating Russians would sooner rather than later return to their country. In the Jewish case, however, this was true only for a small minority of those who had waited so anxiously for many years before they secured permission to leave the Soviet Union. It is not surprising that these few returning exiles were paraded with fanfare before the public for propaganda purposes. They were particularly extolled in the *Sovetish Haimland* by its editor, Aron Vergelis.

A poll taken in several American cities among recent arrivals from the Soviet Union revealed that no more than ten percent had received any Jewish education in their former country. Unlike their ancestors, these new émigrés came to a country in which the Jewish community had become fully matured. Moreover, they brought with them a heritage of destruction caused by the Great Holocaust and a constant denunciation of their Jewish culture by neighbors in their homeland. But one may expect that, before very long, their contributions to American Jewish life will become ever more numerous and creative—a process which in Israel, the other country of large Russo-Jewish immigration, automatically involves absorbing Jewish culture.

In conclusion, I wish to remember gratefully several people, especially my wife, Jeannette Meisel Baron of blessed memory, for the help they extended to me in the preparation and publication of the present work. They are mentioned in the Preface to the First Edition. Here I need only add the name of Ms. Evelyn Ehrlich, a doctoral candidate at Columbia University, who was helpful to me in assembling the materials for this Foreword, which merely intends to emphasize a few pertinent highlights of the history of the last decade, since the publication of the Second Edition.

SALO WITTMAYER BARON

New York, N.Y.
April 30, 1987

Preface to First Edition

The story told in the following pages is both sad and heroic. Rarely was a people subjected to such sustained, unrelenting pressures as were the Jews under the tsarist regime. A powerful autocracy, employing its unlimited powers, combined strict segregation and sharp discrimination with fiscal exploitation and contemptuous treatment to force the Jews to abandon their ancestral mores and faith, and completely to submerge their identity within the religion and culture of the majority. Yet Russian Jewry successfully resisted both pressures and blandishments. Its great vitality came to the fore not only in its constant growth in numbers and intellectual vigor, but also in its ability to nurture from its manpower and spiritual resources the growing Jewish communities of the New World, Western Europe, and Palestine. One need but remember that in the 1920s many a Jewish *Landsmannschaft* in New York City exceeded in size the total population of the town from which its members had stemmed.

Paradoxically, Russian Jewry is at once one of the oldest and one of the youngest communities in Western Judaism. Many peripheral areas of the Soviet Union have been inhabited by Jews from the earliest days of the Christian era; in some cases long before their occupation by their present ethnic majorities. Yet the tsars peremptorily excluded Jews from their rapidly expanding Russian heartland and even after they had willy-nilly taken over hundreds of thousands of Jewish subjects residing in the territories of partitioned Poland in 1772-1795, the tsars succeeded, through the artifice of a Pale of Settlement, in admitting there only a select few to the very end of their regime. The history of Russian Jewry as such thus covers less than two centuries and is actually shorter than, for instance, that of the United States.

By repudiating tsarism and all it stood for, the Revolutions of 1917 seemed to usher in a new glorious era for all the oppressed minorities of the vast empire extending over one-sixth of the earth. Many Jews, in particular, were easily persuaded that the new society would also grant to its numerous ethnic minorities an unprecedented combination of full equality of rights and national autonomy. The new communist Jewish leadership, especially, was prepared to overlook the immediate hardships caused by the Communist Revolution—the undermining of the entire socioeconomic structure of their community, the disfranchisement of about one-third of their people, and the overthrow of their traditional institutions, viewing them all as but a transitional phase toward the fulfillment of their socialist dreams. But few realized that, by giving up their traditional moorings of the Jewish religion, Hebrew culture, and the Zionist ideal, they would sap the very energies which had theretofore maintained the strength of their people in the midst of adversity. Nor did many of them foresee that, even under the totally changed social structure, the anti-Semitic feelings of the Russian masses could reassert themselves under various guises. They also failed to anticipate the sharp reaction of a regime which, growingly nationalistic and imperialist, would look with suspicion upon the "cosmopolitan" connections of the Jewish people dispersed through many lands.

Moreover, before it had a chance to adjust itself to this novel situation, Russian Jewry went through the traumatic experience of the Nazi invasion and extermination. Deeply grateful to the Red Army in which it saw its actual savior, it meekly submitted to the Stalinist terror of 1948-52 which shattered whatever expectations it may have cherished for its postwar reconstruction.

It is small wonder, then, that, facing such world-shaking changes, the Russian Jews have not yet found their bearings. Theoretically still living under the illusion of equality plus autonomy, they face the stark reality of administrative discrimination, governmental and popular animosity , and novel assimilatory pressures. At the same time, taught by their own leaders that they must abandon some of the most essential elements of their millennial heritage, they have not yet found the way of resuming their old cultural progress, interrupted by half a century of alternating exalted expectations and abysmal despair. Yet, despite their numerous shattered illusions, it appears that this is not the "end of the road" for them, and that, in some as yet unpredictable fashion, they will, before very long, recover their ancient vitality to find some unprecedented solutions to the novel, intrinsically contradictory challenges of discrimination by, and assimilation to, one of the great nations of history.

In conclusion it is a pleasant duty for the author to express his thanks to those who have helped him to tell his story in its present form. He is indebted to Professor Michael T. Florinsky who, as General Editor of the Series, read the manuscript and offered a number of valuable suggestions. His secretary, Mrs. Rebecca Fischer, prepared the manuscript with painstaking care and assisted in seeing it through the press. Most of all, the author is indebted to his wife, Mrs. Jeannette Meisel Baron, for her tireless cooperation, encouragement, and constructive criticisms during the entire process of research, writing, and publication. Needless to say, these expressions of gratitude involve no delegation of responsibility.

S. W. B.

Yifat Shalom
Canaan, Conneticut
May 28, 1964

The Russian Jew
Under Tsars and Soviets

[1]

Early Vicissitudes

Like most ancient and medieval origins, those of the Jewish settlement in the present boundaries of the Soviet Union are shrouded in darkness. True, owing to persistent efforts of East European archeologists, we now know a little more about the general ethnology and history of the early inhabitants of that area, particularly of its European segment. Because of the well-known limitations of archeological finds unaccompanied by inscriptions and literary documents, however, these early human settlements in European Russia are subject to conflicting hypotheses and for the most part are completely undatable. Nor can the racial and ethnic composition of that early population be clearly identified. Certainly, if any Jews appeared in those regions before the Christian era without leaving behind any literary or epigraphic traces, they could not easily be isolated as such from the rest of the population.

Nevertheless some early contacts may go back to the seventh century B.C. The vast conglomeration of peoples inhabiting eastern Europe in antiquity and going under the name of Scythians was not unknown to the ancient Israelites. Scythian invaders at one time actually reached the confines of neighboring Syria and, rightly or wrongly, many scholars have seen in them the embodiment of that "peril from the north" of which Jeremiah spoke, when he prophesied, "For I [the Lord] will bring evil from the north, and a great destruction" (4:6). Reciprocally, later Jewish traditions ascribed the first settlements of the Jews in southern Russia to the period of the First Exile. St. Jerome doubtless merely repeated an assertion heard from Jewish contemporaries that "the Assyrians and Chaldaeans had conducted the Jewish people into exile not only in Media and Persia but also in the Bosporus and the extreme north."[1]

Some medieval Jewish legends even spoke of displaced Canaanites at the time of Joshua's conquest of Palestine having gone all the way into Russia, just as others had settled in North Africa. From these legends may have stemmed the medieval Hebrew designation of Slavonic eastern Europe as Canaan, although Canaan's Hamitic descent was clearly contrasted in the Bible with the Japhetite ancestry of the Indo-European peoples. According to another explanation offered by medieval writers, including the famous twelfth-century traveler Benjamin of Tudela, that designation was derived from the slave trade which was so widely prevalent among the "Slav" nations.[2]

ANCIENT SETTLEMENTS

We are on safer ground when we find Greek inscriptions pertaining to Jewish communities settled on the northern shore of the Black Sea in the early centuries of the Christian era. They reveal, as in many other areas within the *limes* of the ancient Roman Empire, the presence of organized communities of Jews who, while professing the Jewish religion, adopted the speech, the names, and even certain rituals from their Hellenized neighbors. A considerable number of Hebrew inscriptions from the Crimea have likewise come to light, but their reading and dating have long been suspect, because their original discoverer, Abraham Firkovitch, is known to have tampered with some texts for the glory of his own, the Karaite, sect which, founded in the eighth century, had increasingly separated itself from the so-called Rabbanite majority of Jews. However, quite a few texts found by this learned and indefatigable traveler probably have greater historical merit than was attributed to them by an oversuspicious and overcritical generation of the late nineteenth century. From these borderlines of the declining Roman Empire venturesome Jewish individuals doubtless explored much of the interior of Russia, just as the Jews of Armenia and northern Persia, including Khiva, had penetrated Asiatic territories adjacent to the Caspian Sea. Jewish émigrés from the more advanced countries of western Asia also early infiltrated the Caucasus, laying the foundations for the so-called Mountain Jews whose peculiar mores and rituals have long greatly impressed travelers and anthropologists.

Early Vicissitudes

The Jewish population in all these regions increased considerably after each of the recurrent Byzantine persecutions and particularly after the total outlawry of Judaism, promulgated in each of the four centuries between the seventh and the tenth. The warlike disturbances accompanying the numerous campaigns between Rome or Byzantium on the one hand, and Persia or the Great Caliphate on the other hand, likewise forced many Jewish refugees to seek shelter in these outlying, more pacific areas. In view of the slowness and perils of personal communication, the settlers around the Black and Caspian Seas often lost contact with the great centers of Jewish learning in Palestine and Babylonia. They harbored among them heterodox elements, including outright sectarians such as Samaritans or Karaites. It was from a Samaritan in Kherson, we are told, that St. Cyril, the apostle of the Christian faith among the eastern Slavs, had learned Hebrew. With the aid of Hebrew one of Cyril's pupils fashioned a new alphabet, the Cyrilitsa, generally used in Russian and other eastern Slavonic languages. Perhaps even more pronounced was the impact of Hebrew on the related Glagolithic alphabet liturgically used by some Slavs, including the Croats, as late as the seventeenth century.

Most decisive was the Jewish influence on the rapidly expanding Khazar Empire, which covered a large segment of southern Russia from the lower Volga to the Crimea and which for a time controlled many Slavonic tribes as well. This influence attracted the attention of distant Arab geographers and literary historians. Muqaddasi did not wish to sound humorous when he described Khazaria as a large arid country, where "sheep, honey and Jews exist in large quantities," while the encylopedic historian of Arabic literature, Ibn an-Nadim, declared bluntly, "The Khazars use the Hebrew script."[3] Not surprisingly, both Byzantium and the Caliphate tried to draw the Khazar Empire into their respective orbits, the best method of securing such an alliance being the conversion of the desirable neighbor to one's own faith. But precisely because the Khazars wished to retain their neutrality, they repudiated both Christianity and Islam. To secure further noninterference, one of the Khazar rulers, Bulan, formally adopted the third monotheistic religion, Judaism (about 740). His example was followed by numerous Khazars, especially among the upper classes, although no effort was made to impose the Jewish religion upon the pagan masses or the Christian and Muslim minorities. In fact, religious toleration went so far that the supreme court of the empire allegedly consisted of two Jews, two Christians, two Muslims, and one pagan.

Nor was the Khazar Jewish faith a monolithic entity. Apart from continuing to embrace numerous sectarians, the Khazar Jews displayed an extraordinary type of orthodoxy which was often at variance with the teachings and rituals accepted elsewhere. For a long time the very classics of Jewish literature were extremely scarce; they were familiar only to a small minority of the educated Jewish Khazars. In time, at least according to one of their kings, Obadiah, they succeeded in importing some eastern rabbis and teachers who helped to reestablish a measure of religious conformity and to raise the level of Jewish education. In any case, Jews, whether of Jewish, Khazar, or other origin, became quite numerous in the Khazar districts and did not totally disappear even after the Khazars lost their imperial power and came under Russian and Tatar domination.[4]

KIEVAN RUSSIA

Upon the destruction of Khazaria, the center of gravity of that entire area shifted to Kievan Russia. Kiev—admiringly called by a Western contemporary, Adam of Bremen, "the rival of Constantinople and the most shining gem of the Greek Church"[5]—entered the scene of world history upon the conversion to Christianity of its ruler Vladimir (980–1015). *The Russian Primary Chronicle* reports the story of this conversion in picturesque detail, relating in particular the debate which allegedly had taken place before the prince between representatives of the three world religions, Christianity, Islam, and Judaism. This is a replica of a similar discussion supposedly conducted two and a half centuries earlier in Khazaria before Bulan decided to adopt Judaism. This time, we are told, Vladimir rejected the Jewish arguments, primarily because the Jewish spokesman had purportedly replied to his question of where the Jews lived by saying:

> We do not [live in Jerusalem] for the Lord was wroth with our forefathers, and scattered us all over the earth for our sins, while our land was given away to the Christians. Thereupon Vladimir exclaimed: How then dare you teach others when you yourselves are rejected by God and scattered? If God loved you, you would not be dispersed in strange lands. Do you intend to inflict the same misfortune on me?[6]

Precisely because Christianity in its Greek Orthodox form was but a recent growth and paganism was still deeply rooted in the Kievan people, the early Russian Church was quite intolerant toward Jews and the adherents of any faith other than its own. Most of its leaders were recruited from Byzantium, where religious intolerance had led to the reiterated outlawry of Judaism, although in other periods the Jewish communities were allowed to persist and at times even to flourish there. The first native Russian Metropolitan, Hilarion, outdid his local predecessors by writing a treatise contrasting "The Mosaic law and the Grace and Truth of Jesus Christ" (after 1051). He probably borrowed most of his arguments from St. Cyril's anti-Jewish polemical tract, since lost. When, under Byzantine pressure, he was deposed from his metropolitanate, he founded the famous Petcherskii (Cave) Monastery in Kiev in 1053, which soon became the main center of Russian Orthodox thinking. In his biography of the Byzantine Theodosius who served as its abbot from 1062 to 1074, the Russian chronicler Nestor tells us that the monk was searching out Jews in order to engage them in theological controversies, hoping to provoke them into inflicting upon him the coveted death of a martyr. That Judaism still represented a serious threat even to that monastery, however, is illustrated by another member, Nikita, who had allegedly tried to spread Jewish doctrines among his fellow monks, though he ultimately repented.

In the meantime Kiev's Jewish community grew in both size and affluence. In the twelfth century, and probably earlier, Jews lived in at least two quarters, in the so-called Podole and in the northeastern section, where in 1124 and 1146 a "Jewish gate" is mentioned in connection with some local disturbances. They were active in both business and politics. We are told that, after the death of Grand Duke Sviatopolk II (1093–1113), some Jews, as well as Kievan grandees, involved in that ruler's machinations, especially his salt monopoly, were attacked by the partisans of the newly elected Grand Duke, Vladimir II Monomakh (1113–25). Upon his tardy arrival Vladimir quickly restored order. Soon thereafter two influential Jews, Ephrem Moisevich and Anbal Yassin, figured prominently in a court conspiracy. But the majority seems to have remained neutral in these court conflicts and we hear of no retribution having been inflicted upon the community at large.

Culturally, too, the Kievan Jews made considerable progress. Although, like most other Jewish peripheral settlements of that period, that of the later Ukrainian capital remained inarticulate, we learn from incidental references in Western letters that it embraced some devotees of Jewish learning who were undoubtedly helped by visitors reaching Kiev from central Europe. Occasionally, Kievan students addressed pertinent inquiries to distinguished rabbis abroad, while one, Moses of Kiev, is recorded in France as a pupil of the leading Western Jewish scholar of the twelfth century, Jacob ben Meir Tam. Moses was apparently also in communication with Samuel ben Ali, head of the important Jewish Academy of Baghdad.

Their relatively advanced educational level enabled the Jews also to exert continued religious influence upon the Russian people. In this period foundations were laid for the spread of those Judaizing Russian sects which were to play so prominent a role in the subsequent history of the Russian Church. Much of the checkered evolution of Russian sectarianism, which understandably shunned the light of day and was largely recorded by its bitter enemies, still is shrouded in darkness. But the presence of a flourishing minority, cultivating its rituals and insisting upon its religious diversity, necessarily helped to nurture deviationist trends among the deeply religious Russian masses. Obviously, this very impact evoked the hostility of the official Church, which increased the vehemence of its anti-Jewish attacks and, before long, sought the complete elimination of this source of "contagion."[7]

MUSCOVITE XENOPHOBIA

After the Mongol conquest we hear very little about Jews in any territories of European Russia, except in the Crimea. Here the Genoese received a concession to develop the harbor of Kaffa (Feodosia) from where they traded with, and even politically controlled, the neighboring areas for about two centuries (1260–1475). Jewish traders soon established there independent Rabbanite and Karaite communities, probably recruited in part from descendants of the old settlers under Khazaria. The Karaite community developed a special Tatar dialect in which a number of its literary documents have been written even in recent generations. However, the figure of 4,000 houses allegedly inhabited by the two Jewish groups in Kaffa, according to Johannes Schiltberger, a traveler who had visited the Crimea between 1396 and 1427, is undoubtedly exaggerated.[8] Conditions became increasingly difficult in the fifteenth century as the expansion of the Ottoman Turks interposed a serious obstacle to the communications between Genoa and its Black Sea colonies. Although in 1449 the republic specifically ordered the local authorities to extend full protection to Jews, as well as to Greeks and Armenians, and the Jewish community soon thereafter expressed special satisfaction with the Genoese chief of police Nicoloso Bonaventura, its economic status constantly deteriorated, causing many Jews to depart.

In the main centers of Russian life, however, particularly Novgorod and Moscow, there seem to have been but few Jews. The prevailing xenophobia of both the Russian masses and their rulers kept out the Jews and other foreigners. True, the Russian liberator from the Golden Horde, Ivan III (1462–1505), made use of some Crimean Jews for his diplomatic negotiations with their khan. Curiously, one such Kaffa Jew, Khoza Kokos, tried to correspond with the tsar in Hebrew, but he had to change, at Ivan's instance, to another language and script ("Russian or Mohammedan," that is, Arabic) which was more readily understood in Moscow. Another Kaffan, Zechariah de Guizolfi, a Judaizer of Italian descent who married a local princess and was styled the Prince of Taman, even thought of settling in Moscow.[9]

Amicable developments of this type were cut short, however, when another Zechariah or Skharia, a Kievan Jew, settled in Novgorod and started engaging in religious propaganda. This great commercial center, which had attracted many foreigners, became the scene of turbulent socioreligious controversies which led to the formation of new sects. The impact of Balkan Bogomilism, to be sure, like that of the ancient Christian gnosticism from which it had stemmed, had many anti-Jewish implications. Yet Skharia quite willingly participated in the raging religious disputations. This mystery man, of obscure antecedents and with unknown objectives, apparently was so successful that under his influence a number of Novgorod nobles and clerics repudiated the divinity of Christ and the Trinitarian dogma, and insisted that the Messiah was yet to come. They also rejected the veneration of icons and adopted a number of other Jewish doctrines. Skharia was supported in these endeavors by two Jewish visitors from Lithuania. From Novgorod the heresy of *Judaizanti* spread also to Moscow. Ivan III himself brought back with him from a visit to Novgorod in 1479 two Judaizing priests whom he placed in two Moscow churches. Among the sympathizers with the new sect appeared such influential personalities as Ivan's daughter-in-law, Helena, and the chancellor, Fedor Kurizin. Alarmed, the Metropolitan of Novgorod, Gennadius, initiated a repressive action which, supported by the revered Joseph Sanin, founder of the Volokolamsk monastery, resulted in the decisions of several synods of the Russian Church between 1490 and 1504 condemning the Judaizing sect. Some apostates were publicly burned at the stake and the sect was again forced underground.[10]

Another characteristic incident occurred when Ivan III invited an eminent Jewish physician, Messer Leon, who because of internal squabbles in his community had been banished from Mantua, to extend medical care to the royal family. To the misfortune of the boastful Jewish physician, he was unable to cure the tsar's son, whereupon he was executed.[11]

Repressive measures of this kind continued under Ivan's successors, Vassilii Ivanovich (1505–33) and Ivan IV, the Terrible (1533–84). Not only did the tsars try to keep out the Jews from their own possessions, but when, in 1563, Ivan IV conquered Polotsk he forced the Jews to adopt Greek Orthodoxy, while three hundred resisters were thrown into the Dvina. For generations thereafter folk tales connected with this incident were being retold by the Jews of that region. Fortunately for the community, the forced converts and other survivors could again publicly profess Judaism after the reconquest of Polotsk by Poland in 1579. Ivan also rejected all advances on the part of the Polish kings that he allow Polish Jewish merchants to visit the Muscovite territories on business. He explained his refusal by claiming that the Jews were in the habit of importing "poisonous herbs" (medical?) into Russia and also of influencing the Russians to question their faith. In fact, in 1550 Ivan begged the Polish king, Sigismund Augustus, never to raise that question again.

Nor was this merely a personal animus of the tsar. His aversion to Jews and Judaism was shared by the empire's grandees who wished to maintain the homogeneous Orthodoxy of their population against any foreign influences. International considerations reinforced that intolerant mood. At least Dimitrii Gerasimov, sent by Vassilii to Rome to try to coordinate the activities of the Greek Orthodox and the Roman Catholic worlds against the Turkish menace, explained to the famous Renaissance publicist, Paolo Giovio, that Jews were not only thieves and generally harmful persons but that they also were responsible for teaching the Turks the art of manufacturing gunpowder and cannons. During the great interregnum after Ivan IV's death, the rumor that the false so-called second Dimitrii (1607–1608), a pretender to the Russian throne, was really a Jew was widely spread by his opponents and helped undermine his claims. When in 1610 the Polish Prince Vladislav was elected to the tsarist throne, his adherents stipulated with him in advance that no churches or chapels of the Catholic or any other non-Orthodox denomination should be allowed in Russia and no one should be induced to observe the Roman or any other ritual. "Jews must not be admitted to the Muscovite Empire whether on business or for any other purpose."[12] This anti-Jewish and antiforeign agitation, including the rumors about Dimitrii's Jewish descent, emanated in part from the native Romanov family (distantly related to the previous Rurik dynasty), who, partially through these methods, succeeded in 1613 in securing the throne for themselves. It is small wonder, then, that the new tsars staunchly adhered to their predecessors' policy of keeping the Jews away from their domains.

More serious were the anti-Jewish moves initiated by Alexei Mikhailovich (1645–76). Drawn into the Cossack uprisings against Poland, Alexei invaded the neighboring provinces of Poland and Lithuania, where his troops found long-established and populous Jewish communities. No sooner did the Russian army enter Moghilev than the commander banished all Jews. Expecting the return of the Polish regime, the Jews tarried in leaving the city, but upon the approach of the Polish troops many were massacred by the Russians. Their Vitebsk coreligionists, perhaps forewarned, helped put up a staunch defense. However, the city was captured and most Jews were taken prisoner and sent back to the interior of Russia. Ironically, these deportees formed the nucleus of a new Jewish settlement, for even after the peace treaty of 1667 provided for an exchange of war prisoners, some of them decided to remain in Russia. True, the government renewed in 1676 the prohibition of Jewish settlement in Moscow, but it could not quite prevent Jewish survivors of the Cossack massacres and the Russian invasion in the borderline areas, now permanently annexed by Muscovy, from remaining in these localities.[13]

No significant change occurred even during the Westernizing regime of Peter the Great (1682–1725). On principle, Peter might have welcomed Jews, as he did many other foreigners in order to introduce Western methods of production and Western science. However, he felt that his people were not yet ripe for their admission. A story, perhaps apocryphal, is told about Peter's interview with the pro-Jewish mayor of Amsterdam, Nicolaes Witsen, during his visit to the Dutch city in 1698. When Witsen transmitted to him a petition from leading Amsterdam Jews for the admission of their coreligionists to his country, the tsar readily conceded the advantages of such a move but he claimed that "the time has not yet come to bring these two nationalities together." He also felt that, if admitted, Jews would greatly suffer from the hostility of the Russian people.

Behind these rationalizations were concealed Peter's own anti-Jewish prejudices. On another occasion, he is supposed to have exclaimed, "They are all rogues and cheats; I am trying to eradicate evil, not to increase it." The tsar may have been influenced also by the rumors concerning a ritual murder, allegedly committed by Jews of Gorodnia near Chernigov, in 1702. On the other hand, when during the Great Northern War with Sweden, the Russian troops approached in 1708 the city of Mstislavl, Peter, if we are to believe a contemporary Hebrew entry in the local communal register, personally entered the synagogue and stopped an incipient attack on Jews by ordering the execution of thirteen ringleaders.[14]

Nor was Peter averse to making exceptions, especially in favor of converted Jews. At least one Courland banker, Lipman Levy, though a professing Jew, was not only allowed to come to Moscow on business, but as the Court's fiscal agent he was also able to play a considerable political role. Other foreigners included Iberian New Christians (Marranos), like Peter's court jester, Ian Lacosta (Acosta), whose biting satire helped the emperor to expose to public ridicule some of the boyars' "backward" mores. Of greater importance were two other converts: Baron Peter Shafirov and Count Anton Devier. Shafirov was baptized in his childhood by his converted Polish-Jewish father who had settled in Moscow. Because of his extraordinary linguistic ability and diplomatic skill he rose quickly in the ranks of Peter's bureaucracy, achieving the titles of baron and privy councillor. He also served as vice-chancellor and senator of the empire, accompanied Peter on his journeys to the West, and was largely responsible for achieving, in 1711, an honorable peace with Turkey after the Turkish army had surrounded Peter and his outnumbered troops. Devier was a young Portuguese Jew living in Amsterdam when Peter arrived there on his first trip in 1698. He so impressed the tsar that he was immediately taken into Peter's services after accepting Christianity. Before long he was given the responsible position of police commissioner in the new capital of St. Petersburg; he performed administrative wonders in helping build up the new metropolis.

Both these men, however, ran afoul of Prince Alexander Menshikov, Peter's favorite, doubly influential because the tsarina (later Catherine I) had been his maidservant and mistress before she married Peter. Shafirov appeared to Menshikov not only as a dangerous rival, but also as a quarrelsome partner in a joint business venture at Archangel. After a brief trial the vice-chancellor was deprived of all his honors; only moments before his scheduled execution he was taken off the scaffold and sent to Siberia. Devier decided to marry Menshikov's old-maid sister and finally achieved his aim by informing the tsar that the lady was pregnant with his child. Before long Menshikov found an opportunity to take his revenge. Devier, too, was deprived of all honors and exiled to Siberia, where he performed important administrative duties with his usual competence. After a few years a rapid turn in the wheel of fortune, characteristic of early eighteenth-century Russia, brought both men back to St. Petersburg. They were rehabilitated, but, with their health ruined, they did not live long enough to enjoy their renewed influence. Independently, Menshikov was now sent off to Siberia.[15]

Perhaps as in other countries such influential converts might have paved the way for the admission of professing Jews. But these promising beginnings were cut short under the brief, intolerant regimes of Catherine I, Peter II, and Anna Ivanovna (1725–40). In 1727 all Jews were formally banished from the country. Even one Zundel Hirsh, who had contracted to supply silver for the Russian mint, had difficulties in securing delay until the completion of this transaction.[16] In the border district of Smolensk, long a battlefield between Poland-Lithuania and Muscovy, a few Jews maintained a precarious foothold after its permanent incorporation into the Muscovite Empire. However, when in the small community of Sverovich one Baruch Leibov dared to erect a synagogue across the street from a church and to influence a retired naval captain, Alexander Voznitsin, to study the Bible in the Jewish vein, and finally to undergo formal conversion to Judaism, the ensuing outcry reached Anna's ears. Both culprits were brought to St. Petersburg and condemned to death. Their burning in a public square before a very large crowd on July 15, 1738, sounded a permanent warning against the possible heterodox implications of the admission of other Jews to the Empire. In the following year the Senate decreed the expulsion of all Jews from the Ukrainian and White Russian territories annexed by Russia. Though postponed because of the then raging Russo-Turkish war, this decree was executed in 1740, affecting 292 men and 281 women scattered through 130 manorial estates.

This exclusive policy was pursued with even greater vigor by the new Tsarina Elizabeth Petrovna (1741–62). Generally, a religious fanatic who also ordered the quiet demolition of many mosques in the southern districts (she refrained from publicizing this ukase only out of fear that it might provoke reprisals by the Ottoman authorities against their Christian subjects), she ordered in 1742 that

> all Jews, male and female, of whatever occupation and standing shall, at the promulgation of this Our ukase, be immediately deported, together with all their property, from Our whole Empire, both from the Great Russian and Little Russian cities, villages, and hamlets. They shall henceforth not be admitted to Our Empire under any pretext and for any purpose, unless they be willing to adopt Christianity of the Greek persuasion. Such baptized persons shall be allowed to live in Our Empire, but not to leave the country.

Elizabeth strictly adhered to this policy, and, according to an undoubtedly exaggerated Russian report of 1753, 35,000 Jews had been deported from Russia during the preceding decade. Even a Marrano physician, Antonio Sanchez, who had lived in St. Petersburg since 1731 and been in charge of the medical department of the army, was forced by the empress in 1748 to give up his honorific post at the Academy of Science and leave for Paris.[17]

Intervening developments in the industrial and commercial fields, to be sure, induced many enlightened Russians to abandon their traditional aversion to Jews. A number of petitions reached the Court, especially from merchants in the Ukraine and Riga, who felt that these restrictive policies played havoc with their international trade. They clamored for the readmission of Jewish merchants who otherwise were diverting much trade to Germany to the detriment of these border provinces. In 1743 the Senate was induced to advocate such a readmission at least "to the border localities." But Elizabeth simply jotted down on the Senate report: "From enemies of Christ I wish neither gain nor profit."

As a result of such constant pressures, no organized Jewish community could function even in the territories on the left bank of the

Dnieper taken over from Poland after 1654. Leibov's tragic experiment with erecting a Jewish house of worship demonstrated the intensity of anti-Jewish feelings permeating Moscow's society and government. It was only after 1772 that the Jewish presence became a permanent, indeed an ever growing, factor in the evolution of the Tsarist Empire.

[2]

Under Catherine II and Alexander I

1762–1825

So deep-rooted were the Russian majority's anti-Jewish prejudices that even Catherine II (1762–96), despite her own more rationalistic attitude, proceeded gingerly in the Jewish question. The problem came up during the first weeks of her regime when she was still uncertain of the legally questionable dethronement of her husband, Peter III. The Senate unanimously favored the admission of Jews. Yet remembering Elizabeth's sharp declaration, Catherine felt that, since she had become tsarina for the defense of the Greek Orthodox faith and since she had to consider the wishes of a predominantly pious people and a powerful clergy, she could not approve such a far-reaching reversal of earlier policies. She could but slightly relax the existing prohibition and, through specific administrative measures, admit some Jews particularly to the newly conquered southern provinces which actually cried out for new settlers. By 1769 she was indeed ready formally to open the Neo-Russian territories to Jewish arrivals.

A new era began with the partitions of Poland in 1772, 1793, and 1795. Each annexation of Polish territory brought into the expanding empire ever-larger masses of Jews. In 1795 these were joined by coreligionists inhabiting the duchy of Courland which, long under Polish overlordship, had been for some time a Russian satellite but now was directly incorporated into the imperial structure. The Neo-Russian territories, on the other hand—greatly enlarged in 1774 in the treaty of Kuchuk-Kinarji with the Ottoman Empire—embraced but few Jews. Only the Crimea included some centuries-old Karaite communities, whose allegiance to Rabbanite Judaism was rather loose and who at the whim of the Russian authorities could be declared a separate sect with a political and legal status of its own. It was, indeed, to the interest of both the government and this relatively small sectarian minority that it be legally separated from the main body of the Jewish people (including some Rabbanite "Krimchaks"), whose integration into the ethno-religious structure of the empire was so greatly to preoccupy the imperial authorities.

Complications arose immediately after the first partition of Poland. For example, Catherine II and many of her advisers were sufficiently influenced by the spirit of French Enlightenment for her to invite Denis Diderot to come to St. Petersburg and complete the Great Encyclopedia in peace. Realistically, too, the traditional exclusion of Jews from the Russian Empire no longer made sense (in her letter of 1773 to Diderot Catherine mentioned, indeed, the residence of three or four Jews in her capital). So long as the empire consisted principally of Russians and small "backward" minorities whose speedy absorption by the Russian nation appeared assured, an ethno-religious group of known perseverance and an ancient history could appear as a menace to homogeneity. Now, however, Catherine's dominions included millions of Poles, Lithuanians, Baltic Germans, and Tartars, whose faiths—Catholic, Lutheran, and Muslim—and well-established cultures could not be expected to be completely absorbed in the Russian language and Church.

Among these heterogeneous groups, in part inhabiting the economically most advanced provinces, Jews constituted at first but a relatively minor element, since the first partition had brought only some 27,000 Jews under the scepter of the tsarina. Western doctrines and Catherine's personal religious tolerance tended to moderate the imperial policies toward the Jewish minority, at least until it began clashing with some deep-rooted vested interests. Here, too, the methods of enlightened absolutism, as practiced in Prussia and Austria by Frederick the Great and Joseph II, promised effectively to mold the lives of this extraordinary, and hence somewhat difficult, minority according to the plans of the empire's central authorities.

Not surprisingly, like most of their contemporaries in that Age of Reason, Catherine and her immediate successors believed that human affairs could be regulated from above by well-thought-out and well-intentioned plans without reference to traditions and established institutions. It was not until 1803 that the level-headed statesman Mikhail Mikhailovich Speransky argued for gradualness also in the treatment of

Jews. Although not yet the influential minister that he was to become a few years later, Speransky insisted at a meeting of the Committee for the Amelioration of the Jews that

> reforms enacted by state power are, for the most part, unstable; they are particularly ineffective when they run counter to centuries-old customs. It is preferable and safer, therefore, to propel the Jews toward perfection by opening to them new avenues for the pursuit of happiness, supervising their activities from a distance, and removing obstacles from their path, but without the use of force. One ought not to establish new special agencies acting in their behalf but rather encourage their own fruitful pursuits. In short, as few restrictions and as much freedom as possible—these are the simple ingredients of an effective social order.[1]

Such ideas, anticipating the nineteenth century historical schools of jurisprudence, were premature even in 1803. They would have fallen on completely deaf ears in Catherine's entourage two or three decades earlier.

JEWISH RIGHTS

At first the empress saw no reason for singling out the Jews for special legislation. In fact, after incorporating the eastern provinces of Poland-Lithuania in 1772, she issued a manifesto welcoming all inhabitants (including Jews) as her new subjects and promising them the continued exercise of the rights they had enjoyed under the previous regimes and equal treatment with the older Russian population. Persuaded by the then dominant mercantilist theories that Jews could help to develop industry and trade, the proclamation actually urged them not to change their occupations of businessmen and craftsmen. Before long they were invited to join the respective three guilds of "merchants," or become "burghers," a category embracing most of the urban population to which by virtue of their occupations and financial strength they would normally belong.

In subsequent years Jews were indeed allowed to participate fully in the public life of their municipalities. In her general constitutional reform Catherine farsightedly tried to decentralize the governmental machinery of her far-flung empire and to place more responsibility upon the self-governmental municipal bodies of two burgomasters and four councillors each (in smaller townships, one burgomaster and two councillors) and, in the countryside, upon the provincial representations of landowners. At first Jews were admitted to these municipal organs on a basis of equality. This was indeed a revolutionary step, for nowhere else in Europe did Jews enjoy such political rights, except in Tuscany, where at about the same time Grand Duke Leopold (later Emperor Leopold II) was also opening municipal offices to his Jewish subjects.

As in many other phases of her administration, however, Catherine found that there was a tremendous gap between intention and fulfillment. In practice, the local burghers often sabotaged the imperial decree relating to the Jewish franchise. More generally, their resistance led to the creation of separate curias of Jewish and non-Jewish voters, whereby Jews were deprived of all influence over the election of the non-Jewish burgomasters and councillors. This separation became doubly meaningful when a decree of 1796 reduced the maximum number of Jewish councillors to one-third. Even that provision was disregarded in practice, many municipalities having no Jewish councillors at all, while in a few others Jews formed the majority of the council. Nor was all this truly significant. Despite Catherine's intentions the seat of power remained with the bureaucracy. The fate of Jews, like that of the rest of the population, depended far more on the decisions, even whims, of local officials or at best of provincial governors than on those of any freely elected municipal or guild councils. Thus a measure which might have been a harbinger of a truly egalitarian treatment evaporated into thin air.

Further complications were caused by the substantial number of Jews living in villages belonging to great Polish and Lithuanian landlords, where they were treated almost on a par with the villeins. At the same time these landowners' income to a very large extent depended on their Jewish agents, who sold their surplus produce on markets in the country or abroad, exercised their monopolistic rights of distilling liquor, sold it in taverns, and extended credit to the farming population. Alcoholism being quite prevalent among the peasant masses, this situation naturally led to much friction between them and the Jewish innkeepers and moneylenders, who on their part were often squeezed dry by the landlords and the state's tax collectors. The government could not shut its eyes to this evil heritage of Poland's anarchical regime, especially since the peasantry in both the old and the new provinces was in a state of more or less permanent unrest. We must bear in mind that serfdom had been a relatively modern institution in Russia and that the peasants had reconciled themselves to it mainly because the landowning aristocracy had largely taken over the defense of the country. That is why when in 1762 Catherine freed the noble class from military service, rumors began spreading among the peasants that she had thereby also abolished the state of serfdom, a fact which the selfish landlords had allegedly concealed from their dependent masses. Certainly, outbreaks like that led by the Cossack pretender, Emilian I. Pugachev, in 1773–74, which spread like wildfire through the Volga and Ural regions, served as a serious warning.

Matters came to a head after Catherine's death under the weak regime of Paul I (1796–1801). In 1799 a severe famine ravaged many western districts. To answer the grievances of the suffering farmers, the government decided to consult the assemblies of landlords in Minsk and other provinces. It may have been well aware that the mismanagement of their estates by those very landlords and the entire institution of serfdom were mainly responsible for these catastrophic shortages. Yet it had to place its reliance on the landed aristocracy, the mainstay of its regime. Understandably, these nobles did not blame themselves, but rather explained the crop failures through natural and other causes, aggravated by the Jewish innkeepers' exploitation of the peasants. Their suggestions culminated in the ousting of Jews from the entire liquor industry and the handing over of all production and distribution thereof directly to the landlords or their appointees. Thus the village Jews, who had long suffered from their intermediate position between nobles and villeins and who as far back as 1648–49 had paid for it a tremendous price in life and treasure during the Cossack massacres in the Ukrainian areas, now found themselves squeezed again between the millstones of aristocracy and peasantry.

INCIPIENT SEPARATION

Another cause of concern to the Russian regime was the traditional Jewish autonomy. From the days of the Babylonian Exile the Jews of the dispersion had developed a vast network of communal institutions of their own which provided not only for the religious needs of their members but also took care of such semisecular requirements as education, the judiciary, and social welfare. Under Polish rule, the *kahal*, as this communal structure was called, served also as a major tax-collecting agency for the government. To many Russian officials this all-embracing separatist institution appeared, as we shall see, incompatible with the desired incorporation of Jews into the various estates to which they belonged by virtue of their occupations or financial standing. The more Catherine herself and her advisers were permeated with the ideas of Western Enlightenment, the more they resented this Jewish "state within the state."

Yet they saw no way of abolishing it entirely. Although little was publicly said about it, one could not overlook the substantial communal debts carried with them by the respective *kahal*s. According to statistical data dating from pre-partition Poland, it appears that at that time the Jewish communities owed the vast amount of 2,305,111 zlotys in capital and 196,478 zlotys in interest. Curiously, only some 900,000 were owed to Jews. The next largest group consisted of the clergy, whose claims of

842,777 zlotys in part dated back to the seventeenth century, while the nobles appeared as creditors of amounts aggregating 737,468 zlotys.[2]

The abolition of the *kahal*, or even a substantial reduction of its authority, would have raised the specter of insolvency, or at least of a protracted forced liquidation of these debts which, for instance, even in more prosperous France engaged the attention of administrators and judges for decades after the Jewish emancipation. In Russia nobody seriously thought of such extreme measures, particularly since there, too, the Jewish communal organs could be put to good use in increasing the governmental revenue from the newly acquired Jewish population. These special contributions could be collected quite apart from the doubling of taxes due from Jewish members of the various estates, which, perhaps in reminiscence of a similar twofold tax previously imposed upon Christian sectarians, was early instituted by Catherine and continued by her successors. The fiscal needs of the empire thus combined with the desires of the Jewish people itself to maintain the old Jewish communal structure fairly intact.

Under these circumstances the government considered it wiser not to let the Jews spread out into the empire's interior provinces. Complex as the situation already was in the west, it did not wish to complicate further the internal conditions in old Russia where Jews faced the perennial hostility of the population, further aggravated now by competitive business factors. The merchant class of Moscow went up in arms against the few newly arriving Jewish merchants who were able to undersell it by importing cheaper goods of higher quality. After a Moscow protest in 1790, the tsarina determined to hold back the influx of Jews from the western provinces. In her decree of 1791, she provided that the rights extended to Jews as members of guilds of merchants and burghers related only to territories newly taken over by her. These included the Neo-Russian provinces which so badly needed new settlers that she even contemplated inviting German colonists from abroad. Here, as well as in her two other decrees of 1783 and 1794, Catherine thus laid the foundations for what was to be styled the Pale of Jewish Settlement, which as such was injurious to Jewish status and in the long run was also detrimental to the best interests of the entire imperial population.

Beset by the complexities of this situation, the Russian regime embarked upon the usual course: the appointment of investigating committees. Especially under Paul and during the early years of Alexander I (1801–25) committees of ministers—for the most part presided over by the minister of the interior, Prince Victor P. Kochubey—went rather deeply into the peculiarities of the Jewish position and collected all sorts of opinions from informed, uninformed, and misinformed officials, groups of landlords, and some Jews. Among the outstanding opinions rendered was that by Ivan Grigorevich Friesel, governor of the Lithuanian province. Of German descent and imbued with the new ideas of the rights of man, Friesel advocated a thoroughgoing reform of Jewish religious and cultural as well as economic life. Curiously, he was seconded therein by some influential Jewish leaders such as Nota Khaimovich Notkin, who often visited St. Petersburg on business. In a similar vein, reflective of the contemporary debates of the Mendelssohnian circle in Prussia, ushering in the Jewish enlightenment movement in central Europe, were also the memoranda written by two other Jewish merchants, Abraham Peretz and Loeb Nikolaevich Nevakhovich. The latter even published in 1803–1804 a pamphlet in both Russian and Hebrew under the characteristic title of "The Outcry of the Daughter of Judah," the first Jewish apologetic work in the Russian language. These voices were not representative of Jewish majority opinion, however. Most communal elders engaged in delaying tactics and usually advocated the postponement of any reforms for some twenty years.

Probably the most influential voice heard in the days of Paul and again under Alexander I was that of Gabriel Romanovich Derzhavin. Quite prominent as a Russian poet of the ultrapatriotic school, Derzhavin was born and educated in the Russian interior and probably had never seen a Jew before he was dispatched by Paul to the western provinces to review the Jewish situation (1799–1800). Here he consulted members of various classes, including Jesuit teachers. He also received a memorandum from an "enlightened" Jewish doctor, Elias Jacob Frank, who, during his earlier Berlin studies, had absorbed much of the ideology then dominant in the progressive Jewish circles of the Prussian capital. Finally, in 1800, Derzhavin submitted a report bearing the characteristic title: "An Opinion on How to Avert the Scarcity of Food in White Russia Through the Curbing of the Jews' Avaricious Occupations, Their Reformation and Other Matters."[3]

Derzhavin was convinced that, although the usefulness of the Jewish people to society at large was questionable, the Jews always managed somehow "to lord it over the nations among whom they lived." Yet he did not believe in their elimination from the country. With pietistic resignation he wrote:

> Since Providence, for the realization of some unknown purpose, has left this dangerous people on the face of the earth and has not destroyed it, the governments under whose rule it lives ought to tolerate it. It is also their duty to take care of them in such a manner that the Jews be useful to themselves and to society at large in whose midst they live.

To achieve this purpose Derzhavin proposed the division of the Jewish group into four classes—merchants, city burghers, rural burghers, and commoners—largely dependent on their occupations and the assessment of their property, ranging from 50 to 1,000 rubles. He advocated the suppression of the *kahal* not only for the benefit of Jews but also as a defensive measure for the protection of Christianity. In its place there should be established purely religious institutions like the synagogues and the rabbinate, headed by a central organ which he called Sendarin (Sanhedrin). He also advocated restrictions of the Jewish franchise in municipal elections and specific economic disabilities. Nevertheless he was convinced that, if accepted, his proposals would make future generations remember Emperor Paul as a benefactor of Jews "who, as fanatic and stiff-necked enemies of the Christians, are destined by fate to remain eternally scattered."

Probably even without Paul's death, Derzhavin's proposals would not have been seriously considered in St. Petersburg. Although as minister of justice he was appointed by Alexander I to another committee in 1803, his influence was not marked; it vanished altogether after his resignation from the ministry. On the other hand, the committee felt the impact of Adam Czartoryski, both because of his strong personality and his intimate friendship with the tsar. Czartoryski, a Western-oriented statesman, was greatly influenced in turn by the debates which had taken place in Poland in connection with the great reforms undertaken, though not fulfilled, by the so-called Quadrennial Diet of 1788–92, and especially by the liberal proposals submitted at that time by the Polish publicists, Count Tadeusz Czacki and Mateusz Butrymowicz. The outcome of the deliberations of Alexander's committee was a mixture of liberal theoretical postulates and highly restrictive practical measures.

Such a mixture greatly appealed to the tsar in the early "liberal" period of his reign, and he readily included many of the committee's suggestions in the decree he issued on December 9, 1804, which may be considered Russia's first fundamental law regarding Jews.[4] This law upheld the admission of the Jews to municipal councils and general courts of justice while maintaining their *kahal* organization. The *kahal's* elders now had to be elected every three years, which would impede the theretofore customary semidictatorial perpetuation in office. Rabbis and communal elders (who had to continue raising the government taxes) were speedily to acquire the knowledge of either Russian, Polish, or German, in which languages Jews were soon to conduct all their business. All schools up to universities were to be open to Jewish students, who, moreover, were to be safeguarded against any violation of their religious scruples. Secondary school pupils, as well as Jewish municipal councillors and travelers beyond the Pale, were to abandon their peculiar Jewish garb. Ironically, some Jews themselves argued that because as a rule they wore beards, they would prefer to be clad in the Russian rather than the German attire. At the same time, the Jewish communities were allowed to maintain their own schools, but these had to adopt the general curricula and use the general languages of instruction employed in public schools, replacing the methods theretofore in use in the old-type schools of rabbinic learning.

If these assimilatory measures were greeted at least by the small progressive minority of Jews with considerable elation, the other provisions of the statute caused general consternation. To cut short the perennial difficulties between Jews and peasants, the Jews were given the choice of either becoming farmers themselves, in which case they could settle not only in the eleven provinces (plus Courland) theretofore assigned to them but also in the more remote provinces of Astrakhan and the Caucasus, or else leaving the rural districts altogether. They were to be evacuated from the villages of Astrakhan and the Caucasus and of Little and New Russia within about two years (by January 1, 1807) and from the other rural areas one year thereafter.

We shall see that some Jews were indeed ready to start a new life in agriculture. But their leaders realized much better than the statesmen in St. Petersburg the enormous practical difficulties confronting such mass resettlement on the land. On the other hand, the cities offered few economic opportunities to the rural evacuees. At the death of Catherine II in 1796, Russia's urban inhabitants were estimated at only 1,310,000 in a total population of some 36,000,000 (including 7,000,000 newly acquired subjects). The cities already included a large Jewish population that was having difficulty eking out a meager existence. The addition of many thousands of displaced persons was bound to play havoc with the entire Jewish economic and social structure.

THE NAPOLEONIC WARS

Implementation of this drastic measure had to be suspended, however, largely because of unexpected developments on the international scene. Internally, too, confronted with the loss of their agents, many landlords submitted petitions arguing at least for the postponement of this threatened removal. Victor P. Kochubey likewise saw the difficulties in transplanting no less than 60,000 Jewish families, or more than 300,000 souls, into overcrowded urban areas.

The decisive factor, however, was Napoleon I's move to reconstitute the ancient Jewish Sanhedrin with the participation of world Jewry. As conceived by the emperor of the French, delegates from all countries were to reestablish this supreme organ of the Jewish people which, discontinued since ancient times, could now serve again as the authoritative interpreter of Jewish religious law. Austria and Russia, embracing masses of Jewish subjects, took fright. The Russian government undoubtedly shared the fears expressed by Count Clemens Metternich, then Austrian ambassador in Paris, in his letter of October 23, 1806. Referring to Napoleon's preparations for an invasion of central Europe, Metternich wrote: "There is no doubt that he will not fail to present himself as a liberator to the Christian people of Poland and as a messiah to its immense Jewish population."[5] The Russian government, too, became apprehensive that French sympathizers among the Russian Jews might adversely affect the prospective Russian military operations on the side of Austria.

Even before Russia's defeat in the "battle of the three emperors" at Austerlitz in December, 1806, Alexander decided to appoint a new committee to review the Jewish situation. In February, 1807, he dispatched Senator Ivan A. Alexeiev to the western provinces, euphemistically instructing him to ascertain to what extent "the military circumstances and the present condition of the border provinces as well as the economic ruin of the Jews, which is inevitable if their expulsion be enforced," made such resettlement difficult or impossible. Jewish deputies, especially Zundel Sonnenberg, a prominent businessman with intimate connections at court, also pressed hard for the suspension of these deportations. True, after concluding the alliance with Napoleon at Tilsit in 1807, Alexander's fears of French intervention receded, and prompted by his new instructions, some local authorities proceeded with the execution of the old order. The difficulties became so immediately manifest, however, that, after the uprooting of several thousand families, the government suspended all further deportations. They were resumed only at the very end of Alexander's regime in 1824–25.[6]

Napoleon's invasion of Russia was, of course, merely postponed. In 1812 he finally embarked upon that fateful campaign which, after bringing his troops all the way to Moscow, ended with the disaster of his *Grande Armée* and spelled the beginning of the end of his meteoric career. To forestall Jewish cooperation with the invading armies—such cooperation was indeed expected on the part of the Poles (including some Polish Jews) craving liberation—the government initiated an anti-French propaganda campaign among the Jewish masses. It did not take at face value the professions of loyalty by Jewish communities which, under both Catherine and Alexander had actually ordered patriotic poems in Hebrew and German from the Berlin poet Naphtali Herz Weisel (Wessely) for presentation to these monarchs on their visits to the western provinces (1780, 1801, etc.). At least one of these panegyrics was translated into German by Moses Mendelssohn himself.[7]

To persuade the population that it was better off under its Russian regime, the government now resumed the arguments already advanced after Austerlitz by the Holy Synod. To arouse Christian public opinion the synod had pointed out that during his Egyptian campaign, Napoleon had associated with the persecutors of Christianity and proclaimed himself a defender of Islam.

> To the greater shame of the Church he assembled in France Jewish synagogues, ordered to pay honor to the rabbis, and reestablished the great Jewish Synedrion, that same godless congregation which once dared to condemn to crucifixion our Lord and Saviour Jesus Christ. He now attempts to unite the Jews scattered by divine wrath over the whole world and to lead them to the overthrow of Christ's Church and to (O horrible impudence overstepping all his wickedness!) the proclamation of a false messiah in the person of Napoleon.

At the same time Jews were informed that by convoking the Sanhedrin, Napoleon had wished to initiate far-reaching religious reforms in order to undermine the very foundations of Jewish Orthodoxy.[8]

Without such governmental pleading most Russian Jews proved loyal to the tsar. Apart from their fears of the French type of emancipation, with all the perils it involved for their traditional religious observance and their vested communal interests, Jews had had a long record of loyalty to their respective governments. Only under extreme provocation or a severe persecution did they occasionally waver. In Russia, in particular, they were told by their own leaders, then and later, that the tsar was really a benevolent ruler of all his subjects and that the repressive measures against the Jews originated either from the evil advice of Jew-baiting counselors or from local officials acting without the tsar's knowledge. To the pro-Russian leaders belonged the outstanding hasidic rabbi, Shneur Zalman of Ladi, who so strongly advocated unflinching allegiance to Russia that upon the approach of the French armies, he had to flee for his life deep into Russia's interior. Another hasidic rabbi, Israel the Maggid (Preacher) of Kozienice, punned on Napoleon's name, using the biblical phrase *napol tippol* (thou shalt surely fall, Esther 6:13). In practice, too, Jews, though not yet formally drafted into the army, performed many useful services for the Russian troops, first during their retreat and then at their triumphant return, through furnishing them necessary supplies and providing useful information about the movements of the French forces.

Alexander I realized the value of that loyalty. Harking back to his earlier liberalism, he became at times a spokesman for Jewish rights beyond Russia's frontiers. He lent a willing ear particularly to Sonnenberg and to another Jewish agent, Eliezer (Lazar) Dillon, who frequently appeared at headquarters before and during the tsar's sojourn at the Congress of Vienna, the Vienna police speaking glibly of "Tsar Alexander's two court Jews." Among other matters, that Congress adopted a "Confederate Act" to serve as the constitution of the newly formed Germanic Confederation; it included certain safeguards for Jewish rights previously enacted by the member states. Alexander felt that as a signatory of the Treaty of Vienna, he had to help uphold the provisions of that act. When after 1815 the growing German reaction led the free cities of Frankfurt, Bremen, and Lübeck to abrogate the rights their Jewish inhabitants had attained during the French occupation, Russia's diplomatic agents joined those of Austria, Prussia, and England in reiteratedly protesting against this infringement of the Confederate constitution. More dramatically, Alexander I lent a willing ear to the British missionary, Lewis Way, who had visited him in St. Petersburg and who later, while the tsar was attending the Congress of Aix-la-Chapelle, submitted to him a memorandum advocating full emancipation of all European Jewry. Alexander ordered his foreign minister, Count Charles Nesselrode, to submit this memorandum to the other members of the Congress and to urge for it sympathetic consideration. This move proved both belated and abortive, however. In the increasingly reactionary atmosphere of the early post-Napoleonic era the European statesmen were in no mood to hasten Jewish emancipation against a growingly hostile public opinion.[9]

Nor was that anti-Jewish mood limited to the western countries. In the patriotic fervor of 1812 the tsarist regime had to fall back on the old national-religious loyalties of the Russian people. Liberals like Speransky had to be discharged and replaced by inferior, but reliably Orthodox, counselors. The tsar's new chief adviser, Admiral Alexander S. Shishkov, reminisced that he and the tsar had often read together selections from the Hebrew prophets which seemed to fit particularly the crisis of the moment; both men allegedly shed "tears of overcharged emotion." At that time a newly founded Bible Society evoked such an echo in the population that it could not "satisfy the hunger of millions of our countrymen," according to the society's president, Prince Alexander N. Golitsin. While this Bible-mindedness of Russian society helped stimulate certain sectarian trends and by 1826 was found to be a danger to Russian Orthodoxy, the newly rising waves of religiosity and mysticism (one need but recall the tremendous influence exercised by the mystic ladies Baroness Barbara Juliane Krüdener and Madame Catherine Tatarinov upon the tsar himself) cut short whatever Western liberal tendencies had made themselves felt in Russian society and the court *camarilla* in Alexander's earlier days.[10]

This general reactionary mood could accrue only to the disadvantage of Jews. Hostility toward them flared up on several occasions soon after the War of 1812. Golitsin, Alexander's lifelong friend, had been placed in 1810 in charge of the religious minorities, although he continued to serve as procurator of the Holy Synod, and as such was the leading lay executive of the Russian Orthodox Church. His and his associates' bent of mind clearly showed itself in a rather minor and unpublicized affair of 1814. During the summer of that year the thirteen-year-old daughter of Rabbi David Slutsky of the then rapidly growing Jewish community of Kiev was kidnapped one Friday night from her home, held incommunicado from her parents for several months, converted to Christianity, and married off to a Christian husband. She succeeded in smuggling out a few notes to her parents, indicating her chagrin about the separation and her unwillingness to abandon Judaism. Once she escaped from her guardians, but was quickly overtaken. When the matter finally reached the synod in St. Petersburg it decided that the conversion was perfectly legal. It apparently even instituted proceedings against the unhappy father for having "maligned" the local churchmen. We do not know from the extant archival documentation the ultimate outcome of that affair, but that there was an obvious miscarriage of justice seems beyond question. Golitsin must have taken a hand in these unfortunate proceedings, although three years later he was to uphold the right of the Jews to be heard through their own deputies.[11]

Even more threatening was the outcropping of Blood Accusations in Grodno in 1816 and Velizh in 1823. These allegations that Jews murdered a Christian (usually a young boy) in order to secure his blood for their Passover ritual, and other manifestations of popular animosity that the government failed to counteract, were symbolic of the steady retrogression in the empire's policies toward the Jews.[12]

More far-reaching was the renewed expulsion of Jews from rural districts. According to a decree of April 11, 1823, all Jews were to be evacuated before January 1, 1824, from villages in the provinces of Moghilev and Vitebsk. In the following nine months some 20,000 Jews were removed into the overcrowded neighboring cities without any provision having been made for their housing or employment. The resulting misery was so great, however, that in 1825 the government had to suspend further deportations and allow many displaced families to return to their prior habitats. On May 1, 1823, the tsar also appointed another ministerial committee, ostensibly to devise means for making Jews more "useful" to the state, but in fact to find new ways to reduce their number. This anti-Jewish reaction was to reach its climax under Alexander's successor.[13]

[3]

Under Nicholas I and Alexander II

1825–1881

Alexander I's latter-day romanticism and his mystic leanings made him increasingly impatient with the Jewish resistance to conversionist efforts. Not only the Bible Society, but also a special Society of Israelitic Christians started with high hopes of converting Jews to Christianity. The results proved utterly disappointing, but the ensuing conflicts added fuel to the existing religious antagonisms. Foreign observers were easily misled. The French playwright Jacques Ancelot wrote to his friend X. B. Saintines from St. Petersburg in June, 1826, that the ordinary Russian is religiously quite tolerant. "Jew, Muslim, Protestant or Catholic arouse no aversion on his part; he may complain about them, but he does not blame them and never persecutes them." This certainly was not true of the governmental circles during the regime of Nicholas I (1825–55).

Throughout the reign, the new tsar concentrated on fostering "Orthodoxy, Autocracy, and [Russian] Nationality," according to the well-known formula suggested by Count Sergei S. Uvarov, his minister of public enlightenment. Personally, too, Nicholas was well characterized by a leading Russian historian, Sergei M. Soloviev, as "a despot by nature, with an instinctive aversion for every movement and expression of individual freedom and independence. Nicholas loved only the soulless mass movement of soldiers under command." Although he had had little contact with Jews before ascending the throne—he had officially been second in line of succession and owed his elevation to the voluntary abdication of his elder brother Constantine—he showed his general prejudice on his visit to the western provinces in 1816, when he observed in his diary, "The ruin of the peasants in these provinces are the *Zhids*. . . . They are full-fledged leeches sucking up these unfortunate provinces to the point of exhaustion." But he added: "Surprisingly, however, in 1812 they were very loyal to us and assisted us in every possible way even at the risk of their lives."[1]

WIDESPREAD MISCONCEPTIONS

Nicholas' observation was characteristic of the then regnant opinion among the Russian intelligentsia. Its large segment of army officers usually came in contact only with Jewish innkeepers, agents, money-lenders, or—spies. None of these represented the cream of Russian Jewry. Apart from occasional words of admiration for the beauty of Jewish women, we hear, therefore, only adverse comments on Jews.

This negative attitude prevailed also among the Decembrists, who during the brief interlude between Alexander I and Nicholas I staged the unsuccessful uprising of December, 1825. Although generally liberal-democratic, these revolutionaries envisaged little improvement in the status of Jews without speedy assimilation. Paul Pestel, intellectual spokesman of the southern section of the party, combined extreme Russian nationalism with his democratic ideals. Hence he saw the future of Russia only in terms of a homogeneous Russian nation which would completely absorb all national minorities including Jews. In his major Decembrist treatise, *Russkaia Pravda* (Russian Truth), he advocated the abolition of Jewish autonomy and the complete integration of Russian Jewry. But he also contemplated the more desirable alternative of transplanting the Jews to an underpopulated area in Asia Minor and establishing there an independent Jewish state. Less extreme were the ideals voiced by the only Decembrist of Jewish descent, Grigorii Peretz, who about 1810 had submitted to conversion to Russian Orthodoxy together with his then wealthy father, Abraham Peretz, the tsar's "commercial councillor" in St. Petersburg. Grigorii, grandson of a Galician rabbi and of a distinguished Lithuanian talmudist-philanthropist, played but a minor role in the movement, and after its failure spent only fourteen years in prison. The Russian Jewish masses, nevertheless, interpreted the conversion of the Peretz family as an additional warning against the pitfalls of Enlightenment. At the same time the predominantly assimilationist policies of the Decembrists, the sole vocal opposition group when they became known in later years, must have confirmed the belief of many Jews that their future lay only in the appeasement of the tsar and his officials.[2]

Russia's bureaucracy was always keenly sensitive to the changes in the central government. Most lower officials were not only generally underpaid (the vast majority even in the early twentieth century had to get along with monthly salaries equivalent to ten dollars or less), but were also removable at the discretion of their superiors. Hence they quickly sensed the winds of intolerance blowing from St. Petersburg. In the religious sphere the new mood lent greater credence to the old Blood Accusation. This perennial source of friction, which had embittered Judeo-Christian relations in many parts of Europe since the twelfth century, resurfaced in the newly acquired western provinces during the days of Catherine. However, the government discouraged the sporadic rumors. In 1817, Alexander I forbade the circulation of unfounded libels of this kind; the officials were to investigate possible murders without reference to the blood ritual.

On the occasion of a new Blood Accusation, however, in Velizh, Vitebsk province, in 1823 the local judiciary was given free rein to introduce this element, which under Nicholas was blown up by the testimony of three local Christian women. At every successive hearing these witnesses elaborated their story and embellished it with incredible and intrinsically contradictory details. The affair drew ever wider circles and finally engaged the attention of the imperial Senate, the majority of which was ready to condemn the accused. In the meantime all synagogues in Velizh had been closed and the alleged culprits kept in prison. Only owing to the efforts of Admiral N. Mordvinov, chairman of the Department of Civil and Spiritual Affairs in the Council of State, who happened to own estates in the vicinity of Velizh, the tissue of lies and fantasies woven by the imaginative witnesses was fully unraveled. In 1834 the department acquitted all accused Jews, offered them compensation for their unwarranted sufferings, and ordered their accusers deported to Siberia. The tsar approved this decision, but noted that while in this particular case the Jews were clearly innocent, he was still convinced that just as there existed criminal sects among Christians, Jews, too, probably embraced sectarians believing in the ritual value of Christian blood.

It is small wonder, then, that the ritual murder libel continued to flourish in Russian folklore. In 1844, Skripitsin, one of Nicholas' advisers on non-Christian faiths, submitted to the tsar an extensive memorandum buttressing that libel by spurious quotations from the Talmud and rabbinic literature, long known from anti-Semitic writings in Germany. This memorandum subsequently served as the basis for a two-volume work by Hippolyte Lutostanski, a Catholic priest defrocked because of many excesses and immoralities (among others he had allegedly raped a Jewish woman), who added further plagiarisms from other sources. At first Lutostanski merely intended to use that work for blackmail, offering not to publish it if the Moscow rabbi, Solomon Zalkind Minor (1827–1900), would pay him 500 rubles. But upon the latter's refusal, he issued the volume in 1876, and followed it up three years later by a comprehensive two-volume work, *The Talmud and the Jews.*

Despite the repudiation of their contents and the revelation of the author's abysmal ignorance of rabbinic literature by such a distinguished Orientalist as Daniel Chwolson, a converted Jew, Lutostanski's works and similar other writings enjoyed a vogue among Russian anti-Semites to the end of the tsarist regime. This literary character assassination received additional nourishment from another ritual-murder accusation in the small locality of Perwisi, near Sacheri in the Caucasus. To be sure, owing to the brilliant defense by two attorneys at the district court of Kutais (hence the designation of Kutais affair), all defendants were acquitted in 1879. But this outcome failed to pacify the contemporary anti-Jewish press and the few pseudoscholarly defenders of the ritual murder myth.

CANTONIST EXCESSES

Far more drastic, though less enduring, was Nicholas I's ukase relating to the so-called *rekruchina.* Until 1827, Jews usually fulfilled their military duty by the payment of a special tax. Now Nicholas, who considered himself primarily a soldier, decided to force the Jews to serve in person. Remarkably, such extension, under discussion since 1800, was treated not as a privilege to be granted to Jews as part of their sharing in all citizens' rights and duties, but rather as a punitive measure to help reduce the size of the Jewish population, to make it pay up tax arrears, or to force it to take up agricultural pursuits. Now Nicholas added another decisive motive. In a confidential memorandum he wrote that "the chief benefit to be derived from the drafting of Jews is the certainty that it will move them most effectively to change their religion." Although unfamiliar with this express statement, the Jewish community sensed the missionary zeal behind the new decree and from the outset repudiated it as a piece of calculated governmental oppression. A group of pietists in Starokonstantinov went so far as to address a bitter complaint against it to God, and to assure its delivery, handed it to a deceased man.

The main regulations were rather simple: At the age of eighteen a specified number of Jews were to be drafted for twenty-five years of service; they could be taken at the age of twelve for several years of preparatory training before that twenty-five-year term. Like other subjects, Jews could still send substitutes, but in their case the substitutes had to be Jews, too. Certain categories, including rabbis, guild merchants, students, skilled artisans, and agricultural workers, as well as single sons and their families' sole breadwinners, were to be exempted, but otherwise the rotation was to affect all Jewish families, beginning with the largest. A curious formula of an oath, apparently taken by many of these recruits in Hebrew as well as Russian, is still extant. The young soldier was made to swear that he would faithfully perform his duties and obey his superiors as if he fought for "the salvation of our own land and our holy Torah." After adding a statement that he had no mental reservations about his oath, the soldier concluded, "But if I should sin, either of my own will or persuaded by someone else, and violate the oath which I am taking today faithfully to serve in the army I, together with my family, shall be excommunicated in this world and the world to come, Amen."[3]

Administration of this draft was handed over to the Jewish communities themselves and soon became the source of endless internal friction. Most cumbersome was the following paragraph: "The community may at any time draft by verdict any Jew who is guilty of irregularity in the payment of taxes, or of vagrancy, or of any offense not tolerated in the community. If a Jew is thus enrolled by an order based on this statute, and is found eligible for service, the community shall be given a receipt to that effect and be credited with it on the following year's quota." Since most Jewish families knew what to expect, many youngsters of draft age fled to forests, mutilated their bodies so as to become physically ineligible, and resorted to all sorts of subterfuges to evade the draft. The communal authorities, implacably pressed to meet their quotas, often employed so-called *khappers* (kidnappers) who seized the required number of youths on streets or by invading private homes. These ruthless agents made use of such illegal methods as forcibly depriving of their certificates young men occupationally exempted from the draft. Most tragically, they often seized children aged eight or nine (one allegedly aged five) and claimed that they were twelve years or over.

As a result, legions of small children were forced to march thousands of miles to reach their destination. Sometimes half the contingent died on the way. One need but cite the telling description by Alexander Herzen, who witnessed what he called "one of the most awful sights I have ever seen" in a small village of the province of Vyatka.

Pale, worn out, with frightened faces, they stood in thick, clumsy soldiers' overcoats, with stand-up collars, fixing helpless, pitiful eyes on the garrison soldiers, who were roughly getting them into ranks. The white lips, the blue rings under the eyes looked like fever or chill. And these sick children, without care or kindness, exposed to the icy wind that blows straight from the Arctic Ocean, were going to their graves. . . . Boys of twelve or thirteen might somehow have survived, but little fellows of eight or ten. . . . No painting could reproduce the horror of that scene.[4]

On the march the process of Christianization began. All means were considered justifiable, including flogging and other tortures. "Get yourselves baptized scoundrels, or else I will flog you to death!" one commander roared. Estranged from their communities, living as outcasts among hostile comrades, removed at a tender age from their families and friends, a great many cantonists sooner or later submitted to baptism. A few resisted and survived all tribulations. Others preferred suicide to conversion. According to a widely circulated story (soon dramatized in a German poem, *Die beiden Matrosen*), Nicholas was once reviewing his troops in Kazan and the commander wanted to impress him with an improvised ceremony of mass baptism of the Jewish cantonists. Yet the children, brought to the Volga to be baptized, by concerted action immersed themselves in the river and drowned.

We have no definite information about the total number of Jewish victims of the *rekruchina* while it lasted—from 1827 to 1856. According to some records, 26,279 were drafted in 11 years. Another estimate mentions some 40,000 in the first 17 years. The total may indeed not have exceeded 60,000 in the entire 30-year period. The Jewish population, which at that time may have averaged some 3,000,000, could sustain such losses without serious interruption in its numerical expansion. However, their psychological impact was most far-reaching and enduring. The class struggle, which had existed in the East European Jewish communities even before the partitions of Poland, now assumed an unprecedented sharpness, since the *kahal* authorities charged with the draft were prone to favor members of the educated and wealthy classes over the "vagrants" and "tax dodgers" mentioned in the decree. Bribery of officials, including the kidnappers, likewise tended to shift the burden of the draft on to the shoulders of the impoverished masses. The populace was never to forget these injustices. A typical folk song bitterly complained:

> *Tots from school they tear away*
> *And dress them up in soldier's gray.*
> *And our leaders, and our rabbis,*
> *Do naught but deepen the abyss.*
> *Rich Mr. Rockover has seven sons,*
> *Not a one a uniform dons;*

But poor widow Leah has an only child,
And they hunt him down as if he were wild.
It is right to draft the hard-working masses;
Shoemakers or tailors—they're only asses!
But the children of the idle rich
Must carry on, without a hitch.[5]

Military service as a means of Christianization proved no more effective than Nicholas' similar efforts to suppress the sectarian deviations of the Dukhobory and Molokani. Forced into the army from 1826 on, these sworn pacifists performed all peaceful tasks, but regardless of tortures, refused to fire a shot. Finally, the tsar, fearing to undermine the discipline of the other soldiers, dispersed these recalcitrant sectarians over the Caucasus (1839–41). Yet, rightly observes Hugh Y. Reyburn, "Nicholas found that to scatter burning coals among combustible material is not the best way to extinguish a fire." The sectarians merely increased their religious propaganda in the new environment. Moreover, the drastic misuse of military service for penal servitude could only prove detrimental to the Russian army, which ever since Napoleonic days had considered itself invincible. When at the end of Nicholas' regime it had to meet the crucial test of the Crimean War, the "degenerate" Western powers proved victorious. Learning the lesson, Alexander II speedily discontinued the cantonist system in 1856.[6]

NEW CODE

Nor was Nicholas any more cognizant of the realities of the Jewish situation when he attempted to codify the laws governing the Jewish status. A passionate legalist, he considered codification a major task of government. By 1833 he had succeeded in publishing a major code of laws, the so-called *Polnoe sobranie zakonov rossiiskoi imperii* (Complete Collection of Laws of the Russian Empire), which served as a basis for all future tsarist collections. He followed it up by a new statute for Jews, published in 1835 after many years of deliberation by a special committee appointed by Alexander I in 1823. The tsar's objective was to introduce order into the welter of often conflicting ordinances which had accumulated since the first fundamental Jewish statute of 1804 and to help eliminate the confusion of which such an informed adviser as P. D. Kiselev was to complain. Without introducing major innovations, the new statute defined more definitively the Pale of Jewish Settlement, which thenceforth was to include the provinces of Grodno, Vilna, Volhynia, Podolia, Minsk, Ekaterinoslav, Bessarabia, Bialystok, Kiev (except for the city of Kiev), Kherson (without Nikolaev), Taurida (with-

out Sevastopol), Moghilev and Vitebsk (without the villages), Chernigov and Poltava (without the fiscal and Cossack villages). In addition,
there were the provinces of Courland and Livonia (Latvia), as well as the
autonomous Kingdom of Poland until its incorporation into the empire
in 1863. These boundaries remained more or less intact until the outbreak of World War I.

It should be noted, however, that the legislation governing Jewish
life in the various provinces was not quite uniform. When Courland and
Livonia were included in the Pale the law provided that only already
established Jewish families should continue living there—a regulation
which could not be strictly adhered to. Bessarabia, an autonomous
province according to the treaty of 1812, was more lenient toward the
Jews than were the other provinces; it granted them, for instance,
exemption from military service. The largest concentration of Jews under tsarist rule, namely those in the Kingdom of Poland, lived on the
basis of separate laws, including certain survivals of the legislation
enacted during the period when it was part of the Duchy of Warsaw.
Though the freedoms of all its population were curtailed after the
unsuccessful Polish uprising of 1831—in which some Jews had joined
the Polish patriots rebelling against the Russian oppression—it retained
much of its autonomy until 1863, when the tsarist armies put an end to
another Polish uprising. But many differences still persisted, and it
would take us too far afield to try constantly to point up these differences until the kingdom became part of the resuscitated Republic of
Poland after World War I.[7]

The law provided further that Jews should not be allowed to settle
anew in the villages along a fifty-verst, or some thirty-mile-wide, strip
along the western frontier, in order to prevent Jewish smuggling. The
specter of illicit imports had already haunted Alexander's government,
which in 1820 had induced the Vilna *kahal* to place smuggling from the
neighboring provinces in Prussia under a religious ban. The Jewish
elders complied despite their own efforts to outlaw bans within the
Jewish community and despite the refusal of the Minsk community to
follow their example. The Vilna excommunication, characteristically,
became the subject of an extensive correspondence within the Prussian
cabinet, the members of which feared that this measure might interfere
with Prussia's exports to the Tsarist Empire.[8]

Evidently the ban did not achieve its purpose, and we hear no more
about it under Nicholas, who in 1843 proceeded to the total elimination
of Jews from the frontier districts. The ukase, uprooting scores of
thousands of Jews from their old habitats, not only caused widespread
consternation in the Russian Jewish community, but also reverberated
through the European press. It even evoked an unpublicized intercession by the Rothschilds, who as early as 1822 had launched a huge

Russian loan of £ 10,000,000, very helpful in that early period of reconstruction and currency stabilization after the Napoleonic wars.[9]

On the other hand, the comprehensive statute of 1835 definitely suspended further expulsions of Jews from villages to cities, acknowledging defeat of a measure futilely carried out for some three decades. The government had come to the conclusion that such expulsions had merely ruined the Jews without benefiting the peasants. The 1835 statute included prohibitions against marriage by Jewish males under the age of eighteen and females under sixteen. It renewed the old medieval restrictions on Jewish employment of Christian domestics and the erection of synagogues near churches. At the same time, it confirmed the Jewish franchise in municipal elections, except that it now demanded a reading knowledge of Russian from each Jewish councillor. A supplementary decree of 1836 restored the old limitation of Jewish council members to but one-third.[10]

In 1836 Nicholas also introduced a special censorship of Jewish books. Censorship had long seriously hampered all Russian intellectual creativity, but here an effort was made to review not only newly published books and pamphlets (no Jewish papers or magazines were as yet appearing in Russia), but also to subject the older Jewish letters to close surveillance. Those allegedly containing statements prejudicial to Christianity or to Jewish loyalty to the Crown were publicly burned, first in St. Petersburg and then in the provinces. In the exercise of its supervision the government had to rely mainly on ignorant converts and corrupt Christian censors. To what extent misinformation ran rampant even in the highest ministerial circles may be noted from the report by Daniel Chwolson that in 1844 the minister of the interior had suggested to the tsar the suppression of a secret Jewish book called *Rambam* (a well-known abbreviation of Rabbi Moses ben Maimon or Maimonides) which allegedly ordered Jews to murder Christian children and drink their blood. Six years later the better informed minister of public enlightenment recommended the publication of the same Maimonidean Code, with a German translation, as a textbook to teach morality to Jewish children.[11] Needless to say, censorship, somewhat refined in the following years, impeded the free development of Jewish learning, especially since Jewish printing presses were allowed to function only in the two localities of Vilna and Kiev or Zhitomir.

EDUCATIONAL REFORM

Nicholas and his advisers soon realized that in order to be effective, their stick would have to be combined with a carrot. In 1840, under the guidance of Sergei S. Uvarov, the minister of public enlightenment, a large-scale action was instituted to induce Jews to establish schools devoted to secular subjects taught in Russian. To be sure, the governmental schools had long been open to Jewish students, a privilege reiterated in the statute of 1835. However, these schools were so completely dominated by Christian ideology and, promises of safeguarding Jewish conscientious scruples to the contrary, so clearly served missionary purposes that they were long shunned by Jewish pupils. In 1835 there were only 11 Jews among Russia's 1,906 university students. More significantly, as late as 1840, the 80,017 pupils in primary and secondary schools included only 48 Jewish students. Now an effort was made to enlist the aid of the growingly vocal minority that preached "enlightenment" and rapprochement with Western culture and that had on its own already begun founding Jewish schools with a general curriculum.

One such school in Riga had invited a young German scholar, Dr. Max Lilienthal, to serve as its principal. Now Uvarov urged Lilienthal to propagate the establishment of such modern Jewish schools throughout the Pale. The young German scholar was duly impressed. In his letter of February 8, 1841, to Rabbi Isaac Loewi of Fürth, he described the cultural "backwardness" of the Russian Jews and added:

> Yet all these fetters are to be removed. His Majesty, the Emperor, has favored the plan of the high-minded Minister of Education to emancipate the Jews. Two hundred schools are to be opened throughout the Empire, elementary, city and high schools. The young people who pass through these schools are to receive all the rights of citizenship without trammel. This is a great and glorious thing, the like of which our history has not yet produced; not a too sudden deliverance from the bonds of the Middle Ages without being able to make use of the freedom, as happened in France; nor a restless exertion and struggle without obtaining the least advantages, as in Germany. No, the exalted desire of the monarch is for education and emancipation, for culture and the rights of man.

In another letter to Samuel David Luzzatto, the distinguished Italian scholar, requesting information about the rabbinical seminary in Padua and about the availability of its graduates for teaching posts in Russia, Lilienthal spoke of no less than eight hundred new Jewish schools requiring teachers. Lilienthal's enthusiasm communicated itself even to Luzzatto, who later was to assume a most reserved and critical attitude toward Jewish emancipation. In his reply, the Italian scholar assured Lilienthal of his perfect willingness to cooperate with him, for "what could be a greater comfort to me than to see the truly philanthropic and paternal zeal with which the Russian government seeks the betterment of those Jews who dwell in its dominion?" Even more enthusiastic were the German Jewish leaders Ludwig Philippson and Isaak Markus Jost, who were in direct correspondence with Uvarov and had already compiled lists of Jewish candidates available for teaching posts in the new Russian schools. More cautious were Abraham Geiger and the Vienna rabbi, Isaac Noah Mannheimer, and still more so the politically experienced West European leaders, Sir Moses Montefiore and Adolphe Crémieux.[12]

For practical reasons it was far more important to persuade the Russian Jews of the government's good will. Equipped with official credentials Lilienthal traveled through the western provinces, trying to interest the Jewish communal leaders in the new scheme. Most Jewish elders rightly suspected that the government was pursuing a conversionist, rather than enlightened, program (this was indeed the tenor of the secret correspondence between Uvarov and the tsar) and viewed the whole undertaking as another attack on their accustomed way of life. According to Lilienthal's reminiscences, the leaders of the Vilna community, which he visited early in 1842, put to him the ominous question:

> Doctor, are you fully acquainted with the leading principles of our government? You are a stranger; do you know what you are undertaking? The course pursued against all denominations but the Greek proves clearly that the government intends to have but one Church in the whole Empire; that it has in view only its own future strength and greatness and not our own future prosperity. We are sorry to state that we put no confidence in the new measures proposed by the ministerial council, and that we look with gloomy forebodings into the future.

In retrospect, this reaction of the level-headed, if politically untrained, traditionalists was far more realistic than the unbounded faith in the government's good intentions among the progressive minority.[13]

The Minsk elders advanced the remarkable argument that pious Jews reared in their old traditions were bearing up well under their inferior social and political status. But no sooner would their children attain general education and be deprived of the traditional solaces than they would resent the discriminatory laws and practices and live an extremely unhappy life. Uvarov and his associates did not notice their inner inconsistency when they tried to force Western education upon the Jewish community while discouraging most of their own people from attending secondary schools altogether. It was the same Uvarov who on June 11, 1845, suggested that the fees in the *gymnasia* be increased "because in secondary schools and universities there is an evident increase of young men born in the lower orders, for whom higher education is useless; it is a superfluous luxury which takes them out of their original condition without profit to them or to the state." This restrictive policy was pursued particularly in the advanced western provinces. As a result, by 1852, 3,458 of 3,790 pupils attending the thirty-three western district schools were children of the nobility. A year later throughout Russia 80 percent of the *gymnasia* pupils were children of nobles or officials, 2.2 percent were the offspring of the non-celibatarian Orthodox clergy, while the rest of the population supplied only 17.8 percent—a decline of fully 10 percent (from 27.8) as compared with 1826. However, the Jewish school was to serve as an instrument of the desired integration of the Jews into Christian society, religiously as well as socially. This could be achieved only clandestinely. In his report of March 17, 1841, Uvarov himself wrote: "In directing the instruction in these schools against the influence of the Talmud, it is not necessary openly to proclaim this intention." Before long, however, Lilienthal realized that he was being duped by the government and departed for the United States, where he was to play a leading role in the nascent Jewish Reform movement.[14]

Practical difficulties were also staggering. To begin with, there were not enough qualified Jewish teachers for the projected schools. The old-fashioned *melamdim* (teachers in the traditional Jewish elementary schools) long obstructed the entire undertaking. But a few attempted to pass the required examination in Russian and many of those who passed it secured the certificate by bribery, rather than knowledge. Appointed by the government, the Christian school principals were much more interested in their revenue than in the quality of instruction. Peter Marek rightly observes that these officials actually occupied two remunerative posts, "one in the service of the ministry of public enlightenment as official disseminators of culture, and the other in the employ of local Jewish communities as the most trusted and effective fighters against the educational policies of that very ministry."

Nevertheless, sustained by the growing desire of Jewish youth to secure general education, the program was making slow but perceptible progress. In 1847 the two rabbinical seminaries of Vilna and Zhitomir opened their gates to a small but eager band of Jewish students. Other Jewish "Crown schools" began enrolling more and more students. By 1857 the number of their pupils had reached the respectable figure of 3,293, and seven years later that of 5,711 (in addition to 1,561 Jews attending Russian schools) which, though still a small minority of the Jewish school population, laid the foundations for the subsequent large-scale entry of Jewish youth into the Western pursuits. Little did the government foresee that it was thus opening the gates for a youth which was later to furnish important recruits to the revolutionary movements. This myopia of the authorities was doubly remarkable because as mentioned before, during that very period they were discouraging peasant children from going beyond primary schools and if possible from attending schools altogether. It is but another illustration of the contradictory and confusing tsarist policies toward the Jewish subjects, based upon both misinformation and ill will.

Even foreign interventions proved completely futile. Sir Moses Montefiore, the distinguished British philanthropist and communal leader, who had submitted a memorandum on the Jewish question to the tsar on his brief visit to London in 1844, journeyed to Russia two years later in order to help persuade the government of the need of more salutary reforms. As an important London banker and Nathan Meyer Rothschild's brother-in-law, he was courteously received by the tsar, had several conferences with Uvarov and other influential officials, visited many communities, and upon his return to England submitted a number of proposals to Nicholas—all to no effect. The Russian police, who kept him under close surveillance and reported all Jewish visitors he received, was irked by hearing Russia compared with Turkey as objects of his intervention. On the other hand, Sir Moses was startled by the Russian officials' constant harping on the backwardness of the Russian Jews, their excessive adherence to the Talmud, and even their starving "themselves all the week in order to have candles and fish for the Sabbath." When the Rothschild firm tried to secure a residence permit in St. Petersburg for one of its agents, W. Davidson, the British ambassador, Lord Bloomfield, did not even dare to press the subject with the tsar during his visit of a few days to the Peterhof. On this occasion Nicholas told him, to cite his report of June 28, 1847, "that he [the tsar] had no great feeling for the Jews and was resolved not to change the law of Peter the Great or make any concessions in favour of Mr. Davidson or any person professing the same religion." Similarly negative were the results of a visit by a French Jew, Jacob Isaac Altaras, who likewise in 1846 proposed to the tsarist authorities the resettlement of a number of Russian Jews in Algeria, which, then under French suzerainty, was supposedly prepared to extend hospitable treatment to these newcomers. At first the Russians demanded from Altaras a per capita ransom for their exit permits. But anxious to get rid of some Jews, they offered to make a gratuitous exception from their general prohibition of emigration for Jewish families in groups of one hundred or more. Only young men of draft age were not to be allowed to leave. Yet Altaras left Russia without completing any arrangements, and the entire scheme came to naught.[15]

Characteristically, during those very years tsarist law deprived even Jewish businessmen traveling abroad of their Russian citizenship if they failed to return within the term of one to two years stated in their passports. This law affected particularly Russian pilgrims to the Holy Land, who after a brief sojourn found themselves in the position of stateless citizens, a situation fraught with great dangers under the unsettled conditions of the Ottoman Empire. Because of these uncertainties the Russian Jewish community of Jerusalem, led by its rabbi, Isaiah Burdaki, applied in March, 1849, to the British consul for British protection under the then-existing system of capitulations. According to Lieutenant Colonel Hugh Henry Rose, the British consul-general in Beirut, he was told by his Russian counterpart, C. Basily, "that it is probable that from henceforward every year some two or three hundred Jews will leave Russia for ever for Palestine; but I perceive that Mr. Basily thinks and hopes that the whole Jewish population in Russia will eventually do the same." Whether or not formally approved by the Porte, this arrangement was largely acted upon by British consular officials for several decades.[16]

WHIFF OF LIBERALISM

A new epoch in Russian history, though far less in that of Russian Jewry, began with the accession to the throne of Alexander II (1855–81). Of a far more hesitant character, the new tsar was willing to lend his ear to advisers who under his father's regime had ineffectually pleaded for reforms. By conviction he was a staunch conservative. Reading in a report the word "progress," he noted, "What is progress?" and forebade its further use in official documents. Yet the growing industrialization of Russia, which made free labor far more remunerative to factory owners, helped force the government to proclaim, in 1861, the general emancipation of the peasants, earning for Alexander the designation of "Tsar-Liberator." Many Jews shared the general enthusiasm which greeted the new regime; they hailed the emancipation decrees and looked forward to their own speedy liberation as well. In 1858 a typical young scholar, Emanuel Borisovich Levin (who was to evince a lifelong concern for Jewish rights), submitted a memorandum to Alexander II on the subject of the "kidnappers" and the evils which had arisen from the cantonist system, now gone into discard. In another memorandum, addressed to the Jewish elders, Levin urged concerted action to secure full equality of rights for Jews. Alexander's reign also saw the rise of a Jewish press (*see* below).

Except for the abolition of the cantonist system, however, and the submission of Jews to the general draft laws, the removal of Jewish disabilities was quite slow. Probably more important than the few specific alleviations of Jewish status was the toning down of the government's conversionist policies. Religious instruction in the government schools, still obligatory, was now left to the discretion of the parents, who, if they so desired, could engage private tutors for their children (1859). The tsar forbade the conversion of Jewish children under fourteen without the consent of their parents (1861). Such small chicaneries as the reduction of a Jewish criminal's penalty if during the trial he embraced Christianity, or the monetary gifts theretofore given to Jewish soldiers accepting baptism, were now stopped by the decrees of 1864–66. There was also a slight liberalization in the Jewish rights of settlement. Cities like Kiev, which though located within the Pale, were officially closed to Jews, were now opened, at least to their upper classes. Other cities had to give up their residential restrictions of Jews to specific ghettos.

However, legislation aiming at ultimate Jewish equality was never adopted. True, it now found eloquent champions in the minister of interior, Count S. S. Lanskoi, and the governor-general of New Russia, Count Alexander G. Stroganov, and it began looming as an important public issue in the contemporary press and literature. Before long, the Jews found vigorous publicists of their own, such as Osip Rabinovich and Yoakhim Tarnopol, who demanded emancipation not as a gift for good behavior but because of the inherent rights of all men. "History has proved," Rabinovich wrote in an editorial of his new journal, Razsvet (The Dawn), "that our legal equality never depended on the level of our education, but rather on the political development of the nations among whom we lived." He was of course not against the quest for better education. But, as he claimed, "we should strive after perfection out of pure love for the highest ideal of perfection." He could readily point to the general progress of Western education among the Jewish youth, who in those years had begun entering the Russian secondary schools en masse. From the small percentage of 1.25 in the secondary school population in 1853, the ratio of Jewish male students rose to 13.2 percent of the much larger enrollment twenty years later.[17]

Nevertheless, the tsar's chief advisers were still adhering to the old doctrine that Jews should be granted equality only after they had proved their usefulness to the country. The Jewish committee, headed by the jurist Count D. N. Bludov, rejected the suggestions submitted by Lanskoi and Stroganov and decided only in favor of a slow extension of Jewish rights "in proportion to the spread of true enlightenment among them, the transformation of their inner life, and their induction into useful occupations." The only difference from Nicholas' approach was that instead of emphasizing the harm accruing to Russian society from the unproductive or "useless" Jews, the stress was now laid on enlarging the rights of the "useful" Jewish citizens. Accepting that governmental distinction, a group of leading Jews, headed by Joseph (Yozel, Evzel) Günzburg (1812–78), petitioned the tsar to permit at least merchants of the first guild, graduates of Russian schools, and skilled artisans to move freely beyond the Pale. Although crowned with success,[18] this petition revealed that the Jewish leaders were prepared to accept, at least temporarily, the continued discrimination against the majority of their people.

A turning point away from these semiliberal policies came with the outbreak of the Polish insurrection of 1863. The Poles now fraternized with Jews, pledged them full emancipation, and in return received much support from them. True, the Polish nobility could not quite overcome its traditional feeling of superiority. We are told of a Jewish innkeeper who at the risk of his life hid a fleeing aristocrat in his cellar. When he brought the fugitive some food he was greeted with the shout: "Remove your hat, you dirty Jew!" Yet the ruling circles in St. Petersburg were frightened at the prospect of a Judeo-Polish alliance; doubly so, since the empire was also threatened by the intervention of Napoleon III and other foreign Polonophiles. With considerable effort and much cruelty the Russian army suppressed the revolt and inflicted severe retribution on participants and onlookers alike. Contrary to the prediction of the Austrian consul-general in Warsaw, Baron Lederer, that the Jews would utilize their intermediary position between the Russians and the Poles to wrest from the former some egalitarian legislation, this uprising made a lasting "anti-alien" impression upon Russia's governing circles. They felt that thenceforth they should rely only on the Russian Orthodox population, to which the minorities should be assimilated as speedily as possible. While the main assimilatory pressures were now exerted on the Ukrainian and other Uniates—whose submission to the pope had become doubly irksome as the papacy had taken the side of the Polish rebels—and to a lesser extent on the Lutherans of the Baltic provinces, the new religio-ethnic intolerance necessarily affected the Jews as well.[19]

Anti-Jewish feelings were further intensified in official circles by the publication in 1867–70 of essays and a book, the *Kniga Kahala* (The Book of the Kahal), by a converted Jew, Jacob Brafman. In this volume Brafman reproduced many excerpts from the minute book of the Minsk community from the years 1795–1803 which, torn out of context and considerably doctored by him, revealed a degree of Jewish xenophobia which seemed to bear out the old Jew-baiting accusations.[20]

The change in public opinion was equally noticeable. The leading Russian papers, including the *Novoe Vremia* (New Time), which before long became the Russian equivalent of the London *Times*, turned increasingly reactionary, particularly in Jewish affairs. There also were popular riots in Odessa in 1871. Largely instigated by the Greek population of that cosmopolitan harbor city (truly developed only under Duke Armand Richelieu after 1803, Odessa embraced 17,000 Jews as early as 1857), these disturbances lasted for three days without any police interference. Rather than blaming the attackers, who had beaten many Jews and looted stores and apartments, some of the local Christian intelligentsia placed the blame on Jewish "exploitation."

As a result of these changes in attitude, the interventions of such influential Jewish leaders as Baron Horace Günzburg (son of Joseph-

Evzel, 1833–1909) had little effect. Minor restrictions were added to the recruitment of Jews for the army. The new municipal law of 1870 renewed the limitation of the Jews' membership on municipal councils to but one-third and confirmed their ineligibility to the post of burgomaster. Only the admission of Jewish students to secondary schools remained unrestricted. Alexander II himself reminded the superintendent of schools in Odessa, who had suggested some sort of *numerus clausus*, that but recently the government itself had "sought to break down Jewish separatism by attracting them to Russian schools." Because of the growing need, Jewish physicians were even taken into government service in the interior of Russia without a full-fledged M.D. degree.[21]

Governmental hostility to Jews came to the fore also in Russia's foreign affairs. After the conclusion of the Russo-Turkish War, in which some Jewish soldiers distinguished themselves, Prince Alexander M. Gorchakov argued at the Congress of Berlin of 1878 against including provisions for Jewish equality in the treaties with Rumania and Serbia. He contended that one must not compare the Jews of these countries or of Russia with their Western European coreligionists, who alone, because of their cultural and economic attainments, merited equality. But all these unfriendly acts were mere skirmishes presaging the major clashes which were to come after the assassination of Alexander II in March, 1881.

[4]

Under Alexander III and Nicholas II

1881–1914

As in many other autocracies, the succession of a Russian ruler by his son often led to a reversal of previous policies. The general revolt of youth was reinforced here by the varying autocratic propensities of father and son or two brothers. Such reversals had been manifest in the transition from Alexander I's to Nicholas I's regime, and again from Nicholas I's reign to that of Alexander II. However, these reversals were neither sudden nor complete. The reactionary policies of Nicholas I had been well initiated during the last years of his father's reign. Similarly, ever since 1863 strong reactionary forces had made themselves felt under Alexander II, and they only came to fuller fruition during the regime of Alexander III (1881–94).

All pretenses at liberalism were now dropped. The new tsar had long been deeply imbued with the old authoritarian ideals, especially by his mentor Constantin Petrovich Pobedonostsev, a former professor of the University of Moscow and now overprocurator of the Holy Synod. A well-trained jurist and logical thinker, Pobedonostsev was an unbending doctrinaire who considered the old ideals of Russian nationalism and Orthodoxy the only safeguards for Russia's greatness. He and the tsar did not hesitate to promote obscurantism among the peasant masses and to seek to suppress both religious dissent and the nationalist movements among the peoples of foreign stock. They did not realize that they were thus playing into the hands of the rising revolutionary parties, of which the successful assassination of Alexander II should have served them as a warning.

As a matter of fact, that assassination was used as an excuse for anti-Jewish legislation. Although the terrorists included only one Jewish woman, Hesia Helfman, whose contribution had consisted merely in providing shelter for her fellow conspirators, officially inspired rumors were spread that Jews had played a leading part in the revolutionary upheaval. The newly organized secret league of nobles (*Sviaschennaia Druzhina*) for the defense of the existing order engaged in large-scale anti-Jewish propaganda. It stirred up sufficient resentment among the peasants to lead to bloody outbreaks in many communities, particularly in southern Russia.

Equivocal hints dropped by such officials as the anti-Semitic governor-general of Kiev, Alexander Romanovich Drenteln (seemingly a member of the *Druzhina*), persuaded would-be attackers that the tsar wished to see the Jews suffer retribution. They disregarded such appeals for peace as were issued by Governor-General P. D. Sviatopolk-Mirskii of Kharkov, who pleaded that "only enemies of the Fatherland can sympathize with the disturbances and only thieves and robbers can hope to gain from street riots." As a result, a series of pogroms swept over the Ukraine and its neighboring provinces; the first was at Elizavetgrad, a city of some 32,000 inhabitants (April 27, 1881). Next to Kiev or Berdichev the greatest sufferers were the hundreds of smaller settlements completely helpless to stave off the disorders. The local police and military forces reacted with painful slowness, whether because they were unprepared for this sudden epidemic of attacks or because of the reluctance of their military and civil commanders to use force against their coreligionists in the defense of hated Jews. In most cases the authorities tolerated assaults and looting of Jewish quarters for two days before effectively intervening on the third day. Quite a few policemen and Cossacks mingled with the looters; they speedily vanished on the approach of troops. Only in the northwestern provinces did the authorities stop the disturbances at their very inception. As if to prove to the world that this was a spontaneous reaction of the masses against their Jewish exploiters, the Russians rejoiced when on Christmas Day, 1881, a similar outbreak occurred in Warsaw, where but two decades earlier Jews and Poles had marched together against their tsarist oppressors. Here, too, some Russians were the chief instigators; one of the arrested, a former Russian colonel, was found in possession of a detailed list of Jewish shops singled out for pillage.[1]

Psychologically, the impact of these pogroms was even greater than the physical and material damage. Russian Jewry, and with it world opinion, awoke with a start at the sight of this revival of what had long been considered an extinct method of settling Judeo-Gentile controversies. Eastern Europe had not been the scene of large-scale massacres since the Cossack rebellion in 1648–50, except for some local disturbances in White Russia in 1744 and under the leadership of Gonta in 1768. That is why even the loss of a few-score lives and much property (estimated in Kiev alone at 2,500,000 rubles), almost irreplaceable for impoverished Russian Jewry, mattered less than the feeling of insecurity which pervaded the entire community. It was but partly mitigated by the Western expressions of sympathy. On the other hand, the protest meetings in London and New York, the parliamentary debates in the American Congress and the British Parliament, as well as the extensive reportage in the foreign press (for instance, a series of articles anonymously published by Joseph Jacobs in the London *Times*), could not fail to make some impression even upon the most obdurate Russian leaders. Alexander may have on occasion voiced utter disdain for the Western press. On a visit to Marienbad in 1888, where he willy-nilly became acquainted with some liberal Austro-Hungarian newspapers, he complained that the press had fallen into the hands of self-seeking journalists. "It is hard to imagine," he contended, "a despotism more irresponsible and violent than the despotism of printed words." Yet even he admitted that the press had become a great power in the world, and he tried, at least at home, to control it by an ever-stricter censorship, which he reinforced by a decree of 1883. With respect to the pogroms he was personally shocked and perplexed by the bloody turn of events, and on one government report he noted: "Someone must have had a hand in inciting the people against Jews. A careful investigation of all such cases is imperative." Yet he deplored more the necessity for the government to prosecute some "patriotic" Greek Orthodox assailants than the losses in Jewish lives and property.[2]

Rather than being fearful that once the masses tasted blood, they might turn on their real oppressors (in the initial stages the authorities tried to place the blame for the disturbances on the nihilists), the tsarist regime decided to restrict the rights of its Jewish subjects more and more. It answered both foreign and domestic accusers by echoing the expostulations offered by local officials, guilty of impassivity in checking the disturbances, that this was but a popular reaction to intolerable Jewish "exploitation." During a twenty-minute interview with a Jewish delegation headed by Baron Horace Günzburg, Alexander himself declared, "On the souls of the Jews, too, a sin is burning; they are said to be guilty of exploiting the Christian population." And he added the query: "Why do they so gladly evade military service?" The government considered itself duty bound, therefore, to devise legislative means to protect the populace.

At court the influence of such relatively liberal advisers as Count Mikhail T. Loris-Melikov, the minister of interior, sharply declined. Alexander doubtless shared Pobedonostsev's opinion of Loris-Melikov, as defined in an anonymous memorandum which the overprocurator forwarded to the tsar on April 30, 1881. Here the minister's honesty was acknowledged, but he was characterized as "an extremely ambitious person, thirsting for power, a heartless egotist and of wholly oriental mentality and morality [the count was of Armenian origin]. . . . The count would make a good governor-general of the Caucasus, but he does not understand Russia and the Russian people, whose aspirations do not evoke any echo in his heart." Moreover, behind Loris-Melikov stood, in the memorialist's opinion, the Jewish terrorist Grigorii Davidovich Goldenberg, who often outwitted the gullible minister. Curiously, at the time of the submission of that memorandum the overprocurator seemed unaware that Goldenberg had turned idealistic traitor, repented and committed suicide nine months before. Loris-Melikov—who in 1880 had escaped assassination by Meir (Ippolit) Molodetskii, a recent convert to Christianity—was now removed in favor of Count Nikolai P. Ignatev, master of intrigue and confirmed reactionary. In his explanation of the massacres Ignatev wavered between the attribution of the bloodshed to nihilists and to Jewish "injurious influences" upon the masses. In his August 22, 1881 memorandum to the tsar, he declared that the cause of the pogroms, "so incompatible with the nature of the Russian people," was the rapid economic expansion of the Jews during the preceding regime.

> Having adopted strict measures [Ignatev added] to suppress the earlier disturbances and mob rule and to protect Jews against violence, the government feels justified in pursuing speedily an equally energetic course in order to remove the existing abnormal relations between the original inhabitants and the Jews. It must protect the Russian people against the Jews' injurious activities which, according to local reports, were responsible for the disorders.

This memorandum suggested the enactment of more restrictive laws.[3]

To initiate the new legislation the government, like its predecessors, started with a committee. This time the investigation was handed over to gubernatorial commissions organized in each of the fifteen provinces of the Pale (outside the Kingdom of Poland) in addition to that of Kharkov. Although each commission included two Jewish representatives appointed by the governors, all the cards were stacked against them from the outset. In the very circular sent out by Ignatev to the respective governors-general on August 25, 1881, the aim of these deliberations was defined as relating to "the harmful impact of the economic activity of Jews on the Christian population, their racial separatism, and religious fanaticism." Since some of the governors themselves were implicated in the disturbances, they had every reason to choose members sympathetic to Ignatev's point of view. Under the circumstances it is astonishing that five commissions, or nearly one-third, recommended the opening of the entire empire to Jewish settlement as the only remedy of the existing shortcomings.

Needless to say, their advice was not taken. On the contrary, the government proceeded with great dispatch to issue on May 3, 1882, new "temporary rules" forbidding Jews to settle anew outside towns and hamlets and to carry on any business on Sundays and Christian holidays. In this formulation some of Ignatev's extreme demands were toned down, and if the "May Laws" had been properly administered, the hardships they caused the Jewish people might have been mitigated. Strict observance of both Christian and Jewish holidays, to be sure, would have made Jewish business less competitive. But in many smaller towns Jews had little to fear from Christian competition; elsewhere they could purchase "protection" from the local police.

Corrupt Russian bureaucrats interpreted even more freely the clauses relating to new settlement. Sometimes they refused to readmit Jews to their old residences after an absence of but a few days (for instance, in order to attend synagogue services on high holidays in a neighboring city), declaring them to be "new settlers." On occasion they expelled Jews who merely changed their residence from one house to another in the same locality. Not surprisingly, these administrative persecutions, coming on top of the sanguinary persecutions by hooligans, convinced Russian Jewry that it was unwanted in its centuries-old habitat. It knew what was in the minds of an Ignatev and his ilk, whether or not it had heard Ignatev's hypocritical explanation offered in April, 1882, to the American chargé d'affaires, "We have on the one hand 5,000,000 Jews, Russian subjects, clamoring to be freed from all special restraints, and we have on the other, 85,000,000 Russian subjects clamoring to have the 5,000,000 expelled from the Empire. What is to be done in such a case?"[4]

STIMULATED EXODUS

The temporary rules were supposed to be replaced by permanent legislation to be passed, as the legal custom demanded, by the Council of State. In February, 1883, Alexander III appointed a "High Commission for the Revision of the Existing Laws relating to Jews" under the chairmanship of Count Constantine I. Pahlen, a former minister of justice. The so-called Pahlen Commission reviewed thoroughly the century-old legislation, the debates of the gubernatorial commissions, and many other data. It took five years to complete its labors and submit its proposals, which because of their moderation did not find favor with the tsar and his chief advisers. Unperturbedly, the administration not only continued to enforce the May Laws, but superimposed upon them a number of further restrictions, among them a *numerus clausus* for secondary schools and schools of higher learning. Under the excuse that Jewish students were "quick in joining the ranks of the revolutionary workers," a quota of 10 percent was established in 1887, for all such schools within the Pale, 5 percent outside the Pale, and 3 percent in St. Petersburg and Moscow. This quota was subsequently reduced to 7, 3, and 2 percent respectively. As a result, Jewish university students often had to overcome serious legal and financial difficulties to obtain their higher education at foreign universities. Upon their return to Russia, such disgruntled foreign graduates were doubly likely to disseminate the liberal doctrines current in the Western lands.

In 1889 a decree restricted the admission of Jewish, Muslim, and Karaite lawyers to the bar, requiring in each case special permission from the minister of justice on the recommendation of the presidents of local bar associations or judicial institutions. While the few Muslim and Karaite candidates had little difficulty in securing such permits, numerous Jewish applicants were rejected and for some fifteen years had to make their living through formally assisting Christian colleagues and by other evasions. Even after admission, a Jewish lawyer could be subject to special chicaneries. According to an anecdote told in her memoirs by Countess Mariia E. Kleinmichel, General Cherevin, head of the secret police under Alexander III, had pacified a lady friend who was losing a lawsuit to a party represented by a Jewish attorney by assuring her that he would deport the Jewish lawyer to Siberia under some trumped-up political charge. Although brought back before his appeal would reach the higher authorities, the latter would in the meantime be prevented from pleading on the next day and thus lose his case. When the countess protested, Cherevin explained, "I cannot hold the scales impartially between intimate friends of mine and a dirty Jew who, if he is not guilty to-day, may have been yesterday, or will be tomorrow." The story has it that during his absence of three months, the attorney not only lost his case but also his pregnant wife, who had been so frightened by her husband's arrest that she immediately miscarried and died.[5]

Chicaneries of various types, legal and extralegal, multiplied from day to day. In another sensational move the government banished the Jews from Moscow on the first day of the Jewish Passover of 1891. Only a small group of old settlers was allowed to remain, while the newly constructed beautiful synagogue was closed down and ultimately, under constant governmental pressure, turned into a charitable institution. The authorities paid little heed to the plight of thousands of Christian workers who lost their employment in Jewish factories and commercial establishments (the important silk industry almost entirely suspended operations) and to the protests of Christian merchants and manufacturers in 1893.[6]

It became increasingly manifest that the government was trying to make the Jewish position in the empire altogether untenable. Although emigration from Russia without an exit permit continued to be strictly forbidden, the authorities placed few obstacles in the way of would-be Jewish émigrés who in ever-swelling numbers fled across the border, particularly to the Galician frontier city of Brody, whence they expected to be rescued by their Western coreligionists. We shall see, in another connection, that the majority of these refugees found their way to Hamburg or Liverpool and were ultimately shipped to the United States and other countries. Needless to say, such mass emigration also created considerable difficulties in the countries of immigration. Notwithstanding the general reluctance of Western statesmen to interfere in the internal affairs of other lands, President Benjamin Harrison reported in his Third Annual Message to the Congress of the United States of December 9, 1891, that

> this Government has found occasion to express in a friendly spirit, but with much earnestness, to the Government of the Czar its serious concern because of the harsh measures now being enforced against the Hebrews in Russia. . . . It is estimated that over 1,000,000 will be forced from Russia within a few years. The Hebrew is never a beggar; he has always kept the law—life by toil—often under severe and oppressive civil restrictions. It is also true that no race, sect, or class has more fully cared for its own than the Hebrew race. But the sudden transfer of such a multitude under conditions that tend to strip them of their small accumulations and to depress their energies and courage is neither good for them nor for us.
>
> The banishment, whether by direct decree or by not less certain indirect methods, of so large a number of men and women is not a local question. A decree to leave one country is in the nature of things an order to enter another—some other. This consideration, as well as the suggestion of humanity, furnishes ample ground for the remonstrances which we have presented to Russia while our historic friendship for that Government cannot fail to give the assurance that our representations are those of a sincere wellwisher.

One million was a rather conservative figure. People were prepared to accept as true a statement allegedly made by Pobedonostsev to the

Jewish publicist Alexander O. Zederbaum that the only solution for the Jewish question in Russia was that one-third should emigrate, one-third become Christianized, and one-third should perish.[7]

Such an exodus of Jews seemed to be directed into more orderly channels after the organization in 1891 of the Jewish Colonization Association by Baron Maurice de Hirsch. Confirmed anti-Semites like Pobedonostsev and Alexander III were not averse to dealing with Jewish big business. Even in St. Petersburg the great railroad builder Samuel Poliakov had free access to the overprocurator, who on several occasions reported to the tsar Poliakov's schemes to secure for Russia a foothold in railways being built in Turkey and Persia. The Russian government was even more inclined to maintain relations with such leading Jewish bankers abroad as Gerson Bleichröder, Bismarck's trusted adviser. They were taken aback when under the impact of the Russian pogroms, the Paris Rothschilds withdrew from a consortium negotiating a half-billion-franc loan for the Tsarist Empire.

It was somewhat easier to deal with a genuine philanthropist like Baron de Hirsch, before whom one did not have to conceal one's conviction of the desirability of Jewish mass departures from Russia. In his first attempt to help his Russian coreligionists, Hirsch offered to pour 50,000,000 francs into a scheme for establishing trade schools within Russia so as to train Russian Jewish youths for crafts and farm work. He actually advanced 1,000,000 francs which was used for the training of Russian youths for the Orthodox priesthood, however. Thereupon Hirsch withdrew his offer when the government insisted that the full amount be placed at its disposal without any strings attached. Undeterred, the Belgian banker continued the negotiations, but now asked for an arrangement to evacuate, as he hoped, fully 3,250,000 Jews from Russia over a period of twenty-five years, and to settle them in colonies overseas, particularly in Argentina. That location must have appealed to Pobedonostsev, who had previously evinced interest in the spiritual welfare of several thousand Greek Orthodox settlers in Buenos Aires and its vicinity and had repeated the observation of the minister of the navy that "these little known southern harbors might offer shelter to our navy in case of war." The government therefore instructed its local officials to extend full cooperation to Arnold White, a member of the British Parliament and a known champion of anti-alien laws there, who was twice sent by Hirsch to Russia to conduct the negotiations. Pobedonostsev personally gave him an autographed letter of introduction describing his mission. But, as we shall see, for reasons beyond either Hirsch's or the tsar's control, this colonization scheme attained but meager results and the overwhelming mass of émigrés continued to flow in the direction of North America.[8]

Nor could the Jews count on the support of an enlightened public opinion. The great Russian writers of the interior had little personal familiarity with Jewish life, especially in the crowded western ghettos which they knew only from occasional visits. That is why most of their descriptions of Jewish characters are stereotyped and lifeless. They also readily shared the prejudices of their environment. The great masters— Pushkin, Lermontov, and even the better-informed Gogol—of the earlier decades in the nineteenth century knew only of such characters as Jewish poisoners, spies, and cowardly traitors.

Later in the century, particularly after the pogroms of 1881–82, the conscience of the people began bestirring itself. Even then some liberals were deterred from voicing loud protests against the pogromists. Many had grown to believe in the righteous instincts of the masses and looked with abhorrence on violent measures taken by the police against the "people." Yet the circle around the distinguished thinker Vladimir S. Soloviev and the eminent writer Vladimir G. Korolenko marshaled enough dignity and courage to voice sharp protests against massacres of innocent Jews. To be sure, Leo Tolstoy appended his signature to Soloviev's petition to Alexander III only because, as he said, he had sufficient confidence in his friend that he could subscribe to anything that Soloviev would write. When the philosopher finally assembled one hundred signatures of distinguished intellectual leaders the petition was suppressed by the government, together with Soloviev's foreword accompanied by a number of philo-Semitic letters attached to a booklet by his long-time friend, Rabbi Feivel Goetz. This fate was also to befall Soloviev's efforts in 1892 to persuade Pobedonostsev to tone down the persecution of Christian sectarians. There is no evidence that the over-procurator ever answered that remarkable epistle, in which the writer frankly indicated his personal dislike of the recipient, who unbeknown to him had already unfavorably commented to Alexander III in 1888 on Soloviev's influential work on *The Russian Idea*. In his novel *Yom Kippur*, Korolenko actually depicted some Jewish characters sympathetically. The pogrom in Nijni-Novgorod in 1884 made so strong an impression on one youthful bystander, Maxim Gorki, as to cause him to relate these happenings on the occasion of the later massacres.

Somewhat more equivocal was Anton Chekhov's attitude. A southerner like Korolenko, he had had a much greater opportunity to observe Jewish life. Chekhov's Jewish characters vary with his changeable views alternately conservative and liberal. But at least during the Dreyfus Affair of the 1890s he broke off with his long-time friend A. S. Suvorin because of the latter's outright anti-Semitic and anti-Dreyfusard stand. Even generally liberal Ivan S. Turgenev, who had been rather friendly in his early story *The Zhid*, kept his peace in 1881–82. So probably would have Fiodor M. Dostoevsky (who died just before the Elizavetgrad riot), since he could never fit the Jew into his dream of a messianic Russian people. At best he suggested that Jews be given equal rights, provided they would not thereby become stronger than the native population, a condition which no one could guarantee. In the very year, 1877, when he asserted that he had never been an enemy of the Jews (*see* below), Dostoevsky entered quite a few derogatory remarks about Jews and Judaism into his *Journal of an Author*. His mood became quite bitter toward the end of his life. In a "Note" written shortly before his demise in February, 1881, he vehemently asserted:

> All the Bismarcks, Beaconsfields, the French Republic and Gambetta, etc., are all for me only a façade; their master, the master of all, and of the whole of Europe, is the Jew and his bank. The Jew and his bank now dominate everything: Europe and enlightenment, the whole civilization, especially socialism, for with its help the Jew will eradicate Christianity and destroy the Christian civilization. Then nothing is left but anarchy. The Jew will command everything.

Next to these equivocal masters there was a growing host of lesser writers, for the most part rabidly anti-Semitic, who had the ear of the majority of the Russian readers. As against this wall of hatred, indifference, or at best sympathetic misunderstanding, the pleas advanced, as we shall see, in both fictional and publicist works by the growing number of Russo-Jewish writers passed largely unnoticed. Works by these apologists were as a rule read mainly by Jews, who needed no convincing. This situation began changing but slowly after the death of Alexander III in 1894.[9]

THE LAST TSAR

The accession to the throne of Nicholas II (1894–1917) involved no immediate change in the governmental system or detailed policies. Although Pobedonostsev's personal influence declined somewhat, his spirit continued to dominate the thinking of the tsar and his court *camarilla*, some members of which, supported by the reactionary tsarina, attained an ever greater influence. Quite early in his regime (January, 1895) Nicholas announced in a public address: "Let it be known by all . . . that the principle of autocracy will be maintained by me as firmly and unswervingly as by my lamented father."[10]

Nevertheless, some Jews seemed to detect harbingers of a better future. Nicholas' declaration in his imperial manifesto that his sole aim was to seek "the happiness of all his loyal subjects" and the invitation extended to three rabbis to participate, at government expense, in the coronation ceremonies seemed promising gestures. The St. Petersburg community reciprocated by commissioning Mark Antokolsky to produce a silver angel handing the crown to the new tsar and presented it to Nicholas. However, the entrenched Russian bureaucracy successfully resisted any relaxation of pressures on the Jewish population. Indeed, so conservative was the prevailing trend in the first decade of the new reign that no substantially new policies were adopted, while the old screws of legal and administrative discrimination were turned more tightly. In 1898 the only justification for these discriminatory policies Pobedonostsev knew to offer to a Paris delegation of the Jewish Colonization Association was that Jews were natively more gifted, better educated, and more aggressive than the average Russians and that the latter therefore needed legal protection against being wholly dominated by Jews. This faked humility, already adumbrated by Dostoevsky, served as a ready excuse even for such a relatively liberal minister of interior as Prince Peter Dimitrevich Sviatopolk-Mirskii to do nothing during his short tenure of office (1904–1905).

Among the principal administrative restrictions was a further lowering of the *numerus clausus*. The aforementioned reduction of the Jewish quota to 3 to 7 percent was now interpreted to refer to each particular department in the universities and colleges. Since Jews knew in advance that they would not secure government appointments in teaching or civil service, they naturally tended to select training for the liberal professions of medicine or law. According to the new interpretation, therefore, the total number of Jews in the academic enrollment was bound to fall below the general quota.

Governmental animus was directed particularly against the legal profession, which enabled Jews not only to display their forensic talents, but also to use them in the defense of their coreligionists appearing in court. At times, the brilliant defense of Jewish defendants by Jewish attorneys and their role in uncovering the machinations behind anti-Jewish attacks proved extremely embarrassing to governmental officials. It is small wonder, then, that in 1897 a special committee deliberated the introduction of a new *numerus clausus* for Jews in the legal profession beyond the restrictions in admission to the bar enacted in 1889. No such law was issued but the ratio of Jews in the legal profession constantly declined. Physicians, too, were now restricted to private practice and excluded from all government posts. Obviously, no clearer illustration of tsarist inconsistencies was required than the early drive under Nicholas I to force the Jewish youth to attend general schools, as contrasted with the persistent governmental efforts half a century later to discourage Jewish participation in the country's general educational system.[11]

Similarly old, but more intensive, was the enforcement of the settlement restrictions relating to Jews, although many more voices were now heard pointing to the adverse economic effects of these laws. A pamphlet on "The Effects of Antisemitism," published in 1897 by

Professor N. Shmerkin, submitted detailed evidence about the fall of both state revenue and grain exports, especially of the finer grades, in those provinces outside the Pale from which Jews had been exiled since 1881. The allegedly high interest rates of 15 to 25 percent charged by Jews were raised by Christian usurers to 75 to 200 percent after the departure of these competitors. In 1895 the Cossacks of the Don, Terek, and Kuban regions successfully protested the contemplated expulsion of Jews, because the latter were the sole distributors of their produce. For similar reasons even the governor-general of the Caucasus persuaded the central authorities to revoke an impending decree of banishment of newly settled Jews from that area.[12]

In most other cases, however, the combination of bureaucratic inertia and bias prevailed. Time and again the police staged regular night raids on Jews found beyond the Pale, in rural districts or even in such southwestern towns as Kiev. Whenever seized, sometimes in their night attire, such illegal residents, men, women, and children, were imprisoned or speedily deported. In some cities the police actually set rewards twice as high for information concerning illicit settlers as for the denunciation of hardened criminals. To add insult to injury, the Kiev police paid its large personnel mainly devoted to the detection of Jewish lawbreakers from the revenues of the Jewish meat tax. Regressing further back into the Middle Ages in his 1895 report to the tsar, Pobedonostsev complained of the pernicious religious influence exerted by Jews upon their Christian household help. Of course, the overprocurator did not bother to submit full documentation for his sweeping accusation.

All these chicaneries added fuel to the resentment on the part of the Jewish masses and, without stopping their constant growth, merely increased their self-assertiveness and political consciousness. Economically, to be sure, the pauperization of Jews proceeded apace. According to an economist, A. Subbotin, the number of Jewish paupers increased by 27 percent in the four years between 1894 and 1898. In many communities fully 50 percent of the Jewish population depended on charity, particularly during the Passover week. The flight abroad likewise continued, notwithstanding objections raised by some Jewish leaders who saw in it a sign of weakness or lack of patriotism.

These very assertions illustrated, on the other hand, the progressive integration of Jews into the political fabric of the empire; more and more of them now believed that their ultimate future lay with political action which would force the government to grant full equality of rights to all citizens. Indeed, this became the heyday of newer Jewish ideologies and the formation of Jewish parties. We shall see that in 1897 both the Jewish-Socialist *Bund* and the World Zionist Organization were founded. True, the latter was led by such Westerners as Theodor Herzl and Max Nordau. But its chief source of manpower and much of its spiritual and ideological energy came from Russian Jewry. In addition, there also were all sorts of combinations of Zionism and Socialism. Many other Jews preferred to join the general Russian parties, both liberal and socialist. The government reacted sharply to all these movements, regarding them as equally subversive of the established order. Even Zionism, which ultimately was to contribute to the further evacuation of Jews from Russia, was soon outlawed because it unavoidably contributed to Jewish militancy against the prevailing oppression.

Aided by the government, the conservative groups went over to a counteroffensive. Through machinations of the secret service agents, especially one Peter Rachkovskii, a tale was concocted—out of an old French story and a German story—relating to an alleged Jewish conspiracy to take over the world. In essence, this story was prepared in 1895, but it was not published in Russia until it appeared in serial form in the newspaper *Znamia* (The Banner), for a while edited by a well-known pogromist, P. A. Krushevan, in St. Petersburg (in nine successive issues of August and September, 1903). In 1905 this apocryphon was reprinted by the government press in Tsarskoe Selo, the imperial residence. It was appended to a book by an alleged "mystic saint," Sergei Nilus, entitled *The Great and Little: The Coming of the Antichrist and Satan's Rule on Earth,* as an illustration of the saint's predictions. By that time its origin was more or less forgotten, and some circles began attributing the plot to the World Zionist Organization and its first Basel Congress of 1897. Another edition, under a different title, was published by another anti-Semite, G. Butmi, in 1906. This editor denied the specific connection with the Basel Congress, but insisted upon the origin of that conspiracy from an alliance between Herzl, the Bund, the Russian Masons, and the British Foreign Office. He wrote:

> England, through its agents, the Russian Masons, is cooperating for the internal enslavement of Russia by the Jews, by Jewish Zionists, by means of stirring up internal sedition, paralyzing the potential resistance of Russia to the wiles of British foreign policy. The agreement on this subject between the Zionists and the Masons was apparently arrived at in 1900, at the initiative of Dr. Herzl, founder of modern Zionism. Thus Jewish Zionism, working in Russia under the protection of Russian Masons, is well-organized and spread throughout Russia by the treacherous agency of the British foreign policy, which is always inimical to Russia but friendly to the Jews.

Although this fabrication thus was semiofficially promoted and another version was published and widely distributed by the Army staff of the St. Petersburg Military Region, it did not play a major role in the history of Russian anti-Semitism. Only years later, under the impact of the revolutionary changes occasioned by the First World War, did this product of the Russian secret service attain its worldwide notoriety under the title of *The Protocols of the Elders of Zion*.[13]

NEW POGROMS

At the same time there was increased violence in both the governmental repression and popular attacks. The pogroms of 1881 were a mere prelude to the greater bloodshed which took place in 1903 and 1905. The chief organizers now were members of the *Soyuz ruskago naroda* (League of the Russian People), founded in 1904. This paramilitary group, forming cadres of fanatical Jew-baiters, frequently collaborated with the even more militant "Black Hundreds." They included much army personnel and were often led by generals like Eugene Bogdanovich. Next to Jewish "exploitation," the new rationale blamed the Jews for the strength of the subversive movements. After investigating on the spot the Kishinev pogroms of 1903, Michael Davitt came to the conclusion that they had been planned "with the passive connivance of the Chief of Police and the active encouragement of some of his officers." This contention was fully borne out by the personal investigation of Bessarabia's new governor-general, Prince Sergei Dmitriyevich Urussov, a fair-minded, though conservative, official.[14]

This time the tsar himself viewed with equanimity the crimes perpetrated on his Jewish subjects and actually encouraged them by occasional hints. His acceptance of an honorary membership in the League of the Russian People for himself and his son was tantamount to a public demonstration. According to a widely believed story, Nicholas II was supposed to have said to a general holding an important post in southern Russia, "I had expected that a much greater number of Jews would perish." On another occasion the tsar allegedly reassured a pogromist leader, Count Konovnitsin, "I know that Russian courts are too severe toward the participants in the pogroms. [This assertion is clearly controverted by such a travesty of justice as occurred in 1904 in the investigation of the Gomel pogrom by the Kiev Court of Appeals.] I give you My imperial word that I shall always lighten their sentences, on the application of the League of the Russian People, so dear to me." The tsar had effective collaborators in several successive ministers of interior, particularly the overtly anti-Semitic Vyacheslav Konstantinovich von Plehve (1902–1904). To a Jewish delegation from Odessa Plehve was supposed to have unabashedly declared, "We shall make your position in Russia so unbearable that the Jews will leave the country to the last man. The Jews constitute in southern Russia ninety, in the interior forty percent of all revolutionaries." This was, of course, a gross exaggeration;

it was part of the government's campaign to discredit the revolutionary movement by identifying it with Jews. On the other hand, according to Prince Urussov, all he had to do in 1904 was show the Kishinev chief of police a telegram sent by Plehve ordering the maintenance of public order. The chief exclaimed, "Be at ease, your Excellency: there will not be any disturbance in Kishinev."[15]

Contemporaries realized that many of the incendiary leaflets had been printed in the official press of the Russian gendarmerie and distributed by these supposed upholders of public peace. In fact, this was the most significant innovation of the Russian regime; it far exceeded anything known about anti-Jewish massacres during the "dark" Middle Ages, when governments as a rule had tried to fulfill their primary duty of preserving public order. If a medieval regime wished to get rid of its Jews, it proceeded with a formal decree of expulsion, a procedure recognized as lawful by both Jews and Gentiles. By methods now introduced by the tsarist regime (and later greatly elaborated and refined by the Nazis), the government itself instigated public disorders.

In 1903 the Kishinev pogrom made a tremendous impression in and outside of Russia. Instigated by P. A. Krushevan, a former petty official and editor of the reactionary local newspaper *Bessarabets* (heavily subsidized by the government), this pogrom affected a community of some 50,000 Jews living side by side with some 60,000 Christians. In two days (April 6–7/19–20) 45 Jews were slain, 86 were seriously wounded, and 500 less severely hurt. More than 1,500 houses and shops were plundered or destroyed. This outbreak was followed by a somewhat lesser attack on the community of Gomel, which actually had a Jewish majority of 20,400 in the total population of 36,800. Undeterred by the ensuing universal outcry, a much larger wave of pogroms took place in 1905 in connection with the First Russian Revolution. This time some 660 Jewish communities were affected in the course of a single week (October 19–25/November 1–7). Among them was the community of Odessa, which had by that time became one of the great intellectual centers of Russian Jewry. Of the 160,000 Jews residing in that city no less than 300 victims lost their lives, thousands more were wounded and crippled, while 40,000 were economically ruined. In all, this pogrom wave cost the Russian Jews about 1,000 dead, 7,000 to 8,000 wounded (many of them permanently crippled), and property losses of 62,700,000 rubles (*ca.* $31,000,000).

In contrast, however, to many earlier massacres, the assailants now often encountered a determined Jewish self-defense. Taught by previous experiences, the Jewish youth, now politically far more sophisticated, organized itself in defensive detachments, which would have met the unorganized, often drunken, pogromists on more than even terms, were it not for the intervention of the Russian military. Rather than protecting the peaceful Jews against their bloodthirsty assailants, the troops often stood passively by until the Jewish self-defense appeared on the scene. At that moment it was greeted by a salvo from the Russian soldiers, some of whom, encouraged by their own commanders, actually participated in the murders and looting. Subsequently, too, many a young Jew was dragged before the courts because of his part in the defense. At times these Jewish detachments were accused of having started the riots by attacking Christians. While most courts did not subscribe to such nonsense, many had gradually lost their judicial independence under the corrupt administration of the new minister of justice, I. G. Shcheglovitov, and proceeded against the defenders rather than the attackers.

In the meantime, there was a natural revulsion against these barbaric methods among some of Russia's intellectual leaders. To be sure, the staunch Russian nationalists for the most part remained quite unfriendly to the Jews. But Kishinev forced Tolstoy to take a public stand. "The outrages at Kishinev," he declared, "are but the direct result of the propaganda of falsehood and violence which our Government conducts with such energy." While some intellectuals, like the upper classes generally, tried to wash their hands of any responsibility for these manifestations of mob hatred, young Maxim Gorki was not alone in contending that "cultivated society is no less guilty of the disgraceful and horrible deeds committed at Kishinev than the actual murderers and ravishers. Its members' guilt consists in the fact that not merely did they not protect the victims, but that they rejoiced over the murders."[16]

REVOLUTION AND REACTION

Such occasional expressions of sympathy inspired some leading Jews to believe that ultimately Russian society would extend its brotherly embrace to the Jewish minority. The majority of Jews, however, were increasingly convinced that they could rely only on their strength. This feeling was clearly expressed by a leading Jewish poet of the age, Simeon Samuel Frug (1860–1916), who had absorbed enough of Russian culture to contribute some distinguished poetry in the Russian language. But he also wrote beautiful Hebrew and Yiddish poems. One of these read:

> *The wholly dead may patient wait,*
> *But there's a people sick and gray,*
> *Not wholly dead, not wholly living;*
> *Are saviors sent to such as they?*

No savior from without can come
To those that live—and are enslaved.
Their own Messiah they must be,
And play the savior and the saved.[17]

Out of this recognition Jews not only organized their own self-defense but entered the broad stream of Russian politics, particularly during the Revolution of 1905. When in October, 1905, under the pressure of strikes and public demonstrations, Nicholas II finally issued a manifesto promising basic freedoms to the whole population, he passed over the Jewish question in silence. But the Jews were determined to use their newly won franchise to wrest full equality of rights from the government by constitutional means. In a 1905 "Declaration of Jewish Citizens" the six thousand signers wrote with great dignity:

> We expect to secure civil equality not because it would make the Jews more useful citizens and benefit others. Nor do we look forward to equality as a reward for the blood our brothers are shedding on the Manchurian fields, just as their brothers had shed their blood in former wars. We do not even demand civil equality because of our centuries-old residence in lands which now form part of the Russian Empire. We demand civil equality and equal submission to general laws as men who, despite everything, are conscious of their human dignity, and as conscientious citizens of a modern state. We do not expect these rights to be bestowed upon us as an act of grace and magnanimity or because of some political expediency, but as a matter of honor and justice.[18]

Jews actively participated in the elections to the First Duma (Parliament), voting wherever advisable for Jewish candidates and elsewhere throwing the weight of their ballots on the side of liberals and moderate labor leaders. The Jewish socialists, however, boycotted the election because they saw in it but a reactionary tool of pacification of the discontented masses and they expected the ultimate solution of the Jewish question only from direct revolutionary action.

Despite this boycott the Jews succeeded in electing twelve of their own coreligionists to the Duma, including the distinguished leaders Maxim M. Vinaver, Shmarya Levin, and Leonty M. Bramson. Although the League for the Attainment of Jewish Rights, which sought to unite the Jewish factions for common action, was run by nationalistic Jews who would have preferred to see the formation of a Jewish bloc similar to the Polish bloc in parliament, the deputies themselves decided to join the two leading parties of the Cadets (Constitutional Democrats), a left-of-center liberal party, and the Trudoviki (Labor Party), still further to the left. The 9 Jewish Cadets, though a small minority of the party's 179 deputies, made their influence felt beyond their numbers. Similarly, the

3 Jewish Labor members (out of 94) often spoke up. Together the two parties formed a majority of the 476 deputies, and though refraining from calling the Duma a Constituent Assembly, planned to write a new egalitarian constitution. The plenary debates of May, 1906, raised the Jewish issue almost immediately. But the Octobrist conservatives urged slow motion, and persuaded the Duma to hand the matter over to a committee of thirty-three, including five Jews.

In the middle of the deliberations the news arrived of the Bialystok pogrom of June 14–16. After a number of outspoken addresses by both Jewish and non-Jewish deputies, including Prince Sergei D. Urussov, a former governor of Bessarabia and assistant minister of interior, who submitted a well-documented accusation of the regime partly based on his own experiences, the Duma elected an investigating committee of three deputies, including a Jew, V. Jacobson, to institute an inquiry on the spot. The committee brought back a devastating report which made the following main points:

1. That there was no hatred of a national, religious, or economic character between the Jews and Christians in Bialystok.
2. That hostility to the Jews existed only among the police, who exerted themselves to promote ill-feeling in the army by accusing the Jews of taking part in the movement of freedom.
3. That the pogrom was previously planned and prepared by the administration and that the local population was quite cognizant of these matters.

After a lengthy debate the Duma adopted, on July 7/20, the following resolution:

That the only remedy for this situation unparalleled in the history of civilized countries, and the only means to prevent further pogroms, are to be found in an immediate judicial investigation and the punishment of all officials, high and subordinate, without regard to their position, who were responsible for the pogroms, and the dismissal of the Ministry.[19]

However, this resolution came too late to do any good. Recovering from the revolutionary shock, the tsar disbanded the Duma on the following day. The liberal deputies, including all the twelve Jews, protested vigorously. At a meeting at Viborg, Finland, they urged the population to retaliate by passive resistance, such as refusing to pay taxes or submitting to the military draft. In reprisal, the government denounced all signers as traitors, condemned several to prison terms of three months, and withdrew their franchise. In the election to the Second Duma, therefore, these prominent leaders were not eligible, and only four unknown Jewish deputies were elected. M. J. Herzenstein, a

Cadet deputy of Jewish descent, and the Jewish deputy G. Iollos were assassinated by the Black Hundreds. By a *coup d'état*, the tsar dismissed the Second Duma, too, and altered the basic electoral law, disfranchising a large majority of the population. As a result, the Third Duma (1907–1912) was wholly dominated by the reactionary forces, and except for occasionally serving as a forum for Jewish and liberal, as well as Jewbaiting and reactionary, pronunciamentos, it was of little assistance to the Jewish cause. Its Jewish membership was reduced to two, to be raised to three in the Fourth Duma (November 1912–February 1917).

Parliamentary institutions thus proved of little avail to the Jewish minority. Tsarism resumed its cold war against its Jewish subjects with renewed vigor, though it was frightened enough by both the domestic and the world reaction not to continue with the hotter forms of warfare, the governmentally instigated pogroms. Nicholas II resisted any amelioration of Jewish status. He was abetted therein by the nobles, who saw in any forward step a diminution of their own power. When in October, 1906, the reactionary Council of Ministers, presided over by Peter A. Stolypin, submitted to the tsar modest proposals for the improvement of Jewish status, Nicholas, after hesitating for two months, entered the following characteristic note:

> Despite most convincing arguments in favor of adopting a positive decision in this matter, an inner voice keeps on insisting more and more that I do accept responsibility for it. . . . I know that you, too, believe that "A tsar's heart is in God's hand." Let it be so. For all laws established by me I bear a great responsibility before God, and I am ready to answer for this decision at any time.

Not surprisingly, the reaction assumed such force in the following year that N. M. Friedman, one of the two Jewish deputies in the Third Duma, could declare in February, 1910, "In the worst days for the Jews under Minister Plehve there never existed so much cruelty and bestiality as is practiced today."[20]

Nor did the government hesitate to continue with its literary incitation of one group of the population against another, although it generally maintained a tight grip on all publications through its vigorous censorship. In the decade of 1905–16, on which we have some detailed data, it permitted the printing and distribution of 14,327,000 copies of 2,837 anti-Semitic books and pamphlets. The tsar himself allegedly contributed 12,239,000 rubles from his private holdings toward the dissemination of that scurrilous literature, including the aforementioned prototypes of the *Protocols of the Elders of Zion*.[21]

The government itself sufficiently believed in the myth of a Jewish world conspiracy—a myth intimated as early as 1881–83 by the famous Panslavist leader, Ivan Sergeevich Aksakov—for Foreign Minister

Count Vladimir Nikolaevich Lamsdorf to submit to the tsar a memorandum "on the anarchists" (January, 1906). Partly guided by his wish to steer Russia's foreign policies away from the dual alliance with France into pro-German channels, he argued that the threat of the world Jewish conspiracy could be averted only by Russia's concerted action with the German Empire and the Vatican. He suggested that in order to counteract the effort of the Alliance Israélite Universelle, with its "gigantic pecuniary means" and its support "by the Masonic lodges of every description," negotiations be begun with the Kaiser and the Pope "for the purpose of organizing a vigilant supervision, and then also for an active joint struggle against the common foe of the Christian and monarchical order of Europe." The gullible tsar noted on the memorandum, "Negotiations must be entered into immediately. I share entirely the opinions herein expressed."[22] Nevertheless, calmer counsels prevailed and no action was taken. Since Lamsdorf's anti-French policy held out little promise of success against the Triple Alliance, he himself was dropped from the foreign ministry.

As a final coup Nicholas II and his advisers resorted to the time-honored method of blackening the Jewish name by a new Blood Accusation. Sporadic instances of the ritual murder libel made their appearance throughout the nineteenth century. The accusation of a Vilna barber, David Blondes, in 1900, led to a protracted trial, an appeal, and retrial, and ended in 1902 with his acquittal. Even the first unfavorable court sentence condemned Blondes only for an ordinary murder but did not impute to him any ritualistic motives. In contrast thereto the discovery in March, 1911, of the corpse of a thirteen-year-old Russian boy in the vicinity of a Jewish factory in Kiev was blown up by the authorities into a *cause célèbre* through the ritual murder accusation of Mendel Beilis, a minor employee in that factory. The trial conducted in Kiev in 1913 attracted world-wide attention. The minister of justice, I. G. Shcheglovitov, and his assistants marshaled a number of "experts" to prove the persistence of Jewish ritual murders, while the defense, led by the distinguished Jewish lawyer Oscar O. Gruzenberg, produced the testimony of first-rate Oriental scholars like Paul Kokovtsev against the very existence of such a ritual. A great many Russian and Western luminaries—including Dmitrii Merezhkovskii, Leonid Andreev, Anatole France, Jean Jaurès, Gerhard Hauptmann, and Thomas Masaryk—likewise took up the cudgel against this revival of a dangerous folkloristic myth. More significantly, even the Kiev jury of unsophisticated peasants acquitted the defendant. This final defeat should have served tsarism as a warning that its extreme Judeophobia would not, as it had hoped, divert the attention of the masses from their genuine grievances to the Jewish scapegoat.[23]

[5]

Population and Migrations

It was a sign of Russian Jewry's tremendous vitality that despite all outside pressures and occasional losses in manpower brought about by pogroms, it steadily increased in numbers during the entire tsarist period. This was not only an absolute growth in population but—except for the last three decades, which witnessed an extraordinary Jewish exodus from the Russian Empire—also relative to the rest of the population. True, the statistical evidence for these statements is somewhat shaky. To begin with, the very estimates of the total Russian population, despite occasional governmental censuses or so-called revisions, are far from reliable. In the Jewish case we often depend wholly on "guestimates." The first time one can speak with some confidence of Russia's Jewish population is after the census of 1897, only twenty years before the end of the tsarist regime. At that time the imperial population was estimated at 126,368,827, of whom 5,189,401 or 4.13 percent were Jews. Of course, the largest number was concentrated in the Pale of Settlement (including the ten provinces belonging to Congress Poland), whose total population numbered 42,352,039 and included 4,874,636 or 11.46 percent Jews. Without Congress Poland, these figures were reduced by 9,401,097 and 1,316,576, respectively.[1]

The Russian Jew

The best estimates for the Jewish population after the Napoleonic Wars, when the area under tsarist domination had become fairly stabilized, show that in 1820 European Russia's total population (without the Caucasus) of some 46,000,000 (including some 3,000,000 in Poland) embraced approximately 1,600,000 Jews (about 400,000 in Poland). By 1851 the ninth official "revision" indicated (including the Caucasus) a total of 61,000,000 inhabitants, and a Jewish population of 2,400,000 (including 600,000 in Poland). By 1880 the general population increased to 86,000,000, the Jewish to about 4,000,000 (1,000,000 in Poland). This increase continued, and in 1910 Russia had 130,800,000 residents and more than 5,600,000 Jews. In short, in the six decades from 1820 to 1880, the number of Jews apparently increased about 150 percent while the general population grew only 87 percent. On the other hand, in the subsequent thirty years Jewry added only about 40 percent to its numbers, while Russia's general population climbed by 52 percent. The reason for this relative retardation is, of course, the tremendous rate of Jewish emigration, which by far exceeded that of the non-Jewish peoples.[2]

Of equal interest are the internal shifts. Understandably, the Neo-Russian territories, first opened to Jews under Catherine II, showed the greatest ratio of growth. The percentage of Jews in the southwestern provinces, including Bessarabia, rose from 3 in 1844 to 7.4 in 1880 and to 8.9 in 1897. Sixteen years later, however, the ratio of Jewish settlers declined to 7.9 percent, although they increased in absolute numbers by almost 25 percent. During the entire period from 1844 to 1913 the general population of the area increased by 265 percent, the Jewish population by 844 percent. In the older northwestern provinces Jewish growth in absolute numbers was actually larger, although its relative progress was much slower. In the fifty years from 1847 to 1897 Jewry increased there from 947,753 to 2,622,553, or by 177 percent. Yet compared with the rest of the population its ratio of 9.26 percent, which had interveningly grown to 16.88 percent in 1881, was reduced to 13.36 percent in 1897. This proportionate decline continued during the early years of the twentieth century, when it was aggravated by incipient signs of biological retardation because of a declining Jewish birth rate. The Polish provinces showed slightly different trends, owing to the considerable immigration of so-called Litvaks from the northwestern provinces into Congress Poland. During the century of 1816–1913 the general population grew by 381 percent, the Jewish by 822 percent, the Jewish percentage rising from 7.8 to 14.97. Only the decade from 1880 to 1890 showed a temporary dip from 14.1 to 13.7 percent.

In contrast thereto, the Jewish population density outside the Pale was very slight, except in the Baltic provinces of Courland (7.33 percent) and Livonia (2.24 percent), where Jews had lived in substantial numbers before the Russian occupation. Otherwise the province of St. Petersburg, with its 21,270 Jews forming 1.01 percent of the population, showed the largest concentration, owing to the presence of a substantial Jewish community in the capital. The second capital, Moscow, together with its province had only 8,749 Jews or 0.36 percent. In toto, European Russia outside the Pale averaged in 1897 a Jewish population of only 0.34 percent, some provinces having as few as 0.03 percent.

Reasons for this extraordinary fertility of Russian Jewry are not hard to find. During the entire nineteenth century the overwhelmingly Orthodox majority of East European Jews viewed God's blessing to Adam, "Be fruitful, and multiply, and replenish the earth" (Gen. 1:28), as a direct commandment. Early marriages were quite common; with them went large families. During his 1891 visit to the Jewish agricultural colonists in the province of Kherson, Arnold White learned "from the neighboring proprietors—Russians—who employed them, [that] they have no vice, unless early, improvident and fruitful marriages can be deemed a vice."

We have no exact statistics for the Jewish birth rate early in the nineteenth century, but it must have annually averaged some 40 births per 1,000 population. In this respect, to be sure, the difference between the Jews and their neighbors was not very substantial. Russia's general birth rate, particularly among the peasant masses, probably also averaged 4 percent of the population. Russian Jewry gained little by immigration even during the first decades of the century, when a number of Galician Jews, particularly scholars, educators, and writers, settled in the newly opened Neo-Russian areas. Unfriendly observers, including foreign visitors, spoke disparagingly of this influx. For example, Robert Lyall, who had spent a number of years in Russia, commented in his travel book, published in 1825, that from the beginning Odessa had become a place of refuge for the "worst members of society" from neighboring lands. Among the new arrivals were three hundred Jewish families, mostly from Galicia.[3] Nevertheless, on balance Russian Jewry was probably losing more members through clandestine or overt emigration, even before the exodus assumed a mass character in the last three decades of the century. The Jews' relatively higher population increase must therefore have depended mainly on a generally lower mortality.

Once again we have no exact figures, but it is likely that Jews suffered somewhat less than their neighbors from the destructive forces of famine, pestilence, and war. According to the historian Alexander Kornilov, the cholera epidemic of 1848 cost Russia about 3,000,000 lives. It was aggravated by crop failure and the ensuing famine, one of the numerous famines in Russia of the post-Napoleonic era (1820–21, 1833, 1839–40, 1843–46, and so forth). Another major cholera epidemic ravaged Russia in 1869, while a severe famine struck down hundreds of thousands of peasants as late as 1890–91. The Napoleonic Wars, too, seem to have accounted for a loss of some 1,500,000 Russian lives. The Jews suffered a great deal, too, during all these catastrophes, but their losses in manpower were somewhat mitigated by their higher cultural level and strong communal solidarity. Jewish communities, as a rule, strained all their resources to help coreligionists in need, and probably relatively few died of full-fledged starvation. During the epidemics, too, the Jewish losses may well have been minimized by communal aid and the ready availability of medical care in many localities.

Most decisive was the lower Jewish infant and child mortality. While even at the beginning of this century out of each 1,000 newly born peasant children some 450 died before the age of five, the figures for the Jewish community probably were for the same reasons very much smaller. Another factor was the great cohesiveness of the Jewish family, which traditionally went to extremes in saving the lives of its members, old and young. If that hypothesis is correct, one can readily see that in each successive generation a much larger percentage of newly born Jewish children survived to the age of reproduction.

On the other hand, losses occasioned by wars seem to have affected more or less equally the general and the Jewish population. Between 1815 and 1914 Russia enjoyed a relatively prolonged period of peace, interrupted significantly only by the Crimean War of 1853–56, the Russo–Turkish War of 1878, and the Russo-Japanese War of 1904–1905. In none of these wars was the Pale of Jewish Settlement a major battlefield. But among combatants Jewish losses were probably as high as those of their neighbors. It is a matter of record that when the results of the fairly reliable census of 1897 were published, the Russian Jewish community heaved a sigh of relief. For decades before, the Jews whad been accused of shirking their military duties—there is no question that many Jewish and non-Jewish young men successfully evaded their civic obligation through bribery or other methods—and many decrees were issued over the decades to prevent the allegedly "excessive" Jewish evasions. One of them provided that families, even remote relatives, be fined 300 rubles for each "shirker," an amount which was often collected from the poorest by the public auction of their meager household goods. In 1901 it turned out that while Jews amounted to only 4.13 percent of the imperial population, the percentage of their servicemen was 5.73. In other words, Jewish soldiers and sailors, despite all the maltreatment they often suffered from their superiors and comrades in the armed forces and despite their religious scruples arising from the impossibility of observing there the Sabbath and ritual food commandments, exceeded their population ratio by nearly 40 percent. These facts, debated long before the census of 1897, were fully borne out again by the established number of Jewish combatants in the Russo-Japanese War.[4]

Of course, one must not lose sight of Jewish war losses of their own kind: those occasioned by anti-Jewish massacres. Ethically and psychologically, ten human victims of violence are ten too many, but from the point of view of population figures, the loss of several hundred or even a thousand members did not seriously undermine the natural growth of a community numbering four or five million.

More important was another specifically Jewish source of demographic losses, namely conversion to Christianity. Notwithstanding the orthodoxy of the majority, quite a few Jews—whether in the armed forces, among the more easily assimilated intelligentsia, or in the group of straight careerists—joined the dominant faiths. An English visitor, Robert Pinkerton, was told by Archbishop Anatoli of Minsk that in the two years between Pinkerton's visits, he had converted fifteen Jews of that city. According to the slightly exaggerated estimates of the Berlin missionary J. de le Roi, no less than 84,536 Russian Jews found their way to the baptismal font during the nineteenth century. Nearly 70,000 of those joined the Russian Orthodox faith, while 12,000, primarily in Poland, became Roman Catholics.[5] However, the biological vitality of the Jewish people, undiminished during the entire nineteenth century, made up for all these losses, including even the largest drain of them all, the stream of emigration.

URBAN CONCENTRATION

Another important demographic feature was the growing Jewish concentration in large and medium-sized cities. In Russia, though to a lesser extent than in western or central Europe, the nineteenth century witnessed the gradual rise of large metropolitan areas. By 1884 there already were twelve cities with populations of over 100,000 in the empire. Sixteen years later their number had increased to sixteen. Next to the two capitals, the largest of these were Warsaw, Odessa, Lodz, Riga, Kiev, Kharkhov, Vilna, Ekaterinoslav, and Kishinev, each of which had a sizeable Jewish community. Odessa, Ekaterinoslav, and Kiev, where Jews started to settle (or resettle) under Russian domination, showed the most substantial growth. The Odessa community embraced only 246 Jews in 1795; it grew to 17,000 in 1855, 138,915 in 1897, and 152,634 in 1904. Ekaterinoslav's Jewry rose from 320 in 1804 to 3,365 in 1857, 40,009 in 1897, and 69,012 in 1910. Kiev, which had long lost its medieval community, had 207 Jews in 1797, 3,013 in 1863, 31,801 in 1897, and 50,792 in 1910. Odessa thus became the largest Jewish settlement outside Poland, where Warsaw was speedily developing into the largest Jewish community in all of Europe (277,787 in 1908). Lodz, too, because of its extraordinary industrial expansion, witnessed the rise of its Jewish community from 2,775 in 1856 to 98,677 in 1897, to decline during the following eleven years to 88,201.

At the same time, the older Jewish communities likewise grew substantially, if less rapidly. The Jewish population in Vilna, which in the course of the nineteenth century achieved the honorific title of a "Lithuanian Jerusalem," grew from some 7,000 in 1797 to 23,050 in 1847, 63,996 in 1897, and 72,323 in 1910. That of Minsk increased from 2,716 in 1802 to 12,976 in 1847, 47,562 in 1897, but declined to 45,103 in 1910. In each of these cases the decline was due entirely to emigration.[6]

These figures assume even greater significance when one realizes that outside the Polish provinces the Pale embraced a nationally heterogenous population. Among the various nationalities inhabiting the northwestern and the southwestern provinces the Jews often constituted the majority, or at least the largest single group, of the urban population. More specifically, in 1897, 52 percent of the combined urban population of Lithuania and White Russia consisted of Jews. The next largest groups were those of Russians (18.2 percent), Poles (12.8 percent), while the White Russian native majority had a share of only 11.8 percent, the Lithuanians as little as 1.7 percent. In the Ukraine, to be sure, the Russians with 33.5 percent appear in the census as the largest urban group, followed by the Jews with 30 and the Ukrainians with 27 percent. But all these census figures were weighted in favor of the Russians, since undoubtedly many Ukrainians, White Russians, and Lithuanians listed themselves as Russians. Moreover, the "Russians" consisted chiefly of garrisoned soldiers, civil servants, teachers, occasional factory workers, technicians, and managers—in other words, of frequently transient residents. Certainly, in all the urban centers of industry, commerce, education, and the arts, Jews played a preponderant role. Their total contribution, therefore, to the Russian economy and culture, particularly in the most advanced western provinces, far exceeded their ratio in the total population.

Needless to say, these urban communities did not owe their extraordinary expansion to natural growth alone but also to the influx of settlers from the smaller towns and hamlets. Apart from taking full advantage of the opening of the Neo-Russian territories, Russo-Polish Jewry spoke of a "discovery of Volhynia" in the mid-nineteenth century. Although that province had belonged to pre-partition Poland and was densely populated by Jews even then, its growing sugar and other industries offered many new opportunities for Jewish entrepreneurs and workers. Hence Volhynia, which in 1847 embraced 174,457 Jews, witnessed their increase half a century later to 395,782, or by 127 percent.

The agricultural colonization projects also drew some Jewish colonists, primarily to the Black Sea region.

Otherwise the Pale offered a permanent obstacle to internal Jewish migrations. Even the two capitals, which undoubtedly would have attracted a very substantial number of Jews, as they did after the Revolution of 1917, not only rigidly restricted their admission but also frequently saw the police stage raids on the few settlers who had secured entry in one way or another. Urbanization of the few Jews who managed to settle beyond the Pale was even greater than within it. Fully 82 percent of all Jews living in the province of St. Petersburg and 97 percent of all Jewish settlers in the Moscow province were concentrated in the two capitals. Similarly, Kharkov embraced more than 80 percent, Rostov-on-Don, nearly 75 percent of all Jewish residents in their provinces. Reinforced by climatic and economic factors, the law also sharply limited Jewish emigration even to the older Jewish settlements in the Caucasus or the Bukhara region, settlements which reached back to the early Middle Ages. While Russian peasants often found an outlet for their surplus population in Siberia (some 800,000 peasants settled there in the decade from 1886 to 1896 alone, and the annual rate of over 80,000 immigrants continued in the subsequent years as well), only few Jews could or would join that procession. That is why the census of 1897 revealed the presence of only 56,783 Jews in the Caucasus and 48,474 Jews in Siberia and central Asia. It is small wonder, then, that as soon as the Neo-Russian territories began filling up and reaching a Jewish population ratio approximating that of the older provinces, Jews had to look for an additional *Lebensraum* elsewhere.

WESTWARD MIGRATION

Russo-Jewish emigration to other countries faced many obstacles, however. The tsarist system required that travelers carry with them governmental passports which were as a rule refused to would-be émigrés. Jews often had to resort to clandestine emigration even for religious pilgrimages to Palestine with the hope of ultimately being buried in its holy soil. Travelers provided with passports, we remember, lost their Russian citizenship after a brief absence and could not return to their native land.

Nevertheless, beginning with the 1840s the pressure became sufficiently great for substantial numbers of Jews to cross the frontiers to Germany and Austria. On German initiative, Jewish leaders of Frankfurt, Königsberg, London, and Paris submitted, in 1844, a petition to Tsar Nicholas I, asking that Jews be allowed to leave Russia without hindrance. Curiously, among the projected areas of Jewish settlement at that time, Texas loomed large; its German Settlement Association, headed by Prince Karl von Solms Braunsfeld, actually negotiated with Jewish representatives for the inclusion of Russian Jews in its plans to colonize that vast underdeveloped territory with European immigrants. Two years later Zacharias Frankel, a famed talmudic scholar, declared bluntly, "For the Russian Jews there is only one way out: to leave Russia and settle under a sky where the law recognizes human rights." His colleague, Ludwig Philippson, always prone to develop new schemes, suggested the establishment of a German Aid Association to organize the mass transplantation of Jews from Russia to a suitable new territory and to assist them in securing employment. Although premature at that time—such a *Hilfsverein* for East European Jews under this very name was to be organized nearly sixty years later—it did indicate the concern of the Western Jews for the future of their Russian coreligionists languishing under the knout of Nicholas I and his subordinates.

Out of the same concern, we recall, Jacob Isaac Altaras of Marseilles arrived in St. Petersburg in 1846 with his adventurous scheme of settling thousands of Russian Jews in French Algeria. The Russian government was inclined to go along, under the condition that the émigrés would lose their Russian citizenship upon crossing the frontier. François Guizot, the French minister of foreign affairs, however, vetoed the entire undertaking. "Do you mean to Judaize Algeria?" he allegedly asked Altaras.[7]

Nothing came out of these grandiose projects, but there was a growing outflow of Russian Jewish individuals to central and western Europe, as well as the New World. During the first decades of the nineteenth century quite a few "Polish" synagogues were founded in America, indicating a swelling stream of immigration from eastern Europe in general, for in the new lands outsiders paid little heed to the differences between Russian, Polish, Galician, or Rumanian subjects. Only a few decades later, when the emigration from these countries assumed a mass character, was it possible for the natives of these lands to separate themselves into special congregations and *Landsmannschaften*, according to their places of origin.

The turning point came during the great Russian famine and epidemic of 1868–69, from which Jews suffered along with their neighbors. At the same time economic conditions were constantly improving in the United States after the Civil War. News from relatives previously settled in America was at times discouraging, but the pessimistic reports were far outnumbered by glowing descriptions from other expatriates. These high-flown expectations, which in Germany and Austria had reached a climax in the so-called On to America Movement of the revolutionary year 1848 and the early 1850s, were now communicated with even greater fervor to the Jews of Russia and Poland. Mary Antin, who came to the United States in 1891, reminisced about her youth in Plotsk, Russia:

> "America" was in everybody's mouth. Businessmen talked of it over their accounts; the market women made up their quarrels that they might discuss it from stall to stall; people who had relatives in the famous land went around reading their letters for the enlightenment of less fortunate folks, the one letter-carrier informed the public how many letters arrived from America, and who were the recipients; children played at emigrating. . . . A few persons—they were a dress-maker's daughter, and a merchant with his two sons—who had returned from America after a long visit, happened to be endowed with extraordinary imagination (a faculty closely related to their knowledge of their old countrymen's ignorance), and their descriptions of life across the ocean, given daily, for some months, to eager audiences, surpassed anything in the Arabian Nights.

Better informed, though no less prone to exaggerate, were the readers of the Russian Jewish press, which published frequent dispatches from American Jewish correspondents.[8]

It was not altogether easy for reemigrants to return to Russia. Those who had failed to fulfill their military duties were arrested despite their American passports. Generally, the problem of reciprocity in the treatment of American Jewish citizens in the Tsarist Empire increasingly complicated relations between the two countries. The Russians took the position that American Jews should not be treated more favorably than native Jews, whereas the United States claimed that there must be no discrimination between her Jewish and non-Jewish citizens. Russia also debated this issue with other countries whose Jewry enjoyed full equality of rights, but only the United States, after several vain protests, took vigorous action. Under the pressure of public opinion and fair unanimity in Congress, President Taft in December, 1911, abrogated the commercial treaty with Russia which had been in operation since 1832.[9]

Additional incentives to emigrate to America were given by the lower rates for ocean travel (bait extended by commercial agents of shipping companies), the ability of earlier arrivals to send more and more tickets to relatives, and ideological postulates concerning the restratification of the Jewish people from a predominantly mercantile class to one living from "productive" occupations. All these factors were accelerated by the pogrom wave of 1881, the restrictive May Laws of 1882, and later ordinances. Psychologically, we recall, these physical and legislative attacks not only shook Russian Jewry, but also evoked a sympathetic echo among Western liberals. Various international Jewish relief organizations now fostered the emigration of Russian Jews to America or, in a lesser degree, to Palestine. True, good will was not enough. The needs of the ever-swelling stream of émigrés transcended the resources of most relief groups, old and new, and often created much confusion, even resentment. Some American Jews viewed with alarm the possible deterioration of their own status as a result of the arrival of large groups of émigrés totally different in language and mores from the American population. As early as 1878, the American delegates to a Jewish World Conference warned their European colleagues against indiscriminate promotion of Jewish emigration to the United States. But as soon as the enormity of the Russian pogroms struck home, opinion veered strongly toward helping the newcomers at all costs. Even then, however, the Alliance Israélite warned the other organizations that it feared "to provoke by our intervention, an emigration movement which, were it to assume too great dimensions, might entail difficulties so serious that even the united forces of Jewry would be unable to cope with them."[10]

On the other hand, an assembly of forty Jewish leaders in St. Petersburg, under the chairmanship of Baron Horace Günzburg, adopted, in April, 1882, a resolution rejecting "completely the thought of organizing emigration" because it was incompatible with "the historic rights of the Jews to their present fatherland." Among the Jewish youth, especially its new radical segment, the idea of fighting it out with the reactionary regime on the spot was constantly gaining ground. On their part some Orthodox leaders, such as Israel Meir Kahan, opposed emigration because they feared the ensuing neglect of Jewish rituals and customs among the expatriates in a new and strange world.[11]

Because of fears of this kind Russian Jewish leaders long hesitated to take an active part in the promotion of Jewish emigration, or even in extending a helping hand to needy émigrés. This ambivalence came clearly to the fore as early as 1869, at the inception of Jewish mass emigration from Russia. Although the relief activities of the ad hoc Kaunas (Kovno) Committee, organized with the aid of the provincial governor, Prince Evgenii P. Obolensky, proved quite successful (the tsar and tsarevitch contributed 2,000 rubles, Baron James Rothschild of Paris, 24,000 francs, and so forth), many committee members were apprehensive that any public effort to encourage emigration to other lands might be considered unpatriotic. This view was sharply expressed by the committee's secretary, J. Lewy, in an article in the Odessa Jewish periodical *Dien*. Instead, these leaders favored aid to Jewish craftsmen to migrate to the interior of Russia, a course which was legally open to them, despite the risks involved. As a result, the short-lived committee contributed but little directly to Russo-Jewish emigration, though the publicity generated in the Jewish press by its formation seems to have raised pertinent questions among the starving masses.[12]

Nevertheless, emigration proceeded apace in ever-increasing numbers. The best estimates available show that during the entire half-century of 1820 to 1870 only some 7,500 Russian and Polish Jews settled in the United States. During the decade of 1871 to 1880 the number of such arrivals suddenly rose to over 40,000. It increased again to some 135,000 during the following decade, to grow further to 279,811 from 1891 to 1900 and to 704,245 between 1901 and 1910. It continued at a high rate for four more years until World War I shut almost all avenues for emigration from eastern Europe. Needless to say, Jews were not the only ones to leave the Tsarist Empire for the United States. In fact, their ratio among Russian émigrés decreased from decade to decade, and from a majority of 63.3 percent in the 1880s declined to a minority of 44.1 percent between 1901 and 1910.[13] But while the tsar's other subjects often went to the United States only in order to accumulate savings and return to the old country, very few Jews repatriated themselves. In any case, Jews were the most conspicuous protagonists of that dramatic movement to friends and foes alike.

We have discussed at some length the emigration from Russia to the United States because that country received well over 70 percent of all Jewish expatriates and also because its egalitarian structure so sharply contrasted with the conditions at home. However, there was a simultaneous movement from Russia to Canada (in 1914 the annual peak of 11,252 East European Jewish arrivals was reached), South Africa (during the first decade of the twentieth century there were 17,200 Jewish arrivals from eastern Europe) and other British Empire countries. The British motherland herself became a major haven of refuge for some 120,000 Jewish immigrants in the four decades before World War I despite the anti-alien legislation which imposed severe restrictions.[14] Many Russian émigrés found their way to other West European countries. Some of them, to be sure, originally planned to proceed to the United States, but largely because of lack of funds had to remain at one of the way stations. If a number of these "transients" ultimately reached their final destination, a great many others found work and became adjusted to their respective environments.

One of the most fascinating phases of that migratory movement was Baron Maurice de Hirsch's large-scale attempt to colonize Russian Jews in such an underdeveloped country as Argentina. Because of the bankruptcy of one of his firm's debtors, Hirsch personally chanced to possess extensive tracts of land there. He founded the Jewish Colonization Association in 1891, endowing it with the then-enormous philanthropic donation of £2,000,000. Upon his death five years later the association received an additional bequest of £6,000,000. Its objectives were stated broadly in Article iii of its charter:

> To assist and promote the emigration of Jews from any parts of Europe
> or Asia, and principally from countries in which they may for the time

[73]

being be subjected to any special taxes or political or other disabilities, to any other parts of the world, and to form and establish colonies in various parts of North and South America and other countries for agricultural, commercial, and other purposes.

Obviously, the Russian Jews were foremost in the minds of Hirsch and his Western associates. His representative, the Englishman Arnold White, conducted lengthy negotiations with the Russian ministers in St. Petersburg and obtained from them pledges of active collaboration. Hirsch's scheme was, as we recall, to remove on the average 125,000 Jews annually during the following twenty-five years and thus to reduce the biological pressure on them. He apparently overlooked their dynamic natural increase, which to some extent would have nullified the effects of even such a mass exodus. The American minister to Russia, Charles Emory Smith, was more correct in estimating in 1891 that at best 25,000 Russian Jews could leave each year for Argentina; such emigration would absorb only a fraction of their natural increase, which he estimated at 150,000 to 180,000. As it turned out, not even 25,000 Jews ever arrived in Argentina in any single year. The peaks of all East European immigration to that country were reached in 1906 and 1912, in each of which approximately 13,500 Jews settled there, most of them without the support of the Jewish Colonization Association. Nonetheless, this gigantic undertaking of a philanthropic visionary made a lasting impression upon both the Jewish and the non-Jewish worlds.[15]

[6]

Economic
Transformations

ⓘ

With even less precision can one speak of the changes in the economic structure of Russian Jewry during the nineteenth century. The general Russian statistics of that period are largely based upon irregular reports by government officials, men not only untrained in statistical work, but using questionnaires lacking in uniformity even during the same years and greatly differing from one "census" to another. The results are therefore rarely comparable. Nor were Jews or, for that matter, other citizens anxious to cooperate. If the threat of military service (frequently used by the Russian regime as a punitive measure) deterred many parents from registering their children, the specter of excessive and arbitrary taxes made returns concerning one's occupation, income, and other economic data quite unreliable.

Nonetheless, the general contours of a major economic revolution that took place especially in the latter part of the nineteenth century emerge quite clearly from manifold detailed studies made by Russian scholars. Jews participated in that general Russian—indeed, European—revolution, beyond their ratio in the population. In some respects they became major victims of the new transformations, in others, their often unconscious pioneers. While the economic structure of Jews within the Russian Pale before World War I still bore a remote resemblance to that of their ancestors a century earlier, the minority allowed to settle outside the Pale had undergone a total change.

After inheriting Poland's eastern provinces, the tsars found many Jewish subjects settled in rural districts, but only partially involved in agricultural pursuits. Many of them were so-called *arendators* (lessees), a combination of innkeepers and landlords' agents. Apart from distilling and selling liquor and accommodating transients, these small rural entrepreneurs ran village stores, collected revenue from farmers for their frequently absentee landlords, and served as purchasing agents for Jewish grain merchants in neighboring cities. On the side they cultivated small parcels of land, had a few cows, goats, and chickens, and produced vegetables and dairy products mainly for their own and their employees' consumption. These factota played a necessary role in the rural economy and, as later studies were to show, enabled the farmers within the Pale to sell their produce at considerably higher prices than were obtainable in Russia's interior. In return, they supplied the farming population with industrial articles imported from cities, sometimes from foreign countries. These relationships were not always amicable. Since the peasants were permanently exploited by their landlords and the Jews often served as the latter's operative agents, there was much anti-Jewish feeling, aggravated by religious animosities fanned by many priests, Russian Orthodox, Uniate, or Catholic.

Such Judeo-peasant tensions became a major preoccupation of the Russian administration and served as a frequent excuse for its discriminatory policies. In general, the controlling feudal powers looked askance at too close relations between the peasantry and its urban neighbors. In 1782, Catherine II altogether forbade the town burghers to establish themselves in villages, "lest they exploit the peasants." If behind this prohibition lurked the suspicion that urban settlers, bringing with them "enlightened" ideas, might help to undermine the established order, this dread was doubly justified, the authorities believed, if Jews were the disseminators of the new concepts. Overtly, the tsarist organs accused the Jews not only of exploiting the peasants by usurious loans and underhanded mercantile deals, but also of poisoning them by selling them excessive quantities of liquor on credit. With this accusation, repeated with endless variations, the government felt justified to try to eliminate Jewish settlers from the rural districts altogether.

On closer examination these imputations proved unfounded. As early as 1844, Ivan Funduklei, a non-Jewish statistician of the province of Kiev showed, after a close survey of a village community, that after the eviction of Jews both the prices and the consumption of liquor had gone up substantially. A government committee appointed by Alexander II in 1870 reported that most complaints about drunkenness came from the Greater Russian provinces, fewer from the Ukrainian and Neo-

Russian territories, and practically none from the western provinces densely inhabited by Jews. The fullest statistical material was assembled by the so-called Pahlen Commission in 1883–86. When carefully analyzed by distinguished scholars—including Ivan S. Blioch—in a five-volume work devoted to a comparative study of the Great Russian, western, and Polish provinces—these data showed conclusively that there was far less alcoholism among the peasants within, than those in the provinces adjacent to, the Pale. These and other studies also demonstrated that the western peasants (in part owing to the proximity of Jewish traders) were economically much better off than their opposite numbers outside the Pale.[1]

AGRICULTURAL COLONIZATION

Nonetheless many progressive Jews themselves admitted that the Jewish economic stratification was unhealthy. Ever since the middle of the eighteenth century Western thinkers, both Jewish and non-Jewish, insisted on the necessity of making Jews more "productive." Under the influence of the physiocratic school of economics, in particular, which emphasized that only agriculture was genuinely productive, some leaders started preaching the return of Jews to the soil. Others combined that preachment with practical efforts toward teaching Jews useful crafts in order to divert them from their reputedly "parasitic" commercial occupations. These ideas, which found a resounding echo during the grand debate on the Jewish question at the time of the Quadrennial Diet in Poland, also had exponents in Russia among Jews like Nathan Neta Notkin in 1797 and officials like G. R. Derzhavin from 1799 on. Of course, none of these advocates had in mind the occasional Jewish landlord, who like Joshua Zeitlin, owned an estate with 910 "souls" on it. The number of such Jewish landowners constantly dwindled.[2]

Following the example set by Emperor Joseph II in Austria, Alexander I adopted the idea of colonizing Jews in the vast open spaces of New Russia. He and his advisers realized that in order to be successful, such colonization would have to proceed by groups which, when transplanted into new village communities, could combine agricultural pursuits with the continued cultivation of their own religious and cultural mores. When in 1806 the government set aside a tract of land of over 80,000 acres in the province of Kherson for young Jews physically fit and in possession of 400 rubles per family, a sufficient number of candidates responded for several such Jewish colonies to be founded. They had an initial population of some 600 families who gave their new settlements such picturesque names as *Sede Menuche (Sedeh Menuhah* or Field of Rest), and *Har Shefer* (Beautiful Mountain). Many more were willing to come. In the province of Vitebsk alone 867 families registered with the authorities, whose pecuniary means proved wholly inadequate, however, during that period of great fiscal stringency.

Not surprisingly, the settlers' enthusiasm cooled off in the face of stark realities. One of the earliest colonists reminisced later: "It took us four months until we dragged ourselves to Kremenchug. . . . Arriving on the spot, in a dismal land during a severe winter, we started to plough up the virgin land. . . . From time to time it occurred that we did not have the utensils to mill the grain, so we had to pound them with pestles in mortars and bake them with their hulls." Another *Sedeh Menuhah* colonist later recorded that because of overexertion and the inhospitable climate, the colony lost two hundred members in the first three years. Complaints to the bureaucracy, submitted also by the German colonists, went unheeded. Some settlers speedily left, and the news of their misadventures spread through the western ghettos. Under these circumstances it is truly remarkable that in 1810 the Jewish colonies embraced a population of 1,690 families, though not all lived from tilling the soil.[3]

Another step forward was made when a great famine struck the western provinces in 1821–22, and a number of Jews established themselves in new colonies with the reluctant aid of the government. A third wave followed in 1835 when Nicholas I issued a call to the pauperized western Jews to proceed to Siberia, whose cool climate was allegedly favorable to agricultural exploitation. For this purpose the authorities set aside over 40,000 acres in the vicinity of Omsk and Tversk. Unbelievable though it may seem, this governmental invitation was enthusiastically received by so many Jews, then in the throes of a great economic crisis, that the government feared an excessive Jewish influx into those distant areas. Minister of Interior Bludov and General of the Gendarmerie Count Alexander K. Benckendorff argued that not only could a physically weak and undernourished population like the Jewish hardly survive the hardships of the long journey, but also that the moral standards of the local population, largely consisting of deported criminals, would not be improved by the settlement in its midst of an inferior class like the Jews.[4] Nicholas suddenly called off the undertaking in January, 1837, after several hundred Jews had already embarked on the journey to Asia at their own expense. These passengers were forcibly rerouted to the Black Sea region. In the early 1840s this southern movement continued with the arrival there of 5,619 Jews. It grew slowly until the reversal of the government policy in 1865.

Understandably, many colonists could not endure the hardships and departed. They did not have far to go because this was the period of tremendous growth of such industrial centers as Odessa, Elizavetgrad, and others. To be sure, the police tried to stem this unauthorized movement. They occasionally raided these cities and forcibly returned some colonists to their respective villages. On the other hand, the same bureaucracy often made life in the colonies utterly miserable. Promises, however solemnly made, were easily broken. Due to inefficiency houses were not prepared in time for their occupants. Areas set aside for cultivation lacked water which, particularly in drought years, often had to be hauled from a great distance; seed allotted for planting usually arrived too late for sowing. These and other shortcomings had been pointed out in an early official survey of the Jewish colonies, presented to Benckendorff by a Colonel Ossigov, who concluded his observations by saying, "One can, indeed, not blame the colonists if they deeply yearn to return to their earlier conditions in the cities, horrible as these were. For a man must be thoroughly demoralized to wish to live in this misery." Some Russian administrators abused their power. As Bencken-dorff himself observed, the chief administrator in the southern area, Colonel Demidov, forced the able-bodied men to earn money for him by working outside the colonies, while leaving in the latter only women and old men unable to perform the necessary agricultural chores.[5]

Nevertheless, on balance the Jewish rural population kept on in-creasing. True, there were intermittent declines, but in the long run the difficulties were overcome and the total number of inhabitants kept on growing, particularly in the 1840s and the 1850s. Here, too, government statistics are not reliable. As noted by two American officials, the gov-ernment records for 1890 indicated the presence in the seventeen Jewish colonies of the province of Ekaterinoslav of 574 families, consisting of 3,403 men and 3,772 women—altogether 7,175 souls. Such average families of over 12 and a preponderance of women in a colony appeared incredible at first glance. Indeed, closer examination showed that fully 749 Jewish families lived there, including only 2,744 men and 2,398 women, or 5,142 souls in all. This average of a little more than 6 persons per family and a male majority of about 54 percent were far more normal.[6] In any case, the colonies' long-range growth was undeniable. All along, moreover, they attracted an increasing number of individual settlers to their environs. It has been estimated that the total number of Jews living on land at the end of the period of governmentally sup-ported colonization in 1865 amounted to some 33,000.

A complete reversal came about when Alexander II's regime em-barked on its forced pace of industrialization. It now prohibited any Jewish colonization of land whatsoever, and in 1874 withdrew the land reserves previously set aside for this purpose. Alexander III went fur-ther. In his May Laws of 1882 he forbade the Jews altogether to acquire rural property. Nonetheless, the momentum achieved in earlier years, as well as the economic pressures on Russian Jewry, stimulated further Jewish efforts in that direction, and by 1900 the Jewish agricultural population seems to have grown to some 100,000 persons. In Congress Poland, too, no less than seventy Jewish colonies were founded between 1817 and 1870, the Jewish agricultural population there being estimated at 28,391 as early as 1858.[7]

Apart from this quantitative increase of Jewish farmers there also was a constant improvement in the quality of their produce. The generation that had grown up in the colonies had fully adjusted itself to the new life, and with its intelligence and spirit of enterprise, had succeeded in improving upon the methods employed by its neighbors. The new cultivation of tobacco in Bessarabia was predominantly in its hands. The French agricultural expert Tisserand, who in 1908 visited the Russian Jewish colonies in behalf of the Jewish Colonization Association, reported,

> It is impossible to find tobacco and maize plants more attractive than those which I have seen among the Jewish colonists of Dombroveni, reconstructed vineyards more remarkable than those of Resina, a nursery better arranged and better kept than that of Soroki, and cultivation more intelligently conceived than that of the agricultural school of Minsk. Everywhere the colonists show an excellent spirit and are open to agricultural progress. They thus avenge themselves for the strange imputation still weighing on them that they are unable to become farmers. As if industrious, intelligent, enterprising men could *a priori* be considered incapable of exercising the farming profession.[8]

At the same time, the steady removal of Jews from villages within the Pale, crowned by the May Laws of 1882 for Russia and 1891 for Congress Poland, more than outweighed the effects of the Jewish agricultural colonization. As before, therefore, Jewish economic endeavor was largely concentrated in urban occupations, particularly trade and industry.

CRAFTS

Our statistical evidence for the early Russo-Jewish economic structure is greatly complicated not only by the meagerness and unreliability of the extant data but also by their predominantly politico-legal, rather than economic, orientation. Partial records of the Finance Ministry for the year 1818 give the economic distribution of the Ukrainian Jews as follows: 86.5 percent in the two classes of merchants and burghers as against only 12.1 percent of craftsmen and their employees, and 1.4 percent of tillers of the soil. In the Lithuanian and White Russian provinces these percentages appear as 86.6, 10.8, and 2.6, respectively. Such computations, based on the legally significant registration in the prime urban categories of merchants and burghers (*meshchanie*) but paying no heed whatsoever to the mass of unregistered persons, run sharply counter to whatever partial evidence has become available from archival researches in various parts of pre-partition Poland.[9] While conditions may have changed slightly during the first decades of the Russian regime, the Jewish economic structure remained essentially intact. These Polish studies invariably show a preponderance of Jews engaged in industrial occupations, including transportation, over the shopkeepers, merchants, and bankers.

In some areas the former class embraced fully 50 percent of the Jewish population. The following statistical table, representing the developments in the Kingdom of Poland during the course of the nineteenth century, is much more typical of the Jewish occupational distribution throughout the Tsarist Empire. The individual percentages, based upon incomplete censuses, are in themselves none too reliable; yet they offer the best available approximation of the prevailing trends. We need not dwell in any detail on these categories. Certainly, the high peaks reached in industry in 1843 and in agriculture in 1857 were owing more to inexact definitions than to actual increases. But this table illustrates the general trends, best reflected in the census of 1897, which, as in the area of population, has furnished the relatively most dependable data.

Year	Commerce	Industry and Labor, including day laborers	Civil Service and Liberal Professions	Agriculture
1825	28.2	61.1	4.9	5.6
1843	21.6	67.8	2.6	4.8
1857	42.8	35.0	2.6	8.1
1897	39.04	46.7	4.38	2.33

A fuller understanding of these figures may be gained, however, only from a consideration of the qualitative distribution in the various branches of industry and to a lesser extent of commerce. Traditionally Jews were represented most fully in the clothing industry. In partial statistical records dating back to 1807 and covering the Jewish artisans in the provinces of Minsk, Kiev, and Ekaterinoslav, we find that the percentage of Jewish tailors, cobblers, and other clothing workers amounted to 69.7 percent of all Jewish artisans. Next in line were metal workers (6.8 percent), gold- and silversmiths (6.1 percent), and barbers (4.1 percent). In contrast thereto the important building industry engaged only a tiny fraction of 2.6 percent of Jewish craftsmen. Probably these ratios can be generalized for most of the Pale of Settlement.[10]

With the growth of Jewish population there was also an increasing proliferation of Jewish craftsmen, particularly in the traditional Jewish occupations. Osher Margolis has drawn some interesting comparisons between the neighboring provinces of Smolensk and Moghilev, Pskov and Vitebsk in 1861. In Smolensk and Pskov, both outside the Pale, one cobbler provided all the needs for the footwear of 280 and 494 persons, respectively; one tailor sufficed for 542 and 881, and one carpenter for 715 and 1,028 people, while one watchmaker took care of 4,498 and 4,495 inhabitants. In Moghilev (without Gomel, where the statistics are questionable) and Vitebsk (without Dinaburg-Dvinsk, a fortress where members of the armed forces made up an atypical 30 percent of the population), these figures are: one cobbler for 127 and 200, one tailor for 70 and 210, one carpenter for 376 and 680, one watchmaker for 1,109 and 2,070 persons. As a result there was an increasingly sharp competition among the Jewish artisans. A would-be purchaser of material for a suit in Uman in 1810 found himself surrounded by five Jewish tailors, each trying to take his measurements and making exaggerated claims. This constant underbidding was but partially curtailed by the ever stricter regulations of the Jewish artisan guilds, which tried to apportion customers to each craftsman, and otherwise to regulate their respective trades. None of these guilds were monopolistic, however, and except for the right to employ apprentices, any nonmember competed on an almost equal basis.[11]

As time went on stronger non-Jewish competition also emerged. The growth of the urban population tended to bring about an increase of non-Jews also active in the branches of industry theretofore dominated by Jews. The sprawling metropolitan areas now had entire sections inhabited by non-Jews. Even more important was the growing competition from large-scale industry, whether based upon home work or concentrated in mechanized factories. It took time for the Jews to make the necessary adjustments from serving as independent artisans to being home workers or factory laborers. As a result there was a considerable drop both in the ratio of Jews engaged in their traditional occupations and in their average earnings, a decline not entirely compensated by the entry of many other Jews into new branches of industry.

The story of Lodz, which in the course of the nineteenth century grew into the major center of the textile industry for the whole empire, may not be quite typical of the entire Pale of Settlement. Yet it tells a truly dramatic story, illustrative of the basic trends everywhere. In 1810 the Jewish tailors of Lodz successfully fought off the incursion of non-Jewish competitors. Fifteen years later we find the first 2 Christian tailors in the city. By 1862 the 41 Christian tailors almost equal the 49 Jews still engaged in that occupation. Similarly, in 1821 all 8 Lodz bakers were Jews; in 1862 the 38 Christian bakers greatly outnumbered their 15 Jewish competitors. Perhaps the sharpest decline is noticeable in the distilling of liquor, which , as we recall, had for so long been a target of attacks by both the government and non-Jewish public opinion. In 1820 Lodz still had 7 Jewish distilleries; a few years later, none. Part of that process of elimination was owing to the sharp opposition of Christian guilds, which though not quite as monopolistic as their medieval predecessors, were sufficiently powerful to promote the interests of their members at the expense of Jewish outsiders. In part, the Jews suffered from the competition of newly imported well-trained German craftsmen, whose products often were of better quality. The more untrained expellees from villages were crowded into the ghettos of the Pale, the poorer the quality of their products often became. Increased competition likewise led to the lowering of both prices and quality.

In some less densely populated Jewish areas the decline in craftsmanship and the number of craftsmen was less marked. The data for 1887 and 1898 show that in the provinces of Chernigov, Kiev, and Taurida there actually were substantial increases in the number of craftsmen from 12.8, 12.0, and 15.1 to 15.5, 16.1 and 20.0 percent, respectively. But in the other, more congested areas of Jewish settlement, there was a definite decline, accelerated by emigration to other countries. On the other hand, resettlement of Jewish artisans in the interior of Russia was relatively slight. Although a special decree of 1865 opened up the vast expanses of Russia to Jewish craftsmen (in the Caucasus they had been allowed to function even earlier), their status as but temporary residents with no right to pass these residential permits on to their grown sons served as a major deterrent. Coinciding with the suspension of Jewish agricultural colonization, this decree was but a half-hearted attempt to attract some skilled Jewish workmen to Russia's interior as part of the governmental push toward industrialization. After three decades only some 2 percent of the Jewish artisan class lived beyond the Pale, particularly in the neighboring provinces of Smolensk and Pskov or the city of St. Petersburg. Administrative chicaneries made the life of Jewish artisans unbearable both inside and outside the Pale. According to an English visitor, E. B. Lanin, Jewish craftsmen were often forced to take examinations so construed that "even the most clever artisans have no hope of passing" them.[12]

Needless to say, the epochal transformations of Russian society, set in motion by the 1861 emancipation of the peasants, had important effects on the Jewish economy. By bringing masses of liberated but impecunious peasants into the cities, it greatly increased the supply of cheap, unskilled labor, and in time also increased the competition among trained craftsmen. The Jewish inhabitants of the Pale, while rapidly growing in numbers, also suffered from the loss of some of their most talented industrial producers through their emigration abroad, as well as to the interior of Russia, which had lowered its legal barriers to their entry. Before long, moreover, the industrial development in many important centers demanded the services of a new type of laborer—the factory worker. Jewish craftsmen wishing to join the new labor force not only had to make a great mental readjustment, but they also found themselves deprived of the benefits of their hard-acquired special skills and the protective safeguards developed by their guilds over generations. Thus the emancipation of the *muzhiks,* which the progressive Jewish leaders hailed as a step toward a general liberalization of the Russian political structure, proved ruinous in its immediate impact upon many of their coreligionists.

Similarly, the modernization of Russia's communications through the expanding railway system had disastrous effects on another traditional class of Jewish labor: the numerous Jewish transport workers. Jewish porters and coachmen had long been familiar figures on the Jewish street and were subjects of great interest to Jewish folklore and belles-lettres of the period. Together with their non-Jewish counterparts they now suffered severely from the growing competition of the "iron horse." Perhaps it was not mere accident that the same Samuel Poliakov who was one of the leading railroad builders in the country (*see* below) felt prompted in 1880—along with Baron Horace Günzburg and others—to organize a "Society for the Promotion of Crafts and Agriculture among the Jews of Russia." Such societies, already operating in many Jewish communities since the middle of the eighteenth century, now appealed greatly to those segments of Jewry whose respective ideologies stressed, as we shall see, the idea of "productivization" and corresponding economic restratification of the Jewish people.

COMMERCE

Nor were Jewish commercial enterprises immune to the destructive forces. Here, too, the combination of governmental and popular hostility with the inner weaknesses generated by rapid population growth without a corresponding broadening of the economic basis undermined the traditional Jewish preponderance in commerce. Among the aggravating factors one might mention Russia's growing protectionism. In her effort to safeguard her home industries Russia, including Congress Poland, shut her gates to many imports by imposing upon them high customs duties. Jews who had been extremely active in the import and export business found their trade increasingly curtailed by these governmental policies. These restrictions were largely responsible for the decline in the number of visitors to the Leipzig fairs (in 1810 there had been

44 Christian and 296 Jewish visitors from Russia) and in the value of goods traded there.[13]

On the other hand, the Russian bureaucracy was both inefficient and corrupt. Since goods imported from Prussia and Austria were much cheaper, the tendency to evade the tariff by smuggling became irresistible. Count Frederick (Fryderyk Florian) Skarbek commented that "smuggling has been raised to the rank of a regular industry. A whole class of smugglers has arisen which, placed between the peasantry and the Jewish occupations, is engaged in an unceasing war with the frontier guards and the finance officials. At times these conflicts take on the form of overt mutiny." Another official observed that many peasants gave up agriculture in favor of smuggling. Many customs officials collaborated with the smugglers and placed all sorts of obstacles in the way of honest importers who wished to pay duties rather than bribes. It is small wonder, then, that a survey conducted by the Ministry of Interior showed that in 1844, 1,600,000 pounds of yarn entered Congress Poland in a legal, and 591,000 in an illegal, fashion. An even more extreme example was the importation of manufactured cotton goods: according to the same survey, only 57,000 pounds had entered legally, as against 2,000,000 pounds smuggled in.[14] From Congress Poland these wares were reexported to the rest of the Pale and to the interior of Russia, despite the existing customs frontier between these two sections of the empire. Native Polish products likewise became objects of smuggling.

Since Jews were among the protagonists in this game, the government imposed various restrictions on their acquisition of rural land and houses in the vicinity of the Prussian and Austrian frontiers. It also persuaded the rabbis not to adjudicate litigations arising out of smuggling, and as we recall, in 1820 even induced the Vilna rabbinate to pronounce a ban on all smugglers, a ban which some Prussian ministers feared might greatly curtail the exports of Prussian manufactured goods. Finally, to stem this traffic completely, Nicholas I issued his aforementioned ukase of 1843, expelling all Jews residing within fifty versts (about thirty-three miles) from the frontier with Prussia and Austria; only owners of houses were to be allowed two years to dispose of them. "This order is to be executed without any excuses." Such a drastic action, affecting thousands of innocent persons along with the guilty, caused a great outcry in the country and abroad, without in any way altering the basic discrepancy between Russia's insatiable demand for imported goods and the inefficient methods of restricting their entry. The number of Jewish smugglers may have diminished, but their places were taken by others, as is illustrated by the Warsaw statistics of arrested smugglers. From the high ratio of 83–96 percent in 1842–49, the proportion of Jewish defendants on this score declined to 37.4 percent in

1850 and to but 27.1 percent in 1851, or far less than the percentage of Jews in the mercantile population.[15]

More consciously anti-Jewish efforts curtailed the Jewish liquor trade. Ever-increasing excise and license taxes, endless legislative vagaries, and the growing competition of non-Jewish distillers and innkeepers reduced the Jewish share in this business to a minimum. To quote the Lodz experience again: in 1820 eight Jewish tavern-keepers confronted three Christian competitors; ten years later the number of Jews was reduced to three, a number remaining constant till 1862, while the number of Christian saloon-keepers had increased to sixty-four. In Berdichev the Jewish ratio among liquor dealers declined from 24.3 percent in 1789 to 6.3 percent sixty years later. At the same time some wealthy entrepreneurs were allowed to lease liquor concessions extending over large areas; they usually operated these through a hierarchy of subcontractors. One such concessionaire, Joseph (Yosip, Evzel) Günzburg (1812–78), created baron by the Grand Duke of Hesse-Darmstadt in 1874, paid the government in 1859–63 an annual rental of 3,777,440 rubles; two other Jews had contracts calling for rentals of 1,517,440 and 1,243,774 rubles, respectively.[16] While these men often employed Jews, the relative number of Jews engaged in the liquor trade kept on declining. The growth of salt and tobacco monopolies likewise interfered the more harshly with these traditional branches of Jewish commerce, as the local authorities tried to favor Christian over Jewish licensees. Although a decree issued to this effect in 1824 had to be revoked in 1830 because not enough Christian applicants were available for the distribution of salt, in practice what had been an almost exclusively Jewish trade increasingly shifted into the hands of non-Jewish distributors.

The ratio of the Jewish mercantile class within the general Jewish population cannot easily be ascertained. Only a minority of Jewish businessmen was registered in the regular class of "merchants"; still fewer were entered under the first, second, or third guild. The figures are, moreover, distorted by the fact that some Jews, though not really qualified, registered under one or another guild and paid the respective fees merely to secure residential privileges outside the Pale or at least greater freedom in traveling there, as well as exemption from the military draft for their sons. Nevertheless a statistical account for 1852, compiled by Bernard Weinryb from three tables extracted by A. Yuditskii from a Kiev manuscript, is quite illuminating (*see* the next page). None of these figures reflect, however, the great mass of unregistered peddlers, agents, mercantile employees, and others. Their individual transactions may have been extremely small, but in the aggregate their contribution to Russian commerce and their numerical strength within the Jewish population were very substantial. We have a graphic descrip-

Province	Jewish Population	Jewish Merchants (ratio of entire class)	Guild members			Of each 1,000 Jews			
			I	II	III	Merchants	Guilds I	Guilds II	Guilds III
Grodno	101,950	1,268 (96.1)	5	2	132	12.4	.05	.02	1.3
Kovno	98,641	458 (76.1)	6	6	125	4.6	.06	.06	1.27
Minsk	98,330	2,338 (88.2)	9	5	227	23.8	.09	.05	2.31
Vitebsk	57,766	1,397 (42.8)	6	5	141	24.2	.1	.1	2.44
Moghilev	99,088	2,672 (74.7)	4	5	276	27.0	.04	.05	2.79
Volhynia	190,804	7,648 (96.0)	8	12	696	40.0	.04	.06	3.65
Kiev	183,629	12,066 (82.4)	7	20	956	65.7	.04	.11	5.2
Kherson	45,241	704 (23.8)	10	15	679	15.6	.22	.33	15.0
Odessa district	12,657	2,928 (52.3)	10	20	450	231.46	.79	1.58	35.5
Poltava	23,971	2,627 (51.6)	1	2	215	109.6	.04	.08	8.97
Chernigov	28,919	1,704 (23.0)	2	2	111	58.9	.07	.07	3.85

tion of a small Jewish town by the contemporary Yiddish novelist, Isaac Meier Dick, which includes the following paragraph:

> The hamlet looks dead during the whole week; it has the semblance of a gynocracy, that is, a kingdom inhabited only by women. Men spend the week until Friday in the country, they wander from village to village and court to court with all sorts of notions, which they exchange there against flax, linseed, rabbit and calf skins, pig bristles and feathers. They sell all that to . . . the rich man of the community. In the hamlet itself remain only women, children, communal officials, students of the academy and a few *batlanim* [unemployed men].[17]

CAPITALIST PROGRESS

All these processes led to increasing pauperization of the Jewish masses by the middle of the nineteenth century. Not all Jews, however, took these blows calmly. Quite a few enterprising young men, sensing the spirit of the time, looked for novel outlets for their talents. The textile and clothing industries lent themselves particularly well to Jewish enterprise. Traditionally, the Jewish communities embraced for socioreligious reasons numerous tailors of their own. In independent Poland foundations were even laid for small Jewish factories employing a number of Jewish workers. The demand for such religious articles as prayer shawls in the growing Jewish population likewise stimulated the development *in nuce* of mass production methods. On its part, the Russian government, bent on the restratification of the Jewish masses, regarded, next to agricultural colonization, the establishment of factories as the most eminent means for retraining Jews for "productive" occupations. For this purpose, it established in 1809 a specific Jewish industrial school in Kremenchug, where forty families of Jewish pupil-workers could be trained for industrial work in textile factories and could serve as the hard core of a labor force to be used by factory owners in many communities. In the eight years of its existence this school taught the new trade to several hundred trainees (in 1810 their number amounted to 148 men) and also furnished employment to several master artisans serving as instructors.

Jewish entrepreneurs realized the new opportunities offered them by this governmental attitude, the generally growing Russian protectionism, and the rising internal demand for industrial products. Active individuals, like the Vilna merchant Hillel Aronov Markevich, sought official aid in establishing several new factories. Although his 1813 application to the Vilna governor for a government loan for building a textile mill was rejected, he continued to press the authorities for assistance in various industrial projects. In 1818 he petitioned for a six-year lease of two specified tracts of land in the vicinity of Vilna so that he might erect there (1) a factory for the production of artisan tools; (2) a paper mill; (3) an oil press; (4) a sawmill along English patterns; (5) a brass factory; (6) a flour mill; and (7) a textile converting mill for the clothing factories. In this application he described his motivation as follows: "On the one hand, I feel the obligation to do my part for the benefit of my fellow citizens and, at the same time, contribute to the extent of my ability to the welfare of society as a whole. On the other hand, I should like thus to employ my considerable know-how and expertise." Markevich repeated his request to the finance minister two years later. But his petitions were constantly rejected because the authorities considered his resources insufficient for such an ambitious program and also because he had "his own profit, rather than that of society in mind." Nonetheless, neither Markevich nor other Jewish entrepreneurs abandoned their plans. By 1828, 75 Jewish textile mills were in operation in eight western provinces (40 in the province of Volhynia, 13 in Grodno, 10 in Moghilev). Among them these factories employed 2,185 Jewish workers.[18]

From these small beginnings developed a major participation of Jewish entrepreneurs in Russia's industrial development. A remarkable illustration is offered by the Ukrainian sugar industry. In the Ukraine, as elsewhere in the empire, where a sugar refinery had been established as early as 1719, sugar had long been produced largely by landlords who refined their own beets for local or at best district-wide consumption. Israel Brodski, scion of a well-known rabbinic family—Schor, but called Brodski because his father had come from Brody, Galicia—entered that business in 1844, at the age of twenty-one. At that time he arranged with one of the Ukrainian landlords (in the district of Cherkasy) that for the substantial advance of 6,000 silver rubles, he was to become an equal partner in the revenue from the sugar refinery. Brodski was not satisfied with the traditional methods of production. After surveying some mechanized refineries in Germany, he imported the necessary machinery, together with technicians to teach the local workers, and in the following years he built one refinery after another. Before long he had also established an effective sales organization. By the 1870s and 1880s he had sixty agencies in all parts of the empire, including the Caucasus, Siberia, and shortly thereafter also in newly annexed Turkestan. From his new headquarters in Odessa he and his sons successfully exported great quantities of sugar to the Ottoman Empire, Persia, and other countries. After his death in 1889 his sons, Lazar and Leon, owned between them twenty-two major sugar mills. Generally considered to be among the wealthiest Russian Jews, they received high decorations from the Russian government and from the Legion of Honor in France. The

Brodski example was effectively emulated by other Jewish entrepreneurs, including the families Zaitsev, Halperin, and Balakhovsky. As early as 1872 an official report estimated, probably with some exaggeration, that Jews controlled 25 percent of the entire sugar industry in the Ukraine. The various joint-stock companies which in the following decades actively participated in the production and distribution of sugar were likewise often managed by Jewish directors and large stockholders.

It was in part owing to these Jewish sugar refiners that the Russian sugar industry, which as late as 1880 did not supply all the domestic needs, was able shortly thereafter to pile up large export surpluses. According to government statistics, imports of sugar declined from 288,160 quintals (6.1 poods each) in the quinquennium of 1888–93, to 7,642 quintals in 1893–98. At the same time production increased by some 40 percent and exports shot up from 3,650,768 to 6,145,003 quintals. This increase was made possible in part by lower prices, which declined from 28.48 rubles in 1881–85 to 17.95 rubles in 1896–98. To be sure, much of that decrease was picked up in taxes, which played an increasing role in Russia's imperial budget. Characteristically these prices were lowest in the Ukraine and considerably higher in Moscow and St. Petersburg.[19]

Even more important for the Russian Empire was the entry of some Jews into the slowly developing railroad industry. Count Egor Kankrin, long-time minister of finance (1823–1844), was a spokesman for the conservative groups which feared that railways might "encourage frequent purposeless travel, thus fostering the restless spirit of our age." The progress was correspondingly slow. Apart from a short sixteen-mile line from St. Petersburg to the emperor's home in Tsarskoe Selo, opened in 1837, the first important route was that linking Vienna with Warsaw. Although it took nine years for that track to be completed—as it also did for the line from Moscow to St. Petersburg (1839–48 and 1842–51, respectively)—the state-appointed managers soon ran into great difficulties. The Vienna-Warsaw line was salvaged by a private joint-stock company, led by the Warsaw Jewish banker Herman Epstein, who owned more than 40 percent of the company's shares valued at 2,500,-000 rubles. Almost immediately thereafter Epstein formed a new company to build the line from Warsaw to Bromberg in Silesia, while another entrepreneur, the convert Leopold Kronenberg, was responsible for continuing the railway from Warsaw to Brest-Litovsk.

These Polish Jewish railway builders were overshadowed by their Russian compeers, particularly Joseph (Evzel) Günzburg, his son Horace, and Samuel Poliakov. Poliakov gained the reputation of being an efficient builder when he succeeded in setting up the two partial lines from Kursk to Kharkov and from Kharkov to Taganrog, a distance of 763 versts (*ca.* 504 miles), in the record time of twenty-two months, whereas other lines had required many years. The government had such confidence in his ability that when in 1869 it decided to build an economically and strategically needed railroad from Voronezh to Rostov, the tsar accepted a proposal backed by only a minority of his cabinet to entrust its building to Poliakov, although a rival Christian firm had underbid him by some 10 percent. Often aided by Jewish financiers in other countries, particularly the Pereire Brothers in Paris and Gerson Bleichröder in Berlin, Jewish builders were able to help greatly in the expansion of the Russian railway network, which in the twenty years from 1856 to 1876 grew from 982 to 17,418 versts.

These and other Jews were also active in developing water transport on the great rivers of Russia, such as the Dnieper and the Volga. An earlier corporation controlling the Dnieper navigation proved very conservative and inefficient. It was followed by a second corporation, established by Jews in 1883. Within ten years the new group proved so successful that the former company was simply absorbed by its younger rival. Under the management of D. S. Margolin and other Jewish directors, in 1911 this combined company owned 62 river steamboats and leased 16 others, which among them transported more than 70 percent of the cargo carried on that river. Under the direction of Grigorii Abramovich Poliak the water transport on the Volga and the Caspian Sea increased by leaps and bounds; it began to play an ever-increasing role in the transportation of crude oil and other oil products from the expanding Baku oil fields. Also connected with water transport was the growing business of marine insurance, in which, as in other branches of the insurance business, Jews also excelled.[20]

Poliakov was not satisfied with his significant role in Russia's domestic transport system; he also cast covetous glances across the borders to the highly promising areas of the Ottoman Empire. Characteristically, the Jewish industrialist did not approach the regular ministries but contacted the tsar through Constantine Pobedonostsev, to whom Poliakov reported in 1886–87 that he had uncovered a joint Anglo-Austrian scheme to acquire the Balkan railway system and by bringing it out into the open had prevented its realization. He now asked for the government's support of a new Russian corporation, which together with some foreign bankers would negotiate with the Porte. He also suggested that Russian capitalists be encouraged to build a railway in Persia. Alexander III, who apparently considered personal negotiations with a Jewish banker as below his dignity, noted on Pobedonostsev's report: "I am as embarrassed by this affair as you are, and do not know what decision to make."[21] Nevertheless, in many other enterprises Poliakov enjoyed the full cooperation of the Russian administration.

Russian oil fields, particularly in the Caucasus, likewise owed a great deal to Poliakov and other Russian-Jewish industrialists. Here, however, the international oil firms, particularly English and French, played an even greater role. Once again Jewish bankers and industrialists made excellent use of their personal connections with foreign coreligionists. In his negotiations with Pobedonostsev, Poliakov submitted a letter from his own son-in-law, James Hirsch of the well-known German banking family. Baron Horace Günzburg had another Hirsch as a son-in-law. Since Russia had vast unexploited territories and natural resources, foreign capital was readily attracted, so long as its owners had confidence in the management of the new enterprises. The leading Jewish capitalists, personally known to their counterparts abroad, often inspired such confidence, and loans were readily negotiated for investment.

In the oil industry Jews first had to overcome the legal obstacles connected with their residential rights around the Caucasian oil fields. As elsewhere, moreover, Russia's oil industry was extremely competitive and risky. There were extreme price swings dependent on the varying supply, which in turn depended on more or less successful drillings, as well as rapidly changing market conditions. These extremes are well illustrated by the prices of the 1890s. After a sharp price decline during the 1880s a quintal of crude oil could be acquired in June 1892 for 5.5 kopeks and one of petroleum for 27.5 kopeks, both priced far below the costs of production. By December, 1899, the price shot up to 1.05 rubles for the crude and 3.05 rubles for petroleum. Only industrialists with substantial cash resources could weather such crises. Nevertheless, beginning in a small way in the area of distribution of oil products, the Jewish firm of Dembo and Kagan expanded gradually during the 1870s and the 1880s, particularly through the disposal of by-products, which soon exceeded in monetary value the trade in kerosene itself. Before long, however, some Jews also succeeded in penetrating the production end of the industry. In particular, the well-trained engineer Arkadii Grigorevich Beilin, a doctor of philosophy of Berlin University, made significant contributions to the improvement of the productive processes, the expansion of transport facilities, and the attraction of foreign, particularly Rothschild, capital to Baku and the other oil fields. It has been estimated that by the beginning of the twentieth century Jews controlled some 15–16 percent of the entire exploitation of oil, while their share in the kerosene refineries had risen to 44 percent. Despite residential restrictions, Jewish employees (many of them recruited through engineering fellowships established by Beilin) amounted in 1913 to 7.6 percent of all commercial and administrative employees engaged in the various firms producing and distributing oil products in Russia.[22]

As of old, many Jewish money traders—engaged not only in credit transactions but also in money exchange, holding deposits, and related activities—existed in almost all communities within the Pale. With the expansion of Russian industry and commerce and the transformation of the Russian economy into a money economy after the liberation of the peasants, the number of such local Jewish bankers increased considerably even in its ratio to the ever-growing Jewish population. Suffice it to cite the example of Berdichev, where in 1849–97 the proportion of money traders per 1,000 Jewish residents increased from 33 to 55. However, the main development now took place through corporate banking, to which Jews contributed significantly also outside the Pale. Directorships of joint-stock banking companies often enabled Jews to establish their residences, especially in the two capitals. With the aid of coreligionists in other countries, leading Russo-Jewish bankers founded a large number of regional banks, some of which transferred their headquarters to St. Petersburg. These activities ranged far and wide and included the Moscow International Commercial Bank and several others controlled by the Poliakovs. An Austro-Jewish banker, A. I. Rothstein, who had been influential in the preparation of the Austrian banking laws of 1892, was invited by Sergei Y. Witte, Russia's outstanding finance minister, to help him in the monetary reforms then under way. In 1896 Rothstein organized the important Russo-Chinese Bank, which fourteen years later merged with another bank into the large Russo-Asian Bank. These examples could readily be multiplied.

Expansion of Jewish and general banking was greatly hampered by government intervention and particularly by ever-changing governmental regulations. No sooner was a comprehensive bank statute issued in 1862 when it had to be modified in 1870, 1879, 1883, and in later years. Next to the Bank of Russia and three other governmental institutions, moreover, private banking had to compete with 240 municipal banks, 116 mutual credit societies, 68 charitable loan banks, and other public or semipublic establishments. In 1899, for which these statistics are given, there existed only 39 commercial banks; through their 198 branches and their larger capital resources they had to make up for their inferiority in numbers. In addition, the Russian persecutions of Jews greatly interfered with the influx of foreign capital into the Tsarist Empire. According to a St. Petersburg paper, the anti-Jewish riots of 1881–82 caused a lowering of the value of the Russian government bonds by 152,000,000 rubles. Western Jewish capitalists such as the Rothschilds or the growingly important American firms felt compunctions about extending loans to the Russian government. The importance of the Paris Rothschilds for the credit of the Russian Empire can hardly be overestimated. According to a recent computation, in the short period of 1889–93, Russia secured loans in the staggering amount of 3,390,000,000 francs from the French money market. By 1904 Russian bonds totaling 6,800,-000,000 francs were in the hands of French investors. And yet in 1906 Finance Minister Vladimir Nikolaevich Kokovtsev tried to raise an additional loan of 800,000,000 francs; he often employed unscrupulous intermediaries, such as an undercover agent, Raffalovich, who did not hesitate to bribe many Paris newspaper editors. The Paris Rothschilds were also under the pressure of the French government, which could not view calmly the weakening of its major Russian ally. But largely because of his intense Jewish loyalties, the American Jacob H. Schiff, the senior partner of Kuhn, Loeb and Company, freely underwrote loans for the Japanese government during the Russo-Japanese war. But such compunctions were more readily overcome if the borrowing concerns were controlled by Russian Jews. Witte fully realized the importance of foreign Jewish finance capital for the development of Russia's economy, and largely for that reason tried to exert a moderating influence on the tsarist policies concerning Jews.[23]

Jewish entry into liberal professions also made tremendous strides. Here, too, relations with Jewish communities abroad proved helpful, especially after the enforcement of a *numerus clausus* at Russian universities. The very introduction of that quota system testified to the growth of that class in the Jewish population. True, our statistical data are unclear and, apart from their general unreliability, cloud the issue by generally lumping the free professions together with civil service. In the latter the Jews were sharply discriminated against, except insofar as it related to employment by the Jewish communities themselves. Nor were Jewish professionals free of arbitrary decisions by the Russian administration. To some extent the government itself had fostered that transition from the old rabbinic to modern university studies by its promotion of Jewish "enlightenment" as well as by opening the areas of Russia's interior to Jewish professionals. Before long the two Russian capitals included a disproportionate number of Jewish lawyers, doctors, and other technicians, whose influence on the entire Jewish community of the empire far exceeded their ratio in the population.

PAUPERIZATION OF THE MASSES

Such advances in the higher reaches of banking, industry, and the professions affected only a small minority of Jews. Suffocating in the increasingly crowded ghettos within the Pale, the masses sank ever more deeply into the mire of poverty. In Russia, as in other countries going through the early stages of modern capitalism, the rich grew richer while the poor became more and more indigent. In the Jewish case these trends were further aggravated by the existing legal restrictions on the Jews' residential and occupational rights, social ostracism and discriminatory taxation. These handicaps could much more readily be overcome by well-to-do businessmen and professionals, but the impoverished masses were exposed, partly because of their poverty, to endless bureaucratic chicaneries, legal and extralegal. It has been estimated that in many communities up to 40 percent of the entire Jewish population consisted of families of so-called *Luftmenschen*—that is, persons without any particular skills, capital, or specific occupations. These "breadwinners" of large families had to rely on occasional chores entrusted to them by relatives and friends; their income was unstable and as a rule quite inadequate. A Russian scholar, B. Miliutin, found that already in 1849 only 3 percent of the Jews possessed any capital at all, while the rest led a miserable existence. In the early 1860s partial studies made by other non-Jewish statisticians showed that, for instance, in the province of Kovno (Kaunas) it was quite common for several Jewish families to occupy a single room. In the province of Grodno a three- or four-room house sometimes accommodated as many as twelve families. "In most cases a pound of bread, a herring, and a few onions represent the daily fare of an entire family. . . . The average earning of a Jewish breadwinner amounts to 15 kopeks a day." The situation in the Ukraine was somewhat better, but even there, according to a Russian landowner in the Kiev province, most Jews were even poorer than the peasants; in view of the extreme poverty of the Ukrainian peasantry, that was saying a great deal. More, the average Jew's income, whenever it came, was far less dependable than that of the peasant.[24]

Many of these descriptions date from the era of Alexander II's great reforms. Understandably, though the governmental policies toward Jews became somewhat less oppressive, the far-reaching general economic transformations created ever new difficulties for the Jewish population, hemmed in as it was both geographically and legally. The emancipation of the Russian peasantry, by pushing, as we recall, masses of penniless and untrained peasants into the hamlets and cities, created a large class of new competitors for the limited opportunities to make a living. Russia also suffered from recurrent depressions. Students of the Russian business cycle have shown that there was a decade-long depression beginning in 1858. After a short respite about 1870, there were further depressions in 1873–76, in 1882–87, and in the early 1890s. During these periods, Jewish occupations belonged to the most vulnerable, and unemployment grew among the Jewish masses by leaps and bounds.

Great impoverishment of the Jewish population is also evidenced by the statistics of Jewish charities, however incomplete. According to one record, indigent Jewish families increased in Russia from 85,183 in 1894 to 108,922 four years later. Even the latter figure is far from complete, since many towns had failed to report and a considerable number of "proud" poor, receiving secret support, did not appear in the records. Applicants for Passover charities reached in 1898 an average of 18.8 percent of the Jewish population, or some 7 percent of the total urban population of the Pale. Needless to say, all these charities rested heavily upon the Jewish communities and their philanthropic associations, the government contributing almost nothing. The burden was somewhat alleviated only by contributions from coreligionists abroad, either through the large Jewish welfare organizations like the Jewish Colonization Association or the ORT (initials of the Russian equivalent of Organization for Rehabilitation and Training), or through private subsidies. In the years of mass emigration to the United States it was quite customary for many families to live largely on donations sent to them by relatives who had meanwhile established themselves in their new countries of settlement.[25]

If anything, the vitality of Russian Jewry showed itself in its unconscious but on the whole acceptable method of adjustment to these untold miseries. Apart from large-scale emigration to less oppressive countries, the Jewish masses found an outlet for their energies in the new industries, which were in part developed by their own leaders. The transition was not altogether easy. Not only did Jewish coachmen lose out in their competition with railroads, but even Jewish artisans found that their respective skills in tailoring, shoemaking, or the food industry were of little avail in mechanized factories producing textiles, shoes, or food products. Jewish entrepreneurs, as well as workers, had to pay a high price for the initial errors accompanying this great transition. In Congress Poland and other border provinces industrialization was promoted by the factories built there by German industrialists in order to avoid the impact of tsarist protectionism. Lodz, in particular, developed into an important industrial center for the whole empire. But when this process extended into the interior of Russia, where the region around Moscow became the prime industrial center of the whole country, Jews found themselves handicapped by residence restrictions.

Nevertheless, the Jewish working classes were making steady progress. Here and there they were aided by some of their coreligionists who for idealistic reasons tried to spread employment among their own people. One such outstanding industrialist-philanthropist was Solomon Posner, who as early as 1823 established a textile mill in Kuchary in the province of Plotsk. The Brodskis in their sugar factories also preferentially employed Jews, especially in executive positions. The empire thus witnessed the gradual rise of an industrial Jewish proletariat consisting of both old-line employees of artisans and an ever-growing number of regular factory workers. Needless to say, Jewish laborers, together with the proletariat of other faiths, suffered from the usual ills of the early

Industrial Revolution, particularly the segment recruited from under-paid women and children. We have no detailed statistics for Jews, but the sex and age distribution among them probably did not differ too greatly from that of the Russian workers.[26]

Recent statistical studies based on official records of the Department of Commerce for 1887 have revealed the presence of 24.4 percent of women workers. The percentage of females in the textile mills of St. Petersburg in 1881 was 42.6 percent. More startlingly, 9.2 percent of the half-million laborers employed by 3,316 enterprises surveyed in 1882–83 were juveniles under fifteen. Some factories employed children aged ten. Also the hours of labor (usually in excess of twelve daily), the unsanitary working conditions in the factories, the instability of employ-ment, and the extremely low wages even for adult males were very discouraging. According to a report submitted in 1896 to the Socialist International in London, the average Russian-Jewish worker often earned but two to three rubles a week for six days of fourteen to eighteen hours each. In the Jewish case additional complications arose from the wish of the predominantly Orthodox workers to observe their Sabbath rest and from the mostly unfriendly attitude of their Christian fellow workers. It was also a far greater psychological strain on an artisan or a petty shopkeeper to become a mere cog in a growingly inhuman industrial machine with unaccustomed forms of discipline, often aggravated by hostile and contemptuous Christian foremen. Nevertheless, the Jewish industrial proletariat was increasing from dec-ade to decade, especially wherever it could form associations of its own, and ultimately also a political party in which it found a more brotherly reception and a fuller understanding of its cultural peculiarities.

Notwithstanding all these transformations, the Jewish economic structure on the eve of World War I still was relatively lopsided. The ratio of 2.33 percent of Jewish agriculturists supplied by the census of 1897 was, if anything, lower seventeen years later. It contrasted with the Russian population, in which the farmers exceeded 90 percent of the total. Even within the so-called urban occupations, the concentration of Jews in some, and their relative absence from others, made their eco-nomic stratification quite different from that of their neighbors. A Polish writer, quoting in 1914 the latest data supplied by the statistical annual of Congress Poland, pointed out that while in tailoring and shoemaking the proportion of Polish to Jewish workers was 40:56 percent and in transport 45:51.5 percent, in the lumber industry and carpentry the percentages were reversed, to 73:17. The wool industry employed some 40,000 Jews in all, compared with 127,000 Poles and over 62,000 Ger-mans. Jewish preponderance in commerce was more obvious. Depend-ent on its particular branches, the Jewish share still ranged from 80 to 95 percent despite the growth of a Polish bourgeoisie stimulated by both government and public opinion, especially in the metropolitan areas of Warsaw and Lodz, as well as the presence of a fairly substantial number of both German and Russian merchants in the Polish cities. Similar conditions prevailed, on a somewhat lower scale, throughout the Pale.

In short, all the efforts at "productivization" of Russian Jewry, though enjoying the full support of Jewish leadership itself, were successful only to the extent of transferring Jews from one branch of industry or commerce to another, rather than in changing the entire economic structure of the Jewish people. This "abnormal" stratification aroused much antagonism among the non-Jewish majority and made the Jews doubly vulnerable to the successive catastrophes which befell them after 1914. But in the face of harsh economic realities little could have been achieved even by the efforts of a much more powerful Jewish community than that which existed in Russia under an inimical government and hostile public opinion.

[7]

Communal Autonomy

In the early stages of their economic struggles the Russian Jews, like their ancestors in Poland, drew considerable strength from their communal solidarity. Russia had inherited from Poland, and indirectly from medieval Germany, a strong and all-embracing communal organization which to some extent minimized the external pressures. In the economic sphere the *kahal* (the name, derived from the Hebrew term for community, connoted the all-embracing communal organization) exercised extraordinary jurisdiction in balancing right against right and in helping the individual Jews to fight their battle for survival. Small professional groups, such as those of midwives or town musicians, were completely regulated by the *kahal*, which prescribed, for example, the methods of performance and the fees of musicians serving at weddings. It also regulated the work of teachers, communal scribes, and other professionals. In its heyday it surveyed weights and measures and sought to protect both the consumer and the producer by its general supervision over prices and wages. It also tried to limit competition by invoking the medieval principle of *maarufia*—that is, the specific connection between a customer and his supplier which was not to be infringed upon by any outsider. Sometimes it went so far as to declare that connection hereditary. Most importantly, the *kahal* tried to prevent undue Jewish competition in relations with the outside world. According to the old principle of *hazakah*, a title to land was acquired only with the permission of the communal authorities. Such licenses were often granted particularly in connection with the acquisition of real estate from Christians, so as to prevent Jewish would-be purchasers from unduly raising prices while bidding against one another. These responsibilities often involved the communal elders in extended litigation, but they served as an important line of defense for the Jewish community as a whole.[1]

Side by side with the central communal organization operated numerous voluntary associations which, though working under the general supervision of the communal council, enjoyed considerable leeway in their specialized fields of activity. In the economic sphere such functions were performed primarily by Jewish artisan guilds, whereas the far more competitive merchants, often individually belonging to general merchant guilds, saw little advantage in forming Jewish associations. Continuing the Polish traditions, the artisan guilds revealed the typically medieval interlocking of social and religious with economic factors, many of them maintaining synagogues of their own and meeting a variety of social needs of their members. Like other guilds, they supervised the admission of apprentices and journeymen and often limited the number of master artisans, so as to restrict competition. Understandably, the journeymen, often thus held back in their professional advancement, occasionally formed associations of their own for the defense of their rights. When they tried in Minsk to hold independent religious services, however, the masters' guild invoked the aid of the *kahal*, which forbade the journeymen to secede from the regular artisan synagogues. At the same time it ordered the guilds to arbitrate the journeymen's legitimate grievances. If because of this socioreligious coloring of all such associations, Jews were not admitted to Christian guilds, the difficulty was minimized within the Pale by the fact that in most areas Jews constituted the majority of artisans, at least in the occupations extensively cultivated by them. On the whole, Christian artisans could with equal justice complain of discrimination by Jewish guilds in their nonadmission of Christian members.[2]

GOVERNMENTAL EQUIVOCATION

Under Russian domination the Jewish communal bodies faced in many ways a novel and difficult situation. The authorities were at first more puzzled than disturbed by this unusual phenomenon. Russian society had long been divided into classes from the nobility down to villeins, and each individual could readily be subsumed under one or another of these established categories. Catherine II and her advisers doubtless

glibly believed that they could simply incorporate the new Jewish subjects into these established groups. They soon realized with chagrin that
the Jewish community was an entity of its own kind which could not
easily be dissolved into the majority's corporate groupings.

More, for practical reasons the government found it advantageous
to maintain that organization intact. Jews were better-than-average
taxpayers and the revenue from them was most easily and inexpensively
collected through their own communal organs. In particular, the so-
called *korobka* (chest tax), originally an excise tax on ritually slaughtered
meat but speedily extended to many other objects of mass consumption
as well, and the candle tax could yield greater revenue for the treasury if
they were rigidly supervised by the Jewish communities themselves.

Most of the *kahals*, moreover, had emerged from Polish domination
with a public debt which could only be serviced by a continuously
functioning communal body. Characteristically, their creditors often
consisted principally of Catholic churches, monasteries, and nobles who
considered such communal loans, even if bearing less than 10 percent
interest, a fairly safe and enduring investment. Extant records of seventy communities, principally located in the provinces of Podolia and
Volhynia, reveal that they owed 102,090 rubles on loans, in part contracted as far back as the seventeenth century. This was a fairly universal
problem, common to both the east and the west. The Rhineland community of Worms, for instance, by 1800 owed six times more than the
cumulative value of all its communal property. It took the wealthy
communities of Alsace-Lorraine more than half a century after the
French Revolution to liquidate in an orderly fashion the debts accumulated during the pre-Emancipation era.[3]

Occasionally the communities contested the claims of some lenders
by pointing out that their past payments had covered both the principal
and the interest at moderate rates. On the other hand, some creditors
were more interested in their regular annual income than in the repay-
ment of the principal. True, Russia's national debt was likewise increasing from decade to decade. But unlike the treasury, the Jewish communal organs could not print paper money and repeatedly depreciate
the currency in circulation, a process but partially checked by Count
Egor Kankrin's and Witte's financial reforms of 1823, 1839–43, and 1893–
99. The government could not afford, therefore, to undermine too
radically the delicate structure of Jewish communal indebtedness without incurring great losses in its own revenue and ruining some influential Christian creditors.

On their part, the Jewish communities had to adjust themselves as
best they could to the new governmental structure. In declining Poland
the prevailing anarchy enabled each group to run its own affairs with
relatively little interference. This system led to many internal abuses and

particularly to excessive concentration of power in relatively few families, but there was little outside supervision and the Jewish community did indeed resemble a sort of "state within the state." Now Catherine's enlightened absolutism tended to convert the Jewish community, too, into an agency of the state's totalitarian control. Under Nicholas I the manifold earlier attempts were consolidated into the generally discriminatory law of 1835, articles 67–68 of which demanded that the *kahal* be held responsible for the enforcement of governmental regulations among the Jews, as well as for the collection of taxes due to the Crown and the county treasuries. It also was to render annual accounts of its income and expenditures to both the municipal councils and the central treasury. On assuming office, all Jewish elders were to take an oath of loyalty and to pledge themselves to execute faithfully all orders of the authorities, supply the quota of recruits, collect all state and communal taxes after assessing them justly among members, and generally to enforce obedience to law and order.

Not surprisingly, these extreme regulations broke down in execution and there was little immediate change in the operation of Jewish communal bodies. Almost in despair, Nicholas and his associates embarked upon the radical enterprise of suppressing the traditional *kahal* altogether. In a decree promulgated on December 19, 1844, the tsar declared that "a separate Jewish administration need not exist and all *kahals* and their subsidiaries are hereby declared abolished. Their functions are to be assumed by the municipal councils and assemblies, each according to its competence." The decree further defined in detail the new prerogatives of the municipal councils and other organs, the substitute methods of collecting Jewish taxes, and the means of providing for the residual duties of the Jewish communities. Curiously, Jews had become so inured to governmental persecution that they took this new edict in their stride, too. When Sir Moses wMontefiore visited Russia two years later and transmitted to the tsarist ministers the main grievances of their Jewish population, he emphasized the civil disabilities much more than the restrictions legally imposed upon Jewish self-government. His informants must have felt that with or without governmental cooperation, they could carry on more or less in their accustomed ways. The Russian official who complained to Max Lilienthal about the Jews' extreme tenacity in maintaining their communal life was quite right in asserting that a Polish rebellion could be suppressed with military force, but that the quiet Jewish obstinacy was being fought in vain.[4]

Not that the Jews consciously wished to oppose governmental regulations. Their old rabbinic law had taught them that the "law of the kingdom is law" and that even in litigations submitted to Jewish courts the existing governmental ordinances had to be respected. The only qualification the rabbis had placed on this principle was that such laws must not be discriminatory but must apply to all citizens alike. This principle was now reiterated by one of the outstanding talmudic leaders of the time, Rabbi Isaac ben Hayyim, head of the famed rabbinic academy of Volozhin.

In general, the Jewish masses and their leaders attributed all antagonistic governmental acts to the provincial authorities or to the tsar's advisers, rather than to the tsar himself. Sometimes they tried to outdo one another in professions of loyalty. We recall the patriotic poems recited by welcoming deputations in honor of Catherine, Alexander, and other monarchs. Catherine was sufficiently impressed by one such ceremony to mention it in one of her letters, and to stress that on that occasion Jews and Dominicans stood side by side. Beyond such verbal expressions of loyalty Jews demonstrated their allegiance to the Crown at such critical moments as the Napoleonic invasion of 1812, the Crimean War, and the Russo-Japanese War. In an interesting report to their communities about a conversation they had held with Alexander I, the Jewish deputies Eliezer (Lazar) Dillon and Yehudah Zundel Sonnenberg recorded the emperor's promise to investigate Jewish grievances and urged their constituents sharply to combat Jewish smuggling, of which the emperor had personally complained. "This is contrary to the teachings of our holy Torah," they added, "which orders us to observe carefully the emperor's commands.[5]

Nor did anyone raise the question whether synagogue audiences should continue reciting the traditional prayers for the welfare of their monarchs including even such anti-Jewish rulers as Nicholas I and Nicholas II. This custom caused some embarrassment to Galician Jews during World War I. At that time the Austrian police discovered that many Galicians were using prayer books imported from Russia and containing these liturgical blessings with the full names of the tsar and his family. Since Russia was at that time an enemy country, a search was instituted throughout the Jewish communities so as to expunge the incriminating passages from the "subversive" prayer books.

LAW ENFORCEMENT

Jews saw no conflict in loyalty when, in cultivating their traditional mores, they paid little heed to the governmental efforts to subject them to the jurisdiction of general courts. In her first proclamation after the annexation of the Polish provinces, Catherine II promised to maintain the existing order and religious liberties of all inhabitants, including Jews. One article stated specifically: "The administration of law and justice among Jews shall continue to be entrusted to their present courts, though in the name and under the authority of Her Imperial Majesty."[6]

Within ten years, however, the Russian authorities started to retreat from this pledge and increasingly tried to subsume the Jews under the jurisdiction of the municipal and other courts. They were prompted not only by the general tendency of authoritarian regimes to try to control all facets of their subjects' life but also by the wish to channel the substantial judicial fees to the tsarist or municipal judges. The law of 1804, finally, tried to restrict the operation of Jewish tribunals to purely religious affairs and otherwise to treat them as mere courts of arbitration, if voluntarily accepted as such by the parties. But whatever their status in public law may have been, the Jews respected their own courts of justice and readily submitted themselves to their judgments even after the reiteration of these restrictive provisions in the edict of 1835 and the total abolition of the *kahal* in 1844.

As a rule, Jewish courts administered justice more efficiently and speedily than did the general courts. Having behind them centuries of experience and well-defined legal principles embodied in codes of law, commentaries, and *responsa* by rabbis, all of which were intensively studied by the entire Jewish intelligentsia, their sentences usually met with instantaneous favorable public opinion and often the approval of the very parties against whom judgment was issued. In his autobiography, the Hebrew writer Abraham Jacob Paperna maintained that in his native hamlet there was no Christian court and litigations were largely settled by the law of the fist. In contrast thereto,

> in all monetary litigations, quarrels between husband and wife, or any other controversies they [Jews] usually repaired to the Jewish court, which enjoyed the full confidence of the local Christians as well. Whenever the latter had a controversy with a Jew, they usually turned to the rabbi, who, after listening to any plaintiff, immediately sent his beadle for the defendant, who appeared almost instantaneously. Both parties placed on the table the judicial fee—both having to pay the same amount—and the proceedings began. Shortly thereafter the rabbi pronounced the sentence which as a rule the litigants accepted without demurrer or the help of court marshals.[7]

This somewhat idealized picture reproduces fairly well the informality of Jewish trials, which in financial and family matters often followed the rules of equity and resulted in amicable settlements, rather than in sentences according to formal law. The official Russian machinery, on the contrary, moved very slowly, and in various instances some cases were pending for years on end. It is small wonder, then, that according to an outstanding Russian expert, as late as the 1880s, many Christians repaired to Jewish courts even in litigations with other non-Jews.

Evidently there existed areas of conflict between these rival judicial systems. One of the most effective weapons of Jewish law enforcement consisted in the promulgation, or the mere threat, of a ban which readily forced any recalcitrant party to appear before the court or to accept its unfavorable judgment. Although because of centuries-long abuses the Jewish ban, like its Catholic counterpart, had lost some of its efficacy, the communal elders could still force a rebellious member to his knees by refusing him certain religious services, such as circumcision, rabbinical wedding, or the religious burial in consecrated ground. An excommunication also implied various forms of social ostracism. Jewish guilds, or the *kahal* behind them, could threaten any artisan with the loss of membership, or at least with his demotion from master artisan to journeyman. The tsarist government looked askance at the exercise of this power, which it was unable to control. Time and again it ineffectually tried to outlaw bans but, since their promulgation rested with rabbis backed by a general assembly of members, even the suppression of the *kahal* in 1844 made little of a dent in the continued authority of Jewish courts over Jews.

Conflicting interests of state and community came to the fore also when in order to strengthen its supervision, the government encouraged informing among Jews, sometimes promising to turn over the ensuing fines to the informers. On the Jewish side, on the other hand, informing had long been considered a major crime, because it was likely to embroil not only a few individuals but by the process of generalization entire Jewish communities in serious difficulties with their neighbors and governments. In medieval Spain the Jewish courts had secured the privilege of passing death sentences on informers who were considered guilty of high treason toward their community. This tradition was kept alive in the Polish and Russian communities, although executions became very infrequent and they were treated as murderous acts by the authorities. One such incident in 1836 in the small Podolian town of Novo-Ushitsa actually brought about sharp retribution. For a long time two Jews played the game of receiving payments from the government for informing and from the Jews for not informing until the Jewish elders decided to get rid of the two blackmailers. Although the executions were carried out quietly and the local authorities were effectively bribed, the governor-general ordered a sharp investigation. After a trial before a military court, the majority of the eighty Jewish accomplices was sentenced to hard labor in Siberia, while most of the others had to run a gauntlet between five hundred soldiers; few of these survived the ordeal. The only person acquitted was the hasidic leader, Rabbi Israel Friedmann of Ruzhin, who had fled to Austria, where he founded the subsequently famous hasidic dynasty of Sadagóra, Bukovina.[8]

Even without this severe punishment, such drastic means of disposing of informers would hardly have continued in the subsequent decades. But here always was a source of conflict between the authorities, who saw in informers welcome allies, and community members, who resented them as traitors. In any case, Jewish judicial autonomy began weakening in the latter years of the nineteenth century as part of the general decline in communal solidarity resulting from the newer social and ideological movements. In particular, in preventing some Jewish litigants from invoking the aid of state judges, the Jews' reluctance to appeal to state courts, which was never wholly effective sharply diminished after the great judicial reform of 1864 which tried to reorganize the Russian courts along the long-accepted patterns of the West European judicial systems. Although this reform was but gradually extended to all provinces, and was never fully implemented—there were too many exceptions by law and judicial precedent for the new system to become universal and untrammeled by arbitrary administrative decisions—Jews now had far more confidence in the honesty and impartiality of the Russian judges, at least in civil cases. This was particularly true in the two capitals, whenever the upper class of the Jewish bourgeoisie became involved in some litigation over the far more complicated business transactions of the advancing capitalistic economy. However, many Jews realized that although nothing in the law prohibited the appointment of Jews to judgeships—especially the office of justice of the peace, which was assigned a significant role in the judicial administration (except during the years of 1889 to 1912, when it was abolished)—no Jew was entrusted with any judicial function. We also recall the various chicaneries to which Jews were subjected in the regular practice of law.[9]

SOCIAL WELFARE

The government evinced no opposition to the ramified communal charities. In general the Russian Empire had to leave all philanthropic efforts to the initiative of private individuals or the churches. From time immemorial the Jewish community had concerned itself with the social welfare of its members in an even broader sense than do modern welfare states. Since charity was connected with religion, social welfare embraced moral, as much as physical, well-being. Therefore, not only did the community supervise the morals of its members—exposing cases of rent gouging, of excessive harshness by landlords toward tenants, or of illicit sex relations to public contumely—but it also tried to protect the good names of innocent persons. We even find communal minutes recording attestations for girls who had lost their virginity because of an accident or illness, lest they be subsequently accused of premarital intercourse. Charities were often delegated to special philanthropic associations. Like the professional guilds, which as a rule also tried to assist their members in emergencies, these societies had had a rich history behind them, dating back to ancient and medieval times. Among them the burial society, the so-called *Hevra kadisha* (the holy association), carried the greatest prestige and wielded most power. At times, these societies were strong enough to defy the very *kahal*. Together with the rabbinate, they thus offered some checks and balances within the Jewish communal structure.

Much was also left to individual philanthropies, particularly to alms distributed among beggars. Indeed, mendicancy became a major blemish on the Jewish, as well as on the general Russian, body politic, with the difference, however, that from time immemorial charity had been stressed so strongly by rabbinic moralists and legislators that beggary lost much of its stigma. In his aforementioned autobiography Paperna observed that "the Jewish pauper does not ask for alms, as does his Christian counterpart, standing before the door or near the window and bending down to the ground, but he brazenly enters the room and demands a gift as if it were his due. If he is refused, he becomes abusive and curses." Both on moral and practical grounds even impoverished families felt obligated to contribute their mite to both the communal and individual charities. Since the number of beggars increased by leaps and bounds and many families were unable to meet even their minimal demands, some communities began issuing scrip representing fractions of a kopek which enabled families to give something to all beggars at their doors. Much disturbance was caused by migratory beggars who moved from one hamlet to another and collected alms. The communities found themselves obliged to issue certificates to deserving mendicants, who were then entitled to spend three days in one locality collecting alms before moving on to the next place. Such certificates were also given to the poor, whom various householders had to entertain at Sabbath meals.

Above all, many communities erected a so-called *hekdesh*, a combination of hostelry and hospital, to accommodate both homeless visitors and sick persons. Such institutions were often maintained even by impoverished communities, unable to give them the necessary care. As a result, they often degenerated into overcrowded unsanitary hovels, which, rather than helping diseased persons, actually increased the dangers of infection. Understandably, these institutions, together with the whole system of begging and other outworn methods of social welfare, were subjected to sharp criticisms by visitors from more advanced Western countries and by local Jewish reformers. The Minsk *hekdesh*, for instance, was thus described by a visiting English missionary, Robert Pinkerton:

> In the Jewish Hospital we saw forty-five young and old, of both sexes, seemingly without any classification of disease, placed in several small rooms; they certainly presented one of the most appalling scenes of wretchedness I ever witnessed; filth, rags and pestilential effluvia pervaded the whole place. A small apothecary's shop, with a kind of chapel, occupied one end of the building. The government contributes 16£ per annum towards its support; and the rest of the miserable pittance allowed to this lazar house is derived from the Jewish kahal and from private charity.

Similar harrowing descriptions are offered by the distinguished novelist, Shalom J. Abramovich (better known under his pen name, Mendele Mokher Seforim), all of which made the *hekdesh* a byword of opprobrium among the assailants of the traditional Jewish community life.[10]

CLASS STRUGGLE

As time went on, the inner tensions in the community increased and greatly undermined Jewish solidarity. From the outset the Russian Jewish community had built-in elements of class struggle. Its predecessor, the Polish Jewish community of the eighteenth century, had suffered from the general dissolution of the Polish state and had allowed certain anarchical elements to distort its traditional order. The growing inflation and with it the disproportionate indebtedness of the communities, together with Poland's arbitrary taxation system, had lent undue prominence to the communal plutocracy. Under Russian domination these conditions were in some respects further aggravated by the close alliance between the wealthy groups and the Russian bureaucracy. Russian law itself, by extending certain privileges to members of the merchant guilds and to a lesser extent to registered "burghers," injected a discriminatory factor into the communal relations as well. While the community still remained responsible for the total taxes imposed upon Jews of each district, its wealthiest members, belonging to the first guild, were exempt from the head taxes and certain other imposts. To be sure, it appears that few of them completely shirked their communal responsibilities. Whether voluntarily or under the pressure of public opinion and possible reprisals, they mostly assumed their share in the communal burdens. But such voluntary cooperation always injected an element of uncertainty and frequently lent the voices of such "volunteers" an undue weight in the determination of communal affairs.

Members of this class, moreover, were usually the entrenched leaders, who though formally elected by their respective constituencies, were little despots subject only in extreme cases to deposition by communal will. As a rule these communal tyrants entertained excellent relations with the Russian officials and with the latter's aid nipped most opposing movements in the bud. We have a graphic description of such a small-time despot in the hamlet of Kamenets, Grodno province, from the pen of a modern writer Yehezkel (Ezekiel) Kotik. Although such descriptions by a propagandist for change must be partially discounted, the fact that the elder concerned, Aaron Leizer, was the writer's grandfather who left a strong imprint on his grandson's childhood recollections gives an inkling of what injustices could be perpetrated by a communal autocrat in the middle of the nineteenth century. It all began when some Jews succeeded in outbidding Aaron Leizer for a concession he had held from a neighboring landlord, at a time when he happened not to serve as "the elder of the month."

> When my grandfather learned of it, he journeyed to the *ispravnik* [police official] and told him that he wished to become a tax assessor. Thereupon the ispravnik arrived in Kamenets and took away the books and the seal from the tax assessor B. and handed them to my grandfather. Now grandfather went to work. In the first place, he sent attendants to seize the kitchen utensils, candlesticks, clocks, all that he could find, even bedding to which he had no right, in the houses of the opposition. To whom should grandfather listen? He had the ispravnik on his side. He also detected some old debts owed the community and he now demanded their payment at once. . . . There was great excitement in town and people quickly recognized that it was difficult to tangle with Aaron Leizer. . . . . The outcome was that the group which had intended to obtain the concession and which consisted, according to my grandfather's calculations, of seventy persons, had to take an oath in the Great Synagogue—all clad in praying shawls and holding scrolls of law in their arms, while the ram's horn was blown and candles were lighted—that they would commit no such injustice toward my grandfather. This was a most solemn oath. . . . The next day grandfather sent a letter to the ispravnik resigning from the post of tax assessor. The ispravnik, well informed about what was happening, gave his approval.[11]

On the other hand, in the predominantly tiny communities of the Russian Pale during the early decades after the partition of Poland, these communal elders had to reckon with the force of public opinion; otherwise they might have been boycotted by their own closest neighbors. Some of their acts could also be scrutinized by higher governmental authorities, if some aggrieved groups were aroused enough to invoke such outside assistance. We have, for example, the texts of such applications to the minister of interior from Minsk and a small Podolian community in 1852–53. One could also appeal to the rabbinic authorities. Of course, the rabbis, like the rest of the sprawling, if often grossly underpaid, communal bureaucracy, usually were appointees of those very leaders against whom they were asked to intervene. But there was enough independence of mind, at least among the more important members of the rabbinate, and they were sufficiently obedient to the postulates of rabbinic law, which embraced elements of what the Romans called *fas* as well as *jus*, to adjudicate matters in accordance with the principles of equity. More frequently, overt rebellion against established communal authority was avoided by the elders' own moderation. Some leaders, even if autocratic, behaved like the benevolent despots of the Enlightenment era, who felt that everything should be done for the people, but as little as possible by the people. Stories about communal autocrats who sought to secure justice by humiliating certain powerful but selfish individuals abound in the literature of the age. Nonetheless, as a rule members of the upper classes, mainly consisting of the plutocracy, an aristocracy of rabbinic descent, and one of actual learning, felt closer kinship for one another and in case of conflict sided with their own class rather than with the majority.

Such conflicts became particularly frequent during Nicholas I's *rekrutchina*. No sooner did the edict appear in 1827 than the entire community was plunged into mourning. Since the administration of this barbarous recruitment system was in part placed in the hands of the communal elders, however reluctant, it was obvious that the lower classes would be the main sufferers, and some houses of Jewish elders in Minsk and elsewhere were stoned. Though speedily repressed by the government, these rebellious acts adumbrated the increasing chasm which this new law would create within the community. Having to deliver a certain quota of recruits—we recall that that quota was set higher than the ratio of the Jewish population—the elders had to choose what they considered the lesser evils. Sometimes the recruitment of under-aged children, for instance, sprang from the humane consideration that boys of eighteen or twenty were usually fathers of families and that their forced enlistment would cause even greater hardships to more individuals. The law itself, moreover, exempted sons of merchants of the three guilds from all military service. It was not surprising when from 1825 on, or two years before the enactment of the severe ukase, the number of Jews enrolled under these guilds increased by leaps and bounds. By paying a registration fee (the fee for membership in the third guild was rather moderate), Jews, like non-Jews, could thus secure exemption from military service for their children. Hence, for example, in the province of Kiev where Jews had outnumbered Christian commoners to but a minor extent, 42,910 Jews, as against 17,156 Christians, now suddenly appeared on the rolls, a disproportion which continued until 1845, or during the entire period covered by the records. Communal leadership was also interested in saving young rabbis and rabbinical students, including children who showed special aptitude for rabbinic studies, because of the deep-rooted Jewish reverence for learning. At the same time, uneducated children of illiterate parents could more readily be deceived by the various "kidnappers" who by substantial *douceurs* made them sign slips indicating their willingness to volunteer for armed service.

In general, the Russian administration treated these prospective servicemen almost on a par with criminals; they were often kept in chains until the respective draft boards examined their physical capabilities. Right at the beginning of this system a Kiev doctor, asked by the military authorities for the reasons for the high rate of mortality among the new recruits, replied:

> More than half of the 1,600 new cantonists brought together in 1828 had come from a considerable distance. According to the documents accompanying them, they were supposed to have been ten years of age, but since they were losing their first teeth, it was manifest that they could not be older than eight years. Unfortunately, no funds were available to return them to their parents in the distant localities. Hence the battalion was forced to keep them and to enter their ages according to the documents.[12]

Such frequent miscarriage of justice was blamed at home on the communal elders even if they happened not to be guilty. Ultimately, the government tightened its screws by decreeing that for every recruit the community had failed to deliver, it was to be penalized by an increased quota of three recruits. Combining recruitment with fiscal administration, another edict provided that for every 2,000 rubles of tax arrears, the community had to furnish an additional recruit without being released from its financial obligations. In short, caught between the Scylla of unrelenting government pressures and the Charybdis of an aroused communal membership, the communal leaders often acted like desperadoes and lost whatever prestige they had previously enjoyed among the masses. To many of them the formal abolition of the *kahal* in 1844 came as welcome relief from an impossible burden.

Nevertheless, the heritage of bitterness left behind by the recruiting laws, kept acute by the continued responsibility of the new semivoluntary associations for certain tax revenues, remained as a festering wound within the community. Combined with the rise of the new ideological movements, which undermined the traditional uniform *Weltanschauung,* these inner forces of distintegration augured badly for the future of the Jewish communal organization. Before long, an increasingly powerful chorus of voices demanded the replacement of the traditional communal organization by a novel form of a secularized and more democratically controlled "people's" community.

[8]

Religion and Culture

Survival of the Jewish people under the trying conditions of the tsarist regime was largely contingent on its adherence to its religious teachings which for most of that period dominated both the thinking and the practical way of life of the vast majority. These teachings, and the institutions giving them flesh and blood, had evolved gradually during the more than two millennia of Jewish life in the Diaspora. In pre-partition Poland these forms of Jewish living had assumed a particular coloring; they were continued with undiminished vigor under the reign of the tsars. The relatively minor adjustments necessitated by the new environmental conditions were taken by the Jewish community in its stride. Ironically, the growing hostility of both the regime and the Russo-Polish public merely helped to reinforce the inner solidarity of the Jewish group and its attachment to its ancestral faith and mores. After a few decades, to be sure, certain reformatory trends began emerging, expressed particularly in the so-called *Haskalah* (Jewish Enlightenment) literature. But the fact that these trends received considerable support from the government for a while aroused suspicions among the Jewish masses. Anything that smacked of excessive rapprochement with the Gentile world was suspect as a path ultimately leading to apostasy from

Judaism, a nexus which indeed underlay much of the government favoritism toward the reformatory movements.

Judaism of the old type was all-embracing in both its doctrine and its demands concerning daily observance. One needs but quote parts of the following appeal, issued in 1838 by the Warsaw rabbinate in collaboration with several other communities. Its tenor was that in order to appease the evident wrath of the Almighty, the Jewish communities ought to watch the more closely all phases of their members' behavior, a surveillance which the public was expected to welcome with great joy. They were to supervise most insistently:

1. the *mezuzzot* (door-post scrolls), which are to be placed in every house on all doors, gates and other places requiring them. . . . The supervisor should check them every month in each city, particularly in places where there is suspicion that these *mezuzzot* might be stolen.

2. the owners of bathhouses, so that the water in the pools be sufficiently heated, for on cold days this matter may constitute a danger to life.

3. the butcher shops, lest ritually permitted meats be sold in shops which also distribute non-kosher meats. . . .

4. the removal of the sciatical vein so that it be accomplished without any residuum of doubt . . . for due to excessive greed many butchers sin on this score. Also to see to it that all meat be washed every three days according to Jewish law.

5. in localities which have an 'erub (symbolically cordoned-off areas for Sabbath use), to supervise their proper installation. Communities which do not have an 'erub should be urged to install it in a proper fashion. . . .

9. to see to it that all stores be closed [on Fridays] at least half an hour before the time set for synagogue services so that there should be enough time to light the candles in full daylight.

10. He who has the fear of God in his heart shall be careful to order his clothes from a reliable tailor who would not commit the severe transgression of *shaatnez* (mixing of wool and linen together). All should also be modest in their attire, which is a good piece of advice for many reasons.

11. Since many localities have privies close to synagogues and prayer houses, and this is a great advantage for the population from both the standpoint of health and cleanliness during services, they should see to it that these outhouses be kept clean and have doors in proper condition. They should also urge such localities which do not yet have them to install them. . . .

[113]

15. It is highly appropriate to institute in every town a charitable chest for the poor who are ashamed of asking for their share for the expenses on Sabbaths and holidays. This charity is to be distributed every Friday morning.

16. The teachers in each community should be careful in instructing pupils able to understand the laws of the *Shulhan Arukh* (code of laws) in some section of that code every day. Particularly in the laws relating to prayers, benedictions, ablutions of hands, the Sabbath, and other commandments which every Jew needs in order to know how to behave.

17. Each community is to appoint supervisors for every wedding lest men and women dance together, God forbid. . . . Every man should also see to it that members of his family should not go on Sabbath and holidays to drink in taverns, lest they become exuberant and careless.

18. Every member is to supervise his family and personnel so that men not be alone with women and also that two unmarried boys not sleep in the same bed. . . .

This appeal is cited here at some length because it shows the range of religious supervision of the minutiae of daily living. Because of the public's general willingness to submit to such controls, the life of the individual Russian Jew was to some extent immunized from the effects of hostile governmental regulations and popular interference.[1]

SYNAGOGUE AND RABBINATE

Religious life centered around the synagogue and the school, as well as their main officials, the rabbis and teachers. Despite strong communal controls, individuals and smaller groups were left much leeway in organizing their own places of worship. While "synagogues" consisted mainly of two types, the synagogue in the narrower sense (*bet ha-keneset*) and the prayer and study house (*bet ha-midrash*), there were many private and associational chapels where services were conducted in exactly the same fashion. Sometimes such lesser places of worship were organized for religious reasons, as during the protracted struggle between the new sect of *Hasidim* (Pietists) and *Mitnagdim* (their opponents). Since the former had introduced certain ritualistic innovations, it was but natural for them to hold prayerful assemblies employing these new rituals. Sometimes followers of a certain hasidic leader were at variance with their counterparts of another hasidic school and worshiped in separate quarters. Professional associations of craftsmen also often preferred to worship in synagogues of their own.

At times a wealthy member had only to quarrel with the leaders of a larger synagogue or with the majority of its worshipers for him to organize an independent group in his own home or rented quarters. Occasionally, the quest for synagogue honors, especially for being called to the recitation of the scriptural lessons on Sabbaths and holidays, was potent enough to induce ambitious individuals to organize small congregations in which they could be more frequently summoned for such honorific assignments. Although all these institutions, major or minor, were subject to general surveillance by the communal boards, they enjoyed considerable autonomy and revealed many variations which added much to the community's spiritual richness and afforded vast opportunities for the display of its creative talents.

The same local autonomy was also enjoyed by the rabbinate, which in the two millennia of its evolution had undergone many transformations. The Russian rabbis, too, largely followed the patterns established in independent Poland, where in 1764 the government had closed down the two central organizations of Polish and Lithuanian Jewry. Even more than before, each community and its rabbi now had to rely on their own resources, only occasionally consulting with leaders in other localities. Complete atomization was prevented only by the fact that as before, an outstanding rabbinic authority like Elijah ben Solomon Gaon of Vilna (1720–97) enjoyed such a wide reputation for scholarship and saintliness that most communities accepted his judgments unquestioningly. Even he, however, ran up against considerable resistance in his own community of Vilna when he tried to outlaw the new hasidic movement.

Other distinguished rabbis included Israel Lipkin (better known as Israel Salanter from his residence in Salant, near Kovno [1810–83]), leader of a new ethical movement, and Isaac Elhanan Spector of Kovno (1817–96), both of whom played an outstanding role especially in the northwestern provinces. In many other parts of the Pale, too, rabbis were often approached by their colleagues for decisions on some ticklish problems in ritual or civil law. This was the highest form of recognition given to a rabbi, whose esteem rose with the number and geographic diffusion of his correspondents. If he received inquiries from other European countries or the United States, he thereby secured a seal of approval as an international leader. But apart from professional rabbis, holding office by communal appointment, many private citizens attained the same rank by virtue of their learning and saintly way of life. Salaried rabbis often bowed their heads in reverence before them and accepted their superior judgment. On the other hand, such flexibility and dependence on the more or less arbitrary judgment of a number of individual *cognoscenti* could also become a source of instability and give rise to many communal dissensions.[2]

Not surprisingly, this entire world of synagogue and rabbinate was alien to Russian officials, who correctly sensed that much of Jewish "separatism" was protected by the ramparts of these two institutions. Before long the Russian autocracy tried, therefore, to seize full control of both. In its comprehensive law of 1835, it prescribed that only Jewish settlements of more than thirty families could maintain a prayer house of their own, and only such as embraced eighty families or more could also erect a synagogue. In larger cities Jews could maintain a prayer house for each thirty and a synagogue for each eighty families. Private chapels, even occasional services at private homes, required special governmental permits, unlicensed gatherings being subject to a huge fine of 1,000 rubles. (According to an official report of 1842, there were 604 synagogues and 2,340 prayer houses as well as 3,944 schools and 954 rabbis in Russia.) Each sanctuary, moreover, had to have an executive board to maintain decorum, regulate the income, appoint the personnel, as well as to submit annual reports to both the local police and the rabbi. At the same time the statute devoted fully seventeen articles to the rabbinate, which was to be placed under much stricter governmental supervision. The rabbi was to keep vital statistics for the whole community, perform the necessary ceremonial functions at births, marriages, and burials, and above all see to it that all these activities be performed in full consonance with the existing Russian laws.[3]

One is readily reminded of Napoleon's equally autocratic reorganization of the French community in 1808, aimed at transforming it into a pliable organ of the authoritarian state. Napoleon could prove more successful, however, as French Jewry had partially deluded itself into seeing in the emperor's grandiose gestures an element of the general emancipatory movement. It was this combination of emancipation with assimilation within a generally egalitarian society which had made possible that gradual weakening of Jewish communal bonds in western Europe upon which Russian officialdom looked with such envy. It certainly could not be achieved in the Russian society, with its rigid class distinctions and its sharp discrimination against Jews. In practice, therefore, the governmental effort to undermine Jewish communal self-government and to convert the rabbinate into a state agency failed miserably even after the abolition of the *kahal* in 1844 and the issuance of certain relatively minor amendments in 1850 and after.

The rabbis—whose spiritual function for the community was derived from their talmudic learning, their strict adherence to rabbinic law, their constant teaching and preaching of it in theory and practice, and their adjudication of ritualistic and civil controversies—were often completely inept at serving as governmental registrars, even if they had had the desire to perform such major police functions for the state. In time, the government resorted to the appointment of official crown rabbis, also salaried by the communities. In many cases, however, even such official rabbis served more as representatives of their communities before the authorities than as authoritarian leaders imposing the government's will upon them. That is why later in the century quite a few patriotic Jewish leaders, equipped with the knowledge of Russian and Western culture, accepted such official positions without being condemned by their fellow Jews as police agents. Among them were such men as Rabbi Jacob Mazeh in Moscow, Dr. Judah Leb Kantor in Libau and Vilna, and Shemaryah Levin (1867–1935) in Grodno and Ekaterinoslav, later an outstanding Zionist leader, elected by the Jews themselves to the Russian Duma. The functions of these men were almost exclusively political and organizational, whereas their constituents' genuinely spiritual concerns were under the jurisdiction of their so-called deputies, the "spiritual rabbis," freely elected by the communities from among the learned talmudists.[4]

EDUCATION

A similar variety of forms existed in the Jewish school system. Here even more leeway had to be given to private initiative, for according to Jewish tradition, the primary responsibility for educating the children rested with the parents, while each adult was to pursue his own program of self-education. At the same time the Jewish community, either through its central organs or through a variety of associations and committees, whether or not connected with the synagogue, saw to it that no male child should be deprived of the opportunity of acquiring at least a good elementary education. Girls did not have to study, but most of them were taught how to recite prayers, read Yiddish translations of the Bible, and so forth. The result was a sharp contrast between the Jews and their neighbors. To cite Abraham Jacob Paperna's somewhat romanticizing reminiscences, the situation of the small town of Kopyl, where he had grown up, was typical of the rest of the Pale: "There was no government or secular public school in Kopyl and the entire Christian population was illiterate. The Jews, on the other hand, had a plethora of schools, albeit of a special type, perhaps twenty in all. All Jewish boys aged four to thirteen were taught in *heders* (elementary schools). . . . Not infrequently a poor man sold his last candlestick or pillow to pay the teacher."

Undeniably, there was considerable anarchy in the system. The teachers were often untrained for their jobs; some assumed their responsibilities only because they had failed in other callings. But there also were gifted and devoted instructors who gave their pupils excellent schooling. The curriculum was quite limited. Even the Bible was not studied too intensively, the main emphasis being placed on the Talmud and rabbinics. Nor were the methods of instruction always on the level considered efficacious by contemporary pedagogues. The school facilities were often totally inadequate; a room in a ramshackle building with few sanitary provisions would accommodate a score or more pupils of various ages and different stages of preparedness. Critics had a field day in describing these inadequacies. Typical of many harangues is the following correspondence from Vitebsk, written in 1894:

> Our Talmud Torahs are filthy rooms, crowded from nine in the morning until nine in the evening with pale, starved children. These remain in this contaminated atmosphere for twelve hours at a time and see only their bent, exhausted teachers. . . . Most of them are clad in rags; some of them are almost naked. . . . Their faces are pale and sickly, and their bodies are evidently not strong. In parties of twenty or thirty, and at times more, they all repeat some lesson aloud after their instructor. He who has not listened to the almost absurd commentaries of the ignorant *melammed* [teacher] can not even imagine how little the children gain from such instruction.[5]

Discounting the evident one-sidedness of this portrayal, there is no question that the old school system offered many legitimate targets for critics, whether recruited from the Jewish "enlightened" circles or from outsiders. Yet backed by a millennial experience, the Jewish elementary school as a rule achieved its goals of giving good elementary training in Jewish subjects to the majority of children and preparing a substantial minority for more advanced studies after the age of thirteen. While we do not have solid statistical information concerning the enrollment in Jewish schools, it appears that to the very end of the tsarist regime, a majority of Jewish schoolchildren attended such Jewish schools. According to one unreliable account, in 1887 the Jewish schools in the Pale outside of Poland had an enrollment of 18,799 pupils. Only seven years later the number of enrolled pupils is given more accurately as 95,661, increasing to 115,575 by 1911. If the Jewish students from the ten Polish provinces are added to this number, the figure for 1911 rises to 200,797. At the same time, 126,976 Jews attended general schools in 1911, as against 29,526 in 1886. This marked a radical change from a century earlier, when almost all Jews went exclusively to Jewish schools, communal, associational, or private.[6]

Above the elementary *heder* stood the *yeshivah*, an academy attended by adolescent boys and young men, sometimes even after their marriage. Practically every distinguished rabbi tried to run a school of this type, formally or informally. His prestige rose with the number of advanced pupils he was able to train. The budgets of small academies were as a rule supported locally, the pupils being assigned to individual citizens for all meals on special days of each week. But there also were large national institutions; among them was that of Volozhin in the province of Vilna (founded in 1803 by Rabbi Hayyim, a pupil of Elijah Gaon) and another in Mir in the province of Minsk. Since these were national schools of higher learning, they felt entitled to send messengers out to collect donations from communities all over the Pale. Out of these gifts they were able to allot small weekly stipends of seventy-five kopeks to each of the pupils, while still assigning them to private homes on Sabbaths and holidays. The methods of financing for the most part proved inadequate and entailed great hardships for both teachers and students. Yet the majority of both accepted these difficulties without demurrer, feeling pride in their academies' intellectual achievements and simultaneously considering their own work the fulfillment of Judaism's supreme commandment.

This spirit also animated the unparalleled devotion of adults to continued self-education. In her interesting *Memoirs*, Pauline Wengeroff reminisced about how her father, a busy and wealthy contractor, used to rise at four o'clock every morning so that he could devote several hours to talmudic studies before attending synagogue services and then going about his business. Apart from such individual efforts, there were group studies in the prayer houses which embraced a large part of the population. Even the sharp critic of communal life, Shalom J. Abramovich (Mendele Mokher Seforim), nostalgically reminisced how during the intermission between the afternoon and evening services in the prayer houses, workingmen and others assembled at special tables where they were given instruction in one or another classic of rabbinic literature, including some ethical and homiletical works. Those qualified to do so studied the Talmud. Many adults organized special associations for the study of the Mishnah or Talmud; some tried to cover the entire Babylonian Talmud in a year by assigning a different segment of it to each member for daily study. Typical of this self-imposed discipline are the following provisions recorded in the minutes of the Grodno Mishnah Society: "A fine shall be imposed upon those who interrupt the study with idle chatter. Those finishing the reading of their chapter before the others shall nevertheless remain [in their places] until the Kaddish is recited, or else shall pay a fine."[7]

Among the schools of higher learning the *yeshivot* of Volozhin and Mir were the pride of Jewry in the Pale. Beginning with ten students maintained at his own expense, R. Hayyim Volozhiner developed the school into a major institution with a hundred pupils before his death in 1828. He was succeeded by his son Isaac, his son-in-law Hillel, and Isaac's son-in-law Naphtali Zvi Judah Berlin (*Nezib*; 1854–91), under whose administration the institution regularly taught up to four hundred pupils from many lands—this despite its closing by the Russian authorities from 1879 to 1881. It was shut again in the period from 1891 to 1895. Its strict regimen, its long hours of instruction and self-study, the wretched poverty of most of its students, and their unflagging devotion to learning have frequently been described by some alumni as well as by outside observers. The same conditions also prevailed in Mir and scores of lesser schools throughout the Pale and in the Kingdom of Poland.[8]

Such an extensive self-governing system of Jewish education was understandably a thorn in the flesh of Russian officialdom. On the one hand, it could not deny the right of parents to give their children religious education so long as the Jewish religion was tolerated in Russia. On the other hand, it viewed Jewish schools as the chief instruments of that Jewish separatism which it was trying to undermine. When in 1808 sixteen communities in the provinces of Vitebsk and Moghilev were asked why they did not establish secular schools, they replied succinctly that Jews neither wished to give their children secular education nor could afford any additional burdens. This situation changed but slowly not only under governmental pressure, but also because of the growingly vocal demands for secular studies by the "enlightened" Jews themselves. Yet as late as 1840, we are told, only forty-eight Jews were enrolled in Russian primary and secondary schools, and but fifteen attended universities. This is the more remarkable as twenty years earlier the University of Vilna alone had, under the active sponsorship of Prince Adam Czartoryski, attracted some forty Jewish students in the course of two decades (1803–24). Only from the middle of the century did Jewish youth begin to flock into Russian secondary schools; the number of Jewish pupils then rose from 159 in 1853 to 2,362 in 1870.[9]

NEWER RELIGIOUS TRENDS

Education was but a reflection of the socioreligious and cultural conditions of Russian Jewry. In the first three decades of the nineteenth century it was still a fairly monolithic cultural group fully cherishing its traditional outlook. The largest inner division between *Hasidim* and *Mitnagdim*, inherited from the Polish regime, had lost much of its sharpness during the second and third generations of the hasidic movement. Originating from the East Galician and Podolian semirural communities, this semisectarian group shared, from its inception, some of the anti-intellectualism of the Eastern Churches. Although not quite condemning intellectual distinction as a sign of personal haughtiness before God, as did some of their Greek Orthodox counterparts, the hasidic leaders considered inner piety, ethical behavior, and semimystic communion with the Deity as a far closer expression of the fear and love of God than sheer immersion into the depth of rabbinic lore. Life of the Jewish masses under Polish and Russian domination was full of suffering and sadness. Yet the hasidic leaders—beginning with the founder of the movement, Israel ben Eliezer Baal Shem Tob (1700–1760)—preached *joyous* exaltation of the Lord as the supreme form of worship. Apart from thus offering an anodyne to many miseries of daily existence, Hasidism, through its emphasis on ethical folk tales and religious folk songs as well as the use of down-to-earth similes and parables, appealed directly to the folk psyche. Not only outright adherents of that movement, but also Ukrainian peasants wove legends around the mysterious personality of Rabbi Israel, who had left behind no written works but many dedicated disciples. These disciples carried the struggle into the Jewish communities, and despite the combined opposition of the entrenched communal bureaucracy, leading rabbis, and plutocrats, conquered most communities in the southern areas, and made considerable headway also in the northwestern provinces.

By the first half of the nineteenth century Hasidism's battle had largely been won. But with its victory also passed its truly heroic stage, followed by an almost total reconciliation of the new movement with the traditional rabbinic Orthodoxy. Whatever minor differences in theological doctrines may still have persisted—and these were in part the heritage of older debates among the devotees of the mystical and ethical literature of the pre-hasidic age—Jewish religious practices were fairly uniform. Apart from some ritualistic minutiae relating to the examination of a slaughterer's knife or the hours allowable for divine service, the Hasidim fully subscribed to rabbinic law and observance. Now the negative aspects of Hasidism came to the fore much more clearly. In particular, the belief of many Hasidim in the hereditary charismatic powers of their leaders, the so-called *tsaddikim* (righteous men), not only undermined the original egalitarian and democratic features of the movement, but also opened the gates to many abuses. Regular dynasties speedily emerged; financially supported by their dedicated adherents, these leaders lived in palatial quarters with retinues of servants and displays of many luxuries. Ironically, rather than discouraging their poverty-stricken followers, this "conspicuous consumption" impressed the latter as a sign of divine grace and enhanced the leaders' prestige. In fact, dynastic allegiance often became so powerful that adherents of one family fought the followers of another dynasty with even greater vigor than they did their common enemies on the outside.

Among these long-lived dynasties stood out in the northwest the family of Shneur Zalman of Ladi, whose role during the Napoleonic invasion typified in some respects the political influence exerted by these new leaders. In 1828, Shneur Zalman's grandson Mendel transferred his residence to Liubavichi, which became the center of a special wing of the hasidic movement. Like its founder, it cultivated kabbalistic and rabbinic studies alongside the deep homiletical and ethical teachings characteristic of the movement as a whole. In the province of Kiev arose the dynasty of the so-called Chernobil Hasidim, founded by Menahem Nahum and his son Mordecai (Rabbi Motele). Another important founder of a dynasty, Israel ben Shalom Friedmann of Ruzhin (1797–1850), after having established a fine reputation throughout the Ukraine and Volhynia had, as we recall, to leave Russia and establish his residence in Austrian Sadagóra, whence he and his descendants held sway over thousands of followers in both empires until World War I. In Russian Poland the outstanding dynasty was that established by the Warsaw leader Isaac (Itshe) Meier Alter in Góra Kalwaria.[10]

Independently influential were outstanding individuals such as Nahman ben Simhah of Bratslav or Levi Yitzhak of Berdichev, both of whom were remembered by a grateful posterity through a host of sayings and apothegms conveying profound lessons of Jewish thought and behavior. True, but few of these leaders still adhered to the old self-denial of the original founders. Certainly few of the new *tsaddikim* emulated the example of Nahman of Bratslav, who in 1799, at the age of twenty-six, undertook a pilgrimage to the Holy Land at enormous personal sacrifice. Before starting out he wrote to his eldest daughter: "You will proceed to your future father-in-law, your next sister will become a servant, your little sister will probably be taken into some home out of pity, your mother will become a cook, and I shall dispose of all my household for traveling expenses." No such asceticism was expected from a grand seigneur like Israel Friedmann. Nevertheless, his followers and many outsiders believed in the sincerity of his declaration, "I am part and parcel of Israel's soul; if any Jew, be he at the end of the world, suffers pain, I feel it instantaneously." In another homily, Israel expatiated on the charismatic powers of a hasidic leader, teaching:

> The true *zaddik* influences the material world, such as childbirth, health and livelihood, as well as the spiritual world, namely the spiritual well-being of all Israel, and particularly of his own followers. Even in the world to come all good stems from him. Every one must believe all this in complete faith. "Who is a fool? He who destroys what is given him" [Bab. Talmud, Hagigah 4a] refers to the man who loses his faith that all comes to him from the *zaddik*, thinking instead that he is able to secure it all by himself without the aid of the *zaddik*.[11]

Outsiders, however, including some rabbinic leaders, looked askance at such assertions and at the basic hasidic belief in the chiefs' supernatural powers. But they made their peace with the movement and were prepared jointly to fight the rising waves of Enlightenment and assimilation.

Something like a compromise emerged in the so-called *Musar* (ethical) movement, founded by Israel Lipkin Salanter. Although an outstanding talmudist in his own right, Rabbi Israel increasingly preached the emphasis on ethics rather than learning, while repudiating Hasidism's anti-intellectual and overexuberant features. In fact, his entire movement leaned toward asceticism, eliciting much opposition among other traditionalists who sought to uphold the long-accepted golden mean. This self-denying element of the *Musar* movement was even more vigorously stressed by Israel's pupils and later successors. Apart from founding first in Vilna and then in other communities special chapels for the cultivation of his brand of ethics (the so-called *Musar shtiblekh*), Rabbi Israel established a special academy of learning in Slobodka, in which intensive training in talmudic studies was combined with regular courses in ethical lore. Although he found many adherents and even patrons in Germany, the movement did not spread much beyond the Lithuanian and White Russian provinces, where it penetrated even into the older academies and congregations. The impact of both Musar and Hasidism upon the masses of Russian Jewry is illustrated also by the numerous editions of several older ethical and behavioral classics then republished in Russia. Moses Hayyim Luzzatto's *Mesillat yesharim* (The Path of the Righteous) was in some respects a best-seller, reappearing in forty-three editions. It was followed closely by Abraham Danzig's *Hayye Adam* (Man's Life; a popular summary of Jewish observances) with forty-two editions, and by the medieval classic, *Hobot ha-lebabot* (Duties of the Heart) by Bahya ibn Pakuda, with thirty-six editions.[12]

Not surprisingly, the literary creativity of the Orthodox leaders, both hasidic and antihasidic, grew by leaps and bounds. Regrettably, we have no reliable statistics for their intellectual output in the fields of law, homilies, kabbalah, Bible commentaries, and the like. But it may suffice to peruse the volumes of the Orthodox periodical *Hapeless (Die Wage)*—though published in Berlin in the years 1900 to 1905, it was edited by the Poltava rabbi Elijah Akiba Rabinowitsch—to note how many Russian scholars collaborated in that literary-scientific enterprise. Personally, in later preparing my *Bibliography of Jewish Social Studies, 1938–39* (published in New York, 1941), I was amazed to note that in less than two years (from January 1, 1938 to September 1, 1939, when World War II broke out) East European Jews, particularly in the Polish-Lithuanian areas which had belonged to Russia in 1917, published more volumes of responsa, halakhic and aggadic commentaries, homilies, kabbalistic (and hasidic) works than in any two decades of the seventeenth century, the heyday of rabbinic learning. And this was after the separation of some 3,000,000 Russian Jews, whose voices in these fields were wholly muted under the increasingly totalitarian and professedly godless Soviet regime. Moreover, the quality of the published works was often very high, and if they had been written several centuries before, some of them might have become classics of rabbinic literature.

JEWISH ENLIGHTENMENT

In contrast to this mass appeal of long-recognized Hebrew letters, many new creations, particularly if written by the "enlightened" critics of the existing order, had a hard time reaching an indifferent, often hostile public. The "enlightened" writers and their followers, the so-called *maskilim*, often made up by vociferousness for lack of popular acclaim. Most of them were, indeed, enthusiasts who felt their mission was to spread enlightenment among their coreligionists; they took adversity and even outright persecution in their stride. An early pioneer in this field was Menasseh ben Porat (1767–1831), known as Illier from the town of Illya near Vilna. As a writer, Illier evinced more concern for the general sufferings of humanity than for the discords within the Jewish community. His booklet, *Pesher dabar* (Solution to a Problem), published in 1807, actually used moderate language and advocated reconciliation between the opposing camps. Yet even such a modest appeal was rejected by members of the entrenched Orthodoxy, who succeeded in suppressing practically all copies of that work so that in more recent years only one was found in the British Museum. A larger work was already on the press in Volhynia when a friend persuaded the printer to burn all the galleys together with the manuscript.[13]

Subsequent enlightened writings were far less restrained. The *Haskalah* movement, originating from the Mendelssohnian circle in Berlin and Königsberg, had brought forth some outstanding scholars and writers in Galicia. Some of these aimed their shafts at Hasidism; among them Joseph Perl and Isaac Erter, whose eloquent satirical works were widely read in Russia as well. The Galician influence spread also through a number of distinguished immigrants, including Basilius Stern (1798–1853), the director of the newly founded modern school in Odessa (later elevated to the rank of Russia's honorary citizen), and Simhah Pinsker (1801–64), an outstanding student of medieval sectarian movements. Some Russian visitors to Galicia also came under the influence of the leading nineteenth-century Jewish philosopher, Nahman Krochmal.

One of them, Isaac Baer Levinsohn (1788–1860), tried, in his *Te'udah be-Yisrael* (Learning in Israel), to furnish definite answers to questions then preoccupying many young Jews, such as whether a pious Jew should devote himself to the more modern study of the Hebrew language and grammar; whether he should learn foreign languages and secular sciences; whether such studies were useful at all, and if so, could they avoid being prejudicial to genuine piety? Of course, these were rhetorical questions, and any reader knew from the outset the author's affirmative answers. While Levinsohn wrote in a heavy Hebrew style, his temperate approach found some acceptance even among the moderate Orthodox, in part because of the approval extended to some of his works by the tsarist administration. At times Levinsohn used his connections with the high officials as a subterfuge to overcome Orthodox resistance to the printing of his books. On one occasion he actually invented the name of such an official. On the other hand, when he set out to defend some cherished Jewish traditions, particularly the Talmud, which because of denunciations by converts and Jewish extremists was in ill-repute with the government, he lost much of the bureaucracy's sympathies. Similarly, when in 1834 he wrote his *Efes dammim* (Naught of Blood) in which, on the occasion of a Blood Accusation in Zaslav, Volhynia, he marshaled much rabbinic evidence against the ritual-murder libel, his stock with the bureaucracy fell quite low. In any case, he was refused the governmental subsidy which his disease-ridden body badly needed. At the same time this book enjoyed great popularity among Jews, and in 1840—on the occasion of the Damascus Blood Accusation, which had created an international sensation and even elicited the intervention of several European powers—it was translated into English, while translations into Russian and German followed in 1883–84.[14]

Apart from the educational reforms the progressive circles, as well as Russian officialdom, were deeply concerned about the traditional Jewish costume, which perpetuated Jewish "separatism." Such leading progressives as the scholars Mordecai Aaron Günzburg (1795–1846), Abraham Baer Gottlober (1811–99), and Samuel Joseph Fünn (1818–90) considered the special Jewish attire a main source of degradation of the Jewish communities. In an interesting memorandum, Gottlober argued that such special attire was limited to eastern Europe, while in other countries Jews dressed like their neighbors; on their journeys even Polish and Russian Jews dispensed with their Jewish costume. Historically, this attire was merely an adaptation of earlier Polish clothing which should now be definitely discarded.

> In the present nineteenth-century spirit of the time [*Zeitgeist*], when most Israelites try to achieve rapprochement with the Christians and to accept European and Christian morals, we must consider the different attire as the first source of misfortune and prejudice. It alone is the strongest barrier separating Jews from Christians in social as well as religious life. . . . Indeed the majority of our coreligionists look forward with deep yearning to a new regulation concerning clothing.

When the government finally issued such an order in 1845, giving the Jewish communities a five-year period of grace after which the Jewish attire would be strictly prohibited, a group of Volhynian progressives, led by Gottlober, made a secret compact to appear in European clothing on the same day. To reinforce this determination Gottlober also wrote a satirical poem, most of which, however, remained unpublished.[15]

Among the younger enlightened Hebrew authors one may mention also the skillful writer and effective pedagogue, Kalman Schulman (1819–99), a popularizer in the field of science and history, whose works opened new vistas to many Hebrew readers theretofore trained only in the traditional rabbinic lore. His Hebrew rendition of Josephus, prepared from a German translation and otherwise leaving much to be desired, received accolades even from some outstanding Orthodox rabbis. Deficiencies in accuracy were more than made up by his lucid and attractive style, which along with their novel content converted his works into fascinating eyeopeners for many of his contemporaries.

Most *maskilim*, however, turned into sharp critics of the existing community. Some became regular muckrakers, particularly with respect to Hasidism, to whose mystic and emotional beauties they were completely blind but whose institutional degeneration they described in all its lurid detail. The critics included some outstanding builders of the new Hebrew style and literature. Even by setting his novels in the biblical age, Abraham Mapu (1808–67) made his purpose of contrasting the idyllic life of the ancient Israelitic people with the unsatisfactory present in Russia quite evident to the reader. His two novels, *Ahabat Siyyon* (The Love of Zion) and *Ashmat Shomeron* (Samaria's Guilt), which Joseph Klausner characterized as "the most romantic and the most permanent in the entire new literature," included characters and situations paralleling certain contemporary conditions. They enjoyed wide popularity, the former soon appearing also in German, English, and Yiddish translations. More overtly satirical was his *Ayit Sabua* (Speckled Bird of Prey; a Hebrew idiom for Tartuffe), in which Mapu derided contemporary Orthodox hypocrites.[16]

Towering above all his compeers was the poet Yehudah Leib (Leon) Gordon (1830–92), who used his indubitable poetic gifts to spread the tenets of Enlightenment. Even his early biblical epics carried a contemporary message. Hailing the reforms under Tsar Alexander II, he wrote in 1863 his *"Awake, My People!"* in which he coined the most representative watchword of the whole movement. He exhorted his Jewish reader: "Be a man in the street and a Jew at home, a brother to thy [non-Jewish] countrymen and a [faithful] servant to thy king." But his lofty expectations remained unfulfilled. In 1872 he was given the opportunity to put his doctrines into practice in his new capacity of secretary both of the Society for the Promotion of Enlightenment among the Jews and of the steadily growing Jewish community of St. Petersburg. However, this career was cut short seven years later by a cabal of his Orthodox opponents with the local police which led to his and his wife's imprisonment and deportation for alleged subversive activities against the Russian regime. After a few months he was fully cleared and returned to the capital, but he was not restored to his former posts and had to earn his living as coeditor of the Hebrew periodical *Ha-Melits*. Nevertheless he continued to maintain friendly relations with Baron Horace Günzburg, the society's president and chief financial patron, and he was greatly disturbed when one of the Günzburg enterprises experienced business reversals. Ultimately the Russian government recognized Gordon's services for helping to Westernize his coreligionists by conferring upon him the rank of honorary citizen. Nevertheless, disappointed by the general reaction in Russia and the slow progress of enlightenment among his own people, his mood became increasingly pessimistic, almost nihilistic. As early as 1871 he saw little future for either Hebrew literature or the Jewish people at large. In a poem, "For Whom Do I Labor?" he expressed the belief that he probably was "the last of Zion's singers."[17]

Other influential Haskalah poets included the father and son, Adam (Abraham Dob Baer) ha-Kohen Lebensohn (1789–1878) and Micah Joseph Lebensohn (1828–52). Of the two the son was the more gifted poet, whose early death at the age of twenty-four evoked from the bereaved father a lamentation belonging among the most deeply felt pieces of the latter's poetic creativity. Gordon, too, commemorated the death of his young friend by a poetic cycle.

Enlightenment was not limited to Hebrew writers, however. There arose in Russia, Galicia, and Moldavia a series of Yiddish publicists and storytellers who, turning to best advantage a literary tradition several centuries old, were appealing more directly to the masses, including women, in a language accessible to them. When Mendel Lefin Satanover (1741–1819) published in 1817 his Yiddish translation of biblical Proverbs, he made a studious effort to avoid the theretofore prevalent Germanisms. He was followed by Israel Aksenfeld (1787–1866), who though a busy notary in Odessa, became a prolific Yiddish writer. While but few of his novels and short stories were printed, those which appeared reveal a keen insight into the realities of Russian Jewish life. His greatest difficulty was getting his works published. By decree of October 27, 1836, the Russian government closed all Hebrew printing presses except two which for the following three decades exercised a monopoly over all printing in Hebrew type. Those in Vilna and Zhitomir refused to accept Aksenfeld's works because his sharp attacks on Hasidism and the existing communal institutions would naturally antagonize their main customers. For more than twenty years, beginning in 1841, Aksenfeld bombarded the Russian Ministry of Public Enlightenment and the local Odessa officials with petitions seeking redress for this indirect censorship after the official Russian censor had expressed admiration for Aksenfeld's work. As a moderately prosperous notary public in Odessa, the writer was finally prepared to spread his works in lithograph form or to establish a printing press of his own—all without avail. The result was that before his death at the age of seventy-nine only two of his pieces appeared, followed by three more posthumous publications. Scores of other works have been lost. Nevertheless, recent students of Yiddish letters have discovered in his novel *Shterntikhel* (a feminine headgear) and other writings an inexhaustible source of information and insight into Jewish social life a century ago.[18]

Much better known in his day was Isaac Meier Dick (1814–93), who though writing in a lower key, exhibited his genuine gifts as a story-teller. After he had arranged with a publisher to submit a novelette every week, his literary output soared to more than four hundred items, some of which, despite their author's haste, were significant linguistic and esthetic contributions to Yiddish literature. Much less talented, though even more popular, was Nahum Meier Shaikevich (1849–1905), better known under his nom de plume, Shomer, who both in Russia and in the United States (where he settled in 1889) contributed much to the uplift of servant girls and uneducated workers. Like their Hebrew confreres, these Yiddish novelists invigorated the sharp critique of the Russian Jewish community and furnished many a weapon for the class struggle by the rising Jewish industrial proletariat.

None of these authors approximated the genius of Shalom Jacob Abramovich or Mendele Mokher Seforim (*ca.* 1836–1917), rightly called the father of modern Yiddish letters. With a matchless sense of style in both Yiddish and Hebrew and a profound knowledge of the various aspects of Jewish life within the Pale, Mendele described it in a series of novels which have become classics in both literatures. His satire was always tempered with deep sympathy for even the weaknesses of downtrodden humanity. In his *Kliatshe* (The Old Mare), symbolic of the oppressed people, his *Massaot Binyamin ha-shelishi* (Travels of Benjamin the Third), a sort of *Don Quixote*, and other works, partially translated also into English, he became the most persuasive critic of his environment, because even the advocates of the established order found his general urbanity and humanity utterly disarming. At the same time, Mendele felt called upon to write a popular work on science to spread its knowledge among the majority of his coreligionists, who read no other language but Hebrew or Yiddish.[19]

Even more important than their contributions to literature was the impact these men had on the gradual transformation of the ghetto community. While many of them were devoid of literary talent and often wrote in total disagreement with one another, theirs were the voices which articulated the unconscious strivings of a growing number of Jews who sought ways out of the narrow confines of their traditional life. If they often opened gates which they did not know how to close, their historic achievement was nonetheless very basic in helping to lead their people out of the ghetto into the vast outside world. In these efforts they were often supported by the government, not because it believed in the value of Haskalah letters but rather because it saw in them a method of breaking down the "separatism" of the Jewish community. Many officials hoped that the new movement might ultimately lead to the conversion and final absorption of the Jewish minority and thereby put an end to the ever-troublesome Jewish question.

For this reason even Nicholas I's officials tried from the 1830s on to promote modern Jewish schools in which first the German and later the Russian language, as well as secular subjects, would gradually outweigh the traditional rabbinic curriculum. Such modern schools were established in Odessa, Riga, and other communities. That of Riga, headed by the imported German teacher, Max Lilienthal, was but two years old when the government started to use the young pedagogue for the spread of its educational reforms among Jews. Most enlightened leaders were slow in perceiving the ultimate missionary aims of the government and basked in its much-cherished recognition. But before long they, like Lilienthal, realized the incongruity of siding with a government as oppressive as that of Nicholas I. It was easier for them to entertain great hopes during Alexander II's early liberal regime. Many *maskilim* helped the government establish such new rabbinical schools as those of Zhitomir and Vilna, whose alumni, lacking true rabbinic training, could not possibly hope to obtain legitimate rabbinic posts. Many of them, therefore, used these schools merely as stepping stones for admission to universities and a subsequent professional or business career, while to the Orthodox masses they appeared almost on a par with Christian missionaries. Ultimately, the government had to give up and to convert these theological institutions into teachers' seminaries, whose pupils could secure positions at one or another "enlightened" primary or secondary school.[20]

For a while the government also tried to force the communities to appoint rabbis in command of a Western language, preferably Russian, and to authorize elementary instruction by teachers only after they secured a governmental license. These authoritarian measures broke down completely, however, under the passive resistance of the parents of school children and the large majorities of each community. Only belatedly did many of the Haskalah leaders themselves realize, as had the spokesmen of European Enlightenment a century earlier, that rational schemes, however unimpeachably logical, could not in a short span of time transform a deeply rooted system of living. Hence came the despondency of such leaders as Gordon, who, despairing of any quick rational solution, gave up all hope for the survival of their people.

Superficially no more successful was the first experiment in Jewish journalism in the Russian language, the *Razsvet* (Dawn), a weekly, published in Odessa for one year (1860–61). Although directed by such able journalists and writers as Osip Rabinovich (1817–69), Lev Osipovich Levanda (1835–88), and for a time, Yoakhim Tarnopol (1810–1900), this pioneering effort—addressed to both the small layer of a Jewish intelligentsia and the tiny segment of the Russian public that was sympathetic—appeared at first as a dismal failure. The difficulties were enormous. On the one hand, the effort to reveal many faults in the Jewish body politic and daily life antagonized many fearful readers who, even if they readily tolerated such criticisms in Hebrew or Yiddish letters, were apprehensive about their impact upon Russian public opinion if given wide circulation in the Russian language. On the other hand, in their attempt to defend the rights of Jews and to propagate ultimate equality, the editors had to run the gauntlet of official censorship, sometimes a double censorship from both the local Odessa office and the St. Petersburg headquarters. At the same time liberals of various shades of opinion, including some non-Jews, contributed regularly to the journal, whose editors expressed the hope that

> not belonging to the retrogrades, the extreme rationalists or the reactionaries, we dare hope that from these three categories a fourth will emerge which will have the final say. It will neither unconditionally destroy the old, nor unconditionally admire it in an effort to support it with all the brilliance of dialectics and sophisms. This will be the golden mean that will join what is reasonable in the past with what is necessary in the present.

Such a program was definitely premature in 1860–61, and the journal could not even marshal the minimum of eight hundred subscribers considered necessary to maintain it financially. The editors decided to suspend publication, since as Rabinovich commented, "honorable death remained the only end for my journal." Although they themselves referred to the pun that their *Dawn* had "lapsed into *eternity* instead of turning into *morning*," the editors had wrought better than they thought. Their magazine ushered in an era of Russian Jewish journalism which lasted throughout the last half-century of tsarist rule and had many significant accomplishments to its credit. Before very long the Jewish press embraced many publications in Russian, Hebrew, and Yiddish. In 1886 no less than three Hebrew dailies (*Ha-Yom, Ha-Melits,* and *Ha-Sefirah*) made their appearance. However, this pace could not be sustained by the relatively few readers able and willing to pay high subscription rates. Among the Russian periodicals the *Voskhod*, founded and edited by Adolf Landau from 1885 until his retirement in 1899 (it continued until 1906), exerted the greatest influence on the Russian Jewish intelligentsia.[21]

[9]

Ideological and
Partisan Strife

❀

The regime of Alexander II, which gave the impression that liberalism
had come to Russia to stay, marked a turning point in the history of its
Jewish community. Until that time Russian Jewry had been a fairly
monolithic structure, notwithstanding the internal divisions between
the Hasidim and their "opponents," the "enlightened" and the old-
fashioned. Even some radical spokesmen of Enlightenment were con-
formists in their private life. Not until the days of Alexander II do we
hear of timid attempts at introducing Russian into the synagogue
proper. The adoption of sermons in the vernacular had long been the
touchstone of even moderate religious reform in the West. In Russia the
very spokesmen of Enlightenment knew little Russian and derived most
of their Western culture through the medium of German. When they
founded their Society for the Promotion of Enlightenment among the
Jews, they considered a principal part of its program to be the publication of a Bible provided with both a German translation in the Hebrew
alphabet and Mendelssohn's commentary.[1]

For ordinary Russian Jews this emphasis upon German made the
entire Enlightenment doubly alien and artificial. It made more sense to
build bridges to the living Russian language and culture. However,
religious reform of the Western type never gained ground in the Russian

Jewish community. Essentially it was a post-emancipatory phenomenon after the Jews felt themselves to be more or less equal citizens in the larger society, different from the majority only through their faith. Russians of the Mosaic persuasion, such as began emerging in the 1860s, were still a tiny minority and an obviously foreign growth on the body of Russian Jewry. Such individuals, moreover, were for the most part religious agnostics, prepared to abandon all traditional observance; they cared very little for what was happening within the synagogue precincts.

The sterility of the Enlightenment movement with its predominantly negativistic emphases gradually became manifest to its devotees themselves. One of the first insiders to submit it to a sharp critique was Moses Leib Lilienblum (1843–1910), a brilliant, if erratic, writer who often changed his mind. From the outset he had come under the influence of Osias (Joshua Heschel) Schorr, the learned radical Galician critic of the Talmud. Soon thereafter he felt the spell of the new Russian positivist philosophy, especially as expounded by the then popular writer Dimitrii Pisarev. Many members of the new generation replaced the old idealism by a rather crude utilitarianism while pushing Enlightenment's superficial cosmopolitanism to even further extremes. In Lilienblum's case this was but a passing episode. He soon turned to Jewish nationalism and Zionism, for which he became an eloquent spokesman.[2]

FAMOUS CONVERTS

A different direction was taken by Abraham Uri (Arkadii Grigorevich) Kovner (1842–1909), who in his poverty-stricken home—his father was an elementary Hebrew teacher—had imbibed a deep hatred for the wealthy and learned members of his community. Personally unstable, prepared at the drop of a hat to abandon his wife and children, he joined the Haskalah movement almost immediately as its sharpest critic. In two volumes of essays entitled *Heker dabar* (Observations; 1865) and *Tseror perahim* (A Bouquet of Flowers; 1868), he submitted contemporary Hebrew letters to a devastating critique. In his second book he vented his ire especially on Alexander Zederbaum (1816–93), editor of the Hebrew periodical *Ha-Melits*, who, upon Kovner's arrival in Odessa, had given him a good deal of work but who became frightened by the hostile reaction of many readers to the writer's destructive criticisms. Kovner also came under the spell of Pisarev's works and imitated the Russian's "demolition" of Pushkin and Lermontov by a similar "debunking" of the great Italian Hebrew scholar and poet Samuel David Luzzatto. In a letter to a fellow writer, Paperna, this *enfant terrible* of Enlightenment literature prided himself on not being a Belinskii, that is, a writer interested in art per se, but only in its utilitarian aspects. "This is the main difference between us," he exclaimed. "You are an admirer of beauty and the sublime, I of the mundane and the useful." Not surprisingly, Kovner soon decided that he ought not to waste his talents on a dead language like Hebrew. After sending a copy of his "Bouquet" to Y. L. Gordon as his "final" gift to Hebrew literature, he observed,

> Let our writers not imagine that they can create through Hebrew a living and enduring literature. This will never happen. Their task should much rather consist in using Hebrew and Yiddish to awaken in our youth a thirst for knowledge. But to quench that thirst our youth will have to resort to the aid of European languages. Hebrew and Yiddish shall thus serve the Jewish reader as steps to the temple of living languages, and only there will he perceive the true light.

Kovner's transition to Russian literature was hastened by a rash criminal act; employed in a minor office by the Jewish banking house of Abraham Zak in St. Petersburg, he forged a large check and tried to escape with that amount and a newly married sickly wife to the United States. He was caught and sent to Siberia, whence he returned to St. Petersburg as a convert to Christianity and a fairly prolific Russian publicist. But even in these later writings he could and would not deny his deep attachment to the Jewish people.[3]

Kovner's career is sketched here at somewhat greater length because it was quite typical of a certain wing of progressive Russian Jewish youth of the period, many of whom likewise found their way to the baptismal font. Among Kovner's contemporaries were such men as Yehudah (Julian) Klaczko (1825–1906), who started in his native Vilna as the son of an influential Jewish merchant and as an ardent poet of the glories of Zion, and wound up as a leading Catholic literary critic of Polish poetry and folklore.[4] Another convert, J. E. Salkinson (died in 1883), also born in Vilna as the son of a Hebrew poet and teacher, moved to Scotland where he served as a Presbyterian minister in Glasgow. He did not lose his love for Hebrew, however, and produced some of the best Hebrew translations of Shakespeare and Milton.

Ivan Stanislavovich Blioch (Jean Bloch, 1836–1901) became one of Russia's most distinguished economists and railroad builders. His five-volume work *Vliianie zhelieznikh dorog* (The Impact of Railways on Russia's Economic System), published in St. Petersburg in 1878, was speedily translated into French and Polish after it was awarded a gold medal at the Paris Exposition of that year. Another large six-volume work, published twenty years later, on future wars was translated into English, German, and French and seems to have stimulated Nicholas II to convoke the Hague Conference of 1899. Although a convert from his youth, Blioch left behind a testament which began, "My entire life I was a Jew and I die as a Jew." Similarly, Daniel Chwolson (1819–1911), a leading Orientalist, never concealed his Jewish origin. Once asked whether he had undergone conversion out of conviction, he was supposed to have answered bluntly, "Yes, I was *convinced* that it was much better to live as a Christian professor than as an elementary Hebrew teacher." Throughout his life, Chwolson had many occasions to defend the Jews against accusations and calumnies. His works on Christ's Last Supper and the Blood Accusation were translated into German and enjoyed a European reputation. Among his Orientalist studies several like the *Corpus inscriptionum hebraicarum,* his monographs on the Khazars, and the catalogue of his own large Hebrew library which included many incunabula represented significant contributions to Jewish learning. However, Abraham Eliyahu (Albert) Harkavy (1835–1919) was able to make even more significant contributions to Jewish scholarship while serving as custodian of the important Near Eastern collections at the Imperial Library in St. Petersburg without giving up his Jewish faith.[5]

Among the other prominent converts was physiologist I. F. Tsion (Elie de Cyon, 1843–1912), who while still a Jew received an award from the Academy of Sciences in Paris for an important physiological work. After his conversion his professorial career was cut short by his unpopularity with colleagues and students, whereupon he turned to diplomatic service. As an agent of the Russian Ministry of Finance he secured the first French loan for Russia and in 1893 assisted in the conclusion of the Franco-Russian alliance. Considerable influence was also exerted by the convert Osip Notovich (1849–1914) who served for many years as the editor of the *Novoe Vremia* and founded the important political periodical *Novosti* (News). Among the distinguished poets of Jewish descent was A. F. Fet, whose love lyrics written in his old age are described by the literary historian Prince Dimitrii S. Mirsky as "among the most precious diamonds of our poetry." Unbeknown to many of his contemporaries, but fully realized by Fet, was the fact that he was born to a Königsberg Jewish woman who had deserted her innkeeper husband while pregnant and had run away with a Russian officer.[6]

Of international fame were the brothers Anton and Nicholas Rubinstein (1829–94 and 1835–81 respectively), both converted by their grandfather in their infancy. Even Pobedonostsev was Anton's great admirer. In trying to persuade Alexander III in 1886 to attend some concerts given by Rubinstein, he wrote:

> It is undeniable that today Rubinstein occupies the first place in the musical world and has no equal since the death of Wagner. According to unanimous opinion, no musician has ever demonstrated such a musical technique and such perfection in execution. His name is

popular in Europe and America. Wherever he appears he receives the homage of the best representatives of music, art, and literature. It is pleasant to contemplate that this artist of the first order belongs to Russia. By birth, education, social relations, and family, his habits and way of life, Anton Rubinstein is a Russian and remains in Russia despite enticing offers from abroad.

(Rubinstein himself was less certain; he once complained to a friend: "The Russians consider me a German, the Germans—a Russian. Jews regard me as a Christian, the Christians—a Jew.") The tsar did not require much urging, since in 1885 he had attended the performance of Rubinstein's opera, *Neron*. Alexander also conferred upon the musician the title "Excellency," which evoked the following comment by Rubinstein to his mother: "I have a presentiment that I shall require this 'Excellenz' some day against the very powers which conferred it upon me. For all your baptism at Berdichev, we are Jews, you and I and sister Sophie." Perhaps because of this awareness of his Jewish descent, Rubinstein chose quite a few Old Testament topics for his musical compositions.[7]

Few baptized writers dared, however, to defy public opinion to the extent indulged in by Constantine Shapiro (1841–1900). Although after settling in St. Petersburg he joined the Russian Orthodox Church and married a Christian woman, this talented author continued to write distinguished Hebrew poetry filled with nostalgia and compassion for the life of his former coreligionists (*Shire Yeshurun* and *Kinnor Yeshurun*; that is, Poems and The Lyre of Jeshurun—Israel). Even more passionate were such sentimental declarations as that made in his letter to Y. L. Gordon of February 20 (March 5), 1877: "If you knew, sir, how great my love for my people and my fatherland is, you would laugh. For, indeed, a man deserves to be ridiculed, if he exchanges his [religious] dignity for no good reason, while his former dignity is still much alive within him. But what can I do? My heart cries out to my people! Can I tear out my heart and replace it by a stone?"

POLITICAL STIRRINGS

At the same time Russia slowly opened her gates to professing Jews who achieved eminence in many fields, especially in law and medicine. Among the jurists one need but mention Herman Trachtenberg (1839–1895), who participated in the important judicial reforms of 1864 and despite his faith was appointed to an important post in the Ministry of Justice. Alexander Passover (1840–1910) achieved international fame through his numerous legal publications and the juridical periodicals he had founded. The number of Jewish doctors serving in the army was so

large that as early as the Russo-Turkish War of 1877–78, many received
military decorations. An active public servant, physiologist Nicholas
Bakst (1842–1904) was also an important contributor to contemporary
scholarly journals. Irked by the unceasing attacks on Jews, Bakst published a collection entitled *Russkie liudi o Evreiakh* (Opinions of Russians
about Jews). He was also instrumental, together with the banker Samuel
Poliakov, in founding an organization for the promotion of crafts and
agriculture among the Jews which later became known as the ORT.[8]

Bakst's booklet was typical of the concern of the Russian-speaking
Jews about the opinion of their non-Jewish compatriots. As before, the
large masses of the Jewish population were much more fortified against
anti-Semitic assaults than the more sensitive Russified intelligentsia,
who often greeted every favorable statement by a distinguished non-
Jew with excessive acclaim. We recall that few of the eminent Russian
writers were friendly to Jews. Fiodor M. Dostoevsky said many unkind
words about Jews and Judaism, although in a private letter of February,
1877, to Kovner, he asserted, "I am by no means, nor have I ever been,
an enemy of the Jews." In contrast, on one occasion Leo N. Tolstoy sang
a paean of praise of the Jewish people, which though included in a
private letter, achieved wide circulation several years before his death in
1910. To quote only a few of the highlights of his answer to the query he
had put to himself, What is a Jew?

> The Jew is that sacred being who has brought down from heaven the
> everlasting fire and has illumined with it the entire world. He is the
> religious source, spring and fountain out of which all the rest of the
> peoples have drawn their beliefs and their religions. The Jew is the
> pioneer of liberty. . . . The Jew is the pioneer of civilization. . . . The
> Jew is the emblem of civil and religious toleration. . . . The Jew is the
> emblem of eternity. . . . The Jew is everlasting as is eternity itself.

Even more outspoken in public was the distinguished philosopher
Vladimir Soloviev. We recall his joining with other leading writers in
protesting against the pogroms and the reactionary policies of the
Russian regime. Such collective protests also reappeared in other periods of crisis, giving some comfort, at least, to the distressed Jewish
intellectuals.[9]

Some brilliant young Jews born during Alexander II's reform era
joined the Russian liberal movements. Particularly the great jurists,
Maxim M. Vinaver (1862–1926), Henry (Genrikh) B. Sliozberg (1863–
1937), and Oscar O. Gruzenberg (1866–1940), played an influential role
in the development of the Cadet Party, while Leonty M. Bramson (1869–
1941) became an important member of the farmer-labor *Trudoviki* Party.
They persevered in their political activities despite severe discouragement on the part of the Russian bureaucracy. Even a relatively liberal

prime minister like Sergei Witte once complained to a Jewish delegation consisting of Baron Horace Günzburg, Vinaver, and others that "of late years the Jews have come to the fore as leaders of various political parties and advocates of the most extreme political ideas. Now, it is not your business to teach us. Leave that to Russians by birth and civil status and mind your own business." While the others allegedly acquiesced, Vinaver replied that in view of the forthcoming equality of all Russians it was indeed the business of the Jew to "offer every possible support to those Russians who were fighting for the political emancipation of the country." At the same time Vinaver and Sliozberg were very active in inner Jewish affairs, Vinaver being the founder and presiding officer of the Jewish Historical-Ethnological Society, the League for the Attainment of Complete Equality, and other organizations. Gruzenberg achieved international fame as the defender of Beilis against the ritual-murder accusation. Bramson became a leader in Jewish social welfare, particularly through his untiring espousal of the ideals of Jewish self-help through the ORT and similar organizations.[10]

Some segments of the Jewish youth were attracted particularly to the Russian exponents of radical ideas. Once again it was a Jewish convert to Christianity, Nicholas Utin, who as early as 1861 participated in a student demonstration and soon played a major role in the first *Zemlia i Volia* (Land and Freedom) organization. Having to flee Russia, he served as editor of Michael Bakunin's periodical in Geneva, although in the well-known conflict between Karl Marx and Bakunin he sided with Marx. There is no evidence that his relations with Bakunin were in any way influenced by the latter's occasional anti-Jewish remarks, such as that the Jews were sworn enemies of the Slavs. In Russia proper the majority of young Jewish radicals, whose number multiplied in the 1870s, were attracted by the ideas of the *Narodniki* and their slogan, "Go to the people." But instead of going to their own, the Jewish people, they preferred to join their non-Jewish compatriots in propagandizing their new ideals among the peasants. Most of them actually had little use for their own people; they saw the Jew as predominantly a petty bourgeois, the very artisan being as a rule the employer, and as such an exploiter of workers.

Later on Aaron Zundelevich, a leading revolutionary writer, reminisced about the 1870s: "For us Jewry as a national organism did not present a phenomenon worthy of support. Jewish nationalism, it seemed to us, had no *raison d'être*. Religion, that cementing force of Jewish unity, represented to us complete retrogression." Some of these early leaders, including Pavel Borisovich Akselrod (*ca.* 1848–1928) comforted themselves with the thought that the liberation of the Russian masses would automatically bring about also the freeing of Jews from tsarist bondage. Not even the Russian pogroms immediately affected this view. At the most, some of the Jewish radicals made despairing comments, as did Lev Daitsch, who wrote to Akselrod:

> A revolutionary can indeed give no practical answer now to the Jewish question. What should he do, for instance, in Balta where they beat Jews? Take their part? This would mean, as [the geographer] Jean Jacques Reclus stated, bringing down the wrath of peasants on the revolutionaries: "Not enough they have murdered the tsar but they also defend the *zhids!*" The revolutionaries thus find themselves on the horns of a dilemma; this is a simple cul-de-sac for both the Jews and the revolutionaries.

According to a plausible story, a Jewish *narodnik* joined the pogromists in Kiev to attack the wealthy Jews. But when he noted that the hooligans destroyed poverty-stricken Jewish homes, but spared rich Christian merchants and officials, he suffered a nervous breakdown.[11]

Curiously, many of these extremists were recruited from among the students of the Vilna rabbinical seminary and *Realgymnasium*. Having lost any real contact with the overwhelming majority of their people, they went all the way in their negativism. Ironically, this was the revenge the Jewish people took on the Russian regime for having forcibly implanted in it these alien educational institutions. A story told by the folk poet Eliakum Zunser has it that in 1872, after the arrest of forty young Jewish "nihilists" in Vilna, Governor-General Potapov asked the leaders of the Jewish community why they had so many subversives in their midst. To which one of the Jewish representatives, Jacob Baritt (better known as R. Yankele Kovner) is supposed to have replied, "As long as we educated our children there were no nihilists among us; but as soon as you took the education of our children into your hands they became so." According to Zunser, it was the tenor of this reply, transmitted by Potapov to St. Petersburg, which helped to bring about the closing of the two governmental seminaries.[12]

As a matter of record, however, the Jewish ratio among the *narodniki* did not exceed 4.4 percent in 1878, and declined to 4.1 percent two years later. This percentage roughly corresponded to the demographic strength of the Jewish community. In the subsequent decades the situation changed, and as more and more Jewish youth went through the Russian and foreign colleges and universities, their proportion grew even beyond their percentage of the urban population. They were far more attracted to the urban-centered Western-type socialist movements, as exemplified by the "Land and Liberty" party founded in 1876 by disillusioned *narodniki* and others, including the Jew, Mark Natanson. One of its offshoots was the more truly Marxist "Black Repartition" movement. Many of these latter-day revolutionaries may not have consciously sympathized with the sufferings of their own people; subconsciously, however, they could not help but seek release from their accumulated resentments by fighting the established order.[13]

Not that they were all welcomed with open arms in the radical camp. In trying to accomplish their main mission of teaching the Russian peasants both culture and socialism, they had to use all sorts of disguises, lest their Jewishness antagonize the listeners. Time and again these masks were unveiled and the preachers of universal brotherhood were rebuffed not only by unlettered peasants but to some extent also by their ideological comrades. Female revolutionaries often resorted to the simple expedient of marrying Russian Gentiles and converting themselves to Christianity.

THE "BUND"

Other Jewish socialists found such denial of their ancestry utterly unpalatable. Another pupil of the Vilna seminary, Aaron Samuel Liberman (1845–80), was perhaps less negativistic because, unlike most of his confreres, he grew up in a relatively "enlightened" household. His father, a modern Hebrew teacher, had instilled enough reverence for the Jewish tradition in him so that, although he rejected the Jewish religion, he remained a lifelong devotee of the Hebrew language. From the outset he and his friend Zundelevich started propagating socialism among Jews. Fleeing from the police, Liberman had to leave Russia and spend many years in London, Berlin, and Vienna. In each of these capitals he tried to organize Jewish socialist clubs and actually issued a socialist periodical in Hebrew, the first publication of its kind. This periodical, of which only three small issues appeared in 1876, bore the programmatic title *Ha-Emet* (The Truth), as explained in the prospectus, "Champions of justice are found among all peoples. Our Jewish literature alone has lacked *emet* [truth]; for since prophecy had ceased among the Jews, our writers have lost interest in the miseries and needs of our people." With all his sincerity Liberman really had a split personality, full of theoretical and practical inconsistencies. After his arrest in Vienna, he was asked in court about his religion; he proudly proclaimed: "I am a socialist." Yet when a socialist club which he organized in London was to hold a scheduled meeting on the Ninth of Ab (a fast day commemorating the destruction of the Jerusalem Temple), he suggested postponement with the somewhat disingenuous argument that "as long as the social revolution has not taken place, political freedom is of prime importance to every people." Hence the Jews may legitimately mourn the loss of their national independence eighteen centuries before. A generally mercurial individual, Liberman ended as a suicide in Syracuse, New York, at the age of thirty-five.[14]

Like Liberman, Chaim Zhitlowsky (1865–1943) preached his social-ism mainly to the Russian Jewish intelligentsia from abroad. First from Switzerland, and later from the United States, in a number of Russian and Yiddish writings effectively smuggled into the Tsarist Empire, he addressed himself to the thoughtful young Jews of his mother country, pressing a combination of socialist and national demands. His "A Jew to Jews," disseminated in 1892 in both Russian and Yiddish, sounded the clarion call for national Jewish minority rights which a quarter century later were to receive basic international recognition in both Soviet legislation and the Paris Peace Treaties. These ideas were more fully developed, apparently in complete independence, by the distin-guished middle-class publicist and historian Simon M. Dubnow (1860–1941), particularly in a series of "Letters on Old and New Judaism," published in Russian in the influential journal *Voskhod,* in 1897–1906.[15]

Other Jewish socialists, particularly Arkady Kremer (1865–1935), were more practical and better organizers. Many of them belonged to the second generation of Jewish socialists who grew up in the era of Russian pogroms and tsarist reaction after 1881. It was much harder now to turn one's back on the downtrodden Jewish people, among whom, moreover, there had begun growing up a regular industrial proletariat. From the outset Kremer was a pragmatist. In his pamphlet, *Ob Agitatsii* (On Propaganda), written in 1893, he argued against the socialist propaganda couched in abstract Marxian terms. In his opinion the proletariat was to be brought to the concrete realization of its own plight and shown how the victory of socialism would benefit it directly. Needless to say, Kremer and his associates were far removed from purely practical trade unionism and the exclusive emphasis on the economic betterment of the working classes, although they were ac-cused of such leanings by Lenin and others. His pragmatic approach also persuaded Kremer that agitation among Jewish workers had to be conducted in Yiddish, the only language they understood, and in terms approximating their daily experience.

Out of such considerations he and other Jewish socialists working independently in various communities decided to pool their resources and to found an all-embracing Jewish socialist organization. Thus origi-nated the *Bund,* or The General Jewish Workers' League, established at a Vilna conference in 1897. Kremer delivered the keynote address and defined the program of the new organization as follows:

A general union of all Jewish socialist groups will have as its goal not only the struggle for general Russian political demands; it will also have the special task of defending the specific interest of the Jewish workers, carry on the struggle for their civic rights, and above all combat the discriminatory anti-Jewish laws. That is because the Jewish workers suffer not only as workers but also as Jews, and we dare not and cannot remain indifferent at such a time.

This program found a resounding echo among the radical Jewish youth. It was completely in line with the thinking of Yulii Osipovich Martov (1873–1923), grandson of Alexander Zederbaum and an outstanding Jewish leader of general Russian socialism, particularly of its later Menshevik wing, who had delivered a speech along similar lines in 1895. In that stage of his career Martov had bluntly declared, "A working class content with the lot of an inferior nation, will not rise up against the lot of an inferior class. . . . The growth of national and class consciousness must go hand in hand."[16]

Even before the formation of the Bund, the issue of Jewish identity and national interests loomed ever larger in the discussions among the Jewish socialists. At first in the 1880s and early 1890s the leading Vilna group—as later recorded by an early participant, Lev Daitch—"wanted the Jewish masses to assimilate as quickly as possible; everything that smelled of Jewishness called forth among many of us a feeling of contempt, if not more." In a similar vein, another of these pioneers, Tsemakh Kopelzon (Grishin), reminisced: "In practice, almost all of us were declared assimilationists." However, in time they had to yield to the pressure of the less-educated workingmen and the so-called half-intellectuals, whose attachment to Jewish customs and outlooks was reinforced by their daily experiences with anti-Semitism, especially discrimination in employment and hostility on the part of many non-Jewish fellow workers. They resisted full-fledged Russification, and although they admitted the advantages of being able to read the existing Russian revolutionary literature, they preferred Yiddish translations, which they sometimes forced their leaders to prepare for them. A leading exponent of this point of view, as early as 1893, was the "half-intellectual" A. Litvak (Chaim Yankel Helfand).[17]

While Martov was moving away from this position in serving, together with Lenin, as editor of the *Iskra,* the Bund became increasingly nationalistic. At first it saw as its main objective the propagation of Marxian internationalism in the Yiddish medium, but after a few years of growing nationalist strife in the Russian Empire it began advocating Jewish national autonomy, along with that of the other national minorities. This programmatic change, which became manifest in 1903 and reached its full clarification during the Revolution of 1905, evoked a hostile reaction among the Russian socialists, including Lenin, who stubbornly denied the very existence of a Jewish nationality. Since the opposition based its main argument on the lack of a Jewish territorial concentration, the Bund was forced increasingly to stress the cultural foundations of Jewish nationalism.

The decisive break came at the Second Congress of the Russian Social Democratic Workers' Party, which met in Brussels in July–August, 1903. While the debate raged over the party's organizational structure, the victory of Lenin and his associates essentially indicated the rejection of the Bundists' contention that the Russian Jews were a nationality apart, analogous to the Poles, despite their lack of a majority status in any geographic area. It also reflected Lenin's constant drive for exclusive centralized control over the party apparatus, rather than a federative system as demanded by the Bund. In several votes, the Bundists' proposals were rejected, and after the final confrontation of August 18, 1903, the Bund felt obliged to leave the Russian Party. It was done "with heavy heart. It was a real catastrophe," according to Medem. At the same time, Martov, the chief spokesman for the majority, was immediately to feel the heavy hand of Lenin's despotism, when at the same Second Congress he and his associates found themselves in the minority during the vote over the historic resolution which resulted in the victory of Lenin's "Bolsheviks" over the "Mensheviks" headed by Martov.[18]

Curiously, it was Vladimir Medem (1879–1923) who most clearly defined this part of the Bund ideology. Medem, whose father, an army doctor, had baptized all his children (stationed in Libau, he first converted them to the Lutheran faith, but the youngest, Vladimir, grew up in the Russian Orthodox religion), gradually found his way back to the Jewish people, although not to religious Judaism. Without making a fetish out of nationalism, he came to the conclusion, as he wrote in 1909, that "all attempts to combat nationalism through the old method of ignoring and hushing up the very facts of national differences and national characters have proved to be useless, mouldy and outworn." Medem and the Bund tried, therefore, to combine class struggle with recognition of national rights. They found a sufficient following in the Jewish proletariat to enlist some 40,000 members in their movement at a time (1906) when the major Russian Socialist Party had no more than 150,000 members, and the Polish Socialist Party only 23,000. This became possible only after the Revolution when the socialists could more openly profess their credo. According to the *Large Russian Encyclopedia*, at the beginning of 1905 the whole Russian Party embraced only 8,400, contrasted with the Bund's 23,000 members. The Bund's strength was also recognized in international gatherings. At the Paris Congress of the Second International, the Russian delegation of twenty-nine representatives included twelve Bund delegates. When Russia's Social Democratic Party and Social Revolutionaries were assigned one vote each on the Central Committee, the former had to share this vote equally with the Bund. It was, therefore, of great importance that at its Sixth Convention, held in Zurich in October, 1905, when the revolutionary movement was reaching its crest, the Bund adopted a program demanding not only full civil and political emancipation for Russian Jewry but also

> national-cultural autonomy: to withdraw from the authority of the state and its local and territorial self-governing organs all functions associated with cultural affairs (education and the like) and to entrust them to the nation itself operating through separate institutions, central and local, elected by all members through a universal, equal, direct and secret vote.

The Bund basically adhered to this program also after its reunification with the Russian Socialist Party in 1906 and in the years of its general decline during the ensuing period of tsarist reaction.[19]

ZIONISM

In the dynamism of Russian Jewish society, the emergent socialist movement was not the only, in fact not even the most powerful, novel trend. Zionism not only increasingly became the dominant passion of the middle-class majority, but it also penetrated deeply the plutocracy and the aristocracy of learning on the one hand, and the working classes on the other hand. The messianic ideal had long been the keynote of Jewish religion. Under one guise or another even the antireligious movements in nineteenth-century Judaism were unable to cast off their messianic yearnings for an ultimate redemption of their people, or of mankind at large. The growing secularization of modern Jewry made the transition from religious messianism to political Zionism appear as but another link in that long chain of evolution. The rise of nationalism throughout eastern Europe during the latter half of the nineteenth century and the Pan-Slavist preachment of the liberation of all Slavonic peoples exerted a considerable influence also on thinking young Jews. Not only the participants in the two Polish uprisings of 1831 and 1863, but many other Jews began asking why the liberation movements of the younger nationalities should not apply to their own older people as well.

Not surprisingly, Russian Jews living abroad reached a more mature understanding of the peculiar position of their people than did those who were absorbed by the routine of their life within the Pale. It was no mere accident that after settling in Vienna, Perets Smolenskin (1842–85) became the most articulate spokesman of the new national movement. Austria was at that time, and for many decades thereafter, the main laboratory for national problems in Europe. In the neighboring Balkan Peninsula one people after another clamored for, and often achieved, national independence. From 1868 until his premature death in 1885, Smolenskin published in Vienna a distinguished Hebrew periodical, *Ha-Shahar* (The Dawn), for which, with an uncanny instinct for discovering new talent, he enlisted the collaboration of almost all young and promising Hebrew writers. While still lacking in clarity and subject to diverse interpretations, his ideas significantly influenced his contemporaries across the border. Above all, he insisted upon the unity of the Jewish people, based not on the usual criteria of territory, language, or statehood, and not even on the binding force of Jewish law and ritual, but rather on the somewhat vague, but to him perfectly tangible, "national spirit." In a series of programmatic essays, entitled "It Is Time to Plant" and published in his periodical during the years from 1875 to 1877, he taught that "no matter what his sins against religion may be, every Jew belongs to his people so long as he does not betray it." In another impressive work, *Am Olam* (The Eternal People), he argued for the reconstruction of Jewish life in the socioeconomic, as well as political, sense. This designation was adopted by a new movement which in the 1880s sought to transplant thousands upon thousands of Russian Jews to the New World and to settle them on land.

To Smolenskin himself and to many of his associates this solution appeared half-hearted. From the outset they felt, along with such non-Russian thinkers as Rabbis Yehudah Alkalai and Zvi Hirsch Kalischer, that for Jews only Palestine could be the promised land of the future as it had been in the past. The Russian pogroms of 1881 strongly reinforced that feeling. M. L. Lilienblum now toned down his positivist rejection of the Jewish tradition and dedicated the rest of his life to the struggle for the Zionist ideal. In his numerous essays he penetratingly analyzed the position of the Jew in the East European world and found it wanting. Among his fellow writers he appeared as a stark realist. He allegedly once squelched an enthusiast who tried to assure him of his readiness to sell his last shirt and to plow the Holy Land with his nose by simply asking how much money could be raised by such a sale and how many dunams of land could be plowed up with a nose. In a remarkable passage written in 1883, Lilienblum described the utterly contradictory, and hence essentially irrational, arguments underlying the growth of anti-Semitism in Europe.

> Opponents of nationalism see us as unflinching nationalists, with a national God and a national Torah; to the nationalists we are cosmopolitans, whose fatherland is wherever we prosper. Religious non-Jews consider us devoid of any faith, while freethinkers accuse us of being orthodox and believing in all sorts of nonsense. The liberals call us conservative and the conservatives denounce our liberalism. Some bureaucrats and writers view us as the promoters of anarchy, insurrection and revolt, whereas to anarchists we are capitalists and bearers of the biblical civilization, based, in their view, on slavery and parasit-

ism. . . . Musicians like Richard Wagner charge us with destroying the beauty and purity of music. Even our virtues are turned into faults; "Few Jews are murderers," they explain, "because all Jews are cowards," which does not prevent them from accusing us of murdering Christian children.

Hence, Lilienblum concluded, the Jewish people ought to live its own natural life rather than pursue the unrewarding course of trying to appease outside opinion.[20]

Anti-Semitism, which in those very years had become a potent force in German and French letters and thereby achieved a certain respectability in Russian intellectual circles as well, was evoking different reactions among Jews. Some cringed and tried to obliterate the memory of their Jewish ancestry. Others, like the socialists and nihilists, believed that only a total revamping of the existing social order would solve the Jewish question, too. Still others, like Smolenskin and Lilienblum, decided that Jews must resort to self-help. The most influential spokesman of that idea was Leon Pinsker (1821–91), son of the distinguished scholar, Simhah Pinsker. As a busy physician, Pinsker had only occasionally participated in Odessa's Jewish communal undertakings. Under the shattering experience of the Russian pogroms, however, he published in 1882 his famous German essay *Auto-Emanzipation,* in which he submitted anti-Semitism, so to speak, to a clinical dissection. He declared roundly:

> Judeophobia is a form of demonopathy, with the difference that the Jewish ghost has become known to the whole race of mankind, not only to some peoples, and that it is not disembodied like other ghosts. As a being of flesh and blood, it suffers the most excruciating pain from the wounds inflicted upon it by a timorous mob who imagine themselves threatened by it. Judeophobia is a psychic disorder. As such it is hereditary, and as a disease transmitted for two thousand years, it is incurable.

Since this malady of the Gentile nations was bound to last for the duration of Jewish life in the dispersion, he called for the "self-emancipation" of his people through its return to the land of its forefathers. As a practical man, he immediately proceeded with the organization of the "Lovers of Zion" movement, whose headquarters he established in Odessa. He presided over that organization until the end of his life in 1891, during which time he and his associates succeeded in establishing a few new colonies in the Holy Land. Under their inspiration a number of youthful pioneers, adopting as their watchword the battle cry BILU (abbreviated from *Bet Iaakov lekhu ve-nelkha* or O, house of Jacob, come ye and let us go, Isa. 2:5), formed a first group in Kharkov in 1882 and proceeded to the Holy Land. These were very small beginnings, but they opened up a new era of Palestine colonization. They also increasingly served as the yeast which kept the Russian Jewish community in a permanent state of creative fermentation.[21]

A new impetus to the Zionist movement was given by Theodor Herzl and the foundation of the World Zionist Organization. Its first congress in Basel in 1897 was well attended by a delegation from Russia, despite the tsarist government's generally jaundiced view of any Jewish international activities. The official antipathy was but slightly mitigated six years later by Herzl's appearance in St. Petersburg and his negotiations with the Minister of Interior Vyacheslav von Plehve. This dramatic visit with the man who was widely blamed for the Kishinev massacres caused much resentment, especially in the revolutionary circles. Yet bent upon promoting the scheme for Jewish emigration to Palestine under a Turkish charter, Herzl did not hesitate to invoke the aid of the Russian tsar. Unable to obtain an audience with Nicholas II, he negotiated with Plehve and Witte in terms which he defined in a memorandum to Plehve after their first interview of August 8, 1903. Herzl asked the minister's approval of the text of the following declaration he was to read at the forthcoming Zionist Congress in Basel and which was to sum up the tenor of these negotiations:

> I am authorized to declare that the Imperial Russian Government has the intention to support the Zionist movement. The Imperial Government proposes to intervene in our behalf with his Imperial Majesty the Sultan in order to secure a Charter of Colonization. In addition, the Imperial Government will place at the disposal of the Zionists conducting the emigration [to Palestine] certain amounts drawn from Jewish taxes. In order to prove the humanitarian character of these measures, the Imperial Government proposes at the same time to enlarge in the near future the Pale of Jewish Settlement for those who do not wish to emigrate.

Plehve, who in his discussions with Herzl contended that rather than being an anti-Semite, he fondly remembered his Jewish playmates during his family's sojourn in Warsaw when he was five to sixteen years old, wished to avoid sharp denunciations by the Basel Congress of the government's role at the Kishinev atrocities. On the other hand, the majority of Russian Jews, despite the Bundist propaganda, hailed Herzl as the great savior of their people.[22]

Nonetheless, the practical outcome of these negotiations was almost nil. Although the Russian administration was far from disinclined to see a large-scale exodus of Jews from the country—we recall its earlier support to Baron de Hirsch's scheme of transplanting millions of Russian Jews to Latin America—these talks proved no more fruitful than Herzl's similar dramatic *pourparlers* with the sultan, Emperor William II, the Pope, and other leaders. When finally, through Colonial Minister Joseph Chamberlain, Great Britain offered the Zionist Organization the opportunity of colonizing Jews in African Uganda, it was preeminently the opposition of the Russian Zionists, led by the iron-willed Menahem Mendel Ussishkin (1863–1941) and the youthful Chaim Weizmann (1874–1952), which defeated the project. To Russian Zionists no country other than Palestine, hallowed by a millennial tradition, could offer a genuine home for the Jewish people.[23]

Some radical Zionists had their eyes so firmly fixed upon the Holy Land that they were prepared to neglect the homefront. Negativistic about the future of Jews in the dispersion, they considered the building of any permanent Jewish communal or cultural institutions in Russia a waste of national energies that would better be concentrated on building up the Palestinian settlement. From the outset, however, one of the most influential Zionist thinkers countered that argument. Asher Zvi Ginzberg (1856–1927), better known under his nom de plume of Ahad Ha-Am (One of the People), pleaded that Palestine, with its limited natural resources, could not even absorb the future increase in the world Jewish population. Hence the overwhelming majority of Jews would have to remain in their respective countries. Yet he believed that a fairly strong Jewish community in Palestine, where it would not be subject to assimilatory pressure and could develop an independent modern culture of its own, could serve as a cultural center for the whole Jewish people. Such a program clearly involved a continuous building of Jewish culture in the dispersion as well. In a clear-cut argument against "The Negation of the Diaspora," then prevalent in certain Zionist circles (1909), he declared succinctly:

> The Jews as a people feel that they have the will and the strength to survive whatever may happen, without any ifs or ands. They cannot accept a theory which makes their survival conditional on their ceasing to be dispersed, because that theory implies that failure to end the dispersion would mean extinction, and extinction is an alternative that cannot be contemplated in any circumstances whatever.

At the same time he viewed the emancipation achieved by Western Jewry at the price of a high degree of assimilation as mere "slavery within freedom," perhaps an unconscious inversion of Alexander Herzen's well-known characterization of Nicholas I's regime as a period of external slavery and inner emancipation. This was, indeed, the tenor not only of his own brilliant essays, written in a fine Hebrew style, but also of the highly influential monthly *Ha-Shiloah* (called after a slow-moving Palestinian river) which he founded in Odessa in 1896 and edited for six years. This organ served as the most important focus of Hebrew literary activity until the First World War.[24]

The difference between the cultural and political Zionists was not quite so sharp as it appeared to some contemporaries. Especially after Herzl's grandiose schemes to secure an internationally recognized Ottoman charter had proved unworkable, the Zionist Organization itself returned to the slower and more patient development of a vigorous Jewish settlement in Palestine. At the same time, the spokesmen of cultural Zionism, including Weizmann, played an increasingly larger role within the organization. In Russia proper the struggle for Jewish rights became ever sharper. Partly under the pressure of public opinion, the Russian Zionists, like the Bundists, had to give up their aloofness from the domestic political struggles and to adopt, after a series of preliminary conferences during the stormy period of the First Revolution, the Helsingfors Platform of November, 1906, which included clearly defined postulates of national Jewish minority rights throughout the empire. Suggesting free democratic elections of representatives to Jewish local, provincial, and national bodies, the convention demanded that these organs "possess the right to found, conduct and support all kinds of institutions which would serve the end of (1) national education, (2) national health, (3) mutual and labor aid, (4) emigration, and (5) matters of faith." While taking into account the fact that Russian Jewry was internally divided between Hebraists and Yiddishists, the convention still insisted upon the recognition of the rights of each nationality to use its own language also in official communications to and from governmental organs in all localities where its members exceeded a certain legally defined percentage of the population. These postulates remained the guide lines of domestic policies for the Russian Zionists during the following years of reaction, as well as during World War I.[25]

Apart from these areas of agreement, the Russian Zionists also had many internal divisions. On the one hand, many socialists were attracted to the Zionist idea and hence could not share the Bund's anti-Zionist stand. Under the prompting of such influential socialist thinkers as Nachman Syrkin (1867–1924) and Ber Borochov (1881–1917), a Zionist socialist wing gradually emerged and was finally organized in 1906 under the name of Poale Zion (Zionist workers). The greatest difficulty, of course, consisted in reconciling Jewish nationalism, particularly of the Zionist variety, with Marxist internationalism. In an essay on the "Anti-Zionist Front" published in 1911, Borochov emphasized that "within Jewry the chief struggle is not between the proletariat and the bourgeoisie, or between the urban and agrarian population, but between Zionists and *Galut* [Diaspora] champions of all classes." The Poale Zion believed, therefore, that Jewish workers must ally themselves on the one hand with the Zionist World Organization and on the other with the Socialist International. They thus followed the program enunciated as early as 1901 by Syrkin in his "Call to Jewish Youth." Here Syrkin declared that the Jewish question could be solved only along the following lines: "(1) Social-democratic movements must be joined in those countries where the Jewish masses live; (2) a Jewish socialist commonwealth must be founded in Palestine and the neighboring lands; (3) Jewish clericalism must be fought through its replacement by a socialist, nationalist ideal." This policy was pursued with a measure of consistency except that the anticlerical propaganda was gradually toned down. There were splinter movements, too, such as those of the Socialist Zionists (S.S.) party who admitted the *raison d'être* of a Jewish nationality, but accepted the Territorialist ideology à la Israel Zangwill, postulating Jewish colonization of any territory which could serve as a Jewish homeland. There also was a "Seymist" party of non-Marxian socialists. Independently, Aaron David Gordon (1856–1922), taking over some ideas from the early Russian socialists and Tolstoy, soon propagated a new brand of Zionist socialism which was to replace the class struggle by the idea of mutual love and devotion to "a religion of labor." Personally moving to Palestine, Gordon, through example, as well as through the propagation of his brand of national socialism in the magazine, *Ha-Poel ha-sair* (Young Worker), succeeded in raising a large number of disciples and in significantly influencing the growth of the Palestinian settlement.[26]

On its part Orthodoxy long remained opposed to both socialism and Zionism. In terms of numbers of followers it still had behind it the majority of Russian Jewry. Averse to political struggles, however, it remained largely inarticulate. Not only did most of the Orthodox bitterly resent the secularization of Jewish life preached by both socialists and Zionists, but they also had long viewed any political action, and particularly one directed against the established regime, as a serious danger to Jewish survival. Typical of that attitude was a proclamation issued in 1902 by a Minsk rabbi when the news of a Jew's assault on the governor of Vilna reached him. He wrote:

A shudder passes over us when we hear the terrible story of what happened in the theater. How do we Jews, who are likened to a little worm—the worm of Jacob—come to get messed up in such matters? How do we Jews, who, according to all sense and reason, are always obligated to pray for the well-being of the sovereign power, without which we would long since have been swallowed alive—how do we Jews dare to climb up to such high places and meddle in politics? Oh, beware, Jewish children! Look well at what you are doing! God only knows what you may bring upon our unfortunate nation, upon yourselves, and upon your families. Our people always were proud of one thing—that they never had any rebels among them; and now you desire to wipe out this virtue, too. We hope you will think well about all this and you will not wish to place in jeopardy the happiness of our whole nation, your own fate, and the fate of your parents and families.

Zionism, in particular, appeared to many Orthodox as the betrayal of the genuine messianic idea, a belief in the redemption of the people only after the advent of the supernatural Messiah.

However, within Orthodoxy itself there soon emerged a group which accepted the temporary solution of a politically secured Jewish state. As we recall, such rabbis as Alkalai and Kalischer belonged to the earliest exponents of the Love of Zion movement in its pre-Herzlian stage. In Russia the outstanding spokesman of Zionism before Pinsker was the Orthodox rabbi Samuel Mohilever (1824–98). By 1902—that is, but five years after the first Basel Congress—a number of Russian leaders had made efforts to organize an Orthodox wing within the Zionist movement. These efforts led to the development, in the following years, of the so-called Mizrahi Organization, under the chairmanship of Rabbi Isaac Jacob Reines of Lida (1839–1915). This faction, seeking to attain the Zionist aims on the basis of the Jewish religious tradition, or as its motto has it, "the Land of Israel for the people of Israel based on the Torah of Israel," has ever since played a great role in the destinies of the Zionist movement and in the development of Jewish settlement in Palestine.[27]

Perhaps this very formation of an Orthodox group within Zionism stimulated the anti-Zionist Orthodox to independent political activity. The initiative, to be sure, came from Germany. Many Orthodox rabbis, including some hasidic leaders, joined Jacob Rosenheim of Frankfurt in organizing a world-wide countermovement under the name of Agudath Israel. A constituent meeting in Katowice, held in 1912 with the participation of a large delegation of Russian rabbis and laymen, proclaimed to the world that Jewish life could be organized only on the basis of the Jewish religious tradition. It also aimed "to represent Orthodox Jewry as a whole before the outside world and to defend the Torah and its adherents against attacks." While little time was left before the outbreak of World War I to develop this new organization, it injected an additional factor into the checkered political picture of Russian Jewry.[28]

LITERARY RENAISSANCE

Unavoidably, the new ideologies also penetrated the national literature in both Hebrew and Yiddish. Jewish nationalism of the late nineteenth century, as the earlier ones in Germany, Poland, or Italy, was then entering its heroic stage. Like the other European movements, led by Herder, Mickiewicz, or Mazzini, the new Jewish national sentiment generated a cultural renaissance which found its outlets in great poetic and prose creations. This became, indeed, the golden age of modern Hebrew and Yiddish letters. Just as Jewish life had become more diversified and the cultural attainments of individual Jews more heterogenous and multifarious, so did the creative literature of the age reflect the much greater vitality and abundant richness of Jewish thought. The rather shallow rationalist critique of the Jewish past, characteristic of the Enlightenment era, now gave way to a new appreciation of the rich heritage of the Jewish spirit in its manifold manifestations. At the same time there were strong literary echoes of the new appreciation of labor as the mainspring of social creativity. Nor was the gate shut to rebels and heterodox seekers of new truths.

Some of these novel attitudes came to the fore in the work of Chaim Nachman Bialik (1873–1934), a native of a Volhynian village who achieved eminence as a poet while living in Odessa. After World War I he was allowed, through Maxim Gorki's intervention, to leave the Soviet Union and settle in Palestine. A great master of language and a bard who expressed his generation's innermost feelings, he raised Hebrew poetry to a level of attainment unsurpassed since the Spanish poets of the eleventh and twelfth centuries, whose works he now toiled to recover for the benefit of the twentieth-century Hebrew public. Unlike his immediate "enlightened" predecessors, Bialik revered rabbinic learning. His poem *Ha-Matmid* (The Talmud Student) became a classic of Hebrew letters because it erected a monument to the poor, industrious student who found in his devotion to talmudic studies some basic answers to the riddles of his life. Other well-known classics were his *Be-Ir ha-haregah* (In the City of Slaughter) and *Megillat esh* (The Scroll of Fire), in which he lent immortal expression to his people's mourning over its dead during the Russian pogroms. Certainly, the traditional "lachrymose conception of Jewish history" nowhere found a more eloquent, if qualified, expression. He also wrote some of the most touching verses on the sanctity of labor.[29]

A different type of romanticism permeated the often paradoxical stories and learned works of Micah Joseph Berdichevski (Bin Gorion, 1865–1921). This semi-Nietzschean admirer of individual strength and exalter of such historic heroes as Cecil Rhodes had a tender heart for the teachings of Hasidism and for the extraordinary piety of some hasidic leaders. He who in some respects placed the Old Testament nature cults above the ethical monotheism of Moses nevertheless spent a lifetime in collecting and reinterpreting biblical and rabbinic legends (mostly under the pseudonym of M. J. Bin Gorion). More consistently "pagan" was another outstanding poet of the Hebrew Renaissance, Saul Tchernichovsky (1875–1943). After a stint in Germany, Tchernichovsky returned to Russia to serve as a practicing physician in small Russian villages. Unlike Bialik and Berdichevski, he had but slight roots in the Orthodox Jewish tradition: his training was largely Western and his ideals were taken from world literature, of which he was an outstanding translator. Not undeservedly he was called the "Greek" in Hebrew letters, a designation borne out by such poems as "Before the Statue of Apollo" or "Sonnets of a Pagan." He also published fine Hebrew translations from Homer and Plato. Yet in moments of crisis his deep moorings in the Jewish past came to the fore. In reaction to anti-Jewish massacres he once wrote in his "This Be Our Revenge,"

> *We are small.*
> *We shall not rise up against you,*
> *To cleave pregnant women with axes*
> *(As you do); nor shall we set fire*
> *To your roofs over your heads, and with iron bars*
> *We shall not shatter the skulls of babes!*
> *Not until with your brute hand you have uprooted,*
> *Not until with your contaminated palms you have erased*
> *   altogether*
> *The image of God stamped upon us,*
> *The tokens of ancient nobility of spirit,*
> *And of descent from princely generations.* [30]

A similar revulsion took place in Yiddish literature, particularly in works by its greatest writers, such as Isaac Leib Peretz (1852–1915) and Sholem Aleichem (pseudonym for Solomon Rabinovich; 1859–1916), who together with Mendele have rightfully been considered the chief stars in the firmament of modern Yiddish letters. Peretz was not an ivory-tower thinker. As a lawyer for some ten years in his native Zamość and later as secretary of a Jewish communal agency in Warsaw, he had many opportunities to observe Jewish life in action. Although he had been writing in Russian, Polish, and Hebrew before he found his way to Yiddish literature (in fact, he and Sholem Aleichem usually corresponded in Hebrew), and although he was an almost total agnostic, he came under the spell of Hasidism. The drama *Di goldene Kait* (The Golden Chain), which he himself considered the best of his works, was in many ways an apotheosis of that mystical movement. So was his most popular story, "And Even Beyond," extolling the extraordinary charity of a hasidic rabbi. But Peretz's versatile pen turned out many other short stories in which a variety of Jewish types was described with masterful characterization and unmatched beauty of expression. For instance, he depicts how Bontshe Shveig, meek and unassuming in life, is ultimately recognized in Heaven in his truly tragic grandeur. [31]

Sholem Aleichem has charmed readers for three generations with his humorous and melancholy presentation of "average" Russo-Jewish types. Although through marriage and inheritance he came into a large fortune at the age of twenty-six (he lost his money rather quickly), he rarely depicted wealthy Jews with any degree of sympathy. His Tevye der Milkhiker (Tobias the Dairyman) has become a byword for a type of uneducated Jew full of malapropisms, but attractive through his deep sentimentality and milk of human kindness. His Menahem Mendel is the incurable dreamer who pursues his quixotic career without any loss of hope or dignity. Described with vivid humor, these and other characters in his stories and plays have acquainted the Western world with the daily life of the Russian ghetto, as had no other works. Descriptive of his life's work is the epitaph Sholem Aleichem had prepared for his own tombstone long before his death in New York in 1916.

> *Here lies an ordinary Jew*
> *Who wrote in Yiddish, it is true;*
> *And for wives, and plain folk rather,*
> *He was a humorist, an author*
> *Poking fun at all and sundry;*
> *At the world he thumbed his nose.*
> *The world went on swimmingly*
> *While he, alas, took all the blows*
> *And at the time his public rose*
> *Laughing, clapping, and making merry*
> *He would suffer, only God knows,*
> *Secretly—so none was wary.*[32]

Needless to say, next to these giants, there was a whole array of talented Hebrew and Yiddish writers who testified to the great internal diversity, and creative vigor of the Russian community at the turn of the century.

So did the incipient Yiddish theater. Going back to early modern Purim plays, which in their artistic crudity and directness if not in their theme and purpose reminded one of the medieval mystery and passion plays, and to groups of singers enlivening Jewish weddings and other festive occasions, a Yiddish theater gradually emerged in 1878. Curiously, it was called into being by a Russian Jewish playwright and director, Abraham Goldfaden (1840–1908), who used a predominantly Russian cast to present plays to a predominantly Russian audience—on Rumanian soil. This ironic situation arose in the wake of the Russo-Turkish War, which turned northern Moldavia, particularly the city of Jassy, into a base of operations for the Russian military forces and their suppliers. Jassy had attracted a sufficiently large Russian colony at that time for one of the publicists, who later turned theatrical entrepreneur, to publish a Russian magazine for it. In 1879, Goldfaden, who like many leading literary and communal figures of the period had been a graduate of the Zhitomir Seminary, returned to Russia. He and his troupe transferred their headquarters to Odessa, but they also visited Moscow and various cities throughout the Pale. Despite their utter lack of training and the popular, rather than artistic, vehicles they had at their disposal, Goldfaden's and other troupes attracted wide and enthusiastic audiences for both their dramas and their operettas.[33]

Temporarily, to be sure, the Russian Jewish theater was stifled by a governmental prohibition of Yiddish public performances, issued, as a result of an Orthodox denunciation, by the reactionary Minister of Interior Count Dmitrii A. Tolstoi on August 17, 1883. Although obviously illegal, on appeal this ukase was confirmed by the Senate in 1904 and reconfirmed by the Ministry of Interior in 1906 and 1909, despite the freedoms guaranteed by the Constitution of 1905. Nevertheless, once set in motion the movement could not be denied. Under the guise of performing "German" plays a number of theatrical groups, with the connivance of local police officials, pursued their ever more creative, if precarious, careers.

The greatest flowering of this branch of Jewish art, however, though carried on for the most part by Russian personnel, came on American soil, until the 1917 abrogation of the government prohibition formally reopened the gates of Jewish theaters in Russia. On both sides of the Atlantic Ocean, memorable plays—like that by Peretz and many more by prolific playwrights Jacob Gordin (1853–1909), Perets Hirschbein ([1880–1948] who had established in 1908 a Jewish art theater in Odessa), and David Pinski (1872–1959), all performed with extraordinary devotion to art by an array of distinguished actors like Boris Tomashevski, Jacob Adler, and their feminine counterparts—raised the Yiddish theater almost overnight to the level of the best of the European theatrical arts. What the distinguished German historian Karl Lamprecht wrote about his impressions at the New York Yiddish theater in 1904 was equally true of similar achievements of the Russian-Jewish theatrical arts on their native soil. Lamprecht compared his New York experience to his visit to the Cologne Cathedral or the ruins of Paestum and concluded: "I now realize what the ancient Hellenic drama must have been so long as they played it with such religious consecration."[34]

Such was the great *élan vital* and creativity of the five million Jews of Russia when the country entered the titanic conflict of World War I.

[10]

The First World War

❁

At the outbreak of the World War in August, 1914, Russian Jewry found itself directly involved, as Russians and as Jews. Not since 1812 had the Pale been invaded by a foreign enemy. Unlike that Napoleonic campaign, however, which was of short duration and largely limited to a few existing roads in the direction of Moscow, the war of the twentieth century lasted for several years and extended over fronts of hundreds of miles. The devastation of the theaters of war was incomparably greater; it was further aggravated by a conscious scorched-earth policy pursued by the retreating Russian armies in supposed emulation of their ancestors a century earlier. Moreover, Jews were now made to serve in the Russian armed forces to the full extent of their able-bodied manpower. It has been estimated that the six hundred thousand Jews who wore Russian uniforms between 1914 and 1917 exceeded their ratio in the empire's population. This high percentage was doubly significant as beginning with the summer of 1915, the German occupation effectively withdrew most of the Jewish population (including that of Congress Poland) from later Russian drafts. Yet such repeated statistical proofs of loyalty during the war failed to silence anti-Semitic accusations of alleged Jewish shirking which ultimately induced Count Alexis Tolstoi to institute a formal investigation.

Jewish willingness to offer sacrifices for the Russian mother country was the more remarkable, as for a long time the Russian administration unflinchingly pursued its old discriminatory policies. The press reported cases of Jewish soldiers who had distinguished themselves in the Russo-Japanese War and had thereby earned residence permits in the interior of Russia. When they were now again drafted for active service their families were ordered to leave, since the fathers had departed. Soldiers wounded on the battlefield were often taken to hospitals in the interior, but upon their discharge, were told to return immediately to the Pale. Yet just as in the dark years of Nicholas I's regime so now did the Russian Jewish soldiers fulfill their duty. What an editorialist (Colonel Peter S. Lebedev?) of the army organ *Russkii Invalid* had written in 1858 was doubly true during the world war.

> How can the Army slander the Jew, when tens of thousands of Jews are serving in the ranks and performing honestly and faithfully their duty to the Tsar and the Fatherland? Were not the ramparts of Fort Sebastopol colored with the blood of Jewish, as well as Russian soldiers, of Jewish soldiers who fought in the many battles for that stronghold even against their coreligionists in the enemy ranks? Let us be worthy of our century, let us denounce the unfortunate custom in our literature to mock and disdain the Jew.[1]

MASS EVACUATION

From the outset the attitude and actions of the Russian High Command toward Jews left much to be desired. True, since Russia was allied with Britain and France, she tried to spread news about the inner rapprochement between the various segments of her population. Undoubtedly stimulated by the idea of the *Burgfrieden* so eminently serving the purposes of the German war machine, Russian foreign propaganda eloquently depicted a fraternization between Jews and known anti-Semites. According to one story circulated abroad, the deputy V. M. Purishkevich, a notorious leader of the anti-Semitic Black Hundreds who in 1911 had personally ordered the printing and wide dissemination of leaflets inciting to pogroms, visited a synagogue, kissed the scroll of law, and amidst copious tears, embraced the rabbi. In fact, however, anti-Semitic accusations were given free rein even under the strict war censorship.[2]

At the beginning of the war the commander in chief, Grand Duke Nicholas Nikolaevich, though a member of the League of the Russian People, issued an appeal to the Poles, promising the unification of their country under the tsar's scepter with full civil and national rights. By implication Jews, too, expected to benefit from the new liberal trend in Russian policies. One can imagine how great the disappointment was when the news of sharp anti-Jewish actions began arriving from Galicia, most of which was overrun by Russian troops in the first three months. General N. J. Ivanov, the commander of the Russian troops occupying Lvov and, after a prolonged siege, the fortress of Przemyśl, behaved as if that territory had always belonged to Russia and been only temporarily estranged from it. The large Ruthenian population of the country, overwhelmingly Uniate, was simply declared to be part of the Russian people and told that Russian Orthodoxy was its proper religion. The Uniate Metropolitan, Count Andrew Szeptycki, was deported to Russia.

Jews were treated with even greater cruelty. Since most of them were loyal Austrian citizens, they were constantly suspected by the Russians of espionage for the Austrian army. Many individuals were imprisoned and executed. Quite apart from the usual atrocities committed by conquering armies on the civilian population, sharp measures were adopted in many localities against the entire Jewish population. Typical of many such military ordinances was one issued by the local commander, Prince Lobanov Rostovskii, during the occupation of the city of Kolomea in southeastern Galicia, and another promulgated by Nicholas Nikolaevich himself and sent to the respective military commands. Rostovskii's ordinance read:

> I announce to the entire Israelitic population of the city of Kolomea that if in the environs of the localities of Delatyn, Kolomea, and Sniatyn, the railroad, the telegraph, or telephone services are damaged in the slightest, a large contribution will be imposed on the entire Jewish population of the city of Kolomea. Should that contribution not be paid within three days, the entire Jewish population of the city will be expelled from the territories occupied by our troops.

The Grand Duke's circular letter began:

> Our experience during this war has clearly revealed the hostile attitude of the Jewish population, particularly of Galicia and the Bukovina. As soon as some substantial change in the locations and movements of our troops occurs, and whenever we temporarily evacuate one or another district, the enemy, because of the intervention of Jews, adopts cruel measures against the loyal non-Jewish population. In order to protect the population faithful to us from the reprisals by the enemy and to safeguard our troops against the treason which the Jews employ along the entire front, the Supreme Commander of the Russian armed forces considers it necessary that Jews be banished as soon as the enemy retreats. It is necessary to take hostages from among the rich or well-to-do and other persons holding important positions. One must also seize the most influential rabbis of the respective communities and deport them all as prisoners to the interior

of our country. (At first to the province of Kiev, where they are to be held in concentration camps.)[3]

This policy of mass evacuation soon began to be practiced also on Russian territory at the approach of German and Austrian troops. As early as March, 1915, the Russian military authorities began with their large-scale expulsions of Jews from the border provinces of Poland, Kovno, and Courland. Particularly during the great Austro-German offensive of May through September, 1915, which ended not only in the recapture of most of Galicia and the Bukovina but also in the occupation of vast Russian territories from the vicinity of Riga down to the Rumanian border, forcible evacuation of Jews assumed enormous proportions. These moves were officially justified by alleged Jewish spying for Germany, although whenever courts had a chance to probe the accusations, they usually turned out, as in a famous case in Kuzhi, Kovno province, to be completely groundless. Many Poles were involved in that anti-Jewish spy hunt, in part because they wished in this way to divert attention from their own often disloyal attitude toward their tsarist oppressors. Alleged widespread pro-German spying also offered defeated Russian commanders a ready excuse for their campaign failures.

True, Jews were not the only evacuees. Apart from voluntary refugees, many other inhabitants of these border areas were forced to leave their residences, for the most part within twenty-four hours. The result was that an incomplete registration of the refugees being cared for in the territory still under Russian control showed that there were 2,700,000 such unfortunates in December, 1915, and 3,300,000 five months later. But Jews were both more suspect and more easily forced out of their concentrated habitations in cities. It has been estimated that more than 600,000 Jews were thus uprooted. Only because of the lightning speed of the Austro-German invasion, which overtook some two-thirds of these exiles, were many of them able to return to their homes. This ebb and flow also caused extensive economic damage. A subsequent survey showed that only some 5 percent of the evacuees were able to take their movable possessions along with them; 22 percent were removed with such speed that they had to leave everything behind; the rest salvaged varying parts of their holdings. In all, these refugees, voluntary as well as forced, sustained losses estimated at $350,000,000 to $400,000,000—a huge amount, indeed, in view of the dollar's still high purchasing power.

Nevertheless, the community of Vilna, for instance, in the summer of 1915 found itself forced to accommodate thousands of evacuees from the provinces of Kovno, Grodno, and Suwalki before its own turn came to be occupied by the Germans. Jewish refugees had to be sheltered not only in private homes and various public institutions but also in synagogues and prayer houses. The food shortage was equally lamentable. The Russian railroads, unable to cope fully with peacetime transportation, broke down completely when they were faced with the tremendous logistic problems of the Russian fronts. Hence local shortages developed even before there was a large-scale famine. National competition, for instance, between the Vilna Poles, White Russians, and Jews for the purchase of whatever food could be brought in from the countryside aggravated an already existing state of tension between these various minority groups. Trying to exonerate the people and to place the entire blame on the government, Maxim Gorki wrote in 1929:

> In 1915, the most shameful anti-Jewish propaganda was started in the army; all Jews in Poland and Galicia were declared the spies and enemies of Russia. A disgusting pogrom broke out in Molodechno. It has been established that this Jew-baiting originated at headquarters, and, of course, it could not but contribute to the disintegration of the army, in which there were about half a million Jews. The people, enraged and blinded by want, were unable to detect their true enemy. If the authorities sanctioned the killing and robbery of Jews—why not kill and rob them?[4]

GERMAN OCCUPATION

By the end of 1915, most of the Pale had come under German domination. Those Jews who had hoped that the new masters would bring alleviation of their distress were quickly disillusioned. The German High Command, led by the later notorious anti-Semite General Erich von Ludendorff, started out with a proclamation to its "dear Jews" in which high-sounding promises were made for their liberation from the Russian yoke.[5]

In practice, the German army pursued its usual policy of exploiting the local population including the Jews not only for the benefit of the occupying forces, but also for that of the German homeland. As the British blockade became increasingly effective and shortages of food and raw materials began to throttle the German war effort at home, the German commanders in the occupied areas ruthlessly seized foodstuffs, gold, silver, and other metals which could be used in German armament factories. Synagogues, like churches, were deprived of their candlesticks and other objects of worship accumulated over generations.

None of this was specifically anti-Jewish. The German authorities soon began issuing their official proclamations in Yiddish, as well as in German, Polish, and Lithuanian. They also allowed many refugees previously concentrated in a few large cities to return to their homes or to seek shelter in hamlets and villages where the food supply was somewhat more ample. For a while they even enabled some Jews to emigrate to the United States, then still neutral. It is estimated that 2,500 such émigrés departed from Russia in 1915–16. (As the American attitude toward Germany became increasingly hostile, the German military authorities suspended all further emigration to the United States.) For instance, the total of some 22,000 refugees found in Vilna at the time of the German entry in 1915 was reduced by these manifold measures to but 1,000 fifteen months later.

Orderly bread rations likewise mitigated some hardships of the lower classes who could not afford black-market prices. But the situation was going from bad to worse, and by the end of 1916 many Jewish communities throughout the occupied area had to extend charitable support to more than half of their members. They were able to do so only because the newly organized American Jewish Joint Distribution Committee found ways and means of getting some materials through to both sides of the Russo-German front. As a result, some city councils withdrew all support from destitute Jews under the excuse that they were getting sufficient help from their American coreligionists.

In time the Germans set in motion a westward movement of the Jewish population. Since the war placed increasing demands upon German manpower and since almost all able-bodied young men were sent out to the man-devouring fronts, many more laborers were needed in the factories at home. More and more Jews, as well as non-Jews, were therefore drafted for labor battalions either to serve in an auxiliary capacity in the occupied zone or to replenish the working class in Germany itself. In the course of the war no less than 70,000 Jews were more or less forcibly transferred to Germany, swelling the number of foreign-born Jews in that country and thus serving as additional targets for German anti-Semites, particularly during the 1920s.[6]

The Jews, whose Yiddish language was more readily understandable to the Germans than any Slavonic tongue, and who upon arrival in Germany could expect a more brotherly reception from the German Jewish communities, were the preferred objects of this disguised manhunt. At the same time, such "favoritism" on the part of the occupation forces served to embitter still more the always tense relations between the Jews and their neighbors. The September 17, 1915, decree of the German authorities ordering the opening of schools with Polish the language of instruction for Polish children, and with German as the language to be used in the case of German and Jewish children, raised the specter of "Germanization" of Poland and added fuel to the existing fire of resentment. Understandably, most Jews preferred the employment of either Hebrew or Yiddish in their own schools, and this clause had to be altered in October, 1916.

As the war progressed, Jewish sufferings kept growing, affecting even the mortality figures. True, the cholera epidemic raging in western Russia earlier in 1915 was successfully stamped out by the German forces, for their own sake, by November of that year. But because of malnutrition and overcrowded quarters in Warsaw (which at one time accommodated 80,000 Jewish refugees), Vilna, and other major centers, Jews were decimated by recurrent attacks of typhoid. In Vilna, for example, where before 1914 the annual Jewish death rate had ranged from 20.4 to 22.6 per 1,000 inhabitants, it increased to 34.4 in March, 1916, 41.5 in December, 1916, and 68.2, in 1917. In March, 1917, it reached the staggering total of 97.5 per 1,000. At the same time the number of births dwindled from 1,502 in 1913 to 489 in 1917. Similar conditions also prevailed in other occupied territories. On the Russian side of the front, too, the Jewish birth rate declined sharply while mortality went up and up. In Elizavetgrad, where symptoms of biological retardation had become noticeable before the war, the Jewish increase in population, as a result of the excess of births over deaths, was reduced from 201 in 1913 to 164 in 1914 and 77 in 1915. This surplus turned into a deficit of 87 to 88 souls each in the subsequent two years.[7]

Undaunted, the Jews pursued their religious and cultural life with increased zest since the German military administration was much less restrictive than had been Russian officialdom. The Jewish parties were now free to build their educational institutions in accordance with their respective ideologies. The Zionists laid the foundations for a school system with modern Hebrew as the language of instruction, which was later to develop into the noteworthy *Tarbut* structure in newly reconstituted Poland. The Bund, on the other hand, established the first secular schools with the Yiddish language of instruction; these were later also to develop into the important CISHO school system in Poland. The Jewish theater, too, now coming out into the open, attracted major talents, and before long the so-called Vilna Troupe achieved great renown for its high artistic accomplishments.

IN RUSSIA'S INTERIOR

On the other side of the front the much-reduced Pale of Settlement could no longer accommodate the large numbers of Jews. Their very evacuation, though inspired by suspicions of Jewish loyalty or temporary military exigencies, contributed to breaking down the historic barriers. Many evacuees had to be transplanted into the interior of Russia; for instance, the city of Saratov attracted an important new Jewish settlement. Jewish soldiers, too, were sent for training to various localities beyond the Pale. Willy-nilly the Russian administration had to relax the old residence restrictions; by the decree of August 4, 1915, most Jewish war sufferers were permitted to move into the interior of Russia, with some specific exceptions which betrayed the usual lack of logical consistency. Not surprisingly, as a part of its war propaganda the Russian government widely publicized this decree in the Western countries, naturally omitting to mention that this was but a temporary relaxation for the duration of the war only. In the general liberalization of admissions to schools the Jewish quota was substantially enlarged. In particular, Jews connected with the war effort were allowed to register beyond their usual allotment. As a result in 1915 the University of St. Petersburg admitted some 600 Jews who helped swell its total enrollment from an average of about 1,900 in the preceding three years to 2,600.[8]

However, the total relief was not as great as one might have expected. Bureaucratic chicaneries often made life very difficult for many newcomers. In Saratov even long-established artisans and guild members, who had theretofore pursued their callings on the basis of pertinent passports, were now told that since passports were no longer being issued under the terms of the August decree, they were not allowed to work in these restricted occupations. Although the movement out of the Pale was greatly stimulated by the Revolutions of 1917, the Central Committee for the Relief of Jewish War Sufferers (EKOPO) found only 211,691 such Jewish residents in the interior. Yet many Russian peasants and city dwellers now had their first opportunity to become acquainted with living Jews, rather than with the distorted image of them presented by Jew-baiting preachers and officials. To some extent this breakdown of the Pale seemed to presage the possible coming of better times, although during the great retreat of 1915 the demoralized soldiers often perpetrated untold brutalities upon the civilian population, and especially on the helpless Jewish segment, behind the front.[9]

News of these atrocities and the generally arbitrary and cruel behavior of the Russian military commanders could not escape the attention of the Russian political leaders and the intelligentsia in the two capitals. The Duma, rather than losing power because of the increasingly centralized controls characteristic of war emergencies, now gained in prestige. In the Jewish question, to be sure, even the Progressive Bloc—consisting of Cadets, Octobrists, and Right Nationalists—was fearful of arousing the internal antagonisms and proceeded at a snail's pace in demanding the removal of Jewish disabilities. Nonetheless, it now became possible for Alexander F. Kerensky and N. M. Friedman to investigate the alleged high treason committed by the Jewish inhabitants of Kuzhi, "in Courland," which the High Command had widely publicized as a warning to all Russian armies. Seconded by Friedman, Kerensky announced to the Duma, "I declare now from this rostrum that I personally went to the town of Kuzhi to verify the accusation . . . and I feel it my duty to reiterate that this is but an ignominious slander. There was no such case, and under local conditions there could be none." Beyond that incident the Committee on Interpellations, representing all major parties, reported out (and thus gave an indirect indication of approval) an inquiry concerning the illegal acts committed by the armed forces and the bureaucracy against Jews. This interpellation of August 30, 1915, singled out eleven major illustrations of serious misbehavior and asked: "If the illegal acts of the authorities are known to the indicated individuals, what steps were taken by them towards the punishment of the guilty and the prevention of similar breaches of law in the future?"[10]

The Duma also dared to voice the growing grievances of the entire population against the confusingly arbitrary actions of the ever more chaotic administration, particularly when the tsarina and Rasputin began exercising their inordinate control over the ministries during Nicholas II's frequent absences at the front. The replacement of Generalissimo Nicholas Nikolaevich by the tsar himself in August, 1915, merely helped to further undermine the dynasty's prestige because of its obviously inept efforts to stem the German advance and its equally clear mismanagement of the domestic economy. Apart from its organizational shortcomings, the administration showed itself totally incapable of mitigating the ever-sharpening contrasts between the war profiteers and the hungry masses.

On the other hand, as early as 1915 some of Russia's leading intellectuals felt obliged to publish "An Appeal for the Jews," in which they stressed the evil effects of the governmental anti-Jewish discrimination. Although in connection with the partial removal of the barriers of the Pale there also was some relaxation of the *numerus clausus* and other educational restrictions, these intellectuals argued that owing to the war, Jewish students could no longer repair to schools abroad while the home institutions continued to limit their admission to a small number. Wives and children of wounded soldiers were not permitted to visit their husbands and fathers in hospitals beyond the Pale.

> Russian Jews have rendered honest service in all domains left open to them. They have given ample proof of their sincere desire to offer utmost sacrifices for their country. Hence, the curtailment of their civic rights is not only a crying injustice but also a condition injurious to the best interests of the state. The Russian Empire can and must derive its sustenance only from the union of all its nationalities. Only when Russia will accord its citizens equal rights will its power become indestructible. Fellow Russians! Remember that the Russian Jew has no other fatherland than Russia and that nothing is more precious to a

man than his native soil. You must realize that the welfare and strength of Russia is inseparable from the welfare and freedom of all its constituent nationalities.

Among the signers were such internationally famous writers and scholars as Leonid Andreev, Maxim Gorki, Alexander Kerensky, Dmitry Merezhkovsky, A. Rimsky-Korsakoff, Mikhail Rostovtsev, Mikhail Ivanovich Tugan-Baranovsky, M. Fedorov, and many others. The deep sense of guilt animating these intellectuals found a vivid expression in Andreev's rhetorical exclamation: "All powerlessness, if it is unable to prevent a crime—becomes complicity; and this was the result: personally guiltless of any offence against my brother, I have become in the eyes of all those not concerned and those of my brother himself, a Cain." Even the rather stodgy State Council had to listen to a less eloquent but equally well-reasoned address by Baron R. R. Rosen, former Russian ambassador to the United States, who among other matters pointed out the dangers to Russia's war effort emanating from a negative foreign public opinion. Discussing the general effectiveness of German propaganda, Rosen added:

> It is inconceivable that the framers of our policy should fail to realize that the propaganda directed against us, conducted under official auspices and equipped with the amplest resources, will scarcely cause our own interests and the interests of our Allies one-tenth of the harm which is caused to these interests by our attitude towards the Jewish population of Russia and our systematic violation of the legal conscience of the Finnish population—an attitude which smacks of the dark times of medievalism.

In short, the feeling was constantly gaining ground that once the war was over, the Russian constitutional system would have to be rebuilt from its foundations and that Jewish equality would be an indispensable ingredient in that reconstruction.[11]

Nor were protests from abroad effective. England and France were embarrassed by the news of Russian atrocities toward Jews, especially since British diplomacy made strenuous efforts to draw the United States into the war against Germany. In its American propaganda Britain often encountered the argument, at times advanced by Germanophile American Jews, that its ally, Russia, was much more barbarous than Germany since she committed atrocities against her own citizens, while the German armies only mistreated conquered populations. At first Britain tried to whitewash the Russian military. It was aided and abetted by its Petrograd envoys, civil and military, some of whom were personally anti-Jewish. They merely transmitted to London official handouts from the Russian Ministry of Foreign Affairs or High Command. Only when a collection of documents assembled by a Jewish committee in Petrograd, under the leadership of Vinaver and Dubnow, reached London via Stockholm and when another such collection was brought by the revolutionary A. Shliapnikov to New York in 1916, did the British give more serious consideration to Lucien Wolf's reiterated petitions for intervention in Russia in favor of both Jewish equality and a modicum of national self-government. However, this was a touchy situation among the Allies. By the time the British diplomats had bestirred themselves to effective action, Russian anarchy and the February Revolution of 1917 rendered all verbal intervention quite meaningless.[12]

Nor can one attribute, as is sometimes done, these anarchical conditions, including the misfortunes of Russian Jewry, to the evil influence of the notorious Rasputin and his henchmen at the tsarina's court. True, some of Rasputin's followers may have felt like his erstwhile friend, the monk Iliodor, who once exclaimed: "In the last resort the world would be safe from ruin only by the holy Russian people and not by accursed advocates, journalists, and all the rest of the Jews!" A number of corrupt and mercenary agents were in Rasputin's entourage, including one Manasevich-Manuilov, son of a Jewish merchant, then employed at the Ministry of Interior. However, on at least one occasion Rasputin himself is supposed to have scolded the wife of a Russian factory owner who had asked him blandly why he had not driven the Jews out of Russia. The mystic courtier is supposed to have replied, "*You* should be ashamed to talk like that. The Jews are as good people as we are. I am sure that each of you knows an honest Jew, even if he is only a dentist!"[13]

With its accustomed vigor and pliability, Russian Jewry undertook an ambitious program of self-help. On either side of the front Jewish communities had from the outset organized a Central Relief Committee to take care of both the local indigent and the waves of refugees and deportees. Known under the abbreviation EKOPO (*Evreiskii komitet pomoshtchi* or Central Committee for the Relief of Jewish Sufferers), this organization from its headquarters in Petrograd did all it could to stimulate the local relief activities. In the relatively brief period of its operations it disbursed some 50,000,000 rubles.

Politically, too, the Jewish leaders were quite active in defending Jewish rights, as well as in preparing for the hoped-for approaching day of complete Jewish emancipation. The Jewish organizations formed a Political Committee in the capital; consisting of their representatives and the elected Jewish Duma deputies, this committee courageously took up the cudgel for its coreligionists. As early as 1915, it suggested that the communities submit to the prime minister a joint petition inquiring about the government's plans for the postwar reconstruction of Jewish status. Fear of the government was too deeply ingrained in the hearts of most local communities, however, for their elders to speak openly and unequivocally. The majority refused to sign this petition, so none was presented.

Nonetheless, the agitation for equality of rights now assumed new dimensions. But while the majority still entertained hopes that upon the cessation of hostilities, the tsar himself would grant the Jews their well-earned rights, a growing radical minority looked for a revolutionary upheaval as the only means of salvation.

[11]

Era of Revolutions

1917–1923

With the majority of the Russian people and the subject nationalities, Jews welcomed with joy the so-called February (March) Revolution of 1917. The government, first headed by Prince George E. Lvov and later by Alexander F. Kerensky, promised to introduce into Russia Western democratic institutions based upon the equality of all citizens and basic freedoms for both individuals and groups. On March 20 (April 2), 1917, a short time after the tsar's abdication, the provisional government published a decree removing all disabilities stemming from differences of race or religion and thus declaring Jews equal citizens of the empire.

All organized Jewish parties, bent on also securing national autonomy for their people, decided to convoke an all-Russian, democratically elected, Jewish Congress. A committee, embracing the various parties and charged with the preparation of the election, appealed to the Jewish communities:

> Citizens, Jews! The Jewish people in Russia now faces an event which has no parallel in Jewish history for two thousand years. Not only has the Jew as an individual, as a citizen, acquired equality of rights— which has also happened in other countries—but the Jewish nation looks forward to the possibility of securing national rights. Never and nowhere have the Jews lived through such a serious, responsible

moment as the present—responsible to the present and the future generations.

This rhetoric was followed by a seven-point program to be submitted to the Congress; its first two paragraphs again stressed the principle of national self-determination and the legal safeguards for the Jewish national minority.[1] The election was indeed held by direct, secret, and proportionate ballot in the autumn of 1917. Owing, however, to the grave internal disturbances, the inroads of the German armies during the summer of 1917, and finally, the successful Communist Revolution of October (November), the Congress never met.

COMMUNIST UPSURGE

The second stage of the revolution, headed by Lenin, opened a new chapter in Jewish as well as in world history. From the outset, there was considerable equivocation in the communist attitude toward the Jewish question. The presence of many Jews in the top echelon of the Communist Party made it appear to outsiders that the new regime would reform the Jewish status in a spirit acceptable to the Jewish people. In fact, anti-Semites in and outside Russia glibly equated communism with the alleged Jewish world conspiracy. They could easily point out that the first president of the Central Committee of the Party was Jacob Sverdlov, a Lithuanian Jew, that this committee included four other Jews in its total membership of twenty-one, and that the long-time president of the Third International was Grigorii Evseevich Zinoviev (Radomislsky). Among the leading diplomats of the period was A. A. Yoffe, Russia's chief delegate at the Brest-Litovsk Peace Conference and subsequently ambassador in Berlin. Yoffe unabashedly used his diplomatic immunity to spread communist propaganda in Germany, then in a desperate mood because of its defeat in the World War I. Later Maxim Litvinov (Wallach) worked in various capacities to reassert the position of the Soviet Union as one of the great world powers. A Galician Jew, Karl Radek (Sobelsohn), helped reorganize the Russian press and laid the foundations for communism's highly effective world-wide propaganda. From the scholarly point of view, it was N. Riazanov (David Borisovich Goldendach) who as head of the new Marx-Engels Institute in Moscow became the outstanding historian of the Marxist movement, editor of the chief classics of the Marxist school, and in many ways founder of the new Russian historiography. Above all these men towered Leon Trotsky (Leo Davidovich Bronstein), second only to Lenin in the leadership of the revolution. As commander in chief and minister of war he reorganized the Russian army and successfully defended the new regime in many battles against its foreign and domestic enemies.[2]

The preponderance of Jews in the early communist leadership, which may even have irritated some of these leaders themselves,[3] is not at all surprising when one realizes how long the Bolshevik party had been an outlawed underground movement with a number of eminent leaders but a relatively small following among the masses. Many Jewish intellectuals were attracted to its professed international ideals, as well as to its socialist radicalism which promised to put an end to the tsarist oppression. Perhaps in subconscious retaliation for the many years of suffering at the hands of the Russian police, a disproportionate number of Jews joined the new Bolshevik secret service. At least when in December, 1937, *Pravda* published a list of 407 officials of that service decorated on the twentieth anniversary of its existence, forty-two names, or some 11 percent, were identified as Jewish. The impression these facts made upon the ordinary Russian is rightly stressed by Leonard Schapiro: "For the most prominent and colourful figure after Lenin was Trotsky, in Petrograd the dominant and hated figure was Zinoviev, while anyone who had the misfortune to fall into the hands of the *Cheka* stood a very good chance of finding himself confronted with, and possibly shot by, a Jewish investigator."[4]

To the casual observer the intrinsically Russian, rather than international, mainsprings of the Bolshevist ideology and practice were far less apparent. Nor did he know, as a rule, that the attachment to Judaism of these Jewish communists was nil. At best some, like Litvinov, classified themselves as members of the Jewish nationality. Most others followed Trotsky's example in considering themselves nothing but Russians and believing that even the Russian nationality would ultimately give way to some sort of international culture. In his autobiography, Trotsky greatly played down his Jewish upbringing and antecedents. In many cases this revulsion from the Jewish past bordered on outright self-hatred and greatly contributed to the revolution's destructive methods in dealing with the established Jewish institutions. Of course, to outsiders, particularly anti-Semites, such self-denial availed very little. When, for example, Zinoviev debated socialist issues with a leading anti-Bolshevik, Yulii Martov, the German Jew-baiter, Count Ernst zu Reventlow, underscored Zinoviev's alleged Jewish name Apfelbaum (given him by the Russian secret police), but he failed to inform his readers that Martov's name had really been Zederbaum.

A closer examination of the record showed that this numerical preponderance in the leadership did not reflect actual Jewish participation in the rank and file of the Party. Our information for the early years after the revolution is incomplete. But data made available for the period of 1922 to 1930 showed that Jewish membership was gradually declining from 5.2 percent in 1922 to 4.3 percent in 1927, and 3.8 percent in 1930, although among the Komsomol youth the decline was somewhat less precipitous: from 4.6 to 4.4 and 4.1 percent respectively. Moreover, even if this median percentage of 4.5 in the Party membership exceeded by some 150 percent the Jewish ratio of 1.8 percent in the Soviet population, this disproportion was characteristic of many non-Russian nationalities, including the Poles and Latvians, the latter actually surpassing their population strength by some 1,100 percent. Even Ukrainians and White Russians, who in their own lands lagged in membership by more than one-third behind their percentage of the population, exceeded that ratio by 233 percent and 873 percent while living as minorities in each other's republics. The leadership of all parties, moreover, had to be largely recruited from the urban population, since the large majority of the peasantry was completely illiterate. Among the city dwellers only 2.25 percent of Jews had joined the Communist Party in 1927, while 3.24 percent of non-Jews had joined.[5] As time went on, the leadership positions, as well as the lower echelons, were gradually filled by non-Jews (Sverdlov, for instance, was replaced by Mikhail I. Kalinin), and as we shall see, most of the early Jewish leaders died violent deaths at the hand of their fellow communists.

Estrangement from their own people by the majority of Jewish communists helped to set the course of the revolutionary regime's policies in a direction running counter to the wishes of the Jewish majority. In the long run, this divergence carried in itself elements of great tragedy. Lenin, too, had long misread the overt signs of the Jews' national will. On principle, as well as for tactical reasons, he had demanded, as early as October, 1903, that the Bund give up its "separatism" and join the ranks of the Russian Socialist Party. At that time he wrote in the *Iskra* that the idea of a Jewish "nationality"

> is definitely reactionary not only when expounded by its consistent advocates (the Zionists), but likewise on the lips of those who try to combine it with the ideas of Social Democracy (the Bundists). This idea of a Jewish nationality runs counter to the interests of the Jewish proletariat, for it fosters among them, directly or indirectly, a spirit hostile to assimilation, the spirit of the "ghetto."

More generally, he insisted, in a much-quoted passage, that "a nation must have a territory on which to develop, and, in our time at least, until a world confederation has extended this basis, a nation must have a common language." He adhered to this point of view (long held by the Bundists themselves but abandoned at the turn of the century) in his other essays written in the following decade.[6]

NATIONAL MINORITY RIGHTS

Upon coming to power, however, Lenin realized that there was almost complete unanimity among the Russian Jews of that time that they must be treated as a national minority. Realist that he was, he did not mind reversing his previous stand and including the Jews in the new Declaration of the Rights of Nationalities, issued by the Council of People's Commissars on November 15, 1917, but a few days after he had achieved power. This declaration promised to all nationalities equality and free self-determination, including the right of secession. The latter privilege was, of course, quite meaningless in the case of the dispersed Jews. But they must have greatly appreciated the pledge of the government to guarantee: "3. the removal of every and any national and national religious privilege and restriction; 4. the free development of the national minorities and ethnographic groups living within the confines of Russia." Hopes rose very high that for the first time Russian Jewry would be in a position to control its own religio-cultural and educational affairs.

Such hopes seemed to be fully confirmed by the reproduction, in the *Pravda* of 1922, of an interview Lenin gave to a Jewish correspondent of the *Manchester Guardian* and the London *Observer*. Here the Soviet leader assured this foreign correspondent that the experience of the preceding five years had fully convinced the Soviet government that the only way to eliminate nationalist strife was to offer maximum satisfaction to the aspirations of all nationalities. True, keener observers could have noted even then a discrepancy between the theory and the practice. Certainly, Simeon Dimanshtain, who soon was to assume the official leadership of the Russo-Jewish community, could clearly remember his own activities as minister of labor in the Lithuanian government during the short span of Soviet rule there in 1917–19. Whatever pledges for the evolution of the national Lithuanian culture may have been made by the new rulers, they themselves, Dimanshtain included, preferred to use the Russian language in their mutual exchanges. But these deviations from the rules could be dismissed as matters of simple habit, and the Jewish community, like the other minorities, could confidently expect to be able to develop an autonomous cultural life of its own, unhindered—indeed, aided and abetted—by the regime.[7]

Careful readers of the subsequent governmental pronunciamentos must have noticed, however, that these pledges of national rights were aimed less at granting to groups of citizens complete freedom to develop their national cultures than at their more effective indoctrination in the new *Weltanschauung*. A few years later (in 1923) the nationalities were bluntly informed by the influential Commissar for Public Enlightenment Anatolii V. Lunacharskii, that educators must refrain from teaching history in a way stimulating the children's national pride. "For I do not know what kind of thing is a healthy love for one's fatherland." More, Joseph Stalin, who even before his rise to supreme power was the Party's chief theorist on the Marxist doctrine of nationalism, consistently preached that national minority rights, like nationalism in general, were to serve only as a temporary measure for the prevention of national strife during the era of building a socialist society. Just as the concentration of state power through a dictatorship of the proletariat was intended merely to pave the way for the ultimate "withering away" of the state, as Marx taught, so was the promotion of national cultures to be but an intermediate link toward the ultimate submersion of all nationalities in a world nation. In his famous address to the Sixteenth Congress of the Communist Party of 1930, Stalin made it clear that "the flourishing of cultures, national in form and socialist in content, in the conditions of a proletarian dictatorship in one country, for the *purpose* of their fusion into one common socialist culture, common both in form and in content, with one common tongue, . . . in this lies the dialectical quality of the Leninist way of treating the question of national cultures."[8]

Vague as these formulations must have appeared even to trained Marxists—Lunacharskii's version was soon to be totally reversed in the crucible of World War II, when the Russian regime had to appeal to the inbred patriotism of the masses—Jewish leaders could nevertheless entertain some hopes for developing their own culture. Few anticipated the hostile reaction to traditional Jewish culture on the part not only of those communist leaders who had severed all connections with Judaism, but also of those who were entrusted by the new government with the erection of the Jewish "sections" (*yevsektsiias*) in the various local governmental bodies. These sections were headed by a Jewish department in the Commissariat of Nationalities of the Council of Commissars. Perhaps the venom with which the Jewish communists approached all traditional institutions and the parties which had theretofore determined the course of Jewish communal life may in part be explained by the bitterness long generated within the community by the divisive policies of the tsarist regime, its fiscal administration, and the cantonist system.

At any rate, no sooner did they attain power than the Jewish communists persuaded the government to outlaw all existing Jewish parties, especially the Zionist organizations. Under Nicholas II the Zionist movement had become the most potent force in Jewish public life despite the necessity of long operating underground. By 1918, when it was out in the open, it included no fewer than 1,200 local Zionist groups with some 300,000 members. But in June, 1919, the Second Conference of the Jewish Communist Sections in Moscow adopted the following resolution:

> The Zionist party plays a counter-revolutionary role. It is responsible for strengthening, among the backward Jewish masses, the influence of clericalism and nationalist attitudes. In this way the class self-determination of the Jewish toiling masses is undermined and the

penetration of communist ideas in their midst seriously hindered. Owing to its Palestine policy, the Zionist Party serves as an instrument of united imperialism which combats the proletarian revolution. In consideration of all these circumstances, the Conference requests the Central Bureau to propose to the pertinent authorities the promulgation of a decree suspending all activities of the Zionist Party in the economic, political, and cultural spheres. The communal organs, which are the mainstay of all reactionary forces within the Jewish people, must be suppressed.

A little later (July 1, 1920) a secret circular of the Central Political Police argued that since Zionism was well received in Western countries and was persecuted nowhere, it must *eo ipso* be inimical to the Soviet Union. The government the more readily followed suit as Lenin had as far back as February, 1903, attacked the Zionist "fable about anti-Semitism being eternal." It speedily outlawed the movement under severe sanctions, arrested some three thousand Zionist leaders, and deported many to Siberia's political labor camps.[9]

With the general Zionists were also outlawed the smaller groups of Labor Zionists, Young Zionists, and similar organizations. The other recognized Jewish groups, such as the People's Party (Folkisten) and the Bund, shared the same fate. In the totalitarian structure of the new regime there was no room for diversity of political organizations. All had to fit into the one mold of the communist-controlled Jewish Commissariat and its subdivisions.

YEVSEKTSIIA

Not surprisingly, the organizers of the Jewish Commissariat had difficulties in recruiting the necessary personnel. This is admitted by its first leaders, Samuel Agurskii and Simeon Dimanshtain. It all began when on January 18, 1918, six Jewish communists met and asked for the appointment of Dimanshtain as a Jewish commissar. Appointed two days later, the new commissar presided on January 21 over a poorly attended public meeting which included some hecklers from the Bund and other parties. He was greeted by such epithets as "Jewish bureaucrat" and "Jewish *pristav* [petty police official]." The opposition aimed its shafts especially at Dimanshtain's avowed program *not* to promote specific Jewish interests. "As internationalists we do not pursue any special national tasks but only proletarian programs." Similarly hostile was the reaction of the Jewish press, which, to quote Dimanshtain's recollections, "greeted the commissariat with venom in its mouth."[10]

The commissariat's first major step was indeed illuminating. The first meeting of the thirteen regional sections theretofore established, held on October 20, 1918, consisted of thirty-one communists and thirty-three hand-picked "impartial" delegates. It passed a resolution, succinctly stating that "all institutions hitherto operating in the Jewish quarter, like the 'communities' and the rest, no longer have any place in our life. . . . All such institutions and establishments are harmful to the essential interests of the broad Jewish masses whom they lull by saccharine songs of alleged Jewish democratism. The Jewish worker relies upon the victory of the proletariat during the October Revolution. He takes power into his own hands and declares the dictatorship of the proletariat within Jewish society." In the spirit of this resolution the government soon began liquidating all existing Jewish institutions. In June, 1919, the Jewish communal organizations were abolished by a decree signed by both Agurskii and Stalin. In justification they wrote that around these organizations were grouped the enemies of the working class and the October Revolution and that these organizations' policies and educational work nurtured an antiproletarian spirit among their members. Included in the general expropriation of all communal possessions were the real estate and funds held by such national organizations as the EKOPO, the ORT, and the OZE, an important health organization.[11]

In practice, to be sure, many difficulties emerged. In one nationalized Jewish home for the aged, for example, the administration had at one time only pork at its disposal. The predominantly Orthodox inmates not only refused such ritualistically prohibited meats but also all other foods which had come in contact with them. As a result, a rumor spread throughout the town that the old men and women received from the revolution the blessings of starvation rather than liberation. Always conscious of such propaganda effects, the Jewish commissars organized a central "Committee of Jewish Associations" (IDGESKOM) in July 1920, to which they admitted a number of old-time social workers. But this effort to placate public opinion failed, for the latter soon found out that their views were totally disregarded by the communist majority. They resigned six months later, rendering the committee itself quite meaningless. It was formally abolished in 1924.

Most important were the anti-Judaistic policies of both the government and the Jewish commissariat. Convinced that all religion was but an "opiate" for the masses, Lenin and his associates had long proclaimed their opposition to any theistic faith. In an essay on "Socialism and Religion" written in December, 1905, Lenin had proclaimed, "Our propaganda necessarily includes the propaganda of atheism." When he came to power, the breach with existing religious bodies was widened by the unyielding attitude of Tikhon, the official head of the Russian Orthodox Church. Without wishing to enter a regular *Kulturkampf* à la Bismarck, the communists nevertheless managed to expropriate churches and synagogues with all their possessions, though allowing their members to form private religious congregations maintaining their own religious personnel. However, instruction in religion to children below eighteen outside their homes was strictly prohibited.[12]

Religious officials were treated as "declassed" members of society, which involved sharp discrimination in securing housing (always extremely limited), in food rations and jobs, and in the admission of their children to schools. Rabbis and other synagogue officials were placed on a par with the other ministers of religion and suffered the more severely since they did not have behind them the backing of a nation-wide, still fairly well-organized, Church. Individually, they also suffered much from the general anti-Jewish feelings and public derision. True, we have no statistics of rabbis executed or otherwise slain during the revolution, while we are told that no less than 32 bishops, 1,560 priests, and more than 7,000 monks and nuns suffered death at the hand of executioners or terrorists. The rabbinic class, too, suffered many losses, but these were largely the result of pogroms which, as we shall see, accompanied the revolutionary upheaval, especially in the Ukraine.

On the other hand, most synagogues were closed by decree. For instance, before the revolution Kremenchug, embracing a community of 40,000 Jews, had a central synagogue and thirty-six lesser sanctuaries. Suddenly, during the Passover holidays, the worshipers arriving at the central synagogue found its gate closed. In general, Jewish communists were among the most vociferous objectors to religion; one of them, Emelian Yaroslavskii, served as president of the Russian Godless Society, which with full governmental support spread atheistic propaganda throughout the country. In 1932 the society had a membership of 5,500,000. The constitutional situation was well expressed by a later decree of 1929, also included in the constitution of 1936, Article 124, which stated: "Freedom for the conduct of religious worship and freedom for antireligious propaganda is recognized for all citizens." It clearly meant that one could not propagate religion in any form, but everyone was perfectly free to spread antireligious propaganda with every means at his disposal. The program of the Communist Party went further. Issued in repeated new editions, it expressed the hope that the realization of its endeavors

> will result in the complete withering away of religious prejudice. The Party strives towards a complete destruction of the relation between the exploiting class and the organization of religious propaganda, thus effecting the actual liberation of the toiling mass from religious prejudice, and towards organizing a most extensive scientific, educational and antireligious propaganda.

At the same time the Party warned its members not to insult the believers' feelings, "since that would only lead to the strengthening of religious fanaticism."[13]

Such antireligious measures affected the Jews even more severely than their non-Jewish neighbors. To begin with, religion had for two millennia been the mainstay of Jewish life. With all the previous progress of secularization within Russian Jewry and the rise of its secularized national movements, it was still open to question whether any Jewish community could long survive without its religious moorings. In practice, too, the large majority of Russian Jews still were ritualistically observant, and few envisaged a full Jewish life without religious ceremonies. Most Russian Jewish children had been attending religious schools; some of the numerous hamlets inhabited by Jews had no other schools, Jewish or non-Jewish. Aggravating these difficulties was the raging ideological battle between Yiddishists and Hebraists about the primacy of their respective languages in Jewish cultural life. Now the Jewish communists, and following them the government, denounced Hebrew as the language of the Jewish bourgeoisie, religion, and Zionism, and hence as an instrument of counterrevolution. If for a while certain manifestations of Hebrew culture were still allowed, its leading spokesmen increasingly realized that they were fighting a losing battle. Within a few years the Hebrew language and literature were largely confined to a few classrooms at universities, where they were taught as part of the ancient dead cultures of the Near East. Remembering with deep bitterness these efforts which proved quite useless against the overwhelming totalitarian pressures, the Hebrew poet Elisha Rodin wrote a sort of epitaph for this dying culture in his native land, the "land of prison":

> *On rivers of sorrow they stifled our song*
> *The song of Zion, crystalline and bright,*
> *Made old and young alike forget our tongue,*
> *Snuffed out its sparkles of splendor and light.*
>
> *On rivers of sorrow our tongue was slain,*
> *How can I ever forget my shame?*
> *The cup of our sufferings, the honor's stain,*
> *All that I swallowed in the sorrow's name.*[14]

This persecution of Hebrew culture and Zionism must have been doubly irksome to the Jewish majority, since 1917 witnessed a great upsurge of both. Next to Odessa, the old center of modern Hebrew creativity, Moscow now attracted many refugee Hebrew writers and scholars from their old habitats in Warsaw, Vilna, and other cities before their occupation by the Germans. Even before the February Revolution the tsarist regime had to moderate somewhat its original wartime prohibition against all publications using the Hebrew alphabet. Originally laid out under the new liberal regimes of Lvov and Kerensky, plans for the publication of important books and journals in both Hebrew and Yiddish continued to be carried out under the early communist rule. Similarly, the repudiation of Zionism by the communist regime came at a time when the movement had attained its highest acceptance among the Jewish masses. This fact was demonstrated by the All-Russian Zionist Convention, which met on May 24 through 30, 1917, and which was attended by 552 delegates elected by 140,000 shekel-paying members in seven hundred localities. In the elections to the Ukrainian Jewish National Assembly in November, 1918, the Zionists polled the largest party vote (33.6 percent) and together with the Zeirei-Zion (Young Zionist, 11.2 percent) and Poale-Zion (Zionist Workers, 8.8 percent) secured an absolute majority of both votes (53.62 percent) and delegates (67 of 125). In September, 1917, no less than fifty-two Zionist periodicals appeared in Yiddish, Hebrew, and Russian. The Balfour Declaration of November 2, 1917, was greeted with tremendous enthusiasm by the large majority of Russian Jews. Although belittled by the non-Zionists as a mere political maneuver of the British government to secure Russian Jewry's help in persuading its government not to make a separate peace with Germany, it contributed greatly to the overwhelming Zionist victory in the November election to the All-Russian Constituent Assembly. According to the best estimates available, 498,198 votes were cast for Jewish parties. Of these, the Zionist and religious parties received 417,215 votes, further augmented by the 20,538 votes obtained by the Poale-Zion. At the same time, the Bundists and other non-Zionist socialist parties garnered no more than 31,123 and 29,322 votes, respectively. In addition, an undeterminate number of Jews voted for general Russian parties. But since the vast masses of Jews living in the German-occupied provinces could not participate in that election, the strong Zionist allegiance of most Russian Jews at that time cannot be denied.[15]

To the argument that Judaism without religion, Hebrew, and its messianic ideal—whether in its old religious or its modern Zionist garb—could not long survive, most Jewish communists replied that assimilation was indeed a desirable goal. While the government soon adopted the policy of settling some Jews in areas where they could form a majority and thus be granted autonomous status (the vicissitudes of Jewish agricultural colonization will be described in later chapters), the official Jewish leaders became increasingly convinced that outside such autonomous regions, Jews would sooner, rather than later, be totally assimilated. This point of view was clearly enunciated by a leading spokesman of the Party in the debates at the All-Union Conference of the Jewish Sections which met in Moscow in December, 1926. Maria Y.

Frumkina, known briefly as Ester, declared:

> Very likely the process of assimilation will engulf all the national
> minorities scattered in the cities. . . . Considering the probability of
> such assimilation, we must, by our approach, indoctrinate the Jewish
> workers and leaders not to judge each particular activity from the
> standpoint of national self-preservation, but rather from that of its
> usefulness to socialist reconstruction.[16]

Assimilation was greatly aided by the dislocations caused by the
revolution and civil war. Many Jews, uprooted from their original
habitats in the Ukraine or White Russia, drifted into Moscow, Leningrad, and other major cities, where they often found little organized
Jewish community life and formed early associations with the uprooted
masses of other nationalities. In fact, the rate of intermarriage was
steadily climbing, reaching within a few years some 25 percent of Jewish
marriages in the interior of Russia. On a visit to the Soviet Union in the
1930s the present writer was told that Jewish husbands were often
preferred by Christian girls because they had a reputation for "not being
drunkards and not beating their wives." True, in the United States with
its separation of Church and state, mixed marriages have not necessarily
resulted in the loss of the Jewish mate to his community. At times, the
gains through conversion to Judaism have balanced the losses entailed
by the conversion of the Jewish partner to Christianity. But in Europe,
including Russia, a powerful tradition of many generations held true
even in the avowedly atheistic environment of the Soviet Union: mixed
marriages would as a rule at least facilitate the raising of non-Jewish
offspring.

ANTI-SEMITISM

Assimilation might have progressed much more rapidly were it not for
various anti-Jewish manifestations. Despite the public fraternization
between the Soviets' ethnic and religious groups, anti-Semitism began
rearing its ugly head again soon after the establishment of the Soviet
Union. These animosities caused concern not only to Jews. Apart from
their running counter to basic socialist ideology, Lenin and his associates sensed in them a great danger to the revolution itself, especially
since the early disproportionate share of Jewish leaders in the Communist Party was being used to excellent advantage by the anti-Soviet
propagandists in and outside the country. Certainly, the temporary
successes of the Ukrainian armies fighting the Soviet troops were in part
accountable to the stirring up of the deep anti-Jewish prejudice of the
Ukrainian peasants by the anticommunist leaders Pavel Skoropadski,
Simeon Petliura, and their henchmen.

For all these reasons the Council of People's Commissars decided to take stern measures against any form of anti-Semitic propaganda. In an announcement published in *Izvestia* on July 27, 1918 (August 9, 1918), the Council argued that in its pogromist agitation the bourgeois counter-revolution was merely making use of an old and tried tsarist weapon.

> The Council of People's Commissars declares that the anti-Semitic movement and pogroms against the Jews are fatal to the interests of the workers' and peasants' revolution and calls upon the toiling people of Socialist Russia to fight this evil with all the means at their disposal.

> National hostility weakens the ranks of our revolutionaries, disrupts the united front of the toilers without distinctions of nationality and helps only our enemies.

> The Council of People's Commissars instructs all Soviet deputies to take uncompromising measures to tear the anti-Semitic movement out by the roots. Pogromists and pogrom-agitators are to be placed outside the law.

Although the latter phrase was rather vague, it was the only item which put some "teeth" into the declaration. Ironically, we have later testimony that while Sverdlov, the Jew, prepared the main text of the declaration, Lenin personally added the final paragraph in red ink. He took the anti-Semitic menace so seriously that in the vein of that declaration, he also broadcast on March 31, 1919, an appeal to the peoples of the Soviet Union and saw to it that it was recorded and replayed on subsequent occasions. However, this address, though vastly publicized abroad, was not published in the Soviet Union until after Lenin's death; it was first included in the second edition of his *Works* in 1932.[17]

Yet as soon as the Civil War and with it the danger of anti-Semitic complications for the Red Army were over, governmental anxiety was greatly allayed. In its execution, therefore, the outlawry of anti-Semitism, which was announced with much fanfare in Western democratic countries—Russia was, indeed, the only country to place anti-Semitism outside the law, a measure later attempted in vain before the League of Nations—left much to be desired. As a matter of fact, the "Statute of Crimes Against the State" of February 25, 1927, subsequently incorporated in the Criminal Code, included only a general provision against arousing national enmities. Even the earlier regular "Collection of Laws and Government Ordinances" and the Criminal Code of 1922 failed to mention specifically either this declaration or anti-Semitism in general. More significantly, the courts treated offenders quite mildly. A detailed review of prosecutions on this score in the province of Moscow in 1927–28, published by the Commissariat of Justice, showed that altogether 38 cases were handled during the entire year. Of the 70 defendants 10 were acquitted, 3 received a public reprimand, 30 were fined, and 12 were sentenced to compulsory labor, which at that time meant that they continued working at their regular jobs and merely forfeited up to 25 percent of their wages. Only 14 were condemned to prison terms, although their crimes included cases of "assault and battery" or "hooliganism," committed against Jewish fellow workers. Russian society had indeed traveled a long distance since the first year of the revolution, when Maxim Gorki had voiced the prevailing opinion among the Russian intelligentsia:

> The emancipation of the Jews is one of the finest achievements of our Revolution. By granting to Jews the same rights as to Russians, we have erased from our conscience a shameful and bloody stain.
>
> There is no reason why we should be especially proud of what we have done. For one thing, the Jewish community has fought for political freedom in Russia with much more honesty and energy than many Russians. For another thing, the Jews have produced considerably fewer renegades and provocateurs. We should therefore not regard ourselves as "benefactors of the Jews," for we have no right to such a claim.
>
> By liberating the Jews of the Pale of Settlement from their shackles of slavery that constituted our shame, we have made it possible for our homeland to make use of the energies of people who know how to work better than ourselves; and each of us knows perfectly well that we need people who know how to work.[18]

For many Jews this reemergence of age-old hostility, doubly significant as it had found strong reverberations in Russia's interior where few people had ever met a Jew before, appeared as a startling confirmation of Zionist predictions that in the dispersion anti-Jewish feeling would persevere under any social order. As usual, such outright hostility helped to cement internal Jewish unity, anti-Semitism thus involuntarily mitigating the assimilatory pressures on the Jewish minority.

UKRAINIAN POGROMS

At first the Jews had to pay a very high price for these "benefits" of anti-Semitism. The initial four turbulent years of the Russian Revolution, which were filled with foreign and civil wars and total instability (Trotsky spoke at that time of the government leaving it to the "élan of the masses" to shape the new realities of Soviet life), also witnessed the renewal of pogroms against Jews in a degree far exceeding anything known in tsarist days. The main seat of these disturbances, as in the earlier pogrom waves, was the Ukraine, which, at this point more than ever before had become the primary center of Russian Jewish life. Its more than one and a half million Jews, who before the War had constituted 66.8 percent of the Jewish population in the area remaining under Soviet domination, shrunk somewhat to 58.7 percent in the census of 1926. Yet what took place in the Ukraine was of decisive importance to all Soviet Jewry.

From 1917 to 1920 the Ukraine became a major battleground for ideologies and rivaling nationalisms. The growing Ukrainian national movement had been sharply repressed by the tsarist regime, but it received much encouragement from Austria and Germany. Now leaders of that movement, including socialists, seized the opportunity for building an autonomous, if not sovereign, Ukrainian state. Combined with this national uprising was a social revolution of the downtrodden peasantry. At the outbreak of the revolution 83 percent of the entire Ukrainian population was illiterate, considerably exceeding even the high general average of 76 percent for the whole Tsarist Empire. Most significantly, the ruling groups in the country were members of non-Ukrainian nationalities, particularly Russians, Poles, and Jews. From these three nationalities were recruited the big landowners, industrialists, and government officials, as well as almost the entire urban population, including the majority of proletarians.

Among the non-Ukrainians, the Jews had least reason to oppose Ukrainian nationalism. Many Jewish leaders, both bourgeois and socialist, viewed the prospect of a Ukrainian state, particularly if federated with other Russian republics, with great sympathy. From the outset the Jews were promised not only equality of rights but also full autonomy. As early as July 1, 1917, while still under the Kerensky regime in Petrograd, the Ukrainian Central Council (*Rada*) appointed three vice-secretaries in charge of Russian, Jewish, and Polish affairs. More definitely, a decree issued on January 9, 1918, provided in its very first article that "each of the nations living within the boundaries of the Ukrainian People's Republic has the right to national-personal autonomy—that is, to independent organization of its national life through the organs of a national association, the authority of which extends over all its members within the confines of the Ukrainian People's Republic. None of the nations can ever be deprived, or be restricted in the exercise, of this right." At the same time the vice-secretariats were raised to the rank of ministries. Arnold Margolin, a distinguished Kiev lawyer and for a time Ukrainian deputy minister of foreign affairs, could assert with some justice in May, 1919, that the Ukrainian Parliament had granted Jews more rights than had ever been given them in any other European country.[19]

Little did Margolin and his associates realize how quickly these promises would be swept away in the crucible of the Civil War, and that the successive armies in power would pay little attention not only to Jewish equality and autonomy but even to the very basic safeguards for Jewish life, limb, and property. In its quest for unexpected freedom, the Ukrainian peasantry knew few restraints. Often proceeding to direct action against its oppressive landlords and bureaucrats, it also attacked with even greater venom the Jews whom it held responsible for much of that oppression.

At the same time the Russian minority, especially the Old Guard, tried its old trick of diverting popular animosity to the Jewish scapegoat. As early as September, 1917, the reactionary groups issued a proclamation: "Russian people, awake from your sleep! A short time ago the sun shone and the Russian tsar used to visit Kiev. Now you find Jews everywhere! Let us throw off that yoke, we can no longer bear it! They will destroy the Fatherland. Down with the Jews! Russian people, unite! Bring the tsar back to us." During the many ups and downs that characterized the Ukrainian Revolution these reactionary forces succeeded in April, 1918, in temporarily seizing control of the government under Hetman Skoropadski. They immediately revoked the January decree and tried fully to restore the *ancien régime,* including the old Jewish disabilities. Their rule did not last long enough to carry out this program, but their point of view was at least partially adopted by the anti-Soviet army led by General Anton I. Denikin and also to a lesser extent by the counterrevolutionary armies headed by Generals Alexander V. Kolchak and Peter N. Wrangel. When in the summer of 1919 Denikin conquered almost the entire Ukraine, some 8,000 Jews were massacred.[20]

As it turned out, Jews were even more seriously endangered by the armies led by the Ukrainian nationalists under the socialist Simeon Petliura, who practically lost all control over his armed forces, bent upon slaughter and pillage of Jews. The atmosphere in April, 1919, is well described by the novelist Nikolai Ostrovskii. To a neighbor's question as to who occupied the town on that day, the reply is given: "Let's wait a bit and see; if they start pillaging the Jews, we shall know it's Petliura's men." As later observed by Salomon Goldelmann, formerly a member of the Ukrainian cabinet,

> the complete dependence of the High Command on the will of the officers' corps and the soldiery caused it simply to fear to stand up publicly against the pogromist mood in the army. It was not brave enough to punish the officers and commanders responsible for the bloodshed of Jews. The High Command was afraid to lose thereby its control over the army. In this fashion the authority of the Ukrainian High Command and that of Petliura, as unbelievable as it may seem, rested upon their sufferance of the destruction of the Jewish people.

According to a fairly authentic report, Petliura himself was supposed to have said, "It is a pity that pogroms take place, but they uphold the discipline in the army.[21]

Compared with these two groups, the Red Army could almost appear as a savior. True, in its initial Ukrainian campaigns it too was guilty of shedding Jewish blood. It has been shown that no less than 106 excesses were committed by Red Army units in the Ukraine, although the majority of these were staged by former members of the Ukrainian or Denikin bands which went over to the communist side. The puzzlement of the average Ukrainian Jew in the face of this hostility from all sides is well described by the distinguished Russo-Jewish novelist Isaac Babel. He puts into the mouth of his *Gedali,* an unsophisticated Jewish sympathizer with the Communist Revolution, the significant query: "The Pole was shooting my kind, sir, because he is—the Counter-Revolution; you shoot because you are—the Revolution. . . . The Revolution is a good deed, done by good men. But good men do not kill."[22]

Before long, however, the Red Army High Command took steps to suppress such pogromist proclivities of its underlings, and it succeeded in reestablishing army discipline. With the progressive consolidation of Soviet power in the interior of Russia and its effective struggle against both the counterrevolutionary armies and Poland, peace and order were also restored in the gradually reoccupied southern territories. Ukrainian Jewry, too, now began achieving a new sense of security which it had lost ever since the departure of the German troops from the Ukraine at the end of 1918.

The upshot was that according to fairly reliable statistical accounts prepared in the 1920s, some 30 pogroms and 50 lesser riots ravaged the Ukrainian communities in the course of 1918. Thereafter, in a constant crescendo, the monthly toll of 24 pogroms and 27 lesser riots in January, 1919, increased to 120 pogroms and 28 lesser riots in May, and reached the record of 127 pogroms and 32 lesser riots in August, 1919. In all, the year 1919 witnessed 685 major and 249 minor attacks on Jews. The number began diminishing during 1920, whose total of 142 major and 36 minor assaults did not greatly exceed the attacks of August, 1919, alone. In the first few months of 1921 the storm blew itself out completely. The direct loss of Jewish lives was enormous, easily exceeding 50,000 slain. Together with those who later died prematurely from wounds and contagious and other illnesses contracted during these disturbances, the number may well have reached 150,000, or some 10 percent of the whole Jewish population. The massacres thus left in their wake some 100,000 new widows and 200,000 orphans over and above the multitude of war widows and orphans. In addition, there was raping of Jewish women and a wholesale destruction of Jewish property, communal as well as private. No less than 28 percent of all Ukrainian Jewish houses were said to have been burned, and 10 percent abandoned by their owners. Ukrainian Jewry would not have recovered from these blows in many years, even if it had not simultaneously faced the great challenges of the new revolutionary order.[23]

Curiously, the very Jews who had effectively fought off pogromists during the tsarist regime were now prevented by their socialist leaders from employing these tactics. Anticipating the difficulties, some old-time Zionist and religious leaders demanded the organization of a Jewish self-defense from among the Jewish combatants returning from the front. But the socialist leadership now in control vetoed this suggestion because it considered it unwise, as well as unpatriotic, to form separate Jewish units. In Odessa, where these counsels were disregarded and a small Jewish force of six hundred men was organized, that combat-ready, well-trained, and fairly well-equipped detachment succeeded in staving off all serious attacks during the two turbulent years.[24]

Next to the Ukraine it was White Russian Jewry which suffered most from the pogromist bands such as those led by Bulak Balakhovich, as well as from the invading Polish armies. But its losses were far less severe and its communities could regain their equilibrium much sooner. Upon the withdrawal of the German army of occupation in November, 1918, there was no White Russian nationalist leadership capable of assuming control. The reentering Red Army was welcomed by the urban population then "in the hands of soviets dominated by Russian and Jewish parties, inclined by seven months of German occupation to be sympathetic to the communists." Nevertheless, here too the Soviet troops found the major centers of Jewish life in a state of abject poverty and total disarray.[25]

It is small wonder that this traumatic experience left a permanent imprint on both Yiddish and Russian letters of the following decade or two. With the usual time lag several years passed before the great creativity of the White Russian and to a lesser extent the Ukrainian Yiddish writers was focused on the tragedy which had befallen their communities at the beginning of the revolutionary era. Perhaps the most permanent expression of the Russians' sense of compassion toward the victims of the massacres was lent a dozen years later by the distinguished writer Nikolai Ostrovskii in his extraordinary novel *Kak zakalialas stal* (How the Steel Was Tempered), published in 1932–34. From another angle, Alexander A. Fadeev extolled Jewish heroism in the struggle against the counterrevolutionary army led by General Kolchak, a struggle in which he had himself participated and been twice wounded. In his oft-quoted novel *Razgrom* (The Debacle), written in 1925–26, the novelist depicts in graphic detail the battles fought on the distant Siberian steppes by an outnumbered Red Army detachment led by a Jew, Levinson. So outstanding, indeed, is the role of this Jewish military leader that some foreign translators renamed the novel *Levinson*. In those years, indeed, it looked as if full-fledged Jewish emancipation would become a reality.[26]

However, there were also some descriptions of Jewish exploiters or of Trotsky-like "internationalists," reminiscent of tsarist days—for example, in A. Puchkov's *The Apple* and S. Malashkin's *The Moon from the Right Side*, issued in 1925 and 1927. But these relatively isolated unsympathetic characterizations of individual Jews did not compare with the anti-Semitic bigotry of Russian writers living in exile, exemplified in the typical comment in the Prague periodical *Volia Rossii* of 1925: "Tell me, please, are there many Jews in the Communist Party?/ No, about 60 percent./ And the rest?/ Jewesses."[27]

[12]

Interwar Consolidation

1924–1939

In 1921 the Soviet Union finally reached a certain measure of stability.
After the secession of Poland, Finland, and the Baltic States and the
inclusion of the Ukraine, its western frontiers became clearly defined
and lasted until the outbreak of World War II. What remained still
covered an area of almost one-sixth of the globe. Its stabilized regime,
though subject to frequent changes in policy and methods, now began
rebuilding the country's shattered economic life, particularly through
the promulgation of the New Economic Policy (NEP) in March 1921.

The Jewish minority, too, began adjusting itself to the new situation. Its catastrophic economic position, to be sure, was officially accen-
tuated when its majority of petty businessmen and artisans was declared
socially undesirable. Even its so-called industrial proletariat consisted to
a large extent of petty craftsmen, "bourgeois" in outlook if proletarian
by income. Since at least one-third of the entire Jewish population was
thus destined to sink into the mire of "declassed" persons, everyone
conceded the need of heroic measures aiming at the restratification of
the people through internal migration, agricultural colonization, and
retraining for "useful" occupations. By reopening limited opportunities
for private enterprise, therefore, the NEP helped create a transitional
period for that necessary readjustment.

Simultaneously the new regime initiated a reorganization of Jewish public life to replace the now outworn patterns of the old Jewish community. It certainly was not aided therein by the aforementioned dichotomy between the small minority of Jewish communists and the large majority of Zionists, members of religious groups, and the Bund. Most Jewish members of the Party, moreover, tended to lose all interest in Jewish affairs and to identify themselves more and more with the broader streams of Russian life. It became incumbent, therefore, on the dwindling number of Jewishly interested communist leaders, largely generals without an army, to devise the means for such communal reconstruction.

NEW COMMUNITY

As a recognized national minority Jews were entitled to their own municipal soviets in towns and villages where they formed a majority of the population. None of the large cities fell into this category. But a great many hamlets in the Ukraine and White Russia and quite a few villages there and in the areas of Jewish agricultural colonization qualified for Jewish councils. In many other localities they, together with other minorities, could form mixed soviets. In all these cases Yiddish was declared to be at least one of the official languages.

Not surprisingly, the largest concentration of Jewish soviets was in the Ukraine. In 1925, 38 of the 250 non-Ukrainian soviets in the Ukrainian Soviet Republic were Jewish, equally divided between town and village. In the subsequent rapid growth until 1932, they reached a peak of 168 Jewish soviets (113 in villages and 55 in hamlets). White Russia on the other hand, handled its national divisions differently. According to Yakov Kantor, the chief student of the Soviet-Jewish national organs, White Russia's program "concentrated not on setting up [separate] national districts, but rather on revamping the entire governmental, cooperative and social machinery so as to serve equally all the principal nationalities." As a result, there were relatively few minority soviets, the Jewish councils but slowly increasing from 7 in 1924 to 27 in 1931; among them, only 4 were located in villages. At the same time, the White Russian regime fostered for a time the use of Yiddish on all governmental levels. With greater difficulty Jews also established soviets of their own in the large Russian Republic. Only its western province of Smolensk had enough Jewish enclaves to justify a few such autonomous councils. At the peak in 1930 there were 11 mixed and 1 purely Jewish soviets among the 26 non-Russian soviets in the province.[1]

From the outset it became obvious, however, that these autonomous organs were not intended to promote the interests of the Jewish community, but rather to serve as organs for the diffusion of the new teachings of Marx-Leninism among the Jews. Once again the difficulties were greater here than in the case of other national minorities, for a larger proportion of the new Jewish intellectual élite trained in the communist *Weltanschauung* preferred to leave its small hometowns and to settle in Moscow. Hence many local Jewish soviets, still rigidly excluding their seasoned old-time leaders, even if they happened to sympathize with the new regime, had to get along with untrained, second-rate personnel enjoying little prestige among their own people.

This shortcoming came to the fore also in the newly organized Jewish courts, which at first were relatively more numerous than those of other national minorities. From the beginning the Party's intention was to teach Jews to repair to such courts, rather than to their age-old rabbinic tribunals. During the tsarist regime, as we recall, the latter, whether employing formal talmudic law or, as was more frequently the case, relying on principles of equity, were much more efficient and judicious than the Russian courts. To break the Jews of this ingrained habit, the Soviet Jewish courts used Yiddish in all their proceedings and likewise tried to employ common sense rather than strict legal standards. By 1931 the Ukraine possessed 46 such Jewish judicial divisions, White Russia, 10, and the Russian Republic, surprisingly, fully 11. To cite Kantor again, these courts had "eliminated the rabbinic administration of justice, formerly so common in the Jewish *shtetl*, and had thus emancipated large groups of the poor people from the influence of their class enemy." Of course, these class objectives did not escape the attention of the Jewish public and helped undermine its confidence in these organs of indoctrination, rather than of judicial impartiality. Nevertheless, at their peak in the early 1930s the Jewish soviets and courts gave a semblance of a flowering Jewish autonomous community.[2]

Nor must we overlook the difficulty facing the Bolshevik movement from the outset because its leaders had few lines of communication with the Yiddish-speaking masses. Most of the old Bolsheviks were completely alienated from Jewish culture. Not only Trotsky, who had grown up in a non-Jewish environment, and Lev Kamenev, whose mother was Russian, but also those whose families had but recently left the ghetto often knew little Yiddish, if they did not altogether refuse to be involved in Jewish affairs. Trotsky, for example, seems to have almost completely ignored the *Yevsektsiia*. It was small wonder that for a time the Jewish Commissariat had difficulty in publishing some of its propagandistic pamphlets in Yiddish. According to S. Agurskii, "among the few Jewish Communists who gathered around the Jewish Commissariat there was none who could write a Yiddish pamphlet for publication. Consequently, translations had to be made from the Russian. . . . [But] no money in the world could produce a Jewish writer willing merely to translate Bolshevik literature."[3]

Jewish, or mixed Jewish and non-Jewish, soviets affected, however, but a small minority of Jews. Even at their greatest Ukrainian concentration only some 14 percent of the Jewish population were represented in these councils. In White Russia, because of the peculiar multinational structure of the republic, their representation was quite minimal. What really mattered, therefore, was the participation of Jews in the general elections to municipal, regional, and national organs.

Here the original Jewish economic structure appeared as a serious drawback. The Constitution of the Soviet Union of December, 1922, basically repeating a text adopted in the original fundamental law of the Russian Republic of 1918, provided that only workers and peasants—that is, persons performing "useful" work for society without employing other workers—could enjoy the full franchise. While the exclusion of policemen and security agents of the old regime affected Jews but little, the denial of franchise to all ministers of religion, landlords, entrepreneurs employing other workers, moneylenders, innkeepers, petty shopkeepers, agents, and persons without clear means of support, disqualified a large mass of Jews. In many communities within the old Pale the proportion of declassed Jews even in 1926–27, or some ten years after the revolution, ranged as high as 45 percent. Children of such persons, even after gaining maturity, were still disqualified so long as they were living with their parents or were financially dependent on them. Such disfranchisement went far beyond political life; it involved exclusion from labor unions and clubs, even loss of these victims' share in the food rations. It also impeded their means of earning a livelihood and of enjoying a modicum of social prestige.

Not until 1927 was there any major relaxation in these stringent laws. A decree of January 28, 1927, allowed exceptions to be made in drawing up lists of voters. Perhaps as the result of this decree, or of a widespread practice which preceded it, in 1926–27 there was a sudden drop in the number of disfranchised Jews in the Ukraine from 44.6 to 29.1 percent, although the proportion of such Jews in the larger Ukrainian cities was still very high. It certainly exceeded by far the Jewish ratio of 5.43 percent of the whole, and of 22.77 percent of the urban population of the republic. Further modifications came in 1929–30, which enabled many small artisans, home workers, and unemployed persons to enjoy the franchise because, the legislators argued, these groups had been prevented from doing productive work by the discriminatory legislation of the Tsarist Empire. Also all Jews who had reached their majority after 1924 and lived from their own productive labor could now qualify. Further concessions were made to those Jews who had fought during the civil war on the Soviet side, to orphans left behind by pogrom victims, and to other limited categories, except former merchants of the first or second guild or religious personnel. Finally, those Jews who, as we shall see, were willing to engage in agricultural labors in the colonies assigned to them in the Crimea or Biro-Bidzhan were forgiven for their past "unproductive" activities and were granted electoral rights together with their associated privileges. The most sweeping enactment of this type was issued in November, 1930, in part stating:

> Among the persons allowed to be registered at labor exchanges are also those belonging to nationalities which under tsarism had been limited in their residential rights and their work opportunities, insofar as they [now] belong to the proletarian population of cities and hamlets, or are engaged in handicrafts, and do not exploit wage labor either by themselves or through their families.

In this fashion, the Soviet leaders felt they could partially right the historic wrong committed against the Jewish people during generations of tsarist oppression. These concessions were reinforced by the administration's actual need of employing more usefully the energies of a large and intelligent population, especially after 1928, when the First Five-Year Plan had begun creating serious shortages of labor.[4]

FORCED PACE

Such socioeconomic integration of Jews into the Soviet fabric did not necessarily entail the promotion of their national identity. While still pursuing, on the whole, a favorable policy toward national minorities, the Soviet regime found that the Jews were in many ways an exception to the rule. Stalin, who by that time had become the undisputed autocrat of the Union, had stated his position very clearly in an early article on "Marxism and the National Question," written in 1912. Although, owing to Stalin's antecedents, this brochure focused on the problem of the Asian minorities, it reflected his basic views, even if he subsequently modified them in some details. Here he defined a nation as "a community of language, territory, economic life, psychological agreement (national character) which, historically created and enduring, expresses itself in the community of culture." Further, he made it clear that if only one of these characteristics was missing, such a community did not merit the designation of a nation. He thus sharply repudiated the more subjective approach to national problems developed by the Austrian socialists, which reflected the different situation in the Habsburg Empire and which was far more akin to the Jewish nationalist ideologies.[5]

Jews certainly neither had a territory of their own, nor could they be considered a single economic entity. On the other hand, most of them were persuaded that they had a common national character and also a national language of their own. To be sure, the use of Yiddish was gradually declining, partly because of the migration of many Jews from the former Pale to the interior of Russia, and partly because the new generation preferred to speak Russian. As a result, the percentage of Jews considering Yiddish as their daily language (*Umgangsprakh*) had declined from some 97.3 percent in 1897 to 72.6 percent thirty years later. Nevertheless, the national sentiment among the Jewish masses was still sufficiently strong to cause the government to disregard this irregularity, at least for a time.

One of the first victims of this anomalous situation was the Jewish national commissariat and its regional and local dependencies. At its inception this commissariat had to take over the numerous Jewish communal institutions in the field of social welfare and education. But as hospitals and other organs of social welfare, even schools, began to be administered mainly on a territorial basis by the local and regional soviets, the personnel of the Jewish commissariats found itself out of work. Hence, as early as 1920 the special Jewish Commissariat was downgraded to a mere Jewish department in the general People's Commissariat for National Affairs. Under its guidance the local commissariats still performed the important ideological function of displacing the traditional Jewish parties. But this task, too, proceeded smoothly under the totalitarian regime and was completed within a few years. By 1923 the Jewish department could be reduced, therefore, to a single official and maintained more for appearance's sake than for actual work.

Liquidation of the old Jewish parties also removed the main *raison d'être* of the Jewish sections of the Party. By 1921 even many of the old Bundists and Left Labor Zionists had been absorbed by the dominant party, whereas all the other prerevolutionary ideologies were silenced or driven underground. Externally, the Jewish sections still carried on, and in 1924–26 they still met in All-Russian Conferences of Jewish Sections. These offered a sounding board for the few leading communists still interested in Jewish questions. But it became ever clearer that these meetings had outlived their usefulness, and none was convoked after December, 1926. Finally, the local Jewish sections were dissolved in 1930, as explained in the 1932 edition of the *Large Russian Encyclopedia:* "In order to overcome once and for all the nationalist tendencies still observable in the activity of the Jewish sections, the latter had been reorganized into a Jewish Bureau, according to a decision of the Central Committee of the Communist Party of the Soviet Union. In January, 1930, the Jewish sections were liquidated at the center, as well as locally."[6]

Although such a statement in the *Encyclopedia* could not have appeared without governmental approval, it did not necessarily represent a clearly defined governmental policy. Evidently, the much-harassed top leadership of the Soviet Union, if it thought at all of the Jewish question, had not yet reached any final decision. Certainly, the so-called President of the Union, Mikhail I. Kalinin, though more a figurehead than a real power in Soviet councils, still enjoyed sufficient prestige within and outside the Union for his reiterated pronunciamentos to carry some weight. In a much-quoted speech he delivered on November 17, 1926, at the Congress of the OZET (in Yiddish, GEZERD), the Organization for Settlement of Jewish Toilers on Land, he declared:

> I believe that the drive for settlement on land animating a large part of the Jewish people's intelligentsia and still larger layers of the Jewish poverty-stricken masses, arises primarily from economic necessity and the desire to secure in one way or another a sound economic basis. But if we view this problem ideologically from the national standpoint, I consider it at least possible that behind this drive is concealed a powerful, unconscious mass manifestation: the wish to maintain one's nationality. To me this trend appears as one of the forms of national self-preservation. As a reaction to assimilation and national erosion which threaten all small peoples deprived of the opportunities for national evolution, the Jewish people has developed the instinct of self-preservation, of the struggle to maintain its national identity. . . . The Soviet government, rather than hindering it, helps this, as any other, nationality with all the means at its disposal (and these are far from ample) to achieve these economic goals and the amelioration of the well-being of the Jewish poverty-stricken masses, in the full realization of the importance which such action possesses for the Jewish nationality. . . . The Jewish people now faces the great task of preserving its nationality. For this purpose a large segment of the Jewish population must transform itself into a compact farming population, numbering at least several hundred thousand souls.

True, between 1926, when these words were spoken, and 1932 when the *Encyclopedia* article appeared, there was considerable deterioration of Jewish status and some weakening in both the national drive within the Jewish community and its recognition on the part of the government. Yet Kalinin's words did represent at least one wing of opinion within Soviet leadership, which found expression particularly in the new Biro-Bidzhan project.[7]

BIRO-BIDZHAN

The conception of a Biro-Bidzhan settlement was quite imaginative and transcended by far the mere scheme of agricultural colonization, such as had long been underway in the European parts of the Union. Devised in

1927 by several communists concentrated around the new governmental office, the so-called KOMZET, it was clearly aimed at the national sentiment of the Jewish masses within and outside the Soviet Union. True, adhering to his own ideology, Simeon Dimanshtain warned, at the very inception of the scheme (March 30, 1928), that "we need a compact Jewish settlement not for any kind of nationalist purposes, from which we are far removed, but for the sake of concrete goals which are connected with the general upbuilding of socialism in our country. Under healthier cultural and economic conditions the Jewish masses will be transformed into competent and exemplary builders of the new socialist life. Toward this goal we ought to work energetically while combating all nationalist tendencies." The KOMZET leaders, without contradicting him publicly, effectively used nationalist arguments in their appeals to Jews in Russia and still more to those abroad. They hoped to undermine the still powerful Zionist sentiment among the Jewish masses by proposing an alternate Jewish homeland in the Far East. While condemning Zionism as a tool of British imperialism, this new effort was presented as a means of helping both to meet the great economic need of Jewish restratification and to normalize Jewish life as that of a territorially rooted nationality, similar to the other nationalities of the Union.[8]

Coming to the somewhat startling conclusion that European Russia, including the region around the Azov Sea, no longer had enough space for the development of a Jewish autonomous republic, the KOMZET leaders drew attention to the availability of vast open spaces in the Far East. They selected a large undeveloped region at the confluence of the rivers of Bira and Bidzhan, an area the size of Connecticut and Massachusetts combined, that appeared to be eminently suitable for their purpose. Its greatest advantage was that the Jewish settlers would not have to displace any native population (in contrast to Zionism, which superimposed Jewish rule upon a large Arab population in Palestine), for there only were some thirty thousand inhabitants in that entire district. Soviet propagandists made considerable use of this contrast.

> That is why [wrote M. Seme in December, 1934] we have in Palestine mutual pogroms between Jews and Arabs, Arab delegations appearing before the English High Commissioner against Jews, and Jewish delegations arguing against the Arabs. At the first assembly in the Jewish autonomous region, [on the contrary,] we had delegates of workers in collective farms from among all the peoples of the Soviet Union, and we thus [generated] a new wave of international brotherhood. For this reason Zionism is a basis for counterrevolution and reaction among Jews, a meeting place for all their black fascist and clerical elements, whereas around the Jewish autonomous region are

centered all the sympathies of the progressive and revolutionary elements in the Jewish masses of capitalist lands.[9]

It apparently required little effort to persuade the government of the worthwhileness of that project. Not only were the propagandistic advantages, particularly among foreign Jews, quite obvious, and not only could this undertaking attract financial aid from American Jewish welfare organizations—we shall see how important were the funds spent by the American Agro-Joint on the Jewish agricultural colonization in Soviet Europe—but this scheme would also help to develop the large natural resources of the Far Eastern region for the benefit of the whole Union. There were also weighty international considerations. In the late 1920s the Union became apprehensive of the growing stream of immigration from across the Chinese border. Overpopulated China had been sending waves of émigrés to all neighboring lands and there was real danger that they would also take over the underpopulated regions of eastern Siberia. Immigration from Korea further deepened these fears.

Before long, it also became clear that a successful Jewish colonization of Biro-Bidzhan would help to reduce the menace of Japanese expansion into the Soviet Far East. As the international situation deteriorated, particularly after the Japanese invasion of Manchuria in 1931, the strategic needs of the Far Eastern provinces became doubly manifest. The Soviet Union had to maintain a fairly large army in the provinces adjoining the Pacific coast. Remembering the causes of Russia's defeat in the Russo-Japanese War thirty years earlier and cognizant of the logistic difficulties of supplying its army with ammunition and food from the industrial and agricultural bases in European Russia, the Soviet government considered it doubly imperative to build up nearby agricultural and industrial centers which would, to some extent, resolve that logistic dilemma.

Once again Dimanshtain was most outspoken. In 1934 he declared: "To every conscious participant in the upbuilding of socialism it is as clear as day that it is important for our entire Soviet Union to protect our Far East against any outside intervention. One of the main elements in this undertaking is the necessity to settle that region as densely as possible with reliable, persevering elements. The stronger we are in the Far East, the more remote becomes the danger of war." On the other hand, it was precisely this danger of becoming involved in a Far Eastern war that discouraged some Russian Jews from proceeding to Biro-Bidzhan and many charitable individuals abroad from extending it their financial support. To appease such compunctions of American Jews, Lord Dudley Marley, vice-chairman of the House of Lords and chairman of the World Committee to Aid Victims of German Nazism, declared that, "speaking as a member of the British General Staff and as one who has been all his life a soldier, I can tell you that no General Staff would ever dream of attacking Biro-Bidzhan, because it would be a sheer waste of time. I should think that Biro-Bidzhan would be about the safest place in the world in case of war, because it is entirely self-contained and, if it were cut off, it could live comfortably on its own produce."[10]

More fundamental difficulties arose from the region's natural conditions unfavorable to speedy mass settlement, its great distance from European Russia, and especially the completely haphazard methods of its colonization. The fierce climate itself, with extremes of cold and heat in winter and summer, would have discouraged all but the hardiest pioneers. But the absence of roads and housing made any development scheme doubly arduous and slow-moving. From the beginning, moreover, the project was bedeviled by poor planning and inadequate financing.

Though the colonization scheme was to start in 1929, the committee sent some Jews on ahead in 1928, without making any reasonable provisions at the receiving end. I. Sudarskii, who in his Yiddish monograph on Biro-Bidzhan offered apologies for the 1928 mistake by arguing that without it the scheme would have been delayed by a year, conceded quite a few other administrative errors. The initial selection of localities, often at a great distance from the Trans-Siberian railroad and almost wholly inaccessible by road or waterway, made the transportation of vitally needed building and agricultural supplies extremely arduous. An expert commission of ICOR, an organization subsidized and provided with personnel from the United States, though generally laudatory about the basic potential of Biro-Bidzhan, admitted that "there are many difficult problems to be solved before the land in its present condition could be transformed into fertile fields." At the same time Sudarskii cited highly optimistic meteorological reports, comparing average monthly temperatures and the average rainfall in Biro-Bidzhan's Birfeld with those of Kharkov, forgetting that averages mean little to a population afflicted by violent extremes. Similarly, he tried to show statistically that during the years 1909 to 1917 a small segment of the Biro-Bidzhan soil had yielded 55 poods (ca. 36 pounds each) of summer corn, 59 poods of summer wheat, and 63 poods of oats per hectare. This production more or less equaled the 59.5 poods produced in the Ukrainian breadbasket, and considerably exceeded the average of 54.2 poods of the entire Soviet Union during 1925.[11]

Such optimistic calculations were clearly controverted by the realities, however. At the end of 1929, the local situation had become so desperate that a sympathetic Soviet writer, Viktor Fink, who accompanied the ICOR mission to the Far East described for the Soviet public the dismal conditions at the Tikhonkaia railway terminal whence the colonists were to spread out to their respective settlements. Originally, new arrivals were to stay there only three days, but since the projected settlements were not yet prepared to receive inhabitants, nor were there roads to reach them, the colonists were indiscriminately crowded into some improvised and unsanitary barracks for several months. It is small wonder, then, that many of the new arrivals returned home, although they found it extremely difficult to secure money for the two-week-long trek to western Russia. Those unable to secure transportation looked for employment in the somewhat closer cities of Khabarovsk and Vladivostok. In toto, we are told, of the 950 Jewish arrivals of 1928, 600 departed. In 1929, 1,875 arrived, 1,125 left. The respective figures for the following years are: in 1930, 2,560:1,100; 1931, 3,250:725; 1932–33, 11,000:8,000. Thus only the years 1930–31 witnessed a proportionately larger increase. In other years more than two-thirds of the immigrants departed. During the entire six-year period the ratio was 19,635:11,450. Although the ensuing slow growth sufficiently satisfied the government for it to proclaim, in May, 1934, that the area was to become a Jewish autonomous region, the Jewish settlers, far from becoming a majority, hardly reached one-fifth of the population. Their immigration had in fact also attracted an influx of many non-Jews, a larger percentage of whom remained in the country.[12]

Undeterred, the KOMZET leaders proceeded with their colonization scheme. Despite many disappointments, they believed in 1932 in the feasibility of carrying out a highly ambitious Second Five-Year Plan. In a brochure published by the New York ICOR in that year, A. Kantorovich proposed the adoption of a long-range plan not only to develop Biro-Bidzhan's agricultural resources but also to lay the foundations for big industry. While the cultivated area was to increase from 35,000 to 230,000 hectares in 1937, a number of factories were to be established for the exploitation of the vast forests, the production of building materials, and so forth. The lumber industry could, in that author's opinion, annually cut and process 2,500,000 cubic meters of lumber, while the building industry was to establish no less than 18 large new state factories with an investment of 30,000,000 rubles. By 1937 these and other improvements were supposed to support a population of three hundred thousand souls (five times the number of inhabitants in 1932), of whom more than 55 percent were to consist of gainfully employed persons.[13]

Characteristically, none of the planners seemed to show any concern about the availability of immigrant manpower. Although this Second Five-Year cycle coincided with the world-wide economic depression from 1929 on and the rise of Hitlerism in central Europe and although millions of Jews in Germany, Poland, and the neighboring lands desperately looked for outlets for emigration, the Soviet Union was reluctant to admit such refugees, even if they were willing to proceed to Biro-Bidzhan. It was but a sop to foreign public opinion that the Central Council of the OZET (GEZERD) adopted in 1934 a resolution reading: "We consider it advantageous to bring from abroad certain contingents of qualified Jewish workers in deficit occupations [that is, where shortages of labor exist], taking into consideration the drive of Jewish workers in capitalist countries to take an active part in the socialist upbuilding of the Jewish autonomous region." Rumors soon spread, particularly in the United States, Britain, and France which, then slowly recovering from the Great Depression, were deeply concerned about the multitudes of refugees knocking at their doors, that Biro-Bidzhan was being prepared for large-scale colonization of Polish Jews. According to releases distributed in 1936 by the American Committee for the Settlement of Jews in Biro-Bidzhan (Ambijan), "100,000 Jews in Poland have signified their desire to emigrate to Biro-Bidzhan." This clearly was but a propaganda and fund-raising gimmick. In fact, but a tiny trickle of communist stalwarts was admitted to the Soviet Union and practically none to Biro-Bidzhan.[14]

NATIONALIST OVERTONES

Contemporaries explained this Soviet reluctance by general xenophobia and the government's fear that these foreigners would draw unfavorable comparisons between the standards of life and cultural amenities of the Soviet Union and the Western lands. Spread by word of mouth, such comparisons might indeed have counteracted the rose-colored propaganda dinned into the Soviet citizens by newspapers and radio. But there also were deeper causes. Behind the international Marxist veneer, Bolshevism had always concealed much of its national Russian heritage. Its victory over the more truly internationalist Mensheviks was in part owing to these hidden nationalist mainsprings. Indeed, during the 1930s came a major turn in the general, as well as in the Jewish, policies of the Union. The rising tide of Nazism in Germany, the fulminations of Hitler and his associates against "Jewish" communism, and the spread of virulent anti-Semitic propaganda in other lands—all revived in Russia the memories of World War I and the German invasion. The leaders realized that sooner or later there would come a showdown in which the weaknesses of the Soviet Union might become glaringly apparent. How uncertain even the intellectual Russian leaders had become was shown by the example of the distinguished historian Eugene Tarlé, who had to make a complete *volte face* in the course of a single year (1937–38). While in his earlier treatment of the Napoleonic invasion of Russia in 1812 Tarlé had readily admitted that quite a few peasants had welcomed the French invaders, he had to reverse himself completely in the following year and to extol the patriotic behavior of the peasant masses during the great national war of the last century. Generally, historians of the modern period had to steer their course between the Scylla of historic determinism, which traced all great historic transformations to basic socioeconomic factors, and the Charybdis of the "cult of personality," according to which the impact of a hero like Stalin deeply influenced the historic evolution.[15]

Almost at once a new emphasis was placed upon Russian nationalism and patriotism, as opposed to the previous stress on Marxian internationalism. The revival of the worship of great national heroes like Dmitrii Donskoi and Alexander Nevskii, who had previously rated but slight mention in history textbooks, was symbolic of the new attitude. When in 1938, the Moscow youth ardently applauded the motion picture *Alexander Nevskii*, *Pravda* intoned: "They did it because the Russian nation is imbued with flaming patriotism and had been imbued with it throughout her history." Such rhetoric did not necessarily adumbrate a reversion to the old intolerance toward national minorities. Yet this return to prerevolutionary loyalties appeared doubly threatening as for other reasons as well the Russian nationality was constantly gaining ground at the expense of the smaller nationalities. The successive Five-Year Plans brought large masses of workers from various parts of the Union to old and new industrial centers, predominantly Russian in character, almost automatically inducing the assimilation of these stray groups to the Russian culture. As an efficient melting pot the Red Army, too, served as an agency of unconscious Russification. The census of 1939 showed that the Russian nationality, which in 1926 had had but a slight preponderance of less than 53 percent, had risen in the intervening thirteen years to 58.6 percent, and could look forward to outnumbering all the other nationalities by two to one within a relatively short time.[16]

This evolution was particularly dangerous to Jews, deprived of the solid territorial moorings of most other nationalities and with more and more of their members leaving their concentrated settlements in the Ukraine and White Russia for the great political and industrial centers of the interior. Anti-Semitism, too, had begun to raise its ugly head more or less publicly; the contagion emanating from Germany at this point could no more be kept out of the Russian territories than had been possible during the rise of German literary anti-Semitism in the 1870s. The government's attitude continued unchanged. In an interview with a foreign correspondent in 1931, Stalin styled anti-Semitism a survival of ancient cannibalism. Although such statements may have been made for foreign consumption and were rarely reproduced in the Russian press, they did reflect a certain basic feeling in Party circles that anti-Jewish prejudice could only serve as a divisive and hence destructive force.

In practice, however, the police and court reprisals for anti-Semitic utterances and deeds continued to be very mild. In his aforementioned speech to the OZET of 1926, Kalinin tried to account for the disturbing phenomenon of the Russian intelligentsia's anti-Jewish feeling, in contrast to its alleged absence among workers and peasants, by the large influx of Jewish public servants and other professionals into Moscow which created ill-will among their Russian competitors. At the same time he considered this influx "of colossal importance" to the Jewish people. Asked why there were so many Jews in Moscow he answered: "If I were an old rabbi whose soul yearns for the Jewish nation, I would curse all Jews going to Moscow to accept Soviet positions, for they are lost to the Jewish nation. In Moscow Jewish blood mingles with Russian blood and the second or, at the most, the third generation converts itself into regular Russifiers." Much as Kalinin exaggerated the impact of intermarriage, his reference to the old rabbi was greeted with sympathetic laughter by the assembled Jewish communists. This particular audience, to be sure, also followed Kalinin's argument that both for the preservation of the Jewish nationality and because of the spreading anti-Semitic prejudice, large-scale agricultural colonization in concentrated Jewish settlements had become doubly imperative. Foreign communist sympathizers, however, such as the German author Joseph Roth and the Austrian Otto Heller, drew the more logical conclusion that such policies in the long run spelled the end of Jewish culture. Roth wrote with enthusiasm:

> If the Jewish question is solved in Russia, it will be half solved in all countries (there are hardly any Jewish émigrés from Russia, but rather Jewish immigrants into the country). The religiosity of the masses decreases rapidly, the stronger barriers of religion are falling down, while the weaker ones of nationalism can hardly replace them. If this evolution continues, the era of Zionism as well as of anti-Semitism will be over . . . , perhaps also that of Judaism. Some will welcome this development, others will regret it. But everyone must view with respect the spectacle of one people being freed from the shame of suffering, and another being released from that of maltreating; of the persecuted being liberated from pain and the persecutor from the curse which is worse than pain. This is the great achievement of the Russian Revolution.

This statement was quoted with elation by Otto Heller, whose theme song was the forthcoming "decline of Judaism," although rather inconsistently he also extolled the Russo-Jewish agricultural colonization, particularly in Biro-Bidzhan. But as early as 1919 had not even a dedicated White Russian Yiddish poet, Kloinimus, praised highly the total break of his generation with its past? He himself had declaimed:

I burned to ashes songs of old
Long chanted in serfdom's day,
Tore to pieces the ancient hold
Of a past, left far away. [17]

Understandably, these major transformations in Russian thinking ultimately affected also the developments in Biro-Bidzhan. With the Japanese in occupation of Manchuria and the Germans knocking at the western frontiers, the Russian leaders were in a hurry to prepare their army for the dreaded two-front war. Biro-Bidzhan was no longer viewed as a primarily humanitarian, or at most domestically useful, scheme of helping to restratify the Jewish masses, but as an urgent strategic plan to help maintain an independent Far Eastern force. That is why the leaders now embarked upon a more indiscriminate colonization of that Far Eastern province, welcoming non-Jews on a par with Jews. They actually preferred settlers with previous agricultural or industrial training who could more speedily develop the local resources. Instead of appealing to declassed persons to seek social and economic rehabilitation through that difficult type of pioneering, the government now turned to gainfully employed Jewish artisans and farmers to proceed to the Far East as a matter of patriotic duty.

In 1934, Dimanshtain claimed that the task of converting the Jewish masses to productive work had already been accomplished. Therefore, "a great proportion of the new settlers in Biro-Bidzhan consists of workers or artisans recruited [by government agencies] to go there in order to assume specific tasks." The colonization leaders raised their sights and hoped to bring 9,000 Jews to that region in 1934, 3,500 families or some 14,000 persons in 1935, and 5,000 families or some 20,000 persons in 1936. The number was to be halved in 1937, but altogether some 50,000 Jews were to be settled during those four years. Actually, the number of new arrivals fell far behind that figure, and while we do not have exact data on the number of reemigrants, the total increase in the Jewish population since 1933 was relatively slight. According to the *Emes* of June 3, 1937, the entire Jewish population of Biro-Bidzhan amounted only to some 18,000 or 23.8 percent of the total population of 76,500. [18]

The Jewish minority status in Biro-Bidzhan was further aggravated, as we shall see, by the relatively small percentage of Jews tilling the soil, thus defeating one of the major objectives of the project. The slow progress had clearly demonstrated how far the Jewish autonomous region was from reaching the original goal of becoming a constituent Soviet republic. It clearly could not expect in any foreseeable future to meet two of the three conditions for deserving that status laid down by Joseph Stalin at the end of 1936 in his famous address "On the Draft Constitution of the U.S.S.R." The dictator insisted that in order to qualify for the designation *republic* "the nationality which gives its name to a given Soviet republic must constitute a more or less compact majority within that republic" and that "it should have a population of, say, not less, but more than a million."[19]

In short, it became quite manifest that this high-sounding scheme which was to outshine the Zionist experiment of Palestine was an almost total failure. Concurrently with the *Emes* report appeared that of the British Royal Commission, headed by William R. W. Lord Peel, which for the first time officially suggested the partition of Palestine into an Arab and a Jewish state. Over and above the declining economic strains on Russian Jews, who now found greater employment opportunities in the rapidly expanding industrial centers in European Russia, there was, of course, the basic difference between the tremendous emotional appeal of the Holy Land to Jewish youth everywhere—in the early years of the revolution even the Soviets tolerated the training of young Jewish *Halutsim* (Pioneers) for the redemption of that ancestral land—and the rather artificial scheme of building a Jewish home in a remote Far Eastern territory, whose very name, Biro-Bidzhan, had to be especially invented for this purpose.[20]

Between 1937 and the outbreak of World War II, the progress of the Biro-Bidzhan colonization was severely impeded by the great purges throughout Russia, which also victimized many leaders of that project on the spot, as well as in European Russia (among them Dimanshtain, Alexander Chemeriskii, Frumkina). Unwittingly, Jews became major objects of that wholesale liquidation of the old leadership. Even in the preceding years the number of Jews in the Communist Party, in the sprawling bureaucracy, and in the Red Army officers' corps was steadily declining proportionately, if not in absolute figures. As education became more widespread and more and more Russians became available for public service (in some respects, membership in the Party could also be considered such), the ratio of Jews steadily declined. We recall that between 1925 and 1930 that ratio had dropped from 5.2 percent to 3.8 percent. Compared with the Jews' percentage of 1.8 of the total population and their generally much higher educational level, these figures certainly were not excessive. Similarly, in the Red Army Jews had their normal ratio of 1.8 percent among the soldiers, but 4.4 percent among the officers, particularly in the medical corps, in the administration, and among the "political commissars." Only in general government service, which in the Soviet Union included all educational posts and jobs in banks and in most other businesses, did the Jewish proportion reach 8.6 percent in 1929.[21]

In the 1930s there was considerable retrogression also in this area. Our information concerning membership in the Communist Party is no longer as detailed as that from the preceding decade. We shall see that even the percentage of Jews in the professions declined. Most illuminating are the statistics of Jews elected in 1938 to the Supreme Soviets of the respective republics. Since such elections were based on single-party tickets, their selection was quite deliberate and centralized. While in the Russian Republic the percentage of Jewish members was 4.1 or almost five times the Jewish ratio in the population (0.9 percent), in the Ukraine only two Jews were elected out of a total membership of 304. This tiny percentage of 0.7, or but one-seventh of the population strength of 4.9 percent, can be explained only by the Party's conscious appeasement of the Ukrainian majority, which was now reverting to its anti-Semitic atavisms. This disproportion becomes doubly evident when one realizes that, for instance, the Supreme Soviet of the distant republic of Tadzhikistan embraced fully eleven Jews, or 3.9 percent of its membership, as against their tiny ratio of but 0.3 percent in the population. Evidently, in this and other Asiatic republics there neither existed any anti-Semitic heritage nor perhaps any conscious differentiation between Russian-speaking Jews and other Russians.[22]

More spectacularly, the great purges of 1936–1938 removed the most prominent names among the Jewish leaders of the Communist Party. After the defeat of Trotsky in his contest with Stalin for succession to Lenin, there still remained a great many "old" Bolsheviki in the highest echelons of Party and government. Now the heads of Zinoviev and Kamenev had rolled in the dust, Radek was sent into exile, and many others simply disappeared, with or without trial. At the time when Marshal M. N. Tukhachevskii was being tried for conspiring with the Germans, the Jewish general Jan Gamarnik, chief of the Political Administration of the Army, committed suicide. Otherwise he would undoubtedly have joined the nine other fellow members of the Central Committee of the Party who were executed, or his thirty-six other colleagues (out of a total of seventy-one) who just disappeared. Even two years later, at the Eighteenth Party Congress of 1939, Gamarnik's successor as head of the Army's Political Administration, L. Mekhlis, spoke of "The Gamarnik-Bulin gang of spies" who had allegedly done their greatest damage by appointing traitors to the high levels of the officers' corps. No less than fifteen thousand Red Army officers were apparently liquidated, greatly contributing to the undermining of the morale and the organizational strength of the armed forces in the face of their approaching emergency. These dramatic trials were highly publicized in the country and abroad, but thousands of lesser officials and Party leaders were executed or banished to Siberia, unsung and even unmentioned except in the closest circles of relatives and friends.[23]

Since in the intervening two decades there had grown up a new generation of Party leaders and executives, the condemned were easily replaced by persons in whom Stalin placed greater trust. At the top of the Party structure and the Council of Commissars there remained only one Jew, Lazar M. Kaganovich, probably spared from the purge by his family relationship to the Russian dictator. All of this did not prevent the German propagandists from shouting from the rooftops about "Jewish" Bolshevism and from constantly reiterating the older, long-superseded data. If the earlier rise of a number of Jewish politicians and agitators, for the most part completely estranged from their people, to positions of leadership in the Party and government had bestowed few benefits upon Russian Jewry at large, their sudden elimination as "traitors" to the cause could only cast aspersion on the trustworthiness of the whole people. It merely added fuel to, and furnished a convenient cloak for, the growing anti-Semitism among the intelligentsia and the masses.

[13]

Socioeconomic Reconstruction

❦

In the first twenty-two years of the Soviet regime the Jewish population underwent great changes, not so much in numbers as in its diffusion through the country. Our information is limited to results of censuses which from the outset contained considerable margins of error. The very definition of "Jew" was based largely upon the personal declaration of each individual telling the enumerator to which nationality he belonged. We know that, like Trotsky, many Russified Jews, particularly if living outside the original Pale of Settlement, considered themselves members of the Russian nationality, even if many of their neighbors still regarded them as Jews.

For the sake of comparison, moreover, the data assembled in 1897 by the last fairly acceptable tsarist census had to be reworked to cover the areas which after 1921 emerged as definitive parts of the Soviet Union. This task was mainly performed by ORT officials, whose inadequate facilities necessarily left a considerable residuum of doubt. An official Soviet census, attempted in 1920, was never carried through because of the unsettled conditions in many areas. We thus have to rely largely on the census of 1926, which has indeed been examined rather carefully by scholars in the Soviet Union and abroad. The next census of 1939 was soon beclouded by World War II, although Soviet scholars still had a chance partially to work up its results before the German invasion of June, 1941.

BIOLOGICAL SLOWDOWN

A comparison between the three censuses of 1897, 1926, and 1939 shows that the Ukrainian segment of Soviet Jewry was constantly shrinking. From two-thirds (66.8 percent) in 1897, it declined to but slightly more than half (50.8 percent) forty-two years later. However, in absolute figures it diminished only by about 100,000 persons between 1897 and 1926, and by another 41,000 in the subsequent thirteen years. On the other hand, the Russian Republic (including the tiny Kazakh and Kirghiz communities) more than quadrupled during these forty-two years (from 209,000 to 969,000). In 1939 this republic embraced 32.1 percent of all Soviet Jewry, overtaking White Russia, whose percentage had dwindled from 18.8 to 12.4 percent. Between them these three republics still embraced 95.3 percent of all Jews in the Union. In comparison with the Union's general population, however, the Jewish percentage had dropped sharply from 2.4 percent in 1897, to 1.82 percent in 1926, and to 1.78 percent in 1939.[1]

The explanation for all these changes is not difficult to find. In the seventeen years before World War I the tremendous emigration to the Western Hemisphere and other lands had drained away a much larger percentage of Russian Jews than non-Jews. During World War I, Jews, living close to the battlefields, sustained greater losses than Russia's population as a whole. This was especially true during the Civil War of 1918–21, when pogroms directly took, as we recall, a toll of well over 50,000 Jewish lives in addition to their generally increased mortality caused by the disturbed conditions in the exposed areas.

More significant was therefore the decline of the Jewish ratio in the peacetime years of 1926–39, when the Union's total population increased by some 16 percent, while the Jews added only some 13 percent to their numbers. In part, this slowing down resulted from their decidedly lower birth rate. Even between 1897 and 1926 the Jewish birth rate had fallen from 35.9 to 24.6 per 1,000 inhabitants, whereas among the non-Jews the decline from 50.2 to 43.3 per 1,000 was far more moderate. True, Jewish mortality was also much lower; in 1926 it was only 9.1 per 1,000, leaving an excess of births over deaths of 15.5 per 1,000. But the non-Jews had an excess of 23.3 per 1,000. These trends seem to have continued in the following thirteen years. Although exact data are not available, it is very unlikely that mortality should have gone much below the 9.1 figure of 1926, whereas natality probably declined further, particularly in view of the growing proportion of Jews living in cities. Unfortunately, the figures are not absolutely comparable, because the census of 1897 recognized three categories—cities, hamlets, and rural districts—whereas the two Soviet censuses assigned the "hamlets" to either the urban or the rural category. According to the 1897 census, of the total Jewish population in the larger area of the Pale 48.84 percent lived in cities, 33.05 percent in hamlets, and 18.11 percent in rural districts. By 1926, the urban population made up 82.4 percent, while the rural Jewish population amounted to only 17.6 percent. Since in 1926 this classification included many inhabitants of the *shtetls*, formerly listed as hamlets, this reduction is doubly meaningful. This process of urbanization continued in the subsequent thirteen years, reaching a ratio of 87 percent of urban as against 13 percent of rural Jews. All this despite the progress of the agricultural colonization, including that of Biro-Bidzhan. At the same time, the Jewish percentage of the entire urban population, then in a period of rapid expansion, was actually declining. Even in the Russian Republic, despite the great influx of Jews from the western areas, the ratio of Jewish urbanites fell from 3.1 percent to 2.2 percent between the two censuses of 1926 and 1939. In both the Ukraine and White Russia that percentage was almost halved (it declined from 22.7 to 11.7 and from 40.2 to 23.9, respectively). In the whole Union the Jews now constituted only 4.7 percent of the urban population, as against 8.2 percent thirteen years earlier.[2]

Nonetheless, in those very years a most significant shift of the Jewish masses to the large cities occurred, particularly to the cities of Russia's interior. While Odessa, with its 153,194 Jews, still retained its preeminent position even in 1926, it had grown in the preceding three decades by only 10 percent. On the other hand, Moscow's Jewry grew from 8,095 in 1897 to 131,244 in 1926; that of Leningrad (St. Petersburg) from 16,944 to 84,480; that of Kiev from 32,093 to 140,256; and that of Kharkov from 11,013 to 81,138. This process continued to accelerate thereafter. Unofficial estimates ranked the Jewish community of 300,000 to 400,000 Jews in Moscow in 1939 as the largest community not only in the Union but in all of Europe. With 250,000 Jews Leningrad likewise belonged among those cities with the largest metropolitan concentrations of European Jewry. Understandably, in such capitals the birth rate tended to sink, as it did elsewhere in that period, while intermarriage and other assimilatory factors operated with redoubled strength. The same was true in a different way in those new industrial centers created by the operation of the Five-Year Plans. Magnitogorsk in the Ural Mountains, for instance, had a community of 40,000 Jews, all of them new arrivals in a strange environment and with relatively few contacts with one another. This feeling of isolation was doubtless responsible for the partial failure of the directed emigration of trained young Jewish workers to the Ural region. At the beginning of the systematic planning in 1928–29 only 538 of 1,220 young apprentices assigned to the planned schools actually reached their destinations, and but 350 remained.[3]

At the same time the Soviet Union was confronted by the problem of Oriental Jews who had lived in the Asiatic areas almost from the dawn of their recorded history—certainly since the early centuries of the Christian era. In the Republic of Uzbekistan, which included the old Jewish community of Bukhara, there still were 38,000 Jews in 1926, the majority of them of Oriental origin. For many centuries they had valiantly fought against assimilation by the surrounding cultures. They developed their own Tadzhik dialect of the Persian language, were for the most part deeply religious, and were intensely attached to Hebrew culture. Now they were told that they had to live without their religious tradition, use Tadzhik rather than Hebrew as their national language, and adjust their economic pursuits to the new demands. According to the communist economist Yurii Larin, an official investigation in 1928 had shown under what abysmal conditions some of these Asiatic Jews (often wrongly equated with the Caucasian Mountain Jews) lived, particularly when they left their old habitats. We are told that "when they arrived in Derbend, they dug holes in the ground which they covered above against rain. In these holes these people still live after ten years. . . . One can easily guess their high rates of mortality and disease."[4] However, these were deep-rooted cultural traits of the ancient Jewry inhabiting the Iranian Plateau and its environs. They appeared equally shocking to the Israeli immigration authorities when the mass influx from those regions came in recent years. But in Israel the acculturation of these Oriental groups proceeded at a much faster rate.

Another interesting demographic phenomenon was the disproportionate excess of women over men in the Jewish population. If in 1926, 1,115 women were counted for every 1,000 Jewish men, in contrast to a ratio of 1,069:1,000 in the general population, one could still explain it by the greater number of males lost during World War I and the subsequent pogroms. But that disproportion was still evident in 1939 when the Jewish ratio was 1,102:1,000, although by this time the general ratio had inexplicably increased to 1,087:1,000. Undoubtedly one of the reasons was that men more readily left their old habitations and moved into the interior of European and Asiatic Russia, where some failed to register altogether or to identify themselves as Jews. This fact is illustrated by the greater preponderance of women in the Ukraine and White Russia than in the other republics. Here the plethora of female members among Jews actually increased between the two censuses. It amounted to 1,140 and 1,122 in 1926, respectively, and rose to 1,160 and 1,139 thirteen years later. On the other hand, by 1939 in the Russian Republic as well as in Uzbekistan the two sexes had become almost fully balanced—1,013 or 1,001:1,000. Only in the Turkmen Republic did both censuses reveal

fewer Jewish women than men, 819 or 844 per 1,000. A similar disproportion also existed in 1939 in the rural districts throughout the Union.
Both phenomena doubtless resulted from a preponderance of male
immigration.[5]

"PRODUCTIVIZATION"

Most complicated and often involving great personal and family trage-
dies was the painful process of economic restratification. Apart from
being ruined by wars and pogroms, the Jewish communities now faced
the task of transferring the majority of their members from "unproductive" to "useful" occupations. The economic structure of prewar Russian Jewry is well illustrated by the results of the census of 1897. We
recall that, roughly speaking, the gainfully employed Jewish population
was divided into three major categories: (1) artisans, home workers, and
factory workers, together amounting to 46.7 percent; (2) merchants,
petty shopkeepers, commercial agents, and others, 39.4 percent; (3) all
the rest, including 2.33 percent farmers and 4.38 percent professionals
and civil servants. In addition, there were a host of unemployed or
persons without a steady occupation.

First to be declared unwanted was the commercial class. This transition was not only difficult for them but also for the Ukrainian and White
Russian Republics, where, as in the rest of the Pale, Jews had constituted fully 72.8 percent of that entire class. That percentage diminished
during the wars and pogroms because many Jews had died or escaped
either to the east or west. In 1921 the NEP temporarily reopened some of
these occupations, but the pressures, especially on the small businessmen, remained in full force. The taxes imposed upon them usually were
quite ruinous. One case revealed by an official investigation during June
and July, 1925, in the district of Proskurov, which had severely suffered
during the pogroms, showed that while the entire stock of merchandise
owned by a poor storekeeper was valued at 17 rubles, his taxes
amounted to 40 rubles. Unable to pay, he was condemned to a six-
month prison term. An incident in the small town of Saratov is another
illustration of persecutions by tax collectors: forty-five persons were
summoned to a court seventeen miles away for alleged tax arrears
ranging from 9 to 30 kopeks. It is small wonder, then, that "the population compares the methods of collecting special debts and taxes with the
activities of the bandits of 1920." The result was that many Jews pursued
their trade clandestinely and in defiance of the law. Naturally, if caught
in illicit trade—including black marketeering or foreign exchange transactions, all of which greatly flourished during that era of great scarcity
and tremendous depreciation of the ruble—they were severely pun-

ished. The frequency of such trials merely added to the zest of the prosecutors and increased the ill-feeling of the population toward Jews. That is why the census figures of 1926, which indicate that only 125,000, or 11.8 (13.3 in the Ukraine alone) percent of all gainfully employed Jews belonged to the commercial class, are undoubtedly an understatement. Many of those classified as pursuing "indefinite occupations" and totaling 7.3 percent doubtless included commercially active persons. Nevertheless, the days of the legitimate private merchant, Jewish and non-Jewish, were numbered. According to the economist Genrikh I. Neiman, private retail trade was reduced from its still dominant position of 57.7 percent of all trade in 1923–24, to but 5.6 percent in 1930, to be almost wholly suppressed from 1931 on.[6]

Apart from its economic consequences, the persistence of the Jewish merchant, whether during the NEP period or later, also created much ill-feeling among the non-Jews. Even after the independent trader had submitted to socialization and become a business agent in a state or cooperative commercial enterprise he, if a Jew, became the focus of many grievances of the dissatisfied population. As late as 1935, Jews may have occupied more desirable positions in the socially controlled Ukrainian trade than the Ukrainians, but they were far outstripped by the Russians. Yet in many areas a NEP man had become synonymous with a Jew, and he was so treated in some of the belles-lettres of the period. When he later served mainly as employee in a state wholesale establishment or a retail store, during the prevailing periods of scarcity, he was accused by the resentful consumers of diverting the scarce merchandise for his own or his friends' benefit. It made little difference that the vast majority of the former Jewish shopkeepers were themselves in a more or less permanent state of starvation. What a Jewish agronomist said at a convention of Jewish farmers in Minsk in January, 1928, about the conditions in the small Jewish communities was doubly valid for the preceding years. He contended that the people of these Jewish hamlets were dying of hunger three times daily, and that their only foodstuff consisted of potatoes.[7]

Nor were artisans clearly separated from traders. Not only had they traditionally engaged in a variety of commercial transactions, such as buying raw materials and selling their own finished products in the market, but some had now found the going extremely difficult and tried to supplement their income by one or another form of trading, mostly clandestine. However, even without such subterfuges the whole artisan class was at first condemned by the communist leadership as "exploiters." This was especially true since many of them employed apprentices and journeymen; in other words, by definition they had lived off the labor of others. But not even craftsmen working only with the aid of their own families escaped the wrath of the impatient reformers.

As a result, the whole class faced enormous difficulties in securing raw materials or credit from the governmentally controlled suppliers; it was also subject to excessive taxation. The general trend was to force artisans into cooperatives, which were given much more favored treatment by the officials and thus could produce wares both of higher quality and at lower prices. This favoritism is well illustrated in White Russia, where in 1926 only 5 percent of all craftsmen had joined cooperatives, which were allotted fully 80 percent of all available raw materials. However, this solution which seemed so easily acceptable in theory had many adverse practical effects. The Moscow *Emes* of February 1, 1923, includes a pathetic description of the economic conditions in the small town of Molev; the correspondent, S. Margolin, wrote:

> In order to evade the strict regulations, some craftsmen tried at the beginning to form cooperatives [*artels*] and to work by themselves without engaging the assistance of any workers. . . . During the season members of these cooperatives have worked beyond their strength, labored twelve hours or more daily, only in order to produce without the aid of outside workers.
>
> To end these evasive methods of the artisans trying to get along without workers, the district office of the professional associations tried to impose the law of an eight-hour day also upon the artisans themselves, and resolved that no craftsman should be allowed to work after 6 P.M. It was thought that in this way the artisans would be forced to maintain hired labor and with its aid keep up the production on its previous levels. But all these means did not save the situation. The artisans preferred to curtail production or even to liquidate it completely, rather than hire workers. . . .
>
> In general the organization of production in our time is connected with so many difficulties that everyone finds it more profitable to trade in merchandise rather than to produce. The result is that the majority of artisans and workers in Molev spend more of their time in the market place than in the factory. There one can find workers, specialists in various branches, and particularly former leather workers. In short, speculation increases at the expense of production.

Similar complaints were also heard from other smaller and larger cities, except that in Odessa a correspondent mentioned a new practice of entrepreneurs distributing work among many home workers, who labored at their homes under difficult and unsanitary conditions from fifteen to eighteen hours a day. In shoemaking alone there existed six hundred such workers. Outwardly, of course, these laborers could be classified as independent artisans working on their own account. In the very capital, according to one plaintiff, the Second State Candy Factory found itself overstocked with products and sent out its best workers to sell them in the market. The *Emes* correspondent described this situation under the sensational title, "A Factory which Produces Agents."[8]

Quality had also suffered from the generally unsettled conditions during the wars and pogroms, which had depleted the available well-trained manpower and opened the road for the entry of substandard producers. The new legislation which discriminated against entrepreneurs employing outside labor strongly affected the very training process of skilled artisans. It has been estimated that in 1897, the approximately 259,000 Jewish artisans consisted of about 50 percent of master artisans and another 50 percent of outside assistants and apprentices. By 1926 the number of such employees had shrunk to 15 percent (even that largely because their dismissal had become very difficult) and in some areas they practically disappeared. For example, in 1924 the city of Minsk had 664 Jewish craftsmen, but only 7 apprentices. According to the census of 1926, in all of the Ukraine there were 126,462 Jews living from crafts, or 20.6 percent of all gainfully employed Jews. Of these, only a small minority of 9,471 (or some 7.5 percent) employed outside help, whereas some 80,000 worked by themselves, while 21,000 others worked together with some 16,000 members of their families. Evidently, the propaganda against the exploiters of labor, combined with the fear of sinking into the status of declassed persons, made the vast majority of Jewish craftsmen wary of engaging the services of even apprentices or journeymen. Understandably, this failure to train qualified apprentices resulted in a general deterioration of all crafts, individual or cooperative, because they fell into the hands of many self-taught and ill-equipped persons.[9]

Such perseverance of Jewish craftsmen was facilitated by communal self-help. From time immemorial Jewish communities have tried to aid their distressed members by extending charitable loans through societies organized by public bodies. Especially from the days of the Jewish Colonization Association's widespread social welfare activities in Tsarist Russia the Jewish communities had inherited a system of charitable loan banks which were very helpful to Jewish artisans. Even in 1926 the former area of the Pale still had some 300 such institutions, embracing 85,000 members. Although now these institutions were dependent on loans from the state banks and their own future was quite dismal—they were to be speedily liquidated by the government—they helped for a time to maintain the Jews' hold on the small private industries. In that year, according to some estimates, 85 percent of all private producers of clothing and 75 percent of all shoemakers in the Ukraine and White Russia were Jews. However, one establishment after another was closed; many individuals found their licenses either revoked or not renewed. Before long most members had to join the industrial proletariat in state factories. Yet as late as 1941 it is estimated that some 14 percent of Soviet Jewry (at that time augmented from the annexed

Polish and Baltic provinces) were still making a living from some craft or other.[10]

When one considers that a great many Jews in the remaining occupations also found themselves in the position of economic undesirables, one may readily gauge the extent of the economic catastrophe which engulfed Russian Jewry. Certainly, not only the former wealthy groups of bankers, industrial entrepreneurs, and landlords, but also the numerous religious officials and teachers who had formed the elite of the earlier generations, now found themselves deprived of the simplest means of earning a living. Because for them the transition was so sudden and because psychologically they were least prepared to face the hardships of the dispossessed, they would have suffered severely even if the law had not specifically singled them out for sharply discriminatory treatment as "declassed" persons.

INDUSTRY AND PROFESSIONS

It was a sign of the tremendous vitality of Soviet Jewry that rather than throwing up its hands in despair, it energetically set about the task of reconstructing its shattered economic basis of subsistence. The immediate remedy was to join industrial labor, which was now not only given the opportunity to earn a fairly decent livelihood, but even became the kingpin of the new society. Of course, there had also been quite a few Jewish factory workers in prewar Russia. In 1897 the Pale of Settlement already included 46,300 Jewish factory workers among the 547,300 Jews classified as "workers" in the census. Although the important industrial centers of Lodz and Bialystok, with their thousands of Jewish workers in textile and other factories, had now been lost to the Soviet Union, a substantial percentage of that Jewish industrial proletariat still remained, particularly in the Ukraine and White Russia. While the numbers of people in the other categories of "workers," under which the original census had included craftsmen and their employees as well, were gradually shrinking, factory labor was speedily increasing even before the First Five-Year Plan of 1928. According to the 1926 census, the number of Jewish factory workers had risen in the Ukraine to 40,149, in White Russia to 10,639, in the city of Moscow to 3,768, and in Leningrad to 3,692. In the latter two cities the Jewish factory workers exceeded in number all other categories of workers among Jews. Together with the still tolerated craftsmen and home workers this "working class" included, according to the census of 1926, 34.3 percent of all gainfully employed Jews.[11]

Of some interest is also the occupational distribution of these various categories of workers. Not surprisingly, most of them still pursued the old trades in one or another branch of the clothing industry. Nearly one-third of all Jewish workers in the Ukraine (31.7 percent) were engaged in the needle and allied trades. To these one must add textile workers (including weavers and dyers), 4.7 percent, and leather and fur workers (including cobblers and furriers), 18.3 percent. In White Russia the percentages were somewhat similar (24.6, 4.0 and 27.2 percent respectively), while in Moscow the respective ratios differed considerably (23.8 percent, 13.6 percent, and 6.3 percent), as they did in Leningrad (30.4 percent, 8.0 percent, and 8.7 percent). The textile workers were, of course, primarily factory hands. On the whole, Jews constituted a very high percentage of all workers in these fields. In White Russia they were fully 72.3 percent of all clothing-industry workers; 74.3 and 65.5 percent of all textile, leather and fur workers. Nor was this their highest percentage; it was exceeded by that of the Jewish printers, who, not very numerous as a class, totaled 88 percent of all White Russian and 75.4 percent of all Ukrainian printers. Other important branches of industry with a more than average Jewish concentration included the food and metal-working industries, although here, and still more so in the building and lumber industries, Jews often lagged behind their ratio in the urban population.[12]

The number of Jews entering new fields of endeavor such as transport and communications also increased at an accelerated pace. Good examples are offered by the situation in White Russia. For many generations past, Jews had played an important role in transporting persons or goods in horse-driven carriages. The *baal agole* had long been a familiar figure on the Jewish street; he had often been depicted as the typical proletarian in Jewish belles-lettres of the prerevolutionary period. The number of Jewish railroad workers and employees in White Russia rapidly increased from 29 in 1926–27 to 82 two years later. During the same two years Jewish postal and telegraph workers in the Republic more than doubled (from 49 to 100 persons), whereas the total of such workers from the other national minorities, Russians and Poles, as well as from the White Russian majority group actually declined. Another statistical table shows that in the rapidly expanding major White Russian workers' cooperatives in ten industrial branches (paper, lumber, leather, metal, printing, foodstuffs, building, textiles, chemicals, and tailoring), the participation of White Russians more than trebled between 1924 and 1927. Yet the Jews still maintained their ratio of about half, dropping from 50.4 to 49.4 percent (they actually increased in absolute figures, from 14,213 in 1924 to 23,452 in 1927), while the percentage of Russian workers declined from 10.7 to 9.0, that of Poles from 7.3 to 4.4.[13]

After 1926, the process of industrialization, which had become the cynosure of all eyes, finally began opening new opportunities for Jewish workers as well. While the available data do not clearly distinguish between wage and salary earners, there was a tremendous leap forward in both categories. Jointly the two groups increased from 394,000 in 1926, to 562,000 in 1930, 787,000 in 1931 and more than 1,100,000 in 1935. The percentage of manual workers in these years rose from 38.8 percent to 40.4 percent, 43.5 percent, and may have ultimately exceeded 50 percent of these totals.

If by the time of the census of 1939 the percentage of manual laborers had declined to 43 percent, out of a total of nearly 1,500,000 Jewish wage and salary earners, this was owing to the increase of Jews endowed with higher technical skills, including many who started as manual laborers and worked their way up to managerial or semimanagerial positions. Although no longer quite so easy as in the early, anarchical stages of the revolution, when councils of workers often seized factories and appointed some members to serve as managers regardless of their lack of technical qualifications, such rise from the ranks continued throughout the years. On the other hand, managers often found themselves in the unenviable position of being blamed for all failures to live up to some preconceived, sometimes wholly unrealistic, plans. The great labor turnover and absenteeism must also have caused many a sleepless night to bewildered managers. In the early 1930s, the average tenure of a factory worker had sunk to but four months, to rise gradually to a little more than a year from 1934 on. Incidentally, this extreme mobility of workers, which has plagued the Soviet economy to the present day, also makes the Russo-Jewish industrial statistics of that period even more dubious. Yet for whatever validity this estimate may have, according to Lev Zinger, the only Soviet Jewish student partially able to analyze the results of the 1939 census, fully 71.2 percent of all gainfully employed Jews belonged to the two categories of wage and salary earners. Together with the other governmentally approved activities in agriculture (5.8 percent), cooperative crafts (16.1 percent) and professions, Jews were thus absorbed in approved economic processes, completely eliminating the original disproportionate number of "unproductive" Jews.[14]

Equally noteworthy was the qualitative change in the types of employment. According to Lev Zinger, the proportion of Ukrainian Jews who were miners, which in 1926 amounted to only 0.1 percent of the Jewish wage earners, had risen to 3.3 percent by 1936, although these men first had to overcome deep-rooted anti-Jewish prejudices of non-Jewish fellow workers, as graphically described in a play by Peretz Markish and a novel by H. Orland published in 1933. Metal workers doubled in that period from 14.1 to 28.3 percent; chemists increased from 0.8 to 2.8 percent, and so forth. This huge increase was made possible by the rapid progress of industrialization under the two Five-Year plans. Overcoming the sharp declines during the early years after the revolution, in 1937 the Soviet Union produced three times as much oil and steel, four times as much coal, and twenty-five times as much machinery as in 1913. A number of Jewish names also began appearing among the Stakhanovite workers in various industries. One Avrom Blidman distinguished himself as a longshoreman. In the Moscow Stalin Automobile Works one Perlshtain succeeded, in 1938, in fulfilling his norm three times over. Summarizing these transformations within a mere decade, Zinger writes:

> The large absolute increase in the number of workers of the Jewish nationality; their heightened specific weight; their migrations from the hamlets and cities of the former Pale to the central industrial regions of the Soviet Union; the numerical growth of Jewish workers in the leading branches of the socialist industry—all this has demanded that the entire class of Jewish laborers should, within an extremely short period, be catalyzed in the socialist industrial cauldron, should free itself from all petty bourgeois, religious, nationalistic prejudices, and should be organically integrated into the general multinational workers' family.

Moreover, this staggering task was accomplished despite the difficulties generated by prejudiced Gentile workers, "through daily educational work in an international vein" which was conducted in every factory and plant. While one may dismiss such propagandistic rhetoric, the factual substratum of Zinger's assertions reflects at least a modicum of reality.[15]

Most of what corresponded to the liberal professions and communal employees before the revolution was now also included in the category of salaried personnel. It has been estimated that in 1897 there were some 1,500 writers and artists, 4,500 doctors and other medical personnel, 10,000 religious functionaries, 16,000 teachers, and so forth. In the following twenty years before the revolution, there was a great onrush of Jews to colleges and universities, both domestic and foreign, and the number of Jewish professionals increased very greatly. Regrettably, no exact statistics are available for 1917. But it is generally known that while the revolution was antagonistic to religious personnel and the legal profession, it sharply increased the demand for doctors, teachers, and government officials of all kinds. The discouragement of the legal profession by the new society, however, did not prevent certain invidious comparisons between the number of functioning Jewish and non-Jewish lawyers. Such complaints were muted under the Soviet regime but came out into the open during the German occupation. A Ukrainian newspaper complained in March, 1942, that of the 250 lawyers practicing in Kharkov only 35 were non-Jews.[16]

Reference has already been made to the considerable percentage of Jews in government employ in the early years after the revolution and their subsequent gradual decline in relative—with a simultaneous increase in absolute—figures. With the progress of socialization more and more occupations fell under the category of government service, including even personnel active in the creative arts, whose livelihood now depended on state stipends. Factories and banks were socialized, and their managerial class belonged to the upper ranks of salaried workers. An interesting statistical account for the Ukraine and White Russia during the mid-1930s showed that the percentage of Jews in managerial capacity was as high as 20.7 and 24.5 percent, respectively. In addition there was a category of so-called experts, who amounted to 35.0 and 31.7 percent. Further information of interest is offered by the following breakdown:

engineers, architects, and builders	25,000
medium technical personnel	60,000
agronomists and other agricultural experts	2,000
scientific workers (university professors, etc.)	7,000
teachers in primary and secondary schools	46,000
cultural workers (journalists, librarians, etc.)	30,000
artists	17,000
physicians	21,000
other medical personnel	31,000
bookkeepers and accountants	125,000

In other words, according to Zinger, from whom these data are culled, there was a two- to five-fold increase in these categories between 1926 and 1939. In short, the 1941 estimate by the Institute for Jewish Affairs in New York may not be too far from the truth. According to this estimate, Soviet Jewry included 1,400,000 gainfully employed persons, of whom no less than 450,000 or 32.2 percent were government employees (this category embraced, of course, the workers in state commercial and industrial enterprises), while 250,000 or 17.8 percent pursued liberal professions. It thus appears that fully one-half of the whole Jewish population in the Soviet Union was concentrated in these two occupational strata.[17]

In all these areas, there was a particularly noticeable increase in the participation of Jewish women, many of whom reached the higher managerial and other influential positions. As a rule, Jewish women progressed much more rapidly than their non-Jewish opposite numbers. For instance, the percentage of women occupying leading positions in the White Russian banking institutions in 1936–37 was 15.4 percent; among the Jews their proportion exceeded 25 percent. In the Ukraine, women experts amounted to only 11 percent; among Jews, over 26 percent. This emancipation of the women, as well as the growing recognition of the value of a well-educated citizenry for both the economy and society, was reiteratedly emphasized by Stalin, particularly in his address to the Eighteenth Congress of the Communist Party of 1939. Jews were merely following their age-old inclinations, as well as responding to inescapable economic needs, when they made effective use of the new opportunities for acquiring higher education.

AGRICULTURAL ADVANCES

Another revolution in Soviet Jewish life occurred at first through the growth of the Jewish agricultural population. Ever since the beginning of the nineteenth century Jewish colonies had accommodated a substantial number of Jewish farmers, in addition to many individual Jewish tillers of the soil scattered through many provinces of the Pale. But World War I, and still more the civil war and the pogroms, had ruined a great many Jewish homesteads, particularly in the province of Ekaterinoslav, where two Jewish settlements had been totally uprooted, with the loss of a thousand lives. Other colonies also suffered severely. Their decline was accelerated by the famine of 1921, which forced many farmers to seek employment in cities. In all, the Ekaterinoslav province, which in 1913 had embraced 10,622 Jewish farmers, saw their number dwindle to 4,263 in the following nine years. Even in 1924, after slow recuperation, these colonies had reached only some 68 percent of their prewar population. Equally catastrophic was the elimination of livestock. The number of horses was reduced by 94 percent in 1913–22, slowly to recover to 28 percent of their prewar strength two years later.[18]

For a while the reentry of Jews into agriculture proceeded without any plan. Nor was it restricted to the former centers of Jewish colonization. From the outset the famished Jewish masses in the Ukraine and White Russia seized the opportunity of securing some of the land which had become available for distribution from the confiscated estates of landowners and churches. It was perfectly natural for families to obtain from the authorities the allotment of a small parcel of land in the vicinity of their own residences. While individual applicants were usually given only lots of about eleven acres, collectives were assigned as much as twenty-three acres per member family. But it was not difficult for several Jewish families to get together and form a collective.

In this respect Jews were treated exceptionally well. According to general rules, only actual tillers of the soil were entitled to a share in the land distribution. Yet since Jews had been discriminated against during the tsarist regime (we recall the May Laws of 1882), they did not have to meet that qualification. This was indeed the tenor of decrees, issued in the summer of 1924 by both the Ukrainian and White Russian authorities, which provided: "During the distribution of the reserve areas of the Republic the requests of individual Jews and Jewish collectives are to be satisfied in the same measure as those of the local population, although the former have not been engaged heretofore in tilling the soil." This privilege aroused considerable resentment among the Ukrainian and White Russian peasants, since the confiscated estates had not sufficed to satisfy their own inveterate land hunger. As a result, moreover, of the general insecurity and economic instability confronting the urban population no fewer than 8,000,000 inhabitants had left the cities for the countryside in 1917–20. Hence the average distribution of land in most Soviet provinces ranged from but one to five quarters of an acre per person. It is small wonder, then, that the Jewish recipients often encountered much ill-will on the part of their neighbors.[19]

Yet starvation in the cities was so great that 22,857 Jewish families, or 112,161 persons, willing to be colonized registered during January and February of 1925 in nineteen western provinces. Up to that year some 6,500 Jewish families had acquired and cultivated more than 122,000 acres of land. All this was done through self-help, with very little propaganda on the part of the Jewish communist leaders and with little direct support from the government. The only encouragement, both financial and professional, extended to the new settlers was that provided by the old Jewish social welfare organization, the ORT, which received most of its funds from abroad.

This relatively successful popular initiative inspired the Jewish leaders to conceive a major plan to help solve the complicated problem of the "declassed" Jews while simultaneously increasing the flow of badly needed foreign exchange into the country. On August 29, 1924, they organized an official committee, known as KOMZET (Committee for the Settlement of Jewish Toilers on Land). Headed by a high-ranking non-Jewish commissar, Peter G. Smidovich, this committee was assisted by a Jewish association pursuing the same purpose, called OZET (Society for the Settlement of Jewish Toilers on Land) and was primarily devoted to propaganda and fund-raising.

After extensive deliberations, the committee selected certain areas in both the Ukraine and the Crimea for concentrated Jewish colonization. In the Ukraine, where the nucleus of old Jewish colonies could easily be expanded, the three districts around Kherson, Zaporozhe, and Krivorog held out considerable promise for a sufficient concentration of Jewish settlements, so that they speedily qualified for the designation of "Jewish administrative regions." To emphasize their indebtedness to the revolution, the Kherson region was renamed Kalinindorf in 1927. Two years later the Zaporozhe area was called the October Region (with its chief settlement in Novo-Zlatopol), while in 1930 the Krivorog region became known as Stalindorf. In all these administrative regions the Jews formed an absolute majority, ranging from 70 percent in the Zaporozhe to 73 percent in Stalindorf and 86 percent in Kalinindorf. But they had close non-Jewish neighbors in large numbers. In this way the KOMZET evidently tried to prevent these administrative regions from becoming wholly Jewish. Otherwise, they feared, the compact settlements might arouse in the colonists those very aspirations for separate national existence which, though postulated by President Kalinin in his afore-mentioned speech of 1926, they found completely unpalatable.

Because of its natural resources and its crying need for population, central Crimea seemed an even more promising area for Jewish coloni-zation. Here the main project was named after its initiator Larin, who optimistically projected the establishment of a Jewish region of about 1,350,000 acres to accommodate 220,000 Jews. He later raised this esti-mate to 400,000 persons. Although by 1928 the Crimean project faced the competition of Biro-Bidzhan, it was decided to pursue both projects independently. In 1931 this new Jewish administrative region, with its chief settlement in Fraidorf, embraced some 610,000 acres, of which more than 57 percent were assigned to Jewish colonization. The rest had to be shared with a cosmopolitan group of Russians, Ukrainians, and Germans amounting to 40 percent of the population.

Devoid as it was of any major ideological appeal, except for meeting the old goal of "productivization," Jewish colonization made excellent progress in the first few years. The Jewish communist leaders made it perfectly clear that unlike their Zionist counterparts, they did not pursue any nationalist aims. Most outspoken in this respect was the chief of the OZET, Yurii M. Larin, who wrote:

> If the purpose of the creation of Jewish agricultural settlements in the Soviet Union were to consist exclusively in the initiation of small national units in order to perpetuate the Jewish people as such, it would not warrant the moving of a finger for such work because of the total absence of any historical prospects for success. . . . We do not believe that every people must exist forever as a national unit; we believe, on the contrary, that ultimately all peoples will be fused together into one people.

With such an ideology it is not at all surprising that at the Conference of Marxist Agrarian Political Scientists in December, 1929, he proposed drastic measures against the so-called *kulaks* (rural plutocrats), including confiscations, deportations, and forced labor. Larin paid no attention whatsoever to the ill-will which such statements were bound to create among influential segments of the peasantry, not only against him personally, but also against him as a Jew and leader of a Jewish organi-zation.[20]

This exclusively socialist, rather than nationalist, emphasis did not prevent these very politicians from extolling the virtues of the Soviet remaking the very character of its Jewish people. After describing how the previously downtrodden, physically weak, and ever nervous and agitated average Russian Jew had become an upstanding, calm, and self-assured citizen, particularly in Biro-Bidzhan, N. L. Semashko, writing under Dimanshtain's aegis, claimed that "nothing of that kind had happened or could happen anywhere else in the world, not even in the fraudulent, Zionist Palestine, for chauvinist narrow-mindedness and capitalist exploitation continue to weaken and cripple the working Jew in Palestine." In practice, nevertheless, the official colonizers stressed the selection of colonists without regular occupations. They tried to retain the "productive" Jews, including artisans, in their old settlements, for the benefit of the Soviet economy. During the first years, to be sure, the New Economic Policy which had driven many artisans into mercantile endeavors did not favor the departure of merchants and other "unproductive" groups. According to a 1924 report in the *Emes*, a majority of 72.8 percent of the colonists actually consisted of former farmers, artisans, and workers. The conditions changed totally under the First Five-Year Plan, which began absorbing the craftsmen and workers into large-scale industry while increasingly dispossessing the mercantile class. In the early 1930s, therefore, the Crimean colonists included only 7.8 percent former farmers, primarily those who had tilled suburban plots assigned to them during the early revolutionary years, and 11.3 percent former workers. The large majority now came from the "unproductive" classes of petty shopkeepers, agents, and similar groups.[21]

Government support was imperative at every stage. Only the government could allot land (in 1925–27 it set aside 259,917 desiatins or some 650,000 acres for this purpose), superficially clear it, and provide transportation. But substantial funds were needed for housing, agricultural machinery, cattle, and other necessities; more money was also needed to maintain the settlers from the time of their arrival to the harvesting of their first crops. If the colonists planted vineyards and orchards, for which the Crimean climate was particularly suitable, the waiting period was naturally much longer. For all these needs the government could extend only limited credit, so that most of the money had to come from foreign Jewish welfare organizations. Next to the ORT and the ICA, long active on the Russian scene, an important new group now appeared, the American Jewish Joint Distribution Committee, working through its specialized subsidiary, the Agro-Joint. The latter's field work was entrusted to a trained American agronomist, Dr. Joseph Rosen. According to a tabulation compiled by Arthur Ruppin who, as a leading executive in the Jewish colonization of Palestine, had much personal experience but also a certain bias in this matter, the government's outright contributions rose from 400,000 rubles in 1924–25, to 1,515,000 in 1927–28, and to 2,600,000 in 1928–29. Credits extended by Russian sources to the colonists rose in these years from 303,500 to 600,000 and 1,000,000 rubles, respectively. At the same time the foreign Jewish organizations, particularly the Agro-Joint, raised their contributions from 1,851,475 rubles in 1923–24, to 7,140,221 in 1927–28, to fall off to 3,782,000 a year later. In toto, the Russian contributions (including credits) during that first five-year period amounted to 9,072,500, contrasted with a foreign share of 20,447,840 rubles. This disproportion is doubly remarkable, as the Agro-Joint was operating in the Soviet Union without the backing of the American government, which had not yet recognized the Soviet regime and entertained no diplomatic relations with it. Equally astonishing is the fact that the Agro-Joint's backers, mainly recruited from the wealthy classes, were discouraged in their humanitarian endeavors by neither the Soviets' avowed aim of fostering the world revolution nor by the no less outspoken Jewish segment of the Communist Party at home.[22]

The decline of foreign contributions in 1928–29 doubtless reflected the growing disillusionment of donors and experts. True, despite great initial difficulties, the number of Jewish farmers was constantly increasing. While the 1926 census counted only 155,400 Jews in the peasant category, the OZET claimed that in 1928 their number had reached almost 220,000. In 1931 the three categories of Jewish farmers were listed in the following order: 21,870 families cultivating some 1,460,000 acres lived in organized colonies outside Biro-Bidzhan; 9,700 families continued to till almost 300,000 acres in the old-time Jewish colonies; 20,340 families still clung to their suburban land, amounting to a little more than 300,000 acres. If these figures are correct, 51,910 families, or approximately 250,000 souls, derived their livelihood from farming in European Russia. This ratio of some 9 percent of the Jewish population was unmatched elsewhere, except among the Jews of Carpatho-Ruthenia, then under Czechoslovak domination, and in the rapidly expanding Zionist colonization of Palestine. If continued, this movement might indeed have revolutionized the Jewish economic structure, a doubly remarkable feat as it would have reversed the general modern historic trend from the village to the city. Such a reversal, long preached by nationalistic Jewish leaders, had nowhere else been attained to any substantial degree.[23]

Nor was it really attained in the Soviet Union, which during the 1930s witnessed a major retrogression. While none of the schemes was formally abandoned, many were allowed to wither away gradually. Doubtless the most important single reason was the progressive industrialization of the Soviet Union during its first two Five-Year Plans, which had drawn a multitude of farmers into the industrial centers. We have seen how actively Jewish workers and intelligentsia participated in the upbuilding of the Russian industries during the 1930s. The gradual absorption of the former declassed persons into the economic stream dried up the major source of manpower for the colonization schemes. The failure of agricultural crops, particularly during the great famine of 1932–34 discouraged Jewish colonists, especially in the more recently established settlements devoid of reserves from earlier years. The disillusionment of the foreign welfare workers and the attrition of the financial contributions from abroad also played a role.

The enforced large-scale collectivization of the Soviet agricultural structure imposed ever new shackles upon the activities of the Agro-Joint, which from the outset had been viewed with a jaundiced eye by some leading Jewish communists in the Union. These doctrinaires resented the Agro-Joint's superior agricultural technology as a demonstration of the superiority of the capitalist system. On the other hand, many democratically inclined officials of that foreign organization, which in its heyday employed more than 3,000 office workers and agents, must have looked askance at the wholesale massacre and banishment to forced labor camps of the *kulaks* (the wealthier peasants) which accompanied the process of collectivization. Ultimately, the ever dwindling Agro-Joint personnel likewise felt Stalin's heavy hand during the "purges" of 1936–38. While the American, Dr. Joseph Rosen, the leading spirit of the Organization, though refusing the shield of diplomatic protection, personally escaped physical retribution, its ranking Soviet officials, Samuel E. Lubarsky, Ezekiel A. Grower, and Aaron E. Zaitchik were arrested and ultimately disappeared without a trace.[24]

As a result, by 1939 there probably remained fewer than 25,000 families or 125,000 persons still qualifying for the designation of a Jewish agricultural population. Notwithstanding the glaring fanfare over more than a decade, Biro-Bidzhan's 3,000 families were not only outnumbered by the 5,000 living in the Crimea and the 8,500 in the three administrative regions of the Ukraine, but also by the 7,000 estimated to have continued tilling the soil in scattered collective farms in the western republics. In short, the share of Jewish farmers had thus dropped back to little more than the 6 percent counted in the census of 1926.

On the other hand, the intervening peaceful years enabled the more recent agricultural population to take deeper roots in the soil and to increase its agricultural production, both quantitatively and qualitatively. Some Jewish farmers again started winning prizes at agricultural displays. For instance, at the All-Union Agricultural Exhibition of 1939–40, no fewer than two hundred Jewish collective farmers from the Ukrainian regions appeared. One of them won the honor prize, another a small gold medal, eight others small silver medals, and so forth.

Ironically, some of the greatest progress was made in the breeding of pigs. In the Kalinindorf region, for instance, during a year and a half in 1935–36 the number of horned cattle rose from 3,363 to 4,223; that of horses from 1,715 to 2,091. In contrast thereto, the respective figures for porkers are 1,990 and 4,798, or an increase of almost 150 percent.[25]

Were it not for a similar upsurge in the breeding of sheep, one might almost have assumed that these Jewish farmers had done it out of spite for their religious tradition. In fact, however, they merely followed the dictates of both economic necessity and the Party. It was precisely during those years of 1939–40 that the entire governmental apparatus was making strenuous efforts to force the collective farmers to increase their production to meet certain very high goals. On May 27, 1939, it was provided that any collective farmer who had not worked the required minimum of 60–100 days a year should be expelled and his property confiscated. Similarly, the previous maximum of 9.6 hours of work during the harvest season was replaced in 1940 by the requirement to start at five or six in the morning and to continue until sunset. Jewish farmers could no more escape that pressure than did their non-Jewish neighbors.

[14]

Cultural Attrition

If in the socioeconomic sphere Soviet Jewry showed a remarkable degree of pliability and creative adjustment, its cultural achievements proved inadequate to meet the new challenge. To be sure, one could argue that the general cultural level among Jews had not declined and that they had merely exchanged their traditional Jewish for new Russian cultural values. Certainly, if there had been little illiteracy in the prerevolutionary community, there was even less of it two decades after the revolution. Women, in particular, whose cultural advance was retarded in the traditional Jewish educational system, were now given full intellectual opportunities. However, any specific Jewish cultural identity was greatly diluted and by 1939 Jewry as such was in a state of intellectual stagnation.

Moreover, the socioeconomic adjustments consisted primarily of the Jews abandoning their traditional middlemen's pursuits in favor of industrial labor, agriculture, and civil service. They thus merely fulfilled the wishes voiced by their own leaders in Russia and elsewhere for two centuries. In the cultural sphere, on the other hand, assimilation to the surrounding cultures was desired by only a small minority of Jews. True, enlightened leaders viewed a modicum of assimilation as an historic necessity. But even many progressive East European thinkers regarded it mainly as a means of modernizing their national culture. Now, however, under the instigation of the Jewish communists with their deep-rooted hatred for the basic traditional Jewish values—religion, Hebrew, and Zionism—the Russian government and society turned quite hostile to the preservation of any of these traditional moorings of Jewish culture.

YIDDISH SCHOOLS

Invoking the fact that Yiddish had been the spoken language of some 97 percent of Russian Jews back in 1897, the new regime now elevated it to the rank of a national language, the official language of the Jewish national minority. The new Soviet-Jewish school, intended to serve that national minority, had to use Yiddish as its language of instruction. There was some conflict in this matter with the Bukharan and other Asiatic Jews, the old-time Krimchaks, and others who had never spoken Yiddish. The aforementioned substitution of the Tadzhik Jewish dialect for Hebrew in Bukharan-Jewish schools elicited immediate protests. After all, unlike Yiddish, Tadzhik had practically no cultural history of its own and no worthwhile literature to replace the Hebrew letters as a proper medium for education. Remarkably, the local Turkestan communists sharply opposed the introduction of either Tadzhik or Yiddish, as was propagated by the local branch of the *Yevsektsiia*. In a joint meeting of the Tashkent Jewish Professional Association and the Fourth Section of the Russian Communist Party of September 14, 1919, the 323 members present adopted a sharp resolution against the introduction of the Farsi or Tadzhik language into the local Jewish schools. They demanded that the pertinent decree be immediately revoked and that Hebrew become the language of instruction; "otherwise not one pupil will be sent to school. We find it necessary to warn in this connection that no manner of force will stifle in us the desire to educate our children in the Hebrew language as we demand." This extraordinary insistence of a communist group prevailed for a time, but ultimately Hebrew instruction had to give way to that offered in Russian and Turkmen schools, which before long were attended by the large majority of Jewish children.[1]

Jewish communist leadership ran roughshod over all such protests. In fact, its purpose was not so much the preservation of Jewish culture through the medium of Yiddish or Tadzhik, but rather the use of these linguistic media for the indoctrination of both children and adults in the communist principles and world outlook. Summarizing the achievements of Soviet Jewish education during the first fifteen years after the revolution, Judah Dardak, a communist educator, contended:

> Assisted by all means at the government's disposal, the school won one victory after another. First, the Sabbath day of rest was abolished. Secondly, all books with a nationalist coloring were removed. These steps enabled the school to raise the level of instruction and to include antireligious and international subject matter in its curriculum. Work in school follows the general program of the People's Commissariat for Education. The very concept of "Jewish history" is alien to the school. Any general course in the history of the class struggles may include sections describing the struggle of Jewish artisans against their employers and of Jewish workers against the Jewish or any other bourgeoisie. All subjects are taught in the [pupils'] mother tongue [Yiddish], and a special course in Yiddish literature is also given.[2]

Naturally, the first victim of this new trend was the old-type religious *heder* and *yeshivah*, the primary, secondary, and schools of higher learning, developed by the Jewish community over a period of two thousand years. True, despite their outlawry they found enough devotees among teachers and parents to keep going for many years. The main organ of the Jewish communists, the Moscow newspaper *Emes*, admitted that as late as 1927 many such schools still operated in smaller towns. In the Ukraine only some 60 percent of the Jewish school population at that time attended either the general or the Yiddish public schools (in a ratio of 51:49 percent), the rest largely consisting of pupils of the traditional types of religious teachers. Elsewhere, however, the *melamdim* were speedily losing ground. In White Russia more than 87 percent of all Jewish schoolchildren between the ages of eight to fourteen went to public schools, almost one-half (47.3 percent) to schools with Yiddish as the language of instruction. Yiddish secondary schools also existed but none of higher learning. While some of the major universities in Moscow, Kiev, Kharkov, and Minsk maintained sectors for Yiddish studies, these were intended only for students specializing in these fields. In all, during 1927, fully 111,377 Jewish pupils were registered in Yiddish schools, as against 180,420 in general public schools. This ratio of 38.2:61.8 percent was sufficiently high for many Jewishly interested communists in the Union and abroad to contrast it with the situation in western Europe and America, where the vast majority of Jewish children attended non-Jewish schools.[3]

In fact, however, the Yiddish school differed from the general Soviet school in form rather than in substance. The basic curriculum was the same, except that the Yiddish language and literature constituted one of the required subjects. Even in the selection of Yiddish literary creations, communist rather than Jewish criteria were employed. If among the great literary figures Sholem Aleichem and Mendele were paid particular attention, this preference was in part owing to their satirical descriptions of the ghetto community which could be used as a foil for contrast with the achievements of Soviet society.

Indoctrination offered by the Yiddish school was considered so valuable that, according to Yakov Kantor's testimony, the authorities forced Jewish children in many localities to attend that school even if their parents preferred a school with another language of instruction. Of course, in some smaller localities in the Ukraine, White Russia, and the Jewish agricultural colonies, where Jews formed the majority of the population, there often was no alternative. In contrast thereto in the Russian Republic, which included the large Jewish communities of Moscow and Leningrad, fully 97 percent of the entire Jewish school population was registered in government schools (there was practically no *heder* or *yeshivah* available there), including some 8 percent who attended Yiddish schools. These were about equally divided between the twenty-one so-called "primary" four-year schools, and the somewhat more advanced eight seven-year schools functioning in the entire republic in 1926–27. Even in the western republics there was a difference between the major cities and smaller localities. In Odessa, for example, where the Jewish minority amounted to 36.4 percent of the population, only 9 percent of all pupils enrolled in Yiddish schools. In Kharkov the discrepancy was even greater: with a population ratio of 19.4 percent that of pupils in Yiddish schools was but 2.9 percent.[4]

The statistics for the large cities are only given for 1933, and no reliable data are available for the later prewar years. But there is no question about the progressive diminution of enrollment in the Yiddish schools during that period. From the outset, the Jewish school system had to contend with a severe shortage of well-trained teachers in both pedagogy and Jewish subjects. From replies to a questionnaire circulated among the White Russian Yiddish teachers in 1925, it appears that only some 14 percent had received any pedagogic training whatsoever. The majority was also so blatantly ignorant of Jewish lore as to give rise to frequent complaints in the Yiddish papers. These deficiencies could not be made up by the newly improvised seven Jewish teachers' seminaries and several university sectors, with their maximum of three hundred graduates a year. Using data scattered over many publications, Jacob Lestchinsky estimated that in the Ukraine enrollment in Yiddish schools had dropped from 94,872 in 1930–31, to 73,412 four years later. The relative decline was even greater: from 46.6 to 32.5 percent. In White Russia, where the registration in such schools had reached the peak of 36,650 pupils in 1932, it shrank to approximately 30,000 during the subsequent five years. This deterioration of the Yiddish school system continued unabated. Even many functioning schools found themselves doomed when their first grades were discontinued because of insufficient enrollment. School boards often tended to merge the Yiddish with the Ukrainian or White Russian schools, while leaving Yiddish as a subject in the curriculum, which really meant that the Yiddish school was abolished. In all, according to Lestchinsky's estimates, in 1940, 85,000 to 90,000 children in all attended schools with the Yiddish language of instruction (including 3,000 in Biro-Bidzhan). This decline was doubly significant as it coincided with the general rapid increase in the school enrollment throughout the Union, which Stalin praised in his address to the Eighteenth Congress of the Communist Party in 1939. It was in part owing to the mobility of the population and the transfer of increasing numbers of Jews from the western republics to the interior of Russia. In part, however, it was the result of progressive assimilation, whether voluntary or under pressure from the growing Russian, Ukrainian and other nationalisms in reaction to the ever more tense world situation.[5]

All along the Jewish enrollment in schools of higher learning increased by leaps and bounds; it rose from 9.4 percent under tsarist oppression to 16 percent in 1926–27. That even here Jews preferred certain branches of study over others is not at all surprising. In White Russia and the Ukraine they constituted no less than 46.6 and 44.8 percent, respectively, of all students attending medical schools. In the Russian Republic, too, their ratio of 11.2 percent of all medical students was wholly out of proportion to their population strength. Next to medicine the most popular subjects were economics (47.8, 32.1, and 18 percent, respectively, in the three republics); industry and technology (no data for White Russia, but 31.9 and 14.6 percent in the two other republics), teaching and art. Curiously, agronomy and related subjects, which played such a tremendous role in the propaganda for Jewish restratification, attracted far fewer students (12.4, 8.0, 3.9 percent). After 1927, the general enrollment in schools of higher learning so greatly increased that the Jewish percentage in most branches of learning decreased substantially. According to Zinger, in 1938, Jews formed only 13 percent of the student bodies at universities and colleges and 5 percent in technical schools. But in absolute numbers, as well as in its ratio to the total Jewish population, Jewish enrollment was still growing rapidly.[6]

HEBREW PUBLICATIONS

Other cultural media, too, claimed much of the government's attention. Books, pamphlets, and periodicals now appeared in ever-greater profusion, largely from the government-owned printing presses and publishing firms. The theater, both in Russian and in the minority languages, also received much greater government support. The Yiddish press, literature, and stage now also achieved a circulation or attendance undreamed of before.

During the first unsettled years of the revolution the people still favored Hebrew publications, which had suffered greatly during World War I. The aforementioned outlawry of any publication in Hebrew letters within the military zone had extended over the entire Pale of Jewish Settlement and beyond. But as soon as the democratic republic was established in 1917, Hebrew writers and publishers made use of the new freedom of the press and issued a substantial number of Hebrew periodicals and books. Characteristically, Moscow, though not yet the official capital of Russia, became, next to Odessa, the greatest center of Hebrew culture. This was owing to the residence there of many Hebrew poets, writers, and scholars, as well as of wealthy Jewish patrons, especially the Hillel Zlatopolsky-Shoshana Persitz family and Abraham Stybel, who lavished much of their rapidly growing wealth on fostering Hebrew-language publications.

Beginning in July, 1917, a Hebrew daily *Ha-Am* (The People) began appearing in Moscow despite the paucity of Hebrew readers in the capital and the difficulties of communication with the provinces. The number of subscribers had never exceeded 15,000, not enough to maintain a daily paper. Nevertheless, after a brief interruption during the October Revolution, the journal resumed publication, first as a weekly and then again as a daily. Its days were numbered, however, especially since it was overtly critical of the new regime. On December 7, 1917, Benzion Katz fearlessly wrote in his editorial: "The Russian Revolution surpasses in its savagery all the negative features of the French Revolution. . . . We have only one hope that the reign of this new Inquisition will not last very long." The newspaper had to suspend publication in June, 1918, while its personnel looked for avenues of emigration.

It was far easier to publish annuals, quarterlies, and other collections. Some of these materials had been available before the war but could not be published owing to the tsarist restrictions. An excellent collection, styled *Keneset* (Assembly) and edited by Chaim Nachman Bialik, had been ready for the printer in 1915. The important periodical *Reshumot* (Sketches), devoted to folklore and ethnography, had actually been set up in the same year. But neither saw the light of day until 1917. As a bibliographical curiosity, a volume on the history of the Lovers of Zion movement appeared in print with the title page bearing the date of 1914, while the book jacket gave the real year of 1919. Probably the most important of these periodical publications was the *Hatekufah*, a quarterly established by Stybel, of which the first three volumes of some 700 pages each appeared in Moscow in 1918. Published in an attractive format, it gathered around it the chief Hebrew literary talents. Unlike most of the other publications, this quarterly survived its suspension by the communist regime; together with its sponsor, it emigrated to Warsaw where it continued to be published, if less frequently, during most of the interwar period. The yearbook *Keneset,* on the other hand, which after a lapse of many years began reappearing in Palestine, was but a spiritual heir to Bialik's original collection.[7]

In regard to Hebrew books, Odessa retained its primacy for a time. True, at first, publication of Hebrew works was extremely difficult. In a pathetic letter of September, 1917, Bialik tried to explain to David Frischman the reasons why his publishing firm, the *Moriah,* was unable to carry out its original program: "The price of paper is two rubles a pound instead of ten kopecks. Good printing font is not available, nor are workers or Hebrew printing presses. There simply is nothing here, and who is able to work under such conditions?" Eight months later he still commented that "the printing of a Hebrew book is more difficult than the parting of the Black Sea." Nevertheless, according to Y. Slutsky's special, probably incomplete, tabulation, 119 Hebrew works were published in Odessa during the period from 1917 to 1919, out of a total of 188 titles in all of Russia. Moscow was second with 25 publications, closely followed by Kiev with 18.[8]

However, Odessa's preponderance stemmed mainly from textbooks and children's literature, the growth of which was truly phenomenal. During the early revolutionary years the Zionist intelligentsia energetically set out to erect a modern school system with Hebrew as the language of instruction. *Tarbut* (Culture), a society founded early in 1917, immediately undertook to establish a number of Hebrew elementary schools to be followed by secondary schools and other educational institutions. Its career was cut short by the suppression of Hebrew instruction by the Jewish communists, but it survived outside the Union, celebrating great victories even under the unfriendly regime of interwar Poland. It was most effective in the new Republic of Lithuania, where the majority of the Jewish school population attended *Tarbut* schools. But as long as it lasted in the Soviet Union, the *Tarbut* society made strenuous efforts to supply the new schools with both trained teaching personnel and textbooks. No lesser a person than Bialik participated in this popularizing effort, he himself authoring ten thin pamphlets intended for children. So sanguine were these Hebrew leaders about the future of their educational system that one of their major efforts, particularly sponsored by the Stybel publishing firm, consisted of a gigantic program of translations into Hebrew of the great classics of world literature. Remarkably, they assumed that their reading public also required translations of the great Russian authors; no less than three volumes by Tolstoy appeared in a Hebrew rendition during that short-lived flowering of the Hebrew book after the revolution.

All these enthusiastic efforts came to naught in 1919, when with the outlawry of Zionism and "clericalism," also came the suppression of the Hebrew book. All Hebrew presses were speedily nationalized and converted to the use of Yiddish publications serving communist aims. Distinguished Hebrew writers now lost their means of subsistence and were deprived of all opportunities for creative work. Only some of them were fortunate enough to join Bialik, who in 1921 had obtained permission for himself and a group of associates to emigrate to Palestine.[9]

Thereafter a limited number of writers found their way to Berlin, New York, or Palestine, but some of them returned to the Soviet Union, where they felt they had their roots. Quite a few became convinced communists and hailed the revolution in their Hebrew writings. Only thus was it possible for a few Hebrew books to appear in print. The largest and most important of these was a collective work, *Be-Reshit* (At the Beginning), which, however, had to be printed in Berlin in 1925, far from the authors and editors living in Moscow and Leningrad. Understandably, the volume is disfigured by numerous misprints. A second volume prepared for publication never saw the light of day. Many authors, then and later, had to be satisfied with a limited distribution of their poems in hectograph form, one of the forerunners of the recent *samizdat*s. The resulting feeling of isolation among many of those writers was well expressed later by Abraham Krivoruchka (Kariv), when after settling in Palestine in 1934, he wrote:

> From afar it is hard to conceive the orphanhood and affliction that comes from writing in a language uprooted from the living soil—a language that found its last refuge on the gravestones of Jewish cemeteries; being cut off from the mines of that language, deprived of an old book or a new one—in a hostile world concealing only dangers and lacking the warmth and encouragement so acutely needed by a writer.

Nonetheless, a number of such quiet, creative minds carried on. Although after 1927 publications in Hebrew were almost totally suppressed—some wags suggested that the *Be-Reshit* should rather have been entitled *Be-Ahrit* (At the End)—they persisted. In fact, some of the greatest Hebrew poems of the period were written by Hayim Lensky while he languished in prison in Siberia. But even they were salvaged from oblivion only by being brought to Palestine by later émigrés from Russia and published there.

Initially, this suppression of Hebrew literary creativity was more the result of Jewish communists' anti-Hebraism than that of the official circles. Jewish communists inherited this negative attitude from the earlier struggle for recognition of Yiddish as the Jewish national language. They condemned Hebrew as a bourgeois-clerical vehicle of propaganda, while Yiddish was obviously "the language of the masses." Of course, one could argue that a large majority of proletarians, especially women, had little acquaintance with books in any language, while most of them recited Hebrew prayers and benedictions, sent their children to Hebrew schools, and even included a great many Hebrew loan words in their daily speech. The proponents of Yiddish exclusivity were also prone to forget that even within the confines of the Soviet Union there were a number of Jewish communities totally unfamiliar with Yiddish. We recall the successful 1919 struggle of the Communist Party in Tashkent for the preservation of Hebrew as the language of instruction in the local Jewish schools.

At first, the government's attitude was ambivalent. The Hebrew language as such was never officially outlawed. It was still taught at universities, especially in connection with linguistic and archeological studies. In a petition to the government submitted in 1927 a number of Hebraists argued that "if our language, for reasons which we are unable to understand, is really harmful and counterrevolutionary, then we demand its suppression by law. But if national policy permits the existence of all languages, then we demand a law forbidding its persecution." Only on practical grounds did the governmental leaders accept the anti-Hebraic arguments. In a conversation with Jacob Mazeh, the "official" rabbi of Moscow, Anatolii V. Lunacharskii, commissar of public enlightenment, declared, "I do not know anyone doubting the value of Hebrew, except the Jewish communists. But they are our allies, and we can hardly reject their contention that Hebrew is the language of the bourgeoisie and not the people." As a result, secular Hebrew writings were effectively prevented from appearing in print, except for the relatively few works which found their way (with or without their authors) to a foreign country. We shall see that in 1926 a similar fate befell the outstanding Hebrew theatrical troupe, the *Habimah*. [10]

Remarkably, the old-type rabbinic literature, which for a time lagged far behind, proved somewhat more enduring. Before 1914 books of this genre (including ethical and hasidic writings) far exceeded in both numbers and readership the other Hebrew or Yiddish letters. However, most of the publishing firms specializing in this branch were concentrated in Warsaw and Vilna, now lost to the Soviet Union. Probably the existing supply—at least of the older classics and handbooks—accumulated in synagogues and private libraries was still sufficiently large. Later, when the needs of the ever-dwindling Orthodox population could no longer be satisfied, zealous men found ways and means to publish some such books, long after the more modern Hebrew letters had been outlawed.

Making use of the small freedoms granted by the New Economic Policy, some enterprising small-town publishers succeeded in distributing many liturgical works (needed in both synagogues and Orthodox homes), calendars, and such. Jacob Ginzburg of Bobruisk was resourceful enough to secure from the reluctant communist authorities not only the necessary permits but also the harder to attain allotment of printing paper. One of his stratagems was to establish printing presses in several localities, including Plotsk, Minsk, and Poltava, so as to require less paper for each press. The April 10, 1928, *Komsomolskaia Pravda* commented, with a sigh bordering on admiration, on Ginzburg's success in distributing no fewer than 100,000 copies of Hebrew liturgical works during the single year of 1927–28. "He has at his disposal alert booksellers who deliver his books directly to the houses of believers. No agent of our publishing firms is able to compete with them in their talent to distribute books." The Hebrew calendars published by these small firms became best-sellers; an alleged 75,000 copies of the calendar for 5687 (1927–28) were sold. However, all such "alarmist" reports of the communist press, though testifying to the continued vitality of the Jewish and other religions in the Soviet Union after a decade of godless propaganda, could not gloss over the constant attrition of the traditional institutions. In the issue of June 22, 1928 the same *Komsomolskaia Pravda* described the "disquieting" religious situation in Kiev and, among other matters, reported that "lately an underhand, hidden Jewish khedera [doubtless referring to the traditional Jewish school, the *heder*] has begun to be widely spread; also so-called 'Tribunals of the Rabbis'; here dozens of Jewish children are being influenced in a certain direction; here also the 'faithful' seek protection, advice, and help!" But in the long run that feverish activity, whether overt or clandestine, led only to a dead-end street; in the 1930s practically no Hebrew works of any kind were allowed to appear in the Soviet Union.[11]

YIDDISH LETTERS AND THEATER

The output of Yiddish letters was incomparably larger. From the outset the Jewish communist leaders felt the need of supplying the Yiddish-speaking public with books and periodicals in their own language. Moreover, since the state took pride in its lavish support of culture, the publishing firms did not have to calculate sales and profit possibilities. Authors, too, were assured of their governmental stipends regardless of the number of copies sold. Those whose sales reached high figures, often going into hundreds of thousands, received additional royalties which frequently placed them in the category of best-paid officials. While such vast distribution was usually attained only in Russian or Ukrainian, the sales of some Yiddish books also exceeded anything known in the West. In this respect the Soviet Yiddish writers could claim primacy over their confreres in the two other great centers of Yiddish culture, Poland and the United States.

Regrettably, the various statistical accounts of Yiddish books published in the Soviet Union are neither complete nor fully comparable. The relatively best data are offered for the years 1932–35 by N. Rubinshtain in annual bibliographical surveys. But published under state auspices in Minsk, they also had to omit books interveningly condemned by the Party as exponents of "Trotskyite and counterrevolutionary propaganda." The constant quantitative rise in titles, sizes of books, and their aggregate circulation came to a halt in 1932–33; it was followed by a steady decline. According to these data, the 1928 total of 238 Yiddish books published, printed on a total of 1,368 sheets (of 16 pages each sheet) with an aggregate circulation of 875,000, rose four years later to 653 titles, 3,087 sheets, and 2,558,585 circulation. In 1933, titles reached the record figure of 668, but we are not told about their sizes or circulation. The reversal came suddenly: in 1934 there appeared only 348 titles printed on 2,424 sheets with a circulation of but 1,551,880 copies. Compared with other languages, moreover, the Yiddish output became disproportionately small. In the Ukraine the 426 Yiddish titles published in 1934–36, and distributed in 1,983,695 copies, amounted to only 3.1 percent of all titles and less than 1 percent of the general circulation, while Jews still made up more than 5 percent of the population.[12]

As in many other fields, the Yiddish publications were often concentrated in large publishing firms. During the five-year period of 1933–37, the single publishing house *Emes* in Moscow could boast of producing no fewer than 852 Yiddish titles with a circulation of 6,240,925. A breakdown in the subject matter of these publications by years and fields is truly illuminating. In the first place, it illustrates the sharp decline of antireligious propaganda. In that entire five-year period the *Emes* published only one such item (in 1937) with a circulation of no more than 4,000 copies. Evidently, neither publisher nor Party was willing to expend much energy on agitating against religion at a time when the Soviet Union was veering toward a gradual reconciliation with the Russian Orthodox Church in the face of the rising Nazi threat. In theory, to be sure, the Communist Party did not abandon its antireligious crusade. In its conference of 1936, the All-Union Party adopted a resolution reading:

> Among the tasks of the cultural revolution, embracing the widest masses, special place is occupied by the struggle against the opiate of the people—religion—a struggle which must be carried on systematically and relentlessly. . . . At the same time the proletarian power, allowing freedom of confession and destroying the privileged position

of the former state religion, conducts by all possible means antireligious propaganda, and reconstructs all upbringing and educational work on the basis of a scientific, materialistic world-view.[13]

In the second place, the largest category consisted of belles-lettres, whose 328 titles with a circulation of 1,147,750 amounted to nearly 40 percent of all publications and to 20 percent of the entire distribution. The political literature (in this listing divided between so-called Marx-Lenin literature, publications devoted to Party politics, and a third section of Soviet political documents) ran a close second in the number of titles (229 or *ca.* 25 percent), but exceeded the belles-lettres in its circulation of 1,941,425 copies, over 30 percent of the entire circulation. Among the other categories the most important was that of textbooks, running to 69 titles and a circulation of 633,750.

Much of that literature consisted of reprints of older classics or translations from foreign languages. The Soviet cultural leaders made a special point of acquainting the national minorities with one another's culture by promoting translations from one minority language into another, as well as from all of them into Russian. For one example, according to the computations of the Soviet bibliographer, A. Finkelshtain, in the first twenty years of the revolution (1917–37) the works of Sholem Aleichem appeared in a total of 2,107,000 copies, of which 1,216,000 were in Yiddish, 405,000 in Russian, and 486,000 in six other languages. With even greater abandon L. Zinger claims that during the years 1917 to 1939, 3,200,000 copies of Sholem Aleichem's works had appeared in ten languages. A Soviet Yiddish writer, Leib Kvitko, was said to have been even more popular; in 1928–39, 6,500,000 copies of his works were published in twenty-two languages. Such figures are beyond any comparison with the publication of Jewish books in the West. However, in the Soviet Union they were easily overshadowed by works of popular Russian authors—indeed, of some written in relatively less prominent minority languages. According to the catalogue of the *Mezhdynarodnaia Kniga* (International Book), the ten Russian translations from the Yiddish, published in 1938 in 2,156 pages, contrasted with twenty-four books and 6,410 pages of such translations from the Gruzhian (Georgian) literature. The number of translations into Yiddish was also large; it actually increased in periods of rapid ideological change, when it appeared safer to translate an old classic than to write an original work.[14]

We have furnished here (perhaps in excess), statistical data pertaining to the publication of Yiddish books. Not that quantitative measurements are decisive in matters of spirit. But the data compiled by Soviet bibliographers stress these measurements, which have at least the virtue of some objectivity. No less a writer than David Bergelson (1884–1952), one of the really distinguished Yiddish novelists, who after many years in Berlin lived and died in the Soviet Union, applied this standard when he claimed that Soviet Yiddish literature had achieved primacy in the world of Yiddish letters. He doubtless had in mind the bibliographical account for 1925, which had appeared in his periodical and which had shown that of the total of 451 Yiddish publications throughout the world, 208 had appeared in the Soviet Union, 163 in Poland, and only 63 in the United States. The author of that list exclaimed with great pride, "This means that during the last year the Soviet Union published almost as many [Yiddish] books as all other countries combined.[15]

On closer examination, however, it turns out that much of the material published then and later in a Yiddish garb was of little specifically Jewish interest. A subsequent bibliography covering the Yiddish publications during 1935 included the respectable number of 437 titles, with an average circulation of 4,320 copies. But the really large editions were devoted to translations from the Russian propaganda literature, such as Stalin's speeches and the Statute of the Collective Farms (in 25,000 copies each), or Molotov's address on the Constitution (18,000 copies). Some pamphlets by Stalin, Molotov, and other Soviet leaders were allotted 15,000 copies each. At the same time, even propaganda works by Jewish communists, such as an information booklet and a speech on Biro-Bidzhan, or descriptions of the new Jewish agricultural colonies of Stalindorf and Novo-Zlatopol, were published in no more than 1,000 to 5,000 copies. It is also interesting that the twelve books devoted to economics, one to geography, one to natural science, and two of the three books in history were all translations. The one original historic work, to be sure, was quite important. It was a collection of documents entitled "Socialist Literature in Yiddish, 1875–1897," edited by S. Agurskii, Volume II, and published by the White Russian Academy in but 1,000 copies. The category of medicine has an original Yiddish book, but it consists only of a popular first-aid guide. Similarly, technology is represented by one original Yiddish book—a handbook of Yiddish stenography, published in 600 copies. There were many other textbooks and children's books, both original and in translation, but they could not claim any major intellectual significance. This entire output could not even remotely compare with the qualitatively rich and highly diversified intellectual harvest of Jewry in neighboring Poland on the eve of its destruction.[16]

The most important branches of Yiddish literature were poetry, novels, and essays in literary history and criticism. The 1935 list shows 141 original Yiddish works of this kind and sixty translations. Apart from the highly popular classics, especially Sholem Aleichem, there were twenty-seven books of new poetry, and a considerable number of novels published for the most part only in editions of 1,000 to 3,000.

Only Bergelson's novel and a collection of short stories appeared in 6,000 copies each. Practically all publications were now limited to Soviet authors. Some eminent Yiddish writers living abroad, such as Sholem Asch, H. Leivick, and Abraham Reisen, had become taboo after their visits to Russia about which they had reported in a critical vein. Typical of the extreme criticisms hurled at these foreign writers is B. Orshanskii's attack on Abraham Reisen. In connection with his discussion of the prewar period of Yiddish literature, whose estheticism had alienated the writers from the masses, Orshanskii referred to a 1908 essay written by Samuel Niger (Charney) which actually blamed Reisen for overstressing the ordinary sufferings and the "gray misery." At that time Reisen had indeed been a "poet of millions," though not Niger's poet. In contrast thereto, Orshanskii contended in 1931 that "now A. Reisen has betrayed the Revolution, the millions of toiling masses, and has sold himself to the yellow *Forward*; he is now in the service of the Nigers and not of the millions." While most of the Soviet authors, too, had been born and trained in the prerevolutionary period, some poems and stories by younger writers also made their appearance in the 1920s and 1930s.[17]

From the standpoint of content the Yiddish letters of the period followed the lead of the contemporary Russian writers. Even lyrics rarely described the personal emotions of individuals perplexed by the difficulties of life and human relations. For the most part, the novels were written in simple black and white, the heroes representing the new type of Soviet worker—upstanding, generous, devoted to the building up of his country—contrasted with the villains harking back to the old order. Distinguished artists like Peretz (Peter) Markish (1895–1952) could not completely suppress their inner sympathy, or at least, some romantic yearnings for the world passed by. But Markish, too, after his return in 1926 from a five-year sojourn abroad, concentrated on the victory of the socialist ideals over the outworn strivings of the past. The writers helped inspire confidence in the future among their Yiddish readers, who even more than most other Soviet citizens faced the harsh difficulties of that era—forced cultural integration, economic scarcity, and constant appeals to sacrifice. Even their heroines are rarely described as persons motivated by the usual human emotions of love or parenthood, but as dedicated workers exceeding all their comrades in organizational zeal and effectiveness.

A highlight of Note Lurye's (1907–   ) significant novel *Der step ruft* (The Steppe Calls), written in 1931 and set in a Jewish farm village in the Ukraine (he himself was a native of a Jewish agricultural colony), is reached with the exhortation, by the nineteen-year-old woman organizer, Elke Rudner, addressed to the Jewish farmers to join a collective. She argues most cogently by comparing their low output with that of a neighboring collectivized farm. And yet Lurye is too genuine an artist to write with unmitigated venom even about the local Jewish *kulak*. He puts into the mouth of this rich Jewish farmer a pathetic description of how he had "lived his whole life quietly and peacefully like a good farmer. Now they want to take away his house. . . . That Jews should slaughter Jews! Where had such a thing ever been heard of before?" On the other hand, Noyakh (Noah) Lurye (1886–1960) does not refrain from extolling the secret service's bloody suppression of counterrevolutionaries in some of his short stories included in his *Brikn brenen* (Bridges are Burning), published in 1929.[18]

In the mid-1930s, when the large purges began and the "cult of personality" was celebrating great triumphs, Jewish authors, like their non-Jewish confreres, were in a precarious position. After much hesitation during the 1920s, when Trotsky and others had advocated a "soft line" toward arts and the creative expression of uncontrollable subconscious feelings, the Party assumed a definite stand for submerging individual creativity to the common purpose of upbuilding socialism. Beginning in 1932, an essay by Lenin, written under totally different circumstances in 1905, began to be cited as a piece of sacrosanct revelation. Here Lenin had stated:

> For the socialist proletariat literature cannot be an instrument of gain for persons or groups; it cannot altogether be an individual matter, independent of the whole proletarian cause. Down with non-Party writers! Down with literary supermen! Literature must become *part* of the general cause of the proletariat, the "wheel and the screw" of a single great Social Democratic mechanism, set in motion by the entire politically conscious vanguard of the whole working class. Literature must become a component part of the organized, planned, united Social Democratic Party work.

So entrenched had Party control become that in 1933, A. V. Lunacharskii completely reversed his previous "liberal" position and declared: "We know very well that we have the right to intervene in the course of culture, starting with mechanization in our country, with electrification as part of it, and ending with the direction of the most delicate forms of art."[19]

Like their non-Jewish colleagues, the Yiddish writers were particularly affected by the constant vagaries in communist ideology. Some preferred to write historical novels going back to prerevolutionary times, even to antiquity or the Middle Ages, because many novels dealing with contemporary subjects, however closely hewing to the momentary Party line, were later condemned for having taken the wrong ideological position. This sense of insecurity affected even literary and scholarly critics. For many a critic who in his review had praised a certain book was later censured along with the author. It was safer, therefore, not to write any criticisms at all, and leading Yiddish literary journals now appeared without their customary review sections.

More permanently debilitating was the constant shrinkage of the Yiddish reading public. Not only were the hundreds of thousands of Jews moving to the interior of Russia increasingly estranged from their mother tongue, but even most Ukrainian and White Russian Jews gradually acquired a good knowledge of Russian and/or the local languages. It made less and less sense now to translate for them speeches by Stalin or resolutions of the Communist Party, which they preferred to read in their Russian originals. In time an unnamed Ukrainian Jewish leader actually suggested to the Yiddish poet Itzik Fefer that perhaps Yiddish poets and novelists would do better if they submitted their Yiddish manuscripts to Russian or Ukrainian translators and had their books published only in such renditions. Since Sholem Aleichem's works were quite popular among non-Jewish readers as well, it could be argued that such Russian translations of works dealing with Jewish subjects would fill a literary void. To some extent such practice was, indeed, adopted in the late 1930s.[20]

This was a complete reversal of the position taken earlier by the Jewish communist leadership. The trend toward concentration on Yiddish came most blatantly to the fore in the field of Jewish scholarship. Before World War I even the leading journals devoted to Jewish history had appeared in Russian (*Evreiskaia Starina*, *Perezhitoe*, and *Voskhod*). Now whatever historical scholarship was still cultivated, for the most part by scholars trained before the revolution, appeared in such Yiddish journals as the Minsk *Zeitshrift*, *Ofn Shprakhfront*, and others. Here, too, there was constant attrition after 1932–33; fewer and fewer works of that Marxist-oriented scholarship saw the light of day. The internecine struggle between the Jewish scholars themselves, filled with denunciations of communist heterodoxy, further increased these authors' feelings of insecurity. Some younger research men in particular, more politicians and Party hacks than genuine students, attacked such an old-time expert as Israel Sosis for his attempts at objectivity in the Western sense and his excessive "nationalism." Even a publicist like Hillel Aleksandrov, who had not only frequently indulged in vehement attacks on "Fascist" Jewish scholarship as represented by the Yiddish Scientific Institute in Vilna but had also published a number of propagandist pamphlets for communism and communist research, became the target of sharp polemics by some younger writers, who detected in his works supposed "deviations" from the "newest" Party line.[21]

Another revolutionary transformation took place in the Yiddish spelling. Long before 1914 one heard suggestions that the Yiddish orthography should be simplified by the transcription of the Hebrew loan words in a phonetic, rather than etymological, form. Some had even recommended the adoption of the Latin alphabet. All such plans had never materialized because of the staunch resistance of the Yiddish readers. Now, however, these proposals were taken up seriously. Even Jewish communists did not dare flaunt the public's wishes to the extent of adopting the Latin, or later, the Cyrillic script, as was done with some two-score other minority languages in the Union. But they unhesitatingly introduced the phonetic transliteration of Hebrew terms. They also eliminated the five final Hebrew letters, which always constituted a minor hardship for beginners, as well as two other letters used only in words of Hebrew origin. January 1, 1932, was set as the deadline for the use of the new spelling. Apart from simplification, this move tended to "dehebraize" Jewish culture, as well as to alienate Soviet readers from the Yiddish literature produced in Poland and America. Its initiators succeeded only too well, but at the price of digging their own graves.[22]

The same phenomenal rise and decline could also be noted in the Yiddish theater. At the outset the democratic revolution opened an outlet for the pent-up creative energies of talented Jewish playwrights and theatrical performers. During World War I, Moscow had become a center of the Jewish stage, as well as of the Jewish book. One of the highlights of all Jewish theatrical history was reached when, under the leadership of Nahum Zemach (1887–1939), a Hebrew theatrical group, the *Habimah*, was organized and received the active guidance of Evgenii B. Vakhtangov, one of Konstantin S. Stanislavskii's brightest pupils. Their performance of S. An-ski's *Dybbuk* in Bialik's unmatched Hebrew translation became one of the high points of the interwar theater in any language. After Hebrew culture was pronounced taboo in the new society, the *Habimah* left in 1926 for other countries, where it was enthusiastically received, and finally settled in Palestine. Its place was taken by the Yiddish theater which flourished in Moscow, Kiev, Minsk, and other centers. Subsidized by the government, as were performances in other languages, the Jewish theatrical groups found themselves, for the first time on Russian soil, freed from nagging financial worries and basking in public recognition by Jews and non-Jews alike. Under the direction of the renowned actor and producer, Salomon Mikhoels, the Moscow Yiddish Theater achieved international fame. There also were Yiddish theatrical schools for the training of Yiddish actors in Moscow, Kiev, and Minsk.[23]

However, here too a process of attrition set in for exactly the same reasons that stymied the development of Yiddish literature. Of the eleven Yiddish theaters which existed in the Ukraine in 1933, no more than four were still in operation five years later. By that time only twelve Yiddish theaters were still open, including one in Biro-Bidzhan and another in a Crimean *kolkhoz*. L. Zinger, in his boasts about cultural achievements under the Soviet regime, speaks of only ten Yiddish theaters in the Union in 1939.[24] Although the Moscow theater still performed plays with a high degree of artistic excellence, its days, too, were numbered.

On the other hand, there was a growing influx of talented young Jews into the general Russian literature and theater. One need but mention names like Isaac E. Babel (1894–1941), Ilya G. Ehrenburg (1891–1967), and Boris Pasternak (1890–1960), in the field of literature; Sergei M. Eisenstein (1898–1948), the outstanding film director, whose 1938 movie *Alexander Nevskii* focused much of Russia's patriotic fervor shortly before the outbreak of World War II, and many others who have added luster to the interwar Russian arts. But most of these men, like the numerous Jews active in science and social studies, evinced little interest in Jews or Jewish affairs.

Some of these writers, to be sure, referred at least incidentally to Jewish characters or reminiscences of their youth. An outstanding example is that of Isaac Babel, whose *Red Cavalry* included many episodes from the Ukrainian Civil War, although he too dreamed of the amalgamation of Jews and their neighbors to the extent of making one of his heroes, a Jew, enlist in a Cossack regiment and in this capacity fight for the revolution. Yet Babel was too much of an individualist to fit into the rigidly controlled Russian literature, especially the literary world of the RAPP (Russian Association of Proletarian Writers) era. During the years 1929 to 1932, when that organization was under the leadership of the young Jewish extremist, Leopold L. Averbakh (1903–1939), the system of repression, often later called Averbakhism, reached such an extent that Babel, together with other writers of his individualistic bent, remained completely silent. In fact, after Averbakh was removed in 1932, to vanish from the scene completely thereafter, the more liberal First Writers' Congress of 1934 featured Babel as one of its speakers. By indirection the novelist spoke exaltingly of the right to write badly. The relaxation of literary controls did not last long, however. During the purges of 1937, Babel, too, was arrested. He died in a concentration camp in 1941 at the early age of forty-seven.[25]

Another distinguished Jewish native of Odessa also remembered his Jewish youth. Eduard G. Bagritskii (Dzhubin, 1895–1934), generally considered one of the outstanding Russian poets of his generation, had also begun his literary career before the war. In his later masterpiece, *Duma ob Opanase* (An Elegy on Opanas), he described how, through a tragic concatenation of circumstances, the farmer Opanas shot down the

Jewish communist Kogan who had tried to requisition his produce for the government. Even more remarkably, Joseph P. Utkin (1903–41), born in far-off Manchuria, depicted Jewish life in that distant province in his outstanding poem, *The Story of the Red-Haired Motele, the Inspector, the Rabbi Isaiah, and the Commissar Blokh*, which attracted wide attention. Less outspokenly Jewish but in their individualism also quite remote from the prevailing revolutionary enthusiasm were not only such older poets as Ossip E. Mandelshtam (1892–1938), but also the youthful Mikhail Golodnii (pseud. for Michael S. Epshtain, 1903–49), and particularly Boris Pasternak, who though reared in the cultured Zionist home of a famous painter, friend of Leo Tolstoy, Rainer Maria Rilke, and Chaim Weizmann, gradually drifted spiritually into both Russian populism and mysticism, and joined the Russian Orthodox faith.

At the other extreme stood out some convinced communist poets who placed the Party and its philosophy ahead of their artistic predilections. Alexander I. Bezymenskii, a native of Zhitomir (1898–   ), professed in one of his poems: "Others may care for a maiden's lips, But I am concerned with smoking factory chimneys." In another poem, quite reminiscent of rabbinic parables, he spoke of a communist cell, whose heart might suddenly appear in the shape of a fifty-kopeck piece. He would consider two of these kopecks as representing the element of bitterness, against forty-five kopecks symbolic of genuine joy. Many other writers, Jewish and non-Jewish, wrote less from conviction than because they had to perform their frequent acrobatic gyrations in order to keep up with the vagaries of communist policies. A most accomplished artist of these *salti mortali* was Ilya Ehrenburg. His return to Jewish interests during World War II inspired many descriptions in the first draft of his novel *Buria* (The Storm). But sensing the changed attitude of the literary dictators during the *zhdanovshchina* (the Zhdanov era), Ehrenburg burned his original manuscript and expurgated most pro-Jewish statements when the novel finally appeared and received the Stalin Prize in 1948. But this extreme pliability evidently saved his life during the Stalin terror.[26]

Perhaps because he himself had felt the pressure of Averbakhism, Mikhail Sholokhov, one of the relatively few Soviet writers to win the Nobel Prize, sensed the feeling of insecurity permeating many of his Jewish confreres. In the *Silent Don* he presented a conversation between a Jewish female soldier and the leader of a machine-gun squad, who assured her that her example was the best answer to the frequent accusation that Jews shirked service on the firing line. This accusation was doubtless promoted by the silent treatment the government gave to the part played by Jews in the Soviet armed services.

For this and other reasons many Jewish writers tried to hide their Jewish background and became what I rather uncharitably call "inverted

Marranos"—a familiar phenomenon in other countries as well. A few even went to the extreme of embracing Christianity, Greek Orthodox or Protestant, although no religious denomination was viewed with particular favor by the ruling circles. Nevertheless, most of these writers unwittingly retained certain peculiar characteristics which distinguished them from their colleagues in many subtle ways. At any rate, the number of Jewish littérateurs in the Russian tongue, already sizable before 1917, increased by leaps and bounds after the revolution. According to Maurice Friedberg, "It would be safe to assume that the number of Jews who entered Soviet Russian literature in the last half a century exceeds that of any other country or historical period"—an assertion which may be controverted by the parallel phenomena in the German Weimar Republic and in the postwar United States.[27]

ANTIRELIGIOUS SHACKLES

Jewish cultural attrition was accelerated, particularly in the 1930s, by powerful antireligious legislation and propaganda. Since Jewish culture had from time immemorial been even more intimately interwoven with the people's religious heritage than that of most other nationalities, the inroads made by communism into Jewish religious life and thought were bound to sap deeply its very vitality. Believers in the communist orthodoxy—and communism from the outset bore many characteristics of a new creed—often demonstrated more zeal and intolerance than practitioners of the traditional faiths. Not unjustly did many Russian Jews compare their fate with that of the Iberian Marranos who could fully cultivate their ancestral rites only in secret conventicles and through the use of one or another subterfuge. Raphael Mordecai Barishensky drew this comparison, for example, in his moving autobiographical record. In 1922 this rabbi of Homel (Gomel) in the Ukraine was condemned to a prison term of two years for having delivered a sermon in defense of the traditional religious school and having thus committed a counterrevolutionary crime. During the High Holiday season, he fell ill and was placed in the prison hospital; together with two Jews arrested because they had tried to resist the government's confiscation of their synagogue's silver implements of worship organized regular services for the Jewish inmates. In order to avoid denunciation by their non-Jewish fellow prisoners, for the most part hardened criminals, they held their services late at night and in the early morning while the others were in bed. In his ruminations about his fate, the rabbi contended that these secretive gatherings were psychologically worse than those of the Spanish Marranos, who had had no alternative, whereas he and his confreres knew that outside the prison walls existed some publicly functioning synagogues which they were not allowed to visit. (His petition for a special permit to worship there under guard had been denied by the communist authorities.) But most galling to him was the reflection that the Marranos could at least take comfort from knowing that they were persecuted by non-Jews, "but we are persecuted by our own brethren . . . in free Russia in 1922. Our brethren have turned into our enemies and torturers, which causes me great pain."[28]

It was, indeed, the *Yevsektsiia*, often in cooperation with Jewish communists among the local officials, that staged some of the public trials to dramatize the shortcomings of the Jewish faith. In one such trial, held in 1921 in the presence of a large Jewish audience in Kiev—by chance in the same auditorium where the Beilis trial had been conducted in 1913—the court pronounced the sentence of death on the Jewish faith. This despite the constitutional guarantees for the freedom of religions proclaimed by Lenin and his associates shortly after their seizure of power. A courageous spokesman for the Jewish community, who had pointed out the great similarity between the anti-Jewish arguments of the Black Hundreds and the accusers of Beilis and those presented by the prosecution against Judaism eight years later, was jailed as a counterrevolutionary agitator. Such sentences by obviously biased courts made little impression upon the Jewish worshipers, however. In the following weeks, more of them are said to have attended the Kiev synagogue services than before the trial.

Far more significant were the practical measures taken by the Soviet authorities against some basic Jewish religious institutions and practices. According to a decree of the Council of People's Commissars of January 23, 1918, all possessions of the existing religious bodies were to be confiscated. They were also to lose their legal status as artificial persons and hence be unable to acquire property in their own name. Because of the permanent housing shortage, the local soviets found it extremely convenient to convert synagogues, *hadarim, yeshivot*, as well as Christian and Muslim religious institutions, into public schools, clubs, orphanages, and the like. Equally aggravating to observant Jews were the expropriation of Jewish bathhouses, making it impossible for women to undergo the required ablutions after their menstrual periods, which cast a shadow on their later offspring; the plowing up of Jewish cemeteries into parks and thus obliterating all identifications on ancestral graves; the closing of Jewish slaughterhouses, which made it almost impossible for Jews to acquire kosher meats except for privately slaughtered fowl; the suppression of Jewish schools, and the proclamation that giving instruction in Hebrew and other traditional Jewish subjects to more than three children under eighteen was a counterrevolutionary crime. Perhaps even more serious was the prohibition of ritual circumcision by *mohelim*—a prohibition which in the days of Hadrian had provoked the Bar Kocheba uprising. So sacred was this ritual in the eyes of most Jews that even many Jewish agnostics and atheists all over the world had continued to have their sons circumcised. In the Soviet Union parents of a circumcised child ran greater and more permanent risks of exposure than if, for instance, they attended a synagogue service. In the case of Jewish Party members and higher officials, both these "transgressions" usually led to expulsion from the Party and loss of jobs. To circumvent that penalty, some parents of a newborn boy would absent themselves on official business for the period of the required ceremony and the child's recovery. In the meantime the grandmother in charge of the baby arranged for the operation and took the blame for acting without authorization. When one such grandmother was summoned before a Jewish court, she audaciously asked the judges whether they themselves were not circumcised.[29]

Understandably, such an heroic course could not be universally followed. A growing number of Russian Jews grew up without circumcision and without any form of Jewish education. It may be true that in 1926, after the temporary relaxation of the NEP period, there still existed 1,103 organized Jewish congregations in the Soviet Union with 137,437 registered members and many more unregistered worshipers (this exceptional bit of statistical information was complained about in a speech by a member of the *Yevsektsiia*), but they doubtless consisted mainly of older persons—diminishing in number from year to year. Certainly, assertions like that made in 1927 by Reuben Breinin, an American Hebrew writer and admirer of the Soviet system, that "the [Jewish] community of Minsk is more religious than that of Vilna," must be taken with a large grain of salt. Yet it was a testimony to the great perseverance of the religious leadership that many Jews were still able to cultivate their ancestral mores at least until the break of 1929.

The rabbis, though suffering from their déclassé status and often sharply persecuted, managed to erect a network of private religious schools and *yeshivot* throughout the land. In 1926 they even dared to convoke a rabbinical assembly at Korosten, Volhynia, which was attended by twenty-five rabbis of the area and by forty-seven others from more distant communities, purportedly participating only as guests. The heroic devotion of numerous teachers and students of the various *yeshivot* was likewise undimmed by the difficulties of their forced migrations from locality to locality. One of the most prominent of these academies, the "Lubavich Yeshivah"—established in 1897 by Rabbi Shalom Dob Schneersohn, leader of the distinguished hasidic movement going under the name of *Habad* (an acronym formed from the Hebrew terms for Wisdom, Understanding, and Knowledge)—moved in 1918 in part to Orel, and in part to Kremenchug. In 1920 it was transferred to Rostov on the Don, where its personnel underwent extreme hardships and suffered many losses during the raging typhus epidemic. In 1923 a number of students moved to the small town of Nevel near Velikoe Luki, where they were immediately thrown into jail. Thereupon the whole academy moved to Kharkov, returned to Rostov, and once more settled in Kharkov. There it flourished for about five years. But after its spiritual leader, Rabbi Joseph Isaac Schneersohn, who had succeeded his father in 1920, left Russia under duress in 1928 and settled in then-independent Latvia, the famous *yeshivah* fell victim to the growing Stalin terror.

While the pressure from above, combined with internal forces of disintegration, thus threatened the survival of the Jewish community, communism's appeal to Jews in and outside the Union began to decline sharply. Especially during the period of the great purges of 1936 to 1938, many of the leaders of the defunct *Yevsektsiia* were liquidated, and even the survivors lost much of their missionary fervor.[30] The Godless Society, too, as we recall, greatly tempered its atheistic propaganda in the face of the new dangers confronting the Union from the expanding power of Nazi Germany. Jews were now caught between the millstones of an incipient revival of Russian anti-Semitism and fear of the spreading violent Nazi racism. The growing disillusionment over the Biro-Bidzhan experiment and the purges of the leading Jewish Bolsheviks must also have paralyzed the terrified Jewish community. Nor were the reports, even if reliably transmitted, about the Western powers' attitude toward both Nazism and the prospective Jewish homeland in Palestine reassuring. Internal Jewish resistance, too, was weakened through the emigration of some of the most gifted leaders, actual and potential, to Palestine, the United States, and other countries. Under these circumstances a do-nothing attitude must have appealed to many Jews as the better part of wisdom, particularly since they had also been deprived of their main organs of public opinion and religio-cultural expression. Russian Jewry thus found itself in a very sorry state at the outbreak of World War II.

[15]

The Second World War

❀

Rumblings of an approaching world war became quite loud after Hitler's rise to power in 1933. After the Nazi occupation of Czechoslovakia early in 1939, *Izvestia* fulminated: "In this struggle we ought to be inspired by the images of our glorious ancestors, Alexander Nevskii, Dmitrii Donskoi, Minin and Pozharskii, Suvorov, Kutuzov and the victorious banner of Lenin. . . . The readiness of the present generation to give everything to protect the Russian country against invaders, the struggle for its independence has deep historic roots. . . . Soviet patriotism is national and historical. National and historical has also been the Russian Revolution, which has continued the tradition of the Russian nation." During World War II this patriotic fervor reached the high pitch of the new national anthem proclaiming to the world the

> *Unbreakable union of free-born republics*
> *Great Russia has welded forever to stand;*
> *Created in struggle, by will of the people*
> *United and mighty, our Soviet land.* [1]

Characteristically, in its constant diatribes against Nazism and its racist doctrines, the Russian press failed to play up the Jewish issue, mainly because of the Nazis' very effective stratagem to weaken the internal unity of their prospective victims by appealing to the anti-Semites of all countries and by placing the blame of the war hysteria on Jewish "war-mongering." Many persons, not just in the Soviet Union but also in France, the Netherlands, and elsewhere, frightened by the steadily worsening international situation, swallowed this Nazi line. The Soviet propagandists therefore avoided the anti-Jewish aspects and merely spoke of the German barbarities against socialists, liberals, and other dissenters. Even Jewish organs no longer had a chance to protest, for the national Yiddish press, especially the Moscow *Emes*, had been suppressed in 1938. What remained were such provincial publications as the Minsk *Oktiabr*, the Kiev *Shtern* (Star), and the Biro-Bidzhan *Shtern*, which had a very small circulation even in their native habitats, and were rarely read in other regions.

NAZI-SOVIET COLLABORATION

In the midst of the sharp Nazi-Soviet exchanges a bombshell exploded: the Molotov-Ribbentrop Treaty of August 24, 1939, a week before the Nazi invasion of Poland. It required all the propagandistic artistry of the Soviet agencies to try to explain this sudden reversal to their own peoples. Among them the Jews must have been the most difficult to persuade that the enemy of yesteryear, who had shriekingly proclaimed the elimination of European Jewry as one of his major goals, should now be considered almost an ally. Yet the Jewish officials active in the "information services" of the Soviet Union, domestically and internationally, strained all their ingenuity to explain this new turn as but a part of Marxian dialectics which, though transcending the reasoning capacities of average men, was fully comprehended by the superior minds of the Soviet regime and the Third International.

Unfortunately, we have no documentary evidence as to the reaction of the rank-and-file Russian Jewish communists to the new policy. While the Soviets were feeding the Nazi war machine supplies of raw materials and foodstuffs (some 500,000 tons of phosphates, 900,000 tons of oil products, 1,500,000 tons of grain, even rubber and zinc purchased from Germany's enemy, the British Empire) in accordance with the treaty, all Russian organs of public opinion observed an enforced silence on the treatment of Jews by the Nazi conquerors in Poland between September, 1939, and June, 1941. Very few Russian Jews had access to the information trickling through from these occupied territories. The ensuing unpreparedness of the White Russian, Ukrainian, and other Jews for the Nazi onslaught when the German steam roller finally started moving into Russia herself astounded even the conquering Nazi commanders. A German military report upon entry into White Russia in

July, 1941, stated:

> The Jews are strikingly ill-informed about our attitude towards them
> and about the treatment Jews are receiving in Germany or in Warsaw,
> places after all not too remote from them. If they were not, they could
> scarcely ask whether we in Germany treat Jews differently from other
> citizens. Although they do not expect to be granted equal rights with
> the Russians under the German administration, they do believe that
> we will let them alone if they apply themselves diligently to their
> work.

This lack of psychological preparedness was partially responsible for the
extent to which the Jewish masses were trapped beyond any ability to
escape at the crucial moment.[2]

At first, even during the period of Russian "neutrality," the war
seemed to bring about a certain relaxation of the antireligious propaganda which might have accrued to the benefit of the segment of Jews
still cherishing their religious tradition. After the Nazi invasion of June,
1941, the government not only tolerated soldiers carrying Bibles into
battle and priests informally accompanying military detachments, but in
a publication *Truth About Religion in Russia*, issued in 1942, various
writers sounded off with the claim that the previous strict separation of
state and Church had benefited the Church. What it lost in number of
adherents, material goods, and external prestige had been more than
made up, they maintained, by the deepening of its spiritual appeal.
True, after recovering from the first shocks of the Nazi invasion some of
the old-time Bolsheviks, such as Kalinin, still spoke of religion as "a
misguiding institution" and contended that the Party must continue to
fight it through education. But even Kalinin admitted in 1943 that "since
religion still grips considerable sections of the population and some
people are deeply religious, we cannot combat it by ridicule." The
number of Russian Orthodox churches was now allowed to grow from
4,225, served by 5,665 priests in August, 1941 (contrasted with 50,960
priests in 1917), to a substantial majority of the 16,000 churches of all
denominations counted in the Soviet Union in June, 1945. The climax of
that reconciliation came when the new patriarch of the Orthodox
Church, Alexis, was installed by the government itself with great pomp
and with the participation of many foreign churchmen.[3]

For Jews, too, this relaxation in the state-Church tensions might
have involved greater freedom of worship, reconstruction of synagogues, and fuller employment of rabbis and religious teachers. In fact,
the godless agitation among them, as among the non-Jews, had long
before been undermined by the government's lukewarm attitude. *Der
Apikoires* (The Epicurean, the ancient Hebrew term for agnostic), the
Yiddish magazine devoted to atheistic propaganda, had suspended

publication in 1935. By 1937, even Emelian Yaroslavskii, the Jewish head of the Russian Godless Society, publicly admitted failure. True, the revival of Russian Orthodoxy entailed some reassertion of traditional anti-Jewish doctrines preached by the prerevolutionary Churches. It thus helped to resuscitate the age-old anti-Semitic feelings, which now manifested themselves with ever-increasing vigor. But the government was still suppressing any overt internal discords, and most Soviet Jews felt far less threatened by this recrudescence of old hatreds. Much as the new processions of the Communist Youth resembled the age-old Church pageants, they were not allowed to degenerate into such prerevolutionary anti-Semitic performances as were recorded in the case of the well-known monk, Iliodor of Tsaritsin (interveningly renamed Stalingrad). At that time the marchers had displayed a large doll dressed in a Jewish caftan which they solemnly burned at the end of the procession.[4]

From the Jewish standpoint the immediate effect of the Molotov-Ribbentrop Treaty had a revitalizing impact, for it soon brought masses of religiously and nationally conscious Jews into the Union. In September, 1939, while the Nazis were subduing the Polish armies, the Soviets occupied large stretches of eastern Poland. In June, 1940, when Germany was fully preoccupied with the conquest of Belgium, the Netherlands, and France, the Soviet Union took over the three Baltic states with practically no resistance. The Jewish population of the Union now increased from over three million in 1939 to more than five million in July, 1940. The accession of two million nationally minded Jews helped revive the national forms of Jewish culture among the older Russian citizens as well.

However, governmental antagonism immediately made itself felt, and the powerful totalitarian machinery quickly suppressed all creative manifestations of the newly annexed Jewish communities. This repression came to the fore clearly in Vilna, which had fully maintained its cultural vitality under the interwar Polish regime, as well as after October 10, 1939, when the Russian army had handed it over to the Lithuanian Republic. The size of its Jewish community had been swelled by some 15,000 refugees from the provinces; among them about one thousand Zionist "pioneers," men and women who had undergone training for work in Palestine. True, material conditions had greatly deteriorated, and with some help from the American Jewish Joint Distribution Committee, the International and American Red Cross, and other foreign relief organizations, the Jewish community had to assume tremendous new financial responsibilities. For the sake of good will it even supported many non-Jewish refugees, including some previously notorious Polish anti-Semites. No fewer than three Yiddish dailies resumed publication; a Jew was appointed vice-mayor, and four streets were renamed in honor of Mendele, Peretz, Dick, and a local communal worker, Zemach Shabad. The same experience repeated itself on a lesser scale in the other communities so long as they remained outside the Soviet Union.[5]

No sooner, however, did the Russian administration take over the Baltic States in June, 1940, than the Yiddish papers had to discontinue publication (they were temporarily replaced in August by a communist daily, *Der Vilner Emes*). Synagogues and schools were starved out of existence, if not formally suppressed. More tragically, in closing all Zionist organizations, the Bund, and other Jewish associations, the Soviet authorities also deported most of their leaders to Siberia. Outstanding Jewish industrialists and businessmen shared that fate, together with some nationalist and business leaders of the Lithuanian people. The proportionate Jewish share, however, was much larger. It has been plausibly estimated that among the approximately 25,000 or more Lithuanian exiles there were some 6,000 to 7,000 Jews, far in excess of their share of the population. Nevertheless, the few Jewish communists who participated in the newly established Soviet regime were conspicuous enough to fan the embers of anti-Jewish hostility among the masses. In a greatly exaggerated form this alleged Jewish preponderance in the communist administration served as an excuse after the world war for some Lithuanian nationalists in the United States and elsewhere to justify the subsequent collaboration of many Lithuanians in the wholesale extermination of Jews during the Nazi occupation. As a matter of fact, during the year of Soviet domination from June, 1940, to July, 1941, Jews had suffered even more severely than their neighbors. The same speedy attrition was noticeable in the course of 1940–41 in the other Baltic communities which had been the scene of vigorous Jewish cultural and religious life before the War.[6]

UNDER NAZI TERROR

All these difficulties were far overshadowed by the stark tragedy which befell Russian Jewry after the Nazi invasion. Although Russia had been forewarned by Hitler's speeches announcing war preparations against world communism and although Soviet and Nazi "volunteers" had already fought many battles during the Spanish Civil War of 1936–37, the Red Army was unprepared to meet the Nazi onslaught. With unprecedented speed the Nazi armies not only occupied the formerly Polish and Baltic possessions which were supposed to serve as buffers for just such an eventuality, but they also occupied all of White Russia, the Ukraine, and many provinces of the Great Russian Republic. By

October, 1941, less than four months after the start of the invasion, Nazi foreposts were a mere six miles from the perimeter of Moscow.

With these conquests the Nazis became the masters of most Jewish mass settlements. The speed of the German advance, combined with the Jews' lack of preparedness, resulted in the overwhelming majority of Jews finding themselves now under the Nazi heel. Only some of the Jewish draftees from the western areas were withdrawn together with the rest of the Russian armies into the deep interior, to be reformed over the winter and to resume hostilities during the second year of the war. However, the four million war prisoners taken by the Germans in the first six months, and their successors during the following two years, embraced many thousands of Jews who, even less than their Gentile comrades, enjoyed the benefits of the Geneva Convention of 1929. In an agreement concluded on July 17, 1941, between the notorious Reinhardt Heydrich of the Reich Security Office and General Hermann Reinecke of the Army, professional revolutionaries, Red Army political officers, "fanatical" communists, and "all Jews" were to be implacably eliminated. Very frequently German officers also condemned Jewish-looking Gentiles to death on the basis of their facial features or because they were circumcised. In the first flush these officers paid little heed to the possible impact of such slaughter of circumcised Muslims upon Turkey, whose good will was being ardently sought by the German diplomacy.[7]

Needless to say, news of these and other atrocities committed on the war prisoners gradually trickled back to the Russian home front, nullifying whatever sympathies the anticommunist segments in the population might originally have felt toward the German "liberators." Even the Jews were at first rather meek and submissive. An officer of the German Economic Commission in the Ukraine wrote in his report of December 2, 1941:

> The attitude of the Jewish population was from the beginning rather shy and willing. They tried to avoid any conflicts with the German Administration. . . . It cannot be proved that the Jews participated in an organized manner in any sabotage action against the Germans. It cannot be asserted that the Jews represented a danger to the German Army. With the work performed by the Jews, which, of course, was stimulated by fear, the German Army and Administration was completely satisfied.

The Jews were quickly disabused, but the vast majority of them were hopelessly trapped behind the advancing German front. That, contrary to news spread abroad, Russian officials did not evacuate entire Jewish communities was quite evident to any informed student of the strategic situation. The Russian railway system had from the outset been inadequate for the tremendous task of moving millions of soldiers and their armaments to the front and then back into the interior. No one could dream of a mass evacuation of any segment of the civilian population, even if the will had been there. Corliss Lamont, an American, was taken in by wartime propaganda when he wrote in 1945: "More than 1,000,000 [Jews] were safely evacuated from these [occupied] regions and were given priority in transportation and care, the bulk of them going to Uzbekistan." The result was that only small groups of Jews and non-Jews, considered particularly valuable for war production or other government services, were sent away in advance of, or together with, the retreating armies.[8]

Even the Jewish collective farms in the Ukraine, whose personnel might have proved very useful for the maintenance of agricultural production in the unoccupied areas, were largely left to their own devices; they suffered nearly total annihilation by the Nazis and their Ukrainian collaborators. Only from the Crimea, which was given a breathing spell before the Nazi conquest, were the inhabitants of some Jewish *kolkhozes* evacuated in large numbers. Otherwise it was left to individual initiative as to how many succeeded in fleeing for their lives by whatever means they had, hiding in forests, being concealed by some non-Jewish friends, or before long, joining the ever-growing partisan detachments who fought the Germans from the rear and tried to cut their supply lines. It was fortunate for the Jews of the western Polish provinces, occupied in the first onrush of the Nazi armies in September, 1939, that hundreds of thousands had succeeded in fleeing into Russia, where most of them were assigned settlements far in the interior, often beyond the Ural. Quite a few hardy souls had traversed the entire Soviet Union and reached China or Japan (much of China was at that time occupied by the Japanese). They formed new Jewish colonies in Shanghai, Tientsin, and Kobe, many proceeding from there to the Americas, Palestine, or Australia during and after the war. In all, the Jewish population in the unoccupied parts of the Soviet Union more than doubled. From some nine hundred thousand in January, 1939, it increased to well over two million by the end of 1941.

The three million left behind suffered all the pangs of hunger and aggravation inflicted upon them by the Nazi autocrats before most of them were finally deported to the gas chambers. Immediately after the occupation they were forced to wear a badge (usually a white armband with the Star of David), segregated in ghettos under the sanction of capital punishment for unauthorized departures, and given food rations far below the prevailing minima. Of course, Jews were not the only ones to suffer. Apart from losses on the battlefields, the Soviet Union had many millions of her citizens liquidated by the Nazis. But in most cases non-Jews were exterminated on individual grounds, some because they had been communist officials (*Bolschewismus—jüdisches Untermenschen-*

tum or "Bolshevism: Jewish Subhumanity" was the title of an early German war pamphlet); others because they were accused of spying or sabotage; still others because they belonged to the native intelligentsia whose destruction was writ large in the Nazi program of enslavement of eastern Europe. As early as May 21, 1930, Hitler had told Otto Strasser that "the Nordic race has a right to rule the world and we must take this racial right as the guiding star of our foreign policy. It is for this reason that for us any cooperation with Russia is out of the question, for there on a Slav-Tartar body is set a Jewish head." Nor did the German dictator refrain from such obvious exaggerations as his reiterated public claims that 98 percent of all leading positions in the Soviet Union in 1937–38 were held by Jews. Ultimately, the aggregate of the Soviet victims of the Nazi occupation forces came quite close to the thirty million persons predicted as desirable by Heinrich Himmler soon after the beginning of hostilities.[9]

Yet Jews were in a category by itself: merely being a Jew was sufficient ground for most brutal treatment and assassination. Many Nazis considered the cold-blooded murder of Jews a meritorious deed. So deeply ingrained had this hatred become that it swept away all utilitarian considerations. Even in White Russia—where Jews monopolized entire branches of handicrafts and where, for instance, a Nazi commander himself reported that with the removal of the Jewish shoemakers, no one was left to repair the shoes of his forced laborers—the progress of the *Einsatzgruppen* proceeded unhampered. The German district commissar of Slutsk complained that although Jewish artisans were "indispensable for the maintenance of the economy," the police had carted off all Jews, claiming "that this purge must take place for political reasons and economic considerations had never yet played a role."[10]

The racialist ideology also came to the fore after the German conquest of the Crimea and parts of the Caucasus. In the Crimea the conquerors drew a line of demarcation between the Krimchaks (old Tartar-speaking Jewish settlers), whom they considered full-blooded Jews and hence subject to extermination, and the Karaims (members of the religious Karaite sect), whom their racial specialists declared to be of non-Jewish origin. Similarly tolerant was the German attitude toward the Tats (the "Mountain Jews") of the Caucasus, whom their neighbors shielded with all means at their disposal and whose outward appearance and dialect sharply differentiated them from Jewish types familiar to the Western conquerors.[11]

All these were minor exceptions, however, to the general plan of extermination of all Soviet Jews on whom the Nazi storm troopers could lay their hands. Their leaders actually gloried in the success of their undertaking. In his well-known address to the SS generals of October 4,

1943—at a time when the fortunes of war had already turned against Germany—Heinrich Himmler thus described the "very grave" matter of the complete extermination of Jews. He declared: "Among ourselves it should be mentioned quite frankly, and yet we will never speak of it publicly . . . I mean . . . the extermination of the Jewish race. . . . This is a page of glory in our history which has never been written and is never to be written."[12]

It has indeed been extremely difficult to assemble full information concerning the Nazi atrocities in the occupied eastern areas. From the outset the German administration divided these territories into a Reichskommissariat Ostland, embracing the northeastern provinces of Poland and the Baltic States, and a similar Kommissariat for the Ukraine, including Podolia and Volhynia. Both these Kommissariats were under the administration of Alfred Rosenberg, the chief ideologist of the Nazi Party, who now served as minister for the East. His subordinates serving as heads of these two Kommissariats, Heinrich Lohse and Erich Koch, outdid their chief in their barbaric treatment of Jews and to a lesser extent of the other inhabitants of these territories. In the Ukraine, particularly, some restraints were imposed by that faction of policy makers in Berlin who, as during World War I, wished to build up a Ukrainian irredenta leading to the formation of an independent Ukrainian Republic under German control. They found many collaborators, and were even able to form Ukrainian auxiliary detachments under the name of the "Ukrainian Liberation Legion." They also encouraged some Russian captives to form a "Russian Army of Liberation" under the command of the collaborationist general Andrei A. Vlasov. Some such local pro-Nazis, though not Vlasov himself, helped their masters uncover hidden Jews and send them to their death. In fact, a leading official in the German Ministry of Propaganda complained of Vlasov's passivity in fighting Jews. As in the past, the White Russian population was far less inclined to stage pogroms, an attitude which German officials attributed to their "political stupidity."[13]

In this great emergency the old religious and national traditions reasserted themselves. An unconfirmed story has it that the Nazi commander of a Crimean town tricked the Jewish population in 1942 by proclaiming that he wished to send them all off to Palestine. The Zionist sentiment in the population was supposed to have been so strong, even twenty-five years after the revolution, that not a single Jew failed to appear at the appointed time. Of course, these train loads had an entirely different destination.

Be that as it may, there is no question about the considerable upsurge of religious feeling. Some heroic rabbis continued to preach to their congregations almost to their last breath. There also was much religious questioning, the ancient debates between Job and his friends being now resuscitated under different guises. A hasidic leader, Kalonymus Kalmish Shapiro, whose homiletical work appeared posthumously in Israel, referred to a talmudic legend concerning the Ten Martyrs executed in the days of Emperor Hadrian. When angels reputedly queried the Lord whether martyrdom was indeed a proper reward for the unflinching devotion of these students of Torah, the Lord supposedly promised that if it were to happen again, the universe would return to chaos. At this point the rabbi asked: "And now innocent children, pure as angels, as well as great and holy men in Israel, are being killed and slaughtered only because they are Jews . . . and the world's space is filled with their heart-rending shouts: 'Save us, save us!' They, too, cry, 'Is this the reward for devotion to Torah?' Yet the universe is not destroyed but remains intact, as if nothing happened." Continuing such preachments all through 1942 and early 1943, the rabbi defied destiny until his body, too, was turned into ashes in September, 1943. Deep religious and national feeling also permeated the numerous melancholy "songs of the ghetto" which have survived to illustrate the unbroken spirit of heroism, however passive, of a whole people facing uncontrollable disaster. Others preferred more active resistance and, whether in partisan groups or individually, fought the Germans. Perhaps one of the most tragic manifestations of the unquenchable anti-Semitism of the period was the occasional rejection of Jewish partisans by their non-Jewish confreres.[14]

SOVIET REACTIONS

Very little of that cataclysm was reported in the Russian press. While all means of communication from the printed word to the radio were set in motion to denounce the Nazi atrocities, the mass murders of the civilian population were not emphasized until very late in the war and postwar periods. Undoubtedly, the propaganda agencies felt that there would have been too much questioning of why the Red Army had retreated so deeply into the interior and left so many millions at the mercy of the Nazi assassins. Even those who believed in the doctrine of "strategic retreat" and approved of the conscious luring of the enemy into the vast open steppes as a means for his destruction often questioned why this method had become necessary and why the Soviet military power could not have halted the German steam roller closer to the frontier. Nor were Russian memories so short as to have forgotten the Molotov-Ribbentrop pact of 1939 and the supplies the Russians had sent into Germany which had helped build up the Nazi military power before the invasion. Only occasionally did a Russian writer find such words of sympathy as those in Boris Gorbatov's novel, *Taras' Family*, written in 1943. Here a Jewish doctor working in a small Ukrainian factory town is depicted as a greatly beloved dedicated physician. When he first appears wearing the Nazi-imposed Star of David, he is greeted with a deep bow by the old worker, Taras, a bow intended "to you and your suffering."[15]

In any case, the specific slaughter of Jews was rarely mentioned in releases intended for domestic consumption. Once again, the Soviet leaders feared that by siding with the Jewish victims of Nazidom, they might furnish "proof" for the Nazi contention of the alliance between the Bolshevists and the Jewish world conspiracy. Even the Soviet soldiers were not immune from the Nazi propaganda. With their accustomed thoroughness the Germans were often able to use specific data in their messages to the Russian combatants. Facing a regiment recruited from a certain area, the Nazis blared over their loudspeakers and radios names of prominent Jews from that area and then asked the Soviet soldiers whether these Jews were among them, or else had shirked their military duty and stayed behind to enrich themselves through war speculations. For the most part these were names of prominent citizens who for that very reason were known to the recruits. The fact that they were overage or badly needed behind the front because of their expertness in the production of war materials or for other vital government services was hardly considered by the unsophisticated *muzhiks* now in uniform. In other effective broadcasts the Nazis warned the Soviet soldiers not to entrust their lives to "Yankel Kreiser"—that is, to Lieutenant General Yakov G. Kreyzer, one of the eminent Jewish war heroes.

Whether because of the efficacy of German propaganda or because of the persistence of atavistic anti-Jewish prejudices, even Jewish partisans often got a lukewarm reception among their comrades in arms. In some areas one heard the saying that Jews "merely eat and spoil the air." When on September 12, 1943, twenty-two young Jews from the Vilna ghetto wished to join a neighboring partisan force, they were asked, "Why have you not come until today? So long as the Germans had not attacked you, you have faithfully worked for them. Only now when they have started exterminating you, you have come to seek refuge among us." Such incidents occurred quite frequently, although the testimony of later writers bears full witness to the heroism of numerous Jewish freedom fighters. Some of them, like the watchmaker Abraham Hirschfeld of Slonim, became quite legendary figures. One of the leading partisans, Colonel G. M. Linkov, devoted an entire chapter in his wartime reminiscences to Hirschfeld. In the regular Russian armies, too, no fewer than 160,772 Jews received decorations for bravery in combat. They were the fourth-largest national group in the Red Army to merit such recognition, although their population ranked but seventh in size. More than a hundred achieved the title of "Hero of the Soviet Union." Among outstanding individuals one need but mention Captain

Israel Fisanovich, who as a submarine commander sank thirteen enemy ships, also earning an American Navy Cross. A woman flier, Lieutenant Lily Litvak, distinguished herself at Stalingrad and shot down six German planes at Orel before losing her own life. At the same time, Jews occasionally suffered from anti-Semitism among both the Soviet officers and enlisted men. The number of decorated Jewish soldiers is doubly remarkable as some of them were passed over "because of the pernicious influence of the late Supreme Army Commissar Shcherbakov, member of the Politbureau . . . [and] dyed-in-the-wool anti-Semite," according to a later report by a Jewish captain.[16]

The story of the Jewish part in the defense of the Soviet Union during World War II is yet to be told in full and illuminating detail. It appears that 420,000 Jews served in the Soviet Army, 65,000 in the Air Force, and 40,000 in the Navy, or a total of 525,000 men and women, a very large number of whom fell on the battlefield, much beyond their percentage of the general population. Although the ranks of Jewish generals were greatly thinned out during the 1936–38 purges, their proportion of all echelons of the Soviet officer corps during the war was exceedingly high. Yet the official Soviet record studiously avoided any mention of Jews. For example, in enumerating the number of Soviet officers in the Army and Air Force, from the outset the five-volume *Soviet History of the Great Patriotic War, 1941–1945* gave exact figures for the respective shares of the various nationalities, but mentioned no figure for Jews, although they were the third-largest group (after the far more numerous Ukrainians and White Russians) among the national minorities. (Only in a supplementary volume published in 1965 were some amends made for this omission.) On a monument for Lev Dovator, the son of a Jewish tailor who became a distinguished general and eventually fell in battle, no reference was made to his Jewish nationality. Commanding 30,000 Cossack cavalrymen in the defense of Moscow, Dovator had devised an effective method for combating the German Panzer divisions by using his mobile forces in marshlands and thick forests where the German tanks were largely stalled. He thus helped stem the advance of the German army in the Battle of Moscow. But he lost his life when Stalin made the erroneous decision to order the Cossacks to dismount and to fight as regular infantrymen.

Similarly Yona (Jan) Davidovich Cherniakovski, holding the highest rank of Marshal of the Soviet Army, who had vanquished the Germans in three important 1943 encounters at Voronezh, Kursk, and Konotop and was the only Soviet general who had never lost a battle, was killed during his drive on Königsberg (now Kaliningrad) by a mysterious explosion of a mine, possibly laid by some of his own anti-Semitic subordinates. He was granted his final wish and was buried in the Jewish cemetery of his native Vilna in the presence of relatives, including two rabbis. But the monument erected in his honor failed to refer to his Jewish nationality, while the official Soviet who's who of leading military commanders called him a White Russian and described his father—who had made a living from selling vodka at a rented roadhouse—as a poor peasant sharecropper. The large number of Jewish generals is doubly remarkable as only a few of the survivors from the purges of 1936–38 were rehabilitated after the outbreak of hostilities because the Soviet high command was short of gifted and well-trained high-ranking personnel. Of the eighteen Jewish generals who died together with Marshal Mikhail N. Tukhachevsky, only two—Yona Emanuilovich Yakir (1896–1937) and Jan Borisovich Gamarnik (1894–1937), head of the political administration of the Red Army who had committed suicide—were rehabilitated many years later. In addition, of course, a great many Jewish scientists and others performed extremely valuable services for the Soviet war machine behind the front.

Only long after the war (in 1965) did *Pravda*, in giving the percentage by nationality of the men awarded the title "Hero of the Soviet Union," mention 107 Jews as recipients of this honor. In fact, there were at least 121, and possibly many more if one adds those Jewish commanders who, like Trotsky, had Russian-sounding names and consistently claimed for themselves a Russian (or some other non-Jewish) nationality. The figure of 121 heroes, along with other data on Jewish combatants, was computed by the well-known Russian-Jewish sociologist Yakov Kantor and written up in several pertinent articles in the Yiddish-language *Folks Shtime*, published in Warsaw. Clearly, this foreign publication came to the attention of but few Jews living in the Soviet Union and remained totally unknown to the Soviet masses. Ironically, even Jewish writers felt prompted to take part in that "conspiracy of silence." For example, in his 1932 novel *Vremya vpered* (Time, Forward), the distinguished novelist Valentin P. Katayev (1897–) sympathetically depicted a Jewish engineer named Margulies as a coworker in the early period of rapid industrialization; in his wartime novels, however, though Katayev glorified fighters of various nationalities, he never chose to glorify a Jew. And Katayev's own wife and children were murdered by the Nazi invaders because they were of the Jewish "race"![17]

No complete statistics of Jewish casualties on Russia's battlefields are available. But the incomplete data at hand indicate that the number of Jewish victims exceeded their ratio in the population. All that may have become known in some official bureaus in Moscow, but no information to this effect was circulated either in the Red Army or among the civilians. If Jews were mentioned at all in praise of the great valor of the Soviet peoples or in deprecation of Nazi methods, this was done either casually or for foreign consumption, especially in broadcasts to Britain or America.

NEW JEWISH COMMITTEE

It was also only with foreign propaganda in mind that a new Jewish organization was called into being: the Jewish Anti-Fascist Committee. The idea of such an organization was first broached by two socialist refugees from Poland, Henryk Erlich and Viktor Alter, who discussed it with Lavrentii.P. Beria, then commissar of the interior and head of the secret service, and subsequently addressed themselves to Stalin himself. Although generally sympathetic to the idea of a Jewish organization, Stalin was evidently annoyed by their letter, which reminded him of the presence in Kuibyshev of these two former leaders of the hated Second International. He immediately noted on the letter the two words: *Rasstrieliat oboikh* (Let them both be shot). They were immediately executed, although in the following year Molotov and Vishinskii continued to reassure correspondents that the two men would soon be set free. Not until January, 1943, did Molotov admit in a reply to Albert Einstein and to labor leaders William Green and Philip Murray that Alter and Erlich had already been executed; Molotov claimed that the latter had engaged in hostile activities toward the Union and incited Soviet soldiers to make speedy peace with the Germans. Until today this calumny has not been formally repudiated by the Soviet government, although Khrushchev has publicly admitted the terroristic crimes committed by Stalin and his associates.[18]

Indirectly, nevertheless, the negotiations initiated by Erlich and Alter may well have persuaded Soviet authorities of the worthwhileness of a Jewish organization to maintain contacts with the Jewry of the Allied lands. While the details of the formation of the Jewish Anti-Fascist Committee have never been fully revealed, by the summer of 1942 it was in operation under the presidency of Salomon M. Mikhoels, the renowned Yiddish actor who was also prominent in the general Russian theatrical circles.[19]

Characteristically, this committee was not intended to be a national organization of Soviet Jewry with any program of domestic activity. It became part and parcel of the Soviet Bureau of Information under the guidance of Solomon A. Lozovskii, director of that bureau and vice-commissar for foreign affairs. Although himself a Jew, Lozovskii specialized in the Far Eastern area and evinced interest in the committee only insofar as it could be used for Soviet propaganda abroad. He defined its task as consisting exclusively in helping the Allies "to stop the bloodthirsty rage of Hitler and the other fascist apes who claim to belong to a master race." In this respect the committee's releases and radio broadcasts to the Jews of the United States and the British Commonwealth served an excellent purpose in Russia's great hour of need.

A highlight of the committee's activity was a 1943 trip to the West undertaken by Mikhoels and Itzik Fefer with Stalin's personal blessings. The two men, known at least to the Yiddish-reading public through their artistic and literary achievements, were hospitably received in the United States and, according to Fefer, raised $2,000,000 to $3,000,000 for the benefit of the Russian people as a whole. Fefer also gloried in having persuaded the American Jewish Joint Distribution Committee to extend charitable aid, through the Russian Red Cross, to the downtrodden of all nationalities. Another oft-repeated early slogan of the committee exhorted the Jews abroad to supply the Soviet Union with one thousand tanks and five hundred bombers. However, with much larger quantities of American governmental supplies reaching the Soviets through Murmansk or Iran, this particular appeal lost much of its significance. In an article of February, 1943, the committee's secretary, Shakhno Epshtain, correctly described its real function:

> The basic activity of the Jewish Anti-Fascist Committee was directed towards enlightening the Jewish popular masses in all countries about the great historical accomplishments with which Soviet reality is replete. The Committee did this in writing, dispatching daily by cable, and frequently through special mailing facilities, newspaper material, reports, short stories, songs and even lengthy plays; and it did it orally by means of four weekly radio broadcasts to foreign countries, especially to England and the United States.[20]

As part of its foreign propaganda the committee undertook to collaborate with American Jewish organizations in the preparation of a Black Book documenting Nazi atrocities, of which Yiddish and English editions were to appear in New York, while a Russian rendition was to be published in Moscow. At first there was considerable excitement within the committee about this project. Many Soviet Jews in high positions, who had previously lost all contact with their people, rediscovered their ancient ties under the blows of Nazism, which did not discriminate between Orthodox or agnostic Jews, nationalists or assimilationists, sending them all alike to gas chambers. Ilya Ehrenburg not only joined the sponsorship of the Anti-Fascist Committee but also personally collected material, mainly eyewitness reports, relating to the Nazi extermination of Jews. In sending such a collection to the prospective copublishers of the Black Book in August, 1944, he wrote in his accompanying note: "I have collected here documents telling of the annihilation of defenseless Jews by the Nazi invaders. Here is no litera-ture. These are genuine, candid stories, letters to relatives, dia-ries. . . . Let all know that defenseless Jews died manfully, with words of contempt and revenge. . . . Let all know that Jews, when they could, killed their executioners. . . . Let this book burn like fire. Let it call for retribution." Active Jewish resistance to the Nazi onslaught, rather than passive martyrdom, was also extolled in Peretz Markish's wartime poems, *For the People and the Fatherland*, and his great postwar epic, *The War*.[21]

As time went on the committee's enthusiasm for the book waned. While the American partners continued with the preparations for publi-cation and even secured a foreword from Albert Einstein, the Moscow committee dragged its feet. It first rejected Einstein's foreword as too Zionist in approach (a later collection of the physicist's essays was to include this "Preface That Was Not Used"), and finally withdrew com-pletely. According to Ehrenburg, the *Black Book* had already been set in type and was to appear at the end of 1948, but was suddenly suppressed by order of the government. Nor did the committee proceed with the implementation of its other major projects. In all these matters the committee had to avoid the appearance of acting as a nationalist Jewish agency, instead of merely following the line laid down by the Soviet Information Bureau. If, as the only functioning nationwide Jewish orga-nization, it unavoidably had to deal with some problems brought to it by various Jewish groups in the country, had to extend support to unem-ployed Yiddish writers and artists, and occasionally engaged in some form of Jewish social work, it actually transcended its permissible range of activity. Curiously, Lozovskii, who if anything had constantly tried to stem any such expansion into the domestic field, was later accused of complicity in this illegal endeavor, an accusation which in part led to his execution in 1952.[22]

One such involuntary Jewish cultural activity consisted in the com-mittee's publication of its own Yiddish organ, *Di Ainikait* (Unity). It was mainly devoted to foreign propaganda, but it also had to report on the activities of the organization itself and on public meetings it held, and otherwise had to mention certain communal or cultural happenings within Soviet Jewry. Needless to say, this was a poor substitute for the ramified press and the educational system which had existed in the Soviet Union but a decade earlier. Even after the German invasion of June, 1941, twenty-two Yiddish books and pamphlets had still appeared in the newly annexed Polish and Baltic provinces. But these had mostly been on the presses before the start of the Russo-German hostilities. In 1942 this output was reduced to a single pamphlet of sketches published in Moscow. Despite a minor recovery during the following three war years in connection with the activities of the Anti-Fascist Committee, the total three-year output was still limited to but fifty-six items, for the most part of minor significance.[23]

In part, to be sure, there existed many purely technical difficulties. Certainly, the Nazi occupation of the main centers of Yiddish printing, the headlong evacuation of Moscow which forced the publishing firm *Emes* to transfer a skeletal force to Kuibyshev, general wartime shortages, the drafting of many writers into active service, and other factors made continued publication of Yiddish works extremely arduous. But these obstacles might have been overcome were it not for the official discouragement of Jewish cultural endeavors, such as had clearly manifested itself during the brief interval of 1938–41. A fairly authentic story has it that when Zelig Akselrod, a prominent Yiddish writer of Soviet Minsk, visited the newly annexed communities of Vilna and Kovno early in 1941, he heard complaints that Soviet authorities were closing down all Yiddish schools. Somewhat rashly, he suggested organized petitions signed by the majority of parents as the only way of saving the Yiddish school system. Evidently denounced for this "nationalist deviation," he speedily disappeared from the scene, never to be heard of again. The totalitarian government simply brooked no interference with its own initiative, especially during the subsequent war years, when it concentrated on its single-minded objective of winning the war.

It may also be noted that only a few years before (in 1934) Fefer had publicly accused Mikhoels of having complained that the Party paid little attention to Jewish culture and of thus having joined the spokesmen of "nationalistic hysteria." Yet when they both arrived in the United States they emphasized the links between Russian Jews and Jews of other countries, with whom, however, they themselves had maintained few contacts for several years. To mollify the American Jewish leaders' anxiety about the fate of Jews in the Nazis' newly conquered Soviet territories, Fefer assured them that the Red Army had saved millions of Jews. The *Ainikait* often harped on the same theme. As early as December 5, 1942, the eminent writer David Bergelson tried to persuade its readers that the Russian evacuation had "saved the large majority of Ukrainian, White Russian, Lithuanian, and Latvian Jews." In fact, these reassurances—which in their helplessness the Western Jews wished to believe and which came, so to speak, from an authoritative source on the spot—helped to deepen the prevailing ignorance in the West of what was actually happening to East Central European Jewry under the heel of the murderous *Einsatzgruppen*. Nonetheless, American and English Jews, though wishing to cooperate with their countries' allies against the Nazis, instinctively gave but half-hearted support to the emissaries of the committee. On its part, this lukewarm attitude must have strengthened the Soviet government's determination to maintain its policy of silence on the Jewish issue.

[16]

Postwar Reaction

When Germany surrendered in May, 1945, Jews and other Soviet citizens looked forward to an era of peace and prosperity of unprecedented dimensions. Jews in particular cherished the hope that once relieved of the great menace from its Western neighbor, the Soviet Union might relax its totalitarian controls and treat them without fear of the world-wide Nazi anti-Semitic propaganda. After the great Holocaust in the western provinces, the Jewish survivors were deeply grateful to the Red Army for saving them from the Nazi extermination squads. Only a few realized that the war had been won by a coalition of great powers, and that without Britain's staunch resistance alone for a whole year and the subsequent entry of the United States into the war, the Nazis would not have been stopped during the invasion of Russia in 1941–42. According to the mythology effectively developed by all domestic propaganda organs, it was the Red Army alone which, with but minor and reluctant assistance from her Western allies, defeated the German war machine. In a *Pravda* article, Ilya Ehrenburg actually contended, without any mention of El-Alamein and the British, that even Palestinian Jewry had been saved from the Nazi onslaught by the Russians. Like the rest of the Soviet inhabitants, Jews rejoiced in the victories of the Red Army and for the most part considered it the savior of their surviving remnant.[1]

The Russian Jew

From the beginning, to be sure, clouds had appeared on the horizon. When many Ukrainian, White Russian, and Baltic Jews who had spent the war years either as combatants or as civilian workers in Soviet factories wished to return to their homes, they not only found their old communities in shambles but they were also received coolly by their erstwhile neighbors. The memories of the German anti-Semitic propaganda were still quite fresh. Many neighbors had been outright collaborationists with the Nazis and had helped them track down prospective Jewish victims. These guilt-ridden individuals looked forward with trepidation to the investigation of their roles during the war in which the victims' surviving relatives might prove to be dangerous avengers.

Many friendly Ukrainians and others in the Nazi-occupied areas also looked askance at the returning Jews, whose homes or posts in industry or government they had interveningly taken over. According to the law, returning refugees, particularly war veterans, could reclaim both their possessions and their prewar positions. But with the growing housing shortage in the devastated occupied cities, most new tenants refused to vacate, for the benefit of such Jewish arrivals, premises which they had acquired with much effort and the bribing of many Nazi or Soviet officials. Some persons allegedly muttered under their breaths that they wished the Nazis had done away with all Jews. Naturally, apologists for the Soviet authorities never lacked excuses. When Ben Zion Goldberg, an American visitor, asked Itzik Fefer whether under similar circumstances a returning Ukrainian war veteran would not be given back his old apartment, Fefer evaded the issue and merely claimed that the Ukrainian's difficulty would be mitigated by the presence in the community of relatives and friends who would extend the hospitality of their homes to him. The Yiddish poet failed to grasp the simple logic that for this very reason Jews had an even stronger case for the return of their former dwellings. A returning prosecuting attorney found that he was demoted to the role of a defense attorney. It was explained to him that since many prosecutions would be aimed at former Ukrainian collaborationists, it would be better for the Jew to be cast in the role of defending the accused, rather than in prosecuting them.[2]

The upshot was that many Jews found life in their old habitations quite unbearable; they preferred to settle in the big cities of the interior and make a fresh start. Even the Jewish agricultural colonies in the Ukraine and the Crimea had been totally wiped out, and no effort was made to rebuild them. Their very names, though connected with Soviet leaders, like Kalinindorf or Stalindorf, were never mentioned again in the official records.

A brighter future seemed to beckon for the Jewish autonomous region in Biro-Bidzhan. Still eager to develop that area, the Soviet regime granted prospective Jewish settlers free transportation and 300 rubles per capita; each family could also secure a government loan of 10,000 rubles. Nor were the conditions on the spot as dismal as they had been when the first colonists arrived there in the late 1920s. Now Tikhonka, renamed the city of Biro-Bidzhan, had become a sizable town of 30,000 to 40,000 inhabitants with broad boulevards and a good deal of free housing made available by the numerous departures during the war, while immigration had been almost totally suspended. Jewish cultural life was also revived; the newspaper *Der Shtern* began to appear two, and later four, times a week. A literary journal, too, was being talked about, as was the founding of a Yiddish university, the only one in the world. It is small wonder, then, that quite a few young Jewish veterans chose to settle in that new land of promise. According to local officials, 20,000 Jews arrived in 1947 and in the first four months of 1948. This figure is greatly exaggerated, but there is no question that more than 6,000 persons were brought in by the government in regular convoys of several hundred Jews, each stemming from a particular western region.[3]

In European Russia things also seemed to be improving. Many assimilated Jews doubtless felt like Ehrenburg, who said: "I grew up in Moscow. My native tongue is Russian. I do not know the Yiddish language. I am a Russian, a Soviet citizen, a man who cherishes the culture of Europe. But now I feel bound to the Jews because of the great misery of my Jewish people." Ehrenburg expressed dissatisfaction with the Jewish Anti-Fascist Committee for being not Jewish enough, although his name continued to appear among the committee's sponsors. In the privacy of his home Ehrenburg allowed himself even such far-reaching admissions as that the Soviet population of the occupied regions, "in particular the youth, had helped the German murderers." To Nathan Rapaport, the famous sculptor of the monument for the fighters and martyrs of the Warsaw ghetto, he conceded in 1945 that he had been unable to write frankly about the persecution of the Jews within the Soviet area because of the prevailing anti-Semitism in the higher echelons of the Party. Nevertheless, immediately after the armistice with Germany he and others could delude themselves into believing that a new era was also dawning for the Russian Jewish survivors.[4]

In 1947 an event took place which must have heartened many devoted Jews. As the Palestinian crisis was drawing to its climax, the Soviet Union suddenly appeared as a champion of a Jewish state. Domestically, Zionism was still outlawed and any Zionist activity was still subject to stringent criminal prosecution. Yet Andrei Gromyko voted, along with the United States and other Western countries, for the United Nations resolution of November, 1947, pledging the partition of

Palestine. After Israel's Declaration of Independence of May 14, 1948, the Soviet Union was one of the first powers to recognize the new state. Keen observers realized, of course, that the main purpose of these moves was to oust Britain from the entire Middle East. Possibly the leaders of the Union expected, as did most outside observers, that the new state would be quickly overrun by the Arab armies and that a British mandatory country would be replaced by a weak Arab alliance, offering many openings for a Russian diplomatic offensive.

When Israel proved victorious and, assured of its independence, for the most part sided with the Western alliance, the tone of the Soviet press became increasingly hostile. Once again the epithet "Zionist" became a supreme insult. The Russian government and public opinion reverted to the old Lenin-Stalinist repudiation of Zionism. One could freely hear the quotation from Stalin's essay of 1913, when in a footnote he described Zionism as

> a reactionary nationalist trend of the Jewish bourgeoisie, which had followers among the intellectuals and the more backward sections of the Jewish workers. The Zionists endeavored to isolate the Jewish working-class masses from the general struggle of the proletariat.

Because of the gradual withdrawal of the Western powers from their Middle Eastern colonies and the rise of Arab nationalism, that area offered a great temptation for the Soviet Union to move into the emerging power vacuum. Certainly, no slogan could appeal more strongly to Arab nationalists than the condemnation of the State of Israel as an outpost of Western "imperialism." The combination of anti-Zionism with general anti-Judaism by many nationalist Arabs further strengthened the inner forces operating in Russia, too, toward the reassertion of the ancient anti-Semitic heritage.[5]

At first, after reading the speeches of the Russian delegates at the United Nations in *Pravda* and *Izvestia*, some Russian Jews assumed that these marked a turning point in the theretofore hostile attitude of the Soviet regime toward Zionism. The Yiddish poet, David Hofshtain, who in his youth had spent some time as a Zionist pioneer in Palestine (1925–26), but had returned to the Soviet Union after the revolution in order to participate in the upbuilding of the socialist society, now deluded himself to the extent of asking the Ministry of Education to introduce instruction in Hebrew into the public schools. He paid dearly for this act of daring, being one of the first of the distinguished array of Yiddish poets and writers to be imprisoned and ultimately executed. Deportation was also inflicted upon hundreds of other Zionist sympathizers who thus misinterpreted the direction of the Soviet policies.[6]

"THE BLACK YEARS"

All along there was growing retrogression of Jewish cultural institutions, particularly in the reoccupied western territories. We must not lose sight of the hundreds of thousands of Jewish survivors who had become Soviet citizens only as a result of the annexations of 1939–40 and the reoccupation of these lands in 1944–45. Most of these more recent members of the Soviet Jewish community spoke Yiddish, had much Hebrew learning, and were of the old type of nationalist and/or religious Jews. Even those who had acquired familiarity with the Lithuanian, Latvian, and Polish languages could now use them to little advantage if they settled in areas dominated by different national majorities. It was quite imperative for their children to attend Yiddish schools and receive instruction in a language familiar to them. We have the eyewitness testimony of Szmerl Kaczerginski, a Yiddish writer who had lived in the Vilna ghetto under the Nazi occupation and had then fought with the partisans against the Nazi armies, that he, together with like-minded Jewish leaders, began rebuilding the Jewish community as soon as the Germans left Vilna in July, 1944. With the aid of Jewish army officers they finally obtained permission from the local Russian authorities to found a Yiddish primary school of four grades. During the following year they applied for permission to open a fifth grade, but they were refused under the excuse that having received the obligatory instruction in the Russian language during the first four years, the children should be able to enroll in a Russian school. In other communities no Yiddish school was opened at all, and the interested parties were dismissed with bland promises for the future.[7]

The same contrast between provinces and capital also appeared in the publishing field. No effort whatsoever was made to revive Yiddish journalism and book publishing in the old Jewish centers of the Ukraine, White Russia, or Lithuania, together with the enlarged territories taken over from Poland, Czechoslovakia, or Rumania. In the entire three-year period of 1946–48 the Ukrainian Academy in Kiev published only one scholarly work in Yiddish—namely, a 64-page study by Elias Spivak of *The Language in the Period of the Great Patriotic War*. This paucity reflected the general growth of the nationalist spirit among Russians and Ukrainians which also prevented the resumption of prewar Ukrainian publications in Polish, Bulgarian, and German. The government publishing house in Minsk brought out in 1947 a literary-artistic collection entitled "With a Firm Step." Not that there was a shortage of Yiddish readers. According to a report in the *Ainikait* of August 17, 1948, no fewer than 5,000 copies of Yiddish books were sold in Odessa in the first six months of that year; among them were 1,500 copies of Sholem Aleichem's writings and 400 copies of a recent memorial volume for

Mikhoels. In the same period Kiev readers spent 67,000 rubles purchasing Yiddish books. A dedicated writer, J. Bukhbinder, succeeded in collecting within four days in the relatively small community of Zhitomir, no fewer than 320 new subscriptions for the literary almanac *Der Shtern*. All these efforts, however, ran up against the passive resistance of the local Russian authorities, with or without prodding from above.[8]

The central authorities had decided at that time to concentrate all major Jewish publishing efforts in the capital. Since open collaboration with Jews abroad was still being encouraged, Moscow could display certain governmentally sponsored Jewish cultural activities to interested visitors. Apart from fine theatrical performances and public lectures, regularly attended by large throngs of people, one could show the *Emes* publishing firm and its ambitious program of publications. Among its more significant projects was a Russian-Yiddish dictionary of some forty thousand words, sponsored by the Yiddish section of the Ukrainian Academy; a comprehensive memorial volume for the Soviet Yiddish writers who had fallen on the battlefields of World War II; and a literary collection entitled "On Soviet Paths," in commemoration of the thirtieth anniversary of the beginnings of the Soviet Yiddish literature. Most remarkably, *Emes* was preparing to publish a collection of Yiddish poems by Bialik, despite the previous fulminations by older communists against this "bourgeois-nationalist" poet. Even if none of these projects was carried through, the *Emes* publications during the three-year period of 1946–48 amounted to some 110,000 copies of Yiddish books and pamphlets. True, this number compares unfavorably with the size and quality of publications of a single year in the mid-1930s. But one could excuse this decline by the prevailing shortage of paper and other technical difficulties. For foreign consumption one could herald these efforts as mere beginnings of a difficult reconstruction period, beginnings out of which would develop a flourishing Yiddish culture. The impression made abroad upon Soviet sympathizers is well described by an academic writer's comment in 1946:

> Meanwhile, with anti-Semitism outlawed by both the Soviet Constitution and public opinion, and cultural autonomy guaranteed where there are Jewish majorities who want it, the Jews in the Soviet Union enjoy a fully rounded ethnic democracy that no other country in the world at present gives to the Jewish people.

A year later an Anglo-Jewish writer subsumed the Jewish people under the general trend: "For all the peoples of the Soviet Union the war not only increased the intensity of their communion, but strengthened the links with their own past, and contributed to a new development of every national community."[9]

At the very moment these lines were written in the West, Jews saw themselves gradually eliminated from all positions of trust and confidence. After the departure of Lev Mekhlis in 1950, the only Jew left in the Politbureau was Lazar Kaganovich. In the course of 1948 to 1953 no fewer than 63 Jewish generals, 111 colonels and 159 lieutenant colonels were pensioned off and no Jew was appointed to any important Army command.[10] More generally, too, a new ice age was descending upon all Russian culture and particularly upon that of the national minorities. Under the system which came to be known as the *zhdanovshchina*, Andrei Zhdanov, with the full concurrence of Stalin, laid down the general rules under which all Soviet writers and artists had to operate. They were to forget their personal inclinations and feelings and put their pens, paintbrushes, and other tools completely at the service of the Party. Great writers like Fadeev, who now became a leading official of the Soviet Writers' Union, were forced to rewrite especially their wartime novels in the sense directed by Party officials. Not a shadow was to fall on the behavior of either the local communists or the Red Army officers during the great retreat of 1941–42. In all cases this was to be presented as a well-planned withdrawal which left behind a Party apparatus able, with almost superhuman wisdom and energy, to organize the partisan groups fighting behind the German front.

It is small wonder, then, that the same Fadeev who had so greatly extolled the Jewish officer Levinson as the hero of the Siberian civil war now had practically no word to spare for the great Jewish tragedy in his Stalin prize-winning novel *The Young Guard*, particularly in its final form published in 1951. The same was true of Valentin Kataev's *For Soviet Power* although the wartime happenings of the book were placed in the center of the old Jewish community of Odessa. Ever-pliable Ehrenburg readily agreed to describe the technique called for in the "production novel." The personal attitudes of the hero and heroine are played down, while their entire energies must be placed in the service of attempting to "over-fulfill their quota." The new rewriting of history did not stop with what might have been considered more or less contemporary history. As early as September, 1946, the new journal *Kultura i zhizn* (Culture and Life), especially founded to serve as a watchdog over the conformity of the Soviet writers, sharply censured the great film artist Eisenstein for his direction of *Ivan the Terrible*. Eisenstein was accused of "ignorance of historical facts in representing the progressive special troops (*oprichniki*) of Ivan the Terrible as a gang of degenerates resembling the American Ku Klux Klan, and Ivan the Terrible himself, a man with a strong will and character, as characterless and weak-willed, a kind of Hamlet."[11]

Fadeev has often rightly been quoted as a typical example of the subjugation of the creative artist to the Party bureaucracy. Although himself involved in Party politics, which had once led to his election to its Central Committee, he had to revise his *Young Guard*, which won the

Stalin Prize in 1946, several times in subsequent editions in order to meet the changing requirements of the officials in charge. This constant insecurity may well have been a factor in Fadeev's suicide at the age of fifty-five (1956). Similarly, Lion Feuchtwanger, for years a most popular writer among the Soviet readers, must have learned with dismay that even his historical novels dealing with Jewish subjects, as well as a film entitled *The Oppenheim Family* for which he had written the script, had been banished from Soviet libraries and motion-picture houses. (The novels were restored to grace during the "thaw" after Stalin's death.) Curiously, even the *Ainikait*, the organ of the *Jewish* Anti-Fascist Committee, especially organized to represent the Soviet Jewish communities in the struggle against their mortal Nazi enemy, quite early sensed the Soviet regime's aversion to any emphasis on the Jewish sufferings. As early as 1946 it censured those Jewish writers who, in the editors' opinion, described "the German fascist crimes against the Jewish population as isolated phenomena, not tied in with the Hitlerite murders of the Soviet people in general." The new pressure also made itself felt in the few surviving Yiddish theaters. Even in remote Biro-Bidzhan the repertory was purged of "all plays which aim merely at amusing the spectator with trivial songs and doggerel, and [the theater] is earnestly concentrating upon the task of creating works of true artistic merit which reflect the heroism of Soviet Jews in fighting the enemy and building a peaceful and happy life."[12]

Under these circumstances what could exponents of Yiddish culture expect? As the cold war grew warmer in 1948, the Soviet leaders began looking askance at any contact between their citizens and foreigners. The American monopoly of the atomic bomb created an abysmal feeling of insecurity. Ever-suspicious Stalin must have spent sleepless nights thinking of what he would have done if for several years the Soviet Union had the sole possession of such an irresistible weapon. In that feeling bordering on panic, every foreigner appeared as a potential spy, and any chat with a foreigner, however casual, became necessarily even more suspect than it had been in the 1930s.

In regard to Jews these suspicions were heightened when the Soviet rulers noted, to their chagrin, how strong the Zionist sentiment still was among the Jewish masses. A spontaneous demonstration at the Moscow synagogue on the Jewish New Year (October 16, 1948) occasioned by the arrival there of Golda Meyerson (now Meir), as the first Israeli envoy to the Soviet Union, a demonstration involving thousands of Moscow Jews openly defying all danger, must have looked like an open rebellion to the secret service men. Even earlier some officials viewed the Anti-Fascist Committee's suggestion that the old Jewish colonies in the Crimea, destroyed by the Nazis, be resurrected as a veiled Russian Jewish intention to create there an autonomous Jewish area where in case of war the Americans could readily establish a bridgehead for the occupation of southern Russia. Unbelievable though it may seem, this canard was still upheld as true in 1956 by Nikita Khrushchev in his lengthy exchange with a Canadian communist delegation, including the provincial deputy Joseph B. Salsberg, although Khrushchev admitted that the execution of Lozovskii on this score was a clear miscarriage of justice. The glorified Biro-Bidzhan experiment itself could be interpreted as an instrument of Western imperialism intended to deliver that base to Japan, although that country was many hundreds of miles away.[13]

TOTAL ECLIPSE

To informed observers such rumblings of anti-Jewish suspicion became quite audible in 1948. The sudden death of Salomon Mikhoels on January 13, 1948, on a trip to Minsk, where he was officially to present the Stalin Prize to the White Russian State Theater, must have raised questions in the minds of wary committee members. Although his death was explained as the result of an automobile accident, he was given a solemn state funeral, and a theater was named after him, some of his colleagues suspected foul play. Suspicions about Mikhoels' loyalty were nurtured by his earlier wartime trip to the United States and his continued correspondence with American Yiddish writers, mostly of pro-Soviet leanings. Not surprisingly, in the prevailing spy scare, someone conceived the idea that Mikhoels had helped to hatch the Crimean and other plots against his native land. Had not that prosaic technician Lazar Kaganovich suspected even Mikhoels' internationally famous presentation of *King Lear* as an oblique criticism of the Soviet order? Mikhoels must have had premonitions of his falling from the grace of the dictator. Stalin frequently liked the great actor to entertain him with private recitations of distinguished dramatic roles. From time to time he even endearingly called Mikhoels his "Solomon the Wise." However, according to a story reported by a Soviet refugee in Israel, Mikhoels' close friend Vasilii I. Kachalov, another well-known Soviet actor, had told him about a conversation with Stalin in which the latter referred to "Solomon the Wise," the caricature of a Jew in Chekhov's *Steppe*. In this connection Stalin had exclaimed: "This is exactly like my Mikhoels, a buffoon and not a king!" That some committee members sensed the real plot against the actor's life could be seen from the eulogy in verse written by Peretz Markish; it stressed the marks of the brutal assault on the deceased man's body and placed him among the Nazi victims.[14]

This was but the beginning. By late November, 1948, the ax fell upon the entire Anti-Fascist Committee. Details of that operation have never been disclosed and are still subject to much guesswork. The

Ainikait seems to have suspended publication soon after November 20, 1948, but the committee's official dissolution was never announced in the Russian press. Inquiries from abroad, as well as those addressed to Soviet representatives in the United States and elsewhere, were answered evasively. For a long time, indeed, foreign Jewish communists simply could not believe the reports about the new terror striking the Yiddish leaders. They finally had to admit the suppression of the Anti-Fascist Committee but explained it simply as a result of the return to normalcy after the war. They were still whistling in the dark about the Soviet recognition of Jewish national culture. But in April, 1949, the shattering news about the jailing of the five most eminent Yiddish writers—David Bergelson, Samuel Halkin, Peretz Markish, Der Nister, and Itzik Fefer—suddenly broke. While Bergelson was accused of pro-Israel sympathies, no particulars were given in the other cases. Certainly one could not accuse Fefer of lack of Soviet patriotism. He who had not only served as a colonel in the Red Army during the war, but had also sung "Siberia, the Urals,/ Kaluga, and Tripolye,/ And wherever I am/ A flaming Komsomol am I," and had outdone any Russian poet in his patriotic diatribes was now lingering in prison as a traitor to the Fatherland. These arrests were followed by a number of others, and before long practically all Yiddish literary leaders were behind bars.

All this was accomplished in extreme secrecy; even the communist organs in other countries were kept in the dark about the fate of these Soviet patriots. Finally, in 1952, most of them were tried and executed on the same day (August 12), except for those who, like Der Nister, had died in prison. Only years thereafter did some survivors of these new purges who succeeded in getting out of the Soviet Union (in part as a result of the Russo-Polish agreement affecting Polish citizens) disclose some of the horrors of that new wave of persecutions. Even they had only fragmentary information, much of it based on hearsay. At any rate, not only were the leaders exterminated, but all organs of Yiddish expression were speedily suppressed. During that bleak quinquennium of the last years of Stalin, no Yiddish paper or book was allowed to appear, except perhaps for the sporadic publication of the Biro-Bidzhan *Shtern*, which reported nothing of Jewish interest—indeed, nothing that had not appeared in the Russian paper of that area, the Biro-Bidzhan *Zvezda* (Star).

While these blows were aimed at the very core of Jewish intellectual life in Moscow, the provinces did not go unscathed. The Baltic countries in particular, which still included important remnants of Jewish communities, felt the brunt of the Stalin terror. It has been estimated that, in the first three years after World War II, no fewer than 371,000 Baltic nationals were deported. Most of these, to be sure, were persons accused of collaboration with the Nazis, and doubtless a great many pogromists who had aided the Nazi extermination squads were included. But others were merely Lithuanian or Latvian "nationalists," a term used at this point as a word of opprobrium; some were Jews guilty of "Jewish nationalism." Perhaps the greatest source of fear was the apparent irrationality of the persecutions. One family was deported because its little daughter had inquired in school where Israel was. A little watch repairman disappeared one day because "his name just happened to be on a list. Maybe it was confused with another name. In any event, he was shot." As a Jewish friend explained it to Harrison E. Salisbury, the correspondent of *The New York Times*, "No one even knew why, and this was what made the terror so much worse."[15]

Even more threatening became the new issue of Jewish "cosmopolitanism." Quite apart from Jewish "nationalism" or "Zionism," the very foundations of the Jews' loyalty to the Soviet Union were now questioned. Through a dialectical combination of such opposites as "cosmopolitan nationalism" Jews could be accused of trying to undermine the allegiance of the Russian people to their Fatherland. To be sure, Jews as such were not usually mentioned, but in the unceasing flow of press releases condemning prominent individuals for "cosmopolitan" associations, a majority of Jewish-sounding names invariably appeared. This proven technique drawn from the days of Nazis and Nazi sympathizers (when Father Coughlin, for instance, fulminated against the "international bankers" he always mentioned at least two or three Jewish banking houses by name) was now used to good advantage. No informed reader in Russia was fooled about the intent of these denunciations, and yet in foreign propaganda one could roundly deny any anti-Semitic aims.

No better illustration of the changed attitude of the Soviet regime need be adduced than the different treatment of Jewish problems and personalities in the successive editions of the *Large Soviet Encyclopedia*, each volume of which was edited with great care and painstakingly attuned to the changing demands and moods of the Party. Like most other semiofficial publications the encyclopedia served as an instrument of communist propaganda. Under the headings of "Jews" (*Evrei*), the edition published in 1932 devoted no fewer than 130 columns to an explanation of the history, literature, religion, and contemporary situation of the Jewish people. In contrast Volume XV of the second edition, published in 1953, reduced the entire treatment to a mere four columns (in addition to some remarks on Biro-Bidzhan), filled with diatribes against "national Jewish culture" which is only "a word of the order of rabbis and bourgeois, a word of the order of our enemies." The very definition of "Jew" follows the Party line. "Jews do not represent a nation," the author contends, "for they do not form a stable community shaped through the course of history on the common basis of language, territory, economic life, and culture. They partake of the economic and cultural life of the peoples among whom they live." Naturally the article emphasizes the great disparity allegedly existing between the fate of Jews in Western countries, where they suffer from anti-Semitism and discrimination (the Soviet propagandists generally like to identify capitalism with fascism and nazism), and their complete equality in the Soviet Union.

> The "American way of life," built upon the oppression of classes and nationalities, also finds its expression in the persecution of Jewish workers. In the United States it is the rule not to admit Jews to public service [these words were written long after the American Jew-baiters had dubbed the New Deal the "Jew-Deal" because it had attracted many Jewish civil servants to Washington and other cities]. In fact, there exist regular quotas for the admission of Jewish pupils to scholarly institutions. The Jewish sub-proletariat, like those of the other national minorities, lives in special closed quarters in particularly unsanitary conditions.

Contrasted with this lowly status, the Soviet Jews "take an active part in the building of communism. In this fashion the Lenin-Stalinist national policy of equality and amity among the people has led to the disappearance of the 'Jewish question' in the U.S.S.R."

All aspects of Zionism are treated with particular venom here and in a few special articles. "The Zionists, agents of American and English imperialism," we are told, "are the sworn enemies of the Jewish workers." The same line is taken in describing Chaim Weizmann, who "had placed himself at the disposal of the American imperialists and transformed Israel into a colony. He pursued the policy of oppressing the Jewish working masses and the Arab minorities in order to extinguish the forces of peace and democracy." Bialik is briefly dismissed as a "reactionary poet," while Herzl, Ahad Haam, Mendele, An-Ski, Sholem Asch, and many others, more or less fairly treated in the first edition, are completely omitted in the second. If some Jewish artists are given considerable space in the new edition, this is merely owing to their sculpting or painting of historic figures from Russia's tsarist or communist past. But in such cases no mention is made of their Jewish origin. A similar silent treatment was extended even to such independent publications as that of the complete works of Maxim Gorki in thirty volumes, finished in 1957. On the whole, every little article by Gorki is included except his manifold attacks on anti-Semitism, his praise of Bialik, and his other pro-Jewish utterances to which reference was made above. Ignoring the Jews and their past was pushed to such extremes that in 1954 an author (Kovalev) could publish a textbook on the history of the ancient world without ever mentioning ancient Israel. Indeed, if the Jewish question could be eliminated by such a "conspiracy of silence," the Russian propaganda machine would have succeeded in disposing of it once and for all.[16]

Inconsistently, however, the Soviet regime itself was guilty of indirectly raising the Jewish issue by referring to conspirators bearing Jewish names. Most dangerous was the so-called doctors' plot, supposedly hatched by nine eminent Moscow physicians, of whom six "happened" to be Jewish—among them Dr. Wofsi, president of the Academy of Medicine and a relative of Mikhoels, whose family name had also been Wofsi. These doctors had allegedly conspired to poison Stalin and other Soviet leaders and thus prepare the way for an internal upset. We need but quote Nikita Khrushchev's secret report to the Twentieth Congress of the Communist Party of February 24–25, 1956:

> He [Stalin] personally issued advice on the conduct of the investigation and the method of interrogation of the arrested persons. He said that the academician Vinogradov should be put in chains, another one should be beaten. Present at this Congress as a delegate is the former Minister of State Security, Comrade Ignatiev. Stalin told him curtly, "If you do not obtain confessions from the doctors we will shorten you by a head."

> Stalin personally called the investigative judge, gave him instructions, advised him on which investigative methods should be used; these methods were simple—beat, beat and, once again, beat.

> Shortly after the doctors were arrested, we members of the Political Bureau received protocols containing the doctors' confessions of guilt. After distributing these protocols, Stalin told us, "You are blind like young kittens; what will happen without me? The country will perish because you do not know how to recognize enemies."[17]

The Russian public, including its Jewish segment, did not have to be informed of what all that meant. It still vividly remembered how the assassination of S. M. Kirov in 1934 had set up a chain reaction resulting in the terrible purges of the old Bolsheviki during the following four years. The doctors' plot, too, was evidently intended to serve as an excuse for new violent purges, except that this time Jews would undoubtedly have been singled out for particular retribution. A foretaste was given, for instance, by the rumored exclusion from the Party of one of its leading publicists, David Zaslavsky (a former Bundist), allegedly because one of his editorial colleagues had declared that he was unable to work "together with the son of a people of traitors and poisoners." Widespread reports had it that Stalin was preparing to deport all European Jewry to the Far East. Since during and after the war various tribes such as the Crimean Tatars, the Kalmyks, and the Volga Germans had thus been physically transplanted from Europe to Asia, where before long most of them vanished as identifiable groups, these rumors enjoyed full credence among many Jews and non-Jews alike. One can easily visualize the terror among the Jewish masses who had but a few years before emerged from the nightmare of Nazi extermination.[18] At that particular moment the old tyrant died, and in the scuffle for succession, the accused doctors were discharged and the entire terroristic campaign was called off.

Not that this relaxation involved the immediate abandonment of the anti-"cosmopolitan" agitation. True, one could now allow himself to deplore the wartime Nazi atrocities without being exposed to a bombastic denunciation of the kind endured in 1949 by the Ukrainian Jewish poet Savva Golovanivskii for a poem describing the infamous massacre of some 75,000 (more exactly, 33,771) Kiev Jews in the cave of Babi Yar in 1941. A critic in the semiofficial *Literaturnaya Gazeta* had accused Golovanivskii of "a terrible defamation of the Soviet nation" because he had described the passive behavior of the Kiev population while the Germans marched Abraham, the old Jew, to his doom.[19]

However, any form of Jewish nationalism was still considered taboo. The American communist writer Howard Fast was glorified in Soviet literary circles even beyond his literary merits. During that period of adulation a complete bibliography of Fast's writings was published in Moscow with the omission of but two items, namely a short history of the Jews entitled *Romance of a People* (1939), and a novel on the Maccabean revolt, *My Glorious Brothers* (1947). Evidently, the compiler feared that by including these two "nationalistic" Jewish items, he might lower the dignity of the writer he and his readers so greatly admired. Naturally enough, when Fast turned his back on communism, his Jewishness was suddenly discovered and made the subject of vicious attacks. All this was symptomatic of the general effort to make the Soviet Jews sever their relations with both the Jewish people the world over and their own past. Howard Fast's comments thereon are indeed pertinent:

> Equality based upon the forcible blotting out of differences and the subjugation of the group memory of minorities is not a pleasant thing to contemplate, and little enough dignity goes along with it. . . . What a bitter thing it is to be robbed of your father's as well as of your own pride!

Yet this was demanded of all Russian Jews who wished to retain their membership in the Communist Party or their offices in one or another governmental agency.[20]

[17]

After Stalin

A conscientious historian will necessarily approach the task of analyzing Jewish life in the Soviet Union during the Khrushchev era 1953–64 with even greater reluctance than in dealing with the earlier periods. All sources of solid, scholarly information had practically dried up. We are limited, for the most part, to fleeting impressions accumulated by foreign visitors, narratives of refugees from some Soviet area, interviews with one or another leading Soviet statesman, and occasional reports from foreign correspondents. We shall see that only after the rise of the new Democratic Movement in the late 1960s and the reawakening of Jewish national consciousness have informative *samizdats*, as well as reminiscences by a growing number of Russian Jewish émigrés in Israel and other countries, supplied the outside world with important new data and insights regarding the situation of Russian Jewry (*see* the next chapter). Yet quite apart from the general bias in evaluating almost anything pertaining to Soviet life, one need but bear in mind how erroneous often are the impressions gathered by foreign visitors to the United States, despite the availability here of a free press and broadcasting media. In the Jewish case, the American community has at its disposal a large network of periodicals and other sources of information which enable a visitor to check and double-check any ambiguous observations. Not to speak of the freedom with which he may circulate among the masses, speak with and listen freely to any casual acquaintance, probe as deeply as he wishes in interviewing responsible leaders, and sift contradictory evidence hurled at him by all sorts of interested parties even without his asking. And yet how often have such visitors gone askew in interpreting the basic trends in general and Jewish life in America!

Most fundamentally, there is a fateful dearth of basic Soviet scientific data. Long before the Jewish lyre was muted with the imprisonment of the Jewish writers and poets in 1948, long before the suspension in that year of the last organs of Jewish public opinion, Jewish scholarly investigations had come to a halt. The last fairly scholarly publication, Lev Zinger's *Dos banaite Folk* (The Rejuvenated People), appeared in 1941 on the eve of the German invasion of the Soviet Union. Much as the underlying data failed to measure up to Western standards of research and greatly hampered as the author was by Party line shackles, this volume at least furnished some statistical data on the population trends and occupational distribution of Soviet Jewry as reflected, in part, by the census of 1939. Even then Zinger's attempt was a singular exception, the other Jewish sociologists and historians having been silenced during the purges of the mid-1930s. After 1941 (except for Zinger's own half-hearted attempt to bring his study slightly up to date seven years later) no effort at all was made by Jews or non-Jews to ascertain the basic facts of Jewish life in the Union until 1965 and beyond.[1]

Everyone working in the contemporary Jewish field knows how difficult it is to evaluate the dynamic changes in any community without the solid cooperation of local Jewish scholars having free access to the archives and libraries of their country. Their interpretation of these data may sometimes be lacking in long-range perspective but it has the virtue of being based on intimate living experience. In a country as vast as the Soviet Union, in a Jewish community which had undergone such a cataclysmic decline during the war and the Nazi occupation, and with a population which had been subjected to the severe strains of inner migration, economic reconstruction, and cultural adjustments in the midst of a growing spiritual vacuum, only the persistent efforts of a whole generation of well-trained and dedicated scholars might have produced some fundamental facts upon which to base general conclusions. As it was, for more than three decades not one Jewish or non-Jewish author has published a book or monograph based upon thoroughgoing research. One need but contrast the vast outpouring of analytical studies probing the Jewish aspects of the census of 1926 in the three or four years after its publication, with the total absence of such Soviet investigations of the censuses of 1959 and 1970, to realize how shaky the ground is over which one may try to erect any structure of scholarly evaluation.[2]

And yet, however reluctantly, one must come to grips with the great enigma of Soviet Jewish life in the last decades. In the following pages we shall try not only to summarize what might be considered the best state of available knowledge but, despite unavoidable minor repetitions, develop certain aspects more fully in the next chapter. In conclusion, we may even cautiously venture into the ever-perilous domain of prediction concerning the shape of things to come.

RADICAL CHANGES

The 1959 census showed how totally the Jewish situation had changed since the preceding census twenty years earlier. To the surprise of many outsiders, no fewer than 2,268,000 persons answered the enumerators' questions by registering as members of the Jewish nationality. While some individuals may have been afraid of giving replies at variance with the national identifications on their passports, others undoubtedly believed the much-publicized promise that these answers would not be divulged to anyone outside the Census Bureau, reinforced by the order to the enumerators to accept the statements of their interlocutors without verification by documentary evidence. In any case, it stands to reason that an unspecified number, perhaps several hundred thousand, preferred to list themselves as belonging to the Russian, Ukrainian, or some other nationality. This doubtless was the case, in particular, of the numerous Jews who had intermarried or who lived in small isolated groups in the scattered mining and industrial areas. Certainly, the countless European Jews employed as executives and white-collar workers in the rapidly expanding industrial enterprises of the Asiatic republics were generally considered by the local population as part and parcel of the "Russian" managerial class, rather than as Jews. Be this as it may, the official figures showed a reduction of the Jewish ratio in the total population from 1.78 percent in 1939, to 1.09 percent twenty years later.

Even more drastic were the dislocations within the various parts of the Soviet Union. Now the largest group of 875,000 Jews, or 38.1 percent of all Soviet Jewry, resided in the Russian Republic. Although declining in absolute figures by some 94,000 (always bearing in mind that perhaps more than that number were among those unidentified as Jews), the percentage of Jews in the Russian Republic had increased from 32.1 percent in 1939. The Ukraine now held second place. Its 840,000 Jews were down from 1,533,000 in 1939 and amounted to but 37.4 percent of the whole Jewish population in the Union. This ratio contrasted with 50.8 percent in 1939, and 58.7 percent in 1926. White Russia lagged even further behind. Its 150,000 Jews, or 7.0 percent of Soviet Jewry, were in sharp contrast with the 375,000 and 12.4 percent of 1939, and the 407,000 or 15.2 percent of 1926. The old Jewish communities of Lithuania, not surprisingly, suffered the greatest devastation, being reduced to a mere 26,700 or 1.2 percent of Soviet Jewry. On the other hand, the newly incorporated Republic of Moldavia retained much more of its prewar Jewish community (95,000 or 4.4 percent of the total). At the same time, Uzbekistan, with about the same number of Jews, revealed how the tremendous wartime influx of Jewish refugees from Poland and other parts had again ebbed away in the fourteen years since the cessation of hostilities. In the list of Soviet nationalities, nevertheless, the Jewish community still ranked as the eleventh largest (it had been the seventh largest in 1939).[3]

These broad figures, incomplete as they appear to be, give us but an inkling of Jewish life in contemporary Russia. Unofficial estimates sometimes give the Jewish populations of Odessa and Kiev as 200,000 each, but the official figures of 118,000 or 17 percent for Odessa, and 154,000 or 14 percent for Kiev are closer to the truth. The other large communities include Kharkov with 80,000 (9 percent) and Minsk with 38,000 Jews (7 percent). With the destruction of the agricultural colonies in southern Russia and the slow development of Biro-Bidzhan, the overwhelming majority of Russian Jewry thus live in the metropolitan areas. Under favorable conditions such local concentration might have favored an intensive development of Jewish cultural life. But in the hostile clime of the contemporary Soviet environment it has merely given an additional impetus to the forces of assimilation.[4]

CONTINUED DISCRIMINATION

Despite official denials few outsiders still doubt that anti-Semitism has continued to play a great role in shaping Jewish destinies in the post-Stalin era as well. Even the most obdurate defenders of the existing system could not deny the fact that in his long indictment of Stalin's crimes, Khrushchev never referred to the crimes committed by the deceased dictator and his henchmen against Jews or the Jewish community. Not even in his denunciation of the handling of the alleged doctors' plot, we recall, did he make the slightest allusion to the Jewishness of the majority of the victims. More, the entire record of his behavior toward Jews seems to betray the atavistic hostility of Khrushchev's Ukrainian environment. True, in 1913, he and other socialists helped quell an anti-Jewish riot in Marinpol. However, in the course of his long-term leadership of the Party in the Ukraine during and after World War II, he did nothing to help Ukrainian Jewry during its greatest hour of trial.

Stalin, too, may have harbored anti-Jewish prejudices from his early days in Georgia; occasionally he may have indulged in such private remarks as were heard by Edward Stettinius during Stalin's conversation with Roosevelt at Yalta. In reply to Roosevelt's statement that he intended to review the entire Palestine question with King Ibn Saud, "Stalin observed that the Jewish problem was extremely difficult. The Soviet Union had tried to establish a national home for the Jews, but they had stayed only two or three years before returning to the cities." Yet publicly the iron-fisted dictator was as a rule on his guard and from time to time even went strongly on record against anti-Semitism, as in his famous reply to the Jewish Telegraphic Agency of January 12, 1931, in which he called it "a survival of the barbarous practices of the cannibalistic period." No such public denunciation of Jew-baiting came from Khrushchev's lips; at the most he publicly denied to foreign journalists the presence of anti-Semitism in his country and pointed out that he himself had a Jewish daughter-in-law, the widow of his son Leonid, who had died as a fighter pilot in the war. On the other hand, during his visit to Warsaw in 1956 for the funeral of President Boleslaw Bierut, he did not hesitate to lecture his Polish comrades on the contrast between the Russian Party, which had been able completely to eliminate Jews from its leadership, and the Polish Party, which still harbored a disproportionate number of Jews in its Central Committee. Almost directly pointing at the chairman of the committee, Roman Zambrowski (formerly Zuckerman), Khrushchev emphasized, "There are among you many leaders named 'ski,' but an Abramovich always remains an Abramovich." He attacked the Jewish leadership even more bluntly upon his arrival in Warsaw during the great Polish upheaval of 1956 which brought Wladyslaw Gomulka to the helm. Having been kept circling over the Warsaw airport until the change in the Polish leadership had become a *fait accompli*, Khrushchev, upon touching ground, delivered himself of his famous three words: *"Zhidam budiete pomagat?"* (Do you wish to help the Yids?). The very term *zhid* had long become a term of opprobrium, rarely used in official statements even by the tsarist administration. Yet at this crucial historical moment, this erstwhile peasant, elevated to a position of undisputed power in the Soviet Union, thus gave vent to his deep-rooted prejudice against Jews.[5]

Khrushchev was too much of a politician, however, to allow these prejudices to be publicly proclaimed as the basic principles of the Soviet international or domestic policies. Espousal of racial and ethnic equality had not only been too integral a part of the Marxist-Leninist ideology, but also the most effective foreign propaganda instrument against Nazi racialism and Western colonialism. Khrushchev and his associates preferred therefore to pursue the postwar Stalinist policy of quietly introducing discriminatory measures while publicly singing the praises of equality and nondiscrimination. To begin with, completing the work begun during the great purges of the 1930s, Jews were completely ousted from the top leadership of the Party and the higher echelons of the governmental bureaucracy. With the removal, in 1957, of Lazar M. Kaganovich, the last Jewish member departed from the Politbureau or Party Praesidium. Only in November, 1962, had a Jew been appointed chairman of the Soviet State Planning Committee and Deputy Premier. But the selection of a largely nonpolitical engineer, Venyamin F. Dymshitz, who had mainly distinguished himself as the builder of the Soviet-financed steel plant in India, indicated that no basic change in policy was intended. These purges of Jewish leaders went down to the lowest local levels. Soviet apologists have often countered this argument by pointing out that in 1960 no fewer than 7,623 Jews had been elected to local soviets. But when one weighs that number against the total of 1,800,000 local leaders then elected, one realizes that the quota of less than 0.5 percent was much below the Jewish ratio of 1.1 percent of the total population. In fourteen of the fifteen republics the Jews were thus underrepresented in the local councils. This was even more true in the supreme soviets of the respective republics: the Russian Republic had only 0.12 percent of Jewish members (population ratio: 0.7 percent), the Ukraine 0.22 percent (as against 2.00 percent), White Russia 0.45 percent (as against 1.90 percent), and so forth.[6]

Apart from Stalin's or Khrushchev's personal leanings, it is quite evident that once again anti-Semitism had begun to be used as an instrument of public policy to divert the disaffection of the people to the Jewish scapegoat. As in tsarist times the far-flung bureaucracy, even larger and more powerful now, had revealed the usual signs of corruption. Lord Acton's famous saying, "Power corrupts, absolute power corrupts absolutely," came true in the case of Soviet officialdom, which despite occasional purges and executions has largely been a self-perpetuating class. Only its constant numerical expansion to provide for new technological and social services, and the ensuing recruitment of younger trained personnel, has thus far prevented its total resemblance to the old tsarist group of *chinovniks*. Nevertheless, connivance of officials in evading the law has become quite commonplace.

Although the economy had progressed markedly from the days of World War II and consumer goods had become much more readily available, especially in the major cities, there still were innumerable examples of persistent shortages, shoddy quality, breakdowns in distribution and other economic ills—all of which encouraged black markets, currency speculation, and other prohibited practices. Since many Jews, especially in the older communities, still engaged in some form or other of merchandising, it was easy enough to place the blame on them as the economic criminals mainly responsible for these shortcomings in the Soviet economy. Such economic "subversion" was now placed among the capital crimes because of its long-range counterrevolutionary effects. While there also were many non-Jewish economic criminals, in all public announcements Jews were singled out with great frequency. Even the numerous culprits who had Russianized their names were cited with their Jewish names in parentheses, so that no reader or broadcast listener could mistake their ethnic identity. According to a contemporary, if incomplete, computation, of the one hundred and sixty-three "economic criminals" condemned to death in eighty-one trials in forty-eight different cities between July, 1961, and August, 1963, no less than eighty-eight (and possibly ninety-six)—that is, 55 to 60 percent—were easily identified as Jews. The lengthy trial of the so-called Shakerman ring, which ended in February, 1964, apparently involved eighteen Jews among the twenty-three defendants. Moreover, many of these trials resulted in the execution of the Jewish culprits while the non-Jewish defendants were usually let off with longer or shorter prison terms. Among the condemned Jews, not perchance, were also leaders of the religious Jewish communities of Leningrad and Moscow, whose arrest achieved wide publicity both in the country and abroad.[7]

Regrettably, reports by foreign observers about anti-Jewish discrimination cannot easily be verified. The government has constantly denied any discriminatory policy. In a recent release it quoted statistics showing that Russian Jewry, constituting but a little more than 1.1 percent of the population, nevertheless furnished 14.7 percent of the country's doctors, 10.4 percent of its lawyers and judges, 10 percent of its scientists, 8.5 percent of its journalists and writers, 7 percent of its workers in graphic and theatrical arts, and 3.1 percent of its university students. If these statistics are accurate, they would indeed attest a considerable measure of equality. Even the obvious decline from 9 percent of the student body in the 1930s to 3 percent in the early 1960s might be explained by the enormous increase of the general student population throughout the country, as for the first time in Russian history, urbanites now outnumber their rural brethren. On the other hand, we are told by informed observers that Jews are discriminated against in admission to the more desirable schools of higher learning or to particular departments.[8]

At the same time there have also been some manifestations of a growing opposition to anti-Semitism among the younger intelligentsia. Evgenii Evtushenko's (Yevtushenko's) poem *Babi Yar*, once again describing the notorious Kiev massacre, has been hailed with extraordinary enthusiasm in the literary circles and in the numerous clubs where it has been recited. This wide acceptance contrasted sharply with the cool reception extended to the similar poem by Savva Golovanivskii a decade earlier. Here Evtushenko identifies himself with the Jewish people:

> . . . *It seems to me that I am as old*
> *As the Jewish people itself.*
> *It seems to me that I am a Jew.*
> *I am tramping through ancient Egypt*
> *I am dying, crucified on the cross*
> *And till this time I have traces of the nails.*
> *It seems to me that I am Dreyfus. . . .*
> *It seems to me that I am a youngster in Bialystok*
> *Whose blood is running over the floors*
> *The victim of the hooliganism of the leaders from the*
>   *saloons. . . .*
> *It seems to me that I am Anne Frank. . . .*
> *Over Babi-Yar there is the hum of the thick grass*
> *The trees look powerful, like judges*
> *Everything screams silently here, and, removing my hat,*
> *I feel that I am growing gray slowly*
> *And that I am myself a totally soundless shriek*
> *Over the thousands of thousands who are buried.*
> *I am each old man that was slaughtered here*
> *I am each child that was slaughtered here.*
> *Nothing in me can forget this.*
> *Let the "Internationale" sound out joyously*
> *When the last anti-Semite on earth will be buried. . . .*

This poem understandably aroused the ire of the authorities, who had long tried to blot out the difference between the Jewish and non-Jewish victims of the Nazis. In fact, in Kiev proper, a monument was erected for the Nazi victims on another hill, while the gully of Babi Yar was allowed to be overgrown by brush and filled with refuse.

Partly in protest against these governmental restrictions, partly as a repudiation of anti-Semitism, and partly out of idolization of the young poet, thousands of young Muscovites gathered to listen to Evtushenko's recitation of this poem in Moscow's Mayakovskii Square on Poets' Day of 1961. Dispersed by the police at midnight, carted twenty miles out of town and dumped on distant roads, many of these youngsters returned the following day to participate in a similar demonstration. The police handled them with equal roughness the second time. The great composer Dmitrii Shostakovich joined the procession of the poet's admirers and included *Babi Yar*, together with Evtushenko's four other poems, in his Thirteenth Symphony. The authorities reacted violently—earlier the composer had already drawn upon his head the censure of musical party hacks—and after the second concert suspended any further performances. At that point both poet and composer yielded and by inserting the two lines: "I am proud of the Russia which stood in the path of the [Nazi] bandits," and "Here together with Russians and Ukrainians, lie Jews," they came close enough to the accepted party position to be allowed to resume their concerts.[9]

ENFORCED SILENCE

Any expression of Jewish national feeling continued to be considered essentially subversive even after the days of Stalin and the ensuing "thaw" (this title of an Ehrenburg novel had become the designation of this new era). Typical of the attitude of littérateurs and literary critics, long after the general relaxation of the Zhdanov system, was a meeting held by a local Writers' Union in Chernovtsy (formerly Czernowitz or Cernauti) early in 1960. That meeting ruthlessly condemned as "an alien voice" the work of Meir Kharatz, a local Yiddish poet whose poem "The Wanderer" was considered an outright anti-Soviet slander. The report in the Bukovina paper did not mention it, but it appears that the Union's Jewish members were among the assailants of the "daring" poet. Although in the somewhat less tense atmosphere of 1960, such denunciations did not spell a death sentence, as they might have a decade earlier, the fate of one so violently attacked could still become extremely unpleasant. Perhaps this rigidity of a provincial group may have merely reflected the usual time lag between the new reformist relaxation in the two centers of Moscow and Leningrad as compared with the unswerving submission to Stalinist directives still dominant in the provinces. Yet Jewish "bourgeois nationalism" continued to be stigmatized as even more unpatriotic than the same sentiments harbored by other nationalities.[10]

Combined with this sharp antagonism to any manifestation of Jewish national feeling was the Soviet Union's unwavering hostility toward the State of Israel, a hostility shared by few of its Jewish citizens. On the contrary, just as the arrival of the first envoy from Israel in 1948 had led to a series of spontaneous outbursts of enthusiasm, a decade later (1959) the Israeli representatives at a Youth Festival were hailed by intrepid Jews at every stop from the Black Sea port to Moscow; this caused great consternation among the local autocrats. It mattered little that from time to time the official propaganda denounced a few of Israel's lower-ranking diplomatic representatives as spies for the United States, and condemned every Soviet citizen's contact with them as part of a conspiracy against the state. Jews and most informed non-Jews, including the authorities themselves, knew very well the baselessness of these accusations. They realized that rejoicing in the rise and growth of the new state did not impinge in the slightest upon Soviet patriotism. At the same time emigration from the Soviet Union was absolutely barred by law. The same Russian press which was vociferously denouncing the American State Department for refusing a passport to Paul Robeson or Howard Fast (in his communist days) considered it perfectly legitimate for its own government to refuse passports to the hundreds of thousands of Russian Jews who wished to go to Israel or to the United States. The extent to which even the assimilated Russian Jews, particularly government officials, were affected by the anti-Zionist line is demonstrated by the following testimony of Howard Fast. He claims to have received a letter from Boris Izakov, a member of the Foreign Department of the Soviet Writers' Union, stating "that he would gladly volunteer to take up arms with Egypt against Israel.[11]

When Nikita Khrushchev was asked in Vienna in July, 1960, why the Soviet Union had refused exit permits even to the few older Jews wishing to join close relatives already settled in Israel, he roundly denied that any Soviet citizen had expressed such a desire. In reply Golda Meir, Israel's foreign minister, informed the Israel Parliament that in the preceding five years alone, no fewer than 9,236 Israelis had applied, through the international Red Cross, to the Soviet authorities for permission for their families to rejoin them in Israel. Under Khrushchev all such requests had been turned down. Nor was there any expectation for a change in this adamant policy in the foreseeable future, unless it were to become the subject of some new international convention. Hopes rose high after the United Nations subcommission on human rights unanimously adopted a resolution, the representative of the Soviet Union alone abstaining, that no citizen ever be forbidden to leave or return to his own country. In the meantime, however, an appeal like that voiced by the Australian delegate H. D. White before the United Nations Assembly on November 1, 1962—"should the U.S.S.R. find difficulty in according the Soviet Jewry full freedom to practice their religion, it should, we believe, permit them to leave the country"—was curtly dismissed by the Soviet delegate as based on "filthy calumnies." An interesting description of a synagogue service held in Moscow on a Saturday morning was given by Yizhar Smilansky, a recent Israeli visitor to the Moscow Peace Conference. No fewer than five hundred Jews had assembled for the services; for the most part they were elderly persons.

> When the members of the Israeli embassy walked in, a spark was lit in the worshipers' eyes. They rose to their feet to honor them. There was

a dramatic contrast between the festive garb of the embassy people and their solemn entry on the one hand, and the drab, beggarly appearance of the synagogue. The guests and the members of the embassy sit on a special dais removed from the congregation. The bond between the guests and the congregants is the bond of the eyes and of glances. This goes on all the time as a silent, shattering experience, which envelops you and does not leave you throughout the whole service.[12]

Curiously, under the vagaries of Soviet policy, the attitude toward Jews had turned full circle. At the beginning of the revolution the "godless" agitators tried to persuade Jews to repudiate their religion and to adopt in its place a purely secular national culture. Now this national culture has been repressed while—even though the reality of the Jewish people remains undeniable—the main mark of identification shifted back to the Jewish religion. With all their cultural institutions, including schools, the press, and the theater, remaining closed, Jews were still allowed to worship in synagogues, of which there probably existed, despite varying official computations, no more than ninety-six in the vast expanses of the Soviet Union. These places of worship are usually located in dilapidated buildings in some fairly inaccessible districts. Manned by frequently unlearned rabbis or cantors, they hold little attraction for the Russian youth. Nevertheless, at least on High Holidays, they are usually overcrowded. More recently, even that modicum of Jewish religious loyalty has annoyed certain official circles. While the godless propaganda has generally been toned down, attacks on Judaism as a religion have been stepped up, especially in the Ukraine, that old focus of anti-Judaism. A professor of philosophy, Trofim K. Kichko, in particular, was given free rein to assail the ethics of the Bible and postbiblical Judaism in several essays and a book, *Yudaizm bez prykras* (Judaism Without Embellishment), published in Kiev in 1963 under the official sponsorship of the Ukrainian Academy of Science.[13]

Most remarkably, while Hebrew had so long been outlawed, in contrast to the Yiddish culture which had been lovingly fostered by the government in the 1920s and early 1930s, the Yiddish authors now remained silent (some observers spoke of a fairly substantial body of letters circulating in manuscript as in the Middle Ages, or even in oral form as in remote antiquity) while a few Hebrew books were allowed to appear. In 1956 Rabbi Salomon Schliefer of the Moscow synagogue was given permission to publish, in a rather inferior photo-offset reproduction, a prayer book consisting of selections from the traditional Jewish liturgical pieces. Some omissions were quite as significant as were such additions as "a prayer for peace," since peace had become a slogan widely bandied about by the Soviet authorities. The prayer begins: "Our

Father in Heaven! Bless the Government of the USSR, the shield of peace throughout the world, Amen." The three to five thousand copies thus reproduced quickly disappeared from the market, satisfying only a small part of a long pent-up demand, especially in the provincial communities. For several years the authorities also permitted the publication of an annual Jewish calendar which not only contained data on holidays, but also reproduced certain prayers such as the Mourners' *Kaddish* or the *Yizkor* services for deceased relatives in both the original Hebrew-Aramaic texts and Russian transliterations.

However, Jews were still forbidden to publish Hebrew Bibles either in the original or a Russian translation (none have indeed appeared since 1917), whereas, for instance, the Baptist denomination, not much larger in size than the Jewish population, was permitted in 1957 to issue a Protestant Bible in an edition of ten thousand copies. Similarly, the Baptist and other denominations were allowed to establish seminaries for the training of religious personnel, the Baptists allegedly maintaining fully five hundred pastors. The Russian Orthodox Church, with which the Soviet regime had made peace during World War II, once again maintained a far-flung, ramified ecclesiastical establishment. In contrast thereto, only with great effort did the Jews succeed in erecting a tiny school for rabbis in the Moscow synagogue. Although it was opened in 1957 with much propagandistic fanfare for foreign consumption, Rabbi Schliefer was allowed to assemble only thirteen pupils at best, eleven of them over forty years old. This number dwindled to four in April, 1962, when the authorities refused some Asiatic students permission to return to Moscow, allegedly because they had no residential permits in the capital. Nor were the Jewish theologians allowed to study abroad or attend any international gatherings of Jewish religious leaders, concessions readily granted to the clergy of the Christian and Muslim faiths. In fact, the Russian Orthodox and other Eastern, as well as the Protestant, Churches were allowed formally to join the membership of the World Council of Churches.[14]

Not that the practice of the Jewish religion and the domestic religious institutions totally escaped the brunt of the new antagonistic policy. In March, 1962, the baking of unleavened bread for Passover was suddenly outlawed, showing how deeply irked the Soviet authorities were by that festival of ancient Jewish national liberation and its immemorial links to Israel. This prohibition was repeated in 1963. Nor was there any official interference with the radio program of a lesser Ukrainian station in which the old Jewish religious doctrine of the Chosen People was held up for public contumely. Taking biblical and liturgical phrases out of their religious context, the broadcaster denounced the Jews for aspiring to world domination—that good old anti-Semitic shibboleth, made doubly popular by the Nazi propaganda. Recurrent vandalism of the Moscow Central Synagogue and other houses of worship led to few official reprisals. In 1961 even the two leading Jewish religious communities of Moscow and Leningrad suffered from another twist of the official policy. This time the major attack was aimed at alleged "espionage" of their lay leaders, who were condemned to long prison terms after a secret trial. The Leningrad dentist Dr. Gedaliah Pechersky's "crime" consisted in his alleged contacts with members of the Israeli embassy visiting the synagogue, while Nathan Tsirulnikov, a Moscow engineer, was sentenced for receiving Hebrew textbooks from abroad. They were not released until 1968 and 1969, respectively. After a waiting period of about two years they were allowed to emigrate to Israel. Nor was there any diminution in either the frequency or the intensity of the perennial attacks on Jewish ritual circumcision as a barbaric custom and a danger to health.[15]

The official strangulation of the only rabbinical school in the Union naturally diminished the supply of younger rabbis to service the old and decaying synagogues. It is noteworthy that neither the number of functioning rabbis nor even that of synagogues (not to speak of private conventicles for worship, so-called *minyanim,* on such occasions as the mourning for deceased relatives) have been ascertained. Generally very cautious, the Moscow rabbi, Yehudah Leib Levin, unwittingly controverted the highly inflated figures quoted by Soviet officials abroad when in 1963 he mentioned a total of ninety-six synagogues, and during his visit to the United States and Canada, spoke vaguely of a hundred or a hundred and two such houses open for worship in the entire Soviet Union. Even Soviet apologist S. Rabinovich knew of only ninety-seven synagogues in the country in 1965. At the same time, the government officially informed the United Nations that four hundred and fifty synagogues existed in Russia. Nor was there any central or regional organ to guide the often blundering synagogue administrators and the public at large concerning details, sometimes controversial, of their daily practices. This absence—in contrast to the presence of 22,000 Russian Orthodox churches and 32,000 ecclesiastics including 100 bishops, all headed by the Holy Synod and a patriarch, while pious Muslims were guided by four regional organs, and the other religious groups had their respective superior authorities—was aggravated by the absence of prayer books and other implements of worship. It was reported that, for instance, prayer shawls had become so scarce that some worshipers were prepared to pay 1,500 rubles for one. Many shipments of articles of this kind by relatives or friends abroad were confiscated on arrival. In short, the government went to great lengths to suppress Judaism in its socioreligious, as well as secular, forms. Its exceptional treatment of the Jewish religion and culture certainly made it open to the accusation of attempted cultural genocide.[16]

Tiny concessions in a few details, combined with large-scale repression, were also finally made to the Yiddish cultural effort. For many years after Stalin's death no Yiddish book or magazine at all was allowed to be printed. But in 1959–60, there appeared one reprint each of Sholem Aleichem's, Mendele's and Peretz's works and a single new volume to commemorate the twenty-fifth anniversary of Biro-Bidzhan. At the end of 1961 a new Yiddish literary journal, *Dos Sovetish Haimland*, made its appearance. Its editor, Aron Vergelis, has become the chief apologist for the Soviet treatment of Jews, insisting also in speeches and interviews in the United States in November, 1963, that there was no anti-Jewish discrimination in the Soviet Union. He and his associates, moreover, interpreted the term "literary" so precisely that they long refrained from including any news item pertaining to Jewish religious, communal, or political life. At the same time another editor, Avron Gontar, reputedly answering a letter from an American, Joseph Hoffman, has gloried in the publication of 25,000 copies of that journal, a circulation never reached by any Yiddish literary magazine in either the United States or Israel. In the same statement Gontar contended that *Dos Sovetish Haimland* "unites over one hundred authors, members of the Soviet Writers' Union. They write in Yiddish. In the last seven years publishing houses in various parts of the country have produced twelve million copies of about two hundred of their works." None of these assertions have been borne out by any other evidence, except if one were to include the Russian translations from Yiddish authors, which in the late 1950s had begun reappearing in the market and which in 1961 suddenly gushed forth from the Moscow and other presses. These translations included some works by Sholem Aleichem, Mendele, and Peretz, as well as by rehabilitated authors like Peretz Markish and new writers whose works had never appeared in Yiddish. As was pointed out, the discrimination against the Yiddish-speaking public, of which 488,000, or 21.5 percent of all those registered as Jews, had formally designated Yiddish as their language, can easily be noted if one compares its treatment to that of the 504,000 backward Asian Maris and 236,000 equally backward Yakuts. In 1961 alone, the Soviet authorities helped to publish 17 Mari and 28 Yakut newspapers, as well as 62 Mari and 144 Yakut books.[17]

Biro-Bidzhan was no exception. Not only were the Jews too few in number—exaggerated earlier estimates were rectified by the total of but 14,269 Jews or 8.8 percent of the 163,000 inhabitants of the region counted in the census of 1959—to develop an independent culture of their own, but they were not even given the opportunity to maintain a single school or to publish a book in the Yiddish language. Apart from the anemic *Shtern*, with a circulation of 1,000, the only reminders of the Hebrew alphabet have been a few signs in Yiddish on street corners and stations, left over from an earlier more friendly era. In his much-quoted interview with Serge Groussard of 1958, Khrushchev admitted that the entire enterprise of erecting a Jewish autonomous region had failed and blamed it on Jewish "individualism." Although subsequent Soviet propaganda tried to tone down that admission, the facts have fully been confirmed by the few foreign visitors allowed into the region in recent years. Perhaps that small Jewish community is a bit more overtly Jewish than any comparable Jewish settlement in European Russia, but the high hopes attached to this "noble experiment" in the Far East in the 1920s and 1930s by Soviet Jewish leaders and their sympathizers abroad have clearly not been fulfilled. [18]

Nor does the frequent official answer that Jews no longer care for their Yiddish or Hebrew letters carry much conviction. Certainly, the twenty-five thousand Jews still found in 1959 in Lithuania must have included a large number of survivors from the Hebrew and Yiddish school systems which had flourished in that country before 1940. After all, more than 80 percent of the Jewish parents of that period had sent their children to Hebrew or Yiddish schools. That they should have suddenly lost all interest in their great heritage is extremely unlikely. On the other hand, some eager youngsters, prevented from acquiring any kind of Hebrew or Yiddish training, could at least partially satisfy their hunger for Jewish values by reading translations. In essence, the Russian Jewish public includes a number of highly intelligent and well-educated groups that have weathered all storms of persecution and discrimination and have succeeded in joining the highest ranks of Russian science, technology, and arts. Perhaps it is indeed symbolic that among the few Russians found worthy of Nobel Prizes in recent years were the poet Boris Pasternak and the physicist Lev Landau, born Jews. [19] Equally Jewish have been the three Russian chess champions of the world in recent decades, Mikhail Botvinnik, Mikhail Tal, and Boris Spassky, the pride of Russia's great national pastime. Yet it is quite evident to any impartial observer that like Polish Jewry in the 1930s, that of the Soviet Union after World War II might have supplied much manpower to the general intellectual endeavors of society at large, while at the same time continuing to cultivate on a high level the ramified domains of its Hebrew and Yiddish learning and letters, both traditional and modern.

[18]

Incipient Revival

◈

More recent Soviet developments have broken the long enforced silence of the Jewish community, resulting in a greater flow of information than was available in the 1950s and early 1960s. The generally somewhat more relaxed atmosphere throughout the Union allowed voices opposing the regime on certain issues to be heard. While dissidence was often severely punished and censorship still held sway over all published utterances, it was possible for a vocal minority to make its views known through *samizdat*s, privately reproduced sheets which often attained wide circulation within the Union; through copies sent out of the country, either in the original Russian or in various foreign translations, these *samizdat*s also reached millions of interested non-Soviet readers. Some of the *samizdat*s were reproduced or summarized in the bimonthly *Khronika* (A Chronicle of Current Events in the U.S.S.R.), which was started in April, 1968, and after a temporary suspension in 1972, began reappearing for a time in the West during 1973 under the title *A Chronicle of Human Rights in the U.S.S.R.* Clandestine within the Soviet Union, occasionally this publication also referred to matters of specific Jewish interest. Beginning with No. 18 (March, 1971) it included a special section on "The Jewish Movement for Emigration to Israel."[1]

Among the most enlightening Jewish documents were letters by Jewish individuals or groups addressed to Soviet leaders such as Brezhnev, Kosygin, and Podgorny, to the Central Committee of the Soviet Communist Party, and to other governing organs of the Union. They courageously demanded the implementation of the human rights provisions in the Soviet Constitution and international covenants. Even more daringly, some Jews appealed to the United Nations and succeeded in making their grievances known through the world organization. Additional sources of information were made available by private letters sent by Soviet Jews to their relatives and friends in Israel, the United States, and other countries. The increasing flow of Western tourists and their slightly greater freedom of movement within the Soviet Union furnished another supply of data unavailable in censored published materials. These personal records greatly supplemented the reports by foreign correspondents in the Western press, especially after they left the Union and could write more freely.[2]

To be sure, all these sources had serious drawbacks. They were largely concerned with the more dramatic events and understandably often gave only one-sided descriptions. However, they opened up new vistas for critical observers, effectively supplemented the official sources, and lent meaning to the published statistical and other data. Most importantly, there were some new stirrings in Yiddish literature, including the enlarged editions of the *Sovetish Haimland*. In recent years this journal has greatly broadened its horizons, and despite its official sponsorship and obvious anti-Zionist bias, has raised some important issues and opened avenues for further investigation. So did the proceedings during hearings by the Soviet secret service and at the trials of courageous Jewish "culprits," insofar as these could be reconstructed from the records or from eyewitness accounts. Finally, the growth of Jewish emigration (*see* below) brought into Israel and several Western countries thousands of informed Soviet Jews. Their earlier experiences, reproduced in memoirs, answers to questionnaires, and the like, have become, despite the usual shortcomings of that kind of source material, an unexpectedly vivid reflection of actual happenings. In this way the ever-alert curiosity of the outside world concerning the Jewish and general developments in the Soviet Union have had much more solid information to draw upon. Yet, the persistent paucity of professional native Jewish scholars dedicated to on-the-spot research in Jewish history, economics, sociology, and political science has despite the few monographs published by Yakov Kantor in Poland or Shloime (Solomon) Rabinovich in Moscow, left serious gaps in our knowledge of many phases of Soviet Jewish life during the last thirty years.[3]

DEMOGRAPHIC STAGNATION

Notwithstanding these signs of a reawakened vitality, the biological strength of Soviet Jewry seems to have been sapped by the adverse developments of the preceding decades. This is well illustrated by an apparent decline in the Jewish population, as reflected by the two censuses of 1959 and 1970. According to the official figures, in 1959 there were 2,267,814 Jews in the Union, forming 1.1 percent of the total population of 208,827,000. Eleven years later the official total was 2,151,300 Jews, or a reduction by some 5.2 percent in a general population which had increased by about 16 percent, to 242,770,000. Many competent scholars have not only doubted the general completeness and accuracy of these figures, but have altogether denied that there was a decline. In the 1960s even official sources such as the *Ethnographic World Atlas* of 1964 had raised the estimates of the Jewish population from the original figure given in 1959. The official estimate for 1964 referred to the presence of some 2,400,000 Jews in the Union, implying an increase of more than 130,000 in the intervening five years. Since no data were available about Jewish birth and mortality rates, Leon Shapiro in his annual review for the *American Jewish Year Book* (despite his own serious reservations), applied the yardstick of general Soviet population growth and estimated the Jewish population of 1971 to be 2,644,000. Curiously, as we recall, that very figure was given by the *Sovetish Haimland* in 1973 without supplying the source. Some more sanguine Jews, especially among the recent émigrés, spoke of the presence in the Union of 3,000,000 to 3,500,000 Jews. One well-informed émigré even gave me the astounding figure of 4,600,000.[4]

Nobody can gainsay that there were more Jews in the country than were counted by the census enumerators. To begin with, in the Soviet Union, as in many other countries, there are uncertainties, both theoretical and practical, in determining "who is a Jew." In the Soviet Union there is also a further dichotomy between the estimates of population based upon passport designations and those based upon information given to the census officials. While the large majority of Jews residing in cities undoubtedly have declared themselves as such when, according to law, at the age of sixteen, they received a passport, this may have been less true in the case of their interviews with census takers. With respect to passports, an offspring of two Jewish parents has had no choice but to indicate the same nationality as his or her own. Only in mixed marriages could the applicant adopt the nationality of either parent, although that of the mother was officially preferred by the administration. Since the passport must be submitted with each application for a job, for admission to a school of higher learning, and on numerous other occasions, the nationality thus registered accompanies the person for life. However, it is known that at times, particularly during the turbulent 1940s many people claimed to have lost their passports, and after moving to other localities, secured new passports with a different national designation. This was especially true of applicants for some position who found their true ethnic designation disadvantageous and preferred to present themselves as Russians or as members of the ruling nationality of the particular republic in which they lived. The census enumerators, on the other hand, were especially enjoined not to require documentation, but to enter the ethnic designation given by the head of each household. It is therefore quite possible that many Jews, bearing passports with the designation "Jew" on the fifth line, misinformed the enumerators or were directed by one or another zealous Russian enumerator to give "Russian" as their nationality.[5]

For these and other reasons the number of "Jews" not so counted in Soviet censuses has been debated from the early census of 1926. So informed an economist-statistician as Yurii Larin (Lurye), whose high government position and general acculturation to the Russian majority must have made him inclined to minimize the number of Jews in the country, estimated that there were some 300,000 Jews not counted in the census. This estimate was largely accepted by most subsequent investigators. For the census of 1939 Jacob Lestchinsky figured on some 250,000 unrecorded Jews. There is a distinct possibility, therefore, that the 1959 and 1970 censuses likewise "overlooked" several hundred thousand Jews. Certainly, during the German occupation of the largest Jewish concentrations in western Russia, many Jews may have tried to save their lives by changing their names and claiming to belong to some non-Jewish ethnic group. If successful, these survivors of the Holocaust doubtless continued to carry passports with the false ethnic designation for the rest of their lives and thus registered their children, even if they (together with some of their close friends) may have regarded themselves as Jews. Hence the real total of the Soviet Jewish population will necessarily remain rather conjectural.[6]

Nonetheless, there are valid reasons to assume that Soviet Jewry lagged far behind its neighbors in the rate of natural growth, and at times may actually have shown symptoms of natural decline. To begin with, unlike the large non-Jewish majority, Jews in the Soviet Union in 1926, and increasingly thereafter, were a predominantly urban group. According to the censuses of 1959 and 1970, more than 95 percent of Soviet Jewry lived in cities, some actually in metropolitan areas: in 1959 Moscow included 240,000 Jews among its 5,085,581 inhabitants; in 1970 the numbers increased to 257,000 and 7,061,000, respectively. Leningrad's comparative figures are 169,000 Jews among 3,321,196 inhabitants in 1959, and 162,600 Jews among 3,949,500 inhabitants in 1970. The ratios in Kiev were 153,500 to 1,104,334 in 1959, and 152,000 to 1,631,900 in 1970; in Baku 29,000 to 971,058 in 1959, and 29,700 to 1,265,500 in 1970; and in Tashkent, 50,500 to 911,930 in 1959, and 55,800 to 1,354,500 in 1970. In other words, these five metropolitan areas—two of them in Asia and only one in the old western settlements—totaling 642,000 in 1959, and 657,100 in 1970, included almost one-third of the entire Soviet Jewish population. Most of the other Jews were living in other major urban centers. Moreover, even Jews listed as inhabiting rural areas were in part thoroughly urbanized. For instance, the 19,682 "rural" Jews listed in the Moscow district doubtless were mainly suburbanites forced to reside outside the capital because the Soviet authorities had proclaimed it and Leningrad overcrowded cities in which residential rights could be acquired only with difficulty. It is a matter of record that in the U.S.S.R., as in other countries, the urban population had a much lower birth rate than rural dwellers. Hence, the Jewish birth rate must likewise have been below the country's average. This biological fact had come to the fore already in the census of 1926, that is, within nine years of the establishment of the Soviet regime. Even at that time the natural increase of the Jewish population had already dropped to 14.97, in contrast to the general population growth of 23.3 per thousand inhabitants. In fact, the Jewish birth rate, which before World War I had already declined to 35.9 per thousand persons, diminished further to 24.6 per 1,000 in 1926. Indeed, even then Jews had the lowest birth rate of any major ethnic group in the Soviet Union.[7]

Another factor lowering the Jews' natural increase was the rise in mixed marriages. From the outset, Jews in Moscow and Leningrad were more prone to marry outside the fold than the inhabitants of the former Pale of Settlement. After World War II, with the center of gravity of the Jewish population shifting to the Russian and Asiatic republics, many more Jews found their mates among the local majorities. After returning from his 1968 visit to Moscow, the well-informed journalist Boris Smolar reported that of 100 Jewish marriages in the Soviet capital 66 were mixed; this meant that one of two Jewish persons had a non-Jewish mate. In the Soviet Union there was also a considerable surplus of Jewish women: according to the census of 1959, there were about 1,200 women for every 1,000 Jewish men in the country. Even in those Asiatic republics, where in 1939 Jewish men had significantly outnumbered the women—in Kazakhstan by almost 2 to 1 (1,000:585)—the 1959 census showed a female surplus of at least 1,036:1,000. In Uzbekistan, with the greatest Jewish concentration in Soviet Asia, the surplus of 159 women (1,159:1,000) came close to the national average, whereas Azerbeidjan's surplus of 251, and Armenia's of 720 women far exceeded that average. As a result, many Jewish women remained unmarried. This factor was further aggravated by the fact that many more Jewish men than women married outside the fold.

While we do not have sufficient information concerning the conditions in the Soviet Union, the evidence from western Europe before the Holocaust invariably showed that mixed marriages were less fertile than intragroup unions. Psychologically, too, the increasing occupational difficulties encountered by Soviet Jews in the years since the Stalin Terror must have persuaded many couples not to bring into the world children who would later be identified as Jews on their passports. In Germany, where assimilation had proceeded apace for several decades before it reached the Soviet Union and where in the 1920s intermarriage had become very frequent (particularly in the big cities like Berlin), the Jewish birth rate suffered considerably. The situation had become so threatening for the survival of German Jewry that even before World War I, Dr. Felix A. Theilhaber, combining expertise in both gynecology and sociology, predicted a speedy decline of the German Jewish population. By 1931, still before Hitler's rise to power, another German Jewish sociologist figured out that under the existing conditions, every Jewish couple then married had to have an average of seven children in order merely to maintain the existing numerical strength of the Jewish population. In the same connection we must also bear in mind that most children born to a non-Jewish mother, after reaching the age of sixteen, doubtless opted for the designation "Russian," or that of the local majority in each republic on their passports. This may have been doubly the case with those being interviewed by census enumerators from the dominant nationalities in the respective republics, who tended to persuade them to register as members of their majority group.[8]

Nonetheless, it still seems likely that even the total of passport bearers with the designation "Jew" was higher than is reflected in either the 1959 or 1970 census. Their number may, indeed, have gone into the hundreds of thousands, but there is no way of telling how large it really was. Still less ascertainable is how many of the truly "hidden Jews" who had avoided that ethnic designation even on their passports found their way back to their ancestral group, or how many continued to live unrecognized as Jews, although they had Jewish-sounding names. Some of them doubtless were confirmed assimilationists who in all sincerity wished to join the majority cultures as fully as possible. Yet under the pressure of the growing outside hostility, even some assimilated Jews increasingly felt "alienated" and ultimately found their way back to their original ethnic identity.

"NEW SOVIET MAN"

Intermarriage among ethnic groups, and particularly among Jews and non-Jews, was favorably viewed in governmental circles. In this way the

Party hoped to overcome the inveterate nationalist leanings of either mate and to help create the ideal "new Soviet man," a type different from all its predecessors. It could be expected, the authorities believed, that, in a relatively short time, such couples would raise completely Russified children and thus fit them into the mold of the new human beings envisaged by the leaders.

This was not a Soviet innovation. Many a totalitarian state had tried to reshape its population according to its own blueprint and to give it a character different from that of other societies. Even after the failure of the original French Revolution and of the attempt to remake the French people into a new nation professing an all-human "Religion of Reason" and thus to overcome all traditional differences between regions and faiths, Napoleon still envisaged the possibility of molding the French people into his own image. He realized that for this purpose he would have to make peace with the strongly entrenched Catholic Church and hence concluded a Concordat with the pope in 1801. Soon thereafter he reorganized the Jewish communities under a new consistorial system. By subjecting them to strict government supervision, he converted them into regular state agencies. Characteristically, despite his general religious indifference, he evinced great interest in assimilating the Jews through intermarriage. By submitting twelve questions to his dramatically convoked Assembly of Jewish Notables and an allegedly revived Jewish Sanhedrin—all performed with great pomp and much international propaganda—he solicited from them authoritative replies which would reaffirm not only the Jews' patriotic feelings but also their willingness to be totally integrated into the French nation. As a typical dictator he even expected that, among other matters, the elders would consider mixed marriages religiously acceptable. Of course, the Jewish elders could neither accept this principle nor urge rabbis to perform the religious rites solemnizing such marriages; they merely declared that according to the old Jewish maxim "the law of the kingdom is law," they would recognize a mixed marriage performed by civil authorities as legally valid. Along similar lines, another authoritarian ruler, Benito Mussolini, tried to integrate the Jews into the mold of Italy's "new man," which he envisaged as the outcome of his fascist mission. Reminiscing in 1941 about his anti-Jewish legislation of the preceding years, he wrote that he had personally "opposed such excesses," for he had found Jews to be patriotic citizens and courageous soldiers, and he also remembered that four of the seven founders of Italian nationalism had been Jews. "I have Aryanized such men of good disposition." With an excess of optimism, he added: "It will be a question of one generation. Mixed marriages will slowly eliminate the Jewish characteristics. A small percentage thereof [of Jewish blood] flowing in the veins of a number of future Italians will do no harm." Needless to say, under Hitler's pressure, the Duce, in adopting the German form of racialism which repudiated intermarriage and discriminated against children and grandchildren of mixed marriages because of their partial Jewish ancestry, had unwittingly promoted greater Jewish segregation and the resulting rejection of assimilation.[9]

Compared with Napoleon and Mussolini the Soviet leaders faced a much more complex situation. After all, France and Italy had had basically homogeneous populations with but small religious and ethnic minorities. The Soviet Union, on the other hand, with more than one hundred and twenty national minorities recognized by law and a number of important republics dominated by ethnic groups at variance with the Russians, could not easily overcome these disparities even by intermarriage. Yet historic continuity made both the tsars and their Soviet successors dream of a nationally monolithic population. If religious diversity proved a foremost stumbling block for the tsars, who could not hope speedily to convert millions of Roman Catholics, Muslims, Jews, and others, they at least made an effort to uproot the Uniate Church in the Ukraine and to assimilate all Ukrainians to the Russian Orthodox Church. Moreover, it could also be denied that the Ukrainians were a nationality apart. By calling them Little Russians the tsarist authorities hoped to absorb them all within the mainstream of Russian language and culture. In principle, the same denial could sooner or later be applied to the White Russians as well. As to the other nationalities and religious groups, the authorities conceded that the process of assimilation of these *inorodtsi* (alien-born) would be far slower. But they tried to promote it by sharp discrimination, thus making the transition to the Russian nationality and religion very alluring. Conversion to the Orthodox faith, often accompanied or followed by marriage with a Russian mate, usually led to the ultimate integration of the offspring into Russian society.[10]

In the early revolutionary era the Soviets, bent upon overthrowing the main tsarist institutions, completely abandoned the religious approach. By trying to substitute for it their own quasi-religion of communism they expected readily to overcome all previous religious separatisms. They dreamed of a world revolution resulting in a new world-wide communist culture, in which nationalities, like states, would ultimately play but a minor role. Interveningly, they not only established separate republics for the major nationalities within the Soviet federation but even granted them the right of secession from the Union—a privilege of which, for example, the Baltic states made immediate use.

In time, however, the old continuity began to reassert itself, and with the new Stalinist emphasis on "socialism in one country," the trend toward progressive Russification became an undeniable fact of life. Three of the four Baltic states have since been restored to Soviet control by the Allied victory in World War II. No one dares now to propagate secession of any republic from the Union, though such a right is still guaranteed by the Constitution, for fear of being accused of high treason. Moreover, from the outset the educational system in the Soviet Union, even if classes were conducted in the local languages, so greatly stressed the common doctrines of Marxism-Leninism that it made little difference in what idiom these doctrines were expounded. They were expected to produce that "new Soviet man" whose intellectual and spiritual make-up would transcend all ethnic diversities. We recall how strongly the *Yevsektsiia* and the leading journalists of the *Emes*, though writing in Yiddish, emphasized that their aim was not the perpetuation of Jewish nationalism, but rather the world-wide embrace of the communist ideals.

From the 1930s on, however, the growing emphasis on Russian nationalism was combined with abandonment of some early innovations designed to undermine the traditional forms of life, such as the new marriage laws and the six-day week. The use of the Latin alphabet to displace the Arabic script in many Muslim areas was speedily followed by a return to the Cyrillic writing. (Only the adoption of the Gregorian calendar proved to be enduring.) This Russophile tendency unavoidably produced a reaction among the other nationalities, who increasingly fell back upon the historic memories of their own national past. True, whatever irredentism now exists in the Soviet Union is not generally aimed at achieving complete national sovereignty. The existing socioeconomic realities, the presence of powerful new institutions, and particularly the irreversible factors operating in the new economic system have persuaded many enlightened leaders of the various nationalities that complete separation from the Union might cause irreparable harm to their social well-being. As a result, the national minority rights have been greatly weakened. But some new compromises have had to be made with the national cultures and occasionally even with their religious elements, particularly in the Muslim-dominated republics. These concessions are reminiscent of some halfway measures adopted by the tsarist successors of Nicholas I. Certainly, the Soviet Union today is far from the monolithic structure which it appeared to be in the days of Stalin's Terror, just as tsarist Russia under Nicholas II had differed greatly from that in the days of Nicholas I's despotism.[11]

Officially, to be sure, the ruling circles pretended that there was no unrest in the population at all. They thought that by consistently denying the problem with the aid of their far-flung propaganda machine, they could make it disappear. Typical of that attitude is an official publication issued in 1967 in connection with the fiftieth anniversary of the Communist Revolution, and entitled *Strana Sovetov za 50 liet* (The

Soviet Land during Fifty Years). Here the accomplishments of its national policies are extolled as follows:

> In our country members of more than a hundred nations and nationalities live and work as a united friendly family. In the U.S.S.R., for the first time in the history of mankind, the nationality problem has been fully solved. . . . An important role in this process [of unification] is played by the Russian language. Many millions of people of various nations regard the Russian culture as their own culture and the great Russian language as their own mother tongue.

In fact, however, many leaders of the dominant nationalities in their respective republics have viewed such linguistic Russification with a jaundiced eye. As far as Jews were concerned, their presence in some of these republics was often resented for two reasons: they were both ethnic Jews and linguistic Russians. More realistically, in 1966 a young Jewish writer admitted in the slightly more independent *Novy Mir* that, though outwardly the anti-Jewish prejudices seem to have entirely disappeared and been forgotten, "at any sharp turn in history, whenever certain difficulties arise, they again make themselves felt, carrying with them the backward sections of the population."[12]

In the Ukraine the local population not only harbored an inveterate enmity toward its Jewish neighbors which was carried over from the days of the Polish domination, but it resented those Jewish officials, especially non-native-born, who helped in the repression of the Uniate Church by the ruling circles of the Russian Orthodox Church, with the blessings of the central Soviet bureaucracy. The Uniates were particularly prone to blame any occasional unfriendly act by a local Jewish official on the Jewish people as a whole. Rarely did a Ukrainian intellectual like S. Karavansky speak up against the anti-Jewish trials, like that of the chairman of the Great Central Synagogue in Leningrad, Gedalia Pechersky. Similarly, the prominent critic Ivan Dziuba, in delivering a memorial address at Babi Yar, went no further than to state that "Babi Yar is a tragedy of all mankind, but it happened on Ukrainian soil, and therefore a Ukrainian, like a Jew, has no right to forget it." More typical of Ukrainian public opinion was the issuance, by the Ukrainian Academy of Science, of Trofim Kichko's savage anti-Jewish work. In the lesser republics of the Union, Jews thus relived the experience of many other Jewish groups in multinational areas of being placed between the anvil of the native national majority and the hammer of the politically and culturally superior ethnic minority controlling the central powers of the state.[13]

Understandably, Russification progressed most rapidly in the Great Russian Republic. Apart from the vast stretches of land originally inhabited by native Russians, the republic has long served as an effective melting pot for the millions of newer settlers from other parts of the Union brought together by the Soviets' memorable industrial revolution. In the speedily growing urban centers—according to the 1970 census the Union's urban population of 135,991,574 greatly outnumbered the 105,728,620 rural inhabitants—the western Slavs and Baltics met Asiatics and other settlers using more than a hundred dialects. For all of them the Russian idiom became the main means of communication. There also was the irresistible allure of the great Russian culture. The government promoted that process of amalgamation by providing few educational facilities in which to cultivate minority cultures. This has been true even in the case of Ukrainians, the second-largest nationality in the Union, many of whom outside the mass settlements in the Ukrainian and Moldavian republics have lost their sense of national allegiance. This failure was clearly demonstrated by the census of 1959, which showed that while in the Ukraine 93.5 percent of those listed as belonging to the Ukrainian nationality also gave Ukrainian as their native tongue, among the 5,000,000 Ukrainians living outside their republic only 51.2 percent reported that language as their native speech. Clearly, in order to implement their policies of denationalization, the Kremlin rulers provided no Ukrainian schools for their internal Ukrainian "diaspora." The progress of Russification even within the lesser republics is well illustrated by Latvia, where the Russians now form 30 percent of the population; in Riga, the capital, they have attained the majority. These factors operated with redoubled force in the case of Jews, whose greatest concentration has shifted to the Great Russian Republic and whose urbanization has long exceeded 95 percent.[14]

POLITICAL WEAKNESS

Behind that general deterioration of Jewish status lurked the continual decline of the Jews' political influence since the 1920s. This came clearly to the fore in their diminishing share of the governing Communist Party. While membership in the Party was no longer so restricted as in the first postrevolutionary years—in the late 1960s it reached the high figure of some 14,000,000—it still played a role in securing desirable employment and in social standing among neighbors. From the beginning, as we recall, the proportion of Jews had been declining, principally because the Party had been admitting more and more members from other ethnic groups. More recently, this process had been aggravated by growing discrimination in the admission of Jewish candidates, and possibly also by some cooling of the ardor of young Jews in seeking admission. At any rate it is estimated that in the late 1960s Jewish membership did not exceed 210,000, or 1.5 percent of the total. True, this number still exceeded the Jewish ratio in the total Soviet population which had dropped to below 1 percent in 1970. But it was definitely less than was warranted by the Jewish proportion of 2 percent in the urban population from which most members were recruited.[15]

Even greater was the decline in the number of Jews in the higher echelons of Party and government. Not only had there been no Jewish regular member of the ruling *Politbureau* since the ouster of Lazar Kaganovich in 1957 but the formerly strong Jewish representation in the sensitive areas of international relations and military defense had continued to dwindle to almost nothing in recent years. Of course, Jews still continued to serve in the Red Army in proportion to their population strength, although no statistical breakdown according to ethnic groups seems to be available. But the last Jew to hold the rank of Army-General of the Army was the wartime hero Yakov G. Kreyzer. On the whole, the glory of a Red Army career, with the numerous distinctions and tangible benefits it conferred upon the soldier and officer, had diminished greatly in the recent period when enforced military service began to be used as a punitive measure against political dissenters and "troublemakers" in civilian life. Even in the two most broadly based so-called parliamentary institutions, the Soviet of the Union and the Soviet of Nationalities, the Jewish representation sank far below the proportion of Jews in the population. Needless to say, the deputies to these bodies— in elections completely dominated by the Party machine, with single lists and no opposition party allowed—have had very little influence on the administration of the country and the shaping of its external and domestic policies. Yet it was truly symbolic when in the summer of 1974, as in 1966 and 1970, only 2 Jews were elected among the 767 members of the Soviet of the Union. One of them was the perennial *Parade* Jew, Venyamin F. Dymshitz, holder for several years of the high-sounding but politically rather innocuous office of deputy prime minister, who has represented the Far Eastern district of Khabarovsk (including Biro-Bidzhan), and the academician Yulii B. Khariton. Characteristically, no Jew was elected from any of the fourteen republics other than the Russian. Similarly, in the Soviet of Nationalities, only Lithuania is represented by, among others, a Jew, Henrik O. Zinonas, an outstanding partisan commander during World War II and more recently editor in chief of the ideological journal *Komunistas*. The other 3 Jews in that body of 750 deputies were elected in the Russian Soviet Republic, namely Aleksander B. Chakovsky, editor in chief of the *Literaturnaya Gazeta*, and 2 of the 5 deputies from Biro-Bidzhan. Only in that remote "Autonomous Jewish Region," does that ratio of 2:5 deputies vastly exceed the 1:12 ratio of the Jews in the total population.[16]

In one area even in government appointments, however, the Soviets could not as effectively discriminate against Jews as in the political sphere. With the Soviet Union's increasing concentration on both the industrialization and the arming of the country, the ensuing shortages of technically highly skilled personnel forced the government to give a somewhat freer rein to talented members of even a disliked minority like the Jewish. Certainly, if the Union, according to Khrushchev's repeated assertion, was to surpass the United States' productive capacity in the foreseeable future and thus help to "bury" the capitalist world, this could only be achieved both by depriving the population of the fruits of its labor in the light, or consumer, industries and by attaining the maximum output in the heavy industries. For this purpose the country had to strain all available intellectual, as well as financial, resources. In the post–World War II era Jews were not only the most urbanized people in Russia but they were also frequently endowed with their traditional zest for learning, further stimulated by their realization that only by being better equipped than their competitors could they mitigate the evils of discrimination. That is why, according to a report in the official Soviet statistical monthly, at the end of 1973, there were fully 4,182 Jews among the 29,806 men and women holding doctoral degrees in the Union. Such a degree can be attained only after several years of serious postgraduate study, going well beyond the requirements for Ph.D. degrees in the United States and most Western countries. That Jews represent some 14 percent of all such most advanced "scientific workers" (*nauchiniie rabotniki*) is noteworthy, even if the occupational statistics based upon ethnic entries in passports may be derived from a larger number of Jews living in the country than is reflected in the census. But assuming that the Union embraced over 2,500,000 Jews (rather than the 2,150,000 recorded in the 1970 census plus a small natural increment over four years), such a number of holders of the highest academic degree would represent about fourteen times the Jewish demographic ratio. This disproportion is further magnified by the greater concentration of Jewish scientific workers of all classes (with doctoral or less intensive training) in such major centers of Soviet political and cultural power as Moscow and Leningrad. Moscow, which in January, 1971, harbored about a quarter of all the scientific workers in the country, accommodated fully 38.9 percent of the Jewish workers in this category. It has been estimated that gainful employment in scientific work was furnishing a livelihood for about one-quarter of the entire Jewish population in the Soviet capital. [17]

Understandably, such a large percentage of Jewish "scientists" (in the broader sense—including specialists in the social sciences and the humanities), almost all of them trained in government institutions and employed by the government, offered to the Soviet ruling circles, and their Jewish apologists in the Union and abroad, material to support their total denial of the existence of any anti-Jewish discrimination in the country. When on December 7, 1959, *Life* magazine published an article describing aspects of Russian anti-Semitism, a Jewish lady in Moscow wrote an irate letter to the editor (which New York's Yiddish communist paper, the *Morgen Freiheit*, reproduced in a Yiddish translation), pointing out that the 15,000 physicians practicing in Moscow included at that time (May, 1960) no less than 6,709 Jewish healers.

A closer look at these statistics, however, reveals a much more complicated situation. The existing numerical ratios of Jews to other nationalities are largely a heritage of earlier, less anti-Jewish attitudes. Interesting data were assembled from a sample of 1,644 physicians and academic teachers in the Ukraine in 1968. The 214 Jews among them amounted to some 14 percent. But among them fully 80, or 37.39 percent, were over 64 years old. In the next oldest category of persons, aged between 55 and 64, the general percentage of 38.38 for the group as a whole contrasted with the Jewish ratio of 41.59. Clearly these two categories, embracing almost 80 percent of the Jews, represent persons born before World War I who had embarked upon their respective careers in the 1920s or early 1930s when their skills were in great demand and discrimination was slight. In contrast, the two younger groups of 45 to 54 and 35 to 44 year old persons reveal a complete reversal. Here the general ratio is 21.66 and 9.18, respectively, as against a Jewish proportion of 16.82 and 4.20. Obviously, the younger Jewish scholars had had far more restricted opportunities for an academic career than their non-Jewish counterparts. Another statistical compilation is even more revealing. It shows that in 1947–55, which included the darkest years of the Stalinist Terror, the number of Jewish "scientific workers" actually declined from 26,186 to 24,620, a loss of more than 1,500 persons. At the same time the total number of workers kept on increasing. Hence the percentage of Jews dropped from 17.98 to 11.00. True, during the following fifteen years (1956–70), the number of Jews increased from year to year, but at a slower pace than their non-Jewish opposite numbers. Consequently, the ratio of Jews continued to diminish until it had reached but 6.94 percent in 1970. In some areas there was actually a decline in absolute numbers as well. For instance, in the Russian Republic the number of practicing Jewish physicians diminished by about a thousand in the years 1958–65. The future appears even bleaker. Because of a variety of discriminatory practices, the ratio of Jewish students at schools of higher learning, which had already declined from some 13 percent to 3.2 percent in the years 1935–61, dropped further even in absolute numbers from 111,900 in 1968–69 to 88,500 in 1972–73, with a loss of 23,400, or more than one-fifth in four years.[18]

SPREADING ANTI-SEMITISM

Discrimination in admission to schools of higher learning also had serious economic consequences, especially for a community so greatly dependent on livelihoods derived from advanced professional work. Certainly, the diminution of the number of postgraduate Jewish students from 4,945 to 3,450 in the short span of three years (1970–1973), in contrast to a fairly stationary total of some 99,000, was a severe blow to the future socioeconomic status of Soviet Jewry. This decline was further complicated by official selectivity, which barred many Jewish students from being admitted to the universities of their first choice, particularly to the most advanced institutions in Moscow, Leningrad, or Kiev. Many young Jews bent on securing higher degrees had to enroll in distant Siberian schools, just as even Jews holding the highest degree often had to take jobs at such lower-ranking institutes or in government offices at some remote locality, where their chances for intellectual advancement and further technical training were greatly reduced. The official explanation that such anti-Jewish discrimination was necessary in order to facilitate a larger enrollment of members of other ethnic groups at the most desirable schools of higher learning was in part controverted by this dispersal of Jewish students to the eastern republics, where the native majorities required much more encouragement to pursue advanced studies. In fact, a case has been made for the contention that such official discrimination was part of a scheme to reduce the general qualifications of Jewish "doctors" and doctoral candidates and thus to reduce their ability to compete with the Russian specialists for positions of greatest trust and influence. After all, as late as at the end of 1973 the 16,603 Russian holders of doctoral degrees outnumbered the 4,182 Jewish holders by only 4 to 1, as against the population ratio of well over 50 to 1. This disproportion is explainable only by the existing shortage of highly skilled scientists and engineers or, as a Moscow Jewish girl student phrased it, it is thus only "because we are needed, not because we are wanted." This situation certainly bodes ill for the future.[19]

We are much less well informed about the other facets of Jewish occupational distribution in recent years. No Soviet Jewish scholar has come forward with a comprehensive analysis of the economic data relating to Jews drawn from the 1970 census, in any way comparable with the studies published by Lev Zinger and Yakov Kantor with respect to the censuses of 1939 and 1959, not to speak of the truly detailed investigations concerning the results of the 1926 enumeration. The general data made available by the census summaries published, or about to be published, by the government itself would have to be supplemented by numerous details appearing only in specialized statistical journals or in a host of local and provincial papers. To be sure, particularly in areas with smaller Jewish populations the local studies may have combined the data pertaining to Jews with those of other minorities in the single category of "others." Yet a conscientious on-the-spot researcher may be able to consult some underlying archival records, access to which depends entirely on the good will of the administration.

However, there is little question that whatever the statistical compilations might yield, the much-publicized trials of alleged Jewish black marketeers and foreign exchange speculators, usually announced with their actual or former Jewish names, served not only to ruin the means of subsistence of the accused individuals, but also to blacken the name of the entire Jewish population. The fact that many defendants were condemned to death under ordinances newly enacted in May, 1961, which placed "economic crimes" of this kind under the sanction of this extreme penalty—though their lives were saved by the sharp worldwide reaction to these Draconian sentences—further heightened the domestic tensions. As a result, the image of the Jewish trader as an exploiter of the masses, inherited from the propaganda of the tsarist period, was thus effectively revived and helped poison all Judeo-Gentile relations. Even Jewish managers and salesmen in state-owned shops did not escape unscathed. In periods of scarcity of consumer goods that perennially plagued the Soviet economy in the 1950s and early 1960s, these officials were often suspected of hiding some of their goods in order to sell them to favored individuals or to divert them to black markets. We are told of a typical episode in a Ukrainian city after the local population lined up in the usual queues before a grocery store. When the would-be purchasers in one queue finally got to a non-Jewish salesman and were told that his supply had all been sold out, they good-naturedly teased him and asked for whom he was hiding his merchandise. But when customers in another line ultimately reached a Jewish salesman who was also sold out, they heaped upon him a torrent of abuse and shouted that all Jews were black marketeers.[20]

Curiously, in these trials many Jewish defendants were accused of high treason not only on account of their "criminal" business deals, but also because of their alleged "cosmopolitanism." This was a noteworthy reversal of the early Marxist international ideals preached by Lenin and Trotsky. At that time, we recall, even Stalin insisted on the provisional nature of national minority rights, which were supposed to enable each nationality to develop its cultural resources to the full before ultimately submerging them in one single communist culture embracing all humanity. Now "cosmopolitanism," as exemplified by intimate Jewish contacts with Jews of other lands, and therefore by implication viewing the world with an international perspective, was considered a menace to the newly established communist order. In the period of the cold war any contact of a Soviet citizen with foreign, particularly American, nationals appeared suspect. Since the United States embraced the largest and most prosperous Jewish community in the world and included in its midst a vast number of relatives of Soviet Jews, the latter could readily be suspected of harboring illicit sympathies for the American system and of thus becoming tools of "American imperialism."

Through these trials, accompanied by a barrage of written and spoken words in the press and pamphlets, radio and television, the regime sought to blacken the honor of the entire Jewish people and its religion. Books of the type presented by Trofim Kichko, we recall, were issued with the censors' blessings as publications of respected institutions such as the Ukrainian Academy of Science. Nor did the Soviet officials abroad hesitate to disseminate virulent attacks on Judaism through the official bulletins of their embassies. One such bulletin quoted, for example, passages from the *Shulhan 'Arukh*, the chief modern Jewish code of laws, ordering Jews to hate non-Jews, a doctrine allegedly instilled in the minds of Jewish children in all Jewish schools.[21]

Paradoxically, attacks on Jewish "rootless cosmopolitanism" were soon combined with assaults on Zionism. Long considered dead and buried by Russian Jews and non-Jews alike, this movement suddenly sprouted again in various parts of the Union. True, in 1947 Andrei Gromyko himself, from the rostrum of the United Nations, delivered a warm pro-Zionist oration advocating the partition of Palestine into a Jewish and an Arab state. But even then few people were misled into believing that the Soviet Union had thus given up its inveterate enmity toward the Zionist movement. Gromyko's speech, the Soviet pro-partition vote, the Kremlin's subsequent recognition of the State of Israel in May, 1948, within two days after the proclamation of its independence, as well as the Soviet acquiescence in Czechoslovakia's furnishing arms to the new state for its defense in Israel's extremely difficult war of liberation—were all readily recognized as stratagems for getting Britain out of the Middle East and opening the way for its penetration by Soviet power. This centuries-old Russian aspiration was, indeed, now fulfilled much beyond anything ever attained by the tsarist imperialists. But very soon the Russians switched to outright support of the Arab nations and their professed desire to liquidate the new state.

As a result, the chorus of accusation of Zionist espionage in favor of the United States grew steadily louder, and the Soviets broke diplomatic relations with Israel for the first time after the discovery, on February 9, 1953, of a bomb placed in the Soviet legation in Tel Aviv by "unknown" perpetrators. Although formal relations between the two countries were resumed on July 20, and their diplomatic missions were raised to the rank of embassies, the enmity persisted and intensified during the wars of 1956, 1967, and 1973. The "Six-Day War" made a particularly deep and lasting impression. All published evidence clearly suggests that the Arabs had prepared for that war with the connivance of the Soviet Union. The Russians not only shipped a tremendous quantity of arms to Egypt and Syria, but after the closing of the Tiran Straits to Israeli shipping—under the existing circumstances as hostile an act as an armed attack—the Soviets threatened with direct military intervention those powers which might feel obliged, by their 1956 promises, to protect Israel against that very contingency. Initially, the Soviet rulers were so sure of a speedy Arab victory that to their own people they merely reported the initial Arab claims of bombings of Tel Aviv and other Israeli localities. They also instructed their chief delegate to the United Nations, Nikolai Fedorenko, to hold off any cease-fire resolution by that body as long as possible, so as to enable the Arab states fully to exploit their victories. One can readily imagine the depth of their disappointment when within two or three days it became manifest that the Arabs had suffered a crushing defeat. Now Fedorenko had to reverse himself and make every effort to hasten the adoption of the cease-fire.[22]

Naturally the Soviet prestige in the world sank rapidly. To mitigate the effects of this miscalculation and to pacify the Soviet people, the Kremlin unleashed an unprecedented propaganda barrage against the Israeli "aggressors" and their "imperialist" supporters. Among the main themes of this propaganda was the alleged Zionist drive for world domination. For this purpose the Soviet media resurrected the slogans of the *Protocols of the Elders of Zion*, which though originating from Russian sources, had made only a slight impression at home, but after World War I had become a "classic" of anti-Semitic literature in the West, and later also in the Arab lands. Some Soviet writers now explained the Zionist program in terms of the old predictions of the prophets concerning the messianic age, when all nations would worship the God of Israel and pay homage to the resuscitated people of Israel.

Needless to say, much as the Zionist idea was indeed rooted in the Jewish people's messianic yearnings, the secularized Zionist movement never went to the eschatological extremes of the prophetic visions of an eternal peace not only among men but also in nature. It was merely determined to build a Jewish state within the confines of ancient Israelitic Palestine. More than seventy years ago, we recall, the Zionist Organization, much as it yearned for any form of international recognition, rejected the British government's offer of land in Uganda. This obvious contrast between visionary prophecies and the realistic Zionist program, which had discouraged some Orthodox extremists from joining the movement and even from recognizing the Jewish state, did not deter Soviet propagandists like Yurii Ivanov from citing the messianic predictions of the ancient prophets as examples of Zionism's ultimate goals. As if Christianity, Islam, and the other world religions had ever relinquished their hope that at the end of days, all humanity would profess their particular brand of universal religion! Certainly, the Marxist-Leninist dream of a world revolution and the withering away of all states to make room for one universal communist empire pursued far more tangible expansionist aims. In this connection Trofim Kichko, in his new book on *Yudaizm i sionizm* (Judaism and Zionism) published in 1968, cited Deutero-Isaiah's enthusiastic predictions—which included the threat to those nations which would reject the universal messianic order: "For that nation and kingdom that will not serve thee shall perish" (60:12)—as an example of Zionism's extremely imperialistic, even genocidal, tendencies.[23]

From here it was but a step to the most ridiculous accusation of all: that Zionism was in alliance with Nazism, the implacable foe and destroyer of Jews. This absurd equation of Zionism with Nazism was seemingly first advanced on an international scale in October, 1965, by the Soviet delegate to the United Nations' Social, Humanitarian and Cultural Committee, which was then preparing a Draft Convention for the Elimination of All Forms of Racial Discrimination. The delegate proposed an amendment condemning Zionism as on a par with Nazism. This theme was enlarged by Fedorenko in the historic 1967 United Nations debate, and repeated in a crescendo of abuse during the following years. The signatories to the Kiev anti-Zionist declaration of March 12, 1970, went so far as to assert that "the tragedy of Babi Yar will forever remain a symbol not only of the cannibalism of the Nazis, but also of the indelible disgrace of the Zionists, their accomplices and followers." These accusations were also echoed in the press of the satellite countries, sometimes reaching utterly fantastic forms. On May 12, 1968, for example, the Lodz workers' journal *Głos robotniczy* informed its readers that Martin Bormann, the fugitive Nazi leader second only to Hitler, was hiding out in Golda Meir's home in Jerusalem and that Moshe Dayan was none other than the notorious Nazi spy Otto Skorzeny.[24]

Such almost irrational denunciations may have carried some weight with gullible masses in the Union, for whom "Nazi" had become a dirty word applicable to almost any hateful person or group. They could at times also be echoed by communists and other leftists in the West. But they understandably evoked the opposite reaction among Jews. Even in Russia, the Jewish survivors of the newly annexed western areas, who included some old Zionists, must have been outraged by such comparisons. Many younger Jews, too, though they had grown up in the Soviet atmosphere, had received all their schooling in the Soviet Union, and were deeply impressed by Russian culture, refused to be taken in by the shrill voices of the accusers of their people. Even so assimilated a man as

Ilya Ehrenburg confessed to a friend that he was elated by Israel's victory. "If, following in Hitler's footsteps," he added, "the Arabs had started massacring all the Jews in Israel, the infection would have spread; we would have here a wave of antisemitism." Persons of this type who for idealistic or opportunistic reasons had severed all spiritual ties with their fellow Jews, were often forced back into the Jewish fold by the Nazis' physical extermination of Jews without any distinction being made between assimilationists and nationalists. What happened in Germany and other countries after Hitler's rise to power was to repeat itself on a smaller scale in the Soviet Union during Stalin's declining years.[25]

Not surprisingly, the reaction was most pronounced among Jews who from the outset had rejoiced about the rise of the State of Israel, some of whom had displayed their enthusiasm about the achievements of their brethren on such occasions as the arrival of the first Israeli diplomatic mission in Moscow, the appearance of Israeli athletes and intellectuals at various international gatherings, and the like. Even persons who had had few ties with the Jewish community in the preceding years reacted as Boris Kochubiyevsky did. Suddenly dismayed by the chorus of accusations hurled at Jews and Judaism at a workers' meeting in the Kiev factory where he worked, he felt impelled to rise and voice his dissent regardless of consequences. Ultimately, in May, 1968, after more than a year of relentless official pressure, he resigned from his factory job and applied for emigration to Israel. At the same time he prepared a *samizdat* to explain to his friends, and perhaps also to himself, *Why I Am a Zionist*. He wrote:

> How is it possible that Jewish boys and girls who know nothing about Jewish culture and language, who are mostly atheists, continue to feel so acutely and be so proud of their national affiliation? The answer is simple: Thanks for that, in large measure, can be given to anti-Semitism—the new brand which was implanted from above and, as a means of camouflage, is called anti-Zionism. . . . More and more Jews are coming to understand that endless silence and patience—lead straight down the road to Auschwitz. That is why the leaders of the Soviet Union have anathemized Zionism.[26]

To be sure, some critics have denigrated the attitude of such "repentant sinners," who discovered their allegiance to their people only after sustained Jew-baiting. Of course, this disparagement runs counter to the well-known talmudic dictum that "the place attained by a repentant sinner may not be reached by a wholly righteous person." Historically, too, such a reaction to outside persecution has often contributed toward strengthening the affirmative forces of continuity. True, the return of numerous assimilated German Jews to the fold in the early years of the Nazi domination led some carping critics to generalize that

Jewish history in the Diaspora has always been but a history of "objects" tossed about by the powerful outside storms in their respective environments, rather than of subjects able to determine their own direction. I have often repudiated that narrow view. Comparing Jewish history with that of even the greatest powers, one must admit that the historic evolution of all of them depended on external and internal forces alike. Just as the history of every nation is influenced by its foreign relations at least as much as, or more than, by its domestic developments, so are the varying reactions of Jews to external anti- or philo-Semitic attitudes just as important as are their internal forces of perseverance. In any case, in the Soviet Union of the 1960s the great transformation of a passive and resigned people into one which again, at least partially, took the direction of its fate into its own hands probably was the most significant, if totally unexpected, effect of both the new prestige of the Jewish people after the rise of the State of Israel and the partial replacement of the Stalinist Terror by the more moderate despotism of the Khrushchev and Brezhnev eras.

DISSENT AND EXODUS

In their quest for a new identity and for individual, as well as national, self-determination the Jews were aided by some new manifestations of dissent among the Soviet peoples. The numerous Soviet nationalities, which had substantial diasporas in other lands, increasingly found ways to evade the strict Soviet antiemigration laws, in many ways resembling those enacted by the tsarist authorities in the nineteenth century. Not only many Ukrainians and Armenians who had their own national republics, but even more ardently members of such uprooted groups as the Crimean Tatars and Volga Germans, who had been deported by Stalin during the war and were subsequently forbidden to return to their old habitats (a Tatar found in the Crimea without authorization was subject to severe punishment), looked yearningly for opportunities to join their fellow nationals in other countries. The dissatisfaction of some of these national groups even found expression in public demonstrations, such as took place in Tbilisi in 1956 and 1973, in Erevan in 1965, in Tashkent in 1969, and in Kovno (Kaunas) in 1972.

At the same time there was the rise of a small but influential Democratic Movement, led by outstanding scientists Andrei D. Sakharov and Valery Chalidze, which demanded the implementation of the human and civil rights provisions guaranteed by the Soviet Constitution, especially that proclaimed in 1936 but never carried out in practice. It also referred to the Soviet Union's adherence to the human rights covenants adopted by the United Nations for all member states and, however reluctantly, accepted by the Soviet delegation and formally ratified by the authorities at home. Although not pursuing a single course of action, this movement—by disseminating its views in *samizdats* and the *Chronicle of Current Events,* reminiscent of the underground literature in the last decades of Tsarist Russia—was reinforced by the resounding echo its utterances found in other lands (including their communist parties), and exerted a far greater influence than was warranted by its relatively small numerical membership in the country.[27]

As in tsarist days persons of Jewish origin appear to have played a disproportionate role in the new Democratic Movement as well. However, this time their interests often diverged from those of the other protagonists of the democratic idea. Generally, the movement was deeply divided ideologically and in practice. One must not forget that Russia had almost no history of democratic institutions along Western lines. The short-lived parliamentary experiences with the tsarist Dumas revealed more about their weaknesses than about any genuine popular appeal such an institution might have among the masses. The Lvov-Kerensky regime was of even shorter duration, besides being beset by the enormous difficulties of a losing war and the growing anarchy in the country.

The new dissenting movement, too, was represented in part by conservatives like Nobel Prize winner Aleksander Solzhenitsyn, who was ultimately deported from the Union since the regime did not dare to defy world opinion and imprison him. His ideas resembled those of some nineteenth-century Panslavists, Dostoevsky, or Tolstoy, rather than those of Western progressives. Nor did he evince any real sympathy for the Jewish characters he depicted in his renowned novels. Even the more truly democratic wing among the dissenters often had little understanding for cultural pluralism as applied to specific Jewish identity. For example, Roy Medvedev, who made a name for himself in the democratic circles in the Union and abroad by his frank analysis in *Let History Judge: the Origins and Consequences of Stalinism,* and even made some sympathetic comments on Jewish rights, nevertheless in his study of "Socialist Democracy" has preached strict adherence to Leninism reformed from within and, in the Jewish case, expected ultimate total assimilation of the Jews to the majority.[28]

However, they all agreed on the importance of human rights. Only a few, to be sure, were quite so outspoken as Sakharov, founder and president of the Soviet Human Rights Society, who exclaimed:

> Is it not disgraceful to allow another backsliding into antisemitism in our appointments policy (incidentally, in the highest bureaucratic élite of our government, the spirit of antisemitism was never fully dispelled after the nineteen-thirties)?

But hampered by the absence of a regular press—the illicit *Chronicle of Current Events* and individual *samizdat*s necessarily had but a limited circulation—and able to propagate its ideas only in small conventicles, often infiltrated by police informers, the Democratic Movement had only a small impact on the general public. Perhaps the popular ballad-eers exerted a more direct influence on the masses, since their satirical and other poems set to music had a considerable following. Among these modern minstrels the Jewish poet and dramatist Aleksander Arka-dievich Galich (originally Ginzburg, born in 1919) has played a major role. "There are few people in our country," wrote the novelist Vladimir Maksimov in his Open Letter to the International P.E.N. Club and the European Association of Writers, "unfamiliar with Galich's songs." Like similar products of his Russian compeers, these songs were widely disseminated in so-called *magnitizdat*s (magnetic tapes), which because they were unlicensed products of independent thinking earned their author an expulsion from the unions of both the Soviet Writers and the Soviet Cinematographers. In these songs Galich not only criticized the prevailing indifference to governmental abuses, the threatened return to Stalinism, and the cruelties perpetrated in the labor camps, but he also referred to the Nazi Holocaust of Jews and commemorated the death of Salomon Mikhoels. In one of his poems written before the outbreak of the Six-Day War, he beautifully expressed his anxiety over the possible annihilation of the Israeli Jews by the Arab hosts.[29]

Like many liberals in the West, however, some of these advocates of human rights by no means opposed the majority's assimilatory pres-sures and often were quite ambivalent about the rights of national self-determination of the ethnic minorities, especially those devoid of territo-rial moorings, like the Jews. Since most of our sources stem from the clandestine channels of the *samizdat*s or from sporadic individual or group appeals to the Soviet authorities, the United Nations, or fraternal communist parties in other lands, it is almost impossible to gauge the numerical strength and the extent of the devotion to their ideals by the representative factions which sometimes cultivated their diverse thoughts in splendid isolation.[30]

Not all Jewish dissenters were of one mind on even the fundamen-tal problem of whether they ought to remain in the Union and fight for their and their compatriots' civil rights or endeavor to leave the country. We recall that such a division of opinion within the Jewish community had also existed in the period of Jewish mass emigration under the last tsars. Remarkably, however, for individual Jews, even more than for other citizens of the Union, emigration, however difficult, was often more readily obtainable than their securing the civil rights denied them by capricious bureaucrats. This was especially true after the Soviet Union had become a signatory of the *Universal Declaration of Human*

Rights and had thus accepted, in particular, the provision that "everyone has the right to leave any country, including his own, and to return to his country" (Article 13,2).

Even before the Soviet ratification of that covenant, Soviet Jews pioneered in the struggle to secure exit visas from a government which, even more than in early tsarist times, considered departures from the country without special authorization a basically treasonable act. Aided and abetted by international public opinion, the Jewish slogan "Let my people go," harking back to a similar demand voiced by Moses to the Pharaoh of ancient Egypt (Exod. 8:16–17), had wrested from Prime Minister Aleksander Kosygin his historic declaration of December 5, 1966: "As regards the reunion of families, if any families wish to come together or wish to leave the Soviet Union, for them the road is open and no problem exists here." Although never formally promulgated in legal form—indeed, the administration still continued to place formidable obstacles in the way of would-be émigrés—this pledge and a few other more equivocal utterances of Soviet leaders visiting foreign countries were used to good advantage by some applicants for exit visas to prove that their requests were perfectly legal. True, the juridical situation was not that simple. Some Soviet jurists and administrators still attempted to hedge that right by all sorts of qualifications. For instance, at a press conference on March 4, 1970, M. S. Strogovich, a leading Soviet jurist, declared:

> Every citizen has obviously the right to choose freely his citizenship, to live in this or another state. . . . This is a democratic, a progressive principle. But nobody is allowed to use it in [furthering] the aims of a racialist and aggressive policy, a policy of hatred, as Zionist circles are trying to do now.

Yet this twilight situation enabled a number of Jews to claim that they were renouncing their Soviet citizenship in order to live as citizens of Israel. Extensively using modern methods of communication, particularly the telephone, which could not easily be controlled even by the otherwise highly efficient Soviet secret service—an increasing number of applicants for exit visas acquired the necessary affidavits (the so-called *vizovs*) from relatives and friends in Israel. In some cases, through special proceedings in Jerusalem the Israeli government granted advance naturalization to certain individuals, thus underscoring their legitimacy to settle in their new home country.[31]

At first the Soviet authorities tried to deny that any Jews were interested in leaving the country. In a 1959 interview Frol Kozlov, First Deputy Premier, bluntly asserted that Jews had a better life in the Soviet Union than in any other country including Israel. We also recall that in the same vein Khrushchev had sweepingly denied that any Jews wished to emigrate to Israel. (Rather inconsistently he had declared somewhat earlier that there were many applications from Jewish émigrés in Israel asking for permission to return to the Soviet Union.) This assertion was controverted by Golda Meir's insistence that no fewer than 9,236 Soviet Jewish residents had received the necessary papers from Israeli citizens and had filed applications for exit visas, which had been denied by the Soviet authorities. Apart from an enormous amount of red tape and many bureaucratic chicaneries, the authorities made exit visas very expensive, gradually raising the fees from 50 to 900 rubles; in some cases this amount was equal to the individual applicant's earnings over 8 to 12 months. For a time they tried to superimpose an additional "education tax" of 20,000 rubles or more, allegedly to recompense the government for the high expenses it had incurred in training a particular applicant at a school of higher learning. But the instantaneous reaction abroad to this roundabout way of denying visas was so sharp that the Kremlin suspended any assessment of that tax. However, the mere application for an exit visa, whether ultimately granted or refused, still automatically involved the cancellation of the applicant's membership in the Communist Party, dismissal from his or her job, and at times immediate arrest. The seriousness of such discharges was aggravated by the possibility that each suddenly unemployed person might run afoul of the existing anti-parasite laws. Going back to 1663, these laws, resembling the old Western anti-vagrancy enactments, made any jobless person liable to deportation to a distant labor camp by a simple administrative order. Nevertheless, an increasing number of Jews defied the officials and through sheer perseverance wore down their resistance. If this harsh policy was at first stiffened in consideration of the Arab allies' demand for complete stoppage of Jewish emigration to Israel—an emigration which necessarily resulted in an increase of manpower available to that country for use in future wars—Jews could counter with the argument that it was the Arab states' enforced exodus of *their* Jewish citizens which to a much larger extent had long swelled the number of Jewish immigrants to Israel.[32]

Under these circumstances Jewish emigration to Israel became very sporadic, with many ups and downs. Following Stalin's death a temporary loosening up of the process allowed 125 Soviet emigrants (for the most part elderly persons from the newly annexed areas) to reach Israel in the period from July, 1953, to September, 1955. During the first years of Khrushchev's tightened regime and the Suez War there apparently was no legal emigration whatsoever. But in the early 1960s a growing number was able to overcome all obstacles and enter the land of their forefathers. Some 1,400 emigrated in the first months of 1967 after Kosygin's aforementioned declaration of December, 1966, but all emigration was again suspended in June, 1967, in the wake of the Six-Day War. It is estimated that during the years from 1948 to 1967 a total of 6,000 Soviet Jews were allowed to join their families abroad. Only when the pressure of both inner dissent and international public opinion mounted, an increasing number of Jewish applicants defied all threats of retaliation and organized public demonstrations before the offices of OVIR (*Otdel Viz i Registratsii* or Department of Visas and Registration of the Ministry of Interior) in Moscow, and many hardy souls staged much publicized hunger strikes, did the authorities decide to permit more applicants to leave the country. The movement was further accelerated by the trend toward a détente with Western Europe and the United States, particularly during the 1972 and 1974 visits of President Nixon to Moscow. The number of Russian Jewish émigrés rose to over 3,000 in 1969, and suddenly jumped (according to divergent reports) to between 13,000 and 15,000 in 1971. It finally spurted to some 35,000 in 1973. Although slowed down by the Yom Kippur War which began on October 6, 1973, and in the following months led to but temporary "disengagements" of the belligerent armies, Jewish emigration from the Soviet Union did not completely dry up. The best figures for 1974 available at this time—they can only be estimated from a variety of journalistic and private sources, since neither Israel nor the Soviet Union have officially published them—seem to indicate that no more than 20,000 Russian Jewish émigrés left the Union, the majority receiving exit visas for Israel. For a while it appeared that, as a result of the passage by the United States Senate of the administration-sponsored Omnibus Trade Reform Bill, which would have enabled the Soviet Union to secure most-favored-nation treatment of its exports to America (Poland and Yugoslavia already enjoy that status), large credits from the Export-Import Bank, and advanced technological assistance, the Soviet government would informally promise to allow the emigration of at least 60,000 of its citizens—primarily Jews—annually. However, because of the worldwide publicity given to these negotiations, magnified by numerous newspaper "leaks," the Soviet government decided to emphasize its sovereign rights in regulating emigration and to repudiate the entire treaty.[33]

If a large-scale exodus should indeed materialize in the coming years, it might repeat the experience of the Russian Jewish emigration to America in the last decades of the tsarist regime. We recall that from a total of some 7,500 Jews who left Russia and Poland during the half-century of 1820 to 1870, the stream swelled to 704,000 in 1901–1910. Of course, the reservoir of Soviet Jewish manpower and its natural increase are much smaller. Yet the number of expatriates would certainly far exceed the figure of 100,000 Jews estimated by Ilya Ehrenburg as the number of Jews willing to leave the Union, though probably it would not come near the total of two-thirds of Soviet Jewry supposedly anxious to depart, according to some oversanguine observers.[34]

Of course, just as in the case of other international migrations there have been quite a few émigrés who could find no employment or who were otherwise maladjusted to life in the new society. In this particular instance the change from a controlled economy to an open and competitive, if semisocialist, society made adjustments doubly difficult. In the Soviet Union people were used to having apartments and jobs assigned them by the authorities. In Israel, on the contrary, with all the aid initially extended to newcomers by Jewish Agency and other officials, sooner or later job-hunting and even finding appropriate housing must have caused much anguish to strangers unfamiliar with either the language or the general conditions of life in the country. Even the far more affluent and diversified society of the United States has long been accustomed to hearing persistent complaints from new arrivals for at least the first year or two. But after the passage of the five years required for an émigré's naturalization as an American citizen, few of them are willing to return to the "old country" unless they had from the outset intended merely to accumulate some savings and return home. On its part, the Soviet Union has rather consistently refused readmission to such émigrés, whom it denounced as traitors. In this way, the authorities hoped to add another deterrent to would-be expatriates (whom their friends refer to as, and they themselves prefer to be called, "repatriates" to Israel). At the same time, the Soviet newspapers have frequently and gleefully published Jeremiads, genuine or spurious, of such maladjusted persons darkly describing the "miserable" conditions in Israel. Moreover, some émigrés used their visas to Israel as a means of getting out of the Union in order to reach some other ultimate destination. Echoing such reports in the Soviet press, even the *Sovetish Haimland* saw new examples of Zionist misdeeds in these difficulties of the Russian émigrés. In an article published under the catchy title "Zionism's Great Swindle: It Does Not Save the Jews from the *Golus* [Exile], But It Drives Jews into a *Golus*," its editor, Aron Vergelis, argued that because of Zionist propaganda, many expatriates "have been uprooted from their home country, where their ancestors had lived for many generations, and placed in a land in which another people had been established and taken roots." Hence there they have felt as though they were "immigrants, that is, as persons living in *Golus*." By April, 1973, the Israeli authorities had admitted that some four percent of Soviet arrivals were leaving the country for some Western land. They prevailed on the HIAS, the old relief organization for Jewish migrants, to discontinue aiding such reemigrants because Israel was not "a country in distress."[35]

A major cause, as well as effect, of this drive for "repatriation" to Israel was the alienation of many young Jews from Russian culture due to their growing feeling of being rejected by many of their classmates, fellow workers, and neighbors. Even among the dissenters, it appears, some individuals resented the Jewish devotion to a foreign country. They may have agreed with the Russian worker who reproached his Jewish friends, saying, "You eat Russian bread, but pray for Jerusalem." Others may have envied the Jews' good fortune in being allowed to emigrate to a free country, a privilege largely denied the other ethnic groups, including the Russians themselves. Not all of them felt with their leader, Andrei D. Sakharov, who in his much-quoted letter of September 14, 1973, to the Congress of the United States, urged it to adopt the Vanik-Jackson Amendment to the aforementioned Omnibus Trade Reform Bill. This amendment was designed to make the treatment of the Union as one of the most favored nations in regard to American customs duties dependent on its allowing its citizens freely to emigrate. Here the eminent physicist spoke up for the "protection of the right to freedom of residence within the country of one's choice," and added:

> There are tens of thousands of citizens in the Soviet Union—Jews, Germans, Russians, Ukrainians, Lithuanians, Armenians, Estonians, Latvians, Turks, and members of other ethnic groups—who want to leave the country and who have been seeking to exercise that right for years and for decades at the cost of endless difficulty and humiliation. You know that prisons, labor camps, and mental hospitals are full of people who have sought to exercise this legitimate right.

Most Jewish activists applauded these sentiments, although there probably were some who would have preferred that the prospective Jewish "repatriates" play a more direct role in the general struggle for human and civil rights. On their part, the applicants for exit visas had to be doubly careful not to give the authorities any additional excuse for condemning them to prison terms of several years, exile to Siberia, or removal to a mental hospital to be cured of what was recently aptly designated the "new mental disease: opposition [to the government]." Any of these forms of detention would have resulted in indefinite postponement of their departure for Israel. A few may even have felt that being on the point of renouncing their Soviet citizenship, they no longer had any right to interfere in the internal affairs of a prospective foreign country. Such men may have preferred another "punishment" occasionally used by the authorities—namely, the call to military service. They may have been comforted by the thought that their good training in the Soviet Army might accrue to some benefit to Israel when they could ultimately settle there.[36]

[321]

SEEDS OF RELIGIOUS AWAKENING

Preparation for emigration to Israel injected a vital new ingredient into the theretofore rather stagnant Jewish cultural activities. There was a sudden new awareness of the importance of the Hebrew language and Jewish history for the understanding of one's ancestral roots. Since public Hebrew instruction was technically outlawed outside the narrow confines of Oriental departments at some universities, the very possession of a Hebrew book seemed to furnish the police cogent evidence of the owner's Zionist, and hence "disloyal," sentiments. In a brief autobiographical sketch an unnamed author described how he had managed to learn the first rudiments of Hebrew. By chance he found an old Hebrew grammar, written in Russian and published in 1889, in a library. He felt that such an innocuous old tract could not possibly be suspect. With great difficulty he thus mastered a rudimentary Hebrew vocabulary and a few basic grammatical rules. This extreme devotion appears doubly amazing when one considers that author's antecedents. His great-grandfather had been one of Nicholas I's enforced recruits, whose family was allowed to live outside the Jewish Pale of Settlement. His father was born in Perm in the Ural Mountains, where at that time only a few Jews lived and where both father and son grew up with little, if any, Jewish education. His father was, moreover, a confirmed atheist, a thoroughly assimilated Russian, and an ardent communist. Yet, after his sudden awakening to his ancestral heritage, the son surmounted all obstacles to acquire a modicum of Hebraic knowledge and ultimately reach Israel, where he put his self-taught Hebrew to good use. Remarkably, even Aron Vergelis, ardent anti-Zionist and pro-Soviet apologist that he is, may well have contributed something to the quest for Hebrew knowledge among the readers of his *Sovetish Haimland* by his interpretation of biblical phrases frequently occurring in Yiddish letters. Further, when he wished to explain the numerous Hebraisms in Sholem Aleichem's Yiddish correspondence which he was reproducing in his journal, he transliterated them into the phonetic Yiddish alphabet, long accepted in Soviet Yiddish letters. Some of the journal's readers may thus have received their first inkling of the pronunciation of certain Hebrew words. It was in such roundabout ways—reminiscent of the method used by the sixteenth-century Swiss humanist Conrad Pellikan in acquiring the first rudiments of Hebrew—that some young and long-alienated Jews found their way back to the ancient language; of course, at the price of an arduous mental effort and the neglect of other more pleasurable pursuits. One cannot help but sadly compare these devoted autodidacts with large segments of Western Jewish youth, to whom a vast educational establishment beckons invitingly, promising to teach them Hebrew within a limited period of time, methodically and with relatively little effort—all in vain.[37]

In the last decade the official attitude toward Judaism as a religion had become even more hostile than before. To be sure, on November 10, 1954, the Communist Party publicly demanded that its members "not offend the feelings of believers and behave toward them in a proper way. They ought to spread the knowledge of science, whereby religion's influence would of itself decline. Restrictions in an administrative fashion and sharp attacks upon religion may merely arouse a reaction among believers." This exhortation was still partially adhered to, at least with respect to the Russian Orthodox Church, since the government found in it an excellent tool of Russification. Particularly in the Ukraine, where the Uniate Church had long been a mainstay of Ukrainian "nationalism," its replacement by Orthodox rituals, churches, and monasteries proved to be an eminent means of denationalization. Not surprisingly, the census of 1970 revealed that the number of "Russians" had increased to some 30 percent of the population of the Ukrainian Soviet Republic.

This relatively moderate religious policy was less strictly observed with respect to other faiths, except perhaps the Muslim Mosque, whose autonomy had to be more carefully safeguarded for both domestic and international reasons. In its report of January 30, 1965, to the United Nations Human Rights Commission the Soviet delegation cited the various legal provisions relating to liberty of conscience and the penalties imposed by the criminal code for disturbing religious worship. Yet the Jewish religion continued to be sharply repressed. Here, too, we find a curious inversion. In the early years of the Soviet regime the Jewish religion, on a par with other faiths, was denigrated by the powerful atheistic propaganda. At that time, the Jewish secular nationalists of the *Yevsektsiia* exerted every effort to dismantle the Jewish religious establishment and replace it with their brand of secular nationalism. Now Jewish nationalism had become even more suspect in the eyes of the ruling circles, and much of the justification for the curtailment of Jewish religious rights derived from the intimate nexus between Judaism as a religion and as an ethnic culture. Time and again the official and semiofficial propaganda pointed out that the Jewish prayer book was filled with the glorification of the Jewish people and the hope of a speedy return to the Holy Land. Under the conditions of the new anti-Israeli antagonism such prayers were declared subversive, especially because they were also recited in Hebrew, a language considered an effective tool for "Zionism."[38]

As a result, the closing of synagogues, which had reached its climax during the years from 1958 to 1964—when, if we are to believe the official announcements of the government abroad, their number shrank from some 450 to 97, or in fact to probably no more than 60—was never reversed by the erection of new buildings. Such contraction was sometimes justified by the statement that the plots on which the buildings stood were needed for other socially useful structures, such as schools, markets, stadiums, or clubs. Other rationalizations were offered by public attacks on the synagogues as alleged centers for black marketeering, exploitation of worshipers, and even espionage. The frequent presence of Israeli diplomats (until the break of diplomatic relations in 1967) and of other Israeli, European, and American Jewish visitors who wished to attend Jewish divine services furnished sufficient excuse for such denunciations. However, after reaching a high point before 1964, the closing of synagogues has declined in the last decade. Even prosecutions of worshipers who gathered together in private conventicles (so-called *minyanim*), which in themselves were a violation of the existing prohibition against any kind of assemblies without special authorization, have now become quite rare. So have the previously frequent official desecrations of Jewish cemeteries. Here, too, the excuse usually given was that the land was needed for some other "useful" purpose. However, the underlying hostility was demonstrated by the removal of the exhumed bodies, including those of famous and revered rabbis whose graves had often attracted pious pilgrims, not to specially assigned new locations, but rather to the general cemeteries. In fact, the majority of Soviet Jews have long since found their final resting place in such unconsecrated local graveyards.[39]

Because of the increase in international travel and cultural exchanges and the constant arrival of a host of foreign visitors the Soviet government tried to display, at least outwardly, a more tolerant attitude toward Jewish religious institutions. We recall that the Moscow rabbi Salomon Schliefer was allowed to publish a small number of copies of a Hebrew prayer book styled "the prayer book of peace" because it included a collection of rabbinic sayings about peace and a special prayer for peace (as well as the traditional prayer for the country's welfare) to underscore the Soviet contention of being the major peace-loving nation. The government also permitted the publication of Hebrew calendars, though likewise only in a very limited number. But these could readily be reproduced by hand by any Jew wishing to have a manual indicating the dates for Jewish holidays, family memorial days, *bar mitzvah* ceremonies, and the like. These publications were quickly exhibited in a Soviet Book Fair in London as an outward sign of Soviet religious toleration. The old chicaneries concerning the baking of unleavened bread for Passover and the production of prayer shawls and phylacteries were no longer quite so frequently applied, though the availability of such implements of worship still largely depended on the rather irregular deliveries of gifts from abroad to their addressees.

Even prosecutions of circumcisers seem to have become less persistent. Certainly, the dramatic story told by a Russian émigré to Israel of how over the years he had managed to arrange for thirty-five circumcisions by a traveling *mohel* in the Lvov area, though each such act technically involved an "illegal surgical operation" punishable by lifelong imprisonment, referred mainly to conditions prevailing before 1964. Most significantly, the resurgence of interest in their faith among many Jews, especially the youth seeking to recover its ancient roots, brought about a certain rejuvenation of the synagogue. Once again, in reversal from earlier precedents when secular Yiddish schools were made to replace synagogues as centers of Jewish life, with the total disappearance at this point of a publicly tolerated Jewish school system, the few remaining synagogues became the foci of Jewish communal life. Reference has already been made to the *Simhat Torah* celebrations in Moscow and elsewhere which attracted thousands of Jewish youths. Social motivations may have prompted many of them to attend these spectacular performances in front of synagogues. Nevertheless the synagogue as such assumed a new meaning in their lives. Many also attended services on Sabbaths (facilitated by the spread of a five-day workweek) and on High holidays, even if they happened to fall on weekdays. The Soviet ambassador in Vienna may have exaggerated when he claimed that the Moscow synagogue attracted 500 worshipers for daily prayers, 1,500 on Sabbaths, 3,000 on the New Year, and 5,000 on the Day of Atonement. But there is no question that the number of participants, especially among the youth, was increasing from year to year, particularly after the Six-Day War.[40]

BURGEONING CULTURAL REVIVAL

Less pronounced was the renewed Hebrew creativity. Yet that a new 700-page Hebrew-Russian dictionary could be published by Felix Lvovich Shapiro in Moscow in 1963 and that other means of learning the Hebrew language became somewhat more readily available were unexpected gains for those who wished to acquire some rudimentary knowledge of that idiom. The 1964 International Congress of Oriental Studies, which met in Moscow and at which the non-Jewish Professor Vasilii V. Struve spoke glowingly of the resurrection of Hebrew from a dead ancient language into a modern cultural medium in Israel and emphasized that the Hebrew University had become a major center of Mid-Eastern research, must also have given new courage to many would-be students of that language. Similarly the presentation there of several pertinent papers on medieval Hebrew learning by other non-Jewish scholars like K. B. Starkova and Grigorii S. Sharbatov widely publicized the fact that both the subject and the work of such Jewish professors as Benzion Grande, Yitzhak Vinikov, Iosif Amusin, and Abraham Rubinshtein were receiving full-fledged academic recognition. Most astounding of all was the survival of Hebrew education among the Georgian Jews, whose unflinching Orthodoxy helped them surmount all obstacles placed in their way by antagonistic bureaucrats. The publication in Jerusalem in 1969 of Boris Gaponov's (Isaac Davitashvili's) Hebrew translation of the Georgian classic *The Knight in the Panther's Skin* by Shota Rustaveli made a deep impression. Its admirable Hebrew style, ranking high among all Hebrew poetry of this generation, astounded even the most optimistic Hebrew literary critics outside the Union. No comparable achievement, however, seems as yet possible from the main Ashkenazic community, where the Hebrew muse had become silent after the fine poems written by Hayyim Lenski and Elisha (Abraham) Rodin thirty or more years ago.[41]

Boris Gaponov's extraordinary feat has demonstrated to the outside world how persistent Hebraic culture remained among the Georgian Jews. The history of these small Jewish communities in Georgia and the neighboring Asian republics, many non-Jewish inhabitants of which claim descent from the Lost Ten Tribes of Israel, goes back to remote antiquity when Jews from Palestine spread into Armenia and fanned out into the areas around the Caspian Sea and Central Asia. We recall that offshoots of the Herodian dynasty settled in Armenia and that Moses of Khorene and other Armenian chroniclers of this early Christian nation referred to the Bagratuni family, second only to the kings, as claiming descent from the ancient royal family of Israel. Later on, farther north and east the Jews lived among predominantly Muslim peoples. Although their legal status was often unenviable, they were able to maintain their Hebrew culture in unbroken continuity until the present day. To be sure, the Soviet occupation made serious inroads into that culture and since the days of the Stalinist Terror from 1948 on, they, like their Ashkenazic brethren, were deprived of their Jewish schools. But they were able to maintain both their synagogues and their biological strength. Only some western wings of these Oriental Jewries had directly suffered from the Nazi Holocaust, while the vast majority was outside the reach of the *Einsatzgruppen*. As a result, their percentage within the Soviet Jewish community has greatly increased. Between the censuses of 1926 and 1959 (that of 1939 does not furnish enough pertinent data) their proportion of the Jewish population increased from 2.5 to 4.2 percent. According to the 1970 census, their number grew further—for instance, in Uzbekistan from some 85,000 to 93,000, or by nearly 10 percent.[42]

The three major groups of Georgian, Bukharan, and so-called Mountain Jews were almost equal in strength; in 1959 according to the census they numbered respectively, 36,000, 28,000 and 30,000, although local estimates raised these figures by almost 100 percent. While the Georgians have had no language of their own and next to the local dialect cultivated mainly Hebrew, the other two groups spoke peculiar West Iranian dialects, a Judeo-Tadzhik and Tat (there also were some small Muslim and Christian groups speaking Tat, but this fact was not recognized as a national criterion by the Soviet census administrators, who listed the Muslims as Azerbeijanis and the Christians as Armenians). At first the Soviet authorities propagated the publication of some writings, even journals, in these local dialects, for which in 1928 they first replaced the Hebrew or Arabic alphabet by Latin characters. When in 1938 the general move was made to substitute the Cyrillic script for the Latin, the Tadzhik dialect was omitted from that transformation and thus after two years lost all possibilities for literary expression. Samarkand had likewise had a Bukharan Jewish Museum and a Jewish theater (in which was also performed a Tadzhik play by a member of a Central Asian secret Jewish community forcibly converted to Islam in the nineteenth century), but they, too, were closed after the Stalinist purges of the late 1930s. Nevertheless these groups overcame the difficulties placed in their paths by the Soviet legislation and administration and retained their unadulterated Jewish identity. The Georgian Jews especially, often abetted by friendly local authorities—the proud Georgians, Muslim and Christian as well as Jewish—staunchly maintained their relative independence from the Kremlin center and were able to continue their accustomed way of life and the cultivation of their religious holidays and rituals. Nonetheless, they unavoidably felt the impact of the new Soviet industrialization and urbanization. By leaving their hamlets and villages and moving to such major cities as Tashkent, Baku, Samarkand, and Derbent, they lost their clannish cohesiveness and thereby also some of their power of resistance to the steam roller of Russian culture. Yet they were far superior to their Ashkenazic compatriots in adherence to their native customs, family life, and synagogue attendance.[43]

At the same time the magnet of the State of Israel, with occasional broadcasts emanating from Jerusalem, surreptitiously listened to by natives as well as visitors in some southern, geographically less remote areas, inspired many Georgian Jews to look for ways to emigrate to their long Promised Land. Frustrated by Soviet officials who constantly rejected their applications for visas to Israel, they courageously appealed to the United Nations and the Israeli leaders. On August 6, 1969, eighteen Georgian families submitted an eloquent appeal to the United Nations Human Rights Commission. After paying due obeisance to the Soviet regime which had put an end to anti-Jewish pogroms, the Pale of Settlement, and the *numerus clausus* at schools of higher learning, and had made it possible for Jews to occupy high government posts, they nevertheless insisted that they wished to go to their homeland, Israel.

> They say there is a total of twelve million Jews in the world. But he errs who believes there is a total of twelve million of us. For with those who pray for Israel are hundreds of millions who did not live to this day, who were tortured to death, who are no longer here. They march shoulder to shoulder with us, unconquered and immortal, those who had handed down to us the traditions of struggle and faith. / This is why we want to go to Israel. / We will wait months and years, we will wait all our lives, if necessary, but we will not renounce our faith or our hopes. / We believe our prayers have reached God. / We know our appeals will reach people. / For we are asking—let us go to the land of our forefathers.

In one of the three accompanying letters addressed to the Israeli representative at the United Nations Joseph Tekoah, they emphasized: "The time of fear is over—the time of action has come!" Not receiving any reply for the subsequent hundred days, they addressed another appeal to the United Nations Secretary General U Thant couched in even stronger terms. Before long the Soviet authorities yielded and allowed an increasing number of Georgian Jews to emigrate to Israel. Thus the relatively few Georgian settlers in Palestine at the beginning of this century were converted into fairly large, self-assertive, and proud communities in the State of Israel. Here, too, they tried to maintain their traditional cohesiveness and even attempted to live in closely knit colonies of their own. Naturally, these new Israeli settlers have maintained close relations with the majority of their brethren left behind in the Soviet Union, thus greatly contributing to Georgian Jewry's powers of resistance and its continued pride in its Jewish heritage.[44]

In passing, one may also mention two other small groups: the Karaites and the Krimchaks. Although an old Jewish sect going back to eighth-century Babylonia, with antecedents reaching back to the ancient Sadducees, the Soviet Karaites lived under a cloud of suspicion. During the Nazi occupation of almost all Karaite settlements in the Union, including the Crimea, Lithuanian Troki, and West Ukrainian Halicz, the Karaites—with the humanitarian cooperation of some Jewish scholars—persuaded the Nazi authorities that despite their religious affinities with Judaism, they were not racially descendants of Jews. They thus escaped the Nazi Holocaust. After the war, many Soviet Jews rejected them as both non-Jews and alleged collaborators with the enemy. This traumatic experience seems to have undermined their morale, and their cultural creativity, which was flourishing during the nineteenth century, completely dried up. They thus fell ready prey to the Russian assimilatory pressures. On the other hand, the Krimchaks, indubitably Rabbanite Jews who before World War II had cultivated their peculiar Tatar dialect and used it effectively as a literary medium, had been badly decimated during the Holocaust. From 7,500 in 1914 and 6,383 in 1926, their numbers dwindled to some 3,000 in 1939. Their remnant after the Holocaust was too small and weak to resist the Soviet bureaucracy and defiantly to resume their self-assertive stance. In 1959 only 189 persons declared the Krimchak dialect as their native language.[45]

YIDDISH LANGUAGE PROBLEMS

Quite different is the story of the revival of Yiddish culture. Outwardly this rejuvenation found expression in a small growth of publications in that language. After years of total silence under the Stalinist Terror, any new publication caused Yiddish-speaking persons to heave a sigh of relief. To be sure, the number of such persons was constantly declining. Even those Jews who to the census enumerators declared themselves as of Jewish nationality mostly professed to speak Russian as their "native tongue." According to the census of 1959, only 488,000 of professed Jewish nationals considered Yiddish their native tongue—that is, only 21.5 percent of the total. In 1970, with their nationality diminished by some 117,000 members, that of Yiddish-speaking persons declined by 107,000 members to 381,000—that is, to 17.7 percent. We must note, however, that the figures for Yiddish-speaking persons in the two censuses are even less reliable than those for Jewish nationals. To begin with, the definition of "native tongue" (*rodnoi iyasik*) is so ambiguous that it could readily be confused with the definitions of the terms for "mother tongue" and "spoken language," or what the Germans called *Umgangssprache,* the equivalent of which has frequently been used by Western census takers. Many Jews who may have spoken Yiddish at home, but Russian in their occupational contacts, almost arbitrarily chose one or the other language. Dependent on the enumerators, too, Russian officials were likely to try to persuade hesitant heads of households to declare Russian, whereas those belonging to national minorities, especially in one of the autonomous republics, may have preferred to enter Yiddish in the pertinent column. Often accused by the local majorities of serving as Russifiers, some Jews living in these republics may have consciously steered clear of identifying themselves as Russians by nationality or speech and may have preferred to choose the more "neutral" designation of Yiddish. At the same time, other Jews may have demonstratedly chosen their national language rather than Russian, although most of their friends and even their own children usually spoke Russian to them. In view of these manifold possibilities the census figures can serve only as educated approximations.[46]

Not surprisingly, Jews in the newly annexed territories had a much higher percentage of Yiddish-speaking persons than those in the prewar Russian areas. In the census of 1959, 68 percent of Lithuanian Jews declared themselves as Yiddish-speaking; Moldavian Jews had a ratio of 50.5 percent, Latvian, 48.6 percent; while even in the Ukraine the percentage was only 16.9, and in the Great Russian Republic, a mere 11.9. If Uzbekian Jewry revealed the very high ratio of 42.4 percent, the reason evidently was that the majority of Jews residing in Uzbekistan were relative newcomers from western Soviet areas, where the original census of 1897 had shown that some 97 percent of the Jewish population spoke Yiddish. It is also noteworthy that in 1959 in the metropolitan areas, where the largest concentration of Jews was found, relatively fewer persons indicated Yiddish as their native tongue than in the respective republics as a whole. The ratio in Moscow and Leningrad was 8.5 percent as against 11.9 for the entire Soviet Russian Republic. In the Ukrainian Republic, Kiev, the capital showed only 12.9 percent of such persons, contrasted with the republic's 16.9 percent. Similarly, Minsk's 14.7 percent compared with the Belorussian Republic's 22 percent. Even in Uzbekistan only 36.6 percent of Tashkent's Jewish nationals declared Yiddish as their native language, whereas the whole republic had 42.4 percent. A further demonstration of the progress of linguistic assimilation was furnished by an age-group breakdown of the total 1970 figure of 94,971 Yiddish-speaking Jews in the Russian Republic. It showed that 37,710, or nearly 40 percent of those listed in that category, were over sixty years old, whereas only 22,603, or about 24 percent, were below the age of thirty. Remarkably, however, the Jews' linguistic assimilation was less rapid than among some other national groups deprived of their own territorial moorings. For one example, while the number of Poles in the Union dropped in 1959–70 by about one-sixth, that of Polish-speaking persons declined from 624,000 to 379,000, with a loss of 245,000 or almost 40 percent.[47]

Nonetheless, interest in Yiddish letters and other forms of communal expression grew irresistibly. At first the government made but grudging concessions, as when it allowed in 1961 the establishment of the *Sovietish Haimland* as a bimonthly. This permission and the necessary governmental subsidy were designed to pacify the aroused public opinion in foreign countries, but in 1965 internal as well as external pressures brought about the change of the periodical into a monthly, and its subsequent growth in size and quality from year to year. More significantly, its content began assuming an increasingly Jewish cultural coloring. At first its editor, Aron Vergelis, and his associates rather closely followed the Stalinist slogan that minority publications should be "national in form and socialist in content." This line has still largely been maintained with respect to articles referring to political and economic affairs, which have invariably adhered to the Party line. At the same time, however, a growing number of Yiddish poems and short stories have made their appearance in the journal. Some 150 Yiddish writers have thus been provided with the possibility of publishing their works and a source of supplementary income. Most remarkably, the journal now freely analyzed and cited not only the old long-accepted classics like Sholem Aleichem and Mendele, but also the great Soviet writers purged by Stalin, including Peretz Markish, David Bergelson, Der Nister, David Hofshtein, and Leib Kvitko (millions of copies of whose children's books had appeared in Russian translation). Even publicists like Moshe Litvakov, who had never been formally rehabilitated nor publicly mentioned since the 1930s, could now be admiringly quoted in the magazine. Some of the distinguished prewar literary critics like Max Erik and Meir Wiener could also now be glorified as trail blazers in the new appreciation of eighteenth- and nineteenth-century Yiddish letters. There also was an increasing output of Yiddish books (including a volume of poems by David Hofshtein), as well as translations from Yiddish into Russian, Ukrainian, Belorussian, Moldavian, Uzbekian, Armenian, and so forth, and even into such foreign languages as Spanish, English, and Bengal. No less than 283 such translations appeared in the single decade from 1955 to 1964. This trend continued after 1964. True, some of the more creative and independent writings by Soviet Jewish authors still had to be published abroad, especially in Israel. The recent wave of Jewish emigration also brought to Israel a few outstanding Yiddish poets who were able to take along some of their unpublished manuscripts. After their publication in Israel, a few of these writings found their way back into the Soviet Union and thus reached at least a segment of the ever-dwindling Yiddish-reading public there. The greatest remaining lacuna consisted of any truly scholarly investigations, historical, sociological, or linguistic, of Jewish life in the Union, formerly contributed mainly by Yiddish-writing scholars. The aforementioned pamphlet by Shloime (Solomon) Rabinovich, *The Jews in the Soviet Union*, published in 1965 by the Soviet Agency Novosti in thirty-six small pages, and almost immediately translated from the Yiddish into Russian, Hebrew, English, and French, offered but a superficial portrayal of Soviet Jewry, evidently intended for foreign consumption.[48]

Evidently also under foreign pressure the Soviet authorities allowed the resumption of some amateur Yiddish theatrical performances, concerts of Jewish music and folk songs, and the like. These events not only attracted vast audiences of local Jews even if they did not understand Yiddish, but also could be shown to tourists and other visitors interested in Jewish culture. Although various efforts made in 1956–62 to reestablish a state-supported Yiddish theater were unsuccessful, even the sporadic amateur performances, especially in Lithuania and Moldavia, kept the interest in Yiddish culture alive even among the youth which otherwise had no access to Jewish media. The publication in 1968 of a volume of thirty Yiddish folk songs included an admiring introduction by one of the leading Russian composers, Dmitri Shostakovich. Not that the Soviet authorities looked with favor upon the revival of such Jewish sentiments. More typical of their attitude was the Third Congress of Soviet Writers, held in May, 1959, which discussed various minor national literatures but made no reference to Yiddish whatsoever. A curious incident, dramatically reported by eyewitness Arie L. Eliav, well describes the real attitude of the Soviet Writers' Union. When in 1959 the authorities decided to celebrate the centennial of Sholem Aleichem's birthday, the Union staged a major literary event in Kolonnyi Zal (Moscow's renowned Colonnade Hall). Among the invited guests happened to be Paul Robeson, the black American singer, who was visiting Moscow. After the recitation of certain selections from Sholem Aleichem's work, Robeson was invited to speak and sing. In his address the singer glorified Mikhoel's performance of Shakespeare's *King Lear* as one of the greatest performances he had ever seen and added: "But don't imagine that you are the only ones who love Jewish literature and culture. In the United States the Jews have great cultural institutions, seminaries, teachers, schools, academies of literature, poetry, drama, and Jewish song." Finally he chose to sing, among others, some songs in Yiddish, "a language I love," announcing:

> I shall now go from folk songs and cheerful tunes to a special kind of song, sad but wonderful, which I heard from Jewish partisans when I visited the ruins of the Warsaw ghetto. As you all know, the Jewish heroes of the ghetto fought a battle which was probably the most desperate and courageous of all peoples' wars for independence and honor. I learned this partisan song from the survivors who sang it on the barricades and in the bunkers as they fought their people's war. I'll sing for you "The Song of the Jewish Partisans"!

All this grated on the ears of the two presiding officials of the Writers' Union, as did his comparison of Jews and blacks as the two most persecuted peoples. But their repeated attempts to interrupt and divert the singer failed and all they could do was to see to it that nothing about this incident appeared in the Russian press.[49]

On the other hand, Jews were enabled to continue writing in Russian. The 1961 Soviet Writers' Union Directory showed that at least fifty-eight members wrote their works in Yiddish (some of whom had a bilingual or even trilingual creativity writing also in Russian and/or in the language of another local national majority), while some 300 members wrote only in the majority idioms. Although none of the new generation of Russian Jewish authors in all fields achieved the stature of Isaac Babel, Boris Pasternak, or Ossip Mandelshtam, a number of them earned high decorations and prizes. Even the former Bundist, David Zaslavsky, who as early as the 1920s served as an important commentator on foreign affairs in the *Pravda* and *Izvestia* (he was also a leader in the campaign against Pasternak's *Dr. Zhivago*), received the Order of Lenin on his eightieth birthday early in 1960. Only a few of the new crop of Russo-Jewish writers dealt with Jewish themes, however. One who ventured into this field, Yulii Daniel (son of the Yiddish writer Mark Naumovich Daniel, originally Meyerovich), was accused of maligning the Russian nation for its anti-Semitism. Together with other transgressions, this accusation served to put Daniel into jail for several years. On the other hand, his colleague Andrei Siniavsky, curiously writing under the Jewish-sounding pseudonym of Abram Tertz, was denounced in the same trial for alleged anti-Semitism, although the anti-Jewish passages in his books were all attributed to villainous characters. At the same time, free rein was given to Stalinist non-Jewish writers to present Jewish characters in an extremely unfavorable light. Great emphasis was also laid upon ignoring the Jewish aspects of the Holocaust, which had to be generally presented as but part and parcel of the massacre of all Soviet peoples. We recall that Evtushenko had been reprimanded by Khrushchev himself as well as by a number of Soviet writers like Aleksei Markov for singling out the Jewish victims in Babi Yar. In reply Anatoli Kuznetsov wrote a lengthy novel on Babi Yar, describing as he contended, not only the first few days, when Jews had been singled out for slaughter ,but the whole period of 778 days, "when Babi Yar became a monstrous symbol of Nazi occupation." Even the *Diary of Anne Frank* was not allowed to appear in a Russian translation until after several years of negotiations a grudging permission was wrested from the government. The play based upon that *Diary* was finally presented by an Italian company during two evenings only. If in 1969 a Jewish artist was decorated for his paintings of the notorious German concentration camps in Auschwitz and Maidanek, he doubtless deserved it in the eyes of the Presidium of the Ukrainian Republic because of the "socialist realism" in which he depicted indiscriminate martyrdom of all Soviet prisoners. In other words, the Jewish people had to be treated as nonexistent. The old myth that there was no Jewish question in the Soviet Union had to be staunchly maintained, even after its fallacy had been clearly demonstrated by the general Democratic Movement and by Jewish activists' agitation for opening the gates to Jewish emigration to Israel.[50]

[19]

No End of Road

Ever since the beginning of the communist regime voices were heard that it spelled the end of the Jewish people in Russia. Some spoke of it joyously in the messianic terms of an approaching end of days when all peoples would lose their identity and be submerged within one common ocean of humanity. Others regretfully commented on the forthcoming disappearance of that ancient people with its ancient civilization as the unavoidable price of the great liberation of the toiling masses. Still others spoke of the mere revival of Russian anti-Semitism under a new guise. But the clamor that history was writing the final chapter in the long annals of the Jewish people was sounded by many observers, both friends and foes of the new regime.

VANISHING PEOPLE

Its friends, particularly West European communists like Otto Heller, theorized that such a "decline of Judaism" was but the realization of an old Marxian prediction and the necessary consequence of the final victory of Marxian ideology. By referring to Marx's own bitter comments on the Jewish question of 1843, and by selecting a few appropriate interpretations of Marxism by both Lenin and Stalin, while disregarding all contradictory utterances by the three men—the accepted technique of dialecticians of all ages—Otto Heller and, less bluntly, some leaders of the *Yevsektsiia* asserted with extreme confidence that Jewish history was drawing to an end. Heller said that in Marxian terms, throughout recorded history diaspora Judaism had been but a "superstructure" of Jewry's social contributions as a merchandising agent, and with the disappearance of merchandise as a vital social function, there was no longer any future for the Jewish group as such. Only such a small remnant might survive as might settle in the Jewish autonomous territory (or ultimately Jewish state) in Biro-Bidzhan. After assimilating even there to the mores and modes of living of the other nations, this remnant might retain sufficient linguistic and cultural identity to continue in some residual fashion the traditions of the ancient people.

Opponents of the communist experiment, on the other hand, viewed the assimilatory pressures exerted by the Soviet regime upon its Jewish subjects as a telling denial of human freedoms. Unblinded by the Soviets' early repudiation of anti-Semitism and their recognition of the Jewish nationality, which was to enjoy the full protection of minority rights, these opponents freely predicted that this new "nationality" could not long survive after being deprived of its traditional moorings in religion, Hebrew culture, and old or new messianic-Zionist goals. They insisted that no matter how many Jewish children might attend schools with Yiddish as the language of instruction, no matter how many local soviets or courts of justice might use Yiddish as their official medium of communication, in the end that new secular nationality would still have to discard some three millennia of its Hebraic history and religious *Weltanschauung;* it would still have to limit itself to a small cultural segment of its heritage, created in the form of belles-lettres by a few outstanding poets and writers of two or three prerevolutionary East European generations. At the same time this Jewish minority would be exposed to the powerful impact of the great cultural attainments of the Russian people of both the tsarist and the communist era. Combined with the indoctrination in the new communist *Weltanschauung*, this overwhelming pressure of the great outside culture could not possibly be resisted long with the meager survivalist tools at the disposal of the downtrodden community.

These dire predictions seemed to come true as early as the 1930s when the autonomous cultural Jewish structure, built up with so much devotion in the 1920s, had begun to crumble in the severe clime of the Nazi-Communist controversy. Beginning in 1934, fewer and fewer Yiddish books were allowed to be published, Yiddish school attendance declined sharply within a few years, and more and more of the Yiddish cultural institutions were dismantled. Moreover, the terror spreading through all classes of society in that early era of purges muted the protests of communal organs and thus deprived them of even the negative solidarity engendered by such complaints in unison. This process of attrition was briefly interrupted by the Soviet occupation of eastern Poland and the Baltic countries, whose Jewish communities, together with some hundreds of thousands of refugees from Nazi-occupied Poland, injected a powerful rejuvenating factor into Soviet Jewish life. But the situation was completely reversed when Nazi armies overran all these and many additional Soviet territories, physically exterminating millions of Jews they now controlled. Even among the remaining segments of the Soviet Jewish communities all manifestations of cultural vitality were quickly expunged by the enforced silence imposed upon them during the "black years" of the Stalinist Terror. There seemed, indeed, to be little hope for any Jewish survival, certainly for any meaningful survival based upon the cultivation of one's religio-cultural heritage.

RIVAL RELIGION

Far beyond these external pressures the intrinsic forces of Jewish survival were seriously sapped by the new communist ideology. It has long been recognized that while presenting itself as a scientific, materialistic movement, communism had in itself all the features of a new religion, promising its believers a glittering messianic future and threatening all infidels or sectarian deviationists with fire and brimstone. No less a student of the Russian mentality than Nicholas Berdyaev, a former Marxist become one of the leading Russian philosophers of religion, once observed:

> Communism, both as a theory and as a practice, is not only a social phenomenon, but also a spiritual and religious phenomenon. And it is formidable precisely as a *religion*. It is as a religion that it opposes Christianity and aims at ousting it. . . . It has its dogmas and its dogmatic morals, has even the beginnings of its own cult; it takes possession of the whole soul and calls forth enthusiasm and self-sacrifice.

It is this religious exclusivity which has accounted for both the great expansive power of the communist credo and its severe denominational limitations. At the outset, its basically universalist message greatly appealed to members of all nationalities and in the minds of many easily displaced all particularist, or historically and nationally confined, religions. To many younger Jews especially, who had grown impatient with the "narrow" particularist traditions of their own Orthodox mode of living, this universalist message sounded like the long-expected clarion call to a boundless humanitarian embrace and the ultimate liberation movement for all men.[1]

If in the past Judaism had effectively resisted the encroachments of other faiths, although it had at one time or another surrendered segments of its population to the onrushing universalist waves of early Christianity or early Islam in their truly heroic stages, it now faced a rival religion which seemed the more persuasive as it denied being a religion. By emphasizing secularism, fully in consonance with the secularist trends of the modern era, and by refraining from demanding any particular religious initiation which necessarily placed upon each convert the formal sign of betrayal of his former faith, communism could indeed appear as the all-human new civilization to which Jews, and others, might readily surrender their identity.

As time went on, however, Russian communism was forced by historic circumstances to shed more and more of its universalist features and to emphasize its particularist Russian characteristics. In the titanic Second World War its very survival depended on the appeal to traditional Russian patriotism, and in a far lesser degree to that of the minorities. The Great Patriotic War thus clinched an evolution which had become increasingly evident after the death of Lenin and the defeat of Trotsky: the Soviets' return to the traditional moorings of the Russian soil and the Russian national spirit.

By the last years of Stalin the wheel of history had made a complete turn. Despite the tremendous revolutionary changes which seemed to have transformed society and its outlook from the bottom up, the early 1950s were not so different from the early 1850s as they appeared to superficial observers. Uvarov's famous guidelines for Nicholas I's regime, "Orthodoxy, Autocracy and [Russian] Nationality," applied now to Stalin's Russia under new guises. Of course, Orthodoxy now meant not conformity with the teachings of the Russian Orthodox Church, but conformity with the even more inviolable dogmas of the Communist Party and their exclusively valid interpretations by the Holy Synod of its Politbureau. Autocracy was even stronger than it had been because it was buttressed by the state's full control over the means of production, its far greater ability to uproot and deport entire populations, and its much more pervasive police surveillance than that of the tsarist gendarmerie. Only with respect to Russian nationalism was the Stalinist regime less explicitly demanding in theory. In practice, however, Russification was progressing in gigantic steps, and notwithstanding all the mouthings of the principle of minority rights, it celebrated far more rapid victories than it had in any such short span of time during the Romanov era.

Above all, under both regimes there has been an overriding, allbenumbing terror. What the keen French observer Marquis Astolphe L. de Custine wrote about the Russia of 1839 applied no less to the "black years" of the Stalinist Terror:

> The affectation of resignation is the lowest depth of abjectness into which an enslaved nation can fall: revolt or despair would be doubtless more terrible, but less ignominious. Weakness so degraded that it dare not indulge itself even in complaint, . . . fear calmed by its own excess—these are moral phenomena which cannot be witnessed without calling forth tears of horror.[2]

Jews, too, found themselves facing an implacable regime quite reminiscent of that of a century earlier. As under Nicholas I, the aim remained to denationalize and completely absorb the Jewish minority, if need be with the aid of the mailed fist. Under Nicholas it was the combination of the seizure of Jewish children for long-term military service, the removal of Jews from frontier districts, and the closing of the *kahal*, along with the liberal admission of Jews to Western-type schools and other measures, both overtly forcible or deceptively friendly, which was to lead to the Christianization of the Jewish masses and their ultimate disappearance as an identifiable group apart. On its part, the Stalinist regime in its last phases tried to achieve substantially the same result through the deportation of recalcitrant individuals for long-term forced labor, the uprooting of large groups of temporarily declassed persons, the suppression of all Jewish communal organs, the physical destruction of their intellectual leadership, and the total silencing of any cultural form of expression, combined with the promises of full self-determination in distant Biro-Bidzhan. Instead of having to turn Christian in order to become good Russians, Jews now had to become devout communists, equally forgetful of their own heritage. Even less than in the days of Nicholas were Jews free to choose the alternative of leaving the country. Once again the frontiers were closely watched, and except for the flight of a few individuals, most Jews, and for that matter non-Jews, felt permanently immured behind invisible but no less impregnable walls under the watchful eyes of a capricious dictator.

NEW MARRANOS

It did not escape the keen eyes of outsiders that this denial of one's heritage forced a great many Russian Jews to live a double life, reminiscent of that of the Spanish and Portuguese Marranos. In the Iberian Peninsula, too, Jews had long cherished the hope of being able to develop their autonomous culture under conditions of relative freedom. But an intolerant regime, even more nationalistically than Church oriented, finally told them that they had to conform and be assimilated by the majority through adopting the latter's beliefs and modes of life. If in 1492 Spain still left the Jews the alternative of a harried, unhappy, and dangerous departure, Portugal five years later gave them no such choice but forced them all to adopt Christianity. The result was that, particularly in the smaller kingdom, the Jews maintained their secret life for generations thereafter.

Nor was this a singular exception. Throughout medieval and early modern history it happened time and again that while individual Jews converted to Christianity or Islam were rather quickly absorbed by the body politic of the majority, any mass conversion of Jews resulted in the perpetuation within that body of an alien group retaining memories of its Jewish past. Four centuries after the so-called expulsion from Portugal thousands of Marranos living in and around Oporto still retained sufficient traces of their former Jewishness for many to find their way back to the Jewish community during the 1920s. Nor, one could argue, would any Russian secret service be more enduringly effective in ferreting out all secret forms of nonconformity than had been the Iberian Inquisition.

Fortunately, it appears that no generations of secret living will be required before the Soviet regime will realize that its methods are totally self-defeating. Khrushchev and his associates have already conceded many grave errors committed during the Stalinist Terror; they have already purged the Lenin mausoleum of Stalin's body, and either physically or at least in the memory of men, they have rehabilitated at least some of the dictator's victims. In some respects the Khrushchev era resembled that of Alexander II, whose initial liberal reforms reversed many dominant trends under Nicholas I's extremely conservative regime. But in the end ever new compromises were made with the old system. Similarly, in the 1960s many modified Neo-Stalinist tendencies reasserted themselves. Yet the Brezhnev era is no replica of Stalin's regime. Despite some misleading appearances of inner consistency, the nearly six decades of the communist regime have witnessed many far-reaching political upheavals which are reflected even in the Soviet historiography, despite its rigid limitations by the overwhelming Party controls. Lenin's own reversal through the introduction of the New Economic Policy in March, 1921, was followed by the gradual atrophy of that system in the following years. The subsequent practical, if not ideological, abandonment of the world revolutionary aims in favor of "building socialism in one country" culminated in Trotsky's banishment from the Soviet Union in February, 1929, and the ruthless suppression of the Trotskyite "heresy." Pointedly summarizing in 1969 the prevailing outlook of authoritative Soviet historians on the past of the Union,

No End of Road

Zbigniew Brzezinski stated:

> Of the forty-five years since Lenin, according to offical Soviet history, power was exercised for approximately five years by leaders subsequently unmasked as traitors . . . ; and, most recently, for almost ten years, by a "harebrained" schemer. On the basis of that record, the present leadership lays claim to representing a remarkable departure from a historical pattern of singular depravity.

Perhaps history has repeated itself once again through the emergence of the Democratic Movement in recent years. At first weak and subject to various ups and downs and deep internal splits, this movement may duplicate the rise of the revolutionary currents under the last two Romanovs. Andrei Amalric, a member of this dissenting group, ventured to pose the challenging question, "Will the USSR Survive until 1984?" Without endorsing the underlying idea of Soviet instability one may indeed expect further major changes in the Soviet policies over the next decade or two.[3]

In the Jewish case, to be sure, the latest reversals have thus far been painfully slow and incomplete. But the unexpected breakthrough of the Soviet opening of the gates for Jewish emigration, however hedged by individual repression and a mass of bureaucratic obstacles, shows that the situation of Soviet Jewry is not quite so abysmally "frozen" as it appeared only a few years ago. Internally, too, the present administration may still persist in a slightly modified late Stalinist denial of any legitimate outlets for Jewish education, literary or artistic creativity, and even simple religious observance or daily modes of life. But the emergence of a number of dedicated, self-sacrificing—to speak in religious terms—witnesses for Jewish culture, the regained articulateness of some representative spokesmen of the long-silent people, and the incipient signs of a cultural revival of Soviet Jewry open up new vistas for the possibilities of a new Russian-Jewish renaissance.

Nor are these isolated phenomena. There appears to be a general stirring among the numerous national minorities in both the European and Asiatic republics and autonomous regions which, even if not—or not yet—pursuing outright irredentist aims, may enforce major changes in the total structure of Soviet society. The world-wide national liberation and anticolonial movements appear to be catching up with the Soviet situation, long obscured by an ideological anticolonialist phraseology.

More significantly, in the titanic struggle for control over humanity, both physical and mental, the Soviet Union can no more afford to waste the great human energies potentially dormant in a suppressed people like the Jews than can any Western power consistently pursue discriminatory racial policies. All keen observers of our modern scene understand that it is not the possession of ever-growing chunks of property, or its denial—those overriding issues of the nineteenth century—but rather the possession of knowledge, of imaginative, creative knowledge of the universe and its potentialities, that has become the real source of power. These factors may have been partially obscured by the recent energy and food crises. But they were, in fact, reinforced by the very need of new technologies to prevent the impending disasters. To dispense in the long run with the fullest contribution that the Jewish people of Russia can make to the widening of the frontiers of human knowledge because of some atavistic desires for discrimination would clearly be even more self-defeating than the persistent racial segregation of the Southern blacks in the United States. Even now there is less anti-Jewish discrimination in the basic fields of Soviet science and technology, especially nuclear physics and space exploration.

True, our prognosis may turn out to be overoptimistic. We need but remember the tremendous eruption of irrational forces into all human affairs in our generation. Yet we must not overlook the very basic assumption of both American democracy and Russia's materialistic conception of history, namely, that in any long historic process reason must ultimately prevail.

Notes

[1]

Early Vicissitudes

1. St. Jerome, *Commentary* on Zechariah 10:11, in Migne's *Patrologia latina*, XXV, 1568 f.

2. The equation of Slavs with Canaanites had a long tradition in the Middle Ages and has been the subject of numerous discussions in modern Jewish historical literature. *See* Samuel Krauss, "Die hebräischen Benennungen der modernen Völker," *Jewish Studies in Memory of George A. Kohut*, ed. by Salo W. Baron and Alexander Marx, New York, 1935, pp. 379–412, especially pp. 397 ff. On the parallel claims of the North-African and Spanish descendants of Phoenician settlers, which at one time even had serious political implications, *see*, for example, Alexander H. Krappe, "Les Chananéens dans l'ancienne Afrique du Nord et en Espagne," *American Journal of Semitic Languages and Literatures*, LVII (1940), 229–43. *See also* the additional controversial literature on both subjects briefly discussed in my *A Social and Religious History of the Jews*, 2d ed. rev., Vols. I–XV, New York, 1952–71, especially Vol. III, pp. 90 f., 271 n. 23, 335 f. n. 53.

3. Muqaddasi, *Descriptio imperii islamici*, ed. by De Goeje, Leiden, 1877, p. 355; Ibn an-Nadim, *K. al-Fihrist* (Book of the List: a Bibliography), ed. by G. Flügel, 2 vols., Leipzig, 1872, I, 20. On the complex problems of the Khazars and the Khazar origins of East European Jewry, *see* the vast literature, cited in my

Social and Religious History of the Jews, Vol. III, pp. 196 ff., 323 ff. Some new material as well as new insights into the history of the Khazars and their relationship with the Karaite sect in eastern Europe have been supplied by the large documentary collection in Jacob Mann's *Texts and Studies in Jewish History and Literature*, Vol. II: Karaitica, Philadelphia, 1935; Arthur Szyszman's various essays, esp. "Die Karäer in Ost-Mitteleuropa," *Zeitschrift für Ostforschung*, VI (1951), 24–54; the numerous studies reviewed by Irène Sorlin in "Le Problème des Khazars et les historiens soviétiques dans le vingt dernières années," *Travaux et mémoires* of the Centre des Recherches d'histoire et civilisation byzantines, III (1968), 423–55.

The complex problems of the origins and mutual relationship of the Glagolithic and Cyrillic alphabets, which have given rise to numerous debates over several generations, have recently been succinctly reviewed by Herbert Scheleskiner in his "Konstantinisches Alphabet und glagolitisches und kyrillisches Schriftzeichensystem," *Wiener Slawistisches Jahrbuch*, XVIII (1973), 96–99.

4. To be sure, in "The Beginnings of East-European Jewry in Legend and Historiography" in *Studies and Essays in Honor of Abraham A. Neuman*, Leiden, 1962, pp. 445–502, Bernard D. Weinryb has subjected all the earlier theories of the origin of Russian Jewry to a sharp critique, coming to the totally negative conclusion that "any remnants which remained [in the areas to which Russia spread] until the middle ages were wiped out by the Mongol invasion in the thirteenth century" (pp. 500 f.). This theory, however, suffers from both the all-too-easy skepticism concerning hypotheses relating to the generally obscure origins of many peoples with their extreme paucity and ambiguity of existing archeological and other documentation and the assumption of the totality and finality of the destruction caused by the Mongolian invasion—an assumption long discredited in other areas devastated by the Mongols.

5. Adam of Bremen, *Gesta Hammaburgensis ecclesiae pontificum*, ii. 19, ed. by Johann M. Lappenberg, Hanover, 1846, in *Monumenta Germaniae historica*, Scriptores, VII, 312 f.

6. *The Russian Primary Chronicle*, Laurentian Text, English trans. by Samuel H. Cross and Olgerd P. Sherbovitz-Wetzor, Cambridge, Mass., 1953 (Publications of the Mediaeval Academy of America, LX), pp. 96 ff.

7. See George Vernadsky, *Kievan Russia*, New Haven, 1948, especially pp. 60 ff., 160 f.; the critique of his and other theories by Nicholas Zernov in his "Vladimir and the Origin of the Russian State," *Slavonic and East European Review*, XXIII (1942–50), 123–28, 425–38; and other data and literature presented in my *Social and Religious History of the Jews*, Vol. III, pp. 215 ff., 336 ff. nn. 54–56.

8. Johannes Schiltberger, *The Bondage and Travels . . . in Europe, Asia and Africa, 1396–1427*, English trans. by J. Buchan Telfer, with notes by P. Brunn, London, 1879 (Works issued by the Hakluyt Society, LVIII), pp. 49, 176 n. 7.

9. Julius Brutzkus, "Zechariah, the Prince of Taman" (Russian), *Evreiskaia Starina*, X (1918), 132–43. Guizolfi's Jewish origin or faith, long widely accepted, has been denied by recent scholars. See the sources cited by B. D. Weinryb (in his essay, quoted above, n. 4), pp. 488 ff.

10. The origins and evolution of the important sect of Judaizers have long intrigued scholars. See the extensive older literature cited by George Vernadsky

in "The Heresy of the Judaizers and the Policies of Ivan III of Moscow," *Speculum*, VIII (1933), 436–54; and D. Oljancyn in his "Aus dem Kultur- und Geistesleben der Ukraine, I: Was ist die Häresie der 'Judaisierenden'?" *Kyrios*, I (1936), 176–89. Ever since the middle of the nineteenth century, influential voices have been heard insisting that this sect sprang from purely internal forces without any Jewish influence. This thesis has more recently been elaborated, with the aid of much new archival material, by Soviet scholars, especially S. J. Lurie. See N. Kazakova and his *Antifeodalniie ereticheskiie dvizheniia na Rusi* (Antifeudal Heretical Movements in Russia from the Fourteenth to the Early Fifteenth Century), Moscow, 1955; and his short French summary, "L'Hérésie dite de judaïsants et ses sources historiques," *Revue des études slaves*, XL (1966), 49–67. However, in his "Jewish Influence on the Religious Ferment in Eastern Europe at the End of the Fifteenth Century" (Hebrew) in *Yitzhak F. Baer Jubilee Volume*, ed. by S. W. Baron *et al.*, Jerusalem, 1960, pp. 228–47, Samuel Ettinger has convincingly argued for the presence of many genuinely Jewish ingredients in the "judaizing heresy" (*zhidovstvuiushchie*), most likely planted by Jewish individuals upon fertile ground among some leaders in Novgorod and Moscow, despite the generally prevailing local xenophobia. *See* Marc Szeftel, "La Condition légale des étrangers dans la Russie Novgorodo-Kiévienne," *Recueils de la Société Jean Bodin*, X (1958), 375–430. There may also have been some importation of West European Christian elements which, because of their divergence from the prevailing Byzantine concepts, appeared as Judaic teachings. *See* Rudolf M. Mainka, "Judaizanten als Bezeichnung westkirchlicher Eigenheiten in Russland des 16. Jahrhunderts," *Annales Instituti Slavici* (Salzburg-Regensburg), III (1967), 150–54. *See also* John L. I. Fennel, "The Attitude of the Josephians and the Transvolga Elders to the Heresy of the Judaizers," *Slavonic and East European Review*, XXIX (1950), 486–508; and other studies reviewed by Jan Juszczyk in his "On Researches in Judaizantism" (Polish), *Kwartalnik Historyczny*, LXXVI (1969), 141–51; and by Edgar Hösch, "Sowjetische Forschungen zur Häresiengeschichte Altrusslands. Methodologische Bemerkungen," *Jahrbücher für Geschichte Osteuropas*, n.s. XXVIII (1970), 279–312. Nonetheless, many problems still await clarification, especially in connection with the underground survivals of the sect beyond the early sixteenth century and their impact on the continued hostility of the Russian leaders to the possible missionary effects of the admission of Jews to Russia. Some additional data are mentioned in the forthcoming Vols. XVI and XVII of my *Social and Religious History of the Jews*.

11. Vittore Colorni, "Note per la biografia di alcuni dotti ebrei vissuti a Mantova nel secolo XV," *Annuario di studi ebraici*, I (1934), 172 ff.

12. Julius Hessen, *Istoriia evreiskago naroda v Rossii* (A History of the Jewish People in Russia), 2 vols., Leningrad, 1925–27, I, 39; *idem*, "Jews in Courland (XVI-XVIII Centuries)" (Russian), *Evreiskaia Starina*, VII (1914), 145 ff.; *idem*, "Jews in the Muscovite States in the XV-XVII Centuries" (Russian), *ibid.*, VIII (1915), 1–19, 153–72. In this exclusivist policy the Muscovite ruling circles were encouraged by the ecclesiastical establishment at home and abroad. According to the merchant and pilgrim Vasilii Pozniakov, in 1558 he visited the ecumenical patriarch in Istanbul. Upon learning from the visitor that no Jews were allowed to come to Muscovy even on short business trips, the heresiarch "stood up,

recited a prayer, twice prostrating himself, and exclaimed, 'God will forgive the sins of the tsar . . . and his sons . . . for their expulsion of the infidel Jews like wolves from Christ's herd.' " See "Pélérinage du marchand Basile Pozniakov (1558–1561)" in Sofiia Petrovna Khitrovo, ed. and trans., *Itinéraires russes en Orient*, Paris, 1889, Chap. XVI, especially p. 290. *See also* Samuel Ettinger's judicious and well-documented analysis, "The Muscovite State and Its Attitude toward the Jews" (Hebrew), *Zion*, XVIII (1953), 136–68. On Ivan IV's execution of Jewish resisters to conversion in Polotsk, *see* some contemporary reports and other data, cited in my *Social and Religious History of the Jews*, Vol. XVI. Ironically, to justify such ruthless measures, the tsar liked to quote biblical passages, particularly the example set by King David (for instance, II Sam. 5:6 ff.). *See* his (somewhat dubious) letter to Andrei Mikhailovich Kurbsky of July 5, 1564, in *Ivan IV, the Terrible, Czar of Russia, 1530–1584. The Correspondence between A. M. Kurbsky and Tsar Ivan IV of Russia*, ed. with a trans. and notes by J. L. I. Fennell, Cambridge, 1955, pp. 12 ff., 38 ff. On this and other phases of Russian Jewish history, *see also* the older sources and studies listed in the *Sistematicheskii ukazatel literatury o Evreiakh* (A Systematic Guide to the Literature on Jews), St. Petersburg, 1883.

13. On the widespread massacres of Jews by the Muscovite conquerors of Lithuanian and Polish cities as distant as Lublin, *see* the contemporary reports cited by S. Ettinger in *Zion*, XVIII, 141 ff. The spirit of religious intolerance, which converted the Muscovite invasion of Poland and Lithuania of 1654 into a war of religion, reinforced the extreme conservatism characterizing most governmental acts during Alexei's regime. It had found expression in the tsar's *Ulozhenie* (code of laws) of 1649, enacted in cooperation with an advisory diet (*zemskii sobor*), which in its preamble explicitly invoked the patristic injunctions and the laws of the Greek emperors as examples to be followed. Its provisions were so restrictive of the freedom of movement even of the burghers—not to speak of the ever more enslaved rural villeins—that settlement in Muscovite territories must have offered little attraction to most Jewish merchants even if they could evade the existing stringent anti-Jewish laws. However, a few hardy souls seem to have managed to live in the very capital, with the aid of the influential convert, Stephen (Danilo Ilich) von Hagen, who served as court physician until his assassination in 1682, when he was accused of having poisoned the young Tsar Fedor (1676–82). On the ever-deteriorating condition of the Russian villeins *see* Boris D. Grekov, *Krestianie na Rusi* (The Peasants in Rus from Earliest Times to the Seventeenth Century), 2d ed., Vols. I–II, Moscow, 1932–34 (also in a German trans.).

14. *See* J. van Esso, "Tsar Peter the Great and the Jews of Amsterdam" (Dutch), *Historia* (Utrecht), XV (1950), 60–67; "From the Archives of the Yiddish Scientific Institute (YIVO)" (Yiddish), *YIVO Historishe Shriftn* (Studies in History), II (1937), 667 f.

15. More details about these two noteworthy social climbers are furnished by Saul M. Ginsburg in his *Historishe Verk* (Historical Works), new series, Vol. II: "Converts in Tsarist Russia: Studies in the History of Russian Jewry," New York, 1946, pp. 11–33. *See also*, more generally, Robert Stupperich, *Staatsgedanke*

Notes

und Religionspolitik Peters des Grossen, Breslau, 1936 (Osteuropäische Forschungen, n.s. XXII).

16. Jacob Gurland, "An Episode from the History of the Expulsion of the Jews from Russia in 1727" (Russian), *Evreiskaia Starina,* II (1909), 246–50. The sad story of the repeated cycles of entry and forced departure of individual Jews, including such royal favorites as the gifted financier Lipman Levi (or Isaac Liebman), who had performed valuable services to Empress Anna Ivanovna and her friend Duke Ernst Johann Biron of Courland, is briefly retold by Joseph Meisl in his *Geschichte der Juden in Polen und Russland,* 3 vols., Berlin, 1921–25, especially II, 74 ff.

17. Hessen, *Istoriia,* I, 51 f. It should be noted that Elizabeth, authoress of that much-quoted statement about the "enemies of Christ," owed much to one Grünberg, son of a German-Jewish convert, who though a lowly sergeant of the palace guard, played a significant role in the *coup d'état* that had secured full imperial power for her. See Michael T. Florinsky, *Russia,* I, 452 f.; and Chap. 2, n. 1.

[2]
Under Catherine II and Alexander I

1. Mikhail M. Speransky, *Proekty i zapiski* (Projects and Memoirs), ed. by A. I. Kopanev *et al.,* Moscow, 1961 (U.S.S.R. Academy of Science, Historical Section), pp. 86 ff. *See also* Marc Raeff, *Michael Speransky, Statesman of Imperial Russia, 1772–1839,* The Hague, 1957, especially pp. 204 ff., 222 ff. Speransky's views sharply contrasted with those of Catherine II, who at the very beginning of her rule in 1764 instructed Prince Alexander Viazemsky that the Ukraine, the Baltic provinces, and Finland, though separately administered, "should be easily reduced to a condition where they can be Russified and no longer, like wolves, look for the woods. This can be achieved without effort if reasonable men are put in charge." Cited by M. T. Florinsky in his *Russia: a History and an Interpretation,* 2 vols., New York, 1947, I, 555.

The number of 27,000 Jews taken over by Russia in the first partition of Poland is somewhat uncertain. The three Polish provinces (*województwa* or palatinates) of Vitebsk, Polotsk, and Mtislav covered an area of some 93,000 square kilometers (or 35,900 square miles) with a population of 1,300,000. The Jewish ratio of a little over 2 percent was clearly far below the average of more than 5 percent in all of Poland-Lithuania. Yet in 1764 the census takers there counted only 21,263 Jews aged one year or more. Even adding the infants the total number of Jews could hardly amount to more than 23,000, except for the evident incompleteness of those estimates, which ought to be raised by at least 20 percent. *See* Raphael Mahler's careful and comprehensive analysis of the results of that census in his *Yidn in amolikn Poiln in likht fun tsifern* (Jews in Old

Poland in the Light of Numbers), accompanied by a Volume of Tables, Warsaw, 1958; and in an abbreviated Polish trans. in *Przeszłość demograficzna Polski* (Poland's Demographic Past), II (1967), 131–80; and other data discussed in my *Social and Religious History of the Jews*, Vol. XVI. The partition of the once powerful Polish-Lithuanian Commonwealth proceeded so swiftly and encountered so little armed resistance that few Jews had a chance to leave their residences before they suddenly found themselves facing a new sovereign.

2. See my study of *The Jewish Community: Its History and Structure to the American Revolution*, 3 vols., Philadelphia, 1942 (or later impressions and a recent photo offset ed., Westport, Ct., 1972), II, 274 f.; III, 190 ff. n. 31; and such monographs as Jacob Galant, "The Debts of Jewish Kahals in Podolia and Volhynia" (Russian), *Zbirnyk prats* (Collection of Papers) of the Jewish Historical and Archaeological Commission, II (1929), 119–27. See also below, Chap. 7, n. 3.

3. Gabriel R. Derzhavin, *Sochineniia* (Works), 2d ed. with notes by Yakob Grot, 7 vols., St. Petersburg, 1868–78, VI, 688 ff.; VII, 261–355. See also ibid., VI, 122 ff., 688 ff., 761 ff., etc. The early memorandum by Dr. Frank bore the characteristic title "How Can a Jew Become a Good and Useful Citizen?" which implied an admission of the current Jew-baiting accusation that Jews were exploiters, rather than useful members, of society. It was even more outspoken than Christian Wilhelm Dohm's well-known tract, *Über die bürgerliche Verbesserung der Juden*, new ed. rev., Berlin, 1783, 761 ff., etc. In their "investigations," moreover, Derzhavin and his successors also had to take account of some such exceptional situations as existed, for example, in Courland. Jews who had been living in that duchy under Poland's overlordship, had been treated there as tolerated aliens with a legal status far inferior to that of their Polish-Lithuanian coreligionists. Nonetheless some of their enemies resented their very presence in the country, which gave rise to a major debate in 1787. See G. von Rauch's rather colored analysis in "Eine Polemik zur Judenfrage in Kurland (1787)," *Jomsburg* (Leipzig), V (1941), 84–95. After Courland's annexation by Russia in 1795, the local Jews found themselves free to settle anywhere in the emergent Pale and to enjoy the much greater opportunities open to all Jews in the empire's western provinces. See also below, Chap. 3, n. 7.

4. The text of this law is reproduced in the *Polnoe sobranie zakonov rossiiskoi imperii* (Complete Collection of Laws of the Russian Empire), 1st ser. XXVIII, No. 21,547; and, from there, in Vitalii O. Levanda's *Polnyi khronologicheskii sbornik zakonov* (Complete Chronological Collection of Laws and Ordinances Relating to Jews, 1649–1873), St. Petersburg, 1874, pp. 53 ff. No. 59. Characteristically, despite these efforts to weaken the *kahal*, Alexander failed to abrogate the law of 1796, thus perpetuating the Jewish minority status and separation on the city councils. On Russia's experiments with its municipal system, see W. Bruce Lincoln, "The Russian State and Its Cities: a Search for Effective Municipal Government, 1786–1842," *Jahrbücher für Geschichte Osteuropas*, n.s. XVII (1969), 531–41.

5. N. M. Gelber, "La Police autrichienne et le Sanhédrin de Napoléon," *Revue des études juives*, LXXXIII (1927), 137, App. 2.

6. Alexeiev's report, cited by Simon M. Dubnow in his *History of the Jews in Russia and Poland from the Earliest Times until the Present Day*, English trans.

from the Russian by Israel Friedlander, 3 vols., Philadelphia, 1916, I, 347 f. Sonnenberg and Dillon, theretofore unofficial representatives, were later to play a considerable role among the elected "Deputies of the Jewish People." *See* Julius Hessen and D. G. Maggid's pertinent essays cited below, n. 11, and Chap. 7, n. 5.

7. Chaim Borodiansky, "Poems of Eulogy in Honor of Catherine II and Their Authors" (Yiddish), *YIVO Historishe Shriftn*, II (1937), 531–37; "From the Archives of the Yiddish Scientific Institute (YIVO)," *ibid.*, pp. 680 f. (reproducing in facsimile the title page and first Hebrew page of a poem published by the Vilna community in 1802 in honor of Alexander I). On Mendelssohn as a German translator of Hebrew patriotic poems, *see also* Alexander Altmann's *Moses Mendelssohn: a Biographical Study*, Philadelphia, 1973, pp. 67 f.

8. Saul M. Ginsburg, *Otechestvennaia voina 1812 goda i russkiie evreii* (The Patriotic War of 1812 and the Russian Jews), St. Petersburg, 1912, p. 30; Asriel Nathan Frenk, *Yehude Polin bi-yeme milhamot Napoleon* (Polish Jews during the Napoleonic Wars), Warsaw, 1912.

9. August Fournier, *Die Geheimpolizei auf dem Wiener Kongress. Eine Auswahl aus ihren Papieren*, Vienna, 1913, p. 164 n. 2; Max J. Kohler, "Jewish Rights at the Congresses of Vienna (1814–1815) and Aix-la-Chapelle (1818)," *Publications of the American Jewish Historical Society*, XXVI (1918), 82 ff., 116 ff. *See also*, more generally, my *Die Judenfrage auf dem Wiener Kongress auf Grund von zum Teil ungedruckten Quellen dargestellt*, Vienna, 1920.

10. *See* Stuart R. Tompkins, "The Russian Bible Society—A Case of Religious Xenophobia," *American Slavic and East European Review*, VII (1948), 251–68; and Francis Ley, *Madame de Krüdener et son temps, 1769–1824*. With a Foreword by Alphonse Dupront, Paris, 1961 (Civilisations d'hier et d'aujourd'hui). The tsar may also have been discouraged by the news reaching him beginning in 1814 from the province of Orel about the spread there of a Sabbatarian sect among the peasants—shades of the old Judaizing sect of the fifteenth century. According to a later report of the archbishop of Voronezh, these dissenters also adopted the ritual of circumcision and other Jewish ceremonies. Their number at that time allegedly amounted to 1,500 souls. By 1823, Alexander's trusted adviser, Prince Victor Kochubey, suggested that all Jews of the area be expelled—there hardly were any Jewish residents in the area—and that, in order to discredit them, the sectarians be officially designated as *zhids* (a term of opprobrium not used in official documents even with respect to professing Jews). Despite those and other repressive measures, the sect grew in number, counting some 20,000 followers later in the century. It was finally relieved of official persecution during the Revolution of 1905. *See* S. M. Dubnow, *History of the Jews in Russia*, I, 401 ff.; and Antoine Scheikevitch, "Alexandre Ier et l'hérésie sabbatiste," *Revue d'histoire moderne et contemporaine*, III (1956), 223–35.

11. The Slutsky affair is described on the basis of the synod's own archival data by Saul M. Ginsburg in "A Forced Conversion of a Rabbi's Daughter" (Yiddish) in his *Historishe Verk*, III, 162–77. On the deputies, *see* Julius I. Hessen, "The 'Deputies of the Jewish People' in the Days of Alexander I" (Russian), *Evreiskaia Starina*, II (1909), 17–29, 196–206; and below, Chap. 7, n. 5.

12. *See* Julius Hessen, "On the Origin of the Ritual Murder Literature in the

Russian Language" (Russian), *Evreiskaia Letopis*, I (1923), 3–17. *See below*, Chaps. 3 and 4, n. 23.

13. The decree of April 1, 1823, is reproduced in the *Polnoe sobranie zakonov*, XXXVIII, No. 29,420; and in V. O. Levanda's *Sbornik* (above, n. 4), pp. 119 f. No. 111. The sufferings of the exiles of 1824 seem to have given rise to a remarkable hasidic folk tale of how, through the use of magic, Rabbi Joshua Heshel of Apta (Opatów) succeeded in nullifying two of the tsar's anti-Jewish decrees. Apart from other details taken over from old Jewish folklore, this tale unhistorically connected the rabbi's intervention with Nicholas I, whose accession to the throne and subsequent enactment of the *rekruchina* (*see* below) occurred after Joshua Heshel's demise on March 24, 1825. *See* Israel Halpern's analysis of both the tale and the underlying historical facts in his "R. Joshua Heshel of Apta and the Anti-Jewish Ordinances at the End of Alexander I's Reign" (Hebrew), reprinted in his *Yehudim ve-Yahadut be-mizrah Eiropa* (Eastern European Jewry: Historical Studies), Jerusalem, 1968, pp. 348–54.

[3]

Under Nicholas I and Alexander II

1. Jacques Ancelot, *Six mois en Russie: lettres écrites à M. X.-B. Saintines en 1826*, Paris, 1827, p. 184; Nicholas I's diary reproduced by N. Schilder in "The Grand Duke Nicholas Pavlovich" (Russian), *Russkaia Starina*, VI (1901), 465 f. It may be noted that the term *zhid* (Jew) had long had a pejorative connotation and ever since Catherine II's time had been replaced by *evrei* (Hebrew) in official parlance. *See also* S. Beilin, "From Historical Journals, IV: a Statement of the Grand Duke Nicholas Pavlovich about the Jews" (Russian), *Evreiskaia Starina*, IV (1911), 589–90. On the meaning of "nationality" in Uvarov's terminology, *see* N. V. Riasanowsky, *Nicholas I and Official Nationality in Russia, 1825–1855*, Berkeley, 1959; and James T. Flynn, "S. S. Uvarov's Liberal Years," *Jahrbücher für Geschichte Osteuropas*, XX (1972), 481–91.

2. *See* Saul M. Ginsburg, *Historishe Verk*, n.s. II, 34 ff.; and, more generally, Mikhail Osipovich Zetlin, *The Decembrists*, English trans. by George Parin, with a preface by Michael Karpovich, New York, 1958. Needless to say, the Jews knew nothing about the brewing palace revolt of December 14, 1825. But after its suppression rumors about it must have reached the Jewish leaders. Later on some of them may actually have read Pavel Ivanovich Pestel's chapter on "The Tribes Inhabiting Russia," in which he preached the amalgamation of all these "tribes" into one Russian nationality. V. O. Kluchevsky, in emphasizing the difference between the Decembrist uprising and the earlier palace revolts in St. Petersburg and stressing the generation gap, correctly stated that the fathers "had been Russians educated to become Frenchmen, the fathers' sons were French-educated men longing to become Russian." See his *A History of Russia*, English trans. by C. J. Hogarth, 5 vols., New York, 1960, V, 172. Those few who

may have heard about Pestel's proposal to transplant the Russian Jews to a state of their own that was to be carved out of the Ottoman Asian possessions must have dismissed it with a shrug. Even a later, more receptive Jewish generation reading his assertion that the two million Russian Jews "will in their quest for a fatherland easily overcome all obstacles placed in their way by the Turks and reach Asia through European Turkey. There they will occupy a sufficient territory to establish a separate Jewish state" (*Russkaia Pravda* [Russian Truth], St. Petersburg, 1906, pp. 50 ff.) must have sensed behind this prediction not only an echo of Russian imperialist ambitions in the Middle East but also an effort to get the Jews out of Russia. In this respect the leader of that early Russian radical movement resembled the Jacobins of Champagne, who during the French Revolution suggested the banishment of Jews from France, or the later French socialist thinker, Charles Fourrier, who (in *La Fausse Industrie*, 2 vols., Paris, 1835–36, especially II, 660, 783 ff.) proposed the restoration of the Jews to Palestine, which would "be a glorious success for Messrs de Rothschild." It was quite different in nature from Napoleon I's dramatic appeal to world Jewry during his Egyptian campaign of 1799. See Edmund Silberner, "Charles Fourrier on the Jewish Question," *Jewish Social Studies*, VIII (1946), 245–66, especially pp. 250 ff., 259 ff.

In contrast, baptized Grigorii Peretz, former member of one of three Jewish families allowed to live in St. Petersburg, preached emulation of the Western constitutional systems in the name of *Herut*, a Hebrew term for freedom, which he used in his communications with fellow conspirators. He merely envisaged the formation of a society to gather the dispersed Jews and to settle them in the Crimea or in the Orient as "a separate people." See Mark Wischnitzer's brief survey, "Die Dekabristen und die Judenfrage," *Die Welt*, no. 31 (1906). See also N. M. Lebedev's recent biography of *Pestel, Ideolog i rukovoditel dekabristov* (Pestel, Ideologist and Leader of the Decembrists), Moscow, 1972; and H. Lemberg, *Die nationale Gedankenwelt der Dekabristen*, Cologne, 1962 (Kölner Historische Abhandlungen, VII).

3. The text of this remarkable oath, followed by signatures of Jewish witnesses and judges, is reproduced by Saul M. Ginsburg in his *Historishe Verk*, II, 10. The text of the law of August 26, 1827, is reproduced from the *Polnoe sobranie* in Levanda's *Polnyi . . . sbornik*, pp. 102 ff. No. 154, while Nicholas I's lengthy instructions to the priests in charge of cantonist institutions concerning the conversion of Jews are published in the Appendix to Ginsburg, III, 357–69.

4. Alexander Herzen, *Byloye i dumy* (Reminiscences and Meditations) in Constance Garnett's English trans. entitled *My Past and Thoughts*, 6 vols., New York, 1924–26, I, 270 ff.

5. This Yiddish folk song, included in Saul M. Ginsburg and P. Marek's collection of *Evreiskie narodnye pesni* (Jewish Folk Songs), St. Petersburg, 1901, No. 50, is cited in an English trans. by Isaac Levitats in *The Jewish Community in Russia, 1772–1844*, New York, 1943, p. 65. In general, compared with the *rekruchina*'s relatively slight demographic effects, its socioeconomic and psychological impact was thus very great. For example, the Jewish community as a whole was held responsible for any individual harboring a cantonist deserter. The sanction was compulsory military service for the host and a fine of 1,000

rubles for the community even if the elders knew nothing about the transgression. According to Count Pavel Dmitrievich Kiselev's computation, in 1827 the debts of the entire burgher class including its Jewish members amounted to 1,141,710 rubles. By 1845, the Jewish indebtedness alone had increased to 4,363,438 rubles, and in 1854 to 7,722,029 rubles. At the same time, the bitterness created by the enforced discriminatory actions of the communal leaders immeasurably sharpened the class struggle within the Jewish community, a struggle which theretofore had been overshadowed by the internal solidarity of the communal membership facing common external enemies in state and society. Nonetheless, there is a kernel of truth in Samuel Joseph Finn's sweeping assertion that the tsar's cantonist policies greatly strengthened the religious sentiments of the Jewish masses, who often viewed governmental harassment as divine punishment for their sinful behavior. *See* Finn's "The Generations and Their Spokesmen" (Hebrew), *Ha-Karmel*, IV (1879), 195 f.; Saul M. Ginsburg, *Historishe Verk*, II, 18 f.; and more generally, A. Yuditskii, *Yidishe burzhoazie un yidisher proletariat* (The Jewish Bourgeoisie and the Jewish Proletariat in the First Half of the Nineteenth Century), Kiev, 1930. Reprinted from *Historisher Zamelbukh*, II, Part I (1931), which volume may never have appeared. *See* below, Chapter 7, nn. 11–12.

6. Hugh Y. Reyburn, *The Story of the Russian Church*, London, 1924, pp. 8 f. It is not surprising, on the other hand, that the Allied armies combating Russia in the Crimean War included some Western Jewish soldiers. *See* Abraham G. Duker, "Jewish Volunteers in the Ottoman Polish Cossack Units during the Crimean War," *Jewish Social Studies*, XVI (1954), 203–216, 357–76. Moreover, it is possible that the much-discussed draconian measures, to which the tsar had to resort to force young Jews to serve in the Russian army, helped to lower the dignity of military service in Russia and, in the long run, even affected the morale of the Russian combatants. *See*, in general, John Shenton Curtis's succinct observations on "The Army of Nicholas I: Its Role and Character," *American Historical Review*, LXIII (1955–56), 880–89, especially p. 882.

7. *See* Eliyahu Feldman, "The Legal Status of the Bessarabian Jews in the First Half of the Nineteenth Century" (Hebrew), *Heawar*, XII (1968), 102–20; Ignacy Schipper, *Żydzi Królestwa Polskiego* (The Jews of the Kingdom of Poland during the November Uprising), Warsaw, 1932; Nathan M. Gelber, "The Jewish Problem in Poland in the Years 1815–1830" (Hebrew), *Zion*, XIII–XIV (1948–49), 106–43, with an English summary, pp. v–vi; and particularly, Artur Eisenbach's detailed analysis of the *Kwestia równouprawnienia Żydów w Królestwie Polskiem* (The Question of Jewish Equality of Rights in the Kingdom of Poland), Warsaw, 1972. *See also* below, n. 18.

8. *See* my Hebrew article, "A Vilna Excommunication and the Great Powers," *Horeb*, XII (1956), 62–69. The text of that ban could not be located in any Russian archive. Even its German translation used in the internal exchanges in Prussia, still available to me at the Geheimes Preussisches Staatsarchiv between the two wars, seems to have disappeared during World War II. The Jews' intensive participation in all branches of trade including that across the Russo-Prussian border is well illustrated, for instance, by Max Ashkewitz's data in "Der Anteil der Juden am wirtschaftlichen Leben Westpreussens um die Mitte des 19. Jahrhunderts," *Zeitschrift für Ostforschung*, XI (1962), 482–91.

9. Jacob Jacobson, "Eine Aktion für die russischen Grenzjuden in den Jahren 1843/44," *Festschrift* . . . *Simon Dubnow*, Berlin, 1930, pp. 237–50; N. M. Gelber, "The Intercession of Baron Salomon Rothschild of Vienna in Behalf of the Russian Jews in 1846" (Yiddish), *YIVO Historishe Shriftn*, I (1929), 803–10.

10. The provisions here cited form but a small selection of the 121 articles included in the statute of 1835 and printed in the *Polnoe sobranie*, 2d ser. X, No. 8,054. The text is reproduced by Levanda in his *Polnyi* . . . *sbornik*, pp. 359 ff. No. 304. Rumors, often vastly exaggerated, about the forthcoming prohibition of early marriages played havoc with the family life of Russian Jews. To avoid the draconian penalties provided in the decree (parents and other relatives failing to prevent such early unions were to be punished by prison terms of two to six months), thousands of families rushed to marry off their minor children down to the age of eight in advance of its formal promulgation. The period of that *behalah* (shocking calamity) made a deep impression on the Russian Jewish public and was graphically described in Hebrew and Yiddish belles-lettres for decades thereafter. See Israel Halpern's analysis of " 'The Rush' into Early Marriage among Eastern European Jews" (Hebrew), *Zion*, XXVII (1962), 36–58, reproduced in his *Yehudim ve-Yahadut*, pp. 289–309, especially pp. 304 ff.

11. Pinhas Kon, "The Attitude of the Tsarist Authorities to Maimonides" (Yiddish), *Yivo Bleter*, XIII (1938), 577–82. Needless to say, Jewish authors were not the only victims. According to Nicholas I's early decree of 1826 the censors were obliged to direct public opinion according to "the views of the government." Modified in 1828, this decree was again sharpened in reaction to the French July Revolution of 1830, particularly under the aegis of the reactionary Minister Uvarov. The conflicting interpretations and biases of the ever-growing army of censors—which led one of them to observe that "if one were to count all officials in charge of censorship their number would greatly exceed the number of books published annually"—made life doubly arduous for authors and publishers among the religious and ethnic minorities. See S. Beilin's brief chronology of pertinent official documents in his "Censorship of Hebrew Books (1833–1842)" (Russian), *Evreiskaia Starina*, IV (1911), 416–18; and more generally, M. T. Florinsky, *Russia*, II, 812 f.

12. David Philipson, "Max Lilienthal in Russia," *Hebrew Union College Annual*, XII–XIII (1937–38), 829, 833, 838; *idem, Max Lilienthal, American Rabbi, Life and Writings*, New York, 1915, especially pp. 12 ff.; Julius Hessen, "Die russische Regierung und die westeuropäischen Juden (Zur Schulreform in Russland 1840–44). Nach archivalischen Materialien," *Monatsschrift für Geschichte und Wissenschaft des Judentums*, LVII (1913), 257–71, 482–500 (also reprint). It may be noted that according to Lilienthal, all of Russia had only one candidate, Salomon Salkind, qualified to serve as a teacher in the projected new school network of some two hundred institutions. Before long no less than one hundred and forty-two applications were received from Germany and Austria. Initially Uvarov insisted that all candidates would have to be recommended by either Philippson or Jost. But later he and his associates became apprehensive that both these men, as well as a majority of the applicants, were advocates of the "new" Reform movement in Germany, which had few adherents in the Tsarist Empire. Apart from the general slowness of the Russian bureaucratic machinery, this apprehension, as well as the coolness of Montefiore and Crémieux (from whom

Uvarov seems to have expected some fund-raising among the English and French Jews in support of the new school system), contributed to the officials' procrastination and Lilienthal's ultimate departure. See the documentation in Hessen, *ibid.*

13. Philipson, *Max Lilienthal*, p. 264. The Vilna community went so far as to address, on July 10, 1842, a letter to Lilienthal's father, Judah, in Munich, trying to induce him to restrain his overzealous son. This letter was intended to counteract another sent to that father by some progressive leaders of Berdichev which had been full of praise for young Lilienthal's endeavors. Published in a German trans. in the *Allgemeine Zeitung des Judentums* (VI, 1842, 715 f.), the Berdichev epistle had helped reinforce the erroneous impression among the Western Jews that these endeavors enjoyed wide popular support in Russian Jewry. See Philipson, pp. 33 ff.; Saul M. Ginsburg, "Max Lilienthal's Activities in Russia: New Documents," *Publications of the American Jewish Historical Society*, XXXV (1939), 45 ff. *See also* below, Chap. 8.

14. Nicholas Hans, *History of Russian Educational Policy (1701–1917)*, London, 1931 (Diss. University of London), pp. 73 f., 85 ff., in part based on Beletskii's "Jewish Education under Nicholas I" (Russian), *Russkaia shkola*, IV (1893).

15. *Diaries of Sir Moses Montefiore and Lady Montefiore*, ed. by L. Loewe, 2 vols., Chicago, 1890, I, 317 f., 328 ff.; Saul M. Ginsburg, *Historishe Verk*, II, 163–202, 292–305 (on Montefiore), 203–19, 304–5 (on Altaras); Theodor Schiemann, *Geschichte Russlands unter Kaiser Nikolaus I*, 4 vols., Berlin, 1908–19, IV, 79 f., also quoting another English official's exaggerated statement, "As to the poor Jews themselves, they consider him [Montefiore] and actually call him their Messiah" (p. 80 n. 1). *See also* below, Chap. 5, n. 7.

16. Albert M. Hyamson, ed., *The British Consulate in Jerusalem in Relation to the Jews of Palestine, 1838–1914*, 2 vols., London, 1939–41, I, pp. xlviii ff., 109 ff. Nos. 68 and 71, 130 f. No. 80, 146 ff. No. 96. The data briefly summarized in this chapter give only a slight inkling of the vast and ramified legislation concerning Jews under the reign of Nicholas I. It has been estimated that during these three decades, no less than six hundred laws governing various aspects of Jewish life were promulgated, in addition to more than a hundred ordinances and countless administrative and judicial decisions which had not been made public. This is not even to mention the often endless negotiations and committee deliberations which preceded the issuance of many ordinances. Despite the considerable work done in this field by historians and jurists (beginning with Ilya Grigorevich Orshanskii's pioneering study, *Russkoe zakonodadelstvo o Evreiakh* [Russian Legislation Concerning Jews], St. Petersburg, 1877), many documents doubtless still lie dormant in the various archives, particularly provincial and local, which might shed some new light on this significant aspect of Russo-Jewish relations.

17. Osip Rabinovich's editorial in *Razsvet*, 1860, vi. 85; his other publicist writings and programmatic stories, collected in his *Sochineniia* (Works), 3 vols., St. Petersburg, 1880–88; Louis Greenberg, *The Jews in Russia*, 2 vols., New Haven, 1944–59, I, 83, 85.

18. In 1859 merchants of the first guild (those paying 1,000 rubles or more in annual taxes) and in 1861 holders of degrees from schools of higher learning

could reside and trade everywhere in Russia outside the Pale. *See* Greenberg, *ibid.*, I, 75 f.; and below, Chaps. 6, n. 12; 9, n. 19.

19. *See* N. M. Gelber, *Die Juden und der polnische Aufstand 1863*, Vienna, 1923, especially p. 165; Jacob Shatzky, "Jews in the Polish Uprising of 1863" (Yiddish), *YIVO Historishe Shriftn*, I (1929), 423–68; D. Fajnhauz, "The Jewish Population in Lithuania and White Russia in the Uprising of January 1863" (Polish), *Biuletyn* of the Zydowski Instytut Historyczny in Warsaw, XXXVII (1961), 3–34; XXXVIII (1961), 39–68; and the telling anecdotes reported by Ezekiel Kotik in *Maine Zikhroines* (My Reminiscences), 2 vols., Berlin, 1922, I, 271. Some Jews, both in Russia and abroad, were cognizant of the perils of the Jewish position between the Polish "rebels" and the Russian oppressors. In his appeal to Alexander II in behalf of certain Jewish prisoners in Minsk, Adolphe Crémieux, president of the then newly founded Alliance Israélite Universelle, observed that if the Jews "remain Russian patriots they will suffer at the hands of the [Polish] revolutionaries, if they side with the rebels they will be regarded as enemies of Russia, and if they remain neutral they will become the victims of both sides." *See* Zosa Szajkowski, "The Alliance Israélite Universelle and East-European Jewry in the '60s," *Jewish Social Studies*, IV (1942), 139–60, especially p. 149. *See also* Artur Eisenbach, "Le problème des Juifs polonais en 1861 et les projets de réforme du marquis Aleksander Wielopolski," *Acta Poloniae Historica*, XX (1969), 138–62; Eligiusz Kozłowski, *Bibliografia powstania styczniowego* (Bibliography of the January Uprising), Warsaw, 1964, especially pp. 475 f. Nos. 8,819–46; and, more generally, the comprehensive and well-documented Polish study by Stefan Kleniewicz, *Powstanie styczniowe* (The January Uprising), Warsaw, 1972.

20. Jacob Brafman, *Kniga Kahala* (The Book of the Kahal), 2d ed., 2 vols., St. Petersburg, 1875–82. With its motto taken from Friedrich Schiller's statement, "The Jews form a state within the state," this book furnished much ammunition for Jew-baiters in the following decades. It was published for the same purpose in a German trans. by Siegfried Passarge, under the title *Das Buch vom Kahal*, 2 vols., Leipzig, 1928. On the modicum of its trustworthiness, *see* Isaac Levitats, "The Authenticity of Brafman's Book of the Kahal" (Hebrew), *Zion*, III (1938), 170–78.

21. *See* the firsthand observations by Genrikh (Henry) B. Sliozberg in his "Baron G. [H.] O. Günzburg and the Legal Status of Jews" (Russian), *Perezhitoe*, II (1910), 94–115; the full-length biography cited below, Chap. 6, n. 23; and Julius Hessen's "On the Lot of Jewish Physicians in Russia" (Russian), *Evreiskaia Starina*, III (1910), 612–23.

[4]

Under Alexander III and Nicholas II

1. Much documentation on the Russian pogroms has been assembled by A. Linden (pseud. for Leo Motzkin) *et al.*, in *Die Judenpogrome in Russland*, ed. by the Zionistischer Hilfsfond in London, 2 vols., Cologne, 1910; G. Krasnii-Admoni (with the cooperation of Simon M. Dubnow), ed., *Materialy dlia istorii anti-evreiskikh pogromov v Rossii* (Materials for the History of Anti-Jewish Pogroms in Russia), 2 vols., Petrograd, 1919–23; in the three Yiddish essays by Elias Tscherikower, "New Materials about the Pogroms in Russia at the Beginning of the 1880s"; N. M. Gelber, "The Pogroms in Russia in the Light of Austrian Diplomatic Correspondence"; and I. L. Lipshitz, "The Intervention of the United States about the Pogroms in Russia in 1881–1882" in *YIVO Historishe Shriftn*, II (1937), 444–65, 466–96, 497–516. See also Mina Goldberg's dissertation, *Die Jahre 1881–1882 in der Geschichte der russischen Juden*, Berlin, 1934.

2. Alexander III's marginal notations on these government reports have been published from archival sources after the Revolution by R. M. Kantor in his "Alexander III on the Anti-Jewish Pogroms of 1881–83" (Russian), *Evreiskaia Letopis*, I (1923), 149–58.

3. Constantin Pobedonostsev, *L'Autocratie russe. Mémoires politiques, correspondance officielle et documents inédits (1881–1894)*, Paris, 1927, pp. 61 f.; Nadezhda Jaffe, "Molodetskii's Assault on the Russian Dictator Count M. Loris-Melikov in 1880: From New Sources" (Yiddish), *Di Zukunft*, XLIII (1938), 89–93; Nikolai P. Ignatev's memorandum of August 22, 1881, more fully cited, in a somewhat different English trans., in Dubnow's *History*, II, 271 f. On Goldenberg, see his "Confession," published in Russian by R. Kantor in *Krasnii Arkhiv*, XXX (1928), 117–83; and other sources cited by Elias Tcherikower in his "Jews—Revolutionaries in Russia in the 1860s and 1870s" (Yiddish), *YIVO Historishe Shriftn*, III (1939), 145 ff., 815 f. See also ibid., pp. 142 ff. At the same time, it must be noted that Pobedonostsev was not a racist. True, when it suited him, he could use a racialist argument, as when he opposed the appointment of Koniard to the post of governor of Kishinev. He stressed "the inconvenience of appointing a descendant of a family of Jewish bankers to serve as governor of a Jewish district." On the other hand, he made good use of a convert, J. F. Tsion (Élie Cyon), a former professor of physiology in St. Petersburg who was living in Paris, in explaining his reactionary policies to the West-European public and in paving the way for the Franco-Russian alliance. See Cyon's *Histoire de l'entente franco-russe*, 3rd ed., Paris, 1895; other sources cited in my *Modern Nationalism and Religion*, New York, 1947 (or subsequent reprints), pp. 176 ff. ("Integral Orthodoxy"), 324 ff.; Gerhard Simon, *Konstantin Petrović Pobedonoscev und die Kirchenpolitik des Heiligen Sinod 1880–1905*, Göttingen, 1969 (Kirche im Osten. Monographienreihe, VII); and Robert F. Byrnes's *Pobedonostsev: His Life and Thought*, Bloomington, Indiana, 1968.

4. Wickham Hofman's report to the Department of State of April 29, 1882, in *Papers Relating to the Foreign Relations of the United States*, 1882, p. 452. The figure of 5,000,000 Jews at that time was exaggerated. See below, Chap. 5. Characteristically, a well-substantiated rumor had it that Ignatev himself delayed the issuance of the May Laws until he made certain that the Jewish managers of his estates in the Kiev province had signed new twelve-year contracts and thus became exempt from the operation of these laws. See Harold Frederic, *The New Exodus: a Study of Israel in Russia*, London, 1892, p. 130. Ignatev's devious policies, his attempt to use the Jewish leaders for his pur-

poses, and his expectation to receive a *douceur* of 2,000,000 rubles are analyzed in Benzion Dinur's Hebrew essay, "Ignatiev's 'Projects for the Solution of the Jewish Question' and the Meetings of Representatives of the Jewish Communities in St. Petersburg in 1881–82" *Heawar*, X (1963), 5–82; and in Vladimir Grossmann's "On Count Ignatiev and the Temporary Rules" (Hebrew), *ibid.*, I (1917), 67–86. Although issued as "temporary" enactments, intended to meet an immediate emergency, the May Laws remained as long-term statutory provisions and in 1891 were extended to the Kingdom of Poland. The effects of the ensuing geographic and economic dislocations not only proved disastrous for the Jews but adversely affected also the Russian economy as a whole. *See* below, n. 12, and Chap. 6 toward the end.

5. Countess Mariia E. Kleinmichel, *Memories of a Shipwrecked World*, English trans. by Vivian le Grand, London, 1923, pp. 129 f. Although doubtless atypical, the incident with the countess illustrated the extent to which lawyers could be exposed to the arbitrary treatment by Russian officials. Nonetheless, beginning with the judicial reform of 1864, Jews entered the legal profession in increasing numbers. *See* Baruch Genkin's brief sketch, "Jews as Practitioners of Law in Tsarist Russia" (Hebrew), *Heawar*, III (1951), 111–15; and Samuel Kucherov, "Jews in the Russian Bar," in Jacob Frumkin *et al.*, eds. *Russian Jewry (1860–1917)*, pp. 219–52. *See* below, n. 20. A survey of Russian Jewry's disabilities in the 1890s was offered by the Belgian professor, Leo Errera, in *The Russian Jews: Extermination or Emancipation?* With a Prefatory Note by Theodor Mommsen. Trans. from the French by Bella Löwy, London, 1894. Of course, Errera advocated complete emancipation in preference to its sole alternative: extermination. A more detailed legal analysis of the conditions in the following decade is found in Genrikh (Henry) B. Sliozberg's *Pravovoe i ekonomicheskoe polozhenie Evreev v Rossii* (The Legal and Economic Status of the Jews in Russia: From Materials on the Jewish Question), St. Petersburg, 1907. *See also* below, n. 11.

6. The protracted Jewish struggle to salvage the Moscow synagogue in 1891–1906 is described by A. S. Katsnelson in his "From the Martyrdom of the Moscow Community" (Russian), *Evreiskaia Starina*, I (1909), 175–88. Regrettably, the precise number of Jews forced to leave Moscow in 1891 has never been ascertained. Since merchants of the first guild, professionals, and honorably discharged soldiers were not affected by the decree of expulsion, the number of exiles was subject to vastly divergent estimates. A single person like the British ambassador, Sir Robert Morrier, could inform his government that the imperial order was going to affect, "on good Jewish authority, 14,000 heads of families," and yet not long thereafter estimate that the total number of victims amounted to only 1,500 persons. Perhaps the smaller figure was but an erroneous restatement of the 15,000 Jewish sufferers reported to Morrier by the British consul in Moscow. On the other hand, Samuel Wermel, himself an eyewitness, later ventured to assume that, because between the official census of 1871 and that of 1882 the Jewish population was said to have increased from 5,314 to 15,085, it trebled again to some 45,000 souls in the following nine years, to drop back to 8,095 persons according to the census of 1897—clearly an unwarranted assumption. Remarkably, the immediate impact of this event on the Russian Jews and non-Jews was less strong than it turned out to be in retrospect a few years later.

This was probably the result of the stringent Russian press censorship which prevented the facts from becoming widely known in the country. When Wermel attempted to enlist Vladimir Korolenko's assistance in having his article on the subject published in a general newspaper, he received the eminent author's acute reply: "If it were possible to write about such events, they would never have taken place. The same power which allows these atrocities to happen, will also prevent them from being [publicly] criticized." *See* the series of articles published by Wermel *et al.* on the eightieth anniversary of the Moscow expulsion in *Heawar* (Hebrew), XVIII (1971), 3–68, especially pp. 5, 60–62.

7. Benjamin Harrison's Third Annual Message to Congress of December 9, 1891, in James A. Richardson's *A Compilation of the Messages and Papers of the Presidents, 1789–1908*, 11 vols., Washington, D. C., 1909, IX, 188; Dubnow, *History*, II, 408 ff.; III, 10.

8. Pobedonostsev's letter to Alexander III of February 11, 1888, in *L'Autocratie russe*, p. 523; Arnold White, "Jewish Colonization and the Russian Persecution," *New Review*, V (1891), 97–105. Hirsch himself explained, in part, his personal motivations in "My Views of Philanthropy," reprinted from the *North-American Review* of July, 1891, in Samuel Joseph's *History of the Baron de Hirsch Fund*, Philadelphia, 1935, pp. 275–77.

9. D. Zaslavskii, "Jews in Russian Literature" (Russian), *Evreiskaia Letopis*, I (1923), 59–86; Joshua Kunitz, *Russian Literature and the Jew: a Sociological Inquiry into the Nature and Origin of Literary Patterns*, New York, 1929 (Diss. Columbia University); Feivel Goetz's analysis of *Der Philosoph W. Solowioff und das Judentum*, Riga, 1927; F. Häusler, "V. G. Korolenkos Kampf gegen den Antisemitismus," *Wissenschaftliche Zeitschrift der Martin-Luther-Universität*, X (1961), 237–48; M. Comitet, "V. G. Korolenko et la question juive en Russie," *Cahiers du monde russe et soviétique*, X (1968), 228–56; Yitzhak Maor, "Turgenev and the Pogroms of the 1880s" (Hebrew), *Heawar*, II (1918), 105–11; Henri Granjard, *Ivan Turguénev et les courants politiques et sociaux de son temps*, Dissertation Paris, 1954 (*Bibliothèque russe* of the Institut des Études Slaves, XXVI); Hans Kohn, "Dostoyevsky's Nationalism," *Journal of the History of Ideas*, VI (1945), 385–414, especially p. 412, n. 27; R. Sliwowski, "Jewish Motifs in Chekhov's Creative Writings" (Polish), *Biuletyn* of the Żydowski Instytut Historyczny, nos. 47–48 (1963), 79–92; Shlomoh Breiman's recent Hebrew review of "The Image of the Jew in the Russian Literature of the Nineteenth Century," *Heawar*, XVIII (1972), 135–73; and below, Chap. 9, n. 9. One must admit, however, that Soloviev, though one of the outstanding religious philosophers of the generation, was not typical of the thinking of even a substantial minority in the Russian Church. After reviewing the three stages in the evolution of the master's religious thought, Robert Haardt has shown that Soloviev had "at first tried to understand Israel. Once he had perceived its meaning, his heart beat strongly for this people which, under the viewpoint of eternity, appeared to him identical with the Church. For this reason even on his deathbed he prayed in Hebrew for the people of Israel." *See* Haardt, "Vladimir Solovjevs Stellung zum Judentum," *Judaica*, X (1954), 1–30. Even he, however, never relinquished the hope that the Jews would ultimately see the light and join Christianity, at least in the final, truly universal form envisaged by him for the end of days. His general attitude was best defined by

his declaration, "I am just as far from Judeophobia as I am from Judeophilia." Cited, together with other excerpts in an English trans. in Paul Berline's review of "Russian Religious Philosophers and the Jews (Soloviev, Berdyaev, Bulgakov, Struve, Rozanov and Fedotov)," *Jewish Social Studies*, IX (1947), 271–318, especially pp. 273 ff.; and below, n. 16.

10. Alexander Kornilov, *Modern Russian History*, 2 vols., New York, 1917, II, 278.

11. Dubnow's *History*, III, 26 f.; above, n. 5. When after the Revolution of 1905 there was some relaxation in practice and a new law of 1909 raised the quota to 5 to 15 percent, another ukase of 1911 extended the *numerus clausus* to "externs," thus shutting an opening which had enabled many Jews to secure degrees by examinations without attending classes. *Ibid.*, pp. 158 f.; and below, Chap. 8, n. 8. It is doubly remarkable, therefore, that human ingenuity, abetted by bureaucratic corruption or study abroad, enabled Russian Jewry in the decades preceding World War I to include an ever-growing and highly educated professional class. Jews now formed a large segment of that "outwardly active element of the Russian intelligentsia" which Georg Brandes observed during his three-month-long visit in 1887. He characterized it as "a world by itself, with its own moral qualities, precarious at times, but always of more value than the mercantile compound, which in other parts of Europe goes under the name of moral." *See* his *Impressions of Russia*, trans. by Samuel C. Eastman and reprinted from the 1889 ed. with an Introduction by Richard Pipes, New York, 1966, p. 40. *See also* Pipes's ed. of essays analyzing *The Russian Intelligentsia* (New York, 1961) in both the tsarist and Soviet periods.

12. N. Chmerkine (Shmerkin), *Les Conséquences de l'antisémitisme en Russie*, with a Foreword by M. G. de Molinari, Paris, 1897; Martin Philippson, *Neueste Geschichte des jüdischen Volkes*, 3 vols., Frankfurt, 1907–11, III, 172 ff.

13. Herman Bernstein, *The Truth about "The Protocols of Zion": a Complete Exposure*, New York, 1935, pp. 36 f. *See also* V. L. Burtsev, *Protokoly sionskikh mudretsov* (The Protocols of the Elders of Zion), Paris, 1938; John Shelton Curtis, *An Appraisal of the Protocols of Zion*, New York, 1942; and, more generally, Mark Vishniak, "Antisemitism in Tsarist Russia: a Study in Government-Fostered Antisemitism" in Koppel S. Pinson, ed., *Essays on Antisemitism*, 2d ed., New York, 1946, pp. 121–44. One of the apologists for Nicholas II's regime went so far as to attribute the authorship of the *Protocols* to the renowned Hebrew essayist Asher Zvi Ginzberg (Ahad Ha-Am). *See* A. Netchvolodow, *L'Empereur Nicolas II et les Juifs. Essais sur la Révolution russe dans ses rapports avec l'activité universelle du Judaïsme contemporain*, trans. from the Russian by I. M. Narischkina, Paris, 1924, p. 377.

14. Michael Davitt, *Within the Pale: the True Story of Anti-Semitic Persecution in Russia*, New York, 1903, p. 126; *Memoirs of a Russian Governor, Prince Serge Dmitriyevich Urussov*, ed. and trans. into English by Herman Rosenthal, New York, 1908, especially pp. 42 ff., 142 ff. *See also* above, n. 1. On the reaction in other countries, *see* especially Cyrus Adler, *The Voice of America on Kishineff*, Philadelphia, 1903; and Taylor Stults's more recent archival study of "Roosevelt, Russian Persecutions of Jews, and American Public Opinion," *Jewish Social Studies*, XXXIII (1971), 13–22, mentioning, among other matters, that while John

Hay, the Secretary of State, contributed five hundred dollars to the relief of the Kishinev victims, the President himself was dissuaded from following that example (p. 14).

15. Alexander B. Tager, *The Decay of Czarism: the Beiliss Trial,* Philadelphia, 1935, pp. 10 f.; Urussov, *Memoirs,* p. 55.

16. Maxim Gorki, "Kishineff Mob Were Led by Men of Cultivated Society" in the English trans. by William Curtis Stiles in his *Out of Kishineff: the Duty of the American People to the Russian Jew,* New York [1903], pp. 276 ff. *See also* Leo Tolstoy's comment, *ibid.,* pp. 274 f.; and below, n. 19. Of considerable interest also is the material brought to light by the subsequent trial in Gomel. *See* B. A. Kreverom, comp., *Gomelskii protsess* (The Trial of Gomel: a Detailed Account), St. Petersburg, 1907.

17. Simeon Samuel Frug, "The Resurrection," in the English trans. by Maurice Samuel in Edmond Fleg, *The Jewish Anthology,* New York, 1925, pp. 387 f. It may be noted that, in order to live in St. Petersburg, Frug had to register with the police as a valet to one of the local attorneys.

18. *Pravo,* 1905, No. 19, here cited, with some variations, from the English trans. by L. Greenberg in *The Jews in Russia,* II, 114. *See also* L. Rubinov, "The Jewish Self-Defense in Southern Russia during the First Revolution" (Yiddish), *Fun Nuenten Ovar* (From the Recent Past), I (1938), 322–32; and on the Jewish part in the revolution, S. Dimanshtain, *Di revolutsionere bavegung ba yidishe masn in di revolutsie fun 1905 yor* (The Revolutionary Movement among the Jewish Masses in 1905), Moscow, 1929. *See also,* more generally, Ludwik Bazylow's comprehensive study, *Polityka wewnętrzna caratu i ruchy społeczne w Rossji na początku XX wieku* (Tsarism's Internal Policies and the Social Movements in Russia at the Beginning of the Twentieth Century), Warsaw, 1966; and Gottfried Schramm's critical observations in his review of that work in the *Jahrbücher für Geschichte Osteuropas,* XVIII (1970), 601–10.

19. These developments are well summarized from the Stenographic Protocols of the Duma and the contemporary Russo-Jewish press by Sidney S. Harcave in "The Jewish Question in the First Russian Duma," *Jewish Social Studies,* VI (1944), 155–76. The report concerning the Bialystok pogrom, the Duma debates, and resolution are reproduced here from an English trans. in the *American Jewish Year Book,* 5667 (1906–1907), pp. 70–89. *See also* Jakob Jaffé's dissertation, *Ursachen und Verlauf der Juden-Pogrome in Russland im Oktober 1905,* Bern, 1916, which includes a number of references to expressions of non-Jewish leaders (pp. 69 ff.). On Sergei D. Urussov, who as a high Russian official was intimately acquainted with the anti-Semitic operations of the various police organs, *see* Israel Berman, "Plehve's Opponent, Prince Urussov and the Jews" (Hebrew), *Heawar,* V (1957), 74–84.

20. Nicholas' statement reported by the then finance minister Vladimir N. Kokovtsov in his *Memoirs,* trans. into English by Laura Matveev and ed. by H. H. Fischer under the title *Out of My Past: Memoirs of Count Kokovtsov,* Stanford, California, 1935 (Hoover War Library Publications, VI), p. 167; A. B. Tager, *The Decay of Czarism,* p. 14. The Third and Fourth Dumas not only had a strong representation of the nobles' class bent upon the preservation of its privileged status, but also embraced a considerable number of reactionary Russian Orthodox priests. While even in the short-lived Second Duma—altogether it lasted some three and a half months in 1907—8 of the 13 ecclesiastical deputies belonged to the Opposition, the 45 clerical members of the Third Duma and the 46 of the Fourth Duma all belonged to the Right. See M. T. Florinsky, *Russia*, II, 1200 n. 11; and Warren B. Walsh's twin essays, "The Composition of the Dumas," *Russian Review*, VIII (1949), 111–16; and "Political Parties in the Russian Dumas," *Journal of Modern History*, XXII (1950), 144–50. Most of these men were staunch defenders of the established order and viewed any move toward equality of rights of "infidels," particularly Jews, with a jaundiced eye. On his part, Nicholas II personally even more undeviatingly tried to preserve the existing class structure and to encourage the progressive Russification of the ethnic minorities. This tendency is quite manifest in both the published and unpublished documents concerning his reign. *See*, for instance, Vladimir Lazarevsky's *Archives secrètes de l'Empereur Nicholas II*, Paris, 1928. On his anti-Jewish policies and other aspects of Jewish life before World War I, *see*, in addition to Dubnow's *History*, Jacob Frumkin *et al.*, *Kniga o russkom evreistve*, Vol. I, trans. into English by Mirra Ginsburg under the title, *Russian Jewry (1860–1917)*, New York, 1966. *See* below, n. 23; and, on the continuation in Vol. II, *see* below, Chap. 11, n. 1.

21. Tager, *The Decay*, pp. 20, 58; A. Chernovskii, *Soiuz russkago naroda* (Union of the Russian People: According to the Materials of the Extraordinary Investigating Commission of the Provisional Government of 1917), Moscow, 1929, *passim*.

22. Ivan Sergeevich Aksakov, "Judaism as a World-Wide Phenomenon" (Russian), reprinted in his *Polnoe sobranie sochinenii* (Complete Collection of Works), 7 vols., Moscow, 1886–87, III, 725–35 (also his attacks on the Alliance Israélite, *ibid.*, pp. 819 ff., 827 ff., 843 ff.); Lamsdorf's memorandum trans. (from the Russian text published in the Secret Documents issued by the Soviet Commission of Foreign Affairs, Vol. VI) by Lucien Wolf in his *Notes on the Diplomatic History of the Jewish Question*, London, 1919, pp. 57–62. On the earlier activities of the Alliance in Russia and Poland and its attitude toward the Russian government, *see* Zosa Szajkowski. "The Alliance Israélite Universelle and East-European Jewry in the '60s," *Jewish Social Studies*, IV (1942), 139 ff., 148 ff.

It was ironical that Aksakov, the journalist who gave wide publicity to the old myth of the Jewish drive for world domination—as well as to his conviction of the alleged incompatibility of Judaism with Russian culture—also was one of the leading Panslavists who viewed the unification of all Slavs under Russian leadership as his country's overriding historic mission. This was to be a first step toward the unification of all humanity under the aegis of Russia and its Church. He and his fellow Slavophiles "thus ascribed to their nation a messianic role which invested Russia's imperial expansion with qualities redemptive of mankind at large." It is small wonder, then, that both Alexander III and Pobedonostsev deeply mourned Aksakov's demise in 1886. *See* my *Modern Nationalism and Religion*, pp. 189 ff. However, not all Panslavists were of one mind on the Jewish question. In fact, from the 1870s on, some young Jews, too, were deeply impressed by the Slavophile ideology. *See*, for instance, A. E. Kaufman, "The

Jews in the Russo-Turkish War of 1877. On the Basis of Contemporary Sources and Personal Reminiscences" (Russian), *Evreiskaia Starina*, VIII (1915), 57–72, 176–82. *See also*, more generally, F. Fadman, *Seventy Years of Panslavism in Russia. Karazin to Danilevskii, 1800–1870*, Georgetown, 1962. Hence, a careful monograph on the various aspects of Panslavist-Jewish relations would be highly welcome. As a curiosity, we may mention that in contrast to the Panslavism of the tsarist era and its more recent secularized communist variant in Soviet imperialism, the query, "Are the Russians Slavs?" was answered in the negative by Henryk Paszkiewicz in a pertinent essay in *Antimurale*, XIV (1970), 59–84.

23. *See* the amply documented story of the Beilis affair in A. B. Tager, *The Decay of Czarism*. Interesting sidelights are also thrown by the reminiscences of the chief defense counsel Oscar O. Gruzenberg in his *Vchera* (Yesterday), Paris, 1938. Of more general interest are the essays, in part based upon personal reminiscences, on various aspects of Russian Jewish life between 1860 and 1917, published by the Union of Russian Jews in New York under the title *Kniga o russkom evreistve* (Book on Russian Jewry), New York, 1960, with the comments thereon by Elias Hurwicz in his "Zur Psychologie und Problematik des russischen Judentums," *Zeitschrift für Politik*, VIII (1961), 256–70. *See also* E. Lifshitz, "Repercussions of the Beilis Trial in the United States" (Hebrew), *Zion*, XXVIII (1963), 206–22; Zosa Szajkowski, "The Impact of the Beilis Case on Central and Western Europe," *Proceedings of the American Academy for Jewish Research*, XXXI (1963), 197–218; the more recent review of the trial by Maurice Samuel in his *Blood Accusation: The Strange History of the Beilis Case*, Philadelphia, 1966; and more generally, S. Kucherov's observations on *Courts, Lawyers and Trials under the Last Three Tsars*, New York, 1953.

[5]

Population and Migrations

1. The results of the 1897 census are comprehensively analyzed in the *Sbornik materialov ob ekonomicheskom polozhenii Evreev v Rossii* (Collection of Materials relating to the Economic Conditions of the Jews in Russia), published by the Jewish Colonization Association, 2 vols., St. Petersburg, 1904; and briefly summarized by J. G. Lipman and Herman Rosenthal in "Russia: Census Statistics," *Jewish Encyclopedia*, X, 529–34. The figures differ slightly in Jacob Lestchinsky, *Dos yidishe folk in tsifern* (The Jewish People in Numbers), Berlin, 1922, whose pioneering effort in this field, though subject to some corrections in detail, still offers the most acceptable data, some of which are utilized in this chapter.

2. The data for European Russia's population, quite unreliable as they appear to be, are cited here from Ludwig Elster's computations in his section of the article "Bevölkerungswesen, III" in the *Handwörterbuch der Staatswissenschaften*, 4th ed., Vol. II, Jena, 1924, pp. 688 f. Somewhat different estimates are given by Paul N. Miliukov and Alexander Kornilov. *See* the latter's *Modern Russian History*, II, 123 ff. On the Jewish population and its growth in the nineteenth century, *see also* the additional data supplied by Benzion Dinur in "The Historical

Image of Russian Jewry and Problems Connected with Its Study" (Hebrew), *Zion*, XXII (1957), 93–118 (with an English summary, pp. ii–iv), especially pp. 94 ff. We must never forget, however, that all Russian population data before the 1890s have to be handled with much caution. This is particularly true of the figures relating to religious minorities. *See*, for instance, H. Virinnis, "Russische Bevölkerungszahlen zu Ende des 18. Jahrhunderts nach dem Tabellenwerk von Johann Friedrich Storch, Riga, 1795," *Geographische Zeitschrift*, L (1944), 124–28; J. J. Zatko, "The Catholic Church and the Russian Statistics, 1804–1917," *Polish Review*, V (1960), 35–52; and Kazyz Pakištas, "Earliest Statistics of Nationalities and Religions in the Territories of Old Lithuania, 1861," *Commentationes Balticae*, IV–V (1958), 169–211.

3. Arnold White in *New Review*, V, 98; Robert Lyall, *Travels in Russia, the Krimea, the Caucasus and Georgia*, 2 vols., London, 1825, I, 162; and more generally, E. Lifshitz, "English Travelers at the Beginning of the Nineteenth Century on East European Jews" (Yiddish), *Yivo Bleter*, XVI (1940), 59–66.

4. These problems were discussed also outside Russia as early as 1887. In a statistically documented essay, "Les Juifs dans le service militaire," included in his collection *Les Juifs de Russie: Recueil d'articles et d'études sur leur situation légale, sociale et économique*, Paris, 1891, pp. 321 ff., an anonymous author proved that Jews were drafted beyond their ratio in the population. *See also ibid.*, pp. 346 ff.; and other passages listed in the Index, *s.v.* Service militaire. It may be noted that, after the Russo-Japanese War and the Revolution of 1905, a reactionary Vilna deputy to the Third Duma suggested the complete elimination of Jews from the armed services. *See* the counterarguments offered by the Jewish deputy, Leonid N. Nisselovich (Nisselowitsch), trans. into German under the title, *Die Judenfrage in Russland*, Berlin, 1909, pp. 15 ff.

5. Robert Pinkerton, *Russia, or, Miscellaneous Observations on the Past and Present State of that Country and Its Inhabitants. Compiled from Notes Made on the Spot . . .* , London, 1833, pp. 88, 101 f.; J. de le Roi, "Judentaufen im 19. Jahrhundert. Ein statistischer Versuch," *Nathanael*, XV (1899), 65–118. A major incentive to conversion consisted in its opening the gate to appointment to public office, from which professing Jews were barred. A bureaucratic career appeared at times to be not only lucrative, but also highly desirable socially. *See* the data analyzed by Erik Amberger in his "Behördendienst und sozialer Aufstieg in Russland um 1900," *Jahrbücher für Geschichte Osteuropas*, XVIII (1970), 127–34; and Daniel Chwolson's witty remark quoted below, Chap. 9, n. 5.

6. The figures here cited follow J. Lestchinsky's computations. *See* above, n. 1. Needless to say that this astounding growth of the Odessa community was part of the meteoric rise of the city which, founded in 1784, by 1863 had become the third largest city in Russia outside Congress Poland. *See* Patricia Herlihy, "Odessa: Staple Trade and Urbanization in New Russia," *Jahrbücher für Geschichte Osteuropas*, XXI (1973), 184–95. It may be noted that Odessa Jewry's rapid expansion attracted the attention of its distant American coreligionists as early as 1857. *See* the *Jewish Messenger*, I (New York, 1857), 38. Even more startling was the fact that in a great many lesser towns Jews formed the majority of the population. In the provinces of Grodno and Kaunas (Kovno) nearly two-thirds of all Jews resided in municipalities in which they outnumbered all other ethnic groups. *See* the detailed computations of H. (G.) Aleksandrov in "The

Jewish Population in the Cities and Hamlets of White Russia" (Yiddish), *Zeitshrift*, II–III (Minsk, 1928), 307–378; and Dinur in *Zion*, XXII, 96 f.

7. *See* above, Chap. 3, n. 15. *See also* Zosa Szajkowski, "The Struggle for Jewish Emancipation in Algeria after the French Occupation," reproduced in his *Jews and the French Revolutions of 1789, 1830 and 1848*, New York, 1970, pp. 1119–32, especially p. 1123 n. 7.

8. Mary Antin, *From Plotzk to Boston*. With a Foreword by Israel Zangwill, Boston, 1899, pp. 12 f.; Leo Shpall, "A List of Selected Items of American Interest in the Russian-Jewish Press, 1860–1932," *Publications of the American Jewish Historical Society*, XXXVIII (1948–49), 239–48, 305–16; XXXIX (1949–50), 87–113.

9. *See* the pertinent documentation in Cyrus Adler and Aaron M. Margalith, *With Firmness in the Right: American Diplomatic Action Affecting Jews, 1840–1945*. New York, 1946, pp. 281 ff.; and the analyses by Louis Marshall (the main architect of the abrogation) and Max J. Kohler in the "American Supplementary Chapters" appended to Luigi Luzzati's *God in Freedom: Studies in the Relations between Church and State*, New York, 1930, pp. 705 ff., 714 ff. *See also* Naomi W. Cohen, "The Abrogation of the Russo-American Treaty of 1832," *Jewish Social Studies*, XXV (1963), 3–41; *idem*, *Not Free to Desist: the American Jewish Committee, 1906–1966*, with an Introduction by Salo W. Baron, Philadelphia, 1972, pp. 37 ff., 54 ff.; Nathan Fainberg's juridical analysis of "A Controversy with Czarist Russia Concerning the Discrimination against Jews of Foreign Nationality" (Hebrew), *Zion*, XXXIII (1968), 77–95 (with an English summary, pp. v–vi). The abrogation of the commercial treaty of 1832 was the culminating episode in the diplomatic exchanges between the United States and Russia concerning the tsarist discrimination against Jews. An early, very timid approach in this area, provoked by petitions from American Jewish organizations to the State Department, is described with ample documentation in the two complementary essays by Evelyn Levow Greenberg in "An 1869 Petition in Behalf of Russian Jews," *American Jewish Historical Quarterly*, LIV (1964–65), 278–95; and by Eliyahu Feldman in his "First Attempt at American Intervention on Behalf of the Russian Jews, 1869–70" (Hebrew), *Zion*, XXX (1965), 206–23, with an English summary, pp. iii–iv. *See also* Zosa Szajkowski, "The European Aspects of the American-Russian Passport Question," *Publications of the American Jewish Historical Society*, XLVI (1956–57), 86–100.

10. Cited by Zosa Szajkowski in his "How the Mass Migration to America Began," *Jewish Social Studies*, IV (1942), 309 n. 93. *See also* Esther L. Panitz, "The Polarity of American Jewish Attitudes towards Immigration (1870–1891): a Chapter in American Socio-Economic History," *American Jewish Historical Quarterly*, LIII (1963–64), 99–130.

11. Cited by S. M. Dubnow in his *History*, II, 304 ff. This resolution was partially inspired by the minister of the interior Nikolai Ignatev who, in a conversation with Poliakov, had declared that promotion of Jewish emigration was tantamount to "incitement to sedition," because "emigration does not exist for Russian citizens."

12. *See* the data culled from the contemporary reports by Gregory Aronson in his "On the History of the Conference in Kaunas in 1869" (Yiddish), in *Lite*

Notes

(Lithuania), ed. by Mendel Sudarsky *et al.*, Vol. I, New York, 1951, cols. 209–218: and below, Chap. 6. It was, therefore, not until December 1907, at the height of the migratory movement, that a number of activist spokesmen organized in St. Petersburg a "Society to Regulate Jewish Emigration" which, however, exerted but little influence on the great, if rather chaotic, movement. *See* the statutes of that society, published from a manuscript extant in New York by Leo Shpall in "The Society to Regulate Jewish Emigration from Russia" (Yiddish), *Yivo Bleter*, XLII (1962), 289–93; and more generally, my *Steeled by Adversity*, pp. 274 ff., 628 ff. nn. 10 ff. and the literature listed there.

13. These figures follow the computations by Samuel Joseph in his *Jewish Immigration to the United States from 1881 to 1910*, New York, 1914 (Columbia University, Studies in History, LIX), p. 164 Tables xii–xiii. *See also* Mark Wischnitzer, *To Dwell in Safety: the Story of Jewish Migrations since 1800*, Philadelphia, 1948, especially pp. 288 ff. and the additional bibliography listed there.

14. Lloyd P. Gartner, *The Jewish Immigrant in England, 1870–1914*, new ed., London, 1973.

15. *See* above Chap. 4, n. 8.

[6]
Economic Transformations

1. Ivan S. Blioch, *Sravnenie materialnago i nravstvennago blagosostoiania* (A Comparison of the Material and Moral Well-Being of the Western, Greater Russian and By-Vistula [Polish] Provinces), 5 vols., St. Petersburg, 1901 (analyzed by A. Subbotin in *Evreiskaia Biblioteka*, X [1903], 63–123); and other sources listed by Louis Greenberg in *The Jews in Russia*, I, 170 f. *See also* the memorandum submitted in 1894 by Sergei Y. Witte and published by the editor (Simon M. Dubnow) in "The Jewish Question or the Introduction of the Alcohol Monopoly" (Russian), *Evreiskaia Starina*, VIII (1915), 405–10. Ivan Ivanovich Funduklei, who as civil governor of the Kiev province in 1839–52 contributed much to the statistical investigation of the area under his jurisdiction, made a number of other pertinent observations on Jewish life there that ran counter to the general assumptions of Nicholas I's administration. *See* the *Statisticheskoe opisanie Kievskoi gubernii* (A Statistical Description of the Kievan Province), ed. under Funduklei's sponsorship by one of the provincial officials, Dimitri Petrovich Shuravskii, 3 vols., Kiev, 1852, especially I, 257, 434, 522; III, 256, 369, 507. These passages are excerpted in a German trans. by August Scholz in *Die Juden in Russland. Urkunden und Zeugnisse russischer Behörden und Autoritäten*, Berlin, 1900, pp. 88 ff.

2. *See* above, Chap. 2. Among the later eloquent exponents of a Jewish return to the soil was the influential Hebrew writer Isaac Baer Levinsohn, especially in his *Te'udah be-Yisrael* (Admonition unto Israel), Vilna, 1828 (written in 1823), which, partly for this reason, received a government prize of one thousand rubles.

3. The fullest information on Jewish agricultural colonization in tsarist

Russia and to a lesser extent on Jewish individual farming is supplied by V. N. Nikitin in his *Evrei zemledeltsy* (Jewish Farmers, 1807–1887), St. Petersburg, 1887; and by Saul Y. Borovoi, *Evreiskaia zemledelcheskaia kolonizatsiia v staroi Rossii* (Jewish Agricultural Colonization in Old Russia: Politics, Ideology, Economics, Daily Life. From Archival Sources), Moscow, 1928. *See also* below, n. 5.

4. It should be noted that Benckendorff was not personally a Jew-baiter. On more than one occasion he is said to have calmed down the tsar's outbursts against Jews and Poles. *See* Sidney Monas, *The Third Section: Police and Society under Nicholas I*, Cambridge, Mass., 1961, p. 92. Curiously, some thirty years after the suspension of the Jewish agricultural colonization in Siberia, a Russian author, Sergei Vasilevich Maksimov, extolled the Jewish *commercial* contributions to the economy of both western and eastern Siberia. He concluded: "For Siberia the Jew is both needed and useful. Siberia offers him a vast field of endeavor." *See* Maksimov, "The Unfortunate: a Description of the Life of Exiles" (Russian), *Vestnik Evropy*, 1868, No. 9, pp. 162–63. On the other hand, later on I. Neiman reminisced about "How the [Government] Regulations Bound the Siberian Jews to the Cities: From Personal Experiences" (Russian), *Evreiskaia Starina*, VIII (1916), 381–85. *See also*, more generally, Yulii Ostrovskii, *Sibirskiie Evrei* (Siberian Jews), 1911.

5. *See* J. M. Isler, *Rückkehr der Juden zur Landwirtschaft. Beitrag zur Geschichte der landwirtschaftlichen Kolonisation der Juden in verschiedenen Ländern*, Frankfurt, 1929, pp. 14 ff.

6. J. B. Weber and W. Kempter, *Report of the Commissioners of Immigration upon the Causes which Incite Immigration to the United States*, Washington, D. C., 1892, pp. 34 ff. This section relating to Russian Jewry was also published in a French trans. entitled *La situation des Juifs en Russie*, n. p., n. d.

7. *See* the "Official Correspondence on the Discontinuation of the Jewish Colonization in Neo-Russian Territories (1862)," published with his comments by I. Galant (Russian), *Evreiskaia Starina*, V (1912), 330–34. On the Jewish colonization movement in the Kingdom of Poland, to which we could but briefly allude here, *see* Jacob Shatzky, "Contributions to the History of Jewish Colonization in the Kingdom of Poland" (Yiddish), *Yivo Bleter*, VI (1934), 209–32. Outside the colonies, too, Jews in the Pale worked on land in increasing numbers. This is also evident from the occupational statistics in the Lithuanian provinces of Kaunas, Vilna, as well as in Suwalki. According to the (probably underestimated) ratios given in 1897, 5.5, 6, and 9.2 percent of the local Jews lived from agriculture, cultivating the soil in areas amounting to between 60,000 and 100,000 acres in each province. In Suwalki (which at that time belonged to Congress Poland), where the legal situation was more favorable, a number of Jewish landlords owned between them almost 15 percent of the area belonging to the large estates. *See* Jacob Rassein, "Agriculture and Gardening among Lithuanian Jews" (Yiddish), in *Lite*, ed. by M. Sudarsky *et al.*, I, 997–1010.

8. Tisserand's report, reproduced in the Jewish Colonization Association's *Rapport* for 1908.

9. In general, Jacob Lestchinsky lends excessive credence to these computations, but he himself shows that a similar listing in the province of Minsk alone in 1808 gives Jewish artisans a ratio of 19.9 percent. *See* his study in *YIVO Shriftn*

far ekonomik, I (1928), 56 f. During the decade of 1808–18 there was a general increase in the Jewish artisan class.

10. Philipp Friedmann, "Wirtschaftliche Umschichtungsprozesse und Industrialisierung in der polnischen Judenschaft 1800–1870," *Jewish Studies in Memory of George A. Kohut,* New York, 1935, p. 185. *See also* the interesting, though fragmentary data presented by S. Rambach in "The Jewish Artisans in Russia in the First Half of the Nineteenth Century" (Yiddish), *Zeitshrift,* I (Minsk, 1926), 25–30.

11. Osher Margolis, *Geshikhte fun Yidn in Rusland* (A History of the Jews in Russia: Studies and Documents), Vol. I: 1772–1881, Moscow, 1930, pp. 42 ff., 246 ff. Nos. 32–37. On the Jewish guilds as part of the communal structure, *see* Isaac Levitats, "The Jewish Association in Russia in the First Half of the Nineteenth Century" (Yiddish), *The Jewish Review,* I (1943), 83–112. *See also* Boris Brutzkus, "Die wirtschaftliche und soziale Lage der Juden in Russland vor und nach der Revolution," *Archiv für Sozialwissenschaft und Sozialpolitik,* LXI (1929), 266–321, especially pp. 275 ff.

12. E. B. Lanin, "Jewish Colonization and the Russian Persecution," *New Review,* V (1891), 113 f. *See* Vasilii Rosenthal's succinct analysis (largely based on the *Sbornik* cited above, Chap. 5, n. 1) in "Russia: Artisans," *Jewish Encyclopedia,* X (1905), 534–38, especially the illuminating breakdown of the various branches by provinces (p. 537); and S. B. Weinryb, *Neueste Wirtschaftsgeschichte der Juden in Russland und Polen,* Vol. I: 1772–1881, Breslau, 1934 (Historische Untersuchungen, XII), pp. 93 ff., 115 ff.

13. Gheron Netta, *Die Handelsbeziehungen zwischen Leipzig und Ost- und Südosteuropa bis zum Verfall der Warenmessen,* Diss. Zurich, 1920, pp. 40, 139 ff. On some conflicting data *see* Weinryb, *Neueste Wirtschaftsgeschichte,* p. 32 n. 2.

14. Count Fryderyk Florian Skarbek, *Dzieje Polski* (History of Poland), Vol. III: Congress Poland after the November Revolution, Poznań, 1877, p. 96; Friedmann in *Jewish Studies . . . Kohut,* pp. 214 ff.

15. S. B. Weinryb, *Neueste Wirtschaftsgeschichte,* p. 41.

16. Margolis, *Geshikhte fun Yidn,* I, 276 No. 63.

17. A. Yuditskii, *Yidishe burzhoazie un yidisher proletariat* (Jewish Bourgeoisie and Jewish Proletariat in the First Half of the Nineteenth Century), Kiev, 1930, pp. 103 ff. App. 8; Weinryb, *Neueste Wirtschaftsgeschichte,* I, 52 n. 1; Isaac Meier Dick, *Feigele der Maggid* (Feigele the Preacher), Vilna, 1860.

18. *See* the data assembled, from archival sources, by Yuditskii in his *Yidishe burzhoazie,* especially pp. 17 f., 35 ff., 56 f., 96 ff. App. 5. On the bureaucratic difficulties generally placed in the way of would-be industrialists, despite the government's professed desire to promote manufacture, *see* G. V. Rimlinger, "Autocracy and the Factory Order in Early Russian Industrialization," *Journal of Economic History,* XX (1960), 67–91.

19. H. Landau, "The Jewish Share in the Russo-Ukrainian Sugar Industry" (Yiddish), *YIVO Shriftn far ekonomik,* I (1928), 98–104. As early as 1868 the government recognized that Jews often were the only entrepreneurs competent to develop that industry in the western provinces and for this purpose relaxed the existing prohibition against landlords leasing their facilities to Jews. *See* the decree of January 29, 1868, reproduced by V. O. Levanda in his *Polnyi khronologi-*

cheskii sbornik, pp. 1092 f. No. 1004. *See also* P. Tchefranoff's (Chefranov's), "Industrie sucrière," included in the semiofficial publication prepared for the Paris Exposition, *La Russie à la fin du 19ᵉ siècle*, ed. by M. W. de Kovalevsky, Paris, 1900, pp. 365–74.

Jews were also active in a variety of other industrial undertakings. For example, Hayyim Frankel, originally a yeshiva student rather than a tanner or cobbler—two age-old Jewish crafts—helped transform the small town of Shauliai (Shavle), Lithuania, into a major center of Russia's leather and shoe industry. *See* the slightly colored Yiddish narration by his son Jacob Frankel (transcribed by Uriah Katzenelenbogen), "The Pioneer of the Leather Industry in Lithuania, Hayyim Frankel" in *Lite*, ed. by M. Sudarsky *et al.*, I, 941–70.

20. P. Friedmann in *Jewish Studies* . . . *Kohut*, pp. 230 ff.; H. Landau, "Jews and the Development of the Credit and Transport System in Russia" (Yiddish), *YIVO Ekonomishe Shriftn*, II (1932), 93–105.

21. Pobedonostsev, *L'Autocratie russe*, pp. 364 ff., 427 f., 473 ff., 477 ff. The project of helping build Persian railways also had important political implications. *See* Firuz Kazemzadeh, "Russian Imperialism and Persian Railways," *Harvard Slavic Studies*, IV (1957), 355–73. It may be noted that in the early stages of railroad building, in which Russia fell far behind the Western Powers, including neighboring Austria—where incidentally the Rothschilds and other Jewish financiers played a significant role—Russian Jewish builders still were a relatively minor factor. But they blossomed forth later in the century. *See*, in general, Edward Ames, "A Century of Russian Railroad Construction, 1837–1936," *The American Slavic and East European Review*, VI (1947), nos. 18–19, pp. 57–74; and J. N. Westwood, *A History of Russian Railways*, London, 1964. *See also* below, Chap. 9, n. 5.

22. H. Landau, "The Jews in the Oil Industry and Trade in Tsarist Russia" (Yiddish), *Yivo Bleter*, XIV (1939), 269–85; A. A. Fursenko, "The Paris Rothschilds and Russian Oil" (Russian), *Voprosy istorii*, 1962, No. 8, pp. 29–42; and, more generally, the twin essays by D. Mendéléeff (Mendeleev), "Industrie du naphte et des produits chimiques" and by S. Goulichambaroff (Gulichambarov), "Industrie du naphte," in M. W. de Kovalevsky's *La Russie*, pp. 333–42, 510–21.

23. A. Goloubeff (Golubev), "Etablissements de banque," in Kovalevsky, *ibid.*, pp. 804–22; Pierre Renouvin, "Finances et politique. L'emprunt russe d'avril 1906 en France," *Etudes suisses d'historie générale*, XVIII–XIX (1960–61), 507–15 (in part based on an unpublished archival study by Jean Servonnat); the correspondence cited by Cyrus Adler in his biography of *Jacob H. Schiff: His Life and Letters*, 2 vols., New York, 1929, I, 212 ff. (quoting a long memorandum by Korekiyo Takahashi, vice-governor of the Bank of Japan). Schiff's anti-Russian activities, starkly exaggerated, form a major chapter in A. Netchvolodov's anti-Semitic study, *L'Empereur Nicolas II et les Juifs*. Understandably, the subsequent Triple Entente between Russia, France, and England caused much grief to the Western Jewish patriots. *See*, for instance, Max Beloff, *Lucien Wolf and the Anglo-Russian Entente, 1907–1914*, London, 1951. On one of the leading Jewish bankers, as well as communal leaders of the period, *see* Henry (Genrikh) B. Sliozberg, *Baron Horace O. de Gunzbourg, sa vie et son oeuvre*, trans. from the Russian by Prince Vladimir Bariatinsky, Paris, 1933; and above, Chap. 3, N. 21.

Notes

In short, under Witte's fiscal administration, it appeared that Russia might follow in the footsteps of the West European countries, and through progressive industrialization and commercialization, embrace the dominant patterns of Western capitalism. However, the specific factors characterizing the empire's earlier sociopolitical evolution created numerous cross-currents and prevented a unilinear development. Some of these factors are analyzed by Samuel H. Baron in "The Weber Thesis and the Failure of Capitalist Development in 'Early Modern' Russia," *Jahrbücher für Geschichte Osteuropas*, XVIII (1970), 321–36. *See also* C. C. Aronsfeld, "Jewish Bankers and the Tsar," *Jewish Social Studies*, XXXV (1973), 87–104; and, more generally, I. M. Dijur, "Jews in the Russian Economy," in J. Frumkin *et al.*, *Russian Jewry (1860–1917)*, pp. 120–43; and T. H. von Laue, "The Witte System in Russia," *Journal of Economic History*, XIII (1953), 425–48.

24. B. Miliutin, *Ustroistvo i sostoianie evreiskiikh obshchestv v Rossii* (Structure and Status of the Jewish Communities in Russia), St. Petersburg, 1849–50, pp. 225 ff.; and other sources cited by L. Greenberg in *The Jews in Russia*, I, 160 ff.

25. *See* above, Chap. 5, n. 1; and this chapter, n. 12.

26. The inadequacy of Russo-Jewish labor statistics is well illustrated by the older, yet still valuable, study by Leonty Soloweitschik, *Un Prolétariat méconnu: Etude sur la situation sociale et économique des ouvriers juifs*, Brussels, 1898, where many more data for the Western than the Russian Jewish proletariat are given. But of some interest still are particularly the tentative statistical tables for Jewish artisans (p. 93) and for the Bialystok workers (p. 100). Once again the more detailed statistical data from Lodz, though not quite representative of the less dynamic developments in smaller centers, shed much light on both the positive and negative aspects of the Jewish economy in Russia's Pale of Settlement. See Philipp Friedmann, "Industrialization and Proletarization of Lodz Jewry in the Years 1860–1914" (Yiddish), *Lodzer Visenshaftlikhe Shriftn*, I (1938), 63–132. One important obstacle for the greater growth of a Jewish industrial working class was the deeply ingrained anti-Jewish feeling among all classes of the Russian, Ukrainian, Polish, and other nationalities. As a result, non-Jewish entrepreneurs frequently refused to employ Jewish workers, who also often found their Christian fellow workers totally uncooperative. *See* Ezra Mendelsohn, "Jews and Christian Workers in the Russian Pale of Settlement," *Jewish Social Studies*, XXX (1968), 243–51; and below, Chap. 9.

[7]
Communal Autonomy

1. The millennial history of Jewish self-governmental institutions, which helps explain their great tenacity and vast range, is described in my *The Jewish Community: Its History and Structure to the American Revolution*, 3 vols., Philadelphia, 1942. It is to be regretted that Isaac Levitats's comprehensive work, *The Jewish Community in Russia, 1772–1844*, New York, 1943 (Columbia University

Studies in History, No. 505), as yet has no counterpart for the period of 1844–1917, when under various guises Jewish self-government continued to operate with great vigor. In fact, because of the rapid growth of the Jewish population and its great vicissitudes under a generally hostile government and society, the functions of the various religious, educational, charitable, and ultimately also political Jewish organizations were increasingly significant in Russian Jewish life. I understand, however, that Dr. Levitats is now working on a comprehensive study of Jewish community life in the period of 1844–1917.

2. *See* Isaac Levitats's "The Jewish Association," *Jewish Review*, I, (New York, 1943), 83–112; and with fuller documentation, *idem*, "Jewish Societies in Russia" (Hebrew), *Heawar*, IV (1956), 95–103; VII (1959), 123–35; XIV (1967), 236–46. The samples here reproduced, as well as Levitats's careful analysis of "The Minute Book of the Dubno Kahal" (Yiddish), *YIVO Historishe Shriftn*, II (1937), 80–114, give us but an inkling of the great richness and variety of the data on all aspects of Jewish socioeconomic and cultural life supplied by the numerous documents emanating from these voluntary associations. For one example, the Jewish Historical-Ethnographic Society in the Name of Solomon An-ski (Rappaport) alone possessed no less than twenty-five manuscripts of this kind. *See* the brief description by A. J. Goldschmidt in "The Pinqasim of H.-E. S. Archive" (Yiddish), *Fun Nuentn Ovar*, I (1937), 21–27. Only relatively few of these important sources have thus far been published and carefully scrutinized. Many local and regional communal histories also exist, some going back to Poland-Lithuania's pre-partition period; these offer extremely valuable historical information culled from communal, municipal, and provincial archives. In the last quarter of a century such publications of local interest have been prompted by nostalgic and filiopietistic sentiments of Jewish groups trying to preserve the memory of their vanished or vanishing communities. A number of these publications meet the high standards of contemporary historical research. There also exist many letters, personal reminiscences, and biographies of individual leaders published in *Reshumot, Heawar*, and other periodicals. But we still have a long way to go before these accumulations of primary and secondary materials will be adequately reexamined and integrated so as to offer opportunities for comprehensive historical generalizations and syntheses.

3. I. Galant, "The Debts of Jewish Kahals in Podolia and Volhynia" (Russian), *Zbirnyk prats* of the Jewish Historical Archaeological Commission, II (1929), 119–37; my *The Jewish Community*, II, 273 f.; III, 190 ff. nn. 31–32; Robert Anchel, *Napoléon et les Juifs*, Paris, 1928, pp. 579 ff.; Zosa Szajkowski, *Autonomy and Communal Jewish Debts During the French Revolution of 1789*, New York, 1959.

4. *Polnoe sobranie zakonov*, X, No. 8,054; XIX, No. 18,545; Levanda, *Polnyi khronologicheskii sbornik zakonov*, pp. 355 ff. No. 301, 577 ff. No. 509; Max Lilienthal, *Allgemeine Zeitung des Judentums*, XI (1847), 226; and other data analyzed by Isaac Levitats in *The Jewish Community in Russia*, especially pp. 35 ff. *See also* above, Chap. 3, n. 20.

5. David G. Maggid, "From My Archive" (Russian), *Perezhitoe*, IV (1913), 188 ff.; above, Chap. 2, nn. 7 and 10.

6. *Polnoe sobranie zakonov*, XIX, No. 13,850 (omitted by Levanda in his *Polnyi . . . sbornik*, p. 23); Levitats, *The Jewish Community in Russia*, pp. 24 ff., 198 ff.

7. Abraham Jacob Paperna, "From the Era of Nicholas I: Reminiscences" (Russian), *Perezhitoe*, II (1910), 1–53. *See also* his *Zikhronot* (Memoirs) in *Sefer ha-Shanah* (Yearbook), ed. by Nahum Sokolow, I (1900), 60–75 (on his student years in Zhitomir).

8. Saul M. Ginsburg, "The Ushitsa Case" (Yiddish) in his *Historishe Verk*, III, 178–87.

9. *See* above, Chap. 4, n. 5.

10. Robert Pinkerton, *Russia; or Miscellaneous Observations on the Past and Present State of That Country and Its Inhabitants*, London, 1833, p. 90; Mendele Mokher Seforim, *Fishke der Krumer* in *Kol kitbei* (Collected Works), 7 vols., Berlin, 1922, I, 69 f. On the ancient origins of that institution and its gradual degeneration even before the nineteenth century, *see* my *The Jewish Community*, II, 328 f.; III, 211 n. 44.

11. Yehezkel (Ezekiel) Kotik, *Maine Zikhroines* (Memoirs), 2 vols., Warsaw, 1913, I, 189 f. *See also* A. J. Paperna's reminiscences in *Perezhitoe*, II, 38 ff.

12. Cited, from documents published by the Ukrainian Academy, by Saul M. Ginsburg in his *Historishe Verk*, III, 20. *See also* Ezra Mendelsohn, *Class Struggle in the Pale: the Formative Years of the Jewish Workers' Movement in Tsarist Russia*, Cambridge, 1970; D. Fajnhaus, "Social Conflicts among the Jews of Lithuania and Belorussia in the First Half of the Nineteenth Century" (Polish), *Biuletyn* of the Żydowski Instytut Historyczny, no. 52 (1964), 3–16; and below, Chap. 9. Some Soviet Jewish historians in particular were prone to overstress the perennial elements of class struggle within the Jewish community. *See*, for instance, T. B. Heilikman, *Geshikhte fun der gezelshaftlekher bavegung fun di Yidn in Poiln un Rusland* (A History of Social Movements among the Jews of Poland and Russia), Vol. I, Moscow, 1926; and Israel Sosis, *Di Geshikhte fun di yidishe gezelshaftlekhe shtremungen in Rusland in XIX yorhundert* (The History of Jewish Social Trends in Russia during the Nineteenth Century), Minsk, 1929. However, not until the emergence of the modern labor movements with their crystallized socialist ideologies did these internal differences assume the character of conscious class militancy. In the earlier periods even the downtrodden Jewish masses shared with their better-situated coreligionists the conviction that they jointly faced the bitter hostility of the Gentile majorities who were a far greater menace to their survival. Jewish solidarity in the face of the common external enemies thus greatly overshadowed the internal differences. This attitude gradually changed under the impact of the socialist calls for the unity of the proletariat of all nationalities against their internal exploiters.

[8]

Religion and Culture

1. The text of the Warsaw ordinance of 1838 is reproduced in the Hebrew original in Saul M. Ginsburg's *Historishe Verk*, I, 301 ff. App. iii. On the general background, *see* Jacob Shatzky, *Geshikhte fun Yidn in Varshe* (A History of the

Jews in Warsaw), Vols. I–III, New York, 1947–53. Similar regulations were also enacted from time to time by other communities within the Pale.

2. *See* Abraham Menes's brief survey of "Learning in Lithuania in the Nineteenth Century" (Yiddish), *Lite* (Lithuania), ed. by Mendel Sudarsky, *et al.*, Brooklyn, New York, 1951, pp. 483–526. The only other method of establishing over-all communal unity in a large area, such as was achieved by the medieval synods, the occasional country-wide chief rabbinates, or even the provincial and central councils, which proved very effective in medieval Spain, Sicily, and particularly in early modern Poland and Lithuania, seemed to have lacked both popular Jewish and governmental support. The rabbinical conferences occasionally recorded in Russia were too sporadic and too lacking in any sustained support from either the rabbis or the public, to play a major role in the history of Russia's Jewish self-government. *See* Simon Dov Yerushalmi's "Conferences and Assemblies of Rabbis in Russia" (Hebrew), *Heawar*, III (1951), 86–94.

3. *Polnoe sobranie zakonov*, X, No. 8,054; Levanda, *Polnyi . . . sbornik*, pp. 359 ff. No. 304; *Allgemeine Zeitung des Judentums*, VI (1942), 185; Levitats, *The Jewish Community in Russia*, pp. 148 ff., 178 ff.

4. *See* Levin's highly informative autobiography in 3 parts entitled *Childhood in Exile, Youth in Revolt*, and *The Arena*, New York, 1929–32 (also in a one-volume ed., abridged by Maurice Samuel and called *Forward from Exile*, New York, 1967). Not surprisingly, the regular Orthodox rabbis looked condescendingly down upon their "official" confreres because of their own generally superior talmudic learning. An interesting anecdote, however, illustrates the refutation of such a generalization by Rabbi Jacob Mazeh, who was a learned rabbinic scholar and in this capacity distinguished himself by his eight-hour-long testimony at the Beilis trial. On one occasion, we are told, his interpretation of a talmudic passage in the tractate Taanit was challenged by a cantankerous old-fashioned talmudist. But Mazeh showed that his interlocutor had been misled by uncritically accepting the textual reading in the Warsaw edition of the Talmud, which had been arbitrarily altered by a Christian censor, rather than consulting the uncensored Amsterdam or even the Vilna edition. *See* A., "Rabbi Jacob Mazeh" (Hebrew), *Heawar*, XIV (1967), 247–49.

5. A. J. Paperna's aforementioned reminiscences in *Perezhitoe*, II, 31 f.; the correspondence from Vitebsk in *Voskhod* of 1894, cited by J. G. Lipman in the *Jewish Encyclopedia*, X, 547.

6. Benzion Dinur, "The Historical Image of Russian Jewry and Problems Connected with Its Study" (Hebrew), *Zion*, XXII (1957), 107, n. 46. A somewhat different computation, likewise incomplete, prepared by the Jewish Colonization Association in connection with its work on the census in 1897, showed that at that time some 370,000 Jewish children attended the various types of Hebrew-Yiddish schools (the *heder, Talmud Torah, yeshivah*), while only 60,000 went to schools with Russian as the language of instruction. *See* the *Sbornik materialov* (above Chap. 5, n. 1.), II, 297.

7. Pauline Wengeroff, *Memoiren einer Grossmutter Bilder aus der Kulturgeschichte der Juden Russlands im 19. Jahrhundert*, 2d ed., 2 vols., Berlin, 1913–19, I, 5, 9, 143 ff.; minutes of the Grodno Mishnah Association, cited from a Jerusalem MS by Levitats in *The Jewish Community in Russia*, p. 192. In this connection

Notes

Levitats also reproduced, from several manuscripts, interesting passages relating to the various forms of adult education pursued by the less learned members of the public.

8. *See*, for instance, Moshe Eleazar Eisenstadt's "From the Memories of My Youth: the Yeshivah of Volozhin" (Hebrew), *Heawar*, XIV (1967), 159–72; L. I. Mandelstam's comments on Mir cited by L. Greenberg in *The Jews in Russia*, p. 58; Louis Ginzberg, *Students, Scholars and Saints*, Philadelphia, 1928; Samuel K. Mirsky, ed., *Mosedot torah be-Eiropa* (Torah Institutions of Higher Learning in Europe in Their Flowering and Their Destruction), New York, 1956; and other writings cited by Samuel Ettinger in his article "Volozhin," *Encyclopaedia Judaica* (1971), 214–18. *See also* the pertinent Yiddish essays by A. Menes and others in *Lite*, ed. by M. Sudarsky *et al.*, I, 483–686; Mark Wischnitzer, "Material for the History of Yeshivot of Eastern Europe" (Hebrew), *Talpiot*, V, nos. 1–2 (1950), 151–75; nos. 3–4 (1952), 603–18; VI, nos. 1–2 (1953), 359–69; nos. 3–4 (1955), 739–49; Abraham Menes, "Yeshivahs in Russia," in J. Frumkin *et al.*, *Russian Jewry (1860–1917)*, pp. 382–407; and such monographs as cited below, Chap. 9, n. 18. It is high time, indeed, that a number of comprehensive scholarly, rather than nostalgic, monographs on the East European *yeshivot* be published by competent students with the aid of whatever documents and personal recollections may still be salvaged after the Holocaust.

Needless to say, not all was peaceful in the academies. One frequent discussion concerned the use of the dialectical ("pilpulistic") versus the ordinary method in interpreting the Talmud. While most schools generally preferred to adhere to one or the other tradition, the Volozhin academy did not escape a serious conflict on this score in the 1860s. Here it was intertwined with a struggle between two strong personalities, Joshua Heshel Lewin, married to one of R. Hayyim's great-granddaughters, and her uncle, Berlin. The controversy ended in Berlin's victory and Lewin's departure from Russia. *See* Samuel Leib Citron (Zitron), "A Dynastic Struggle in the Volozhin Yeshivah: Reminiscences" (Hebrew), *Reshumot*, I (1918), 123–34. *See also* Chaim Zalman Dimitrovsky's penetrating analysis "On the Pilpulistic Method" (Hebrew) in *Salo Wittmayer Baron Jubilee Volume*, ed. by Saul Lieberman and Arthur Hyman, 3 vols., New York, 1974 [1975], III, 111–81.

9. S. Posner, *Evrei v obshchei shkole* (Jews in the General Schools), St. Petersburg, 1914; Jacob Shatzky, *Kultur-Geshikhte fun der haskole in Lite* (Cultural History of Jewish Enlightenment in Lithuania), Buenos Aires, 1950, p. 58; Elias Tcherikower, *Istoriia Obshchestva dlia raspostraneniia prosveshcheniia mezhdu evreiami v Rossii* (A History of the Society for the Promotion of Enlightenment among the Jews of Russia), 2 vols., St. Petersburg, 1913, I, 129. *See also* the figures for the later years, cited above, this chapter, n. 5; and Chaps 3, nn. 10–11; and 4, n. 5.

10. Mordecai Teitelbaum, *Ha-Rab mi-Ladi u-mifleget Habad* (The Rabbi of Ladi and the Habad Faction), 2 vols., Warsaw, 1910–13; Simon M. Dubnow, *Toledot ha-hasidut* (A History of Hasidism), 3 parts, Tel Aviv, 1930–32 (also in a German trans. by A. Steinberg, entitled *Geschichte des Chassidismus*, 2 vols., Berlin, 1931–32); Gershom G. Scholem, *Major Trends in Jewish Mysticism*, Jerusalem, 1941 (and subsequent editions), especially pp. 321–45, 414–16, 426–28. The

English reader may get an inkling of R. Shneur Zalman's teachings by perusing his *Liqqutei amarim* (Selected Sayings from His *Tanya*), trans. with an Intro. by Nissan Mindel, Brooklyn, N.Y., 1962. *See also* Wolf Zeev Rabinowitsch, *Lithuanian Hasidism from the Beginnings to the Present Day*, London, 1970; Yaffa Eliach, "The Russian Dissenting Sects and Their Influence on Israel Baal Shem Tov, Founder of Hassidism," *Proceedings of the American Academy for Jewish Research*, XXXVI (1968), 57–83; and Eisig Silberschlag's perceptive analysis of the "Interpretations and Reinterpretations of Hasidism in Hebrew Literature," *Yearbook of Comparative Criticism*, 1971, pp. 218–58. It may also be noted that, because the village Jews, among whom Hasidism took roots first, were in close contact with their Ukrainian neighbors, some hasidic doctrines, folk tales, and homilies found a perceptible echo among the local peasants. *See* Ch. Chajes, "Baal Shem Tob among the Christians" (Polish), *Miesięcznik Żydowski*, IV (1934), 440–59, 550–65.

11. Nahman ben Simhah of Bratslav, *Shibhe ha-Ran* (On His Life and Teachings), new ed., Lwów, 1901, Chap. on his journey to Palestine, vi; Israel Friedmann of Ruzhin, *Irin kaddishin* (Holy Angels: Selections of Homilies by Him and His Son, Abraham Jacob of Sadagóra), Warsaw, 1885, pp. 105, 92, also cited by Levitats in *The Jewish Community in Russia*, p. 166. On Nahman's enthusiastic praise of the Holy Land, *see also* the excerpts included in Louis I. Newman (in collaboration with Samuel Spitz), *The Hasidic Anthology: Tales and Teachings of Hasidism*, New York, 1934, p. 299.

12. Louis Ginzberg, *Students, Scholars and Saints*, especially pp. 145 ff., 278 (on Israel Salanter); Kopul Rosen, *Rabbi Israel Salanter and the Musar Movement*, London, 1943; Dov Katz, *Tenu'at ha-musar* (The Musar Movement: Its History, Leaders, and Ideas), 4 vols., Tel Aviv, 1952–57; B. Dinur in *Zion*, XXII, 109 f.

13. Israel Zinberg, *Di Geshikhte fun der literatur bay Yidn* (The History of Jewish Literature), 8 vols., Vilna, 1929–37, VIII, Part 2, pp. 13 ff., 251 f. App. i.

14. The extraordinary difficulties under which Levinsohn labored throughout his literary career, as did many of his progressive confreres, come to the fore in various letters. *See*, for instance, that written on Shebat 18, 5603 (January 19, 1843), to Jacob Reifmann, in which he expressed his satisfaction over the sympathy evinced for his struggles by so distant a colleague as Abraham Geiger in Breslau. This letter is included in the collection *Be'er Yizhak* (Isaac's Well: Letters by and to Levinsohn), ed. by David Baer ben Yehudah Nathanson, Warsaw, 1899, pp. 93 ff. *See also* Louis S. Greenberg's brief study, *A Critical Investigation of the Works of Rabbi Isaac Baer Levinsohn*, New York, 1930. Diss. Columbia University.

15. Zinberg, *Geshikhte*, VIII, Part 2, pp. 104 ff., 254 ff. App. iii. On the resistance of the Jewish population to any changes in attire also in Congress Poland, *see* J. Shatzky, *Geshikhte fun Yidn in Varshe*, II, 81 ff. With the onset of Alexander II's more liberal era, the *Haskalah* movement progressed at a rapid pace. In 1863 its protagonists organized a Society for the Promotion of Enlightenment among the Jews, which in the following decades played a considerable role in Russo-Jewish affairs. *See* Yehudah Leon Rosenthal, *Toledot Hebrat Marbei ha-Haskalah be-Yisrael be-Eres Rusiah* (A History of the Society for the Promotion of Enlightenment among Jews in Russia), 2 vols., St. Petersburg, 1885–90; and

Notes

for later years Elias Tcherikower's aforementioned *Istoriia Obshchestva dlia raspostraneniia prosveshcheniia mezhdu evreiami v Rossii*. Also of great interest in this connection is the correspondence between two leading protagonists of the movement, Lev Osipovich Levanda and Judah Leb Gordon. See Moshe Perlmann, "L. O. Levanda and J. L. Gordon: Levanda's Letters to Gordon, 1873–5," *Proceedings of the American Academy for Jewish Research*, XXXV (1967), 139–85 (reproducing thirty-six Russian letters).

16. See Reuben Brainin's extensive biography of *Abraham Mapu hayyav u-sefarav* (A. M. His Life and Works), 2 vols., Pietrków, 1900; and, more generally, Joseph Klausner's comprehensive *Historiah shel ha-sifrut ha-ibrit ha-hadashah* (A History of Modern Hebrew Literature), 6 vols., Jerusalem, 1930–50, to be consulted also in connection with the other Hebrew writers discussed in this and the next chapter. See also the pertinent chapters in Meyer Waxman, *A History of Jewish Literature*, new ed. rev. and enlarged, 5 vols., New York, 1960.

17. Much light on Gordon's personality and his time is shed by his letters, collected under the title *Iggerot YeLaG*, 2 vols., Warsaw, 1894–95; his reminiscences, picturesquely entitled "*Al nehar Kebar* (By the River Chebar; with reference to Ezek. 1:1, etc.)" (Hebrew), *Reshumot*, I (1917), 69–96; V (1927), 61–85; and his brief diary (*Yoman*), ed. by Saul M. Ginsburg in *Heawar*, I (1917), 1–32; II (1918), 3–33, especially II, 8, 32. The episode of "Y. L. Gordon's Arrest and Deportation" is described by S. M. Ginsburg in his *Historishe Verk*, I, 121–39. *See also* the brief biographical sketches of Gordon by Abraham Benedict Rhine in his *Leon Gordon: An Appreciation*, Philadelphia, 1910; and by Shalom Spiegel in his *Hebrew Reborn*, New York, 1930 (paperback, Cleveland, 1962), pp. 174–87; and more generally, Jacob S. Raisin, *The Haskalah Movement in Russia*, Philadelphia, 1913; and Jacob Shatzky, *Kultur-Geshikhte fun der haskole in Lite* (Cultural History of the Haskalah in Lithuania; From the Earliest Times to the Love of Zion Movement), Buenos Aires, 1950. *See also* above, n. 13; the interesting profiles of some representative writers drawn by Moses Kleinman in his *Demuyot ve-Qomot* (Portraits and Personalities: Essays on Modern Hebrew Literature), London, n.d.; and Eisig Silberschlag's Preface to his *From Renaissance to Renaissance: Hebrew Literature from 1492–1970*, New York, 1973, which succinctly analyzes some "New Approaches to the Study of Hebrew Literature." Though long convinced of the general artificiality of dating major literary movements, I have, as far back as 1937, insisted that there was an Italian and Dutch Haskalah before that of the Berlin, Galician, and Russian periods. *See* my *Social and Religious History of the Jews*, first ed., II, 205 ff.

18. *See* Meir Wiener *et al.*, bio-bibliographical sketches in the Intro. to Aksenfeld's *Verk* (Works), ed. by Wiener, 2 vols., Kharkov and Moscow, 1931–38 (the editor tries in vain, however, to explain away the religious overtones in Aksenfeld's letter to Levinsohn of 1840, congratulating the latter on the publication of his *Bet Yehudah*, pp. 345 ff.); S. M. Ginsburg, *Historishe Verk*, I, 75 ff.; Zalman Reisen's (Rejzen's) comprehensive *Leksikon fun der yidisher literatur, prese un filologie* (Lexicon of the Yiddish Literature, Press and Philology), 3d rev. ed., 4 vols., Vilna, 1928–29, I, 159–62; and, more generally, the essays assembled in *Tsu der geshikhte fun der yidisher literatur in 19tn yorhundert* (On the History of Yiddish Literature in the Nineteenth Century: Studies and Materials), Kiev,

1940. On "The Social Import of Aksenfeld's Creativity" *see* Max Erik's pertinent Yiddish article in the Minsk *Zeitshrift*, V (1931), 125–69, with additional documents reproduced by J. Riminik, *ibid.*, pp. 171–80.

19. Reisen, *Leksikon*, I, 8–37; Samuel Niger, *Mendele Mokher Seforim*, New York, 1937. The numerous Soviet publications on Mendele are listed in Khone Shmeruk, ed., *Pirsumim yehudiim be-brit ha-moesot* (Jewish Publications in the Soviet Union, 1917–1960), Jerusalem, 1961, under the numbers listed in the Index, p. 474. On the large earlier literature *see* especially the informative review article by A. Gurstein, "Bird's-Eye View of Mendele Studies" (Yiddish), *Zeitshrift*, II–III (1928), 485–524.

20. *See* the well-documented outline by Peter S. Marek, *Ocherki po istorii prosveshcheniia Evreev v Rossi* (A Survey of the History of Jewish Enlightenment in Russia), Moscow, 1909 (on the period of 1844–73), with Simon M. Dubnow's remarks thereon in his review of that volume entitled "Echoes of the Last Century" (Russian) in *Evreiskaia Starina*, I (1909), 302–308. It may be noted that despite governmental assistance, all efforts at injecting Christian doctrines into some sectarian movements within the Jewish community achieved but minor results. *See* the twin essays by N. A. Bukhbinder, "From the History of Sectarian Trends among Russian Jews" (Russian), *ibid.*, XI (1924), 238–65; XIII (1930), 116–30.

21. Moshe Perlmann, "*Razsvet* 1860–1861: the Origins of the Russian Jewish Press," *Jewish Social Studies*, XXIV (1962), 162–82 (with extensive bibliographical references); and, more generally, S. L. Zinberg, *Istoriia evreiskoi pechati v Rossii* (A History of the Jewish Press in Russia), Petrograd, 1915. *See also* the same author's Yiddish essays on "The History of the Russo-Jewish Press (1860–1880)" and "The *Kol mebasser* [Voice of the Herald, ed. by Alexander Zederbaum] and Its Time" in his *Kultur-historishe Shtudien* (Studies in Culture and History), New York, 1949, pp. 87–158, 159–81; and A. Kirzhnitz's bibliography, chronologically arranged, of *Di yidishe presse in der gevezener ruslendisher imperie* (The Yiddish Press in the Former Russian Empire, 1823–1916), Moscow, 1930. The first periodical here mentioned is *Der Beobakhter an der Vaiksel* (The Observer on the Vistula), a weekly published in Warsaw from Dec. 3, 1823 to Sept. 29, 1824; it suspended publication after the appearance of the thirty-ninth issue. A little-known effort in 1871 to found a new Russo-Jewish periodical for the combating of anti-Semitism is described by its initiator, Jacob Teitel, in "Aus meinen Memoiren," *Festschrift Moritz Schäfer*, Berlin, 1927, pp. 237–40. *See also* Yehuda Slutsky's comprehensive work, *Ha-Ittonut ha-yehudit-russit ba-meah ha-tsha-esreh* (The Russian Jewish Press in the Nineteenth Century), Jerusalem, 1970; and G. Elkoshi, "The Hebrew Press in Vilna in the Nineteenth Century" (Hebrew), *Heawar*, XIII (1966), 59–97; XIV (1967), 105–52.

[9]
Ideological and Partisan Strife

1. The history of that society was described by one of its founders, Leon Rosenthal (1817–87), in his *Toledot* reproducing the early protocols of the society and more fully, by Elias Tcherikower in his *Istoriia Obshchestva*, both cited above in Chap. 8, nn. 9 and 15.

2. Moses Leib Lilienblum, *Hatot he'urim* (Sins of Youth; an autobiographical sketch) in his *Kol kitbe* (Collected Works), ed. with an Introduction by Joseph Klausner, 4 vols., Cracow-Odessa, 1910–13, II, 201–410; Klausner, *Yotserim u-bonim* (Creators and Builders; biographical sketches), 3 vols., Jerusalem, 1925–29, I, 80–123; below, n. 20.

3. Abraham Uri Kovner, "Letters to Paperna and Y. L. Gordon" (Hebrew), in *Hed ha-zeman*, 1909, p. 132; Leonid Grossmann, *Die Beichte eines Juden in Briefen an Dostojewski*, ed. by René Fülöp-Miller and Friedrich Eckstein, Munich, 1927; S. M. Ginsburg, *Historishe Verk*, n.s. II, 157–93; J. Bronstein, "Avrom Uri Kovner (1842–1909)" (Yiddish), *Zeitshrift*, V (1931), 211–43.

4. Of the extensive literature on Klaczko we need but refer to Count Stanislaw Tarnowski's comprehensive Polish biography, *Julian Klaczko*, 2 vols., Cracow, 1919.

5. Herman Rosenthal, "Blioch (Bloch), Ivan Stanislavovich," *Jewish Encyclopedia*, III, 250–52; S. M. Ginsburg, *Historishe Verk*, n.s. II, 119–56, 209–21; Daniel Chwolson, *Corpus inscriptionum hebraicarum*, St. Petersburg, 1882; *idem, Das letzte Passamahl Christi und der Tag seines Todes*, new impression revised, Leipzig, 1908 (based on a Russian ed. of 1875); *idem, Die Blutanklage und sonstige mittelalterliche Beschuldigungen der Juden. Eine historische Untersuchung nach den Quellen*, German trans. from the 2d Russian ed., Frankfurt, 1901; A. E. Harkavy's works listed in the *Festschrift* in his honor published in St. Petersburg, 1908.

6. Dimitrii S. Mirsky, *A History of Russian Literature*, ed. and abridged by Francis J. Whitefield, new impression, New York, 1958, pp. 223 ff.; and other literature listed by L. Greenberg in *The Jews in Russia*, I, 172 ff., 182 f. *See also* A. D. Briggs's London Diss., *A Critical Study of the Original Lyric Poetry of A. A. Fet*, London, 1968 (typescript).

7. Pobedonostsev, *L'Autocratie russe*, pp. 359 f.; Catherine Drinker Bowen, *"Free Artist"*: *the Story of Anton and Nicholas Rubinstein*, Boston, 1939, pp. 308 f. *See also* pp. 73, 151, 183, 222 f. The story of the conversion of the Rubinstein family beginning with the grandfather Roman Ivanovich (formerly Reuben) in 1830—he had thus evaded the penalty for bankruptcy provided by Russian law—is described in detail, on the basis of archival materials, by Saul M. Ginsburg in his *Historishe Verk*, n.s. II, 279–308.

8. Henry B. Sliozberg, *Dela minuvshikh dnei* (Affairs of Days Past: Notes of a Russian Jew), 3 vols., Paris, 1933–34, I, 132 ff., 207, 267 f.; *80 Years of ORT: Historical Materials, Documents and Reports*, Geneva, 1960, emphasizing that much of the original archives was lost during the Russian Revolution and the Nazi occupation.

9. Fiodor Mikhailovich Dostoevsky's letter to Kovner of February, 1877, reproduced in a German trans. by L. Grossmann in *Die Beichte eines Juden*, p. 119; other literature listed by Avrahm Yarmolinsky in his *Dostoevsky: a Life*, New York, 1934, pp. 156, 342, 436; Leo Nikolaevich Tolstoy's letter, cited from an earlier English trans. by Joseph L. Baron in his *Stars and Sand: Jewish Notes by Non-Jewish Notables*, Philadelphia, 1943, pp. 45 f. Otherwise Tolstoy generally avoided the Jewish issue in his writings. *See* Joshua Kunitz, *Russian Literature and the Jew*, pp. 139 ff.; and above, Chap. 4, n. 9.

10. Sergei Y. Witte, *Memoirs*, trans. from the original Russian manuscript and ed. by Abraham (Avrahm) Yarmolinsky, Garden City, 1927, pp. 381 f.; the biographical and other essays included in the memorial volume, *M. M. Vinaver i ruskaia obshchestvennost* (M. M. V. and Russian Society at the Beginning of the Twentieth Century), ed. by P. M. Miliukov *et al.*, Paris, 1937; Vinaver's own *Nedavnee* (Not Long Ago: Reminiscences and Characteristics), 2d ed., Paris, 1926; H. (G.) B. Sliozberg, *Dela minuvshikh dnei;* O. O. Gruzenberg, *Vchera; idem, Ocherki i rechi* (Sketches and Addresses), ed. by Alexander Goldenweiser, New York, 1944; Julius Brutzkus "Bramson—Organizer of Russian Jewry" (Russian), *Evreiskii Mir,* II (New York, 1944), 14–24; and other essays in that volume. *See also* Gregor Aronson, "Jews in Russian Literary and Political Life," in J. Frumkin *et al., Russian Jewry (1860–1917)*, pp. 253–99; and, more generally, the documents reproduced in German trans. in Peter Scheibert, ed., *Die russischen Parteien von 1905 bis 1917. Eine Dokumentensammlung,* Darmstadt, 1972; and Victor Leontovich, *Geschichte des Liberalismus in Russland,* Frankfurt, 1957 (Frankfurter wissenschaftliche Beiträge, X). It should be noted, however, that Witte himself had long perceived the real reason for the disproportionate number of Jewish members of the radical parties. In a conversation with Theodor Herzl in 1903, he first complained that although Jews numbered only 7,000,000 persons in Russia's total of 136,000,000, they constituted 50 percent of Russia's revolutionaries. (All three figures were exaggerated.) But when asked by the Zionist leader about the causes of this disparity, he admitted that "it is the fault of our government. The Jews are too oppressed." *See* Herzl's *Complete Diaries* (below, n. 22), IV, 1530; and above Chap. 6, n. 23.

11. Pavel B. Akselrod (Paul Axelrod), *Perezhitoe i peredumanoe* (Experiences and Meditations), Berlin, 1923; *idem, Die russische Revolution und die sozialistische Internationale. Aus dem literarischen Nachlass,* Jena, 1932; Abraham Ascher's recent analysis of *Pavel Axelrod and the Development of Menshevism,* Cambridge, Mass., 1972 (Russian Research Center Studies, LXX); Samuel Leib Zitron (Citron), *Drai literarishe doires* (Three Literary Generations: Reminiscences concerning Jewish Writers), 4 vols., Vilna, 1920–23, II, 104 ff. Even the distinguished early socialist Peter Lavrov, who though denying the existence of a Jewish nationality, was sympathetic to the Jewish workers' demands, nevertheless advised against too sharp protests against the Russian pogroms of 1881–82 on tactical grounds. He persuaded Akselrod to desist from publishing an intended pamphlet on this subject, lest it interfere with the party's objective "to establish closer contacts with the [Russian] people and to arouse them against the government." *See* his letter of April 11, 1882, cited by E. Tcherikower in his "Peter Lavrov and the Jewish Socialist Emigrés," *YIVO Annual of Jewish Social Science,* VII (1952), 133. *See also* S. Agurskii's ideologically interesting reconstruction of "The Character of the Socialist Movement among the Jewish Workers until the Rise of the Russian Social Democratic Labor Party" (Yiddish), *Zeitshrift,* IV (1930), 237–54 (also citing Lev Daitch's postscript to Peter Lavrov's letter to Akselrod, p. 248); with the interesting editorial comment thereon, *ibid.,* pp. 254–55; Lev Deich's (Daitch's) own *Rol Evreev v russkom revolutsionnom dvizhenie* (The Jews' Role in the Russian Revolutionary Movement), 2d ed., Moscow, 1925. *See below,* n. 19.

It is not surprising that blinded as most of these early Jewish populists were to religious factors, including those relating to their own Jewish faith, they were completely unaware of "The Religious Sources of Russian Populism," on which *see* G. P. Fedotov's pertinent essay in the *Russian Review*, I (1941), 27–39; F. Venturi's comprehensive review of *Il Populismo russo*, 3 vols., Turin, 1972 (Piccola Biblioteca Einaudi, nos. 188–90). *See also* other eyewitness accounts and reminiscences reproduced in *Revolutsionnoe dvizhenie sredi Evreev* (Revolutionary Movement among Jews), with an Intro. by Simeon Dimanshtain, Moscow, 1930; Yitzhak Maor's careful analysis of *She'elat ha-Yehudim ba-tenuah ha-liberalit ve-ha-mehapakhtanit be-Rusiah* (The Jewish Question in the Liberal and Revolutionary Movements in Russia, 1890–1914), Jerusalem, 1964; the literature listed below, nn. 14 and 19; and, more generally, Avrahm Yarmolinsky, *Road to Revolution: a Century of Russian Radicalism*, London, 1957.

12. Eliakum Zunser, *A Jewish Bard*, Yiddish text of his autobiography with an English trans. by Simon Hirsdansky, New York, 1905, pp. 43 (Yiddish), 32 (English). On this eminent folk poet *see also* Sol Liptsin's biography, *Eliakum Zunser: Poet of His People*, New York, 1950. Equally paradoxical were the results of the otherwise well-intentioned tsarist legislation which in order to help restratify the Jews economically had opened up much of Russia's interior to Jewish professionals and craftsmen. With the growth of the assimilationist trends among the new Russo-Jewish intelligentsia came also a certain rapprochement of Jews with like-minded Christians. Jewish populists and socialists now gained ready access to non-Jewish circles. If some Jewish sufferers from the *numerus clausus* were forced to dispense with higher education and become craftsmen, they also could more effectively vent their dissatisfaction by agitating among their non-Jewish compeers in behalf of their socialist ideals. Jewish populists and socialists could perform extraordinary services for the revolutionary cause in such centers as Vilna, Vitebsk, Gomel, and Odessa. Residing in a great international harbor city or in proximity to the western frontier, they could also help endangered comrades flee abroad as well as clandestinely import forbidden books and pamphlets. But many of them, both intellectuals and manual laborers, were increasingly attracted to the great centers of industry in the interior of Russia where they found a far more promising field for their agitation among the genuine industrial proletariat, rather than among the employees in the small individual workshops of their home communities. Quite early, therefore, Jewish propagandists began playing a large role in the all-Russian socialist movement. *See* the data assembled by Allan K. Wildman in his "Russian and Jewish Social Democracy" in *Revolution and Politics in Russia: Essays in Memory of Boris I. Nicolaevsky*, ed. by Alexander and Janet Rabinowitsch, Bloomington, Ind., 1972 (Russian and East European Series, XLI), pp. 75–87.

13. The absence of any consciously Jewish motivation among the Jewish *narodniki* is well illustrated by a small Yiddish hectograph paper, entitled *Arbeter-Tsaitung*, published in a few copies in January, 1881. It is essentially a trans. of a similar sheet in Russian and does not even mention Jews. *See* L. Greenberg, *The Jews*, pp. 148 f.; Elias Tcherikower, "The 'Arbeter-Tsaitung' of the Narodnaya Volia (1881)" (Yiddish), *YIVO Historishe Shriftn*, III, 604–609. *See also* the other valuable essays by Abraham Menes, Elias Tcherikower *et al.* in that comprehensive volume devoted to the history of "The Socialist Movement among the Jews

up to 1897"; and below, n. 17. From another angle, *see* the somewhat exaggerated account by Osher Margolis of "The Participation of the Jewish Masses in the Famine 'Disturbances' of 1891" (Yiddish), *Forpost*, VII (1938), 127–45.

14. The facsimile of Liberman's prospectus, reproduced by S. Ts. in *Evreiskaia Starina*, XIII (1930), 164–70; G. E. Gurevich, "The Trial of Jewish Socialists in Berlin (1878–79)," *ibid.*, X (1918), 151–74; N. M. Gelber, *Aus zwei Jahrhunderten*, Vienna, 1924, pp. 185–92. *See also*, more generally, Elias Tcherikower, "The Beginnings of the Jewish Socialist Movement" (Yiddish), *YIVO Historishe Shriftn*, I (1929), 469–532, together with "The Minute Book of the Society of Hebrew Socialists in London (1876)," *ibid.*, cols. 533–94; Boris Sapir, "Liberman et le socialisme russe," *International Review for Social History*, III (1938), 25–88 (includes several letters to and by Valerian Smyrnov, secretary of the small but influential *Vpered* [Forward] movement); *idem*, "Jewish Socialists around Vpered," *International Review of Social History*, X (1965), 365–82; *idem*, "Unknown Chapters to the History of 'Vpered,'" *ibid.*, II (1957), 52–77; Dov (Bernard) Weinryb, "The Ideological Evolution of A. S. Liberman" (Hebrew), *Zion*, IV (1939), 317–48. *See also* Lloyd P. Gartner, *The Jewish Immigrant in England, 1870–1914*, new ed., London, 1973 (Studies in Society), especially pp. 100 ff., 283; and above, n. 11.

15. Chaim Zhitlowsky, *Gezamelte Shriftn* (Collected Works), 10 vols., New York, 1912–19 (VI, 11–55: "A Jew to Jews"); Simon M. Dubnow, *Nationalism and History: Essays on Old and New Judaism*, ed. with an Introductory Essay by Koppel S. Pinson, Philadelphia, 1958 (paperback, Cleveland, 1961). On the early hesitant moves of these two founders of Jewish diaspora nationalism, *see also* their autobiographical descriptions in Zhitlowsky's *Zikhroines fun main leben* (Reminiscences from My Life), Vols. I–III, New York, 1935–40; Dubnow's *Kniga zhizni* (Book of Life: Reminiscences and Reflections. Materials for the History of My Time), 2 vols., Riga, 1934–35 (to 1922; also in a Hebrew trans.); and letters by and essays on him, ed. by Simon Rawidowicz in *Sefer Shimeon Dubnow*, London, 1954. *See also*, Aaron Steinberg, ed., *Simon Dubnow, The Man and His Work*, Paris, 1963.

16. Koppel S. Pinson, "Arkady Kremer, Vladimir Medem and the Ideology of the Jewish Bund," *Jewish Social Studies*, VII (1945), 233–64; and, more generally, Jacob Sholem Hertz, ed., *Doires Bundistn* (Generations of Bundists), New York, 1956 (including more than 300 biographical sketches with a listing of the main biographies); *idem*, *Di Geshikhte fun Bund* (The History of the Bund), Vols. I–III, New York, 1960–66; *idem*, *The Jewish Labor Bund: a Pictorial History, 1897–1957* (English and Yiddish), New York, 1958. *See also* Henry J. Tobias's brief report on "The Archives of the Jewish Bund. New Materials on the Revolutionary Movement," *American Slavic and East-European Review*, XVII (1958), 81–85; *idem*, *The Jewish Bund in Russia from Its Origins to 1905*, Stanford, Cal., 1972. Nor must we overlook the contribution made to the Russian revolutionary movement by the large Russian diaspora in the Western countries. In this respect the *numerus clausus* for Jews in Russia's schools of higher learning which forced many eager young Jewish students to enroll at foreign universities, greatly enhanced the resources in talented manpower for formulating and disseminating ideologies "subversive" of tsarist absolutism. The Russian secret police early realized the importance of that menace to the country's established order and

sought to minimize it by having its agents infiltrate the respective groups, report any new developments in detail and, on occasion, discredit the revolutionaries by actions inspired by especially planted *agents provocateurs.* The story of these machinations is yet to be told in full and illuminating detail. Thus far our knowledge is limited to data discussed in a few monographs, such as L. Mysyrowicz's "Agents secrets tsaristes et revolutionnaires russes à Genève, 1879–1903," *Schweizer Zeitschrift für Geschichte,* XXIII (1973), 29–72. *See also,* more generally, the well-documented study by Robert C. Williams, *Culture in Exile: Russian Emigrés in Germany, 1881–1941,* Ithaca, 1972 (with special reference to Germans and Jews).

17. *See* Lev Daitch's and Tsemakh Kopelzon's reminiscences in the former's "The First Jewish-Socialist Propagandist" (Yiddish), *Di Zukunft,* 1916, No. 8, pp. 677 f.; Kopelzon's "The First Burgeonings [of the Jewish Socialist Movement]: Reminiscences from the Years 1887–1890" (Yiddish), *Arbeter-luakh,* III (1922), 66; both cited by Tobias in *The Jewish Bund,* pp. 17 f. They undoubtedly were also encouraged by the example of the Polish socialists, for whom, too, Vilna was a major center of activity. Many Poles had grown up while the memories of the Polish uprising of 1863, its bloody suppression by the Russians, and the subsequent curtailment of Congress Poland's autonomy were still much alive.

18. See the graphic description of the debates at the congress by H. J. Tobias in *The Jewish Bund,* pp. 207 ff.; and by I. Getzler in his *Martov,* as well as the numerous sources cited by them. The former Zederbaum thus immediately paid the price for his retreat from his original position of 1895. Had the Bund stayed in the party—its exodus was a tactical mistake, as was generally recognized—the five Bundist votes would have helped Martov to secure a majority.

It may be noted that Lenin's drive for dictatorial control within the party did not cease even after the failure of the 1905 revolution and the decline of the socialist movements in Russia until World War I. At that time the fate of the party largely depended on the strength of the exiled leaders and their ability to train underground party workers abroad. Yet Lenin, aided and abetted by such Jewish associates as Kamenev and Zinoviev, "apparently was more interested in developing loyal Bolshevists who were ideologically consistent with his point of view than he was in training workers in the arts of the underground." *See* Ralph Carter Elwood, "Lenin and the Social Democratic Schools for Underground Party Workers, 1909–11," *Political Science Quarterly,* LXXXI (1966), 370–91, especially p. 387. Nonetheless, the socialist agitation among the Jews in Russia continued to make progress, and like the *Haskalah* before, even penetrated the academies of Jewish higher learning. *See* B. Shulman, "The Revolutionary Spirit in the Yeshivot (Telzh and Shadov [Sheduva] in 1906–1909)" (Hebrew), *Heawar,* XII (1965), 134–47.

19. *Encyclopédie socialiste, syndicale et coopérative de l'Internationale ouvrière,* 8 vols., Paris, 1912–13, V, 377, 385 f., 397 f.; articles on "Bund" and "VKP(B)" (All-Russian Communist Party), both in Russian, in *Bolshaia sovetskaia entsiklopedia,* 1st ed., VIII, 113; XI, 531; Vladimir Medem, *Fun main leben* (An Autobiography), 2 vols., New York, 1923, II, 86 ff.; and, more fully, Oscar I. Janowsky, *The Jews and Minority Rights (1893–1919),* with a Foreword by Julian W. Mack, New York, 1933 (Diss. Columbia University), pp. 72 ff., 88 n. 1, 122 ff. *See also,* more

generally, Lev Deich (Daitch), *Rol Evreev v russkom revolutsionnom dvizhenii* (The Jews' Role in the Russian Revolutionary Movement), Vol. I (only), 2d ed., Moscow, 1925 (partly recording personal experiences); A. L. Patkin, *The Origins of the Russian-Jewish Labour Movement*, Melbourne, 1947; the articles on "The Jewish Socialist Movement in Russia and Poland (1870s–1897)" and "(1897–1919)" by Abraham Menes and Raphael R. Abramovich in *The Jewish People, Past and Present*, II (1948), 355–68 and 369–98; and Leonard Shapiro's perceptive lecture, "The Role of the Jews in the Russian Revolutionary Movement," *Slavonic and East-European Review*, XL (1961), 148–67. Additional data may be gleaned from Arieh Tartakower's comprehensive review of *Toledot tenuat ha-obdim ha-yehudit* (History of the Jewish Labor Movement), 2 vols., Warsaw, 1929–30; and the recent English dissertations, J. Frankel, *Socialism and Jewish Nationalism in Russia 1897–1907*, Diss. Cambridge, 1960; H. Shukman, *The Relations between the Jewish Bund and the RSDRP* [Russian Social-Democratic Labor Party], *1897–1908*, Diss. Oxford, 1960; and Ezra Mendelsohn, *The Jewish Labor Movement in Czarist Russia: From Its Origin to 1905*, Diss. Columbia University, 1966 (all three in typescript).

Of the vast number of primary sources we need but mention the large collection of documents assembled in the Bund Archive in New York; and the biographical and autobiographical records of some early pioneers of the movement, including Raphael R. Abramovich's *In tsvai revolutsies* (In Two Revolutions: the History of a Generation), 2 vols., New York, 1944, esp. I, 117 ff.; *Arkady: Zamelbukh* (Collection of Essays and Reminiscences in Memory of Arkady Kremer, the Founder of the "Bund"), New York, 1948; Vladimir Medem, *Fun main leben* (From My Life: an Autobiography), 2 vols., New York, 1923; *Vladimir Medem tsum tsvantsigstn yorsait* (V. M. on the Twentieth Anniversary of His Death), New York, 1943; and John (Joseph) Mill, *Pionern un boiern* (Pioneers and Builders), with an Introduction by Franz Kursky, 2 vols., New York, 1946–49. In short, despite its numerous defeats and its ultimate eclipse in Russia after the Communist Revolution of 1917, the Bund's early activities have left behind a rich heritage in both Jewish politics and culture, particularly in Poland and the United States—a factor insufficiently recognized by Bernhard K. Johnpoll in *The Politics of Futility: the General Jewish Workers Bund of Poland (1917–1943)*, New York, 1967. *See*, for example, W. Glicksman, "The 'Bund' as Reflected in Yiddish Fiction in Poland, 1914–1939" (Yiddish), *Yivo Bleter*, XLIV (1973), 217–30.

20. Moses Leib Lilienblum, "The Future of Our People" in his *Kol Kitbe* (Collected Works), 4 vols., Cracow-Odessa, 1910–13, cited here, with variations, from Arthur Hertzberg, *The Zionist Idea: an Historical Analysis and Reader*, with a Foreword by Emanuel Neumann, New York, 1959, p. 173 (also paperback). *See also* Zalman Epstein, *Mosheh Leib Lilienblum, shittato ve-halakh mahshevotav* (M. L. L.: His Doctrine and the Evolution of His Thoughts on Religion and the Rebirth of the People of Israel in the Land of Its Fathers), Tel Aviv, 1935.

21. Leo Pinsker, *Auto-Emancipation*, trans. from the German by David S. Blondheim, New York, 1906, p. 2 (here cited with variations in the English rendition). *See also* the rich collection of *Ketabim le-toledot hibbat Siyyon* (Documents for the History of "Love of Zion" and Palestine Colonization), ed. by A. Druyanov, 3 vols., Odessa-Tel Aviv, 1910–32.

Notes

22. Theodor Herzl, *Tagebücher*, 3 vols., Berlin, 1923, III, 460 ff.; in the English trans. by Harry Zorn, entitled *Complete Diaries of Theodor Herzl*, ed. by Raphael Patai, 5 vols., New York, 1960, IV, 1517 ff. *See also* Alex Bein, *Theodor Herzl: a Biography*, trans. from the German by Maurice Samuel, Philadelphia, 1941 (also paperback, Cleveland, 1962), pp. 447 ff.; and Saul Ginsburg, "Theodor Herzl's Trip to St. Petersburg" (Russian), *Evreiskii Mir*, II (1944), 197–209. Of interest in this connection is also the subsequent interview by the non-Zionist Lucien Wolf with Plehve, reported by Wolf in his "Mr. Plehve and the Jewish Question," *The Times* (London) of Feb. 6, 1904. That Plehve was well informed about the developments in the Russian Zionist Organization is attested by Chaim Weizmann's memorandum to Herzl of May 6, 1903, reproduced in his *The Letters and Papers*, Vols. I, London, 1968 (in progress of publication), II, 301 ff. which generally deplored the unsatisfactory situation of the movement and the ambivalence of the tsarist administration toward it. This ambiguity came to the fore also in later years when David Wolfsohn, Herzl's successor as President of the World Zionist Organization, negotiated with the Russian authorities for a formal recognition of the Russian branch of that body. *See* Nathan Michael Gelber, "David Wolfsohn's Attempt to Secure Legal Recognition for the Zionist Organization in Russia" (Hebrew), *Heawar*, V (1957), 73–80. *See also* above, Chap. 4, n. 15.

23. *See* especially Joseph Klausner, *Menahem Ussishkin: His Life and Work*, New York, 1942, pp. 65 ff. Interesting data on the intellectual evolution of a young Russian Jew who ultimately became an outstanding Zionist leader are offered by Shmarya Levin in his autobiographical *Childhood in Exile* and *Youth in Revolt*; both in the English trans. by Maurice Samuel, New York, 1929–30. On Nissan 20, 5664 (April 26, 1904), the veteran Zionist propagandist Moses Leib Lilienblum addressed a pathetic appeal to Herzl not to abandon Zion for Uganda. See the text published by Alter (Asher) Druyanov in "A Bundle of Letters: From the Archive of Hayyim Yonah Gurliand" (Hebrew), *Reshumot*, II (1927), 405–34, especially pp. 433 f. In 1903 the outcry of the Russian Zionists carried the greater weight in Zionist circles, as the preceding five years (1898–1903) had witnessed a remarkable growth in the number of Zionist societies in Russia from 373 to 1,572. *Cf.* the respective reports in the *Protokolle* of the Second and Sixth Zionist Congresses of 1898, p. 47; and 1903, p. 22. On the early Zionist activities of Chaim Weizmann, who was later to serve as the first President of the State of Israel, *see* his *The Letters and Papers*.

24. Ahad Ha-Am (pseud. for Asher Zvi Ginzberg), "The Negation of the Diaspora," in his Hebrew essays collected under the title *Al parashat derakhim* (At the Crossroads), 4 vols., 3d ed., Berlin, 1921, IV, 106 ff., 108; here cited from the English trans. by Leon Simon in his *Ahad Ha-Am: Essays, Letters, Memoirs*, Oxford, 1946 (East and West Library), p. 215. *See also* Ahad Ha-Am's *Iggerot* (Letters), 6 vols., Tel Aviv, 1923–25; his *Pirqe zikhronot ve-iggerot* (Memoirs and Letters), Tel Aviv, 1931; and in an English trans., *Basic Writings of Ahad Haam*, ed. with an Introduction by Hans Kohn, New York, 1962. Regrettably, many of Ahad Ha-Am's personal papers, left behind in Odessa when he moved to London in 1908, were lost during the subsequent revolutionary period. *See* Ahad Ha-Am's "Memoir—Fragments (from Old Notes)" (Hebrew), *Reshumot*, V

(1927), 86–144, especially p. 95 n. *See also,* more generally, Aryeh (Leon) Simon and Joseph Eliyahu Heller's biography of *Ahad Ha-Am ha-ish, poalo ve-torato* (A. H., the Man, His Work and Teaching), Jerusalem, 1955. Ahad Ha-Am did not limit himself to the literary espousal of his ideas, but in 1889 also founded an elitist secret society *Benei Mosheh* which in the following dozen years trained many gifted Russian activists to play important roles in the Zionist movement. Of interest also is Noah Rosenbloom's "Ahad Ha-am and the Knowledge of Historiography" (Hebrew), *Salo Wittmayer Baron Jubilee Volume,* 1975, III, 331–52.

25. Oscar I. Janowsky, *The Jews and Minority Rights,* pp. 106 ff. *See also* Moses Nachman Syrkin's report on the earlier "Zionist Conference in Minsk" of 1902 in his Hebrew essay in *Sefer ha-Shanah,* ed. by Nahum Sokolow, IV (1902–1903), 11–24.

26. Nachman Syrkin, *Geklibene tsionistish-sotsialistishe Shriftn* (Selected Zionist-Socialist Writings), 2 vols., New York, 1925–26 (with a biographical sketch by Isaac Zar); *idem, Kitbe* (Writings), ed. by Berl Katzenelson and Judah Kaufmann, Vol. I, Tel Aviv, 1939; Marie Syrkin, *Nachman Syrkin Socialist Zionist: Biographical Memoir. Selected Essays,* New York, 1961 (*see* especially p. 304); Ber Borochov, *Geklibene Shriftn* (Selected Writings), 2 vols., New York, 1920–28; *idem Ketabim* (Works), in the Hebrew trans. by D. Ben Nahum *et al.* in L. Levita's and his ed., 2 vols., Tel Aviv, 1957–58 (II, 399 ff. includes an interesting documentary appendix relating to the early history of the Labor-Zionist movement); *idem, Nationalism and the Class Struggle: a Marxian Approach to the Jewish Problem,* ed. by Moshe Cohen, New York, 1937 (includes Abraham G. Duker's essay on "Ber Borochov's Theories and Their Place in the History of the Jewish Labor Movement"); Aaron David Gordon, *Kitbe* (Writings), 5 vols., Tel Aviv, 1925–28 (includes a biographical sketch by Joseph Aronowich); *idem, Selected Essays,* trans. from the Hebrew by Frances Burnce and ed. by N. Teradyon and A. Shohat. With a biographical sketch by Eisig Silberschlag, New York, 1938. On the antecedents of those movements, *see also* Israel Ritov's *Peraqim be-toledot "Seire-Siyyon"* (Studies in the History of the S.S.), Tel Aviv, 1964.

27. On the beginnings of the Mizrahi (or Mizrachi) movement, *see* especially Judah Leb Fishman, "The History and Evolution of the Mizrahi Organization" (Hebrew), *Sinai,* I (1937), 260–67, 361–68; II (1938), 63–72; III (1938), 301–15, 478–81. *See also* Isaac Jacob Reines's *Or hadash al Siyyon* (New Light on Zion), Vilna, 1902, expounding the principles of the new movement; and the essays ed. in memory of Reines by J. L. Fishman under the title *Sefer ha-Mizrahi* (The Book of Mizrahi), Jerusalem, 1946. On Mohilever, *see* the collection of Hebrew essays by I. Nissenbaum *et al., R. Shemuel Mohilever,* Warsaw, 1938. Other early Russian Zionists belonging to the various groups are included in Samuel L. Citron's *Leksikon siyyoni* (Zionist Handbook: Biographies of Leaders Who Distinguished Themselves in the Zionist Movement), Warsaw, 1924. *See also* Samuel Rosenblatt, *History of the Mizrahi Movement,* New York, 1951.

28. Jacob Rosenheim, *Ausgewählte Aufsätze und Ansprachen,* 2 vols., Frankfurt, 1930, esp. II, 159–318; Issac Breuer, *25 Jahre Aguda,* 1937; *idem, Am ha-Torah ha-meurgan* (The Organized People of the Torah), 1944. In any case, it appears that most of Russia's Orthodox Jews were not yet prepared to join any organized political movement. Quietist by tradition, they accepted even adverse govern-

mental decrees as a divinely inflicted punishment for the sins of their generation. Orthodox Jewish leaders turned most of their energies to the cultivation of
the Torah, particularly its ramified rabbinic letters, including homiletical and
ethical writings. Regrettably, the rich history of nineteenth- and twentieth-
century rabbinic literature has not yet been made the subject of those modern
analytical as well as synthetic historical investigations which it so amply deserves. Certainly, most of the "histories of modern Hebrew literature" concentrate almost exclusively on the story of modern belles-lettres and ignore the very
significant achievements of many outstanding "old-fashioned" rabbinic authors
whose impact, direct or indirect, on the masses at that time greatly exceeded that
of many celebrated Hebrew or Yiddish poets and publicists.

   29. Chaim Nachman Bialik, *Kitbe u-mibhar targumav* (Writings and Selected
Translations), 4 vols., Berlin, 1923, especially 1, 287 ff., 320 ff., 341 ff.; *idem,
Iggerot* (Letters), assembled and ed. with notes by Fischel Lachover, 5 vols., Tel
Aviv, 1938–39. Some of his poems are available in the English trans. by Leonard
Victor Snowman, entitled *Poems from the Hebrew,* with an Introduction by
Vladimir Jabotinsky, London, 1924, especially pp. 66 ff., 77 ff.; and by Maurice
Samuel in Bialik's *Selected Poems,* New York, 1926, especially pp. 45 ff., 67 ff. The
full-length Hebrew biography by Fischel Lachover, *Chaim Nachman Bialik* (C. N.
B.: His Life and Works), Tel Aviv, 1936; the perceptive Hebrew essays on *Ch. N.
Bialik u-bene doro* (C. N. B. and His Contemporaries) by the distinguished poet
Zalman Shneur, Tel Aviv, 1953; may be supplemented by the general histories
of modern Hebrew literature by Joseph Klausner, Lachover, and Shalom Spiegel
(*Hebrew Reborn,* pp. 295 ff.); and by a host of monographs. *See* especially the
penetrating essay by Moses Kleinman in his *Demuyot ve-komot* (Portraits and
Personalities: Essays on Modern Hebrew Literature), 2d ed., London, n.d., pp.
279 ff.; and Eisig Silberschlag's even more independent evaluation of Bialik's
work in his *From Renaissance to Renaissance,* pp. 181 ff. Of considerable interest
are the miscellaneous materials assembled in the year book *Kenesset* issued in
his memory, Jerusalem, 1936–46 and 1960; and his own *Debarim she-be'al peh*
(Oral Dicta), 2 vols., Tel Aviv, 1935, a collection of sayings uttered by or
attributed to the poet on various occasions. While some of Bialik's poems now
appear dated and others have lost their luster owing to the passage of time and
changes in the circumstances of Russian and world Jewry, one cannot overesti-
mate the impact of his flaming exclamations, such as the verse "We are the last
generation in slavery, the first in freedom," upon many of his contemporaries.
Their appraisal of his genius and their oft-reiterated view that Bialik was the
greatest Hebrew poet since the Golden Age of medieval Spanish Jewry will still
find few objectors among the *cognoscenti* and the public alike.

   30. Micah Joseph Bin Gorion (Berdichevski), *Kitbe* (Writings), 2 vols., Tel
Aviv, 1960; *idem, Yiddishe kesovim* (Yiddish Writings), 6 vols., Berlin, 1924; Rachel
and Emanuel Bin Gorion, *Gedächtnisschrift zum zehnten Todestage von Micha Josef
Bin Gorion,* Berlin, n.d.; Yeshurun Keshet (Koplowitz), *Mikhah Yosef Berdichevski*
(biography, in Hebrew), Jerusalem, 1959; Saul Tchernichovsky, *Shirim* (Poems),
collected by the author, 12th ed., Tel Aviv, 1959, especially pp. 317 ff.; Leonard
V. Snowman, *Tchernichowsky and His Poetry,* London, 1929 (includes English
translations of poems, such as that cited, with variations, in the text); Joseph

Klausner, *Shaul Tchernikhovsky: ha-adam ve-ha-meshorer* (S. T.: the Man and the Poet), Jerusalem, 1947; Eisig Silberschlag, *Saul Tschernikowsky, Poet of Revolt*, Ithaca, New York, 1968. Of interest are also Jacob ben Yeshurun's (Kitaiksher's) succinct observations on *Ha-Shirah ha-russit ve-hashpaatah al ha-shirah ha-ibrit* (Russian Poetry and Its Influence on Hebrew Poetry), with an Introduction by Joseph Klausner, Tel Aviv, 1955.

31. Isaac Leib Peretz, *Ale Verk* (Complete Works, in Yiddish), 11 vols., New York, n.d.; *idem, Kol kitbe* (Collected Works, in Hebrew), 8 vols., Tel Aviv, 1948–52; *Briv un Redes* (Letters and Addresses), ed. and trans. by Nachman Meisel, New York, 1944; *idem, Yizchok Leibush Peretz un zein dor shreiber* (Y. L. P. and Contemporary Writers), New York, 1951; Reisen, *Leksikon*, II, 974–1043; A. A. Roback, *I. L. Peretz, Psychologist of Literature*, Cambridge, Mass., 1935; Maurice Samuel, *Prince of the Ghetto*, Philadelphia, 1948; and the rich special Yiddish issue devoted to Peretz in the *Yivo Bleter*, XII (1937), 1–384, which includes Jacob Shatzky's "Addenda to the Bibliography of I. L. Peretz," supplementing the earlier bibliographies by Ber Borochov and A. Gurstein and raising the total number of bibliographical entries to 555. A great many more biographical and critical studies have since seen the light of day; among them Nachman Meisel's comprehensive Yiddish work, *I. L. Peretz. Sein Lebn un Shafn* (I. L. P. His Life and Creativity: Essays and Materials), New York, 1945 (with a good selected bibliography, pp: 355 ff.; also in an updated Hebrew trans., 1961). Nevertheless, some of the lacunae in our knowledge stressed by A. Gurstein in his Yiddish essay "The Present State of a Peretz Biography (On the Published Biographical Materials)," *Zeitshrift*, I (Minsk, 1926), still await filling.

32. Sholem Aleichem's works appeared in many editions and translations. *See* especially his *Ale Verk* (Collected Works), 28 vols., New York, 1923; Melech Grafstein's illustrated *Sholem Aleichem Panorama*, London, n.d. (includes translations of selected stories and essays by various authors on S. A.); and Maurice Samuel, *The World of Sholem Aleichem*, New York, 1943. *See also* Reisen, *Leksikon*, IV, 673–736; below, Chaps. 14 and 17; Dan Miron's comprehensive summary, "Shalom Aleichem" in the English *Encyclopaedia Judaica*, XIV (1971), 1272–86 (with a good selected bibliography). In recent years the play *Fiddler on the Roof*, a dramatized presentation of Tevye and his circle, has given an inkling of Jewish life in an old Russian *stetl* to untold multitudes of viewers and record listeners in the Western world, while numerous translations of his works have become best-sellers in the various Soviet republics. *See* below, Chaps. 16, n. 8, and 17, n. 17; and, more generally, A. A. Roback, *The Story of Yiddish Literature*, New York, 1940.

33. Jacob Shatzky, ed., *Goldfaden Bukh*, published by the Yiddish Theater Museum in New York, 1926; Nachman Meisel, *Abraham Goldfaden, 1840–1908* (biography, in Yiddish), New York, 1938; and, more generally, B. Gorin (J. Guido), *Di Geshikhte fun yidishen teater* (History of the Jewish Theater: Two Thousand Years of Theater among Jews), 2 vols., New York, 1918; and the various essays included in the *Arkhiv far der geshikhte fun yidishen teater un drame* (Archive for the History of the Jewish Theater and Drama), ed. by J. Shatzky, Vol. I, Vilna, 1930.

34. Karl Lamprecht, *Americana. Reiseeindrücke, Betrachtungen, geschichtliche Gesamtansicht*, Freiburg i. B., 1906, pp. 61 f.

Notes

[10]

The First World War

1. *Russkii Invalid,* 1858, No. 39, cited by Joseph L. Baron in *Stars and Sand,* pp. 227 f.

2. Purishkevich's gesture was the more remarkable, as this notorious rabble rouser did not always follow his government's directions. In fact, in an open session of the Duma he had accused the somewhat less reactionary Prime Minister Peter Arkadievich Stolypin of violating the constitution. This independence earned him the designation of the "Duma's *enfant terrible*" in some court circles. See C. E. Brancovan, "Grand Duke Nikolay Mikhailovich on the Ministerial and Parliamentary Crisis of March 1911. Five Letters to Frédéric Masson," *Oxford Slavonic Papers,* VI (1973), 66–81, especially pp. 79 f. No. v.

3. These Russian edicts are reproduced in a German trans. in *Die Juden im Kriege. Denkschrift des Jüdischen Sozialistischen Arbeiterverbandes Poale-Zion an das Internationale Sozialistische Bureau,* submitted in The Hague, November, 1915, pp. 49 ff. A dramatic story of these ruthless acts of the conquerors was told, partly on the basis of direct observation, by the famous playwright S. An-Ski (pseud. for Salomon Rapoport) in his *Hurban ha-Yehudim be-Polin, Galitsia u-Bukovina* (Ruin of the Jews of Poland, Galicia and the Bukovina), trans. into Hebrew by S. L. Citron, 4 parts, Tel Aviv, n.d. To be sure, some of the Galician Jewish hostages found ways of securing freedom through douceurs to the proper Russian authorities. But the majority were sent to Russia and were held in prison there, regardless of age or physical condition. What was worse, almost immediately some commanders also started removing Jewish hostages from Russo-Jewish communities near the frontier with Germany. Jews resented not only the manifold sufferings inflicted on their respected coreligionists but even more the aspersions thus indiscriminately cast on the loyalty of the entire Jewish people under the tsars. See A. Litai, "A Chapter from the 'Scroll of Destruction': Events Affecting Russian Jewry during the World War, August 1914—April 1916" (Hebrew), *Reshumot,* II (1927), 199–254. N. M. Friedman, a deputy to the Fourth Duma, rejected, however, the proposal that Jews should deliver hostages in return for the suspension of wholesale expulsions (*see* below). In his letter to Prime Minister Ivan L. Goremykin he wrote: "Jews will never consent to this astounding condition imposed by the authorities on their own subjects. . . . The Jews have honestly fulfilled their obligations to the fatherland and they will continue to fulfill them. . . . But all the persecutions will not force them to proclaim a falsehood to be truth, and through their acceptance, confirm the dastardly libel spread against them." Cited *ibid.,* pp. 217 f.

Jews suffered not only from governmental ruthlessness, but also from the growing anti-alien frenzy and ethnoreligious fanaticism which had seized a large segment of the Russian population. The raging xenophobia found expression, for instance, in the Moscow riots of May 27–29, 1915, directed against individuals bearing foreign-sounding names and their property. Curiously, as it turned out, the majority of the sufferers were not enemy aliens, but rather Russian citizens (489 against 113). In Galicia, too, the Uniate Ruthenians probably sustained more losses in life and limb than the Jews, while their intellectual leader Michael Hrushevsky, the distinguished nationalist historian of the Ukraine, was like Metropolitan Szeptycki deported into the interior of Russia. *See* Gregor Prokoptschuk, *Metropolit Andreas Graf Scheptyckyj. Leben und Wirken des grossen Förderers der Kirchenunion,* 2d ed. rev., Munich, 1967.

4. Maxim Gorki, "Anti-Semitism" (1929) in his collection of essays entitled *Culture and the People,* English trans. from the Russian, New York, 1939, p. 67; Litai in *Reshumot,* II, *passim;* and the graphic description of one such local expulsion (from Shavle) by one of its victims, reproduced in trans. in "The Expulsion of 1915" (Hebrew), *ibid.,* V (1927), 230–72 (with photographs). In their anti-Jewish fervor, the Russian commanders often disregarded the havoc played with the local economy by the sudden removal of the Jews. In Kovno, for example, only two Christian shops (selling leather goods and metal objects) and a few food stalls remained open, while all doctors and most apothecaries, as well as the aforementioned Duma deputy Friedman, were banished. Although many Jewish soldiers distinguished themselves on the battlefields, Russian censorship forbade the mention in the press of any decorations for valor bestowed upon them. *See* Litai, pp. 218 ff., 248 f.

5. Ludendorff's and other manifestos were reprinted by J. Barkai in his "Proclamations Issued by the German and Austrian Armies to the Jews of Poland" (Hebrew), *Reshumot,* VI (1930), 459–65. *See also* the Hebrew and Yiddish texts of the leaflets dropped from airplanes over Warsaw and other cities and reproduced in An-Ski's *Hurban,* I, 39 ff., and, more generally, Paul P. Roth and Wilhelm Stein, *Die politische Entwicklung in Kongress-Polen während der deutschen Okkupation,* Leipzig, 1919, especially pp. 170 ff. (by Stein); and Janusz Pajewski, "The Policy of the Central Powers toward Poland during the First World War" (Polish), *Roczniki historyczne,* XXVIII (1962), 9–56.

6. A partial story of that semivoluntary labor enlistment is told by Julius Berger, who had made valiant efforts to mitigate its hardships, in his *Ostjüdische Arbeiter im Kriege. Ein Beitrag zur Arbeitervermittlung unter Juden,* Berlin, 1919 (reprinted from *Volk und Land,* a Jewish weekly).

7. Zalman Reisen, ed., *Pinkos far Geshikhte fun Vilne* (Record Book of the History of [the Jews of] Vilna in the Years of War and Occupation), Vilna, 1922, pp. 133 ff. (article by Z. Shabad); Israel Cohen, *Vilna,* 1943 (Jewish Communities Series), pp. 361 ff.; S. Weissenberg, "Zur Biotik der südrussischen Juden," *Archiv für Rassen- und Gesellschafts-Biologie,* IX (1912), 200–206; *idem,* "The Russian Jews during the War and Revolution" (Yiddish), *Bleter far yidishe demografie,* I (1924), 17–20, especially Table I. *See also* the interesting data on "Births, Deaths, and Marriages among the Jews of Odessa, 1892–1919" (Yiddish), assembled by Jacob Lestchinsky, *ibid.,* pp. 70–74.

8. N. Hans, *History of Russian Educational Policy,* pp. 204 f. The increase in the general and Jewish enrollment at the university, despite the draft of many young men for the armed services, was only part of the large increase in the metropolitan Jewish population contrasting with the country-wide demographic trends. It has been shown that St. Petersburg had 2,100,000 inhabitants in 1914 and 2,465,000 in 1917. Moscow's population increased from 1,600,000 in 1912 to 2,000,000 in 1917. *See* Hugh Seton-Watson, *The Russian Empire, 1801–1917,* Oxford, 1967 (Oxford History of Modern Europe), p. 720.

Notes

9. *See* the data assembled by S. M. Dubnow in his "From the 'Black Book' of Russian Jewry. Sources for the History of the War, 1914–1915" (Russian), *Evreiskaia Starina*, X (1918), 195–296; Louis Stein, "The Exile of the Lithuanian Jews in the Conflagration of the First World War (1914–1918)" (Yiddish), *Lite* (Lithuania), ed. by M. Sudarsky *et al.*, pp. 89–118; and, more generally, Abraham G. Duker's succinct survey of *Jews in World War I: a Brief Historic Sketch*, New York, [1939] (reprinted from *Contemporary Jewish Record*, II, No. 5).

10. *See The National Question in the Russian Duma: Speeches by Professor Milyukoff, Dzubinsky, Tschkeidze, Freedman, Djafaroff, Kerensky, etc., etc.*, trans. and arranged by E. L. Minsky, London, 1915; *The Jews and the War in Russia*, New York, 1916, pp. 81, 84; *The Jews in the Eastern War Zone*, published by the American Jewish Committee in New York, 1916, pp. 49, 70 ff. *See also* the documentary appendix to the aforementioned memorandum of the Poale-Zion (above n. 3); and, more generally, C. Jay Smith, Jr., *The Russian Struggle for Power: a Study of Russian Foreign Policy during the First World War*, New York, 1957.

11. *Shchit* (The Shield), ed. by Maxim Gorki, *et al.*, trans. into English by Avrahm Yarmolinsky, with a Foreword by William English Walling, New York, 1917, pp. 5 f., 8, 24, 57 f., 68, 70 f., 86, 90 f.; *The Jews in the Eastern War Zone*, p. 119. *See also* Gorki's earlier brief description of a "Pogrom" (1901–1903), in his *Sobranie sochinenii* (Collected Works), 30 vols., Moscow, 1949–55, V, 328–33, 486. Baron Rosen's combination of the Finnish and the Jewish questions may have arisen from news about the outside agitation of the *inorodtsi* (peoples of non-Russian origin) against the tsarist regime. In particular, the League of Alien Peoples in Stockholm, under the leadership of the Finn, Hermann Gomerus, tried to bring together representatives of the various minority groups in Russia for joint action against the hostile Russian regime. Its activity culminated in a long cable sent to President Woodrow Wilson, pleading that "Russia had enslaved and turned into derelicts peoples who had been entrusted to it. It has abused its power to torture its own subjects and to destroy their well-being for generations to come. In this fashion Russia itself has repudiated us!" *See* Soppo Zetterberg, "Die Tätigkeit der Liga der Fremdvölker Russlands in Stockholm während der Jahre 1914–1918," *Acta Baltica*, X (1970 [1971]), 211–57, especially p. 220. Yet except for a few individuals sporadically appearing at the league-sponsored assemblies, Jews seem to have absented themselves (the purported Jewish signatory of the cable to Wilson later disavowed his signature), perhaps because of their distrust of the Baltic Germans, particularly Baron Friedrich von Rosen, one of the chief German spokesmen at the league, who was suspected of being a German agent. Even American Jews had to proceed warily, lest their anti-Russian stance be interpreted as sympathy for the Central Powers and as such resented by the Allies. *See* Zosa Szajkowski, "Jewish Diplomacy: Notes on the Occasion of the Centenary of the Alliance Israélite Universelle," *Jewish Social Studies*, XXII (1960), 131–58, especially pp. 134 ff., 149 ff.; and on the special relations between the German invaders and the ethnic Germans in Latvia and Estonia, *see* L. Lawrenz, *Die deutsche Politik im Baltikum, 1914–1918*, Hamburg, 1969.

12. D. Movshovitch, "A Page of Modern Jewish History (1915–1917)" (Yiddish), *YIVO Historishe Shriftn*, II (1937), 549–62 (with a note by E. Tcherikower).

13. René Fülöp-Miller, *Rasputin, the Holy Devil*, trans. from the German by F. S. Flint and D. F. Tait, Garden City, N.Y., 1928 (A Star Book), pp. 61, 227 ff., 282. His general anti-Jewish stance did not save the monk from aspersions, later spread by Nazis and others, that he had helped promote Jewish schemes. *See* Rudolf Kummer, *Rasputin—ein Werkzeug der Juden*, Nuremberg, 1939. *See also* the more judicious appraisal by Elizabeth Judas, *Rasputin, Neither Devil Nor Saint*, 2d ed., Miami, Fla., 1965.

[11]
Era of Revolutions

1. The text of this appeal is reproduced in a German trans. in *Die Judenfrage der Gegenwart: Dokumentensammlung*, ed. by Leon Chasanowitsch and Leo Motzkin, Stockholm, 1919, pp. 35 ff. The government decree of March 20, "On the Revocation of Religious and National Disabilities," included this crucial passage: "All the limitations on the rights of Russian citizens imposed by hitherto existing laws on the basis of religion, creed or nationality are hereby revoked." It was supplemented by a list of some one hundred and fifty such restrictive provisions from the earlier tsarist legislation, all of which were now abrogated. The news about their newly won equality rapidly spread among the Jews, who during the following days were celebrating their Passover holiday, their traditional "festival of liberation." According to Saul M. Ginsburg, some Petrograd families gave vent to their exhilaration by substituting the reading of the decree for the recitation of portions of their traditional *Haggadah*. *See* Yehuda Slutsky, "Russian Jewry during the Year of the Revolution" (Hebrew), *Heawar*, XV (1968), 32–35, especially p. 36. *See also* the essays by Benzion Dinur, Samuel Ettinger *et al.* in that issue; and Gregor Aronson, "Jewish Communal Life in 1917–1918" in his, Jacob Frumkin *et al.*, eds., *Russian Jewry, 1917–1967*. English trans. by Joel Carmichael, New York, 1969, pp. 13–38, especially pp. 14 f. *See also*, more generally, the large documentary collection in English trans., ed. by R. Browder and Alexander Kerensky in their *Provisional Government 1917. Documents*, Stanford, Cal., 1961; M. Ferro's succinct observations on "La Politique des nationalités du Gouvernement provisoire," *Cahiers du monde russe et soviétique*, II (1961), 131–65.

Of considerable importance also was the role of former Russian expatriates who under the lure of Russia's new egalitarianism returned to their homeland. They even included some residents of the United States, whereas in other years Jews had constituted but a tiny fraction of repatriates. They actually seem to have formed the majority of the 10,000 Russians estimated to have gone back to the new Russian Republic in the first flush of enthusiasm after the February Revolution. Upon his return in August, 1917, from his historic mission to Russia, Elihu Root complained that his work had been hampered by Russian extremists who "were aided by thousands who had swarmed back to Russia from America, declaring America to be as tyrannous as the Czar." *See* Zosa

Szajkowski, *Jews, Wars and Communism,* 2 vols., New York, 1972–74, especially I, 270 ff., 283 ff.

In this connection, Professor Dinur has rightly observed that "although the historic evolution of Russian Jewry in the period from February to October 1917 is of great importance for Jewish history in general, it has not yet received any basic scholarly treatment. Even the sources appertaining thereto have thus far not been listed and still less assembled" (*Heawar,* pp. 17 f.). Clearly, this period of transition has been completely overshadowed in the minds of scholars by the more decisive events after the Bolshevik take-over. *See also* Dinur's own meaningful reminiscences in his *Bi-yemei milḥamah u-mahapekhah* (In Time of War and Revolution: Reminiscences and Autobiographical Notes [1914–1921]), Jerusalem, 1960.

2. This preeminence of Jews in the early communist regime understandably attracted world-wide attention from friend and foe alike. The various anti-Semitic movements in the West kept on denouncing the new world-wide revolutionary propaganda as a tool of an alleged Jewish conspiracy to take over the world domination. Among the numerous pamphlets on this theme one need but mention J. F. (Fedor Izmailevich) Roditschew and Alfred Nossig, *Bolschewismus und Juden,* ed. by David Eintracht, Berlin, 1922; Daniel S. Pasmanek, *Russkaia revolutsiia i evreistvo* (The Russian Revolution and Jewry), Paris, 1923; Dimitrii Bulaschow (pseud. for Benjamin Segel), *Bolschewismus und Judentum,* 3d ed. rev. of *Die Nutzniesser des Bolschewismus,* Berlin, 1923; and the later violent Nazi diatribes by Herman Fehst, *Bolschewismus und Judentum. Das jüdische Element in der Führerschaft des Bolschewismus,* Berlin, 1934; and by Rudolf Kommoss, *Juden hinter Stalin: die jüdische Vormachtstellung in der Sowjetunion, auf Grund amtlicher Sowjetquellen dargestellt,* 3d ed., Berlin, 1942. More serious, though also permeated with Nazi bias, are Reinhart Maurach's *Russische Judenpolitik,* Berlin, 1939; and Peter Heinz Seraphim's comprehensive study of *Das Judentum im osteuropäischen Raum,* Essen, 1938. The lengths to which some anti-Jewish and anticommunist rumor mongers were prepared to go is well illustrated by the story spread after the communist take-over that the new leader was not the genuine Lenin, who allegedly had died in Switzerland two years before, but a Jewish imposter named Zederblum (evidently a misspelling of the name Zederbaum-Martov), who assumed Lenin's name. *See* Alexander Dallin, "Bias and Blunders in American Studies on the U.S.S.R.," *Slavic Review,* XXXII (1973), 560–76, especially p. 560; with the general comments thereon by John A. Armstrong, *ibid.,* pp. 577–87.

3. In his purported diary Litvinov referred to a conversation he had allegedly had with Lazar Kaganovich about the appointment of a Jewish communist to serve as Secretary-General of the Party in Kazakhstan. Kaganovich objected because the man had been a member of a left-wing Jewish organization, whereupon Litvinov jokingly suggested that perhaps they ought to introduce a *numerus clausus* into the Party. *See* Maxim Litvinov, *Notes for a Journal.* Introduction by E. H. Carr, and a Prefatory Note by Walter Bedell Smith, New York, 1955, pp. 39 f. True, the authenticity of this document has rightly been impugned. *See,* for instance, Philip E. Mosely's review of this volume in *The New York Times* of November 6, 1955; and Bertram D. Wolfe, "The Litvinov 'Diaries' Literary

Detective Story," *Commentary*, XXII (1956), 164–71. Doubts were voiced by Carr himself in the Introduction. Yet some of these alleged dialogues approximate the truth. *Se non a vero*. . . . On Litvinov (Meir Genokh Moiseevich Wallach, 1876–1952), his Jewish family in Bialystok and his almost exclusive use of Yiddish in his early years, see Arthur Upham Pope, *Maxim Litvinov*, New York, 1943, pp. 35 ff. In contrast thereto, see Leon Trotsky, *My Life: an Attempt at an Autobiography*, New York, 1930, p. 292; and the comprehensive analysis of Trotsky's family background and general attitude toward Jews and Judaism—which not only reflected his complete repudiation of his ancestral religion but often bordered on outright self-hatred—in Joseph Nedava's *Trotsky and the Jews*, Philadelphia, 1972, especially pp. 28 ff., 100 ff. *See also* the judicious weighing of the evidence concerning the general "Extent of Jewish Participation in the October Revolution," *ibid.*, pp. 133 ff.

4. Leonard Schapiro in the *Slavonic and East-European Review*, XL, especially p. 165; E. H. Carr, "The Origins and Status of the Cheka," *Soviet Studies*, X (1958–59), 1–11; and, more generally, S. Wolin and R. Slusser, eds., *The Soviet Secret Police*, New York, 1957. The high percentage of Jews in the secret service contrasted with the even greater ratio of Jewish revolutionaries brought to trial by the tsarist police and condemned to long prison terms with hard labor. Their ratio had risen from 11 percent in the years 1884–90 to 24.8 percent in 1898–99. *See* Elias Tcherikower, "Jews–Revolutionaries in Russia" (Yiddish), *YIVO Historishe Shriftn*, III (1939), 60–172, especially p. 129. These figures are but partially accounted for by the anti-Jewish bias of the tsarist police and courts.

5. N. Gergel, "Jews in the Russian Communist Party and the Communist Youth Organization" (Yiddish), *Yivo Bleter*, I (1931), 62–70. Slightly different data are cited by Abraham Heller in *Die Lage der Juden in Russland von der Märzrevolution 1917 bis zur Gegenwart*, Breslau, 1935 (Schriften der Gesellschaft zur Förderung der Wissenschaft des Judentums, XXXIX), pp. 107 ff. Fuller answers to these and other problems will be supplied only after the enormous number of documentary materials, published and unpublished, extant in the Russian archives are carefully sifted through and analyzed. According to G. A. Below's "Dokumentarische Quellen zur Epoche der Oktoberrevolution in den staatlichen Archiven der UdSSR" in *Die Oktoberrevolution und Deutschland: Referate und Diskussion*, ed. by Albert Schreiner, Berlin, 1958, pp. 369–79, the Central Government Archives of the October Revolution alone had accumulated more than 6,000,000 documents. In addition, there are many more millions scattered in the numerous other archives throughout the Union. Nor is the habit of many scholars to publish individual documents in the daily and weekly press throughout the country really helpful so long as there are no satisfactory bibliographical guides to these scattered publications.

6. Vladimir Ilich Lenin (Ulianov), "The Position of the Bund in the Party" (Russian), reprinted from the *Iskra* of Oct. 22, 1903, in his *Sochineniia* (Works), 4th ed., 40 vols., Moscow, 1941–62, VII, 76–86; in the authorized English trans. of his *Collected Works* published by the Marx-Leninist Institute of the Central Committee of the Communist Party, Moscow, 1960–62, VII, 92–103, especially pp. 99, 101. *See also* his earlier article (in *Iskra* of Feb. 15, 1903), "Does the Jewish Proletariat Need an 'Independent Political Party'?" reproduced in *Sochineniia*,

Notes

VI, 295–300; and *Collected Works*, VI, 330–35; and other communist statements against the Bund, cited by Khatskel Dunets in his *Kegn sotsialfashistishn Bund* (Against the Social-Fascist Bund: Against the Idealization of Bundism), Minsk, 1932.

7. This Declaration of the Rights of Nationalities, signed by V. Ulianov (Lenin) and Joseph Djugashvili (Stalin), is reproduced in the pamphlet *Lenin on the Jewish Question*, issued by the International Publishers in New York, 1936. *See also* Alfred D. Low, *Lenin on the Question of Nationality*, New York, 1958; and Richard Pipes's comprehensive analysis of *The Formation of the Soviet Union: Communism and Nationalism, 1917–1923*, Cambridge, Mass., 1954. Great inconsistencies in the Marxist nationalist doctrines had already been manifest in Marx himself; *see* Solomon F. Bloom, *The World of Nations: a Study of the National Implications in the Work of Karl Marx*, New York, 1941; and my brief review of that work in *Jewish Social Studies*, III (1941), 438–39. On the Lithuanian developments *see* Alfred Erich Senn, "Die bolschewistische Politik in Litauen, 1917–1919," *Forschungen zur osteuropäischen Geschichte*, V (1957), 93–118.

8. N. S. Timasheff, "Russian Nationalism under the Soviets," *Thought*, XX (1945), 443 f.; Joseph Stalin, *Political Report to the Sixteenth Party Congress of the Russian Communist Party*, English trans. from the Russian, New York, 1930, p. 191. Even more "dialectical" was Stalin's position regarding the Jewish nationality. At the height of the Bolshevik-Bundist controversy, he joined Lenin in denying the very national character of the Jewish people. In his pertinent 1913 essay he defined nationality as "a historically evolved stable community of language, territory, economic life, and psychological make-up manifested in a community of culture." The criterion of territory alone ruled the Jews out of that norm. But even culturally Stalin asked: "What national cohesion can there be between the Georgian, Daghestanian, Russian and American Jews?" *See* his *Marxism and the National and Colonial Question*, English trans., London, n.d., pp. 8 ff. Although under the pressure of existing conditions the communist regime had to include the Jews in the protective treatment of the widely heralded Soviet national minority rights, this outlook was never formally abandoned by the Party and its formulation made itself increasingly felt during the years of Stalin's dictatorship. On the ideological vicissitudes of this policy, *see* Jacob Miller's analysis of the "Soviet Theory on the Jews" in *The Jews in Soviet Russia since 1917*, ed. by Lionel Kochan, 2d ed., London, 1972, pp. 44–61; and with reference to the Jewish and other religions, my *Modern Nationalism and Religion*, pp. 197 ff. *See also* Zvi Y. Gitelman's informative study, *Jewish Nationality and Soviet Politics: the Jewish Section of the CPSU, 1917–1930*, Princeton, 1972.

9. The proceedings and resolutions of that Second Conference are extensively reproduced by S. Agurskii in *Di yidishe komisariatn un di yidishe komunistishe sektsies* (The Jewish Commissariats and Communist Sections: Protocols, Resolutions and [Other] Documents, 1918–1921), Minsk, 1928 (published by the *Histpart* at the Central Committee of the White Russian Communist Party), especially p. 228; L. Tsentsiper's *Eser shenot redifot* (Ten Years of Persecutions: a Story of the Persecutions of the Zionist Movement in the Soviet Union), Tel Aviv, 1930, pp. 97 ff., 269 ff. App. iv; Lenin's article of February 15, 1903, cited above, n. 6. In his anti-Zionist fervor, Lenin went so far as to declare that

"Zionism appears to be a greater enemy to Social Democracy than antisemitism. . . . The Zionist Movement is a more immediate threat to the development of the class organization of the proletariat than antisemitism." *See* his *Sochineniia,* 1st ed., Moscow, 1925, IV, 219. This obvious exaggeration is explicable only in terms of the Bolshevik leader's heated controversy with the Bundists and his consistent drive to concentrate all revolutionary activity around his centralized organization.

Typical of the numerous later publicist attacks on Zionism are the pamphlets by "Hadad," *Der Tsionizm vi er iz* (Zionism as It Is), 2d ed., Moscow, 1925; Alexander Chemeriski, *Tsionistishe Traiberaien* (Zionist Cabals: a Collection of Essays), Moscow, 1926; and P. Minski, *Vi lebt un kempt der arbeter in Palestine* (How the Worker Lives and Struggles in Palestine), Minsk, 1932, with such characteristic chapter headings as "50 Years of Imperialist-Zionist Colonization" or "Zionist Cities and Colonies—Strategic Outposts of British Imperialism." *See also* Dan Pines, *He-Halus be-kur ha-mahapekhah* (The Haluts Movement in the Crucible of the Revolution), Vol. I: 1917–1924, Tel Aviv, 1924; Guido G. Goldman, *Zionism under Soviet Rule (1917–1928),* New York, 1960; and below, Chap. 12, n. 18.

10. S. Dimanshtain, "The Beginnings of Communist Work among the Jewish Laborers" (1919), a report in Yiddish, prepared for an intended volume *A yor arbet* (A Year's Work), the proofs of which were destroyed in 1920. This report was later published in Agurskii's *Di yidishe komisariatn,* pp. 1–16. Curiously, Agurskii found it necessary, in the light of intervening developments, to correct Dimanshtain's semilaudatory reference to the more passive opposition of Labor Zionists (p. 4 n.). *See also ibid.,* pp. 423 ff.; and J. Barzilai's "Talks with S. Dimanshtain" (Hebrew), *Heawar,* XVIII (1968), 216–39. These interviews with a personal friend reveal the oft-denounced leader of *Yevsektsiia* as a split personality in relation to Jewish culture. This is the less surprising as in his first twenty-five years this leader of the *Yevsektsiia* had lived an Orthodox Jewish life, attended the Telzhe, Slobodka, and Lubavitch *yeshivot,* was for a while captivated by the *Musar* and hasidic movements, and secured a rabbinic ordination from distinguished Orthodox rabbis. Now he found himself in the position of having to play a major role in the dismantling of the traditional Jewish communal structure and in the serious undermining of the survivalist forces of his people. *See* Z. Y. Gitelman, *Jewish Nationality,* pp. 130 ff. and *passim.* All of these reversals did not prevent Dimanshtain from ultimately sharing the fate of many of the Bolshevik Old Guard. He was executed in 1937 during the era of the great Stalinist "purges."

11. Agurskii, *Di yidishe komisariatn,* pp. 19 ff., 59f.; and more generally his succinct summary on "Evsektsii" in *Bolshaia sovetskaia entsiklopedia,* 1st ed., XXIV (1932), 337–38. Curiously, in the bibliography he was able to cite exclusively Yiddish books.

12. Lenin, "Socialism and Religion," in the English trans. in his *Selected Works,* 12 vols., New York, [n.d.], XI, 658, 661; P. V. Gidulianov, *Otdelenie tserkvi od gosudarstva v S. S. S. R.* (Separation of State and Church in the Soviet Union), 3d ed., Moscow, 1926; William Chauncey Emhardt, *Religion in Soviet Russia: Anarchy,* Milwaukee, 1929; and other literature listed in my *Modern Nationalism and Religion,* pp. 23, 197 ff., 331 ff.

13. Cited in an English trans. from the 16th ed. by Julius F. Hecker in his *Religion and Communism: a Study of Religion and Atheism in Russia*, London, 1933, p. 275 App. I.

14. Elisha Rodin, *Bi-fe'at nekhar* (In Foreign Parts: Poems and Reflections), Tel Aviv, 1938, pp. 23, 38 (my trans.). At the same time, the poet made it clear that he had no use whatsoever for the counterrevolution which "hangs," rather than "shoots," its opponents. *Ibid.*, pp. 63 ff.

15. *See* A. L. Tsentsiper, *Eser shenot redifot*, p. 27; J. Nedava, *Trotsky*, pp. 154 f.; A. Kirzhnitz, *Di yidishe prese in Ratnfarband* (The Jewish Press in the Soviet Union), Minsk, 1928, p. 68; Joseph B. Schechtman, "The U.S.S.R., Zionism, and Israel," in L. Kochan, *The Jews in Soviet Russia*, 2d ed., pp. 99–124; Z. Y. Gitelman, *Jewish Nationality*, especially pp. 75 ff.; and, more generally, Oliver Henry Radkey, *The Election to the Russian Constituent Assembly of 1917*, Cambridge, Mass., 1950. *See also* below, Chap. 14.

16. *Alfarbandishe beratung fun di yidishe sektsies* (All-Union Conference of the Jewish Sections of the Communist Party of December, 1926), Moscow, 1927, pp. 130 f. This greatly abbreviated report of the Conference proceedings is analyzed by Solomon M. Schwarz in *The Jews in the Soviet Union*. With a Foreword by Alvin Johnson, Syracuse, 1951, pp. 122 ff.

17. Lenin, *Sochineniia* (Works), 2d ed., XXIV (1932), 203 (repeated in the new ed. XXIX, 227–28); the translation of the 1918 decree in *Lenin on the Jewish Question*, p. 23; Schwarz, *The Jews in the Soviet Union*, pp. 274 ff., 289 n. 14. *See also* Anatolii V. Lunacharskii, *Ob antisemitizme* (On Antisemitism), Moscow, 1929; and I. Larin (pseud. for M. A. Lurye), *Evrei i antisemitizm v SSSR* (Jews and Anti-Semitism in the USSR), Moscow, 1929.

18. I. Zilberman, "The Court in Its Struggle against Anti-Semitism" (Russian), *Ezhenedelnik sovetskoi iustitsii* (Weekly of the Soviet Judiciary), 1929, No. 4, p. 148, cited in an English trans. by S. M. Schwarz in *The Jews*, pp. 276 ff.; Larin, *Evrei*, pp. 277 f.; Maxim Gorki, cited by Reuben Ainsztein in his "Jewish Tragedy and Heroism in Soviet War Literature," *Jewish Social Studies*, XXIII (1961), 68. *See also* M. Gorev, *Protiv Antisemitov* (Against Anti-Semites), Moscow, 1928; and L. Rodishchev, *Yad* (Poison: On Contemporary Anti-Semitism), Leningrad, 1930. The very appearance of the four volumes (including Lunacharskii's and Larin's) within little more than two years reflects the awareness of both the public and the upper levels of the Soviet bureaucracy that the expected disappearance of anti-Jewish attitudes among the masses after a decade of Soviet rule represented wishful thinking more than reality.

19. The Ukrainian legislation and its practical applications were cited in full and analyzed by some of the most active Jewish politicians who participated in these early Ukrainian liberation movements. *See* especially M. Zilberfarb, *Dos yidishe ministerium un di yidishe avtonomie in Ukraine* (The Jewish Ministry and Jewish Autonomy in the Ukraine: a Page of History), Kiev, [1918] (with an extensive documentary appendix); Salomon Goldelmann, *Juden und Ukrainer (Briefe und Dokumente)*, Vienna, 1921; A. Rewutski, *In di shvere teg oif Ukraine* (In the Difficult Days in the Ukraine: Memoirs of a Jewish Minister), Berlin, 1924. *See also* his informative essay "Patterns of Life of an Ethnic Minority," *Annals* of the Ukrainian Academy of Arts and Sciences in the U.S., VII (1959–Arnold Margolin Memorial Vol.), 1567–85. On their part, through their press service in Western lands, the Ukrainian nationalist leaders distributed a brochure, *Die Lage der Juden in der Ukraine. Eine Dokumentensammlung*, ed. by Wladimir Lewitzkyj and Gustav Specht, Berlin, 1920. Here various decrees, appeals by Ukrainian and Jewish groups, etc., were reproduced in a German trans., including Margolin's and Mark Wischnitzer's interviews published in the *Jewish Chronicle* (London) of May 16, and September 19, 1919. *See also* the extensive documentation supplied by *Di idishe avtonomie un der natsionaler sekretariat in Ukraine* (Jewish Autonomy and the National Secretariat in the Ukraine: Materials and Documents), Kiev, 1920. This volume was ed. for the Secretariat by M. Grossmann *et al.* at a time when most regulations had become obsolete.

20. The proclamation of 1917 is cited, from the *Razsvet* of Sept. 6, 1917, by Elias Tcherikower in his *Antisemitizm un pogromen in Ukraine* (Anti-Semitism and Pogroms in the Ukraine 1917–1918: a Contribution to the History of Ukrainian-Jewish Relations. With a Foreword by Simon Dubnow), Berlin, 1923, p. 52. It may be noted that in reply to a Jewish delegation which contrasted the relative absence of anti-Jewish excesses in Kolchak's army with the disturbances under Denikin, the latter's collaborator, Gen. Shkura, explained Kolchak's restraint by his consideration for "the all-controlling American Jews." Cited from a memorandum by the Jewish Central Committee to the Zionist Actions Committee by Lewitskyj and Specht in *Die Juden*, pp. 75 f.

21. Nikolai Ostrowskii, *The Making of a Hero*, English trans. by Alec Brown, New York, 1937, p. 77; S. Goldelmann, *Juden und Ukrainer*, pp. 49 f.; A. Rewutski, *In di shvere teg*, pp. 290 f. The regime's equivocation came fully to the fore during the Paris trial of Samuel Schwartzbard, the 1926 assassin of Petliura. *See Documents sur les pogromes en Ukraine et l'assassinat de Simon Petlura à Paris*, Paris, 1927, the materials for which were largely supplied by Elias Tcherikower. *See* the next notes.

22. Tcherikower, *Antisemitizm*, pp. 275 ff.; Isaac Babel, *Gedali*, in Alexander Kaun's English trans. in his "Babel: Voice of New Russia," *Menorah Journal*, XV (1928), 412. *See* N. Gergel, "The Pogroms in the Ukraine in the Years 1918–1921" (Yiddish), *YIVO Shriftn far ekonomik*, I (1928), 106–13, especially p. 111. *See also*, more generally, Arthur E. Adams, "The Bolsheviks and the Ukrainian Front in 1918–1919," *Slavonic and East-European Review*, XXXVI (1958), 396–417; and John S. Reshetar, *The Ukrainian Revolution, 1917–1920: a Study in Nationalism*, Princeton, 1952 (Diss. Harvard University).

23. In addition to the studies listed in the previous notes, *see* Elias Heifetz, *The Slaughter of the Jews in the Ukraine in 1919*, New York, 1921 (by the former chairman of the All-Ukrainian Relief Committee for the Victims of Pogroms); A. D. Rosenthal, *Megillat ha-tebah* (Scroll of Slaughter: Materials for the History of the Pogroms and Slaughter of the Jews in the Ukraine, Greater Russia, and White Russia), 3 vols., Jerusalem, 1929–31 (arranged in the alphabetical order of the destroyed communities); and, more comprehensively, Elias Tcherikower, *Yehudim be-ittot ha-mahapekhah* (Jews in Revolutionary Periods). With a Foreword by Ben Zion Dinur, Tel Aviv, 1957. *See also* the additional data and literature supplied by Abraham Heller in *Die Lage der Juden in Russland, passim*. On the economic effects, *see* the succinct summary in Jacob Lestschinsky, *La Situation économique des Juifs depuis la guerre mondiale (Europe orientale et centrale)*, Paris, 1934

Notes

(Cahiers of the Comité des Délégations Juives, XI–XIV), pp. 48 f. More recently, the issue of the Ukrainian pogroms, the more general developments relating to both the position of the Jewish minority under the rapidly changing Ukrainian regimes, and to a lesser extent the internal developments within the Jewish community in the area have been discussed by numerous writers, including some former actors in the great Ukrainian-Jewish political drama. *See* especially Joseph Schechtman's "Jewish Community Life in the Ukraine (1917–1919)," in G. Aronson, J. Frumkin *et al.*, eds., *Russian Jewry, 1917–1967*, pp. 39–57; and Solomon L. Goldelman, *Jewish National Autonomy in the Ukraine, 1917–1920*, Chicago, 1968.

On Petliura's personal role during the massacres, *see* the debate between Taras Hunczak in "A Reappraisal of Symon Petliura: Ukrainian Jewish Relations, 1917–1921," and Zosa Szajkowski in his "A Rebuttal" thereto in *Jewish Social Studies*, XXXI (1969), 163–83 and 184–213, respectively, followed by both authors' extensive "Letters to the Editors," *ibid.*, XXXII (1970), 246–53 and 253–63. In any case, Israel Zangwill was quite right in summarizing the tragic situation of Ukrainian Jewry during those years by stating that "it is as Bolsheviks that the Jews of South Russia have been massacred by the armies of Petliura, though the armies of Sokolow have massacred them as partisans of Petliura, the armies of Makhno as bourgeois capitalists, the armies of Grigoriew as Communists, and the armies of Denikin at once as Bolshevists, capitalists and Ukrainian nationalists. It is Aesop's old fable." *See* the London *Jewish Chronicle* of January 23, 1920, p. 14, cited by Szajkowski, XXXII, 256.

24. On other Jewish self-defense groups which functioned during the pogrom era of 1918–19, *see* the Hebrew studies and reminiscences by Dov Ber Slutsky and others in *Heawar*, XVII (1970), 90–120.

25. Richard Pipes, *The Formation of the Soviet Union: Communism and Nationalism, 1917–1923*, p. 152. *See* the data presented by the anonymous study, *Evreiskie pogromy* (Anti-Jewish Pogroms, 1918–1919: Materials), Moscow, 1926, pp. 22 ff. Dramatic testimony of excesses committed by Polish troops in the occupied territories was presented to Sir Stuart Samuel. *See* his *Report on My Mission to Poland*, London, 1920 (Foreign Office, Miscellanies, X).

26. *See* the illustrations cited by B. Orshanskii in his "Yiddish Poetry in White Russia After the Revolution" (Yiddish), *Zeitshrift*, V (Minsk, 1931), 1–83, especially pp. 39 ff.; Nikolai Ostrovskii, *Kak zakalialas stal* (How the Steel Was Tempered), in the English trans. from the Russian by R. Prokofieva, 2 vols., Moscow, 1952 (Library of Selected Soviet Literature); Alexander A. Fadeev, *Razgrom* (The Debacle), in the English trans. by R. D. Charques entitled *The Nineteen*, New York, 1929; R. Ainsztein in *Jewish Social Studies*, XXIII, 68 ff. Other Jewish heroes are depicted in such early Soviet stories as Marietta Shaginian's *Agit-Car*, published in 1923; and G. Nikifirov's *Grey Days* of 1926. On Babel's *Red Cavalry*, *see* below, Chap. 14, n. 25. Not that these writers were unaware of the widespread anti-Semitic sentiment even among the Red soldiers. In Fadeev's novel the first page records the reaction of Levinson's orderly, Morozka, who upon receiving an unpleasant assignment, thinks silently, "All Jews are scoundrels!" But such responses were dismissed as temporary relapses to a bygone era.

27. See Joshua Kunitz in his Columbia University dissertation, *Russian Literature and the Jew: a Sociological Inquiry into the Nature and Origin of Literary Poems*, New York, 1929, pp. 169 ff., 175 ff., 191 n. 8. *See also* Maurice Friedberg, "Jewish Themes in Soviet Russian Literature," in L. Kochan, ed., *The Jews in Soviet Russia*, pp. 188–207. Contrast, however, his references to Ostrovskii and Fadeev (pp. 191 f.) with his strictures on my treatment in the first ed. of the present book in *Midstream*, XI, No. 1 (1965), p. 193.

[12]

Interwar Consolidation

1. Yakov Kantor, *Natsionalnoe stroitelstvo sredi Evreev v SSSR* (National Reconstruction among the Jews of the Soviet Union), ed. by E. Ostrovskii, Moscow, 1934, pp. 21 ff., 27 f., etc.; S. M. Schwarz, *The Jews in the Soviet Union*, pp. 149 ff.

2. Kantor, *op. cit.*, pp. 29 ff.; Schwarz, *op. cit.*, pp. 156 ff. *See also* Benjamin Pinkus, "Yiddish Language Courts and Nationalities Policy in the Soviet Union," trans. from the Hebrew by Doron Horowitz in *Soviet Jewish Affairs*, 1971, No. 2, pp. 40–60.

3. *See* J. Nedava, *Trotsky and the Jews*, especially pp. 105 ff., 152 f.; S. Agurskii, *Der yidisher arbeter in der kommunistisher bavegung* (The Jewish Worker in the Communist Movement, 1917–1921), Minsk, 1925, p. 9, here quoted in the English excerpt by Z. Y. Gitelman in his *Jewish Nationality*, p. 126. *See also* Gitelman's further observations, *ibid.*, pp. 105 ff.

4. Yakov Kantor, *Ratenboiung in der yidisher svive* (Soviet Reconstruction in the Jewish Environment), Kiev, 1928 (written in July 1927), pp. 18, 51; *idem*, *Natsionalnoe stroitelstvo, passim*; *Yidn in FSSR* (Jews in the Soviet Union: Atlas and Graphs), Moscow, 1930, p. 127; Otto Heller, *Der Untergang des Judentums: Die Judenfrage—ihre Kritik—Lösung durch den Sozialismus*, Vienna, 1931, pp. 192 ff.

5. Joseph Stalin (Djugashvili), *Marxism and the National and Colonial Question: a Collection of Articles and Speeches*, New York, n. d. (Marxist Library, XXXVIII); *idem*, *Political Report to the Sixteenth Party Congress*, English trans. cited above, Chap. 11, n. 8. *See also* S. Dimanshtain's rather tortured review of "Stalin as a Bolshevist Theoretician of the National Question" (Yiddish), *Zeitshrift*, IV (1930), pp. vii–xxi; his ed. of essays on *Revolutsiia i natsionalnyi vopros* (The Revolution and the National Question: Documents and Materials for the History of the National Question in Russia and the Soviet Union in the Twentieth Century), collected by I. Levin and E. Drabkin, Moscow, 1930; and above, Chap. 11, nn. 6–8.

6. *Bolshaia sovetskaia entsiklopedia*, 1st ed., Moscow, 1932, XXIV, 338.

7. Kalinin's speech of November, 1926, first appeared in the stenographic transcript of the proceedings at the *Pervii vsesoiuznii siezd OZET v Moskve* (First All-Soviet Congress of the OZET in Moscow, November 15–20, 1926). Republished, together with his reply to a Crimean community, in both Russian and

Notes

Yiddish in the Izvestia and the Emes of July 11, 1926, it was widely heralded in Jewish circles in the Soviet Union and abroad. It was distributed in a Yiddish trans. by the GEZERD (OZET) under Kalinin's name in a brochure entitled *Yidn Erd-Arbeter* (Jewish Workers in the U.S.S.R.), Moscow, 1927.

8. See Dimanshtain's and other statements excerpted by D. Zalbefert et al. in their *Birobidzhanish* (Biro-Bidzhan Matters: a Small Anthology on the Jewish Autonomous Region), Vilna, 1935, pp. 22 ff. The editors admit not only the general incompleteness of their materials, but also their total disregard of voices opposing that scheme. So enthusiastic had the protagonists of the project become that they not only overruled the serious objections of such experts among the OZET members as the economist Yuri Larin and the agronomist Abraham Bragin, but completely disregarded the elaborate report of their own large mission to the Far East, which consisted of 180 persons, including 85 scientists. They paid no attention, for example, to the emphatic recommendation that the colonization begin in the southern, relatively most fertile part of the area along the Amur River and from there gradually spread into the less promising northern sections. Similarly, in their haste to exploit the public relations and strategic aspects of their project, they took lightly the equally strong suggestion that before any colonists were sent to Biro-Bidzhan, a year's preparatory work be done on the spot so as to provide some housing, tools, roads, and so forth. See Jacob Levavi's (Babitski's) careful study, *Ha-Hityashvut ha-yehudit be-Biro-Bidzan* (Jewish Settlement in Biro-Bidzhan), Jerusalem, 1965; and Solomon Schwarz's "Birobidzhan: an Experiment in Jewish Colonization," in G. Aronson, J. Frumkin et al., eds., *Russian Jewry 1917–1967*, pp. 342–95.

9. See D. Zalbefert et al., *Birobidzhanish*, p. 26. According to the Soviet census of 1926 the area later assigned to Biro-Bidzhan (1927, subsequently somewhat enlarged) embraced 27,344 inhabitants. This population was largely recruited from descendants of the Trans-Baikal Cossacks settled there by the tsarist authorities in the first two decades after their annexation of that area in 1858. It was later augmented by Korean and other immigrants. These "natives" reacted unfavorably to that mass immigration, further complicating the tasks of the new settlers. Of course, under the totalitarian Soviet regime, the local population could neither as frequently nor as vigorously voice its opposition to the new colonization as did its counterpart, the Arab residents of Palestine under the British Mandate. On the other hand, the Jewish officials involved in the Biro-Bidzhan scheme often unwittingly echoed Zionist phraseology, such as the famous Herzlian exclamation, "If you want it, you will achieve it." See Chimen Abramsky, "The Biro-Bidzhan Project," in L. Kochan's *The Jews in Soviet Russia*, p. 69; and on its 1917–18 antecedents in the wider area, James William Morley, "The Russian Revolution in the Amur Basin," *American Slavic and East European Review*, XVI (1957), 450–72.

10. D. Zalbefert, p. 23; Dimanshtain, *Yidishe Avtonome gegend* (Jewish Autonomous Region: a Child of the October Revolution), Moscow, 1934; Dudley L. A. Lord Marley, *Birobidjan as I Saw It*, New York, 1934 (ICOR Library, II). Marley's statement was understandably cited in the propaganda brochure *Birobidjan, the Jewish Autonomous Territory*, published by the American Committee for the Settlement of Jews in Birobidjan (Ambijan), New York, 1936, p. 8.

11. I. Sudarskii, *Biro-Bidzhan* (Yiddish), Kharkov, 1933, especially pp. 19, 22 ff., 66 ff. *See also* ICOR's equally overoptimistic English pamphlet, *Biro Bidjan Today and Tomorrow*, New York, n.d.; and Sol Almazov's review of *Ten Years of Biro-Bidjan*, trans. from the Yiddish by Nathan Farber, New York, 1938.

12. Viktor Fink, "Biro-Bidzhan" (Russian) in *Sovetskoe Stroitelstvo* of May, 1930, p. 117; Sudarskii, *Biro-Bidzhan*, pp. 70, 75 f.; the GEZERD's semiofficial publication *Birobidzhan in itstikn moment* (B. at the Present Time) by A. Kantorovich, Moscow, 1933; and other data carefully sifted by S. M. Schwarz in *The Jews in the Soviet Union*, pp. 174 ff.; *idem*, "Birobidzhan," pp. 360 f. Here Schwarz cautions the reader that the ratios of Jewish immigrants to reimmigrants given for the first six years of the Biro-Bidzhan project seem not to include any data on the natural growth of the Jewish population. Yet he believes that this consideration "could not have much affected the final figure."

The numerous blunders of the colonizing agency are to be attributed not only to the general inefficiency of a far-flung bureaucracy beset by enormous difficulties all over the Union, but also to the great haste with which it tried to accomplish an almost superhuman task within ten to fifteen years in the face of a threatened Far Eastern war. However, Leon Trotsky, biased observer that he was, rightly contended in 1937 that "under a regime of Soviet democracy Biro-Bidzhan could undoubtedly play a serious national-cultural role in regard to Soviet Jewry. Under a Bonapartist regime which nourishes anti-Semitic tendencies, Biro-Bidzhan threatens to degenerate into a sort of Soviet ghetto." On another occasion he even more bluntly dismissed the whole undertaking as "a bureaucratic farce." *See* J. Nedava, *Trotsky and the Jews*, pp. 211 ff.

13. A. Kantorovich, *Tsvaiter 5-yor plan* (The Second Five-Year Plan for Biro-Bidzhan), 2d ed., New York, 1932.

14. *See* especially the statements made by Gine Medem and O. Pressman and excerpted in *Birobidzhanish*, pp. 28, 30 f.; the Ambijan's *Birobidjan*, p. 6.

15. A. Powell, "The Nationalist Trend in Soviet Historiography," *Soviet Studies*, II (1950–51), 372–77; Robert H. McNeal, "Soviet Historiography on the October Revolution: a Review of Forty Years," *American Slavic and East-European Review*, XVII (1958), 269–81.

16. *Pravda* of November 7, 1938, cited by Nicholas S. Timasheff in his "Russian Nationalism under the Soviets," *Thought*, XX (1945), 447; and more fully in his *The Great Retreat: the Growth and Decline of Communism in Russia*, New York, 1946, pp. 151 ff., 168; Frank Lorimer, *The Population of the Soviet Union: History and Prospects*, Geneva, 1946, pp. 137 ff.; and other sources mentioned in my *Modern Nationalism and Religion*, pp. 203 ff., 332 f. nn. 71–73. *See also* Vincas Rastenis's succinct observation on "The Russification of Non-Russian Peoples in the Russian Empire under the Czars and under the Soviets," *Lituanus*, VI (1959), 103–107.

Remarkably, the glorification of medieval religious as well as national heroes did not immediately mitigate the impact of the antireligious laws, least of all in the Jewish religious domain. We recall that the crucial statement in the decree of April 9, 1929, about the freedom of antireligious propaganda was taken over verbatim into the 1936 Constitution (*see* above, Chap. 11, n. 13). To be sure, some observers believed they had seen a gradual relaxation in the iconoclastic fervor which characterized the 1920s and early 1930s. But there is no clear evidence to support that contention. In a recent essay Robert Stupperich has rightly insisted that "dependable sources, useful to the historian, concerning the persistent developments in the years 1930–1945, are practically nonexistent." *See* his interesting survey of "Die deutsche Forschung über Religion und Atheismus in der UdSSR seit 1945," *Kirche im Osten*, XV (1972), 74–88. At the same time, the Soviet rulers did not hesitate, for nationalistic reasons, to favor the Russian Orthodox Church against the Uniate faith in the Ukraine. The same anti-Uniate policy was also pursued by the Russian conquerors in 1939–41 and from 1944 on in the newly occupied southwestern territories. See B. R. Bociurkiw's Chicago dissertation, *Soviet Church Policy in the Ukraine, 1919–39,* Chicago, 1961.

17. Kalinin's speech cited above, n. 7; Joseph Roth, *Juden auf Wanderschaft,* Berlin, 1927 (Berichte aus der Wirklichkeit, IV), p. 104; Otto Heller, *Der Untergang des Judentums,* pp. 198, 238; Kloinimus in *Komunistishe Velt,* 1919, Nos. 3–4, cited by Orshanskii in *Zeitshrift,* V, 15 f. *See also* Larin's *Evrei i antisemitizm v SSSR, passim.*

18. S. Y. Chutskaev, "Ten Years of Biro-Bidzhan" (Russian), *Vlast Sovetov,* April, 1938, p. 18; *Emes* of June 3, 1937; S. M. Schwarz, *The Jews,* pp. 180 ff.; and the literature cited above, nn. 11–12.

19. *See* Stalin's *Leninism,* London, 1940, p. 584, cited by C. Abramsky in L. Kochan's *Jews in Soviet Russia,* p. 73; and below, Chap. 13, nn. 20 ff. As a matter of fact, after 1937 the Jewish population of the autonomous region diminished and twenty-two years later in the census of January, 1959, was recorded as being only 14,269 persons, or 8.8 percent of the region's inhabitants. *See* below, Chap. 17, n. 16.

20. Report of the Royal (Peel) Commission, London, 1937. Cmd. 5479. The pro-Zionist sympathies of a great many Jews in the early years of the Soviet regime had found expression not only in the aforementioned 1917 election but also in the actual preparations made by many groups, especially in the troubled years 1918–19, to emigrate to Palestine. Only under the prompting of the anti-Zionist leaders of the *Yevsektsiia,* the originally fairly neutral attitude of the Soviet authorities—still evident in the mild reply of the All-Russian Central Executive Committee of July 21, 1919, to a petition of the Zionist Organization—gradually turned into overt hostility. The *Yevsektsiia's* reiterated accusation that the Zionist movement was "an instrument of united imperialism which combats the proletarian revolution," as it was denounced in the aforementioned resolution of the Second Conference of the Jewish Communist Sections in June, 1919 (above, Chap. 11, n. 9), the Soviet secret service started to harass individual Zionists, arrest many Zionist leaders, and confiscate the property of their organization. For a while the officials still tolerated some emigration of Jews to Palestine—for the most part clandestine. But during the decade of 1925 to 1936 only a total of 3,045 Soviet Jews reached the Promised Land. *See* the extensive documentation in A. L. Tsentsiper's (Rafaeli's) *Eser shenot redifot;* and his Ma'abaq ha-ge'ulah (In the Struggle for Redemption), Tel Aviv, 1950. *See also* the briefer, but more up-to-date, essays by J. B. Schechtman in L. Kochan's *The Jews,* pp. 99–124; and in Aronson, Frumkin *et al., Russian Jewry 1917–1967,* pp. 406–43; S. Gepstein, "Russian Zionists in the Struggle for Palestine," *ibid.,* pp. 503–20; and Julius Margolin, "Russian-Jewish Immigration to Israel," *ibid.,* pp. 540–56.

21. Otto Heller, *Der Untergang*, pp. 231 ff.

22. *See* the interesting statistical table (IX), largely compiled from official Soviet sources, by S. M. Schwarz in *The Jews*, p. 302.

23. Zbigniew Brzezinski, *The Permanent Purge: Politics in Soviet Totalitarianism*, Cambridge, 1956 (Harvard University Research Center, Studies, XX), especially pp. 65 ff., 106, 217 n. 126.

[13]

Socioeconomic Reconstruction

1. *See* the illuminating statistical table (V) in S. M. Schwarz, *The Jews in the Soviet Union*, p. 15, based on sources listed by him, p. 22 n. 23.

2. Arthur Ruppin, *Soziologie der Juden*, 2 vols., Berlin, 1930, I, 175 Table XX, 240 Table XXXIII; L. Zinger, *Dos banaite Folk* (Rejuvenated People), Moscow, 1941, pp. 33 ff., 40; Jacob Lestchinsky, "The Evolution of the Jewish People during the Last One Hundred Years" (Yiddish), *YIVO Shriftn far ekonomik*, I (1928), 24; Friedrich Hermann Zanders, *Die Verbreitung der Juden in der Welt: Statistische Beiträge zu den Fragen der Zeit*, Berlin, 1937, pp. 63 ff. (somewhat colored and unreliable). *See also* above, Chap. 11, n. 23; J. A. Nillesen's comprehensive review of *De sociale Toestand der Joden in Rusland* (The Social Status of the Jews in Russia under the Tsars and the Soviets: a Contribution to the Study of the Jewish Question), Nijmegen, 1939.

3. I. Koralnik, "Jewry in Poland and Russia according to the Latest Censuses" (Yiddish), *YIVO Shriftn far ekonomik*, I, 211–28; L. Zinger, *Evreiskoe naselenie v Sovetskom Soyuze* (Jewish Population in the Soviet Union), Moscow, 1932, pp. 104 ff.; Schwarz, *The Jews*, pp. 168, 172 f. n. 44.

4. Yurii M. Larin, *Evrei i antisemitizm*, p. 133. *See* H. Lowenthal, "Les Juifs de Boukhara," *Cahiers du monde russe et soviétique*, II (1961), 104–108; and Julius Brutzkus, "History of the Jewish Mountaineers in Daghestan (Caucasia)" (Yiddish), *YIVO Historishe Shriftn*, II (1937), 26–42 with an English summary, p. vi.

5. Zinger, *Dos banaite Folk*, pp. 41 ff.

6. M. Kipper, *Dos yidishe shtetl in Ukraine* (The Jewish Hamlet in the Ukraine), Kharkov, 1929, pp. 97 ff.; Larin, *Evrei*, pp. 68 ff., 156; Yakov Kantor, *Di yidishe bafelkerung in Ukraine* (The Jewish Population in the Ukraine: According to the Census of 1926), Kharkov, 1929; *Evrei v S.S.S.R.* (Jews in the Soviet Union: Texts and Studies), published by the ORT, Moscow, 1929, pp. 10 ff.; Genrikh I. Neiman, *Vnutrennaia torgovliia SSSR* (The Soviet Union's Internal Trade), ed. by E. I. Kviring, Moscow, 1935, pp. 145 f.; above, Chap. 6, n. 10. Even the leading Jewish party organ, the Moscow *Emes*, was forced to report the sufferings of the Jews in the small towns and hamlets. A typical communication by D. Feldman from Stepenitse in the Kiev province, published on January 21, 1925, p. 4, read: "The economic situation in the hamlet is terrible. Altogether, the population of 800 souls embraces forty artisans and thirty petty traders. The rest lives from undefinable occupations, from pennies they receive from America, from service

as porters and the like. Only eighteen families, adding up to one hundred persons, have registered for agricultural labor. Not because of unwillingness to register, but they are so poor that they cannot afford to travel to, and still less to establish themselves on, the land." This communication is reproduced by Jacob Lestchinsky in *Der Emes vegn di Yidn in Rusland* (The Truth about the Jews in Russia), Berlin, 1925, pp. 19 f.

7. *See*, for instance, Mikhail Chumandrin, *Fabrika Rable* (Rable's Factory), Leningrad, 1929; and L. Radishchev's critique thereof, both cited by Bernard J. Choseed in "The Soviet Jew in Literature," *Jewish Social Studies*, XI (1949), 262 f.; Jacob Lestchinsky, "Jewish Commercial Employees in the Soviet Ukraine" (Yiddish), *Yivo Bleter*, X (1936), 197–231 (mainly based on the official *Perepis* published in Kiev, 1936); John A. Armstrong, *Ukrainian Nationalism, 1939–1945*, New York, 1958 (Studies of the Russian Institute of Columbia University), p. 227 n. 2; Boris Brutzkus, "Die wirtschaftliche und soziale Lage der Juden in Russland vor und nach der Revolution," *Archiv für Sozialwissenschaft und Sozialpolitik*, LXI (1929), 266–321, especially pp. 301 ff.

8. Numerous such excerpts from the *Emes* and other Soviet newspapers and journals are reproduced by Jacob Lestchinsky in *Der Emes vegn di Yidn in Rusland*, especially pp. 34 ff.

9. Y. Kantor, *Di yidishe bafelkerung*, pp. 44 f. Table 25. Evidently using somewhat different definitions, a pamphlet, *Evrei v kustarno remeslennoi promyshlennosti SSSR* (Jews in the Home Industry of the Soviet Union), published by the ORT in Moscow, 1928, gave the number of those employed in crafts, home work, and petty industry as being 25.2 percent of all gainfully employed Jews in the Ukrainian Republic. Of those 52 percent worked by themselves, 23.6 percent together with their families (including those family members themselves), and only 6.2 percent employed outside labor. The others consisted of factory workers and office personnel. *See* the summary in Ruppin's *Soziologie*, I, 438 f. *See also* Abraham Heller, *Die Lage der Juden in Russland*, pp. 78 ff.

10. B. Brutzkus in *Archiv für Sozialwissenschaft*, LXI, 302 f.; *The Jews under Soviet Rule*, published by the Institute of Jewish Affairs, New York, 1941. The continued activities of the Jewish communal organs, however reduced in scope, doubtless proved helpful to many individuals in making the extremely difficult adjustments to the new society. For a while some Jewish health and welfare agencies, abetted by both the deep-rooted Jewish philanthropic traditions and financial contributions from coreligionists abroad, must have helped many persons in need to overcome their physical and mental handicaps in entering the labor market. Before World War I the physique of many Russian Jewish young people did not quite measure up even to the generally low standards of health among the Russian workers. After more than a decade of wars, massacres, and famines, a 1927 survey showed that the average Jew was shorter and weighed less than his Gentile counterpart. A slightly earlier study of 1,500 Jewish schoolchildren in Gomel revealed that "a far larger proportion of them suffered from anemia and respiratory and circulatory illnesses than did their Polish and Russian classmates." Cited from the *Natsionalnaya politika VKP (b) v tsifrakh* (National Policy VKP (b) in Ciphers), p. 319, and from S. Palatnik's article in *Emes* of January 13, 1926, by Z. Y. Gitelman in his *Jewish Nationality*, p. 493 n. 12.

11. A. Heller, *Die Lage*, pp. 82 ff. *See also* Brutzkus in *Archiv für Sozialwissenschaft*, LXI, 266–321. At first the rate of entry of Jews into the cadres of Soviet factory workers was exceedingly slow. It has been estimated that in 1926 their total number in this class did not greatly exceed the prewar figure of 46,000. According to a report submitted in 1929 by Ezekiel A. Grower, a well-informed official of the Agro-Joint (*see* below) to that organization's headquarters in New York, only about 14.7 percent of Soviet Jews were employed as factory workers, as against 23.9 percent earning their living as artisans. Together both classes represented a minority of 38.6 percent. *See* Yehuda Bauer, *My Brother's Keeper: a History of the American Jewish Joint Distribution Committee 1929–1939*, Philadelphia, 1974, p. 61 (from the Agro-Joint archives). Conditions were to change rapidly after the NEP period and under the impact of the Five-Year Plans.

12. *See* the telling data summarized by Ruppin in his *Soziologie*, I, 441 Table LII; and by A. Heller in *Die Lage*, pp. 78 f. Table XX, both following the ORT's *Evrei v S.S.S.R.*, pp. 10 ff. Somewhat different statistical computations, based on different classifications, are offered for the Ukraine alone by Y. Kantor in *Di yidishe bafelkerung*, pp. 50 ff. Tables 28 and 30.

13. *See* B. Dunets, *Di dergraikhung fun der natsionaler politik in W. S. S. R.* (The Achievements of the National Policy in the White Russian S. S. R.), Moscow, 1930, pp. 22, 30.

14. S. N. Prokopowicz, *Russlands Volkswirtschaft unter den Sowjets*, German trans. from the Russian manuscript by W. Jollos, Zurich, 1944, pp. 198 ff.; L. Zinger, *Dos banaite Folk*, pp. 49 ff.; *idem, Dos ufgerikhte Folk* (The Reconstructed People: the Socioeconomic Restratification of the Jewish Population in the Soviet Union), Moscow, 1948, p. 39. To be sure, some of these data are highly conjectural and Solomon Schwarz's strictures thereon (in *The Jews*, pp. 169 ff.) are quite justified. But they clearly indicate the tremendous transformations in the Russo-Jewish economic structure within half a generation.

15. Peretz Markish, *Der finfter horizont* (The Fifth Level); and H. Orland, *Aglomerat*, cited by Choseed in *Jewish Social Studies*, XI, 266; Zinger, *Dos banaite Folk*, pp. 63, 68 f.

16. Armstrong, *Ukrainian Nationalism*, p. 242. *See also* P. Kretzer's dissertation, *Die beruflichen und sozialen Verhältnisse der Juden in der UdSSR*, Berlin, 1931.

17. Zinger, *Dos banaite Folk*, pp. 103 ff., 106; Institute for Jewish Affairs, *The Jews under Soviet Rule*. Zinger concedes the tentative nature of these computations and expresses the hope that further detailed investigations of the results of the 1939 census would amplify and modify his findings. Yet he remained, during the portentous years of 1939–41, the sole fairly competent, if biased, student of the Jewish aspects of that census with relatively easy access to the primary materials. There is almost no possibility now for an independent recheck of his statistics. *See also* below, n. 21.

18. B. Brutzkus, *Di yidishe landvirtshaft in Mizrakh-Eirope* (Jewish Agriculture in Eastern Europe), Berlin, 1926, pp. 57 ff.

19. *Ibid.*; Isler, *Rückkehr der Juden zur Landwirtschaft*, pp. 40 ff.; S. N. Prokopowicz, *Russlands Volkwirtschaft*, pp. 63 ff., in the main following the data presented by the Soviet economist, B. N. Knipovich. The ill-will of many peasants toward their new Jewish neighbors is well reflected in such stories as Samuel Persov's *Tog un nakht* (Day and Night), Moscow, 1933, especially p. 150.

Notes

20. Larin, *Evrei i antisemitizm*, p. 308; *Pratsi* (Proceedings) of the First All-Russian Conference of Marxist Agrarian Political Scientists, December, 1929, Vol. I, Moscow, 1930, pp. 74 ff. Yurii Larin who though raised in a traditional Jewish household—his father Solomon Zalman Lurye was an "official rabbi" and Hebrew poet in Kiev—found an early entry into the socialist movement and later played a considerable role in Soviet economic planning, *see* Joseph Barzilai's biographical sketch, "Larin, Founder of Soviet Planning" (Hebrew), *Heawar*, XVIII (1971), 151–61. But perhaps only his death in 1932 at the age of fifty spared him the fate of many other former Mensheviks, as well as old Bolsheviks, during the purges of 1936–38.

21. N. L. Semashko, "A New Man is Born" (Yiddish), in S. Dimanshtain, ed., *Yidn in FSSR* (Jews in the Soviet Union: a Symposium), Moscow, 1935, p. 49; above, Chap. 11, n. 8; *Emes* of December 19, 1924, and other sources, cited by J. Lestchinsky in *Der Emes vegn di Yidn*, pp. 49 ff.; *idem*, "Die soziale und wirtschaftliche Lage der Ostjuden nach dem Kriege," *Weltwirtschaftliches Archiv*, XXIV (1926), 39–62.

22. *See* the ORT's publication *Evrei v S.S.S.R.*, pp. 67 f.; Artur Ruppin, "Die jüdische landwirtschaftliche Kolonisation in Russland," *Palästina*, XI (1928), 2–28. *See also* A. Rovner's report, *The ICOR and the Jewish Colonization in the U.S.S.R.*, New York, 1934 (ICOR Library, III). The original preponderance of grain cultivation in the Ukrainian Jewish colonies is well illustrated by the Statistical Table (36) in Y. Kantor's *Di yidishe bafelkerung in Ukraine*, p. 56. But even then it was less pronounced in the Crimea. On the varying fortunes of the Jewish participants in the American communist movement, see Melech Epstein, *The Jew and Communism: the Story of Early Communist Victories and Ultimate Defeats in the Jewish Community, U.S.A., 1919–1941*, New York, [1959]. In considering the government's readiness, even eagerness, to contribute its share to the Jewish agricultural colonization we must bear in mind the fact that Russian agriculture was in considerable disarray in the late 1920s and that the Soviet leaders expected to benefit greatly from the introduction through the Agro-Joint of some methods employed in the advanced American technology. *See* Richard Lorenz, "Die Stagnation der sowjetischen Getreidewirtschaft zwischen 1927 und 1929," *Jahrbücher für Geschichte Osteuropas*, XVIII (1970), 389–425.

23. L. Zinger and B. Engel, *Yiddish bafelkerung fun FSSR* (Jewish Population in the Soviet Union: Tables and Diagrams), Moscow, n. d., Tables I,2; II,2; III,8, etc. On the frequent inconsistencies in the data supplied by Zinger in his various studies, *see* S. M. Schwarz in *The Jews*, pp. 164 ff., 171 f.

24. See Y. Bauer's *My Brother's Keeper*, especially pp. 71, 90, 98 f., 103; and Dana Dalrymple's succinct observations, "Joseph A. Rosen and Early Russian Studies of American Agriculture," *Agricultural History*, XXXVIII (1964), 157–60. The seriousness of the 1932–34 agricultural crisis is analyzed by Dalrymple in "The Soviet Famine of 1932–34," *Soviet Studies*, XV (1963–64), 250–84; XVI (1964–65), 471–74 (pointing out that the Soviet government never admitted that this man-made famine, one of the worst in all recorded history, had caused such enormous human sufferings).

25. Zinger, *Dos banaite Folk*, pp. 85 ff. In his enthusiasm for the achievements of Jewish agriculturists in the 1930s Zinger mentions that the wheat production of the Crimean colonies had increased elevenfold between 1926 and

1938. He not only fails to indicate that in 1926 Jewish colonization there still was in its infancy, but also that at the same time the number of colonists had increased by 436 percent. Understandably, with the progressive acquisition of both skills and equipment, the productivity of these Jewish farms increased greatly—in 1935–38 alone from 8 to 14 tons of wheat per hectare. In the latter year the Crimean Jews were able to deliver 2,500,000 poods (some 41,000 metric tons) of grain and 1,000,000 tons of fruits to the state.

[14]

Cultural Attrition

1. *See* Elias Tcherikower's interesting Yiddish essay "Communist Fighters for Hebrew in Turkestan" in the collection, *In der tekufe fun revolutsie* (In the Revolutionary Period: Memoirs, Materials and Documents), Vol. I, Berlin, 1924, pp. 356–66.

2. Judah Dardak, "Our Educational Achievements in Fifteen Years of the October Revolution" (Yiddish) in *Tsum 15 yortog fun der Octiabrrevolutsie* (To the Fifteenth Anniversary of the October Revolution: Socioeconomic Essays), Minsk, 1932, pp. 172 f., also cited with variations by S. M. Schwarz in *The Jews in the Soviet Union*, p. 131. It must be borne in mind that, however circumscribed and effectively used for communist propaganda, the very existence of a network of Yiddish schools marked a sharp reversal of Lenin's prewar attitude. In several essays, written in 1903 and 1913, the dictator had sharply attacked the idea of a "Jewish national culture" which he called "the slogan of the rabbis and the bourgeoisie, the slogan of our enemies. Anyone directly or indirectly putting forward the slogan of Jewish national culture is (whatever his good intentions) an enemy of the proletariat, a partisan of the old and the castelike in the Jewish group, an accomplice of the rabbis and the bourgeoisie." He had attacked the idea of separate Jewish schools of any kind even more vehemently. "We must not aim for this," he declared, "but for the unity of the workers of all nationalities in the struggle against all nationalism, in the struggle for a truly democratic public school and for political freedom generally." Quoted here in the English trans. in Elias Schulman's *A History of Jewish Education in the Soviet Union*, New York, 1971, pp. 47 ff., from Lenin's *Sochineniia* (Collected Works), 2d ed., Moscow, 1929, VI, 83 ff.; XVI, 553 f.; XVII, 113 ff., 138 ff.; XVIII, 138 ff.

3. Nahum Gergel, *Di lage fun di Yidn in Rusland* (The Situation of the Jews in Russia), Warsaw, 1929; A. Heller, *Die Lage*, pp. 119 f. *See also* the data marshaled by Bernard Weinryb in "Das jüdische Schulwesen in Sowjetrussland," *Monatsschrift für Geschichte und Wissenschaft des Judentums*, LXXV (1931), 455–62.

4. These and other data have been assembled, with some inner contradictions and obscurities, by Yakov Kantor in his *Natsionalnoe stroitelstvo*, especially pp. 170 ff. *See also* the statistical tables in S. M. Schwarz, *The Jews*, pp. 14 ff.; and the figures quoted by E. Schulman in *A History of Jewish Education*, pp. 90 ff. Claiming that the data for the school year 1930–31 are relatively "most accurate,"

whereas those later announced "have a propagandistic character," Judel Mark states that in that year the 785 Yiddish schools in the Ukraine were attended by 82,000 pupils and that the far fewer (262) White Russian schools had an almost equally large enrollment of 80,000—which on its face is not very likely. See his "Jewish Schools in Soviet Russia" in Aronson and Frumkin's *Russian Jewry, 1917–1967*, p. 253.

The use of Yiddish schools for purposes of socialist indoctrination had been preached by Bundists and others even before World War I. In her Yiddish essay "A Few Remarks about National Education" in *Tsait fragen*, I (1909), 24, for example, Maria Y. Frumkin ("Ester") had written: "When we speak of education in a proletarian spirit, we do not mean that children should recite part of the Erfurt Program [adopted by the German Social Democrats in 1891] instead of the *Shema* [Hear, O Israel] or a chapter of the Communist Manifesto instead of *Modeh ani* [I Confess; part of the morning prayers]. . . . But when we say 'proletarian upbringing' we mean that Marxism is not only a political program, but a *Weltanschauung*." Cited in an English trans. by Z. Y. Gitelman in his *Jewish Nationality*, p. 61. "Ester" continued to work for the expansion of the Yiddish school system under the Soviet regime. On one occasion she complained that some local soviets had failed to implement the government's decree concerning the allocation of funds for the Yiddish school (1919), though she did not hesitate on another occasion (1923) to censure some leaders in the Jewish sections of the Party for being excessively preoccupied with the problems of the Yiddish school. *See* Schulman, pp. 65, 86.

5. Weinryb in *Monatsschrift*, LXXV, 458; Jacob Lestchinsky, *Dos sovietishe yidentum* (Soviet Jewry, Its Past and Present), New York, 1941, pp. 323 ff., largely based on newspaper clippings from the *Emes* and other Soviet papers, since no serious Soviet study of Jewish education after 1933 had appeared. *See*, however, A. Kirzhnitz's obviously overoptimistic evaluation of the progress of Yiddish education during the First Five-Year Plan of 1928–32 in his succinct survey of "The Culture Upbuilding among the Jewish Masses" in *Yidn in FSSR*, ed. by Dimanshtain, pp. 257–67.

6. A. Heller, *Die Lage*, pp. 121 f.; Zinger, *Dos banaite Folk*, p. 108.

7. *See* Yehuda Slutsky's comprehensive bibliographical study of "The Hebrew Publications in the Soviet Union in the Years 1917–1960" in Khone Shmeruk, ed., *Pirsumim yehudiim be-Berit ha-Moesot* (Jewish Publications in the Soviet Union, 1917–1960), compiled by Y. Y. Cohen and M. Piekarz, Jerusalem, 1961, pp. xix–liv.

8. C. N. Bialik, *Iggerot* (Letters), collected and ed. with notes by Fishel Lachover, 5 vols., Tel Aviv, 1938–39, II, 183 No. 327, 189 No. 333; Slutsky, in Shmeruk's *Pirsumim*, pp. xxiii ff.

9. *See* Bialik's *Iggerot*, II, 207 ff. Nos. 348–49. A member of that group of Hebrew émigré writers, Benzion Dinaburg (Dinur), the historian and later minister of education in Israel, dramatically describes these vicissitudes in his autobiographical *Bi-yeme milhamah u-mahapekhah* (In the Days of War and Revolution: Reminiscences and Impressions, 1914–1921), Jerusalem, 1960, especially pp. 285 ff., 320 ff., 476 ff., 519 ff. *See also* above, Chap. 9, n. 29.

10. *Be-Reshit*, though announced as published in Leningrad and Moscow in

1926, was printed by the Gutenberg Press in Berlin, and only three hundred copies were brought into Russia. This despite its clearly procommunist views, as typified in one of the stories in the volume written in Moscow in 1925 by S. H. (Shimon Haboneh). It describes the life in a Ukrainian hamlet during the revolution. There new "poets and storytellers will emerge, the very opposite of the poets" of the previous generation like Mendele. "For Motel Piklini, the Jewish sans-culotte of the Russian Revolution, the Red Maccabean, will until the outbreak of 'the final decisive battle' beget men like himself in all the places of the dispersion: in the markets of Lodz, the streets of Haifa, and the noisy lanes of Whitechapel" (pp. 163 ff.). Much information about the outlook and changing moods of the Hebrew writers of the period may be culled principally from their publications, as compiled by émigrés such as Abraham Kariv (Krivoruchka) in his ed. of *Ha-Anaf ha-gadu'a* (The Cut-Off Branch), Jerusalem, 1954. *See* especially his own Introduction. *See also* Yehuda Slutsky's aforementioned introduction to Khone Shmeruk's ed. of *Pirsumim yehudiim*, which includes an extensive list of works published by Soviet Hebrew writers outside the Soviet Union (pp. xlii ff.); and the fine summaries by Yehoshua A. Gilboa in his "Hebrew Literature in the U.S.S.R." in L. Kochan's ed., *The Jews in Soviet Russia*, pp. 216–31; and Alfred A. Greenbaum, "Hebrew Literature in Soviet Russia," *Jewish Social Studies*, XXX (1968), 135–48.

11. *See* the early bibliographical survey of "Hebrew Printing in the Soviet Union" (Hebrew) by [Saul] B[orovoi] in *Kirjath Sepher*, V (1928–29), 250–54 (of the 53 numbers, representing 35 books, 24 were simple prayer books and only four secular books, including 3 volumes of communist poetry); Slutsky, in Shmeruk's *Pirsumim*, pp. xxxv ff.; and the excerpts from the communist press of 1928 attesting the continued "vitality of religion" at that time, cited by William Chancey Emhardt in his *Religion in Soviet Russia: Anarchy*, Milwaukee, 1928, pp. 281 ff., 293.

12. Nahum Rubinshtain, comp., *Dos yidishe bukh in Sovietfarband* (The Jewish Book in the Soviet Union) for 1932, 1933, 1934, 1935, Minsk, 1933–36, especially yearbook 1934, pp. xxiii f.; Khone Shmeruk, "Yiddish Publications in the Soviet Union, 1917–1960" (Hebrew) in his ed. of *Pirsumim yehudiim*, pp. lv ff., lxi ff., lxxxviii ff., 13 Nos. 97–100; S. M. Schwarz, *The Jews*, p. 139 Table XIV. *See also* the list of Hebrew liturgical and rabbinic works published in the Soviet Union before 1929 in A. A. Gershuni's *Yahadut be-Rusiah ha-Sovietit* (Judaism in Soviet Russia: a Contribution to the History of Religious Persecutions), Jerusalem, 1961, pp. 129 ff. The last rabbinic collection, ed. by Yehezkel Abramski and Shlomoh Yosef Zevin respectively, under the title *Yagdil torah* (May the Lord Enhance the Torah)—its two slender issues appeared in Bobruisk in 1928—was put to good use by the Soviet foreign propaganda. In his interview with the correspondent of the Jewish Telegraphic Agency, Lunacharskii himself stressed the presence of this rabbinic Jewish "monthly" as proof that the Hebrew language was not outlawed in the Soviet Union. Nevertheless, in 1930 the government stopped all such activities and formally outlawed even the importation of Bibles in any language. True, the older liturgical handbooks available in most communities until the German invasion of 1941, amplified in 1939–40 by the collections assembled in the Polish and Baltic lands occupied by the Rus-

sians, could temporarily satisfy most needs of would-be worshipers. But the absence of annual calendars could seriously interfere with the observance of Jewish holidays and memorial services for decreased relatives (so-called *Jahrzeiten*). This difficulty was obviated in part by some zealous worshipers through calendars ordered from relatives abroad; these were subsequently reproduced by hand and distributed in various communities. There also existed some copies of an almanac *Ittim la-binah* (For the Understanding of the Times), which computed the Jewish calendar to the end of the sixth millennium (2240 C.E.). It was doubtless available for reproduction by many communal copyists.

13. Paul B. Anderson, *People, Church and State in Modern Russia*, New York, 1944, p. 62. *See also* Adolf Ziegler, *Die russische Gottlosenbewegung*, Munich, 1932.

14. *See* especially A. Finkelshtain, "The Book Production of the *Emes* Publishing House during the Second Five-Year Plan (1933–1937)" (Yiddish), *Sovietish-literarisher Almanakh*, VII–VIII (1938), 416–27; Zinger, *Dos banaite Folk*, pp. 109 f.

15. D[avid] B[ergelson], "Three Centers" (Yiddish), *In Shpan*, I (Vilna, 1926), 84–96; "Chronicle" (Yiddish), *ibid.*, p. 165, both cited by K. Shmeruk in *Pirsumim*, pp. lxxxviii f. n. 35.

16. *See* the list in N. Rubinshtain's bibliography for 1935 (above, n. 12), summarized by K. Shmeruk in *Pirsumim*, pp. cxiii ff. On the Polish-Jewish publications, *see*, for instance, my *Bibliography of Jewish Social Studies, 1938–39*, New York, 1941. Jewish Social Studies, Publications, I; and my *From a Historian's Notebook: European Jewry Before and After Hitler* (a memorandum prepared for my testimony at the Eichmann trial in April, 1961; reprinted from the *American Jewish Year Book*, LXIII, 1962, 3–53).

17. B. Orshanskii in *Zeitschrift*, V, 21.

18. Zalman Reisen, *Leksikon*, II, 105 ff., 348 ff.; Bernard J. Choseed, "The Soviet Jew in Literature," *Jewish Social Studies*, XI, 277 f. *See also* such monographic studies as Yehezkal Dobrushin's "Benjamin Susskin and the Types in Soviet Drama" (Yiddish), *Forpost*, VI (1938), 205–23; and Noah Isaac Gotlib's more comprehensive review of *Sovetishe shraiber* (Soviet Writers), Montreal, 1945 (a collection of articles published in 1934–44; includes material on non-Jewish Soviet writers discussing aspects of Jewish life). According to Judel Mark, himself a leading Yiddish writer and literary critic, during the interwar period in the Soviet Union there were four major periods in Yiddish literary creativity. Up to 1920 most Yiddish writers were given sufficient leeway to reflect in their diverse ways the great sufferings of the Jewish masses during the civil war and pogroms. From 1920 to 1925 the so-called proletarian culture and its attempt to depict only the virtues of proletarian, as against the vices of bourgeois-clerical, life—all in the service of the "dictatorship of the proletariat"—dominated the scene. At that time even Sholem Aleichem, later one of the most popular authors among Soviet readers, was often denigrated as a petty bourgeois scribbler. But there was enough hospitality extended to like-minded Yiddish writers abroad to have their works admitted to and even reproduced in the country. From 1925 to 1930 there was a growing "sovietization" of Yiddish letters which led to the further alienation of Soviet Jews from the Jewries of other lands, including their Yiddish littérateurs. After 1930 came a general decline in the number of Yiddish readers and in the quantity and quality of the literary output, affected by the pernicious "cult of personality" which reached its climax in the era of the Stalinist purges. During that period of "Stalinization" of the Soviet literature in general, in which sycophantic praise of the dictator became a "must" also for various Yiddish publications, there was little room left for any kind of individualistic "deviation." Ironically, many of the leaders of the "proletarian" school, including Dimanshtain and Moshe Litvakov, the editor in chief of *Der Emes*, were executed long before the ax fell on the "fellow travelers." However, all Yiddish writers were soon completely silenced until the mid-1950s. *See* Yosef Berger-Barzilai, "Moshe Litvakov, Strokes toward His Profile on the Basis of Personal Impressions" (Hebrew), *Behinot*, No. 1 (1970); and, more generally, K. Shmeruk, "Yiddish Literature in the U.S.S.R." in Aronson, Frumkin *et al.*, eds., *The Jews in Soviet Russia, 1917–1967*, pp. 232–68; and his Hebrew Introduction to *Pirsumim yehudiim*, pp. lv-cxxxi. *See also* the earlier appraisal of the "New Trends in Post-War Jewish Literature" by S. Niger in *Jewish Social Studies*, I (1939), 337–58.

19. Lenin's essay of 1905 and Lunacharskii's statement of 1933, cited in the English trans. by Robert M. Hankin in his informative analysis of the "Main Premises of the Communist Party in the Theory of Soviet Literary Controls" in *Continuity and Change in Russian and Soviet Thought*, ed. with an Introduction by Ernest J. Simmons, Cambridge, Mass., 1955, pp. 433–50, especially pp. 445, 449. Developments in the Yiddish literature naturally paralleled those in general Russian letters. On these ever-tightening controls, restored after a brief intermission of the war years in 1946, see Avrahm Yarmolinsky's *Literature under Communism: the Literary Policy of the Communist Party of the Soviet Union from the End of World War II to the Death of Stalin*, [Bloomington, Ind., 1957]. (Russian and East European Series of Indiana Univ., XX). *See also* below, n. 22.

20. This conversation of 1939 is reported in the reminiscences relating to a leading Soviet writer, Der Nister (The Occult, pseud. for Pinhas Kahanovich; 1884–ca. 1948) by H. Bloshtain, which were published under the telling title, "He Would Now Be Seventy-Five Years Old (Some Reminiscences about Der Nister)" (Yiddish) in *Yidishe Kultur*, XXI, No. 8 (1959), 20–23. *See* K. Shmeruk in *Pirsumim*, p. xc n. 54; and Nachman Meisel's introductory Yiddish essay, "Der Nister as a Man and Artist," in his ed. of Pinhas Kahanovitch's *Dertselungen un essaien* (Stories and Essays, 1940–1948), New York, 1957.

21. *See*, for instance, the sharp attack on Sosis's objectivity and nationalism by Leib Holmstock and Yakov Rubin in their "On the Front of Jewish Historiography" (Yiddish) in *Tsum 15tn yortog fun der Oktiabr revolutsie* (On the Fifteenth Anniversary of the October Revolution: an Historical Collection), published by the White Russian Academy of Science, Minsk, 1932, pp. 147, 152; Hillel Aleksandrov, "The Economic and Statistical Research of the Yiddish Scientific Institute" (Yiddish), *Zeitshrift*, IV (1930), 296–331 (attacking in particular Jacob Lestchinsky's demographic studies); his, Sosis's and others' articles in *Fashizirter yidishizm* (Fascist Yiddishism and Its Science), published by the White Russian Academy of Science, Minsk, 1930; Judah Rosenthal, "Jewish Historiography in Soviet Russia and Simon Dubnow" (Hebrew) in Simon Rawidowicz, ed., *Sefer Shimeon Dubnow*, London, 1954, pp. 201–220; and, more generally, Alfred Abra-

Notes

ham Greenbaum, *Jewish Scholarship in Soviet Russia, 1918–1941*, Boston, 1959; *idem*, "Jewish Historiography in Soviet Russia," *Proceedings* of the American Academy for Jewish Research, XXVIII (1959), 57–76; *idem*, "Nationalism as a Problem in Soviet Jewish Scholarship," *ibid.*, XXX (1962), 61–77.

22. See *Yidishe ortografie* (Yiddish Orthography: Projects and Materials Prepared for the Second All-Union Yiddish Culture Conference), Kiev, 1928; A. Zaretski, *Far a proletarisher sprakh* (For a Proletarian Language), Kharkov, 1931, especially pp. 21 ff.; and other writings listed by Uriel and Beatrice Weinreich in their *Yiddish Language and Folklore: a Selective Bibliography for Research*, The Hague, 1959. *Janua linguarum*, X; Shmeruk in *Pirsumim*, pp. cxxv ff. *See also* Judel Mark, ed., *Yuda A. Yofe-bukh* (Studies Presented to Judah A. Joffe), New York, 1958, especially pp. 207–20 (Roman Jakobson, "The Yiddish Sound Structure in Its Slavic Environment") and 236–56 (Yehuda Elzet, "Discourses on Hebrew-Yiddish and Yiddish-Hebrew").

It is nevertheless noteworthy that no serious effort was made to force Yiddish writers and the public at large to abandon the Hebrew script altogether and to replace it by the Latin and/or Cyrillic alphabets. This form of Russification, which was vigorously promoted among many minority nationalities, was reinforced by their frequent voluntary adoption of an increasing number of Russian loan words and grammatical forms. These governmentally supported efforts by many linguistic zealots led, for example, to the total suppression of the Arabic script theretofore used by Azerbaijanis and other Turkic peoples and its replacement first by the Latin and subsequently by the Cyrillic alphabet, with newly invented characters or diphthongs to meet the special requirements of each language. *See* Uriel Weinreich's lucid analysis of the progress of "The Russification of Soviet Minority Languages" in *Problems of Communism*, II, No. 6 (1953), 46–57. That Yiddish escaped that fate, despite the obvious wishes of many Jewish communists thus even more effectively to sever the relations between Yiddish and the hated Hebraic heritage, may have been owing to the realization that as long as Yiddish was the prevailing speech of the Jewish masses, the transition to a foreign script might reduce the effectiveness of communist propaganda among the Jewish workers—a reversion to the old argument of the Bundists and other anti-Hebraist socialists. In the long run, moreover, it became quite evident that Yiddish was steadily losing ground among the Jews and outright Russification was progressing at an accelerated pace without the adoption of a Cyrillic script for the ever-diminishing output of Yiddish letters.

23. *See* the report by Salomon Mikhoels himself, together with Yehezkel Dobrushin, "Jewish Theater Culture in the Soviet Union" (Yiddish) included in Simeon Dimanshtain, ed., *Yidn in FSSR* (Jews in the Soviet Union: a Collection of Essays), Moscow, 1935, pp. 419–62. If I may indulge in a personal recollection, I can testify to the tremendous impression the *Habimah* performance of An-ski's *Dybbuk* made on West European audiences, the majority of which understood no Hebrew. I happened to be in Vienna during the summer of 1926, a few months after that famous theatrical troupe had terminated its six-year stay in Moscow and had left the Soviet Union never to return. Attending its Vienna performance, I noticed the presence of an array of distinguished theatrical experts, among them Max Reinhardt, whose enthusiasm for the play, its staging, and particularly its hasidic dance made them forget themselves and behave almost like a claque, rather than as calm, seasoned observers. The same thing happened in Paris, London, New York, and elsewhere. It is small wonder, then, that the memory of this play and its performance recently inspired Leonard Bernstein and Jerome Robbins to compose a new musical score and a new choreography for it. The fascinating story of the Moscow years of the *Habimah* was told by Isaak Norman in his *Be-Reshit ha-Bimah* (The Birth of the Habimah: Nahum Zemach, Founder), Jerusalem, 1966, with a Documentary Appendix from Zemach's literary collections, pp. 145–209.

On its part, the Jewish Chamber Theater—which from 1919 to 1948 had an equally distinguished career performing Yiddish plays in Moscow and other cities—and its outstanding actor and long-time director, Salomon Mikhoels, have likewise been the subject of unbounded admiration. *See* Josef Shein, *Arum Moskver Yidishn Teatr* (Around Moscow's Jewish Theater), Paris, 1964; Konstantin L. Rudnitsky, ed., *Mikhoels* (Essays, Conversations, Speeches and Reminiscences), Moscow, 1965. *See also* Gershon Swet's succinct analysis of "The Jewish Theater in Soviet Russia (The Jewish Chamber Theater and the Habimah)" in Aronson, Frumkin *et al.*, eds., *Russian Jewry, 1917–1967*, pp. 283–99, with its finale, a quotation from the *Sunday Pictorial* of London: "When you see a Habimah show you regret knowing no Hebrew. It is a great theatrical event; the emotional acting and the artistic perfection of Habimah are worthy of a Rembrandt's brush."

24. Zinger, *Dos banaite Folk*, p. 109.

25. *See* especially Alexander Kaun, "Babel: Voice of New Russia," *Menorah Journal*, XV (1928), 400–413 (includes trans. of Babel's *Gedali*); Lionel Trilling, "The Fate of Isaac Babel," *The London Magazine*, III (1956), 40–58. It is not surprising that some of his realistic descriptions of the *Red Cavalry* did not please participants in the Civil War campaign. Semyon Mikhailovich Budyonny, who in 1919–24 had served as commander of the First Cavalry Army, addressed on October 26, 1928 a sharp "Open Letter" to Maxim Gorki, protesting that writer's praise of Babel's work. The future marshal of the Soviet Union declared Babel unqualified objectively to describe the Cossacks because he had never fought in their ranks and produced his "lampoon" only from observations "in the Backwaters" of the cavalry. Gorki heatedly defended the author's competence, pointing out that Tolstoy, too, was able beautifully to depict the Russian army of 1812, though he had not personally fought against Napoleon (November 27, 1928). *See* the English trans. of that exchange in Babel's *The Lonely Years: Unpublished Stories and Private Correspondence*, trans. by Andrew R. MacAndrew and Max Hayward, New York, 1964, pp. 106 f., 384 ff. Apps. IIa and IIb. *See also* Babel's *Collected Stories*, ed. and trans. by Walter Morrison, with an Introduction by Lionel Trilling, New York, 1955; Petrina Carden, *The Art of Isaac Babel*, Ithaca, 1972; and the Italian rendition of Babel's *Opere*, including Vol. III, *Racconti proibiti e lettere intime*, ed. by Maria Olsonfiera, Milan, 1961, I Narratori di Feltrinelli, X. The extent of "Averbakhism" in 1931 is well illustrated by Mikhail Sholokhov's complaint to Gorki that if he had accepted the RAPP's criticisms of the manuscript of the third part of his *Tikhii Don* (The Silent Don)—published in 1928–40 and frequently celebrated as a classic of the rank of Tolstoy's *War and Peace*—he would have had to discard three-fourths of the volume. *See* Ernest J. Simmons, *Russian Fiction and Soviet Ideology: Introduction to Fedin, Leonov, and Sholokhov*, New York, 1958, pp. 171 f.

26. *See* Gleb Struve, *Soviet-Russian Literature 1917–50*, Norman, Okla., 1951, in the revised and more up-to-date German trans. of this work by Horst Neerfeld and Günter Schäfer entitled, *Geschichte der Sowjetliteratur*, Munich, 1958 (up to 1957), pp. 172 ff., 212 ff., 217 ff., 223 ff., 225 ff.; Mark Slonim, "Jewish Writers in Soviet Literature" (Russian), *Evreiskii Mir*, II (New York, 1944), 146–64; and Ainsztein in *Jewish Social Studies*, XXIII, 72 f.

27. *See* below, Chap. 15, n. 21; M. Friedberg's well-informed twin essays on "Jewish Themes in" and "Jewish Contributions to Soviet Literature" in L. Kochan, ed., *The Jews in Soviet Russia*, pp. 188–207 and 208–15, especially pp. 192, 209; and Vera Alexandrova's profusion of pertinent data in her "Jews in Soviet Literature" in Aronson, Frumkin *et al.*, eds., *Russian Jewry*, pp. 300–327. *See also* Judith Storer, "Pasternak et le judaïsme," *Cahiers du monde russe*, IX (1968), 353–64; and for later developments, Friedberg's *The Jews in Post Stalin Soviet Literature*, New York, 1970.

28. *See* Rabbi Barishensky's reminiscences, which first appeared in Yiddish in the New York *Morgen Zhurnal* of November 19, 1923, and reappeared in a Hebrew trans. by A. A. Gershuni in his *Yahadut be-Russiah ha-Sovietit*, pp. 251 ff. App. ii, especially p. 257. *See also* the recent continuation of this informative work for the period after 1930 in Gershuni's *Yehudim ve-Yahadut be-Brit ha-Moesot* (Jews and Judaism in the Soviet Union: Russian Jewry from the Stalin Era to the Present), Jerusalem, 1970.

29. Gershuni, *Yahadut*, pp. 24 ff., 47 ff., 56 ff., 74 ff., 93 ff., 115 ff. The law of January 23, 1918, and the sharp reaction thereto of many Russian religious leaders, especially the then newly elected patriarch of the Russian Orthodox Church, have often been analyzed. Tikhon, who excommunicated the Soviet rulers for their "satanic deed, for which you shall suffer the fire of Gehenna in the life to come, beyond the grave, and the terrible curses of posterity in the present earthly life," ineffectually fought against its implementation until his humiliating retraction in 1923. *See* the recent careful analysis of that historic struggle, done on the basis of all accessible documentation, by Roman Rössler in his *Kirche und Revolution in Russland. Patriarch Tichon und der Sowjetstaat*, Cologne, 1969 (Beiträge zur Geschichte Osteuropas, VII). On the general conflict between state and Church in the Soviet Union, *see* the literature quoted in my *Modern Nationalism and Religion*, pp. 197 ff., 331 f.; above, this chapter, n. 13; and such more recent publications as Walter Kolarz's *Religion in the Soviet Union*, New York, 1961; and the essays, ed. by Richard H. Marshall, Jr., *et al.*, entitled *Aspects of Religion in the Soviet Union, 1917–1967*, Chicago, 1971. On the peculiar aspects of the Soviet persecution of the Jewish religion *see*, in addition to Tsentsiper's and Gershuni's aforementioned studies, *also* Joshua Rothenberg, *The Jewish Religion in the Soviet Union*, New York, 1971; and his *An Annotated Bibliography of Writings on Judaism Published in the Soviet Union, 1960–1965*, with a Foreword by Erich Goldhagen, Waltham, Mass., 1969. *See also* above, nn. 9–10.

30. In the great purges of 1936 to 1938 Dimanshtain and Litvakov were but minor figures among the many politicians and military leaders who happened to be Jews. They are not even mentioned in the large monograph by Robert Conquest, *The Great Terror. Stalin's Purge of the Thirties*, New York, 1968.

[15]
The Second World War

1. *Izvestia* of April 17, 1939, cited by N. S. Timasheff in *Thought*, XX, 455. *See also* Max M. Laserson's remarks on the Soviet "rehabilitation of national history" in his *Russia and the Western World: the Place of the Soviet Union in the Comity of Nations*, New York, 1945, pp. 138 ff.; and above, Chap. 11, n. 8.

2. The German report cited from an archival source by S. M. Schwarz in *The Jews in the Soviet Union*, p. 310; Ihor Kamenetsky, *Hitler's Occupation of the Ukraine (1941–1944): a Study of Totalitarian Imperialism*, Milwaukee, 1956 (Marquette Slavic Studies, II), especially pp. 19 ff., 35 ff. *See also* the extensive documentation in E. M. Carroll and F. T. Epstein, eds., *Deutschland und die Sowjetunion, 1939–1941*, Washington, D. C., 1948; Angelo Rossi (Tasca), *The Russo-German Alliance, August 1939–June 1941*, trans. from the French by John and Michelin Gullen, Boston, 1954; and, from the legal aspects, George Ginsburg, "The Soviet Union as a Neutral, 1939–1941," *Soviet Studies*, X (1958), 12–35.

In view of the tense Polish-Soviet relations before the war, it appears that the Polish descriptions of the Nazi atrocities against both Jews and Poles, as reflected in the early underground leaflets in the Nazi-occupied territories, were not allowed to circulate within the confines of the Soviet Union. A year before the Molotov-Ribbentrop Treaty the Second Session of the Supreme Soviet of the U.S.S.R. (August 10–21, 1938) resounded with anti-Polish denunciations, including S. A. Korneichuk's fantastic assertion that Polish belligerency against Germany was caused by the fact that "the Polish fascist *szlachta* are covetous of the laurels of the fascist vandals in Germany." *See* Bohdan B. Budurowycz, *Polish Soviet Relations 1932–1939*, New York, 1963 (East-Central European Studies of Columbia University), especially p. 120; Wladyslaw Chojnacki, *Bibliografia zwartych druków konspiracyjnych wydanych pod okupacją hitlerowską* (Bibliography of the Non-Periodical Conspiratorial Prints Published during the Hitlerite Occupation in 1939–1945), Warsaw, 1970; and the additional data supplied by Czesław Gutry in his Polish review of that volume in *Przegląd Historyczny*, LXIII (1972), 275–305, with Chojnacki's reply thereto, *ibid.*, pp. 685–99; and Henryk Sawoniak's "Some More Data for the Bibliography of the Conspiratorial Prints" (Polish), *ibid.*, LXIV (1973), 169–74.

3. *See* my *Modern Nationalism and Religion*, pp. 205 f., 333 f. nn. 77–78; P. B. Anderson, *People, Church and State*, pp. 213 f. and above, Chap. 14, n. 28. The relaxation of the Soviet anti-religious policies was also felt among the minority faiths. *See*, for instance, D. J. Dunn, "Stalinism and the Catholic Church during the Era of World War II," *Catholic Historical Review*, LIX (1973–74), 404–428. *See also* W. C. Fletcher, *Religion and Soviet Foreign Policy, 1945–1970*, London, 1973;

Notes

and E. Winter, *Die Sowietunion und der Vatikan*, Berlin, 1972 (Studien zur Geschichte Osteuropas, VI, 3).

4. René Fülöp-Miller, *Rasputin, the Holy Devil*, English trans. cited above, Chap. 10, n. 13; Ziegler, *Die russische Gottlosenbewegung*, p. 157 n.

5. Israel Cohen, *Vilna*, pp. 469 ff.

6. *See* Samuel Gringauz (Grinhaus), "The Last Year of Jewish Life in Lithuania" (Yiddish) in *Lite*, ed. by M. Sudarsky *et al.*, I, 153–62, also citing from the *Lithuanian Bulletin*, III, No. 5 (1945), 20 ff., the interesting official Soviet listing of the alleged "counterrevolutionary" organizations in Lithuania (compiled in April, 1941). Here, too, the Jewish groups are assigned a disproportionate role. On Latvia, *see* Max Kaufmann, *Die Vernichtung der Juden Lettlands (Churban Lettland)*, Munich, 1947. In addition, some 10,000 Jews were deported from Latvia. Another estimate of the number of Jews the Soviet administration deported from both Lithuania and Latvia in 1940 is some 25,000 Jews among the total of 70,000 exiles. In the elections held during the plebiscite of July 14–21, 1940, only five Jews were elected to the Lithuanian Diet, as against eighty non-Jews, corresponding to 7.6 percent, the original Jewish percentage of the population according to the official census of 1927. This fact did not prevent the subsequent Nazi invaders in 1941 from equating Jews with communists and from thus trying to secure the support of many nationalist Lithuanians. *See* Eugene Kulischer, *The Displacement of Population in Europe*, Montreal, 1943, p. 63; Shimon Redlich, "The Jews in Soviet Annexed Territories, 1939–1941," *Soviet Jewish Affairs*, 1971, No. 1, pp. 81–90, especially pp. 83 f.; Piotr Lossowski, "National Minorities in the Baltic States," *Acta Poloniae historica*, XXV (1972), 82–107, especially pp. 89 f.; D. A. Loeber, *Diktirte Option. Die Umsiedlung der Deutsch-Balten aus Estland und Lettland, 1939–1941*, Neumünster, 1972; Gerald Reitlinger, *The Final Solution: the Attempt to Exterminate the Jews of Europe, 1939–1945*, 2d ed. rev. and augmented, London, 1968, pp. 255 ff.; and, more generally, *idem*, *The House Built on Sand: The Conflicts of German Policy in Russia, 1939–1945*, New York, 1960.

7. Raul Hilberg, *The Destruction of the European Jews*, Chicago, 1961, pp. 219. ff. On the overt mistreatment of Jewish and other Russian war prisoners, which the Germans legalistically justified by the Soviet Union's refusal to ratify the Geneva Convention, *see also* the extensive documentary material assembled by the Soviets in *Dokumenty obviniaiut* (Documents Accuse), 2 vols., Moscow, 1943–45. *See also* the *Soviet Government Statements on Nazi Atrocities*, London, 1946; the German analysis by Karl I. Albrecht, *Sie aber werden die Welt zerstören*, Munich, 1954, pp. 201 ff.; and the graphic description of the shooting of 231 Jewish war prisoners in a camp near Proskurov by Vladimir Bondarets in his "Notes from Captivity" (Russian), *Novy Mir*, Nos. 9–10 (Sept.–Oct. 1959), extensively cited in an English trans. by Reuben Ainsztein in "Jewish Tragedy and Heroism in Soviet War Literature," in *Jewish Social Studies*, XXIII (1961), 57–84, especially, pp. 82 ff. Despite the Heydrich-Reinecke agreement, the German army leaders tried after the war to deny any share in the massacres of East European Jews and other victims. Among many others, General Dwight D. Eisenhower, who had access to a great many intelligence reports, is said nonetheless to have been misled into asserting that "the German soldier never lost his honor" during the

Holocaust. This apologia is clearly controverted by such an order of the day as was issued to the Sixth Army by Field Marshal Walter von Reichenau on October 10, 1941, emphasizing that the German soldier was not only a fighter for his fatherland, but also "the bearer of a ruthless national ideology" and that, hence, "he must have understanding of the necessity of a severe but just revenge on sub-human Jewry." Similar orders were also issued by the commanding generals of the Eleventh and Eighteenth Armies. See Reitlinger, *The Final Solution*, pp. 210 f.

8. *Trial of the Major War Criminals before the Nuremberg International Tribunal,* 42 vols., Washington, D. C., 1949, XXXII, 72 ff.; Corliss Lamont, *The Peoples of the Soviet Union,* New York, [1946], p. 85. See also the critique of similar assertions by B. Z. Goldberg in 1946–47 in S. M. Schwarz, *The Jews,* pp. 228 ff.

9. Philip Friedman, "The Jewish Badge and the Yellow Star in the Nazi Era," *Historia judaica,* XVII (1955), 41–70; *Bolschewismus—jüdisches Untermenschentum,* published by the Reich Security Office; Adolf Hitler's letter to Otto Strasser of May 21, 1930, cited by the latter in his *Ministersessel oder Revolution?* pp. 12 ff. and the address in Nuremberg of 1937–38, summarized in English in Norman H. Baynes, ed., *The Speeches of Adolf Hitler, April 1922–August 1939.* An English trans. of representative passages arranged under subjects, 2 vols., London, 1942, I, 700, 713; II, 988 f.; Himmler's address early in 1941, cited in the *Trial of Major War Criminals,* IV, 482. See also J. A. Newth, "Some Trends in the Soviet Population 1939 to 1956 (with Particular Reference to the RSFSR)," *Soviet Studies,* X (1958–59), 252–78; and Karol Marian Popieszalski, "The Extermination of the Jewish People and the Hitlerite Intentions to Destroy the Slavs" (Polish), *Przegląd Zachodni,* X (1954), 527–41, largely based upon Artur Eisenbach's comprehensive monograph, *Hitlerowska polityka eksterminacji Żydów* (The Hitlerite Policy of Exterminating Jews in the Years 1939–1945 as One of the Manifestations of German Imperialism), Warsaw, 1953.

10. The Slutsk report and other data analyzed by Alexander Dallin in his *German Rule in Russia 1941–1945: a Study of Occupation Policies,* London, 1957, pp. 205 ff.

11. See Rudolf Loewenthal, "The Judeo-Tats in the Caucasus," *Historia judaica,* XIV (1952), 61–82; *idem,* "The Extinction of the Krimchaks in World War II," *American Slavic and East-European Review,* X (1951), 130–36; and on the earlier developments, Julius Brutzkus, "History of the Mountaineers in Daghestan (Caucasia)" (Yiddish), *YIVO Historishe Shriftn,* II (1937), 26–42, with an English summary (p. vi). See also above Chap. 13, n. 4.

12. Heinrich Himmler's address of October 4, 1943, cited by William L. Shirer in *The Rise and Fall of the Third Reich: a History of Nazi Germany,* New York, 1960, p. 966. See also Hilberg, *The Destruction,* p. 652. The number of Jews murdered by the Nazis in the Soviet Union, as in many other lands, has never been satisfactorily computed. Himmler and his associates saw to it that along with the Jewish victims the pertinent records were also immediately destroyed. See also T. Berenstein and A. Rutkowski, "The Hitlerite Statistical Reports concerning the Extermination of Jews in Europe" (Polish), *Biuletyn* of the Żydowski Instytut Historyczny, no. 49 (1964), 7–84. Hence, the precise number of those shot by the Nazi *Einsatzgruppen* and buried in mass graves, or deported

and executed in gas chambers, in addition to those who died of starvation in the newly created ghettos and labor camps, will probably never be fully ascertained. But the most likely global figure is that some 6,000,000, or about one-third of the whole Jewish people, died during the Holocaust. This approximation, calculated by Gregory Frumkin, chief statistician of the League of Nations, was largely accepted (as 5,700,000) by the Nuremberg Tribunal of leading Nazi war criminals in 1946. *See The Trial of German Major War Criminals;* the additional arguments in favor of that widely held hypothesis, briefly presented by me in my testimony at the Eichmann trial of 1961, reproduced in the original Hebrew transcript of the *Eduyot* (Testimonies at the Eichmann Trial), published by the State of Israel, 2 vols., Jerusalem, 1963, I, 5–41; also in my "European Jewry Before and After Hitler," *American Jewish Year Book,* LXIII (1962), 3–53, especially pp. 49 ff.; and my "Queries in Retrospect," *The Colloquium on the Holocaust,* presented by the Dropsie University with Villanova University, Philadelphia, 1973, pp. 11–18; above, Chap. 14, n. 16. *See also* Léon Poliakov's numerous publications, including *Harvest of Hate: the Nazi Program for the Destruction of the Jews of Europe,* with a Foreword by Reinhold Niebuhr, New York, 1954; *Das dritte Reich und die Juden, Dokumente,* with Josef Wulff, Berlin, 1955; and other studies ed. by him for the Centre de Documentation Juive Contemporaine in Paris.

There is less consensus about the number of Jews victimized by the Nazis in the occupied Soviet area as it existed in June, 1941, after the conquests in eastern Poland and the Baltic countries in 1939–40. The most likely total is that close to 3,000,000 of the 5,000,000 Jews inhabiting this enlarged area perished, in one way or another, under the Nazi knout in 1941–45. Perhaps as many as 1,700,000 of these may have lived in the original prewar Soviet territories. The best-known individual massacre is that which took place in Babi Yar, in the Lukyanovka suburb of Kiev, where on September 29–30, 1941, less than a fortnight after their occupation of the Ukrainian capital, the Nazis shot 33,771 Jews and buried them in an enormous mass grave. The figure was ascertained after careful examination of the records by the Extraordinary State Commission for the Investigation of Nazi Atrocities in Kiev and was published on March 1, 1944. Characteristically, although *all* the victims were Jews, this fact is not mentioned once in the report, which merely speaks of "thousands of peaceful Soviet citizens" massacred there by the Nazis. *See* especially G. Reitlinger, *The Final Solution,* pp. 533 ff. App. i, especially pp. 543 ff.; Solomon Schwarz, *The Jews in the Soviet Union,* p. 220; and the various other estimates quoted by them, as well as by Reuben Ainsztein in his "Soviet Jewry in the Second World War" in L. Kochan's *The Jews in the Soviet Union,* pp. 269–87, especially pp. 285 ff.; and more generally, Benjamin West's comprehensive study, *Be-Havle ha-Kelayah* (In the Clutches of Extermination: Russian Jewry during the Nazi Holocaust, 1941–1943), Tel Aviv, 1963. On the general Soviet population losses, which were never officially documented by the government, *see* J. A. Newth's attempted computation in "The Soviet Population: War Time Losses and the Postwar Recovery," *Soviet Studies,* XV (1963–64), 345–51; with "Comments" thereon by Raymond Hutchings, *ibid.,* XVIII (1966–67), 81–82.

     13. Dallin, *German Rule,* pp. 215, 649 f. According to an official German report of December 2, 1941, "the population of the Crimea is anti-Jewish and in

some cases spontaneously brings Jews to *Kommandos* to be liquidated. The *starosts* [village elders] ask for permission to liquidate the Jews themselves." Cited by Hilberg in *The Destruction,* p. 202 n. 76. *See also* J. A. Armstrong, *Ukrainian Nationalism, 1939–1945*; and, more generally, Alexander Dallin's "interim report" on *Popular Attitudes and Behavior under the German Occupation, 1941–1944*, Cambridge, Mass., 1944. (Harvard University Russian Research Center). On the special conditions in the Ukraine, *see also* Ryszard Trzecki's recent study of *Kwestia ukraińska w polityce III Rzeszy* (The Ukrainian Question in the Policies of the Third Reich, 1933–1945), Warsaw, 1972, and the literature listed there.

14. Kalonymus Kalmish Shapiro, *Sefer Or Kodesh* (The Holy Light: Homilies Delivered in Warsaw during the Years of the Catastrophe, 1942–44), Jerusalem, 1960; Shmerke Kaczerginski, comp., *Lider fun gettos un lagern* (Songs of Ghettos and Camps), ed. by H. Leivik, New York, 1948. The great tragedy of Soviet and more generally of European Jewry could be mentioned here only with utmost brevity. It has been the subject of many primary and secondary publications, the bibliographical listing of which alone has been a prodigious task. *See* especially the comprehensive works by Gerald Reitlinger, *The Final Solution* (also in a revised German trans. by J. W. Brügel, entitled *Die Endlösung,* Berlin, 1956); Léon Poliakov, *Harvest of Hate: the Nazi Program for the Destruction of the Jews of Europe,* New York, 1954; and Raul Hilberg, *The Destruction.* A host of other publications are listed by Jacob Robinson and Philip Friedman in their *Guide to Jewish History under Nazi Impact,* with Forewords by Benzion Dinur and Salo W. Baron, New York, 1960; and in Friedman's ed. of *Bibliografiah shel ha-sefarim ha-ibrim al ha-sho'ah* (Bibliography of Books in Hebrew on the Jewish Catastrophe and Heroism in Europe), Jerusalem, 1960, together forming the Bibliographical Series, I-II, of the Joint Projects of Yad Washem and the YIVO. *See also* the other bibliographies in that series, and my memorandum on "European Jewry Before and After Hitler," cited above, n. 12.

15. Boris Gorbatov, *Semia Tarasa* (Taras' Family), English trans. from the Russian by Elizabeth Donnelly, London, 1944, p. 21; Choseed in *Jewish Social Studies,* XI, 281 f. Gorbatov (1908–1954), who also served as a widely read war correspondent, won the Stalin Prize in 1943–44. Although not as popular as his other novel, *The Unsubdued*—more than a million copies of the Russian edition of this book were distributed, and it was translated into twenty-three foreign languages—*Taras' Family* must have made some impression upon the many Russian readers still kept in the dark by the controlled Soviet press about the extent of the Nazi Holocaust of Jews.

16. Moshe Kahanovich (Kaganovich), *Milhemet ha-partizanim ha-yehudiim* (The Struggle of the Jewish Partisans in Eastern Europe), Tel Aviv, 1954, pp. 173 ff., 179; G. M. Linkov, *Voina v tylu vraga* (War in the Enemy's Rear), Moscow, 1947; and other data, cited by Reuben Ainsztein in his "Jewish Tragedy and Heroism in Soviet War Literature," *Jewish Social Studies,* XXIII, 70 n. 2, 73 ff.; Carol Jacobson, "The Jews in the USSR," *American Review of the Soviet Union,* VI, No. 4 (1944–45), 50–68, especially p. 64; the anonymous report of an Army captain summarized by A. R. L. Gurland in *Glimpses of Soviet Jewry: 1,000 Letters from the USSR and DP Camps.* Report on Material Collected by the Union of Russian Jews, Inc., New York, 1948, p. 55. *See also* D. Karov, *Partizanskoe* *dvizhenie v SSSR v 1941 gg* (Partisan Movement during the Years of 1941–45), Munich, 1954. *Posledovaniia* (Texts and Studies of the Institute for Research into the History and Culture of the Soviet Union), 1st ser., XI; and from retrospective evaluations, below, Chap. 16, n. 1. Although superseded in many details, the following Russian studies published in 1944 in the New York *Evreiskii Mir*, II, are still worthy of note: Joseph Schechtman, "Soviet Jewry in the Soviet-German War" (pp. 221–40); and E. Stalinskii, "Jews in the Red Army" (pp. 240–54). The high figure of 160,772 Jewish combatants who are said to have received decorations for valor was announced by the Soviet authorities, according to Boris Smolar, only for foreign consumption, but was not mentioned in any official publication at home. See his *Soviet Jewry Today and Tomorrow*, New York, 1971, p. 68 (also mentioning that fully 50,000 Jews out of a total of 300,000 soldiers and civilians had fallen in the heroic defense of Leningrad during its prolonged siege; p.17). Of some value also are such autobiographical records as S. Katcherginsky's *Ikh bin geven a partizan* (I Was a Partisan), Buenos Aires, 1952. The relatively fullest documentation is available in the *Sefer ha-partizanim ha-yehudiim* (Book of Jewish Partisans), ed. by M. Gefen *et al.*, 2 vols., Merhavia, 1958; and particularly in Reuben Ainsztein's comprehensive description of the *Jewish Resistance in Nazi-Occupied Eastern Europe, With a Historical Survey of the Jew as Fighter and Soldier in the Diaspora*, London, 1974 (with a good bibliography). However, one must not forget that though less numerous than in West European countries, some Russians and members of other nationalities at great personal risk hid Jews and sometimes succeeded in saving their lives for the duration of Nazi rule. See the examples adduced by Philip Friedman in his *Their Prother's Keepers*, with a Foreword by John A. O'Brien, New York, 1957.

17. *See* the dramatic story briefly told by Leo Heiman in his "Khrushchev's Jewish Generals. Exposing the Plot to Obliterate the Memory of Jewish War Heroes," *The Jewish Digest*, VIII, No. 9 (June, 1963), 17–27 (although some of his assertions are unsupported by documentary evidence and may be subject to doubt); and with somewhat fuller documentation, R. Ainsztein's "The War Record of Soviet Jewry," *Jewish Social Studies*, XXVIII (1966), 3–24, quoting, among others, several essays by Y. Kantor in the *Folks Shtime* of 1964–65. Another illustration of total disregard of Jewish national feelings was the conferral on a number of Jewish war heroes of the Order of Hetman Khmelnitsky (Chmielnicki). According to the testimony of a witness before the Select Committee on Communist Aggression of the American House of Representatives on September 22–23, 1954, these valiant fighters were completely unaware that they were wearing on their chests the portrait of a leading anti-Jewish pogromist during the Cossack uprising of 1648–49. So effective had been the total suppression of that aspect of the hetman's career in the Soviet press and historical literature. *See* Joseph L. Lichten, "A Study of Ukrainian Jewish Relations," *Annals* of the Ukrainian Academy of Arts and Sciences of the United States, V (1955–56), 1160–77, especially p. 1162; and B. Krupnycky, "Bohdan Khmelnitsky and Soviet Historiography," *Ukrainian Review* (London), I (1955), 65–75. *See also,* more generally, Seweryn Bialer, *Stalin and His Generals: Soviet Military Memoirs of World War II*, New York, 1969.

18. Léon Leneman, *La tragédie des Juifs en U.R.S.S.*, Paris, 1959. (Questions

actuelles), pp. 103 ff.; the report in *Unzer Tsait* of July 1943, pp. 26 ff. *See also The Case of Henryk Erlich and Victor Adler*, with a Foreword by Camille Huysmans, London, 1943; and Shimon Redlich's more recent study of "The Jewish Antifascist Committee in the Soviet Union," *Jewish Social Studies*, XXXI (1969), 25–36, which includes a good summary of the Erlich-Alter proposal, based on copies of the various drafts and of the final plan in the Bund Archives in New York (pp. 26 ff.).

19. The committee itself traced its origin back to a meeting of Jewish representatives in Moscow on August 24, 1941, at which, among others, Ilya Ehrenburg had made a dramatic declaration about being a Jew: "We are hated by Hitler above all others, and this is a source of pride for us." His speech was reported in *Pravda* of August 25, 1941. *See* the pamphlets *Brider Yidn fun der gantser velt* (Brother Jews All Over the World), Moscow, 1941 (also in Russian), and *The Second Jewish Anti-Fascist Meeting, Moscow, May 24, 1942*, Moscow, 1942. *See also* the Committee's semiofficial report, *Evreiskii narod v borbe protiv fashizma* (The Jewish People in the Struggle against Fascism: Materials for the Third Antifascist Meeting), Moscow, 1945; and the literary anthology, *Tsum zig* (Toward Victory), Moscow, 1944, with significant contributions by Bergelson, Markish, Der Nister, and many others. On Mikhoels, *see* above, Chap. 14, n. 23.

20. Shakhno Epshtain in the committee's organ, *Ainikait*, of February 7, 1943, cited, together with other sources, by S. M. Schwarz in *The Jews*, pp. 202 ff. Like most of the older communists, Epshtain had traveled a great distance from the time he had written on Y. L. Peretz als sotsialer dikhter (Peretz as a Social Poet), New York, 1916, emphasizing, in particular, Peretz's "spirit of freedom" (p. 5). The Mikhoels-Fefer mission to the West was part of a Soviet campaign to enlist the support of foreign groups. For the same purpose the patriarch of the Orthodox Church visited in 1943 Palestine and Egypt, while the newly elected chief of the Sunni Muslims, Abd ar-Rahman Rasuli was sent to Mecca, Medina, and Egypt. *See* Bertold Spuler, "Die Lage der Muslims in Russland seit 1942," *Der Islam*, XXIX (1950), 296–300.

21. Peretz Markish, *Far Folk un haimland* (For the [Jewish] People and the [Russian] Fatherland), Moscow, 1943; *idem, Milkhome* (The War), Moscow, 1948 (a poem of 660 pages). Ehrenburg's note is cited by B. Z. Goldberg, one of the chief American partners in the preparation of the Black Book, in *The Jewish Problem in the Soviet Union: Analysis and Solution*, with a Foreword by Daniel Mayer, New York, 1961, pp. 65 f. Ehrenburg attempted to controvert the accusation, frequently heard then and later, that Jews had too meekly submitted to the Nazi assassins. This accusation has once again been answered in K. Shabbetai's essay *As Sheep to the Slaughter*, with a Foreword by Gideon Hausner, Bet Dagan, Israel, 1962; and more fully, in R. Ainsztein, *Jewish Resistance in Nazi-Occupied Eastern Europe*.

22. See S. M. Schwarz, *The Jews in the Soviet Union*, pp. 202 ff.; S. Redlich in *Jewish Social Studies*, XXXI, 29 ff.; Ilya Ehrenburg's autobiography, in the section devoted to *The War: 1941–1945*, English trans. by Tatiana Shebunina in collaboration with Yvonne Kapp, London, 1964, p. 130. It was undoubtedly under the pressure of the Stalinist censorship that before publishing the final volume of his autobiography, Ehrenburg tried to minimize his part in the preparation of the

Black Book. According to the revised edition ultimately published, Ehrenburg claims to have "brought with me certain published materials and photographs." *See* his *Post-War Years,* likewise trans. by Shebunina and Kapp, Cleveland, 1967, pp. 76 f.

Other signs of pusillanimity of the committee's leaders and of their being used by Stalin for his own purposes was their inability to take any position on the Palestine *Yishuv.* Personally, Mikhoels, like most Russian Jews, had a deep emotional attachment to Zion. In a later interview with the great actor, Abraham Sutskever was told by his host: "When I flew to America in July, 1943, I kissed the air when we passed over Palestine." But when it was repeatedly suggested to him that the delegation visit Palestine, he had to refuse. Equally illusory were the hopes of such American Zionist leaders as Stephen S. Wise and Abba Hillel Silver, that a representative sent to Moscow might persuade the Russian authorities to give up their hostility to Zionism and Hebrew. For this reason they extended a warm public welcome to the delegates despite warnings voiced by the prominent Yiddish writer Menahem Boraisha in his letter to Wise of July 1, 1943, against his "paying homage to a second-rater from the U.S.S.R. [Fefer] . . . who is co-responsible for the course of Jewish Communism in Russia, which led to a cultural mass conversion (*shmad*), the like of which Jewish history has not known." But these Zionist hopes proved completely illusory. See Abraham Sutskever, "With Solomon Mikhoels" (Yiddish), *Di Goldene Kait,* 1962, No. 43, p. 165; Z. Szajkowski, *Jews, Wars, and Communism,* I, 458 f.

23. K. Shmeruk in *Ha-Pirsumim,* pp. xcv ff.

[16]

Postwar Reaction

1. Ilya Ehrenburg, "On the Occasion of a Letter" (Russian), *Pravda* of September 21, 1948, cited by S. M. Schwarz in *The Jews in the Soviet Union,* p. 209; and, more generally, Matthew P. Gallagher, *The Soviet History of World War II: Myths, Memoirs and Realities,* New York, 1963.

2. B. Z. Goldberg, *The Jewish Problem in the Soviet Union,* pp. 61 ff.

3. These figures were given by A. Bakhmutskii, Secretary of the Biro-Bidzhan Communist Party, especially in his enthusiastic report "In the United Soviet Family of Nations" (Yiddish), *Ainikait* of April 10, 1948; S. M. Schwarz, *The Jews,* pp. 185 ff.; and the literature cited above, Chap 12, n. 11.

4. Carol Jacobson in the *American Review of the Soviet Union,* VI, No. 4, pp. 62 f.; Shmerl Kaczerginski, *Tsvishn hamer un serp* (Between the Hammer and the Sickle: a Contribution to the History of the Liquidation of Jewish Culture in Soviet Russia), Paris, 1949; and other data cited by R. Ainsztein in "Jewish Tragedy," *Jewish Social Studies,* XXIII, 72 f. Many thoroughly assimilated Jewish intellectuals and workers could not avoid the impact of the great tragedy of European Jewry, the enormity of which had become known only after the cessation of hostilities. Therefore, many of them, including members of the Communist Party and high government officials, participated in the Day of Mourning for the Holocaust victims, proclaimed by the Moscow rabbinate which had been reconstituted under Rabbi Salomon Schliefer in 1941. That day had been set for March 14, 1945, by the Palestinian Ashkenazi Chief Rabbi Isaac Herzog for all world Jewry, and the fact that Russian Jews could participate fully in that event seemed to demonstrate a newly awakened solidarity of the Jewish people the world over. Of course, the Nazi assassins had not discriminated among Jews and had massacred them all—in many cases even if they had been converted to another faith. Rumor had it that the Jewish wife of Foreign Minister Vyacheslav Molotov fasted on that day. See A. A. Gershuni's *Yehudim ve-Yahadut,* pp. 176 ff., 183 f.

5. Stalin, "Marxism and the National Question (1913)," reprinted in his *Works,* Moscow, 1953, II, 300 f., 418 n. 131. The same position had been taken in 1945 in the semiofficial description of "Zionism" by A. Shainberg in the *Bolshaia sovetskaia entsiklopedia,* LI (1945), 191–92, where it was defined as a "reactionary nationalist-political organization" of the Jewish bourgeoisie, whose aim was, as already observed by Lenin, to divert the masses of Jewish workers from the class struggle, the revolution, and socialism. *See also* below, n. 12.

6. Marc Jarblum, *Le problème juif dans la théorie et la pratique du communisme,* Paris, 1953; Léon Leneman, *La tragédie des Juifs en URSS,* pp. 275 ff., citing anonymous letters in the Tel Aviv *Davar* and other sources. Although overtly written in terms of special pleading and often inaccurate in details, Leneman's volume offers a most comprehensive summary of the anti-Jewish persecutions in the Soviet Union during the first dozen years after World War II. Its author, who had spent some seven years in the Union, several of them in prison and labor camps, was released as a result of the Russo-Polish agreement for the return of Polish refugees to their home country. Some telling illustrations are offered here as eyewitness accounts. *See also* above, Chaps. 11, n. 9; 12, nn. 8–9; and on the prewar flirtations with the Arab world, the pro-Nazi essay by Mohammed Sabry, *Islam—Judentum—Bolschewismus,* Berlin, 1938 (Schriften der Hochschule für Politik).

7. Kaczerginski, *Tsvishn hamer un serp, passim.*

8. Elias Spivak, *Di shprakh in di teg fun der foterlendisher milkhome* (The Language in the Period of the Great Patriotic War), Kiev, 1946; *Mit festn trit* (With a Firm Step: Literary-Artistic Collection by Soviet Yiddish Writers of White Russia), Minsk, 1947; K. Shmeruk in *Pirsumim yehudiim,* pp. xcvii ff. *See also* Robert S. Sullivant, *Soviet Politics in the Ukraine, 1917–1957,* New York, 1962 (Diss. University of Chicago).

9. Corliss Lamont, *The Peoples of the Soviet Union,* pp. 91 f.; Walter Zander, *Soviet Jewry, Palestine and the West,* London, 1947, p. 61.

10. Joseph B. Schechtman, *Star in Eclipse: Russian Jewry Revisited,* New York, 1961, citing a conversation with a "bemedaled former officer" in Odessa in 1959. There is no way to verify these figures.

11. Alexander Fadeev (Fadeyev), *Molodaia Gvardiia* (The Young Guard: a Novel), Moscow, 1959; in the English trans. by Violet Dutt, ed. by David Skvirsky, Moscow, n.d.; Valentin Kataev, *Za vlast sovetov* (For Soviet Power),

Notes

Moscow, 1951; Ilya Ehrenburg, "On the Writer's Work" (Russian), *Znamia*, 1953, No. 10, pp. 160–83; *Kultura i zhizn* of September 10, 1946; and other data cited by A. Yarmolinsky in his *Literature under Communism*, especially pp. 19, 52 ff., 64 ff.; Ainsztein in *Jewish Social Studies*, XXIII, 77 ff. *See also*, more generally, M. P. Gallagher, *The Soviet History of World War II*, especially pp. 57 ff. on the criticisms leveled at the early edition of Fadeev's *The Young Guard*, despite its author's high standing in Party circles; the stimulating papers published in the *Proceedings* of the [Second] Conference of the Institute for the Study of the History and Culture of the USSR, New York, 1953; Harold Swayze, *Political Control of Literature in the USSR, 1946–1959*, Cambridge, 1962 (Studies of Harvard University's Russian Research Center, XLIV); and above, Chap. 14, n. 19. The sharp criticisms of Eisenstein's film can readily be understood in the light of the Party's ever-changing appreciation of the character and deeds of the sixteenth-century tsar. *See* G. H. Bolsover, "Ivan the Terrible in Russian Historiography," *Transactions of the Royal Historical Society*, VII (1957), 71–90.

12. *See* Jerzy G. Gliksman's quotation in his annual review of "The Soviet Union" in the *American Jewish Year Book*, L (1948–49), 403; B. J. Choseed, *Jews in Soviet Literature*, especially pp. 122, 142 f.; M. Friedberg in L. Kochan's *The Jews in Soviet Russia*, pp. 198 ff.; and, more generally, Solomon M. Schwarz, *Evrei v Sovetskom Soiuze* (Jews in the Soviet Union from the Beginning of the Second World War, 1939–1965), New York, 1966; *idem, Antisemitizm v Sovetskom Soiuze* (Anti-Semitism in the Soviet Union), New York, 1952; and William Korey's more up-to-date analysis, *The Soviet Cage: Antisemitism in Russia*, New York, 1973.

13. *See* the widely publicized picture of the Jewish throngs extending their hearty and courageous, though imprudent, welcome to the first Israel envoy to the Soviet Union in L. Leneman, *La tragédie*, illustration No. 288 A, facing p. 280. *See also ibid.*, pp. 130 ff. The surfacing of a strong Zionist sentiment among the Soviet Jews in 1948 in this connection is well described by Yehoshua A. Gilboa in his "The 1948 Zionist Wave in Moscow," *Soviet Jewish Affairs*, No. 2 (1971), 35–39.

14. These and other stories illustrative of widespread Soviet anti-Semitism are included in Mendel Man's *Bai di toirn fun Moskve* (At the Gates of Moscow), New York, 1958; and *Bai der Waiksel* (At the Vistula), Tel Aviv, 1958; Leneman, pp. 130 ff. On Mikhoels, *see* above, Chap. 14, n. 23.

15. *See* the early report (trans. by Aaron Antonovsky from the Yiddish article in *Di Goldene Kait*, Tel Aviv, 1956) by Bernard Turner, "With the Yiddish Writers in Siberia," *Dissent*, IV (1957), 88–91; and other moving testimonies of various survivors cited by Leneman in *La tragédie, passim*; Casimir M. Smogrorzewski, "The Russification of the Baltic States," *World Affairs*, IV (1950), 168–81; "The Sovietization of the Baltic States," *Annals* of the American Academy of Political Science, CCCXVII (1958), 123–29; Roman Smal Stocki, *The Nationality Problem of the Soviet Union and Russian Communist Imperialism*. With a Preface by Lew E. Dobriansky, Milwaukee, 1952, especially pp. 199 ff; Harrison E. Salisbury, *To Moscow—and Beyond: a Reporter's Narrative*, New York, 1959, pp. 65 f., 69, 78 f. *See also* Z. Brzezinski, *The Permanent Purge*, pp. 132 ff. On Stalin's changing attitudes toward even such older nationalist movements as that in White Russia, *see* S. Krushinsky's *Byelorussian Communism and Nationalism: Per-*

sonal Recollections, New York, 1954. (Columbia University's Research Program on the USSR, Mimeographed Series, No. 34). In all such personal reminiscences the individual bias must be discounted. Yet this volume offers insights not available from other sources. *See also* above, Chap. 14, n. 20; and, more generally, Yehoshua A. Gilboa's comprehensive survey of *The Black Years of Soviet Jewry, 1939–1953*, trans. from the Hebrew by Yosef Schachter and Dov Ben-Abba, Boston, 1971.

16. The article "Evrei" in the *Bolshaia sovetskaia entsiklopedia*, new ed., XV (1952), 377–79, is reproduced in a French trans. by François Fejtö in *Les Juifs et l'antisémitisme dans le pays communistes (entre l'intégration et la sécession), suivi de documents et de témoignages*, Paris, 1960 (Les documents de "Tribune libre"), pp. 101 ff. Also reproduced here are the critical comments on that article, courageously published by the Polish Jewish communist Michael Mirski in the Warsaw Yiddish paper, *Folks-Shtime* of January 24–26, 1957 (pp. 107 ff.). It may be noted that the article in the encyclopedia on "Evréiskaia avtonómnaia oblást" (Jewish Autonomous Region = Biro-Bidzhan) occupies an equal amount of space in addition to several photographs (cols. 379–81). A more comprehensive analysis of the Jewish aspects of the two editions of the *Bolshaia sovetskaia entsiklopedia* is offered in M. Jarblum's aforementioned *Le problème juif*, pp. 29 ff., 43 ff. The treatment of the Jews in Vol. IX, pp. 10–14 of the third edition (published in 1972) is no better. Here only 2 columns are assigned to the article "Evrei," while 6 columns deal with "Jewish literature," and 4 columns with the "Hebrew script." But the ramified problems of the Hebrew and Yiddish languages are disposed of in 3 lines each (p. 13). A detailed analysis of that edition, similar to those by Mirski and Jarblum, would definitely be in order, as also would one of the biased treatment of Jews in the various other Soviet encyclopedias, both general and specialized, published before and after World War II. *See* Marianne Seydoux, "Les encyclopédies générales russes. Essai bibliographique," *Cahiers du monde russe et soviétique*, VI (1965), 245–63. *See also* Schechtman, *Star in Eclipse*, pp. 114, 183 f.; and Alexander Weissberg, *Conspiracy of Silence*, English trans. by Edward Fitzgerald, with a Preface by Arthur Koestler, London, 1952. While mainly a dramatic narrative of the author's own experiences during the purges of the 1930s, it also helps explain the public complacency and inactivity of the Jewish masses during the Stalinist terror of 1948–52.

17. *See* the text of Khrushchev's secret report, reproduced and analyzed by Bertram D. Wolfe in his *Khrushchev and Stalin's Ghost: Text, Background and Meaning of Khrushchev's Secret Report to the Twentieth Congress on the Night of February 24–25, 1956*, New York, 1957. While the underlying text is taken from an evidently modified version sent from Moscow to the communist leadership of one of the satellite countries and subsequently used by the U.S. Department of State for its translation, it does represent the essence of Khrushchev's seven-hour peroration. *See* especially pp. 202 ff. Never controverted by the Soviet authorities, it was further amplified by new Khrushchev "revelations" at the Twenty-Second Party Congress of October, 1961, which ended in the removal of Stalin's body from the Lenin mausoleum. How easily Stalin could have persuaded the Russian public of the doctors' guilt may be seen from the following, probably typical, remark of a Moscow taxi driver to Harrison E. Salisbury. When

in April, 1953, the driver learned about the innocence of the alleged plotters, he exclaimed: "Those *svoloch* [rascals]! They got away this time. But their day will come. We will get those yids!" *See* Salisbury's *To Moscow—and Beyond*, p. 77. On the first impression generally made by the public revelation of the "doctors' plot" in *Pravda*, see Salisbury, *American in Russia*, New York, 1955, pp. 140 ff.

18. The allegedly threatened Zaslavsky dismissal cited by Solomon Goldelmann in his "Zur Frage der Assimilierung und Denationalisierung der Juden in der Sowjetunion," *Sowjet Studien*, X (1961), 29–58, especially p. 39; and, more generally, *idem*, *Das Schicksal der Juden in der Sowjetunion*, Jerusalem, 1958. On the threat of the mass deportation *see* Schechtman, *Star in Eclipse*, pp. 41 f.; and the various essays in *Genocide in the USSR: Studies in Group Destruction*, ed. by Nikolai K. Deker and Andrei Lebed, English trans. ed. by Oliver J. Frederikson for the Munich Institute for the Study of the USSR, New York, 1958, especially pp. 20 ff., 30 ff., 49 ff. Next to the groups subjected to complete destruction a number of others suffered partial annihilation. Among these are counted here the Jews too, on whom *see* Solomon Goldelmann's pertinent essay, *ibid.*, pp. 94–110. *See also* Robert Conquest, *The Nation Killers*, London, 1970, analyzing in considerable detail the ruthless methods employed in the wartime deportation of seven nationalities.

19. L. Dmiterko, "The Situation and Tasks of Theatrical and Literary Criticism in the Ukraine," *Literaturnaya Gazeta* of March 9, 1949, cited by S. M. Schwarz in *The Jews*, p. 359. The policy of enforced silence with respect to Babi Yar has continued to the present day. Joseph Schechtman graphically described the obstacles the Russian authorities placed in the paths of foreign visitors wishing to visit that neglected ravine, of which he also supplied a telling photograph. *See* his *Star in Eclipse*, pp. 99 ff., with the illustrations following pp. 120 ff.; and below, Chap. 17, n. 9.

20. Howard Fast, "A Matter of Validity," *Midstream*, IV (1958), 7–18, especially p. 10; also under the title "The Soviet Hatred of Jewish Jews," in the *Jewish Digest*, III, No. 11 (1958), 1–15. *See also* Fast's *The Naked God: the Writer and the Communist Party*, London, 1958; and below, Chap. 17, n. 11.

[17]

After Stalin

1. L. Zinger, *Dos banaite Folk*, Moscow, 1941; *idem*, *Dos ufgerikhte Folk* (The Reconstructed People: the Social-Economic Restratification of the Jewish Population in the Soviet Union), Moscow, 1948 (includes a 23-page superficial survey of "The Soviet Jews in the Years of the Great Patriotic War and the Postwar Period"). The 1965 effort consisted of the rather inadequate description by S. Rabinovich, *Idn in Sovietn-Ferband* (Jews in the Soviet Union), Moscow, 1965.

2. Our information is therefore derived mainly from the few studies and a host of personal observations, necessarily fragmentary, by such foreign scholars as S. M. Schwarz, L. Leneman, B. Z. Goldberg, J. B. Schechtman, K. Shmeruk, and others mentioned in our earlier notes. *See also* Gregorii Y. Aronson, *Soviet Russia and the Jews*, New York, 1949; Elliot E. Cohen, ed., *The New Red Anti-Semitism: a Symposium*, Boston, 1953; "Jews in the Soviet Union." Special issue of the *New Leader*, XXXVI (Sept. 14, 1959); several essays in the Israeli Hebrew periodical *Gesher*; and François Fejtö, *Les Juifs et l'antisémitisme dans les pays communistes*. Some additional sidelights may also be obtained from the studies relating to the Jews of neighboring lands, such as Peter Meyer *et al.*, *The Jews in the Soviet Satellites*, Syracuse, 1953. The extent to which even Soviet Jewry depended on foreign research for information about the basic facts of its own life is illustrated by the figure 2,644,000 for the total Jewish population in the Union given in *Sovetish Haimland*, 1973, No. 4, p. 179. This figure is evidently taken (without acknowledgment) from Leon Shapiro's very tentative computations in the *American Jewish Year Book*. *See* Shapiro's note in his "Soviet Union Today and a Look Back" in that *Year Book*, LXXIV (1973), p. 481. *See also* Shapiro's other annual reports on the Soviet Union in the successive recent vols. of the *Year Book*; his fine summary concerning the developments between 1953 and 1966 in his "Russian Jewry after Stalin" in Aronson, Frumkin *et al.*, *Russian Jewry, 1917–1967*, pp. 444–502; Arieh Tartakower, "The Jewish Problem in the Soviet Union," *Jewish Social Studies*, XXXIII (1971), 285–306; and below, Chap. 18, nn. 1–4.

3. *See* Mark Neuweld, "The Latest Soviet Census and the Jews," *Commentary*, XXIX (1960), 426–29, largely based upon the preliminary reports published in *Pravda*; Mark Geffen, "Jews in the Soviet Union: Results of the Population Census," *Bitfutzot hagolah*, II (1960), 109–17; Zvi Rudy, "The Jews of the Soviet Union as Reflected in Soviet Ethnography" (Hebrew), *Gesher*, VI, No. 4 (1960–61), 47–53; Moshe Abramovich, "Jews in the Soviet Census, 1959" (Hebrew), *Molad*, XVIII, Nos. 144–45 (1960), 320–29; Schechtman, *Star in Eclipse*, pp. 27 ff.; *The New York Times* of October 23, 1962; Alec Nove, "Jews in the Soviet Union," *Jewish Journal of Sociology*, III (1961), 108–20. *See also* the earlier, somewhat overspeculative, observations by Francis Bower on "The Population of Soviet Russia," *Contemporary Review*, CLXXX (1951), 337–43. Some of these studies have largely, but not completely, been superseded by Mordechai Altschuler's comprehensive analysis of *Ha-Yehudim be-mifqad ha-okhlosim be-Brit ha-Mo'esot, 1959* (Jews in the Population Census in the Soviet Union, 1959), Jerusalem, 1963.

Another example of the sharp decline of the Jewish population between the censuses of 1939 and 1959 is offered by Latvia. Despite the fourteen-year period of recovery since the end of the war, the number of Jews had declined from 93,900, or 4.6 percent of the republic's population, to 36,600, or 1.7 percent. *See* the interesting study, going back to the data available since 1750, by Andrios Namsons in his "Nationale Zusammensetzung und Struktur der Bevölkerung Lettlands nach den Volkzählungen von 1925, 1939 und 1970," *Acta Baltica*, XI (1971 [1972]), 61–86, especially pp. 63 ff. *See also* below, Chap. 18, n. 4. The stationary total of Latvian Jewry and its decline to 1.6 percent eleven years later (according to the 1970 census) should serve as a warning against equating the surpluses, if any, of the Jewish birth rate over the death rate with that of the general population, as was frequently done. *See* the earlier *caveat* to this effect, sounded by Joshua Rothenberg in "A Note on the Natural Increase of the Jewish Population in the Soviet Union," *Jewish Social Studies*, XXXI (1969), 37–39.

4. The 1959 census figures of 239,246 Jews for Moscow and 168,641 for Leningrad add up to only a small majority of the Jews in the Russian Republic, while the rest are scattered over many of the 874 other cities listed as such in the census. Yet it appears that the aforementioned general factors operating to reduce the actual numbers of self-acknowledged Jews living in the respective localities, as reported in the census, has led to even lower estimates in the two metropolitan areas. Remarkably, far-off Tashkent with its 50,500 Jewish inhabitants exceeded the old centers of Kishinev (43,000), Riga (30,000), and others. Even Vilna, glorified as the "Lithuanian Jerusalem" during the nineteenth century, had only a little more than 16,000 Jews. At the same time, the 106,000 Jews counted as living in rural districts now amounted to less than 5 percent of the total Jewish population. *See also* the list of cities having a Jewish population of over 5,000 compiled by Ivor I. Millman in his "Major Centres of Jewish Population in the USSR and a Note on the 1970 Census," *Soviet Jewish Affairs*, No. 1 (1971), 13–18; and below, Chap. 18, n. 7.

5. Edward R. Stettinius, *Roosevelt and the Russians: The Yalta Conference*, ed. by Walter Johnson, Garden City, New York, 1949, p. 278; Stalin's reply to the Jewish Telegraphic Agency of January 12, 1931 (not publicized in the Soviet Union until 1936, when it was quoted from a Molotov speech in *Pravda*), cited by S. M. Schwarz in *The Jews*, pp. 292, 305 nn. 4–5; and the data assembled by Leneman in *La tragédie*, pp. 166 ff.; and by Schechtman in his *Star in Eclipse*, pp. 78 ff. Some of the numerous official denials of the existence of anti-Semitism in the Soviet Union, emanating from Khrushchev, Anastas Mikoyan (who bluntly asserted before United Nations correspondents that there existed no Jewish question in the U.S.S.R.), and others are summarized by F. Fejtö in *Les Juifs*, pp. 121 ff.

6. Peter N. Juviler, "Representatives of Nationalities and Occupations in the Soviets," *Annals* of the Ukrainian Academy of Arts and Sciences in the United States, IX (1961), 201–24, especially p. 219; Moshe Decter, "The Status of the Jews in the Soviet Union," *Foreign Affairs*, XLI (1962–63), 420–30; Alec Nove, "A Note on the Proportion of Jews in Republican and Local Soviets, U.S.S.R.," *Jewish Journal of Sociology*, III (1961), 276; and more generally, Anatole Goldstein, *The Soviet Attitude towards Territorial Minorities and the Jews*, New York, 1957. It may be noted that the percentage of Jewish elective officials, as well as of industrial managers, is somewhat higher (relative to population) in the Asiatic republics. Evidently Jews are viewed there primarily as "Russians." However, with the growth of local talent, the gradual process of displacement of these "alien" leaders by native officials and managers is likely to hit the Jews in both capacities, as Jews and as Russians. In fact, in 1963 there were only 13 Jews among the 5,761 members of the supreme soviets of all the fifteen republics. *See also* below, Chap. 18, n. 16.

7. "Soviet Union: 'Show-Trial' or Showdown," *Jews in Eastern Europe*, II, No. 4 (1964), 12–22, especially p. 17; Decter in *Foreign Affairs*, XLI, 429 f.; *The New York Times*, February 27, 1964, pp. 3, 6. The widely publicized trials and their obvious anti-Jewish animus were quickly noted abroad. As early as 1953–54 they evoked such comments as those presented by Joshua Kunitz in *The Jewish Problem in the USSR: on Trials and Purges* by the Editors, New York, 1953 (The

Monthly Review Pamphlet Series, VI); M. Leites and E. Bernaut, *Ritual and Liquidation: the Case of the Moscow Trials*, Glencoe, Ill., 1954; and, more generally, Judd L. Teller, *Scapegoat of Revolution*, New York, 1954. Interesting materials on the various aspects of the situation of Soviet Jewry were also assembled by Moshe Decter in the "Conference Papers" submitted to the *Conference on the Status of Soviet Jews* held in New York on October 12, 1963.

8. The statistics here given are quoted from news dispatches in the *Congress Bi-Weekly*, XXIX, No. 10 (1962), p. 4. Substantially the same figures were supplied by Georgii M. Korniyenko, Counsellor of the Soviet Embassy in Washington, to Moses I. Socachewsky, president of the Jewish Nazi Victims Organization. The variants of 15.7 percent of all doctors, and 3.2 percent of all students are not significant. *See* the report in *The New York Times* of October 11, 1962, p. 6. *See also* some other figures cited in Schechtman's *Star in Eclipse*, pp. 53 ff.; and in *Jews in Eastern Europe*, II, No. 4, pp. 40 f. In the early 1960s the absolute number of Jewish students continued growing, while their percentage was declining. From 77,117 in 1960 they increased to 82,000 in 1963–64, but their ratio dropped from 3 to 2.5 percent. A typical denial of discrimination was issued by Vyacheslav Yelyutin, Minister of Higher and Secondary Schools, in his statement made to *The New York Times* (of September 29, 1959). He asserted that Jews constituted approximately 10 percent of the Soviet student population—obviously a vast exaggeration. *See* the more detailed data analyzed below, Chap. 18, nn. 16–19.

Surprisingly, there have also existed some Jewish apologists for the otherwise restrictive policies. Harking back to the old ideology of "productivization" of the Jewish people, a retired Jewish medical professor in Leningrad told B. Z. Goldberg in 1959: "Look here, on my faculty I had fifty-seven professors and forty-six of them were Jews. Do you think this was natural? Was this good for the Jews? Would you want the Soviet Jews to become a nation of professors? We want fewer Jewish professors and more Jewish plain workers." *See* Goldberg's *The Jewish Problem*, p. 157. On the improvement in Soviet statistical accounts in recent years and the earlier difficulties in their interpretation, *see* Harry Schwartz, "The Renaissance of Soviet Statistics," *Review of Economics and Statistics*, XL (1958), 122–26.

9. Evgenii Evtushenko (Yevtushenko), *Babi Yar* in his *Selected Poems*, trans. with an Intro. by Robin Miller-Gulland and Peter Levi, New York, 1962, pp. 82 ff.; here cited from the somewhat different English excerpts, reproduced in Harry Schwartz's column, "Moscow Papers Assail Writer" in *The New York Times* of September 28, 1961, p. 22; Harrison E. Salisbury, "Fear Grows among Soviet Jews at Resurgence of Anti-Semitism," *ibid.*, February 8, 1962, p. 4; Arthur P. Reed, Jr., "Soviet Culture: Its Ups and Downs," *New York Standard*, February 17, 1963, p. 133. *See also* above, Chap. 16, n. 19; and the interesting report on Evtushenko's encounter with Khrushchev, published from somewhat dubious transcripts, in "Russian Art and Anti-Semitism: Two Documents," *Commentary* of December, 1963 (with a critical analysis by Moshe Decter).

10. Schechtman, *Star in Eclipse*, pp. 38 f. n. 2; Alfred D. Low, "Patriotism, 'Bourgeois Nationalism' and the Nationality Policy of the USSR after Stalin," *Annals* of the Ukrainian Academy of Arts and Sciences in the United States, IX

(1961), 126–46. *See also* the illustrations offered by Leopold H. Haimson in "The Solitary Hero and the Philistine: a Note on the Heritage of the Stalin Era" and by Max Hayward in "The Thaw and the Writers" in Richard Pipes's ed. of *The Russian Intelligentsia*, New York, 1961, pp. 101–10, 111–21.

11. Howard Fast, "The Ordeal of Boris Pasternak," *Midstream*, V (1959), 38–44, especially p. 42. *See* such reports as that published under the telling title, "Israel: 'Hell' or 'Paradise' " (Russian) in *Sovetskaia Kultura* of March 25, 1958; and the other harangues, selected from Russian publications in 1957–59 by F. Fejtö in *Les Juifs*, pp. 155 f. Typical of the official view was a sharply anti-Israel study, published by the State Publishing House in Moscow, 1958, under the title *Gosudarstvo Izrail* (The State of Israel, Its Location and Policies) by K. Ivanov and Z. Sheinis. *See* the facsimile of its title page in Schechtman's *Star*, p. 194. *See also* the *New Leader*, XXXVI (Sept. 14, 1959), 27 ff.

12. *The New York Times* of November 2, 1962, p. 13; Yizhar Smilansky, "Behind the Red Curtain: Impressions of a Sabra Writer," *Jewish Frontier* of January 1963, Section II, p. 32. This report, originally published in Hebrew in Israeli journals, is more fully reproduced in the *Hadoar*, XLIII, No. 2, of November 9, 1962, pp. 19 ff. *See also* below, n. 16. The transition of Soviet policies from the pro-Israel attitude during the United Nations debate on the partition of Palestine in 1947 and the outright hostility which grew from the early 1950s to the break in diplomatic relations after the Six-Day War in June, 1967, is illustrated by Mordecai Namir's well-documented reminiscences in his *Shlihut be-Moskva* (Mission to Moscow), Tel Aviv, 1971. Namir had served there from August 1948 to the end of 1950 as counselor of the Israeli embassy and later as ambassador (he subsequently was a member of the Israeli Cabinet and mayor of Tel Aviv). Another Israeli diplomat, Arie L. Eliav, who was first secretary of that embassy in 1958–60 and visited the Soviet Union on several other occasions has presented a graphic description of many contacts he had had with Jewish communities and individuals in various parts of the Soviet Union from Riga to Biro-Bidzhan. *See* his (Ben-Ami's) *Between Hammer and Sickle*, Philadelphia, 1967, or the paperback ed., New York, 1969. *See also* below, Chap. 18, where the growing Soviet hostility toward Israel, especially after the Six-Day War of 1967 and the simultaneously evolving substantial emigration of Russian Jews to Israel and other lands are briefly described.

13. The storm of indignation which greeted Trofim K. Kichko's book in the West seems to have surprised the Soviet authorities. They tried to explain its publication by an irregular procedure at the Ukrainian Academy and stated that "those responsible for publishing this book have been severely punished." *See* the letter addressed on August 20, 1964, by Ekaterina Kolosova, head of the Presidium of the Ukrainian Friendship Society to the secretary of the Society for Cultural Relations with the U.S.S.R. in London. She also pointed to some adverse criticisms of the book which appeared in the Soviet Union and claimed that Kichko "has never worked in the Academy nor does he now work there." *See* J. Miller, "The Kichko Affair: Additional Documents," *Soviet Jewish Affairs*, No. 1 (1971), 109–113. In his comments on the text Miller clearly demonstrates the fallacy of the Soviet arguments. On the number of synagogues, *see* the next note.

14. M. Decter in *Foreign Affairs*, XLI, 424 ff. The picture of Rabbi Schliefer opening the rabbinical school is reproduced by Leneman in *La tragédie*, p. 16 A. *See also* below, Chap. 18, n. 40; and more generally, Alexander A. Bogolepov, *Tserkov pod vlastiu kommunizma* (The Church under Communist Domination), Munich, 1958. Institute for the Study of the U.S.S.R., Studies, 1st ser., XLII (reviews also the conditions in the satellite countries).

15. *The New York Times* of December 20, 1959 (Kirovagrad broadcast); *ibid.*, of October 23, 1962, p. 11 (an interview with the prominent Moscow rabbi Yehudah Leib Levin). *See also* the attack on "The Reactionary Nature of the Jewish Religion" (Russian) published in the Lvov *Pravda* and trans. into French, together with several other similar press notices, by F. Fejtö in *Les Juifs*, pp. 157 ff.

16. *See* S. Rabinovich, *Idn in Sovietn Ferband*, p. 47; L. Shapiro, "Russian Jewry after Stalin," in Aronson, Frumkin *et al.*, eds., *Russian Jewry, 1917–1967*, pp. 448 ff.; A. A. Gershuni, *Yehudim ve-Yahadut*, pp. 219 ff. and *passim*; Lewis S. Feuer, "The Soviet Jews: Resistance to Planned Culturocide," *Judaism*, XIII (1964), 90–100; and, more generally, *Genocide in the USSR: Study in Group Destruction*, published by the Institute for the Study of the USSR, Munich, 1958.

17. *See* David Miller's extensive report on "Russia's Defense on Jewish Bias Charges" in the *New York Herald Tribune* of November 24, 1962, pp. 1–2; Decter in *Foreign Affairs*, XLI, 421 ff.; and below, Chap. 18, nn. 46–47. On the spurt of Russian translations from the Yiddish in 1961, *see* the list in *Kirjath Sepher*, XXXVIII (1962–63), pp. 79 ff. Nos. 761–79. *See also* S. Goldelmann's studies cited above, Chap. 16, n. 18. This process contrasted sharply with the far slower process of Russification even in recent years, for instance of the Ukrainians, on which *see* Robert S. Sullivant, *Soviet Politics and the Ukraine, 1917–1957*, pp. 294 ff. *See*, however, above, n. 16.

18. *See* Khrushchev's interview with Serge Groussard, published in the Paris *Figaro* of April 9, 1958, and reproduced by F. Fejtö in *Les Juifs*, pp. 124 ff. Although denounced in the Soviet press as a "provocative forgery," this interview clearly reflected Khrushchev's essential reasoning. Of considerable interest also were the rather penetrating observations on the spot by the Polish communist, Dominik Horodynski, published in the Warsaw magazine, *Świat* of December 7, 1958 and trans. into French by Fejtö, *ibid.*, pp. 131 ff. Subsequent reports by several visitors, including direct observations of their own on visits to Biro-Bidzhan in 1934, 1959, and the 1960s are summarized by B. Z. Goldberg in *The Jewish Problem in the Soviet Union*, pp. 170 ff.; and by A. L. Eliav in his *Between Hammer and Sickle*, pp. 184 ff.

19. It is well known that Pasternak's Nobel prize-winning novel, *Doctor Zhivago*, could not appear in Russia, because the editors of the *Novy Mir* (New World) rejected it as too critical of the revolution. In 1958, after the award of the Nobel Prize, the officials of the Writers' Union expelled Pasternak from the Union. At that time the original rejection of the novel was publicized in the *Literaturnaya Gazeta* of October 25, 1958, and therefrom reproduced in an English trans. in the *Current Digest of the Soviet Press* of December 3, 1958. This lengthy document is now readily available in *The Russian Intelligentsia*, ed. by R. Pipes, pp. 208–26. *See also* Howard Fast's perceptive essay on "The Ordeal of Boris Pasternak," *Midstream*, V (1959), 38–44; and above, Chap. 14, n. 27.

[18]

Incipient Revival

1. *See* Philippa Lewis's brief review of these materials in "The Jewish Question in the Open: 1968–1971" in L. Kochan, ed., *The Jews in Soviet Russia*, 2d ed., pp. 337–53; and, more generally, C. Gerstenmeier, *Die Stimme der Stummen, Die demokratische Bewegung in der Sowjetunion*, Stuttgart, 1971.

2. Of special Jewish interest were the *samizdats*, issued in the series *Iskhod*, which in 1972 appeared in an English trans. entitled *Exodus*. The first three series describe the difficulties in securing exit visas, the events during U.S. President Richard Nixon's first visit in Moscow, and the press conference of October 15, 1972. Number four deals with the much-discussed hijacking trial in Leningrad in December, 1970. *See also* the pertinent data assembled in *Jews in Eastern Europe*, IV, No. 6 (April, 1971): "Moscow on Trial: What to Do With Imprisoned Jews?"

3. Among the outstanding publications of this kind are Max Hayward's *On Trial: The Soviet State vs. "Abram Tertz" and "Nikolai Arzhak,"* which contains an English trans. of an almost complete transcript of the 1966 trial of the non-Jew Andrei Siniavskii and the Jew Yulii Daniel, New York, 1967; Frida Maria Vigdorova's similar transcript of the trial of Iosif Brodskii in the *New Leader* of August 31, 1964; a number of appeals to the United Nations and other bodies, with all signatures, in "Soviet Jews Protest at Arrests," *Jews in Eastern Europe*, IV, No. 6 (April, 1971), 84–103; the story of the "Second Leningrad Trial," *ibid.*, No. 7 (November, 1971), 5 ff.; of the Riga, Kishinev, and three other trials, *ibid.*, pp. 76 ff., 160 ff., 185 ff.; and other cases summarized *ibid.*, V, No. 3 (August, 1973). *See also* René Beerman's juridical analysis of "The 1970–71 Soviet Trials of Zionists: Some Legal Aspects," *Soviet Jewish Affairs*, No. 2 (1971), 3–24. One must also bear in mind that the peculiar Soviet conception of justice cannot be simply equated with those long regnant in the West. See Harold Joseph Berman, *Justice in the USSR: an Interpretation of Soviet Law*, 2d ed. enlarged, Cambridge, Mass., 1963 (Russian Research Center Studies, III). Of the numerous noteworthy autobiographical records we need but mention the anonymous "The Road Home: a Russian Jew Discovers His Identity," *Bulletin Soviet Jewish Affairs*, No. 4 (December, 1969), 3–14; and Ilya Zilberberg's "From Russia to Israel: a Personal Case-History," *Soviet Jewish Affairs*, II, No. 3 (1972), 42–65. Further materials are available in the publications listed in Benjamin Pinkus and Abraham Albert Greenbaum's comprehensive compilation of *Russian Publications on Jews and Judaism in the Soviet Union, 1917–1967*, ed. by Mordechai Altschuler, Jerusalem, 1970; and Israel Rudnitsky's more recent "Publications on Soviet and Eastern European Jewry (Bibliography)" (Hebrew), *Shvut*, I (1973), 192–99; II (1974), 206–209.

4. *See Atlas narodov mira* (Atlas of the World's Nations), Moscow, 1964, p. 158; A. M. Maksimov, "Population Movements of 1959–1970" (Russian), *Istoriia S.S.S.R.*, No. 5 (September–October, 1971), 16, with Leon Shapiro's comment thereon in the *American Jewish Year Book*, LXXIII (1972), 536 f., 596; Ivor I. Millman, "Major Centres of Jewish Population in the USSR and a Note on the 1970 Census," *Soviet Jewish Affairs*, I, (1971), 3–12; objected to by Jacob Robinson and L. Shapiro in "Letters to the Editor" of *Soviet Jewish Affairs*, dated March 24

and 21, 1972, respectively, and published there in II, No. 3 of 1972, pp. 148–49; and Millman's reply to them of August 14, 1972, *ibid.*, II, No. 4 (1972), 130–31. Another specialist in Soviet Jewish demography, Mordechai Altschuler, likewise assumed that by 1966 the Jewish population in the Union had increased during the preceding seven years by some 407,000 and totaled 2,675,000. *See* his "Sketches for the Demographic Image of the Jewish Community in the Soviet Union" (Hebrew) in *Yahadut Berit ha-Moesot, Meassef* (Judaism in the Soviet Union: a Collection of Essays), ed. by A. Tartakower *et al.*, Tel Aviv, n. d., pp. 9–30. On the other hand, the general decline of the Jewish population is even more dramatically illustrated by the censuses of the western Soviet republics. For example, in Latvia, where the tsarist enumerators of 1897 found 142,315 Jews forming 7.4 percent of the total population, the censuses of 1925 and 1935, when Latvia was an independent country, showed a diminution of Jews both in absolute and relative numbers, to 95,625 or 5.18 percent and 93,479 or 4.79 percent, respectively. This decline was sharply accelerated during World War II and the German occupation. The Soviet censuses of 1959 and 1970 revealed the presence of only 36,392 and 36,700 Jews in the republic, amounting to only 1.7 and 1.6 percent of the population. *See* Andrios Namsons' essay, cited above, Chap. 17, n. 3. We must bear in mind, however, that all Russian censuses, including that of 1970, were partially motivated by political considerations. Such weaknesses in the 1970 computation were noticed quite early by the American demographer Murray Feshbach in his "Observations on the Soviet Census," *Problems of Communism*, XIX, No. 3 (May–June, 1970), 58–64.

5. René Beerman, "Russian and Soviet Passport Laws," *Bulletin Soviet Jewish Affairs*, 6 (1968), 1–11, pointing out that after a revolutionary break of some fifteen years, the Soviets simply restored an old tsarist practice. They reinstituted passports as obligatory for all urban and many rural settlers under a sanction of a ten-ruble fine for any infraction of the passport regulations. This amount remained constant despite inflation (or occasional deflation) and currency revaluation.

6. *See* Yurii Larin (Lurye), *Evrei i antisemitizm v S.S.S.R.* (Jews and Anti-Semitism in the U.S.S.R.), p. 304; Jacob Lestchinsky, "Jews in the Soviet Union" (Yiddish), *Yidisher Kemfer*, 1946, No. 669, 95; M. Altschuler in *Yahadut Berit ha-Moesot*, p. 13.

7. *See* Mordechai Altschuler, "Sketches for the Demographic Image," in *Yahadut Berit ha-Moesot*, p. 20; Michael Checiński, "Soviet Jews and Higher Education," *Soviet Jewish Affairs*, III, No. 2 (1973), 3–16, especially p. 5; Ivor I. Millman's aforementioned essay (above, n. 4) in *Soviet Jewish Affairs*, I, especially pp. 15 f.; my *Social and Religious History of the Jews*, first ed., II, 365 ff., showing that the decline in natural growth, sometimes followed by an actual diminution in numbers, was a novel characteristic of many Western and Westernized Jewish communities in the twentieth century. To be sure, on occasion some Russian cities had an astounding surplus of births over deaths. In 1938 the ratio was 195:100 in Moscow and 252:100 in Minsk. *See* Harry Schwartz, *Russia's Soviet Economy*, 2d ed., New York, 1954, p. 27. However, this phenomenon may be accounted for by the mass migration of younger persons of both sexes from the villages to the metropolitan areas in search of employment in the rapidly expanding industries.

Notes

In their "Supplementary Note" to "The Jewish Population" in L. Kochan's ed., *The Jews in Soviet Russia*, pp. 357 ff., Alec Nove and J. A. Newth compared the Jewish census figures of 1959–70 with those of other ethnic groups which also diminished in numbers in both population and those speaking their national language. *See* below, n. 47. In these eleven years the Poles registered a decline of 213,000 in total numbers and of 245,000 in those habitually speaking Polish. Among the far fewer Karelians the comparable decline was 21,000 and 27,000; among the Finns, 8,000 and 12,000, respectively. In their comment on these figures Nove and Newth rightly observed that "in each of these three cases the decline in total numbers is far in excess of what could be attributed to natural causes, and we must assume that individuals switched nationality and also claimed a new national language. This is by no means the necessary explanation for the figures concerning the Jews."

8. Boris Smolar, *Soviet Jewry Today*, p. 80; M. Altschuler in *Yahadut*, p. 15; Felix A. Theilhaber, *Der Untergang der deutschen Juden; eine wirtschaftliche Studie*, Munich, 1911.

9. *See* Robert Anchel, *Napoléon et les Juifs*, Paris, 1928, pp. 166 f., 171 f., 214 f.; Yvon de Begnac, *Palazzo Venezia—Storia di un regime*, Rome, 1950, p. 643; Renzo de Felice, *Storia degli Ebrei italiani sotto il fascismo*. With a Preface by Dello Cantimori, 3d ed., Turin, 1972. At times Mussolini was able to combine anti-Jewish with antipapal utterances, as when in 1941 he voiced surprise about Hitler's failure to abolish the celebration of Christmas which "reminds one only of the birth of a Jew who gave the world debilitating and devitalizing theories, and who especially contrived to trick Italy through the disintegrating power of the popes." Quoted by Mussolini's son-in-law, Count Galeazzo Ciano, in his *Diaries, 1939–1943*, ed. by Hugh Gibson, New York, 1946, p. 423.

10. Regrettably, our information about the rate of intermarriage among Soviet Jews is very limited. In "A Statistical Study of Intermarriage among Jews in Part of Vilnius (Vilno-USSR)," *Bulletin Soviet Jewish Affairs*, 1968, No. 1, pp. 64–69, J. A. Newth is able to cite but few pertinent Russian studies, and admits the general inadequacy of Soviet research in the area of intermarriage among the various nationalities. Certainly, his sample, derived from a suburban community of some 12,500 inhabitants, cannot be considered typical of the large majority of Jews residing in the "core" cities. Nor can one generalize from the experience of a locality in an area incorporated into the Soviet Union after World War II and the Holocaust to surmises about the settlements living under the Soviet system for more than half a century, with all the variables arising from the different rates of Jewish migrations during that period. Yet his general conclusion that "Jewish husbands in the area in question have over the years shown a growing tendency (at least to the mid-fifties) to choose their wives from outside the Jewish community and over a steadily expanding spectrum of nationalities, while the reverse is true of Jewish women—they have tended more and more to take either Jewish husbands or none at all" (p. 67), seems to apply to most other localities as well. Such differences in exogamous tendencies between men and women have also been observed among the Soviet Muslims; they had already come to the fore among the Jews residing in the interior of Russia during the early years of the revolution. *See* my *Social and Religious History of the Jews*, first ed., II, 367; and Geoffrey Wheeler's twin essays, "Racial Problems in Soviet

Muslim Asia," *Journal of the Royal Central Asian Society*, XLVII (1960), 93–105; and "The Muslims of Central Asia" in *Problems of Communism*, XVI, No. 5 (September–October, 1967), 72–81. Obviously, intermarriage in the Soviet Union has purely secular connotations and religious disparity per se plays no role in law. In the case of Jews or Muslims, however, ethnic diversity is as a rule little different from the religious variety. Although the general laws concerning marriage and divorce have been considerably tightened in recent years and do not diverge in many areas from those existing during the tsarist period, the legislators saw no reason to make special provisions for ethnically mixed marriages. *See*, more generally, Bernard Duboit's analysis of "Le nouveau droit soviétique du mariage et de la famille," *Annuaire de l'U.R.S.S.*, 1970–71, pp. 11–34.

11. *See* "Nationalities and Nationalism in the U.S.S.R.," *Problems of Communism*, XVI, No. 5 (September–October, 1967), including Zvi Gitelman's brief remarks on "The Jews" (pp. 92–101); Peter G. Stercho, "Soviet Concept of National Self-Determination: Theory and Reality from Lenin to Brezhnev," *Ukrainian Quarterly*, XXIX (1973), 12–27. *See also* Otto Rudolf Liess's thoughtful study, *Sowietische Nationalitätsstrategie als weltpolitisches Konzept*, Vienna, 1972 (pointing out, among other things, that the very definition of nationality, with all the paraphernalia of the "new" discipline of ethnogenetics, enabled the Russians to count the number of recognized nationalities in the Union as ranging from 160 in the census of 1926, down to 62 in that of 1939, and up again to 93 in that of 1959; p. 29); František Silnitsky, "Leninism's National Concepts and the Jewish Problem" (Hebrew), *Shvut*, II (1974), 74–81 (stressing the similarity between the tsarist and the communist theory of nationality [both of which were primarily designed to maintain the integrity of Russia's multinational empire], the paradoxical combination of denial of the existence of and repression of this allegedly nonexistent Jewish nationality, and the beginnings of a scholarly debate in 1964–67 questioning the fundamentals of that theory); Edward Allworth, ed., *Soviet Nationality Problems*, New York, 1971; and other writings mentioned above, especially Chaps. 11–12.

12. *Strana Sovetov za 50 liet* (The Soviet Land during Fifty Years); I. Kon, "The Psychology of Prejudice: On the Social-Psychological Roots of Ethnic Preconceptions" (Russian), *Novy Mir*, 1966, No. 9, cited here in a variant from the English trans. in Jacob Miller's "Soviet Theory on the Jews" in L. Kochan, ed., *The Jews in Soviet Russia*, p. 61 n. 1. On the less tense situation in the Asian republics, *see* Edward Allworth, ed., *The Nationality Question in Soviet Asia*, New York, 1973.

13. *See* Ivan Dziuba, *Internationalism or Russification: a Study in the Soviet Nationalities Problem*, English trans. from the Ukrainian, ed. by M. Davies, with a Preface by Peter Archer, London, 1968; Victor Swoboda, "Ukrainian 'Unpublished' Literature on the Jews," *Bulletin Soviet Jewish Affairs*, 4 (1969), 39–42; and *Ukrainians and Jews: a Symposium*, New York, 1966. Such dichotomies had already emerged in the early interwar period. *See* Janusz Radziegowski's interesting analysis of "The National Question in the Communist Party in the Soviet Ukraine, 1920–1927" (Polish), *Przegląd Historyczny*, LXII (1971), 477–99 (with Russian and French summaries). *See also* the fairly recent evaluation by a White Russian anti-Soviet writer, N. Nedasek, in his "National Self-Determination under the Soviets," *Belorussian Review*, VIII (1960), 3–16.

Notes

14. *See* the United Nation's *Demographic Yearbook* for 1972, p. 208; V. Swoboda in *Bulletin Soviet Jewish Affairs*, IV, pp. 39 ff.; Murray Seeger, "Latvia Loses Its Identity to Russians," *New York Post* of November 28, 1972. Other examples are cited by A. Avtorkhanov in his "Denationalization of the Soviet Ethnic Minorities," *Studies in the Soviet Union* (Munich), IV (1964–65), no. 1, pp. 74–99; and, more generally, by Frederick Charles Barghoorn in his *Soviet Russian Nationalism*, New York, 1956; and above, n. 11.

15. *See* T. H. Rigby, *Communist Party Membership in the U.S.S.R.*, Princeton, 1969; J. A. Newth and Z. Katz, "Proportion of Jews in the Communist Party of the Soviet Union," *Bulletin Soviet Jewish Affairs*, 4 (1969), 37–43; and above, Chap. 11, n. 5. It may be noted, however, that even the Great Russians held only 63.4 percent of Party membership in 1961, although in the 1959 census they figured as representing 65.8 percent of the Union's urban population, while the Ukrainians held their own (14.672 percent of Party members and 14.6 percent of urbanites) and the Georgians exceeded that ratio by 1.77:1.

16. *See* the various newspaper reports, including that in the New York *Jewish Week* of July 13, 1974, p. 7.

17. "Statistical Materials Toward the 250th Anniversary of the Academy of Science" (Russian), *Vestnik statistiki*, 1974, No. 4 (April), p. 92 Table 14, also summarized by Theodore Shabad in his report to *The New York Times* of July 7, 1974 (No. 42,533); Mordechai Altschuler, "The Statistical Data on Jews among the Scientific Elite of the Soviet Union," *Jewish Journal of Sociology*, XV (1973), 45–55, especially p. 48; and, more generally, Vilmos von Zsolnay's succinct review of the rapid growth of schools and institutes of higher learning and their personnel throughout the Union in his "Wissenschaft und Forschung in der Sowjetunion," *Saeculum*, XX (1969), 161–66. This expansion has continued in more recent years.

18. Altschuler, *ibid.*, J. A. Newth, "Jews in the Soviet Intelligentsia—Some Recent Developments," *Bulletin Soviet Jewish Affairs*, 2, No. 7 (1968), 1–12.

19. *See* the "Materials" in *Vestnik statistiki*; and T. Shabad in *The New York Times*, cited above, n. 17.

20. Various trials for alleged economic crimes committed by Jews, often resulting in death sentences, and the press campaigns before, during, and after them, greatly contributed to the spread of anti-Semitism in the Union, especially in the early 1960s. As to the nature of the reportage of these trials, a staff report prepared for the International Commission of Jurists in Geneva (a private organization supported by 50,000 lawyers in 108 countries) and published in its *Journal* characterized it well: Its "style and technique . . . is not to furnish data and information on which to form an opinion, but to form such an opinion." *See* "Soviet Jews as Economic Criminals," reproduced in *The Unredeemed, Anti-Semitism in the Soviet Union*, ed. with an Introduction by Ronald I. Rubin, and a Foreword by Abraham J. Heschel, Chicago, 1968, pp. 115–26. In his "Economic Crime and Punishment," *Survey* (London), No. 57 (October, 1965), 67–72, especially p. 70, George L. Kline is undoubtedly right in stating that the 1961 ordinances were "not specifically antisemitic" in the way the Nazi Nuremberg Laws of 1935 had been. But the merciless application of these laws to Jews, who made up more than one-third of those condemned to death, and the wide publicity given each defendant's former Jewish name or patronymic could have had no other purpose than to cast aspersion on the Jewish people as a whole.

21. One such vitriolic communication bearing the title "L'École de l'obscurantisme," with the by-line of one M. Zandenberg, was included in the official *Bulletin* of the Soviet Bureau of Information, and officially distributed by the Soviet embassy in Paris on September 22, 1972.

22. As late as 1958, Jules Margoline could glibly write about "L'anéantissement du sionisme en Union soviétique," *Problèmes soviétiques* (Munich), I (1958), 74–89, claiming that by 1930 the movement had been definitely eliminated. From the enormous literature dealing with the vicissitudes of the Soviet policies in the Middle East since World War II, we need but mention recent publications by Michael Confino and Shimon Shamir, eds., *The USSR and the Middle East* (from papers submitted to a conference at Tel Aviv University in December, 1971); Aryeh Yodfat in his *Arab Politics in the Soviet Mirror* (The Monograph Series of the Shiloah Center for Middle Eastern and African Studies); and his (in collaboration with Hayim Javets) *Brit ha-Moesot ve-ha-Mizrah ha-Tikhon* (The Soviet Union and the Middle East), both published in Jerusalem, 1973, with the sources cited there. We must, nevertheless, be aware that in this as in other areas, the attitude of the Soviet governing circles has not been quite so solidly uniform as it was in the days of Stalin's undisputed absolutism. Some slight differences in the interpretation of important Middle Eastern developments have been detected even between the *Trud,* the organ of the trade unions, and the *Pravda,* the official voice of the Communist Party. These differences—for example, in the *Trud's* usual omission of the word "all" in the Soviet interpretation of U.N. Resolution 242 demanding Israel's withdrawal from the territories conquered in the Six-Day War; the *Trud* often even omitted the phrase "all territories" in quoting speeches by Arab statesmen—may go beyond the fact that the *Trud's* editors addressed themselves principally to the Soviet workers, whereas the *Pravda* has always been keenly aware of the impression its comments made on other countries. Most remarkably, both organs have been under the direct control of the Propaganda Department of the Party's Central Committee. This divergence may, indeed, reflect some inner cleavage between the exponents of an emphasis on Soviet imperial interests and the proponents of an accent on communist ideology, who have often been perturbed by the suppression of communist parties in some "progressive" Arab lands. *See* Hana Dimant-Kass, "*Pravda* and *Trud*: Divergent Soviet Attitudes Towards the Middle East," *Soviet Union* (Pittsburgh), I, No. 1 (1974), 1–31.

23. Yurii Ivanov, *Ostorozhno, Sionizm* (Beware of Zionism: Notes on the Ideology, Organization, and Practice of Zionism), Moscow, 1969. This booklet of 176 pages was intentionally sold at the minimal price of 27 kopeks, in order to assure the speedy dissemination of hundreds of thousands of copies. Other writings of the same kind included: Vladimir Bolshakov, *Sionizm na sluzhbe antikommunizma* (Zionism in the Service of Anticommunism), Moscow, 1972 (231 pages, yet priced at only 34 kopeks); I. I. Mints *et al.,* eds., *Sionizm, teoriia i praktika* (Zionism, Its Theory and Practice), Moscow, 1973. Even the Yiddish periodical *Sovetish Haimland* was frequently made to join in that anti-Zionist chorus. Among its latest sharply worded outpourings was an article published in its August, 1972, issue (pp. 3–17) bearing the characteristic title "The Great Zionist Swindle," cited below, n. 35. Similarly, the book *Sionizm, vorog molodi* (Zionism, the Enemy of Youth), Moscow, 1973, by the notorious anti-Semite Trofim Kichko (whose earlier vitriolic attack on Judaism is praised by the publisher of his new work, notwithstanding its alleged condemnation by the Party; *see* above, Chap. 17, n. 13) is introduced to the public in a foreword written by a Dr. Bernshtein. Here the Jewish professor denounces Zionism as being imbued with "the decadent ideas of the reactionary philosophers Nietzsche and Spengler, of the founder of eugenics [Francis] Galton, of the racialist theorist Gobineau, of the Malthusians, Social Darwinists and Clericals." *See also* Zeev Ben-Shlomo's earlier review of "The Current Anti-Zionist Campaign in the USSR," *Bulletin Soviet Jewish Affairs*, No. 5 (1970), 3–13; and on the use of the medieval type of Jewish caricatures, as revived by Streicher and other Nazis, *see* the characteristic reproductions in Moshe Decter's compilation, *Israel and the Jews in the Soviet Mirror: Soviet Cartoons on the Middle East Crisis*, New York [1967]; and S. Elisha's "Anti-Israeli Soviet Cartoons" (Hebrew), *Shvut*, I (1973), 119–23.

24. *Jewish Chronicle* (London) of October 23, 1965, cited, together with other relevant materials by Joseph B. Schechtman in "The U.S.S.R., and Zionism and Israel," in L. Kochan, ed., *The Jews in Soviet Russia*, pp. 99–124, especially p. 120; and by Zev Katz in his "After the Six-Day War," *ibid.*, pp. 321–36, especially pp. 323 f.; the Kiev declaration of March 12, 1970, cited by Zeev Ben-Shlomo in "The Current Anti-Zionist Campaign in the USSR," *Bulletin Soviet Jewish Affairs*, No. 5 (1970), 10 (fuller text, *ibid.*, pp. 29 f.); *Głos robotniczy* of May 12, 1968, cited by Benjamin Eliav in his "It Is Possible to Secure a Turn" (Hebrew), *Yalqut magen*, Nos. 47–48 (April, 1969), 5. On the general situation in Poland and its contributions to the fabrication and perpetuation of the myth of a Zionist-Nazi alliance, *see* Maurice Friedberg, "Antisemitism as a Policy Tool to the Soviet Bloc," *American Jewish Year Book*, LXXI (1970), 123–40, especially pp. 126 ff.; and more fully, *The Anti-Jewish Campaign in Present-Day Poland: Facts, Documents, Press Reports*, London, 1968.

25. Ilya Ehrenburg's statement, quoted by Alexander Werth in his *Russia: Hopes and Fears*, London, 1962, p. 242; Zev Katz, in L. Kochan, ed., *The Jews in Soviet Russia*, pp. 321, 334 ff.

26. Boris Kochubiyevsky, *Why I Am a Zionist*, reproduced with other documents in English trans. in Moshe Decter, ed., *A Hero for Our Time: the Trial and Fate of Boris Kochubiyevsky*, with a Foreword by Abraham J. Heschel, New York, 1970, pp. 33 ff.

27. *See*, for instance, the five essays and the ninety documents in English trans. ed. by Abraham Brumberg under the title, *In Quest of Justice: Protest and Dissent in the Soviet Union Today*, New York, 1970; and C. Gerstenmeier, *Die Stimme der Stummen*. Some of these materials came to world attention through sympathetic nations, such as the United States (in the Jewish case, especially Israel), and through some of the more than two hundred private national and international groups accredited to the United Nations, during their frequent debates on human rights. *See* especially Ronald I. Rubin's twin essays, "Soviet Jewry and the United Nations: The Politics of Non-Governmental Organiza-

tions," *Jewish Social Studies*, XXIX (1967), 139–54; and "The Soviet Jewish Problem at the United Nations," *American Jewish Year Book*, LXXI (1970), 141–59.

Some important materials were also brought to public knowledge through their inclusion in the official publications of member nations. For example, after Avraham Shifrin, who had spent ten years (1953–63) in a Soviet labor camp, had settled in Israel, he vividly described his experiences in his "Concentration Camps in the Soviet Union Today: an Appeal to the Conscience of the West"; this narrative appeared in the *Congressional Record* of the United States in February, 1973. Here Shifrin mentioned the sufferings of, among others, Piotr Yakir (son of the influential General Yona Emmanuilovich Yakir), who after the execution of his father on Stalin's order, spent twenty years (from the age of fourteen to thirty-four) in such a camp. Yet after being freed Yakir courageously joined the dissenting movement. Remarkably, even the Ukrainians, the largest national minority of the Soviet Union, often had to resort to appeals to the United Nations or to individual foreign governments for help to redress their far-reaching grievances—with even less immediate effect than did the Jews. *See,* for instance, the editorial "Fifty Years of the USSR: an Anniversary of Fraud and Deceit," *The Ukrainian Quarterly*, 29 (Spring, 1973), 5–11.

28. *See* the brief summaries by Jeri Laber in "The Real Solzhenitsyn," *Commentary*, LVII, No. 5 (May, 1974), 32–35; and by Maurice Friedberg in his "Solzhenitsyn and Russia's Jews," *Midstream*, XX, No. 7 (August-September, 1974), 76–81. The writer's lukewarm attitude toward Jews did not spare him the allegation by some obscurantists that he was of Jewish descent and that his real name was Solzhenitzer. *See* Zhores A. Medvedev, *Ten Years After Ivan Denisovich*, English trans. by Hilary Steinberg, New York, 1973, especially pp. 100 f. On Medvedev's brother, *see* Roy Medvedev's *Let History Judge: the Origins and Consequences of Stalinism*, English trans. by C. Taylor, ed. by D. Joravsky and G. Haupt, New York, 1971; *idem*, "*Samizdat*: Jews in the U.S.S.R.: Documents: Soviet Union," *Survey*, XVII, no. 79 (1971), 169–84; *idem*, *De la démocratie socialiste*. French trans., slightly condensed, by Sybil Geoffroy, Paris, 1972 (the Russian original likewise had to be published in the West, namely in Amsterdam, 1972); and Frederick C. Barghoorn's comments thereon in his "Medvedev's Democratic Leninism," *Slavic Review*, XXXII (1973), 590–94. *See also* Ellen de Kadt's annotated English trans., *On Socialist Democracy*, New York, 1975; and below, n. 50; and Chap. 19, n. 3.

29. *See* Andrei D. Sakharov's famous memorandum, *Progress, Coexistence and Intellectual Freedom*, trans. by *The New York Times*, with Introduction, Afterword, and Notes by Harrison E. Salisbury, New York, 1970, pp. 65 f.; Gene Sosin, "Alexander Galich: Russian Poet of Dissent," *Midstream*, XX, No. 4 (April, 1974), 29–37. A fine analysis of Sakharov's growing involvement in the right of Jews to emigrate and his critique of the Soviet Middle East policies is offered by William Korey in his "Sakharov and the Jewish National Movement," *ibid.*, No. 2 (February, 1974), 35–46.

30. *See also* Roman Rutman, "Jews and Dissenters: Connections and Divergences," *Soviet Jewish Affairs*, III, No. 2 (1973), 26–37; and the chapter on "Jews and Democrats: the Ambivalence of Friends," in Leonard Schroeter, *The Last Exodus*, New York, 1974, pp. 377 ff.

Notes

31. See William Korey, "The 'Right to Leave' for Soviet Jews: Legal and Moral Aspects," *Soviet Jewish Affairs*, No. 1 (1971), 5–12; Leonard Schroeter, "Soviet Jews and Israeli Citizenship: the Nationality Amendment Law of 1971," *ibid.*, No. 2, pp. 25–34; Philippa Lewis, "The 'Jewish Question' in the Open: 1968–1971," in L. Kochan, ed., *The Jews in Soviet Russia*, p. 342. *See also* George Ginsburg's *Soviet Citizenship Law*, Leiden, 1968 (Law in Eastern Europe, XV).

32. Frol Kozlov's interview reported in *The New York Times* of July 2, 1959; the Khrushchev and Meir statements, cited above, Chap. 17, n. 12; the informative, as well as dramatic, presentation of the recent Jewish emigration movement from the Soviet Union in the chapter on "The Right to Leave" in Leonard Schroeter's *The Last Exodus*, pp. 350–96, 418–19. On the enormous difficulties placed by Soviet regulations and bureaucratic red tape in the way of applicants for exit visas, *see* A. S. Karlikow's succinct analysis of "What It Takes to Leave the USSR" in Richard Cohen, ed., *Let My People Go: Today's Documentary Story of Soviet Jewry's Struggle to Be Free*, New York, 1971 (paperback), pp. 212–17. *See also*, René Beerman's brief analysis of the "Soviet and Russian Anti-Parasite Laws," *Soviet Studies*, XV (1963–64), 420–29; and below, n. 36.

33. *See* L. Schroeter's careful review of the often contradictory evidence in *The Last Exodus*, pp. 350 ff., 418; and, as an early example of the numerous, doubtless officially "leaked," reports *The New York Times* of September 8, 1974, pp. 1 and 9. On the vicissitudes of the pertinent amendment to the treaty, sponsored in the United States Senate by Henry M. Jackson and in the House of Representatives by Charles Vanick and Wilbur Mills, *see* William Korey's graphic description in "The Story of the Jackson Amendment, 1973–1975," *Midstream*, XXI, no. 3 (March, 1975), 7–36.

34. *See* my *Steeled by Adversity*, pp. 274 ff.; above, Chap. 5, n. 12; Ilya Ehrenburg's remark, reported in the Jewish Telegraphic Agency's *Daily Bulletin* of May 13, 1959.

35. *See*, for instance, Abram L. Cherches's litany, "Fed Up with Israel: a Jew Returns to the Soviet Union," reproduced in an English trans. from *Vechernaya Moskva* in *Atlas*, 19 (November, 1970), 60; Aron Vergelis, "Zionism's Great Swindle" (Yiddish), *Sovetish Haimland*, 1973, No. 8 (August), 3–17; and, more generally, L. Schroeter, *The Last Exodus*, pp. 359 ff. *See also* Zvi Gitelman, *Soviet Immigrants in Israel*, New York, 1972 (Publications of the Synagogue Council of America).

36. Sakharov's "Open Letter to the United States Congress of September 14, 1973," widely quoted in the press and excerpted in L. Schroeter's *The Last Exodus*, pp. 386 f.; Jean Jacques Marie, ed., *Opposition: eine neue Geisteskrankheit in der Sowjet Union? Eine Dokumentation von Wladimir Bukowsky*, German trans. from the French by Willy Thaler, Munich, 1971. *See also* Bukovsky's noteworthy interview with William Cole of the Columbia Broadcasting Company, broadcast in the United States on July 27, 1970, and reproduced in "Three Voices of Dissent" in *Survey* (London), No. 77 (Autumn, 1970), 128–45, especially pp. 139 ff. (includes interviews with Andrei Amalric and Piotr Yakir). On the growing quest for Jewish identity among the youth and its various novel manifestations, such as the *Simhat Torah* dances in front of synagogues, *see* Boris Smolar's eyewitness account, "The Simhas Torah Mass Demonstrations," in *Soviet Jewry*

Today, pp. 114 ff.; Alexander Voronel and Victor Yakhot, eds., *I Am a Jew. Essays on Jewish Identity in the Soviet Union*, with a Foreword by Moshe Decter and an Introduction by Lewis A. Cosen, New York, 1973; Elie Wiesel, *The Jews of Silence: a Personal Report on Soviet Jewry*, trans. from the Hebrew, with an Historical Afterword by Neal Kozodoy, New York, 1966.

37. See the anonymous reminiscences entitled "The Road Home: a Russian Jew Recovers His Identity," *Bulletin Soviet Jewish Affairs*, No. 4 (December, 1969), 3–14, especially pp. 6 f.; Lazar Lubarsky's case recorded in *Jews in Eastern Europe*, V, No. 3 (August, 1973), 11–28; Moshe Decter, ed., *The Lonely Course of Lazar Lubarsky*, New York, 1973; Aron Vergelis in *Sovetish Haimland*, 1969, No, 1, pp. 138–41; and, more generally, "The Attitudes toward the Hebrew Language in the Soviet Union" (Hebrew), *Yalqut magen*, Nos. 51–52 (April, 1970), 80–83. More recently, Vergelis even published a brief Yiddish "Survey of the History of Modern Hebrew Literature" by the veteran communist scholar, Hillel Aleksandrov, in *Sovetish Haimland*, 1974, No. 3, pp. 146–54. Though necessarily superficial, this sketch gave many eager Soviet Jewish readers a fuller comprehension of the evolution of Hebrew letters, from the days of the Italian Renaissance (beginning with the scholars Azariah de' Rossi and Leon da Modena) than they were able to secure from the pertinent articles in the various Russian encyclopedias.

38. A. A. Gershuni, *Yehudim ve-yahadut be-Brit ha-Moesot* (Jews and Judaism in the Soviet Union), Part II: Russian Jewry from the Stalin Era to the Present, Jerusalem, 1970, pp. 219 ff.; and more succinctly, *idem* in Aryeh Tartakower *et al.*, eds., *Yahadut Berit ha-Moesot*, pp. 157–70. On the repression of the Greek Catholic Church, *see*, for instance, "The Uniate Church: a Case Study in Soviet Church History," *Canadian Slavonic Papers*, VII (1965), 89–113. As in tsarist times, and frequently elsewhere, the oppressive regime tried to buttress its hold on the minorities by sowing discord among them. "Divide and rule" has often proved to be a useful tool in the hands of imperialists since Roman times. The Soviet government certainly did little to reduce the old tensions between Ukrainians, both Uniate and Orthodox, and the Jews. *See* J. L. Lichten, "A Study of Ukrainian-Jewish Relations," *Annals* of the Ukrainian Academy of Arts and Sciences of the United States, V (1955–56), 1160–1167; L. Shankowsky, "Russia, the Jews, and the Ukrainian Liberation Movement," *Ukrainian Quarterly*, XVI (1960), 11–25, 147–63; and some older studies listed in Jurij Lawrynenko's *Ukrainian Communism and Soviet Russian Policy toward the Ukraine: an Annotated Bibliography 1917–1953*, ed. by David I. Goldstein, with a Foreword by John S. Reshetar, New York, 1953 (Research Program of the U.S.S.R., IV). Nor must we overlook the fact that, since it made its peace with the Orthodox Church during World War II, the Soviet government put the Moscow patriarchate to very good use in influencing the ruling circles in the Eastern Churches in favor of its own imperial policies in the Middle East. *See* "Le Patriarcat de Moscou et l'Orthodoxie dans le Proche Orient," *Proche Orient Chrétien*, V (1955), 137–51, 332–45; VI (1956), 317–32.

39. A. A. Gershuni, *Yehudim ve-yahadut*, pp. 224 ff., 236 ff.; above, Chap. 17, nn. 12 ff.; A. L. Eliav, *Between Hammer and Sickle*, pp. 54 ff. (the story of the "three stages in closing a synagogue"—namely that of Lvov in 1962). The same

attitude also dictated the prohibition against Vilna Jews having a shrine in memory of their most revered rabbi, Elijah ben Solomon, known as the "Vilna Gaon" (1720–97). *See* the London *Jewish Chronicle* of June 5, 1959. Among other hostile measures, one that stood out was the quadrupling, in 1961, of the taxes on the income of the synagogue personnel, with assessments to be retroactive for several years, supposedly because the congregants had been overcharged for the ritualistic services rendered. Typical of the rumors spread by the controlled press was a report published in the *Sovetskaya Belorussia* of February 2, 1960, stating that the Minsk cantor received 8,000 rubles in salary and full board, and that the circumciser charged 500 rubles for each operation. *See* below, n. 40.

40. *See* the description of the *Siddur ha-shalom* (Prayer Book for Peace) in K. Schmeruk's ed. of *Pirsumim yehudiim be-Brit ha-Moesot* (Jewish Publications in the Soviet Union), p. 25 n. 186; London *Jewish Chronicle* of September 10, 1960; *The New York Times* of October 2, 1960; above, Chap. 17, n. 14. A noteworthy Hebrew description of a *Yom Kippur* evening service (with the recitation of the well-known prayer *Kol nidre*) in the fall of 1966 by an unnamed official of the Israeli embassy is reproduced in A. A. Gershuni's *Yehudim ve-yahadut*, pp. 282 ff. The story of the thirty-five circumcisions, as told by the protagonist, Mordecai Schenker, is reproduced in Moshe Prager's Hebrew paper "Religious Life and Devotion to Israel's Heritage under Underground Conditions" in *Tarbut yehudit be-Brit ha-Moesot* (Jewish Culture in the Soviet Union: Proceedings of the Symposium Held by the Cultural Department of the World Jewish Congress, Jerusalem, January 30–31, 1972), ed. by Aryeh Tartakower and Zelda Kolich, Jerusalem, 1972, pp. 135–42, especially pp. 136 ff.

41. *See* Felix Lvovich Shapiro's *Ivrit-russkii slovar* or *Millon ivri-russi* (Hebrew-Russian Dictionary of About 28,000 Words), ed. with a brief grammatical outline of the Hebrew language by B. M. Grande, Moscow, 1963; Shota Rustaveli, '*Oteh 'or ha-namer* (The Knight in the Panther's Skin), Hebrew trans. by Boris Gaponov (Isaac Davitashvili) with comments and notes by the translator and the editor Abraham Shlonsky, Merhavia, 1969 (almost simultaneous with the new English trans. by Venesa Urushadze, published in Tbilisi, 1968), with the brief comment thereon by Ben-Zion Yaakov Shavili in *Tarbut yehudit be-Brit ha-Moesot*, ed. by Tartakower and Kolich, pp. 114–18, especially pp. 117 f. *See also* Alfred A. Greenbaum's "Hebrew Literature in Soviet Russia," *Jewish Social Studies*, XXX (1968), 135–49, whose analysis, not unjustly, ends with the early 1940s. The new beginnings here alluded to may, however, be harbingers of a new Hebraic renaissance which at present still is in its hesitant earliest stages.

42. *See* my *Social and Religious History of the Jews*, 1st ed., I, 169; II, 204, 404 n. 56; III, 110, 199 ff. 282 n. 44, 327 n. 35; M. Altschuler, "Sketches for the Demographic Image" in *Yahadut Brit ha-Moesot*, pp. 25 ff. and the sources listed there; and above, nn. 4 and 7.

43. *See* especially the succinct and informative reviews by Michael Zand in his papers and replies to discussants at the 1972 Symposium of the World Jewish Congress in Jerusalem and published in *Tarbut yehudit be-Brit ha-Moesot*, pp. 22–26, 38, 119–29, where the books and journals published before World War II are mentioned. Of considerable human interest is A. L. Eliav's vivid description of his visits to "the Jews of the Asian Borderlands" in his *Between Hammer and Sickle*, pp. 147–73. *See also,* Rudolf Loewenthal, "The Jews of Bukhara," *Revue des études juives*, CXX (1960), 345–51; and, more generally, Edward Allworth, ed., *The Nationality Question in Soviet Central Asia*, New York, 1973. It is to be noted that the Jewish community of Biro-Bidzhan, entirely of Ashkenazic origin, seems to have maintained but few contacts with their fellow Asiatic groups. Similarly, the newly awakened Zionist consciousness and the Democratic Movement apparently evoked no perceptible reactions there, despite the increase in the publication of the *Birobidzhaner Shtern* from three to five days a week. *See* A. Vinokur, "An Ancient Faith Dies Out" (Russian), *Nauka i religia*, 1967, No. 1, pp. 41–43.

44. *See* the widely publicized appeals of the Georgian Jews, also circulated in the Soviet Interior in various *samizdat*s and reproduced, among others, by Moshe Decter in his ed. of *Redemption: Jewish Freedom Letters from Russia*, with a Foreword by Bayard Rustin, New York, 1970. The Hebrew text of the first appeal—reproduced, for instance, by A. A. Gershuni in his *Yehudim ve-yahadut be-Brit ha-Moesot*, pp. 305–307—is even more impressive than the English text.

45. *See* Philip Friedman, "The Karaites under the Nazi Rule" in *On the Track of Tyranny. Essays Presented by the Wiener Library to Leonard G. Montefiore*, London, 1960, pp. 97–122; the valuable documents published by Jacob Mann in his *Texts and Studies in Jewish History and Literature*, 2 vols., Cincinnati, 1931, and Philadelphia, 1935, especially Vol. II; Rudolf Loewenthal, "The Extinction of the Krimchaks in World War II," *American Slavic and East-European Review*, X (1957), 130–36; and other literature listed in my *Social and Religious History of the Jews*, especially Vols. III, V, and XVI.

46. *See* above, n. 7; and the "Supplementary Note" to A. Nove and J. A. Newth's aforementioned essay in L. Kochan, ed., *The Jew in Soviet Russia*, pp. 356 ff.

47. *See* Nove and Newth, *ibid.;* Michael Checiński, "Soviet Jews and Higher Education," *Soviet Jewish Affairs*, III, No. 2 (1973), pp. 6 f. Table 5, also mentioning that of the approximately 95,000 Jews in the Russian Republic who gave Yiddish as their native tongue, some 77,000 indicated Russian as a second language, while the 710,000 Russian-speaking Jews included 86,500 who claimed Yiddish as their second idiom.

48. *See*, for example, Rose Katz-Rabinovich, "Sketches to the Profile of Shloime Rabinovich" (Yiddish), *Sovetish Haimland*, 1973, No. 12 (December, 1973), pp. 104–10; Hersh Remenik, "Studies in Criticism and Critics" (Yiddish), *ibid.*, pp. 131–43 (includes praise of Litvakov as "a leading ingenious personality in literature"; p. 131). The twelve issues of the 1973 volume testify to the advances both in quantity and quality made over the first thirteen years of the journal's existence. Earlier analyses of its contents in English include Joseph and Abraham Blumberg, *Sovetish Heymland—an Analysis*, New York, 1966; Abraham Blumberg's " 'Sovyetish Heymland' and the Dilemmas of Life in the USSR," *Soviet Jewish Affairs*, No. 3 (1972), 27–41; Chimen Abramsky, "Sovietish Heimland and the Anniversary of the Russian Revolution," *Bulletin Soviet Jewish Affairs*, No. 1 (1968), pp. 70–71; *idem*, " 'Sovietish Heimland' Jan.–May 1969," *ibid.*, No. 4 (1969), 44–45. A fuller listing of the first Yiddish publications in the post-Stalin era was compiled by A. Finkelstein in "The Work of Soviet Yiddish Writers in the Years 1955–1964" (Yiddish), *Sovetish Haimland*, 1966, No. 1, pp. 149–55 (no similar compilation for the later years has as yet been made available). Of particular interest also are the lectures delivered at the aforementioned 1972 Symposium of the World Jewish Congress in Jerusalem by the émigré writers Joseph Kerler ("The Soviet-Jewish Literary Creativity in the Post-Stalin Era") and Ziama Telsin ("Contemporary Yiddish Prose in the Soviet Union") in *Tarbut yehudit be-Brit ha-Moesot*, pp. 40–72, 73–84, both with illuminating excerpts from the original writings. *See also*, more generally, Jacob Sonntag, "Yiddish Writers and Jewish Culture in the USSR: Twenty Years After," *Soviet Jewish Affairs*, II, No. 2 (1972), 31–38, referring to August 12, 1952, the date of the aforementioned execution of the great Yiddish writers Markish, Bergelson, and others.

49. *See* the detailed Hebrew report in the most widely read Israeli paper, *Ma'ariv* of December 1, 1968; Arie L. Eliav, *Between Hammer and Sickle*, pp. 40 ff.; M. Kalik, "On Jewish Culture in Theatrical Arts and the Film of the Soviet Union" (Hebrew), *Tarbut yehudit be-Brit ha-Moesot*, pp. 130–34. Of course, these popular nostalgic performances have been but pale imitations of the flourishing Jewish theatrical and musical arts in old Russia. *See* Irene Heskes and Arthur Wolfson, *The Historic Contribution of Russian Jewry to Jewish Music*, New York, 1967; with *A Supplement* by Heskes, New York, 1968.

50. Bernard Choseed, "Categorizing Soviet Yiddish Writers," *Slavic Review*, XXVII (1968), 102–108, especially p. 106; *Sovetish Haimland*, 1960, No. 1; above, n. 3; and Chaps. 14, nn. 25–26; and 17, n. 9; Anatolii Kuznetsov, *Babi Yar*, Moscow, 1960; *idem*, "The Memories," *The New York Times Book Review*, April 9, 1967, pp. 4 f. Only the 1962 publication of the fuller English translation of that work—in which the passages deleted by the censors in the Russian original, about a third of the book, were printed in a boldface type—has shown that from the outset the author had held a more balanced view; he just did not have the strength to resist the Party's dictates more vigorously. *See* his *Babi Yar: a Document in the Form of a Novel*, trans. by David Floyd, New York, 1970, as compared with the original Russian *Babii Yar: Roman-Dokument*, ed. by C. Brodsky, Moscow, 1967. Evtushenko retaliated when, in his 1971 Address to the Fifth Congress of Writers of the U.S.S.R., he exclaimed, "Our generation included both addicts of fashion [*stiliazi*], and those who were moldy. But these individuals can no more be taken as typical of our generation than the pitiful, fawning, pasty face of that Dickensian Uriah [Heep] who uses the pseudonym Monsieur Anatoli [Kuznetsov]." *Literaturnaya Gazeta* of July 7, 1971, pp. 203–209. *See also* Maurice Friedberg, "On Reading Recent Soviet Judaica," *Survey*, No. 62 (January, 1967), 167–77 (mainly concerned with the treatment of Jews and Jewish writers in recent Soviet encyclopedias; *see* above, Chap. 16, n. 15); Max Hayward, "Some Observations on Jews in Post-Stalin Soviet Literature," *Bulletin Soviet Jewish Affairs*, No. 4 (1969), 15–19; and with reference to the smaller republics, Vera Reich's "Heroes and Jews in Byelorussian Literature," *Soviet Jewish Affairs*, III (1973), 80–91. Much pertinent material is available in Aleksander Donat's aforementioned anthology, *Neopalimaya kupina* (The Burning Bush), New York, 1973, including five items by Evtushenko (pp. 429 ff.). Of considerable interest also are the brief yet penetrating remarks by Rachel Baumvol in her "Jewish Themes in the Russian Literature as a Factor in Soviet Jewish Life" and by Vadim Meniker, "Jewish Themes in Unofficial Publications [*Samizdats*]" in *Tarbut yehudit be-Brit ha-Moesot*, pp. 85–92 and 93–103.

Not surprisingly, these underground writings reflect the deep ideological splits in the Democratic Movement and among the Jewish activists. *See* above, n. 28. Of particular significance are Roy Medvedev's *Blizhnovostochkii krisis i evreiskii vopros v SSSR* (The Near-Eastern Crisis and the Jewish Question in the Soviet Union), published in 1970 (*see also* above, n. 28); Grigorii Vladimov's humanitarian *Open Letter to the OVIR*; and particularly Friedrich Gorenshtein's Russian short story "The House with the Small Greek Tower" of 1964. The officially censored publications, on the other hand, are characterized by Rachel Baumvol as follows: "(1) The so-called Jewish theme is rarely treated in Russian letters; (2) most writers on Jews are themselves non-Jews; (3) the Russian literature describes Jews as if they were non-Jews except in a few cases when the treatment is pronouncedly anti-Semitic" (p. 90). All these aspects would certainly merit more comprehensive monographic treatment.

[19]

No End of Road

1. Nicholas Berdyaev (Berdaev), *The Russian Revolution, Two Essays on Its Implications in Religion and Psychology*, English trans. from the Russian with an Introduction by D. B., London, 1931 (Essays in Order, VI), pp. 59 f. *See also* Robert C. Tucker, "Marxism: Is It Religion?" *Ethics*, LXVIII (1957–58), 125–30. Still germinal in Marx's own teachings, despite Ludwig Feuerbach's exclamation in 1842, "Politics must become our religion," the religious brand of Soviet communist fanaticism had become more and more marked.

2. Marquis Astolphe L. L. de Custine, *Russia* [1839], abridged trans. from the French, 3 vols., London, 1844, I, 160 f. *See also* George F. Kennan, *The Marquis de Custine and the Russia in 1839*, Princeton, 1971; and various essays on *Continuity and Change in Russian and Soviet Thought*, ed. by Ernest J. Simmons, including Adam Ulam's "Stalin and the Theory of Totalitarianism," also referring to the use of undercover anti-Semitism in the struggle against Trotsky, Zinoviev, and Kamenev (pp. 165 ff.).

3. *See* Zbigniew Brzezinski, ed., *Dilemmas of Change in Soviet Politics*, New York, 1969, p. 2; Andrei Amalric, "Will the USSR Survive until 1984?" *Survey*, No. 73 (Autumn, 1969), 47–70. The constant reappraisal of Russia's past by Soviet historians has extended even to tsarist expansion into Asia, despite their professed opposition to all forms of colonialism. Some now claim that "tsarist imperialism is a salutary phenomenon inasmuch as it prepared the way to socialism and assured in advance the happiness of the future Soviet peoples." *See* N. G. Gurshi, "Soviet Colonialism" in *Problems of the Peoples of the USSR*, Munich, 1958, I, 18 f.; and N. Nedasek, "National Self-Determination under the

Soviets," *Belorussian Review,* VIII (1960), 3–16. On the internal Jewish aspects, *see also* my "Cultural Reconstruction of Russian Jewry," *The 1971 Allan Bronfman Lecture,* Westmount, Quebec, Canada [1973], especially pp. 26 f.; Roy Medvedev, "Samizdat: Jews in the USSR," *Survey,* No. 79 (Spring, 1971), 185–200; and Maurice Friedberg, *Why They Left: a Survey of Soviet Jewish Emigrants,* published by The Academic Committee on Soviet Jewry, New York, 1972.

Index

Index

Index

Index

Index

Index

Index

Ibn an-Nadim, 3, 343 n.3
ICOR mission, 196, 197
Ignatev, Nikolai, 46, 47, 356–57 n.4, 364 n.11
Iliodor of Tsaritsin, 166, 251
Illier, Menasseh ben Porat, 124
Industrial workers, Jewish, 88–89, 96–97, 209, 211, 213–16, 369 n.26, 403 n.9, 404 n.11
Industrialization, 79, 82, 83, 369 n.23
  Jewish entrepreneurs, 88–94, 96–97, 367 ns.18, 19
  Soviet regime, 213–16, 222–23, 304, 306, 327
Isler, J. M., 366 n.5
Israel, 290, 292. *See also* Palestine
  Arab wars, 310–11, 316, 319, 325, 429 n.12, 436 n.22
  emigration to, 208, 288, 291, 295, 317–21, 327–28, 331
  establishment of, 267–68, 310
  reaction of Russian Jews to, 287–88, 313, 314
  Soviet relations with, 268, 287–88, 310–11, 323, 324, 429 n.12, 436 n.22
Italy, 300–301
Ivan III, 6, 7
Ivan IV, 7–8, 346 n.12
Ivan the Terrible, 271, 423 n.11
Ivanov, K., 429 n.11
Ivanov, N. J., 158
Ivanov, Yurii, 311, 436 n.23
Izakov, Boris, 288

Jackson, Henry M., 439 n.33
Jacobins, 351 n.2
Jacobson, Carol, 418 n.16
Jacobson, Jacob, 353 n.9
Jaffé, Jakob, 360 n.19
Jaffe, Nadezhda, 356 n.3
Jakobson, Roman, 411 n.22
Janowsky, Oscar I., 381 n.19
Japan, 195, 201, 254
Jarblum, Marc, 422 n.6
Jerome, Saint, 2, 343 n.1
Jerusalem, Russian Jewish community in, 38–39
Jewish Anti-Fascist Committee, 261–64, 267, 272, 273–74
Jewish Colonization Association, 50, 53, 73–74, 80, 96, 212
Jewish Commissariat, 174, 175, 189, 192
Jewish communists, 186, 188, 189, 226, 241, 246, 252, 337–38
  anti-Hebraism of, 176, 177, 226, 231–33, 241, 411 n.22
  anti-Judaism of, 169, 173, 175, 176, 244–45

Jewish communists—Continued
  decline of, 202–204, 247, 305
  exterminated by Nazis, 254–55
  as leaders, 169–70, 173, 174, 176, 177, 179, 220, 222, 223, 226, 240, 247, 283, 284, 305, 391 ns.2, 3
  purges of, 203–204, 247, 284, 394 n.10, 405 n.20, 413–14 n.30
  statistics, 170–71, 304–305
Jewish Congress (1917), 168–69
Jewish culture, 123–31, 151–55. *See also* Hebrew; Yiddish
  attrition under Soviets, 225–47, 336–37, 409–10 ns.18, 19
  post-World War II, 269–74, 289, 291–92
  revival of, 295, 330–33, 341, 441 n.41
  Robeson on, 332
Jewish schools, 21, 35–37, 117–20, 129, 246, 289, 291–92. *See also* Education
  Hebrew, 162, 231, 293, 372 n.6
  Yiddish, 162, 226–29, 269, 293, 336, 372 n.6, 406–407 ns.2, 4
Jewish settlement. *See also* specific locations; Pale of Jewish Settlement
  early, 1–6
  expulsions, 21, 25, 33, 57, 350 n.13
  interior Russia, 162–67, 205–208, 281–82, 298, 304
  restrictions, 21, 32–33, 53–54
Jews, in Russia. *See also* Jewish settlement
  assimilation of, 19–21, 178–79, 200, 205, 225–29, 240, 298–301, 303, 329–30, 379 n.12, 411 n.22
  autonomous communities, 17–18, 20, 99–111, 188–90, 370 n.1. *See also* Kahals
  class struggle, 108–11, 371 n.12
  clothing, 125–26, 374 n.15
  Communist attitude toward, 169–79
  "conspiracy of silence" on, 243, 257–61, 264, 276–77, 333–34
  discrimination against. *See* Anti-Semitism
  early marriages, 34, 65, 353 n.10
  franchisement, 16, 20, 34, 59, 190–91
  health, 403 n.10
  landowners, 77, 366 n.7
  literacy of, 225
  loyalty of, to Russia, 22–23, 27, 103, 157, 164, 274, 275
  mixed marriages, 179, 200, 207, 296, 298–301, 433–34 n.10
  nationality issue, 141–44, 171–74, 188, 191–93, 202, 393 n.8, 406 n.2, 434 n.11
  Oriental, 208, 226, 326–27
  origins, 1–2, 344 n.4

Index

Index

Index

Index

Marley, Dudley, 195–96, 399 n.10
Marranos people, 9, 244, 245, 339–40
Martov, Yulii, 142, 143, 170, 381 n.18
Marx, Karl, 138, 173, 335, 393 n.7
Marxism, 149, 169, 283, 312, 335–36
Maskilim, 124–29
Maurach, Reinhart, 391 n.2
May Laws (1882), 47, 48, 79, 80, 218, 356–57 n.4
Mazeh, Rabbi Jacob, 117, 233, 372 n.4
Medem, Gine, 400 n.14
Medem, Vladimir, 143, 381 n.19
Medical profession, Jews in, 53, 94, 136–37, 216, 217, 285, 307
Medvedev, Roy, 315, 438 n.28
Medvedev, Zhores, 438 n.28
Meir, Golda, 272, 288, 312, 318
Meisel, Nachman, 386 n.31
Meisl, Joseph, 347 n.16
Mekhlis, Lev, 203, 271
Mendele Mokher Seforim, 108, 119, 128, 227–28, 371 n.10
    mentioned, 153, 276, 292, 331, 408 n.10
Mendéléeff. D., 368 n.22
Mendelsohn, Ezra, 369 n.26
Mendelssohn, Moses, 22, 349 n.7
Menes, Abraham, 372 n.2
Meniker, Vadim, 444 n.50
Mensheviks, 142, 143, 198, 405 n.20
Menshikov, Prince Alexander, 10
Merchants, Jewish, 86, 87, 209–10, 221, 285, 309
Merezhkovskii, Dmitrii, 62, 165
Metternich, Count Clemens, 22
Meyer, Peter, 426 n.2
Migne, Jacques P., 343 n.1
Mikhoels, Salomon, 241, 270, 277, 332, 411 n.23, 412 n.23, 421 n.22
    death, 273, 316
    political activity, 261, 262, 264, 420 n.20
Mikoyan, Anastas, 427 n.5
Military service. *See* Drafting; Red Army; specific wars
Miliukov, P. M., 378 n.10
Miliutin, B., 95, 369 n.24
Mill, John, 382 n.19
Miller, David, 430 n.17
Miller, Jacob, 393 n.8
Millman, Ivor I., 427 n.4
Mining industry, Jews in, 215–16
Minority nationalities, 292, 314, 438, n.37
    assimilation of, 299–304, 338, 411 n.22
    rights under Soviets, 171–74, 191, 309, 393 n.8
    statistics, 199, 329, 433 n.7, 434 n.11
Minsk, 17, 32, 33, 68
    anti-Semitism in, 41

Minsk—Continued
    economic stratification, 80, 81, 87, 212, 366 n.9
    education, 36, 119, 227
    hekdeshes, 107–108
    mentioned, 100, 109, 210, 234, 246, 249, 273, 355 n.19
    population figures, 68, 282, 330, 432 n.7
    Yiddish culture, 235, 240, 241, 269, 330
Minski, P., 394 n.9
Minsky, E. L., 389 n.10
Mints, I. I., 436 n.23
Mir, 119, 120
Miron, Dan, 386 n.32
Mirski, Michael, 424 n.16
Mirsky, Dimitrii S., 135, 377 n.6
Mirsky, Samuel K., 373 n.8
Mizrahi Organization, 151
Moghilev, 8, 33, 82, 87, 89, 120
Mohilever, Samuel, 151
Moldavia, 154, 282, 304, 330, 332
Molodetskii, Meir, 46
Molokani sect, 32
Molotov, Vyacheslav, 237, 261, 422 n.4
Molotov-Ribbentrop Treaty, 249–52, 257, 414 n.2
Monas, Sidney, 366 n.4
Mongol conquest, 6, 344 n.4
Montefiore, Moses, 36, 38, 102, 353 n.12, 354 n.15
Mordvinov, Admiral N., 28
Morley, James W., 399 n.9
Morrier, Sir Robert, 357 n.6
Mosaic sect, 133
Moscow, 22, 90, 93, 117, 285, 345 n.10
    anti-Jewish activity, 6–9, 12, 18, 48–49, 180–81, 286, 291, 345–46 n.10, 357–58 n.6, 387 n.3
    economic stratification, 211, 213, 214, 216
    education, 48, 227, 228, 308
    Jewish culture, 177, 230–32, 241, 242, 270, 325–26, 330
    as a major center, 96, 177, 287, 306
    population figures, 65, 69, 207, 297, 298, 330, 357 n.6, 388 n.8, 427 n.4, 432 n.7
    Russification of Jews, 179, 200, 298
    synagogue, 288–91, 325, 357 n.6
    World War II, 253, 259, 263, 264
Mosely, Philip E., 391 n.3
Moses of Khorene, 326
Moses of Kiev, 5
Motion pictures, 271, 272
Motzkin, Leo, 390 n.1
Mountain Jews, 2, 255, 327
Movshovitch, D., 389 n.12
Mtislav, 347 n.1

Index

Index

Pahlen Commission, 48, 77
Pajewski, Janusz, 388 n.5
Pakištas, Karyz, 363 n.2
Pakuda, Bahya ibn, 123
Pale of Jewish Settlement, 18, 32–33, 40,
    68, 69, 328, 348 n.3
  alcoholism in, 76–77
  economic stratification, 75–76, 81–83,
    93–98, 100, 209, 213
  Jewish charities, 212
  mentioned, 66, 109, 115, 192
  population figures, 63, 190, 207
  schools, 35, 48, 117, 118, 120
  World War I, 157, 160, 162–64, 230
Palestine, 221, 231, 241, 251, 265. See also
    Israel
  Arabs in, 194, 202, 399 n.9
  emigration to, 39, 69, 71, 147, 232, 247,
    328, 401 n.20
  Jewish colonization in, 148–51, 152, 222
  as Jewish homeland, 145, 148, 202, 247,
    351 n.2, 421 n.22
  partitioning of, 202, 267–68, 283, 310
Panitz, Esther L., 364 n.10
Pan-Slavism, 61, 144, 315, 361–62 n.22
Paperna, Abraham, 104, 107, 117, 133, 371
    n.7
Pasmanek, Daniel S., 391 n.2
Passarge, Siegfried, 355 n.20
Passover, Alexander, 136
Pasternak, Boris, 242, 243, 293, 333, 430
    n.19
Paszkiewicz, Henryk, 362 n.22
Patkin, A. L., 382 n.19
Paul I, 17–20
Pechersky, Gedaliah, 291, 303
Peel, William R. W., Lord, 202
Peretz, Grigorii, 27, 351 n.2
Peretz, Isaac, 153, 155, 292, 386 n.31
Perlmann, Moshe, 375 n.15
Persia, 2, 3, 89, 91, 208
Persov, Samuel, 404 n.19
Pestel, Paul (Pavel), 27, 350–51 n.2
Petcherskii Monastery, 5
Peter I (the Great), 9, 10, 38
Peter II, 10
Peter III, 13
Petliura, Simeon, 179, 183–84, 396 n.21,
    397 n.23
Petrovna, Sofiia, 346 n.12
Philippson, Ludwig, 35–36, 70, 353 n.12
Philipson, David, 353 n.12
Pines, Dan, 394 n.9
Pinkerton, Robert, 67, 108, 363 n.5
Pinkus, Benjamin, 398 n.2
Pinsker, Leon (Leo), 146, 382 n.21
Pinsker, Simhah, 124, 146
Pinson, Koppel S., 380 n.16

Pipes, Richard, 359 n.11
Pisarev, Dimitrii, 133
Plehve, Vyacheslav von, 56–57, 61, 147,
    383 n.22
Plotsk, 71, 96, 234
Poale Zion, 149
Pobedonostsev, Constantin, 43–44, 46, 49–
    54, 91, 92, 135, 356 n.3, 358 n.8, 361
    n.22
Podolia, 32, 101, 105, 109, 256
Pogroms, 44–46, 51, 56–58, 60, 71, 72
  during Civil War, 176, 181–86, 206, 209,
    212, 218
  international reaction, 45, 50, 93, 359–60
    n.14
  Jewish reaction, 57–58, 145, 146, 152,
    185
  outlawed by Soviets, 180, 328
  revolutionary Jews and, 138–39, 185, 378
    n.11
Poland
  Bund influence in, 382 n.19
  communal government in, 17, 99–101,
    115, 372 n.2
  Communist regime, 269, 274, 283, 295,
    319, 422 n.6, 437 n.24
  economic stratification, 76, 77, 81, 84,
    85, 96, 97, 98
  1863 uprising, 33, 41, 144, 355 n.19, 381
    n.17
  1831 uprising, 33, 144
  May Laws extended to, 357 n.4
  19th-early 20th cents., 64, 67, 76, 77, 81,
    98, 118, 120, 122, 357 n.4, 382 n.19.
    See also Congress Poland
  partitions of, 13–15, 347–48 n.1
  population figures, 63, 64, 330, 433 n.7
  pre-partition years, 17, 81, 99–101, 112,
    115
  Quadrennial Diet, 20, 77
  religious practices, 67, 112, 120, 122
  Republic (1918–1939), 33, 162, 184, 187,
    197, 230, 235, 237, 241
  schools, 118, 120
  16th–17th cents., 7, 8, 10, 12, 346 n.13
  World War I, 157, 159, 161, 388 n.5
  World War II, 249, 251, 252, 254, 256,
    263, 282, 337, 417 n.12
  Yiddish culture, 235, 237, 241
Poliakov, Leon, 417 n.12
Poliakov, Samuel, 50, 84, 90–93, 137, 364
    n.11
Polish people, 16, 59, 143, 330, 433 n.7
Political activity, of Jews, 59–61, 136–40,
    166–67, 190–91, 304–305, 427 n.6.
    See also Jewish communists
Orthodox Jews, 384–85 n.28
Polotsk, 7, 346 n.12, 347 n.1

Index

Poltava, 33, 87, 234
Pope, Arthur U., 392 n.3
Popieszalski, Karol M., 416 n.9
Population statistics. *See also* specific
 locations
 birth rates, 65, 162, 206, 262, 298, 299,
  432 n.7
 emigration, 73, 74, 318–19
 Jewish Communist membership, 170–
  71, 304–305
 Jews in interior Russia, 163, 206–207,
  281
 minority nationalities, 199, 329, 433 n.7,
  434 n.11
 19th cent., 31, 47, 63–69, 362–63 ns.2, 6
 occupational data. *See* Economic
  stratification
 Oriental Jews, 326–27
 rural, 21, 79–80, 219, 298, 304, 427 n.4
 school enrollment, 35–37, 40, 118, 120,
  163, 227–29, 307, 372 n.6
 20th cent., 205–209, 281–82, 296–99, 326–
  27, 427 n.4, 432 ns.4, 7
 urban, 21, 67–69, 207, 282, 298, 304, 427
  n.4, 432 n.7
 women, 208–209, 298
 Yiddish-speaking, 192, 226, 292, 329–30,
  442 n.47
Posner, Solomon, 96, 373 n.9
Potapov, Governor-General, 139
Powell, A., 400 n.15
Pozniakov, Vasilii, 345 n.12
Prager, Moshe, 441 n.40
Pravda, 170, 260, 265, 268, 333, 436 n.22
Press, Jewish, 34, 39, 71, 229–40, 376 n.21
 censorship of, 34, 353 n.11
 revival of, 330–31
 in Russian language, 130–31
 suppression under Soviets, 249, 269–70,
  274, 289, 292
 World War II, 263–64
Pressman, O., 400 n.14
Prokopowicz, S. N., 404 n.14
Prokoptschuk, Gregor, 388 n.3
Protocol of the Elders of Zion, 56, 61, 311,
  359 n.13
Prussia, 14, 19, 24, 33, 85, 352 n.8
Purges of 1936–1938, 202–204, 223, 277,
  280, 327. *See also* Stalin Terror
 Jewish communists, 203–204, 247, 284,
  394 n.10, 405 n.20, 413–14 n.30
 Jewish writers, 239, 242, 331, 410 n.18
 Red Army officers, 203, 259, 260, 413–14
  n.30
Purishkevich, V. M., 157, 387 n.2
Pushkin, Aleksandr, 51, 133

Quadrennial Diet (1788–1792), 20, 77

Rabbinate, 115–17, 372 n.2
Rabbinic literature, 123–24, 152
Rabinovich, Osip, 40, 130, 354 n.17
Rabinovich, Shloime, 291, 295, 331, 425
 n.1
Rabinovich, Solomon. *See* Aleichem,
 Sholem
Radek, Karl, 169, 203
Radishchev, L., 403 n.7
Radkey, Oliver H., 395 n.15
Radziegowski, Janusz, 434 n.13
Raeff, Marc, 347 n.1
Railroads, 84, 90–91, 160, 368 n.21
Raisin, Jacob S., 375 n.17
Rambach, S., 367 n.10
Raminowitsch, Wolf Z., 374 n.10
Rapaport, Nathan, 267
Rapoport, Salomon. *See* An-Ski, S.
Rasputin, Grigori, 164, 166, 390 n.13
Rassein, Jacob, 366 n.7
Rastenis, Vincas, 400 n.16
Rawidowicz, Simon, 410 n.21
Red Army, 185, 199, 253
 anti-Semitism in, 397 n.26
 in Civil War, 184, 412 n.25
 Jews in, 202, 243, 258–60, 271, 274, 305,
  419 ns.16, 17
 purges in, 203, 259, 260, 413–14 n.30
 as savior of Jews, 264, 265
Redlich, Shimon, 415 n.6
Reed, Arthur P., Jr., 428 n.9
Reich, Vera, 443 n.50
Reichenau, Walter von, 416 n.7
Reichskommissariat Ostland, 256
Reinecke, Hermann, 253, 415 n.7
Reines, Isaac J., 151, 384 n.27
Reinhardt, Max, 412 n.23
Reisen, Zalman, 375 n.18
Reitlinger, Gerald, 415 n.6
Rekruchina, 29–32, 110, 350 n.13, 351–52
 n.5.*See also* Drafting, of Jews
Religion, under Soviets, 175–79, 244–47,
  301, 400–401 n.16, 408–409 ns.11,
  12, 413 n.29. *See also* specific
  religions
 post-World War II, 289–91, 323–24, 440–
  41 n.39
 World War II, 235, 250–52, 290, 414 n.3,
  420 n.20, 440 n.38
Remenik, Hersh, 442 n.48
Renaissance, Hebrew, 151–55
Renouvin, Pierre, 368 n.23
Reshetar, John S., 396 n.22
Reshumot, 230
Reventlow, Count Ernst du, 170
Revolution of 1905, 57, 59, 142, 143, 149,
  349 n.10, 359 n.11

Index

Index

Index

Index

History/Judaica

SALO W. BARON

THE RUSSIAN JEW UNDER TSARS AND SOVIETS

SECOND EDITION, REVISED AND ENLARGED WITH A NEW PREFACE BY THE AUTHOR

This comprehensive, richly textured history describes the stirring story of how Jews survived—and often prospered—under an irregular succession of despots, humanitarians, and dictators of the proletariat. Beginning with the earliest known settlements of Jews in Russia, Professor Baron discusses the important role Jews played in the evolution of modern Russia and recounts the history of official persecution they have endured under the tsars and their heirs to power.

"Professor Baron . . . take[s] the reader with learning and lucidity through a whole range of topics affecting Russian Jewry. . . . [His] book deals impartially with the lights and shades."   —*The Economist*

SALO WITTMAYER BARON, Emeritus Professor of Jewish History, Literature, and Institutions at Columbia University, is one of the world's foremost authorities on Jewish history. He is the author of more than 500 books and articles including the eighteen-volume *Social and Religious History of the Jews*.

SCHOCKEN BOOKS   62 COOPER SQUARE   NEW YORK CITY 10003

ISBN 0-8052-0838-0   >$14.9!